GREEK TRAGIC POETRY

GREEK TRAGIC POETRY

ALBIN LESKY

TRANSLATED BY
MATTHEW DILLON

YALE UNIVERSITY PRESS
NEW HAVEN AND LONDON

Translated from the German with the permission of
Vandenhoeck & Ruprecht, Göttingen.
Copyright © 1972 Vandenhoeck & Ruprecht in Göttingen.

Published with assistance from the Mary Cady Tew
Memorial Fund

Designed by James J. Johnson
and set in Trump Roman by
Graphic Composition, Inc., Athens, Ga.
Printed in the United States of America by
Vail-Ballou Press, Binghamton, N.Y.

Library of Congress Cataloging in Publication Data

Lesky, Albin, 1896–1981
    Greek tragic poetry.

    Translation of: Die tragische Dichtung der
Hellenen. 3., völlig neubearb. u. erw. Aufl., 1972.
    Bibliography: p.
    Includes index.
    1. Greek drama (Tragedy)—History and criticism.
I. Title.
PA 3131.L413   882′.01   82–1886
ISBN 0–300–02647–1   AACR2

10   9   8   7   6   5   4   3   2   1

AMICO BONNENSI
IOANNI HERTER
AMICIS VINDOBONENSIBUS
RUDOLPHO HANSLIK
WALTHARIO KRAUS
FRIDERICO SCHACHERMEYR

Yet these few grand fragments that have
come down to us are so vast and so important
that we poor Europeans have already been
busying ourselves with them for centuries,
and will for several centuries to come still
have to draw from and work on them.

Goethe to Eckermann, 1 May 1825

CONTENTS

PREFACE TO THE ENGLISH EDITION

This English version of *Greek Tragic Poetry* is a translation of the third and final edition of *Die tragische Dichtung der Hellenen*, which is much expanded from the book's earlier form. There are two reasons why I enlarged the volume. The first has to do with my original intent in undertaking this study; the second reflects a new purpose, and I shall speak of that one first.

Unlike the first two editions, the final one does not restrict itself to treatment of the scholarly debate, but also includes discussion of the surviving plays. I have chosen a procedure I would like to call "descriptive analysis." By means of a close reconstruction of dramatic action, I mean to show the plays' composition, structure, and inner dynamic.

It was not possible in the course of my analyses completely to avoid taking a stand on problems that have a fundamental bearing on the interpretation. Generally, however, I have separated the discussions of particular issues from the analyses, placing them last. In this respect I have preserved the book's original purpose.

Anyone aware of the extraordinary density and international breadth that the discussion of Greek tragedy has attained, especially in the last two decades, will understand that this undertaking posed serious difficulties. I have considered it particularly important to do justice to recent scholarship. The breadth of this continuing discussion is matched by its depth, and in recent years a number of outstanding studies have been produced by younger scholars.

To keep the bibliographical notes as concise as possible, I have adopted this procedure: authors' names—without given name or further information, or with a short title only—refer to the bibliography. An author is cited by initials and surname with the notice "op. cit." when the reference is to a previous note in which the literature on a given topic is gathered together. Such catchall notes occur especially at the beginning of the treatment of individual plays.

Lately we have often been cautioned not to concentrate too exclusively on the masterworks of ancient literature. If this caution is meant as a challenge to keep our horizons broad enough to take in all of ancient literature and its reception, it is to be embraced wholeheartedly. If, on the other hand, it is a suggestion that we move away from the areas of central importance, then—as far as Attic tragedy is concerned—we can only reply in the words of Goethe which I have chosen as my epigraph.

I have gladly followed the publisher's advice and added translations of Greek material; thus we hope to make the book accessible to readers who cannot follow the classical texts in the original.

I would like to express my deep thanks to Eugen Dönt and Walther Kraus for their labors in proofreading this work and for valuable references.

ALBIN LESKY

SELECTED ABBREVIATIONS

APF	*Archiv für Papyrusforschung und verwandte Gebiete*
AUMLA	*Journal of the Australian Universities Language and Literature Association*
CMG	*Corpus Medicorum Graecorum*, Leipzig and Berlin, 1908–65
DK	H. Diels-W. Kranz, *Die Fragmente der Vorsokratiker*, Berlin, 1934–37
DLZ	*Deutsche Literaturzeitung für Kritik der internationalen Wissenschaft*
FCG	A. Meineke, *Fragmenta Comicorum Graecorum*, 1839–57
FGrH	F. Jacoby, *Die Fragmente der griechischen Historiker*, Berlin and Leiden, 1923–
GGA	*Göttingische Gelehrte Anzeigen*
GGN	*Göttinger Gelehrte Nachrichten*
IG	*Inscriptiones Graecae*, Berlin, 1873–
LSJ	H. G. Liddell-R. Scott, *A Greek-English Lexicon*, 9th ed., revised by Sir H. Stuart Jones, Oxford, 1940
PMG	D. L. Page, *Poetae Melici Graeci*, Oxford, 1962
PSI	*Papiri Greci e Latini. Pubblicazioni della Società Italiana*
RE	A. Pauly-G. Wissowa, *Real-Encyclopädie der klassischen Altertumswissenschaft*, Stuttgart, 1893–
TrGF	A. Nauck, *Tragicorum Graecorum Fragmenta*, new ed. B. Snell, Hildesheim, 1964

1

PROBLEMS OF ORIGIN

A reader of the studies of H. Patzer, G. Else, and W. Burkert (published between 1962 and 1964), which attempt to solve the problems of the origin of tragedy, might well conclude, in view of the sweeping diversity of theories they represent, that solid ground is farther off now than ever. The most important task is to sketch out the problems clearly and to leave them open when we have to, not refraining from proposing our own solutions.[1]

In the first decade of our century, the field belonged chiefly to theoreticians who relied upon ethnological material and rejected Aristotle's statements completely. Descendants of this school are with us even today. In the second edition of his *History of Greek Religion*, Martin P. Nilsson still says: "The τραγῳδία takes its name from the singers clad in goat skins (hence the name τράγοι) who once sang the dirge of the god slain in goat form."[2] Like R. M. Dawkins[3] and A. J. B. Wace,[4] Nilsson wants to see the folk customs of modern Macedonia as a reminiscence of a presumed primal form of tragedy. With respect to the dirge, which plays a large role in these ethnological theories, we note appreciatively Patzer's remark that C. O. Müller had already viewed a Dionysian liturgy of this type as the nucleus of tragedy.[5]

Jane E. Harrison had developed the theory that Dionysos as well as the most important heroes of Greek mythology were variations on the pattern of the Year Daimon, who embodied the cycle of life in his death and rebirth.[6] Building on the ideas of Harrison and F. M. Cornford, G. Murray represented the position that tragedy had evolved out of spring rituals that had to do with the fortunes of this Year Daimon.[7] This hypothesis, which attempted to derive even the individual parts of developed tragedy from such dromena, met with thorough and well-founded opposition by Pickard-Cambridge.[8] Murray later conceded that he had assigned too central a place to the cult play of the God of the Annual Cycle, but continued to believe in its fundamental importance.[9] Recently T. B. L. Webster took up this theory and gave it a place in his revision of Pickard-Cambridge's book.[10]

As in the work of these scholars so, too, in Thomson's book on Aischylos, ritual stands in the foreground of explanation. He argues that the Dionysian thiasos was a secret association that with some changes preserved the structure and functions of the totemistic clan;[11] from the initiation rites of this clan customs emerged, which, proceeding from ritual to myth, gave rise to the story of the suffering of Dionysos, eventually providing the way to tragedy. Gaster's methods are connected with the English ethnological school. Citing Ugaritic, Hittite, Egyptian, and Hebrew texts, he argues that the dramatic forms grew out of an interaction of rituals and myths that revolve around the renewal and strengthening of life in the annual cycle.

In all this work the abundance of ethnological material cannot replace the missing links in the assumed connections. The application of matters attested elsewhere to the case of the Greeks in most cases lacks any tenable support, and the derivation of myth from ritual with this confidence arouses grave misgivings.[12] Above all, the ethnological approach has laid itself open to the objection that it has failed to do justice to Greek tragedy as a unique and thoroughly Hellenic creation. M. P. Nilsson, who himself often successfully turns ethnological material to account, has nevertheless warned: "The excesses of the ethnological approach become especially glaring when it is applied to higher and more complicated religious formations."[13] This point is no less true of literature.

Reservations with respect to ethnological methodology are necessary, but it would nonetheless be wrong to regard the material gathered in the works mentioned as worthless for our enquiry. We must simply assign to it its proper place. K. T. Preuss did so when he entitled his abundant evidence for dramatic nuclei in primitive cultures "Der Unterbau des Dramas" (The Substructure of Drama).[14] Greek tragedy and comedy both stand on such a substructure; and what we know of masked dances and daimon imitations at primitive levels of human culture refers to it. In dealing with Greek tragedy we will do well to separate its prehistory from its history, which was shaped by the personalities of the great poets. A scholar as versed in ethnology as in classical scholarship gave pointed expression to this separation when he said of the miracle of tragedy which arose uniquely in Athens: "This one fact alone is proof enough that we are dealing with a creation, not a development."[15]

In Greece as elsewhere the prehistory of both dramatic types leads into the realm of primitive dances, through which man sought to protect himself from daimons or to win the power of their blessing. E. Buschor has stressed the diversity of these dances and collected many of their appellations.[16] Above all, the foundation in dance gave Greek actors the mask, which they wore in every age of tragedy and comedy. Bieber has established (*Maske*, 2083) that it was also used by the chorus beyond any doubt (cf. H. Hommel, *N. Jahrb.* 1940, 282. 47).

In our field the notion of such masked dances primarily suggests satyrs, the ancient wood goblins, who form a natural link with numerous related conceptions among other peoples. We must also mention Dionysos, the satyrs' master, who was regarded as the mask god par excellence.[17] But we must not forget that the mask and the masked dance once ranged over a far wider realm than that of the later theater god. In *Maske*, Bieber gives the evidence for the cult of Artemis and Despoina, in which the animal dancers on the hem on the cult statue of Lykosura's robe clearly continue the tradition of Mycenean daimons with their animal masks.[18] These divinities are always associated with organic growth, and it is to the point to ask whether these dances were not once independent observances, just as the satyrs were originally independent from Dionysos. The ethnological parallels at any rate seem to support this view.

The work of K. Meuli gives a good introduction to such customs.[19] To be sure, the question remains whether the masks are to be interpreted so exclusively as the returning dead or whether, particularly in Greece, they should not rather suggest to us direct imitation of the daimons of nature.[20] Meuli helps us particularly well to realize that a primitive man does not don a mask as an ornament. Rather the mask transforms him, and in this transformation he experiences the uncanniness of those daimonic powers he ventures to represent. A gripping instance occurs when the "Stopfen" and "Perchten" tell of their supernumerary companion, who took part in their leaping but was no longer with them once they removed their masks. The daimon himself had been among them.[21] This is the phenomenon that Meuli, following Frobenius, calls "Ergriffenheit" (raptness). In this primeval phenomenon "are rooted the best and most productive properties of man, understanding and sympathy in the widest and deepest sense, and the true art of the drama, of the play."

Our interpretation of the mask as one of the original elements of drama may seem to run counter to the testimony of ancient sources, which name Thespis as the inventor of the dramatic mask.[22] This tradition has its origin in the ancients' wish to name an inventor for everything. I will return to this point when I discuss Thespis.

The theories examined thus far were all advanced under the assumption that Aristotelian theory should be done without. On the subject of Aristotle, opinion differs. But before we take up the central question of what exactly it is that he said and whether it is credible, let us cast our eye on some proposed explanations that may be loosely brought into connection with those already discussed.

First, there is the work of A. Dieterich, who, in a study published long ago, took a general threnos for the Athenian Feast of the Chytroi as his starting point, but considered that the artistic form of tragedy had been shaped by the influence of the Eleusinian dromena.[23] I mention this because I believe it to be of fundamental importance to keep distinct the world of the mysteries and that of the tragedies. In the latter it is a case of man's λόγον διδόναι (rendering an account) in his fundamentally exposed condition; as for the mysteries, their nature is defined if we recall Aristotle's dictum that we do not enter that realm to learn, but to submit.

In a brilliant attempt, Untersteiner strove to extend the discussion of the problem under consideration into the earliest periods of Greek prehistory.[24] In these early eras he does not find definite dramatic forms, but he does locate the spiritual givens that led to a tragic world view. He finds these in the tension between the heterogeneous elements that gave rise to Hellenism, in the confrontation between the new Indo-Germanic immigrants and the Mediterranean culture of the native inhabitants. This makes a good beginning; and Weber (213) has drawn on this rich tension extensively to clarify the development of tragedy. But of course any attempt to derive particular elements of fully developed tragedy from this early age necessarily results in uncertain speculation. Ancient Aegean features of the Dionysian remain hypothetical, and the Indo-European relatives of the satyrs, such as fauns, "Waldfänke," gente selvatica, and the skougman, make a clear case against these fellows' pre-Greek origin. The great pre-Greek mother-goddess and her paredros certainly exerted a strong influence on Greek religion and myth, but this source determines neither the story of Agamemnon and Klytaimestra nor a series of other Greek tragic materials. The method is obviously overtaxed when Untersteiner tries to use it to reconstruct the *Heraklides* and *Philoktetes* of Aischylos.[25]

The attempt of Schreckenberg proceeds from a highly speculative history of the word δρᾶν (to do), which proposes as its root meaning an "action of the χεῖρες (hands)," and, interpreting the word in terms of mime and dance, comes to the definition of δρᾶμα as an "imitative presentation based on body movement."[26] We should think twice before viewing the original tragedy as no more than a pantomime dance. Words, music, and dance have always been closely connected, as A. Marjorie Dale so beautifully explained at her inaugural lecture at Birkbeck College in London in 1960.

Among the many variations in the treatment of these problems, two principal lines can be distinguished; Lindsay combines them. In the first and larger part of his book he shows himself a follower of Jane Harrison, Cornford, and Cook, boldly drawing connections from shamanism and rites of initiation to the religion of the Greeks; but all the same, he follows Aristotle on the question of origin. The disparity between the two parts of his book proves once more how problematic it is directly to relate the folkloristic prehistory of drama to what is historically manifest.

Every step beyond the general fundamentals is determined by reference to what Aristotle says in the *Poetics* (1449a):[27]

γενομένη δ᾽ οὖν ἀπ᾽ ἀρχῆς αὐτοσχεδιαστικῆς—καὶ αὐτὴ καὶ ἡ κωμῳδία, καὶ ἡ μὲν ἀπὸ τῶν ἐξαρχόντων τὸν διθύραμβον, ἡ δὲ ἀπὸ τῶν τὰ φαλλικὰ ἃ ἔτι καὶ νῦν ἐν πολλαῖς τῶν πόλεων διαμένει νομιζόμενα—κατὰ μικρὸν ηὐξήθη προαγόντων ὅσον ἐγίγνετο φανερὸν αὐτῆς· καὶ πολλὰς μεταβολὰς μεταβαλοῦσα ἡ τραγῳδία ἐπαύσατο, ἐπεὶ ἔσχε τὴν αὑτῆς φύσιν. καὶ τό τε τῶν ὑποκριτῶν πλῆθος ἐξ ἑνὸς εἰς δύο πρῶτος Αἰσχύλος ἤγαγε καὶ τὰ τοῦ χοροῦ ἠλάττωσε καὶ τὸν λόγον πρωταγωνιστεῖν παρεσκεύασεν· τρεῖς δὲ καὶ σκηνογραφίαν Σοφοκλῆς. ἔτι δὲ τὸ μέγεθος· ἐκ μικρῶν μύθων καὶ λέξεως γελοίας διὰ τὸ ἐκ σατυρικοῦ μεταβαλεῖν ὀψὲ ἀπεσεμνύνθη, τό τε μέτρον ἐκ τετραμέτρου ἰαμβεῖον ἐγένετο. τὸ μὲν γὰρ πρῶτον τετραμέτρῳ ἐχρῶντο διὰ τὸ σατυρικὴν καὶ ὀρχηστικωτέραν εἶναι τὴν ποίησιν, λέξεως δὲ γενομένης αὐτὴ ἡ φύσις τὸ οἰκεῖον μέτρον εὗρε· μάλιστα γὰρ λεκτικὸν τῶν μέτρων τὸ ἰαμβεῖόν ἐστιν . . . ἔτι δὲ ἐπεισοδίων πλήθη. καὶ τὰ ἄλλ᾽ ὡς ἕκαστα κοσμηθῆναι λέγεται ἔστω ἡμῖν εἰρημένα· πολὺ γὰρ ἂν ἴσως ἔργον εἴη διεξιέναι καθ᾽ ἕκαστον.[28]

Since these sentences, brief as they are, nevertheless give us our most concrete evidence on the origin of tragedy, their credibility is a matter of prime importance. Here the fragmentation of opinion becomes drastically evident. Obviously the proponents of the ethnological method, just surveyed, must reject Aristotle as untrustworthy. Thus M. P. Nilsson's attitude has remained unswervingly negative. But the detractors of Aristotle's testimony are by no means limited to this one circle. For instance: Schmid mocks in his *Literaturgeschichte* orthodox Aristotelians (2. 775), R. Cantarella in all his remarks on this question has remained adamant in his rejection of Aristotle,[29] and Pickard-Cambridge has assumed a similar position in his book, which is the most careful collection of primary sources for our subject; but it is highly significant that in the second edition of this work (95) T. B. L. Webster makes a much more cautious judgment. When at the end of this chapter we turn to the recent studies of Patzer, Else, and Burkert, we will find there too either total rejection or else a very skeptical appraisal of the passage from Aristotle.

The adversary front is formed by the scholars who follow the interpretation of Wilamowitz, already found in his study of *Herakles*, according full authority to Aristotle's remarks; among these are Kranz, Pohlenz, and Ziegler, and I myself agree with them. H. Koller takes off from Aristotle but ends in conjecture: from the reading of Parisinus ἀπ᾽ ἀρχῆς αὐτοσχεδιαστικῆς (from an origin in improvisational performances) he comes to assume the existence of a stichic prooimion performed by a bard as the introduction to a dithyramb.[30] More recent authors who try to fit Aristotle into their own hypotheses include Untersteiner and Lindsay. In K. Kerényi's ingenious attempt to use the genesis of Italian opera to shed light on our problem he writes: "This is the Greek 'tragédie avant la tragédie' that Aristotle hints at in his sketch; for us, as for him, it forms the concrete basis for a history of the birth of tragedy."[31]

This is one of the cases where we serve scholarship better simply by acknowledging its limitations than by self-confidently proclaiming our personal opinions. As for the question whether Aristotle is giving facts or hypotheses, there is no way to find conclusive evidence. This does not mean that we should not try to achieve as high a degree of probability as we can. First, we must point out that if Aristotle is reporting unfounded hypotheses here, it would contradict everything we know of his working methods in his historical studies. The range and type of his sources on the question of tragedy can no longer be determined, but that does not mean they never existed. The sophists began early to investigate literary forms and certainly must also have posed the question of the origins of tragedy. Kranz has gone so far as to speak of an abundance of theoretical and literary-historical material preceding the *Poetics*. That Aristotle was only about two centuries removed from the processes under discussion, whereas we are more than two millennia from them may seem to some a rather naïve observation, but it is not therefore unimportant. I follow A. Rostagni, who presumes Aristotle to have devoted the same care to the preliminary work on the *Poetics* as he is known to have for the *Politics*.[32] That the notes in the *Poetics* are short and sketchy is because they were intended as the speaker's own lecture notes. But they stem from much richer knowledge, as Aristotle clearly lets us know when he breaks off chapter 5 (1449a 29) saying it would lead too far afield to pursue every detail. As Bywater has already emphasized,[33] there is a passage of special significance in which Aristotle emphasizes his imperfect knowledge of the beginnings of comedy and expressly contrasts it with the evidence for tragedy: αἱ μὲν οὖν τῆς τραγῳδίας με-ταβάσεις καὶ δι᾽ ὧν ἐγένοντο οὐ λελήθασιν (The stages of development in tragedy and whence they arose are not unknown). To doubt him is to accuse him of making many a quite unsupported remark. We would have to do that, nevertheless, if it were proven that his claims contradicted his own or other available data. Therefore the decisive question is whether the *Poetics* allows us to construct a consistent picture that is also supported by other data. First we shall examine the individual elements and then inquire how we may connect them meaningfully.

Earlier scholars caused themselves unnecessary trouble with the phrase ἀπὸ τῶν ἐξαρχόντων τὸν διθύραμβον (from the leaders of the dithyramb). F. Bradac spread confusion by collecting evidence for restricted uses of the verb.[34] Kranz thought of the ἐξάρχοντες (leaders) as the singers of the chorus; Untersteiner followed the suggestion of Lammer and took the questionable phrase to refer to a double chorus. But Aristotle, with the simplicity of his technical terminology, would not have chosen the word if he had not wanted to suggest the chorus leader. Ziegler (1907 f.; 1944, 25) collected Homeric and other evidence that confirms this usage. Patzer (90. 6) shows that the point is now beyond doubt. Apparently Aristotle saw in the relationship of the chorus leader to the chorus a nucleus of the dramatic encounter; unlike Ziegler (1908), however, I do not equate the ἐξάρχων with the first actor in order to explain away Aristotle's silence on this technical innovation. The speaking actor, as we will see, entered from the outside.

In the *Poetics*, the dithyramb is named as one of the roots of tragedy. Every attempt to explain the name of this old cult song has failed; the word was probably borrowed from pre-Greek times.[35] The song is inseparable from the cult of Dionysos. When Archilochos boasts (77D) that he knows how to strike up the dithyramb, the beautiful song of lord Dionysos, whenever wine overwhelms his senses, we already recognize the chorus leader before the chorus. The song is also associated with the gift of Bakchos in the spirited assertion of Epicharmos that with water there can be no dithyramb. Pindar's phrase (*Ol*. 13. 19) βοηλάτης διθύραμβος (the cattle-driving dithyramb) reveals that it was sung as a cult song at animal sacrifice. A vase fragment from the heyday of the red-figured style illustrates the inner connection of the song with Dionysos.[36] This piece, which will interest us later, depicts a silenus playing a lyre, under the inscription ΔΙΘΥΡΑΜΦΟΣ. This Dionysian song, once perhaps no more than cultic cries, was reformed and developed by Arion, as we shall discuss later.

The further history of the dithyramb poses difficult questions. The musical reforms of Lasos of Hermione furthered the form's artistic development under Hipparchos, and the newly founded democracy accepted the dithyramb agon into the program of the Great Dionysia of 509 or 508.[37] The performance was the concern of the κύκλιοι χοροί (choruses dancing in a circle), fifty boys or men who formed a circle in the orchestra around the altar and flute player.

The Alexandrians possessed two books of *Dithyrambs* by Pindar, fragments of which have come down to us. Some of them bore titles (fr. 70b Sn.) that cannot be confidently attributed to the poet himself. These poems, composed antistrophically, treat various stories of gods and heroes, but reveal, especially at the outset, a connection to Dionysos. A special question arises from the *Suda* article on Pindar, which numbers δράματα τραγικά ιζ' (seventeen tragic dramas) among his works. The figure can easily be explained by the erroneous repetition of the sum of all Pindar books given earlier. Yet the questionable phrase has often been taken as a reference to the *Dithyrambs*. Since there is no support for the theory that we are dealing with an ancient anthology title, the expression, which occurs again for Simonides (schol. Aristoph. *Vesp.* 1410; *Suda* s.v.), can be more easily explained by sloppy Byzantine usage. Pickard-Cambridge too (108) considers this possible, but does not rule out that Simonides may have produced genuine tragedies. The author of the *Suda* article on Pindar is presumably responsible for no small confusion, having mentioned the dithyrambs previously in the Pindar catalogue, and thus apparently counting the same poems twice. And in the face of the difficult questions that are connected with τραγικὸς τρόπος (tragic mode) of Arion and the τραγικοὶ χοροί (tragic choruses) in Sikyon (see below) we cannot yet close the debate over the strange phrase in the *Suda*.

The Alexandrians counted six of the poems of Bakchylides as dithyrambs. They treat various myths, have titles, and show only a very occasional connection with the Dionysian element. This intrusion of non-Dionysian elements into a Dionysian art form, already evident in Pindar, is noteworthy, since we must assume that similar processes took place in the development of tragedy.

The dithyramb *Theseus* (18) offers, without preparatory introduction, four strophes of conversation between Aigeus and an undesignated interlocutor, most likely a chorus of Athenian citizens, on the subject of Theseus's arrival, which is upsetting everybody. Not surprisingly, when the poem became known (the Bakchylides papyri came to the British Museum in 1896), many greeted it as the missing link between dithyramb and tragedy: the dithyrambic chorus in encounter with the chorus leader was thought to correspond to Aristotle's descriptions. Ziegler (1909, 1961) remained confident, but we must consider, as Kranz (32) and Schmid (1. 534) do, that the *Theseus* of Bakchylides falls in the time of developed tragedy and could thus have been influenced by it. A certain dialogue element that belonged to the dithyramb from its beginning in its juxtaposition of the chorus leader and the chorus may, of course, also have played its part.

The second half of the fifth century sees the stormy development of the new Attic dithyramb, which released the Dionysian element from the norms of the classical form and secularized the ancient cult song.[38]

Aristotle mentions a second root of tragedy, which we now turn to without first concerning ourselves with its connection to the earlier remarks.

In our passage of the *Poetics*, the two phrases διὰ τὸ ἐκ σατυρικοῦ μεταβαλεῖν (since it was transformed out of the satyric) and διὰ τὸ σατυρικὴν καὶ ὀρχηστικωτέραν εἶναι τὴν ποίησιν (because the poetry was satyric and more suited to the dance) show unmistakably that Aristotle looked on the σατυρικόν as a preliminary stage for the development of tragedy, a view that recurs in the Peripatetic Chamaileon (fr. 38W). Here especially the fronts are divided. Schmid (2. 26, 42) speaks of an unfruitful and tortured derivation attempt; H. van Hoorn believes that the satyr play and tragedy developed separately and were unified only in 501;[39] Pickard-Cambridge was opposed to Aristotle, as we have already seen, while Webster takes the opposite position in his revision of his book. More recently Else, Patzer, and Burkert have radically rejected the testimony of Aristotle. Of course the scholars whom we earlier termed his supporters follow him in this point also. We add to them Lindsay and Guggisberg.

Now we believe here that we can go beyond mere speculation and confirm the evidence of Aristotle. None of his opponents could explain the close bond between the satyr play and tragedy, which is generic and points to genetic connections.[40] The sharp separation of tragedy and comedy stands in eloquent contrast to this. This is a result of what we might term the genre constraints. At the end of Plato's *Symposion*, Sokrates has a difficult time wresting the admission from Agathon and Aristophanes that the tragic poet must also be capable of writing comedies. Leukippos (DK A 9) expressed the general view of the essential difference of the tragic and comic play in this comment: "The same letters can form such different things as tragedy and comedy." Flickinger (202), who emphasizes a sharp line of separation, quotes Dryden: "The sock and buskin were not worn by the same poet."[41] This stands in clear contrast to the fact that the satyr plays and tragedies regularly have as their authors the same poets: We are simply speaking of one and the same genre. At least worthy of mention in this context is a vase painting showing the personified Tragodia being awakened by satyrs.[42]

Of course we must not think of the developed satyr play when speaking of the σατυρικόν of the *Poetics*, but rather of a form of choral performance by satyrs with dramatic overtones.[43]

In the rejection of Aristotle's evidence two arguments were decisive: the ancient assertion that Pratinas was the originator of the satyr play, and the thought that the process designated by ἀποσεμνύνεσθαι (to be formed with sublimity) could never have developed the playful burlesque into high tragedy.

Pratinas is called the creator of the satyr play in the *Suda*, as well as in two Hellenistic epigrams of Dioskorides.[44] *Anth. Pal.* VII 37 introduces a satyr wearing a purple garment and holding a tragic mask. When he announces that Sophokles has ennobled him, this can only refer to the Peripatetic interpretation of the development of the satyr play into tragedy. But that this satyr emphasizes his coming from Phleius, as another (*Anth. Pal.* VII 707) also names this place as the homeland of his brothers, is certainly a reference to Pratinas and may be an allusion to the theory that he was the creator of the satyr play. We cannot expect too much consistency from Dioskorides in these questions. Finally, in the pseudo-Acronian scholia on Horace, there is the conjecture of Fabricius (*Ars Poet.* 216), who inserts "Pratinae" instead of "Cratini" for the originator of the satyr play, which Patzer (23. 5), probably rightly, considers unavoidable.

The evidence is by no means copious, but it suffices to prove that a viewpoint existed in antiquity which contradicted the picture of the development offered in the *Poetics*. Two mutually exclusive ancient interpretations of the origin of tragedy diverge here. M. Pohlenz has correctly characterized and compared these in an investigation whose results one can ill afford to neglect.[45] The first is the Peripatetic interpretation offered in the *Poetics*, which can also be confirmed by Photios's explanation of the proverb οὐδὲν πρὸς τὸν Διόνυσον (see below), the *Suda*, Apostolios (13, 42), and by Chamaileon's work on Thespis (38W; see below). It is the same Peripatetic theory that drew the conclusion for the explanation of the name τραγῳδία from the priority of the satyr play and interpreted it as "goat song." More will be said presently on this and the connected claims of the Peloponnesians to certain preliminary stages of tragedy.

The second theory is rooted in the Attic reaction against the Doric claims, as is clearly expressed in the pseudo-Platonic *Minos* (321a):

ἡ δὲ τραγῳδία ἐστὶ παλαιὸν ἐνθάδε, οὐχ ὡς οἴονται ἀπὸ Θέσπιδος ἀρξαμένη οὐδ᾽ ἀπὸ Φρυνίχου, ἀλλ᾽ εἰ ἐθέλεις ἐννοῆσαι, πάνυ παλαιὸν αὐτὸ εὑρήσεις ὂν τῆσδε τῆς πόλεως εὕρημα.[46]

It may be assumed that references were made to old Attic village custom in connection with this view; in any case the Alexandrians, in their interest in the bucolic, did this often enough. The acceptance of Pratinas of Phleius as the creator of the satyr play must have been decisive for their position against Aristotle. The satyr play then stood not at the beginning but at the end of the development: tragedy had arisen from rural Attic custom, as has been reported for Ikaria, and thus could not be the "goat song." In variations that differ only slightly, a history of the development was given on this basis. The word τραγῳδία was derived from rural festivals at which the participants sang and danced around a prize goat.[47] This theory was connected with another, according to which such peasant customs were the common roots for all drama: tragedy, comedy, and satyr play. Eratosthenes may have introduced this view first in his work *On Old Comedy* and then in the poem *Erigone*, which is rich in explanations. From this work we possess the verse "Ἰκαριοῖ, τόθι πρῶτα περὶ τράγον ὠρχήσαντο" (Ikaria, where they first danced around the goat).[48] Meuli, who even speaks of a theory of Eratosthenes, has collected in the first excursus of his study the passages in which this view occurs, mostly in connection with τρυγῳδία as the designation of this primitive dramatic nucleus. In the process, this parodistic word for comedy derived from τρύξ = yeast has achieved undeserved honor. K. Meuli has also shown well in Vergil, *Georg.* (II 380 ff.) how far this theory of rural Attic Ur-drama influenced the poetry of the Romans.

The explanation of the name of tragedy as deriving from the goat as victory prize is offered by the *Marmor Parium* (ep. 43[49]), recorded in 264/263. Cantarella tried to contest with Pohlenz that this monument could already take into account a Hellenistic theory.[50] The learned character of the chronicle does not make this clear; one could perhaps think of the rudiments of the Alexandrian theory in Attic local patriotism. The goat prize hypothesis is further attested[51] by an epigram of Dioskorides (*Anth. Pal.* VII 410), by Zenobius (5. 40) in the explanation of the proverb οὐδὲν πρὸς τὸν Διόνυσον (nothing to do with Dionysos), and by an especially select witness, Horace (*Ars Poet.* 220). Most of these last named sources (*Marmor Parium*, Dioskorides, and Horace) make Thespis the poet who was first to compete for the goat prize in the original tragic agon. Dioskorides also connects Thespis (*Anth. Pal.* VII 411) with the jocular activity in the rural forest areas; Horace does not mention his name in the given passage, but he appears in 275 ff. as the creator of tragedy, while the immortal Thespis cart came from the σκώμματα ἐκ τῶν ἁμαξῶν (gibes from the wagons) of Attic spring festivals. We shall see later, when we come to speak of the achievements of Thespis, that the Peripatetic school placed the poet later in their history of the development. Long ago Tièche contrasted the "Ikarian clown" to Thespis, who appears in sources of another kind as the founder of tragedy through rather definite achievements.[52] Patzer (37) has excellently termed the Alexandrian theory a disjointed pastiche of disparate elements that are in themselves historical but whose connection remains conjectural. That our paths nonetheless diverge in the judgment of the Peripatetic school will be seen later.

Despite all the variations, this theory produces an essentially unified picture in that it places the creation of the satyr play by Pratinas chronologically after the establishment of tragedy; even in Horace (*Ars Poet.* 221) the satyr play still appears clearly as the later form. The question of how the tradition of Pratinas as its creator came about is, according to Pohlenz, easily answered by the Aristotelian plan of development. Tragedy not only grew out of the satyric, it in fact drove the latter progressively out of the orchestra. The phrase οὐδὲν πρὸς τὸν Διόνυσον, which we have seen often before, indicates a development that must be connected with such processes. A reaction necessarily set in which refused to dispense with the old games of Dionysos's companions. Its leader was particularly Pratinas from Doric Phleius, the opponent of Phrynichos, who was heavily influenced by the Ionian style. Buschor and Brommer have shown how from about 520 onward vase-paintings frequently appear which are obviously influenced by the orchestra. This is clearly connected with the interpretation discussed here of a Renaissance of the satyrs initiated by Pratinas. One can well imagine that Pratinas embellished the play in a way that facilitated his being named its inventor.

The sixteen verses that Athenaios (14. 617B) quotes from a hyporchema of Pratinas have played a continuing role in this question.[53] With ecstatic rhythms, a satyr chorus rushes into the orchestra, lays exclusive claim to the correct method of honoring Bromios, and attacks the flute, which is trying to suppress the correct old song with its artifices. This splendid piece opens up many questions. To ascribe it to a satyr play, as many interpreters have done, remains a probable solution.[54] One must then, of course, reckon with an extremely vague use of the term *hyporchema* in Athenaios, which offers, however, no important difficulty.[55] A. M. Dale, to be sure, thought of a poem independent from any satyr play,[56] and Webster took up the conjecture of Wilamowitz that the work was a dithyramb.[57]

A further difficulty concerns the opponent of this riotous satyr chorus. One thing is certain: the chorus considers its song the correct service to the lord Dionysos as opposed to the flute, which is made contemptible. Does this mean that the chorus turns against its own flute player, or against another chorus that performs with excessively loud flute sounds? The first is conceivable if, following A. M. Dale and H. Patzer (130. 2), we take the χορεύματα (dances) in verse 1 as a reference to the flute sound, which the use of χορεύει (it dances) for the flute in verse 7 does not quite prove but certainly makes possible. On the other hand the chorus in the final verse ⟨ἀλλ'⟩ ἄκουε τὰν ἐμὰν Δώριον χορείαν (but listen to my Doric dancing-song) expressly contrasts its singing and dancing to τάδε τὰ χορεύματα in verse 1, which it combats as hubris at the thymele of Dionysos. Thus the assumption of a second chorus is more probable. It is, however, completely impossible to fit this hyporchema into the literary disputes of the time. That it concerns a protest against the rising importance of accompanying music in the developing tragedy is possible but cannot be proved.

The assumption would find strong support if we could see an allusion to the name of Phrynichos in verse 11: παῖε τὸν φρυνεοῦ ποικίλου πνοὰν ἔχοντα (strike the flute that has the voice of the spotted toad), a hypothesis often repeated since the Athenaios translation of Delecampius (1583; on 14. 617E). But this remains conjecture, and may, of course, exist as such, despite the vigorous attempt of E. Roos to refute it.[58] The idea offered by Buschor (85) and Roos, that the opponent of the flute could be a chorus playing the lyre, remains unfounded. The vase-paintings of lyre-playing satyrs cited by both scholars cannot have any reference to the hyporchema.

That these verses are connected with the processes that led to the modification of the old satyrikon, as Pohlenz thought, remains a vague possibility, which does not of course speak against his interpretation of the note that Pratinas created the satyr play. Lloyd-Jones, in his important study,[59] also considers this interpretation "possible" but places next to it the other explanation, easily reconcilable with the picture developed here, that perhaps Pratinas appears as the creator of the satyr play simply because he was the oldest representative of this dramatic form whose name could be determined.

The second objection to Aristotle denies the possibility of the process designated by him as ἀποσεμνύνεσθαι (to be formed with sublimity). According to this view, a path from the bawdy jests of the satyrs to the gravity of the tragic is unthinkable. Patzer, especially, maintains this opinion. We follow him in this question only in that we also consider misguided the attempts to discover traces of the original γελοῖον (comic) in developed tragedy.[60] That the process described by Aristotle was fully complete by the year 472 B.C., the date of the oldest of our preserved tragedies, does not speak against its historicity. Patzer denies its possibility in his attempt to discover the gravity and religious depth of the tragic in its earliest known origins, an extraordinary study considering the fragmentary evidence.[61] These are fundamental claims, but parallels do exist that document processes of this sort. The most obvious example is the Japanese No drama, which with its serious and often melancholy content grew out of the Dengaku, a form of vegetation rite, and the Sarugaku, a celebration of the temple cult.[62] Both forms were improvisational and jocular at first. Of course no one would wish to prove the correctness of the process described by Aristotle on this ground, but such parallels do speak for its possibility.

If we thus have no occasion to doubt Aristotle's information about the satyrikon as a preliminary stage of tragedy, the same is true of his remark that in the course of tragedy's development iambics replaced the trochaics, which were better suited for the satyric and dancing. It would certainly be too confining to characterize the trochaic measure from this context alone, and certainly it too can raise the tone to the sublime and solemn, but excitement and foot movement do lie in its nature and supplied its very name.[63]

Out of the questions discussed here arises the problem of the meaning of the word τραγῳδία. Of the numerous and partly hybrid attempts at explanation, only two are worthy of serious consideration.[64] Even the interpretation that tragedy was named from a male chorus that wore goat skins can be now put aside along with the extremely folkloristic hypotheses from which it arose and which we discussed earlier.

Still to consider is the "song of goats" or the "song at the goat sacrifice" and the variation "song for the goat prize." The second possibility receives support primarily from those scholars who do not follow Aristotle.[65] But whoever, with Pohlenz, recognizes the position of this interpretation within a secondary Hellenistic speculation that is transparent in its origins, and believes further on the basis of the *Poetics* that the σατυρικόν (the satyric) was a decisive preliminary stage of tragedy, comes necessarily to the view initiated by Welcker and often repeated by Wilamowitz,[66] that τραγῳδία is the "song of goats." Burkert recently has tried to prove this explanation linguistically impossible. But although he was able to correct, with great linguistic skill, details in the argumentation of Kalinka (31) and Patzer (131), the essentials of the case remain valid. To construe the first part of the word τραγῳδία as the singing subject cannot be ruled out, as the examples of μονῳδία (song for a soloist) and κωμῳδία (song of a komos) show. But then κωμῳδοί are not "singers on the occasion of the komos," as Burkert translates, but members of the singing κῶμος. Patzer remarks rightly (131): "It must be admitted that there are no strict formal parallels for the meaning 'to sing disguised as goats,' but there are even fewer for 'singer for the goat prize' or alternatively, 'for the goat sacrifice.'" The late-attested form, ἀρνῳδός, "singer for the lamb prize" is "formed like τραγῳδός" (thus old Pape), that is, in imitation of the latter word, which was construed as a song for the goat prize according to Hellenistic or perhaps already Attic theory.

We are by no means finished with the difficulties involved in this interpretation. If tragedy is the song of goats, and if we follow Aristotle in accepting the satyr play as a preliminary stage of tragedy, then the satyrs must be the goats referred to in the name. But we know since Furtwängler that the goat attributes of Hellenistic satyrs modeled on Pan must be excluded from the debate.[67] The primary sources of the sixth and fifth centuries show us these creatures with features which, in part (like the powerful tail), are derived from horses.

An escape from these difficulties has been sought along three lines. The most popular leads to the Peloponnesus. Here a terminological note is necessary. Brommer (*Satyroi*, 2; *Phil.*, 225) has recently shown, as the articles by Kuhnert and Hartmann proposed, that the terms *silene* and *satyr*, from the archaic period to the Hellenistic, were in use interchangeably for the same creature with equine attributes. But we cannot follow Brommer in his attempt to prove other meanings for σάτυρος and thus exclude the word from technical linguistic usage. There is also nothing to show that the good-for-nothing satyrs, who in Hesiod (fr. 198) belong, with the nymphs and curetes, to the descendants of Phoroneus, were different from those who cavort with the nymphs of Ida in the *Homeric Hymn to Aphrodite* (262). These forest spirits belong to the same ancient Indo-European stock as nymphs and naiads. In this "lesser" mythology, much more of this traditional material has been preserved than in that of the gods, although we cannot rule out contamination by Aegean sources.[68] That silenes and satyrs are identical in the dramas known to us is sufficiently indicated by the circumstance that the satyr chorus consists of children of the silene Pappos, and Pausanias notes (1. 23. 5): τοὺς γὰρ ἡλικίᾳ τῶν Σατύρων προήκοντας ὀνομάζουσι Σιληνούς. (The satyrs already advanced in age are called silenes.)

This leads to another attempt to solve the problem of the "song of the goats." Silenes and satyrs may actually have been different types of daimons at one time, and since the earliest evidence concerning satyrs leads to the Peloponnesus (Hartmann, 50), it was tempting to separate the silenes, as Ionic horse creatures, from the Doric satyrs, who supposedly represented the long-sought-after goats. This was Wilamowitz's view in *Glaube der Hellenen* (1. 199); Ziegler (1919) considers irrefutable the case for Peloponnesian goat daimons from which the goat form of the satyrs was developed in Hellenistic times; and Pohlenz too (2. 12) takes a very firm stand in favor of this separation.

A bronze group, found at Petrovinum in Methydrion and published in 1911, has played an important role in deliberations of this sort.[69] It represents in miniature four joined, standing figures, the stumps of their arms outstretched for a round-dance. Latterman had spoken of ramlike creatures, but then Brommer's thesis of dancing goats, daimons, or disguised humans prevailed. This view is found, among other places, in the first edition of this book (24). Now, however, R. Hampe, on the basis of our expanded knowledge of such pieces, has shown with striking parallels that the group is in all probability a primitive rendition of dancing men.[70] And if they were goats, they would now be Pans. The plural use is attested by Kuhnert (522), following Reisch. The same is true of the lead figures from Sparta, which do actually represent goats and are important for the history of the Pan cult. They cannot be taken for a chorus of goat dancers and must be held separate from the history of tragedy. The explanation of the "goat song" from Peloponnesian goat satyrs cannot be decisively refuted, given our present knowledge, but neither can it be proved, despite the tenacity with which the theory has been repeated.

Another attempt is now merely one more chapter in the history of the problem. In his appendix to Bethe's *Prolegomena zur Geschichte des Theaters* (1896), G. Körte was the first to refer to the choral dancers on the Pandora krater of the British Museum as goat-like satyrs who could solve the riddle of tragedy's name.[71] But E. Reisch soon put an end to this speculation.[72] The tradition of the satyr-silene form is fixed so rigidly in the fifth century that goat satyrs cannot be introduced here. They must be Pans or less probably figures from a comedy such as the Αἰγές (*Goats*) of Eupolis.

A third path was followed by those who wished to prove the identification of the choral dancers as goats from three passages of preserved satyr plays. Thus Ziegler (1921), with erroneous reference to the Pandora vase, and Pohlenz (2. 8). The three passages demand separate interpretations. The complaint of the satyr chorus in the *Kyklops* (79) that it must serve the monster δοῦλος ἀλαίνων σὺν τᾷδε τράγου χλαίνᾳ μελέᾳ (as a wandering slave with the black cloak of a goat) refers to the fact that the satyrs are shepherds in this play and wear as their garment a simple goat skin.

Nor can the existence of goat satyrs be derived from the verses of the *Ichneutai*, in which Kyllene reproaches the satyr chorus: ἀλλ' αἰὲν εἶ σὺ παῖς· νέος γὰρ ὢν ἀνέρ/ πώγωνι θάλλων ὡς τράγος κνηκῷ χλιδᾷς.[73] That the satyrs are compared to goats shows that they are not here perceived as such. There remains the fragment attributed with relative certainty to the *Prometheus Pyrkaios* of Aischylos (fr. 207N =

455M). The context (Plut. *Mor.* 86c) tells us that a satyr wishes to embrace and kiss the newly brought fire. But Prometheus warns him: τράγος γένειον ἄρα πενθήσεις σύ γε (Goat, you will burn your beard). It was an artifice to think here of an otherwise unattested proverb.[74] Ziegler's interpretation is correct: Goat that you are, you will feel it on your beard. Τράγος must be understood as a brachylogy for τράγος ὤν.[75] If one grasps the *Prometheus* passage in this way, then it comes down to a comparison in which, in true Aischylean style, the compared objects merge into one: You with your beard and lust are a real goat! It is clear that the satyrs on stage cannot simply be proved to be goats in this way. Yet we would like to point out that their nature and behavior recall those of goats so vividly that such a mode of expression is possible.

Here we must include the gloss of Hesychios: τράγους· σατύρους διὰ τὸ τράγων ὦτα ἔχειν (Goats: the satyrs, because they have goat ears). The explanation is invalid, since it presumes the Hellenistic form of satyr, but Burkert (90. 5) has rightly emphasized the accusative, which points to a quotation as the source for the word.

No slight confusion concerning the satyr problem was caused by a theory that still exerts a strong influence (e.g. in Patzer, 115). Its originator, G. Löschke, wanted to apply the term *satyr* to those dancers with fleshy buttocks and bellies who often appear on vases from the late seventh century to the middle third of the sixth.[76] The best-known example is the vase in the Louvre that depicts comic scenes involving wine thieves.[77] The inscriptions reveal that the participants and dancers represent daimons. At the time, Löschke could claim the support of an etymology that connected σάτυρος and *satur* and interpreted the word as the designation for Dionysian daimons of plenty. This explanation has long been abandoned, but Brommer and Buschor (*Satyroi*, 21; *Phil.*, 227) have revived the argument that these obese figures could be called satyrs. Buschor simply equates the two and develops a theory that almost totally humanized young satyrs (in Buschor's sense of the word) served the annunciation of myth, while grotesque choruses of horse-formed silenes developed the satyr play. Now it is certain that these obese figures belong to a group of daimons which, in their behavior and in their personal relationship to fertility, exhibit many similarities to the satyrs, but we have not the slightest shred of evidence for calling them satyrs. They are in fact more closely connected with comedy, as H. Herter has rightly emphasized in his important work on the origins of comedy.[78]

For the daimons with horses' tails, the name satyr has been attested in at least one case, since the ΣΑΤΡΥΒΣ on a red-figured bowl in Würzburg is perhaps best construed (as Webster did) as an error for Satyros.[79] Brommer (*Phil.*, 223) mentions the fragment of a Kabeiric vase in Athens (photo of the Germ. Arch. Inst. of Athens KAB 350) that seems to depict a youthful silene; from the inscription, the letters ΣΑΤΥ . . . are legible.

Also lacking a firm basis is Untersteiner's attempt to avoid all difficulty by the projection of the problem into pre-Greek times. The goats of Tragodia supposedly refer to an ancient cult community that arose from the animals of a πότνιος τράγων (master of goats). This πότνιος was associated as paredros with a πότνια τράγων (mistress of goats), a variation of the great Aegean mother deity. It was an act of total desperation when A. von Blumenthal claimed that τράγος was a non-Greek (perhaps Thracian) homonym, whose meaning was purportedly close to κῶμος.[80]

It is important to note that our problem already existed in antiquity in the Peripatetic school. Actually it could be assumed that a doctrine that counted the satyr play among the early forms of tragedy would necessarily find in its name the satyrs understood as goats. We have in fact a source that not only confirms this, but also shows how one tried to deal with the difficulties involved in trying to interpret the satyrs as goats. The *Etymologicum Magnum* has, under the entry τραγῳδία, amid notes based on the Hellenistic theory of the "song for the goat-prize" and other quite misguided speculations on the name, the following important paragraph:

ἢ ὅτι τὰ πολλὰ οἱ χοροὶ ἐκ σατύρων ουνίσταντο· οὓς ἐκάλουν τράγους σκώπτοντες ἢ διὰ τὴν τοῦ σώματος δασύτητα ἢ διὰ τὴν περὶ τὰ ἀφροδίσια σπουδήν. τοιοῦτον γὰρ τὸ ζῷον. ἢ ὅτι οἱ χορευταὶ τὰς κόμας ἀνέπλεκον σχῆμα τράγων μιμούμενοι.[81]

Here we have the question posed in its entirety. Tragedy is understood as goat-song, and the goats are to be seen in the satyrs. But the satyrs, with all their attributes, are not simply goats; this is also clear from the passage, and thus a reason is sought for this name. The explanation of the hairstyle is forced, but the first two attempts are worthy of attention even today.

The satyrs of the fifth-century stage are not simply goats, but neither are they simply horses.[82] They are also never called such, and there is no similar ἵππος analogy for the τράγος comparisons (Aisch. fr. 207N = 455M, *Ichn.* 357 f.). Some time ago Ziegler (1920) and the author (in the first edition of *Griech. Trag.*, 1938) pointed independently to the skin loincloths of the chorus as depicted (with a single exception) on the satyr-play vase in Naples.[83] An attachment made of cloth secures the phallos and horse tail. This shaggy garment can really only be understood as a rudiment of hair covering the entire body. There are also older pieces that depict shaggy-haired satyrs. Webster in Pickard-Cambridge's book (*Dith.*, 114) quickly orients the reader with references to his invaluable list of monuments. We especially should like to point out the incomparable wood daimon in his shaggy dress on a Boiotian clay tripod.[84] But the silene, who, after all, is the father of the good-for-nothing satyrs, wears a μαλλωτὸς χιτών (hairy cloak) on stage, which is supposed to represent the shaggy growth of hair on his whole body. That all this indicates the nature of the goat has been decisively formulated by Webster against any doubt: "Greek artists always represented horses with smooth hair but often represented the rough hair of goats. Therefore the natural explanation of the hairy chiton . . . is that they represent goat-skins. . . ."[85] Ziegler (1923) has further remarked correctly that the large beards of the satyr chorus certainly do not come from horses, but probably from goats.

We come to the conclusion that these creatures were perceived not as half horse but simply as half animal, whose exact zoological designation apparently mattered little. This agrees very well with the fact that the satyrs are referred to as θῆρες (wild animals) three times in the scanty literary fragments.[86] And we learn from Galen (*CMG* V10. 22; 143. 19 ff.) that the Ionians called the satyrs φῆρες. As θῆρες they are thus related to the centaurs, for whom the same word is used. This connection is strengthened by the existence of two vase-paintings: one, the well-known vase with satyrs harassing Iris;[87] the other, a fragment from Florence depicting centaurs in the same attack. The other vases offer vivid and abundant evidence for the voracious sexual appetite of the satyrs. For this reason they could also be called goats, since the goat was the prime example of the lustful animal in antiquity (e.g. Diod. 1. 88) as it is for us, and it is exactly because of this concupiscence that Prometheus in *Prom. Pyrk.* calls one of the satyrs τράγος. Therefore, following this interpretation, we again come to the view that the suggestions offered by the Peripatetic school are the best that we can achieve with our limited means.

In this context the vases that show satyrs and goats together are also worthy of attention. Burkert (99. 25) has collected and arranged these perspicuously.

Up to now we have dealt separately with the two suggestions of Aristotle for the origin of tragedy, dithyramb and satyrikon; now we will examine the possibility of their unification. Our evidence is scanty and has been interpreted in different ways.

Herodotos reports of Arion (1. 23): καὶ διθύραμβον πρῶτον ἀνθρώπων τῶν ἡμεῖς ἴδμεν ποιήσαντά τε καὶ οὐνομάσαντα καὶ διδάξαντα ἐν Κορίνθῳ.[88] The article in the *Suda* lexicon (ς. Ἀρίον) reads much like a broader paraphrase:

λέγεται καὶ τραγικοῦ τρόπου εὑρετὴς γενέσθαι καὶ πρῶτος χορὸν στῆσαι καὶ διθύραμβον ᾆσαι καὶ ὀνομάσαι τὸ ἀδόμενον ὑπὸ τοῦ χοροῦ καὶ σατύρους εἰσενεγκεῖν ἔμμετρα λέγοντας.[89]

There are also the remarks of Johannes Diakonos in his commentary on Hermogenes (ed. H. Rabe, *Rhein. Mus.* 63 [1908], 150):

τῆς δὲ τραγῳδίας πρῶτον δρᾶμα Ἀρίων ὁ Μηθυμναῖος εἰσήγαγεν, ὥσπερ Σόλων ἐν ταῖς ἐπιγραφομέναις Ἐλεγείαις ἐδίδαξε. Χάρων (thus Wilamowitz from Δράκων; Patzer 29, suggests Στράτων) δὲ ὁ Λαμψακηνὸς δρᾶμά φησι πρῶτον Ἀθήνησι διδαχθῆναι ποιήσαντος Θέσπιδος.[90]

There are further passages that name Arion as the originator of the dithyramb: Pindar, *Ol.* 13. 18, with the scholium on v. 19 (more on v. 25); schol. Aristoph. *Av.* 1403, which offers Hellanikos (*FGrH* 4F 68) and Dikaiarchos (fr. 75W) as the sources for this identification and contrasts them with others that name Lasos of Hermione in this role; Proklos, *Chrestomatheia* 12, who follows Aristotle and adds: ὃς πρῶτος τὸν κύκλιον ἤγαγε χορόν (who first led the round-dance).

There is no doubt that Herodotos's report on Arion refers to the development of the dithyramb into a fixed art form. What the *Suda* adds to Herodotos remained subject to modern scholars' caprice until the publication of the Hermogenes commentary introduced Solon as a witness. He confirms for us the connection of Arion with a decisive period in the early history of tragedy. We would naturally like to know Solon's exact words, but this lies beyond our means.[91] We need not doubt that he was able to make a pronouncement on the subject. In this context, the debate about the anecdote related by Plutarch (*Sol.* 29) is quite interesting. The aged Solon, ἀρχομένων τῶν περὶ Θέσπιν ἤδη τὴν τραγῳδίαν κινεῖν (when the circle around Thespis already began to develop tragedy) supposedly was present at a performance by Thespis and reproached him afterward for composing such lies. This may be mere invention, just as Solon was also connected with Kroisos and Amasis, but it is quite plausible that in his later years he was a witness to the beginnings of the development that produced tragedy through the appearance of an actor some time before the first state agon.[92]

Aristotle, *Poet.* 3, 1448a 29 and Ps. Plat. *Minos* 321a bear witness to a dispute in which Attic and Peloponnesian local patriotism both laid exclusive claim to the beginnings of the tragic play. If Wilamowitz correctly restored the name Charon of Lampsakos in the text of Johannes Diakonos quoted above, we could confirm the existence of this dispute as early as the middle of the fifth century.

Our group of sources connects Arion with the beginnings of tragedy, with the development of the dithyramb and with the satyrs. Now the decisive question is whether this evidence refers to one unified achievement or to three separate achievements. Reisch (*Festschr. Gomperz* 1902, 471) and Pickard-Cambridge (*Dith.*, 98) support the latter. Flickinger (10. 2) opposes this, and even Webster in his additions to Pickard would like to refer the three separate notes to the same arrangement. More recently, Patzer has again recommended the separation into three different acts.

It speaks for our interpretation (i.e., that the sources quoted refer to one single achievement of Arion) that even in the *Poetics*, developing tragedy, dithyramb, and satyrikon are mentioned in the closest connection, and that the remarks by our sources, though brief, support each other. Arion had his κύκλιοι χοροί (choruses in the round-dance) sing artful choral poetry that stood in the service of Dionysos and bore the ancient name "dithyramb." As choral dancers he introduced—regularly or only occasionally—the satyrs, who even at that time belonged to the entourage of the god. Thus we find the unification of the two elements mentioned briefly in the *Poetics* by Aristotle confirmed for the satyr dithyramb of Arion. That many doubt the existence of this form lies in the nature of the sources. Patzer (50. 1) offers an abundant bibliography of the opposing fronts. He belongs himself to those scholars, such as Else and Burkert, who recently dispute the interpretation proposed here.

In this difficult field we are grateful for the help offered by the vases that bring together the satyrs and the dithyramb. First of all, there is the fragment of a red-figured Attic krater in Copenhagen (Pickard-Cambridge, *Dith.*, 5). It depicts a Dionysian procession with a lyre-playing satyr, over whom ΔΙΘΥΡΑΜΦΟΣ is written. Webster has further pointed (Pickard-Cambridge, 20, 35, 301, pl. 1a) to an Attic red-figured krater (ca. 425 B.C.) that shows three aged and hairy satyrs with lyres approaching a flute player. The important inscription above, ΟΙΔΟΙ ΠΑΝΑΘΕΝΑΙΑ, marks them as singers at the Panathenaia, and the only known choral agon in this festival was that of the dithyramb.[93] Webster (op. cit., 20, 301) would also like to see a reference to the Panathenaia in a black-figured lekythos with three hairy satyrs playing the lyre (ca. 490 B.C.), which is indeed likely in view of its similarity to the vase just discussed, whose connection with the festival is confirmed by the inscription. A red-figured stamnos in the Louvre (Webster, op. cit., 34, 301, n. 3; ca. 480 B.C.) shows satyrs striking a grave with hammers. A reference to the prizes for the dithyramb agon might be indicated by a bull sacrifice on the opposite side, as well as a goat and amphora under the handles, but the connection remains uncertain.

With a better conscience than in earlier publications, we now would like to omit the apparent difficulty introduced by the *Suda*'s note that Arion introduced Σατύρους ἔμμετρα λέγοντας (satyrs speaking in verse). Every attempt to find in these words satyrs either talking or reciting melodramatically comes to naught. It is simply a question of the same imprecise use of language that occurs in the *Poetics* (12, 1452b 22) when Aristotle speaks of the parodos as ἡ πρώτη λέξις ὅλου χοροῦ (the first speech of the whole chorus). In a fragment of Aischylos, λεγούσας refers clearly to a hymnos and in the scholium on Eur. *Hipp.* 58 the verbs ᾄδειν and λέγειν alternate for the same verse group. Thus also in the case of Arion, only the song of the chorus is meant.

A more difficult question is posed by Herodotos's phrase οὐνομάσαντα (naming), which occurs again in the *Suda*. Schmid (1. 407) thought of individual titles, like those that designate content and are known from the transmission of the dithyrambs of Simonides, Pindar, and Bacchylides. Pohlenz (2. 9) has disputed this without justification and assumed a fixed designation for the new art form. We believe that this is incorrect, since the song's name already existed (Archilochos fr. 77D), and to apply it to the elevated art form could not be considered an achievement worthy of special emphasis. If this was a reference to individual titles, then it is extremely probable that even the dithyrambs of Arion, like the later ones and like the tragedies, had various myths as subject matter.

Besides the testimony of Aristotle, we must include in our picture of developing tragedy two structural elements, the Dionysian and the hero sagas.

Few still deny that tragedy grew out of the Dionysian cult. Schmid (2. 42) is one of these, as is R. Cantarella in his latest writings.[94] Else also comes necessarily to the same conclusion in the course of his theory (see below). In contrast to this view we find already in Aristotle's notes two Dionysian elements: the dithyramb as a Dionysian song, and the satyrs, who soon became associated with the god after their original independence. Other facts can be adduced. The occasion for performances of tragedy was always a Dionysian festival. In the fifth century the eleventh to the thirteenth Elaphebolion (March/April) is reserved for the tragic performances of the Great Dionysia, also called the City Dionysia.[95] Each day featured a tetralogy.[96] The oldest state performance that we can determine, that of Thespis in one of the three first years of the Olympiad 536/535–533/532, belongs to this festival.[97] This goes back to Peisistratos, as does the entire arrangement of the Dionysia. They were celebrated in honor of Dionysos Eleuthereus, who was specially favored by the tyrant, and whose carved image had come to Athens from the Attic-Boiotian border town of Eleutherai. This manifestation of Dionysos stands next to the common Ionic god, in whose honor the Lenaia were celebrated in the month of Gamelion (January/February). This was the festival of comedy, which had been nationalized earlier (487/486) at the more prestigious Great Dionysia. But comedy had long existed as an independent performance at the Lenaia and received its national agon there too about 440. Later, an agon for tragedy was added to the Lenaia, which has been convincingly explained as the result of the increasing number of tragic works. The date 432 for this innovation, however, must be regarded as uncertain.[98]

The location of the Dionysian festival was the sacred precinct of Dionysos Eleuthereus on the southern slope of the Akropolis, which saw theater construction change over the centuries from the primitive orchestra of the sixth century to the Roman theater with its additions for animal-baiting. Photios (v. ἴκρια) tells of wooden grandstands in the agora before the construction of the theater of Dionysos.[99] We cannot exclude the possibility of such early performances in the marketplace, but this is certainly no argument against the Dionysian character of tragedy, since Photios speaks expressly of Διονυσιακοὶ ἀγῶνες (Dionysian agons).

The costumes of the actors, which were probably the same for tragedy and satyr play, show in their essentials a relationship to Dionysos.[100] To be sure, this has been recently disputed for the sleeved chiton, since this is in fact also found outside the realm of Dionysos.[101] But it is attested for the god so early and so well that Bieber seems justified in asserting the cult significance of the garment. The kothurnos, a soft shoe, certainly has this significance; Aristophanes (Ran. 47) confirms it as a piece of characteristically soft Dionysian clothing. It fits every foot comfortably, for which reason a compromising politician like Theramenes is called Kothornos.[102] The grotesque ivory statuette in Paris (Bieber, Hist., fig. 799; Pickard-Cambridge, Fest., fig. 63) cannot be counted as an example of classical tragic costume, which is best illustrated by the satyr-play vase in Naples. Here too the kothurnos is represented as a soft shoe without a fixed sole. It is thus extremely doubtful whether Aischylos, as the Vita 14 claims, increased the stature of the actors by raising the sole of the kothurnos. The mask of course belongs to the substructure of drama and is not Dionysian in origin, but like the satyrs, it was drawn into the service of the mask-god at an early date.

The connection between the Dionysos cult and tragedy is also expressed in the tremendous advancement that both enjoyed through the religious and cultural political measures of the Greek tyrants. More important than all the external factors however is the consideration that in the ecstasy of the Dionysos cult, that mysterious process of transformation occurs which is the single most important presupposition for the origin of drama. Here the "possession" of the primitive daimon actor finds its continuation and exaltation.[103]

The bond between the tragic play and Dionysos is well expressed in the vase paintings where the personified Tragodia appears in the thiasos of the god.[104]

But all this seems strangely contradicted by the predominantly non-Dionysian character of tragic subject matter. This is what was meant by the phrase οὐδὲν πρὸς τὸν Διόνυσον.[105] The ancient interpreters referred it to different phases: to the transition from dithyramb to tragedy with Epigenes of Sikyon, to Thespis, to Phrynichos, and to Aischylos. We cannot decide the point here, but we know for certain that the contrast between the Dionysian festival play and non-Dionysian material was perceived and expressed at an early date. In an effort to prove an originally Dionysian cycle of material, reference has been made repeatedly to the few Dionysian dramas with the nativity story and myths of opposition by Lykourgos and Pentheus. But the sober calculation of Ziegler (1931) makes it quite clear that these dramas form only a small fraction of the whole picture of tragedy as we know it, and that despite many attempts one cannot speak of a stronger emphasis on Dionysian material, even for the earlier period.[106] The subject matter of tragedy, as far as we can trace it, is the hero saga. This must have merged very early into the Dionysian play. It appears that we are still in a position to analyze part of the process of this important development. Herodotos tells us (5. 67) of the cult reforms of Kleisthenes of Sikyon, the maternal grandfather of the Athenian statesman of the same name, who ruled in the first third of the sixth century. The Argive hero Adrastos had a shrine in the marketplace of Sikyon, which Kleisthenes, at war with Argos, wished to remove. Since Delphi would not allow this, he transplanted the cult of Melanippos, archenemy of Adrastos, from Thebes to Sikyon. He gave the new hero sacrifices and a festival, and carried out yet another change:

τά τε δὴ ἄλλα οἱ Σικυώνιοι ἐτίμων τὸν Ἄδρηστον, καὶ δὴ πρὸς τὰ πάθεα αὐτοῦ τραγικοῖσι χοροῖσι ἐγέραιρον, τὸν μὲν Διόνυσον οὐ τιμῶντες τὸν δὲ Ἄδρηστον. Κλεισθένης δὲ χοροὺς μὲν τῷ Διονύσῳ ἀπέδωκε, τὴν δὲ ἄλλην θυσίην τῷ Μελανίππῳ.[107]

First of all, we may be sure that there were ceremonies in Sikyon, dating from very ancient times, at which the fortunes of Adrastos were sung and lamented by choruses. The content of these songs can be more or less imagined from what we know of the epic poetry about the expedition of the Seven against Thebes. We know of dirges of this type for Achilles in Elis, Kroton, and Rhoiteion; for Medea's children in Korinth; for Ino in Thebes and Hippolytos in Troizen.[108] This part of the hero ceremony was then brought into the cult of Dionysos in Sikyon. Although local motives may also have played a part, this reform is still closely connected with the religious politics of the tyrants, who strongly advanced the cult of the great nonaristocratic peasant god. Arion's reform of the dithyramb belongs to the Korinth of Periander, and in Athens tragedy found its festival in the Great Dionysia of Peisistratos. Now Herodotos tells us nothing about the content of the τραγικοὶ χοροί (tragic choruses) that were taken over by the Dionysos cult, but the text invites the assumption not that Dionysos was celebrated in place of Adrastos, but rather that the ancient hero songs remained preserved as a part of the Dionysian celebration.[109] We spoke earlier of the probability that the subject matter of the dithyramb that Arion elevated to an art form was material from the hero sagas.[110] By connecting this to the further point, in Herodotos's report on Sikyon—namely, that the ancient hero songs were absorbed into Dionysian celebrations, we believe that we have found the historical explanation of the phrase οὐδὲν πρὸς τὸν Διόνυσον. If the reports about Arion in Korinth and the reforms of Kleisthenes in Sikyon have the meaning we assign to them, then we have also clarified the path from the hero saga to the actual subject matter of tragedy developed within the context of Dionysos.

The hero mythology offered tragedy a source for material that was full of the highest values and possibilities. The heroes were alive in the people's heart and were certain of their direct sympathy.[111] Not less importantly, this material stood before poet and public at the distance necessary for the subject of all great works of art, and yet still possessed the weight of historical fact. What Schiller said of the objective definiteness of such materials that resist arbitrary change, or Grillparzer said of the consistency and core of reality in events and persons of historical materials—all this is fully applicable to Greek myth. The ancient tragedian was bound to this traditional material but in a way that allowed him a great deal of personal freedom in elaboration and interpretation.[112]

Herodotos's story contains another element extremely important for tragedy. The song that was sung to Adrastos by the choruses of Sikyon was most probably a dirge. In accordance with the nature of the hero cult, the threnos had to claim its place in the development of tragedy along with the material from hero sagas. Tragedy need not be derived simply from the hero cult, as Ridgeway believes, but the special significance of the threnodic element in the surviving works cannot be overlooked.[113] Peretti (passim; see his index) has examined this problem and emphasized that plays like Μιλήτου ἅλωσις (The Capture of Miletos) and the Phoinissai of Phrynichos show the extensive influence of the threnos even on historical material.

We may speculate that Epigenes of Sikyon played a part in the reforms of Kleisthenes as reported by Herodotos, which was similar to that of Arion at the court of Periander. The Suda, under Θέσπις (cf. under Οὐδὲν πρὸς τὸν Διόνυσον) names Epigenes in competition with Thespis as the first tragedian. Historical reality may lie behind the name, even if the chronology is so confused that according to some, Thespis was Epigenes's sixteenth successor, while according to others, his second.

One question remains that cannot be answered with any certainty. Are the τραγικοὶ χοροί in Herodotos to be construed as "tragic choruses" as such choruses occurred in tragedy at the time of the historian or as "goat choruses"? The same question applies to Arion's τραγικὸς τρόπος (tragic mode, Suda) and his τραγῳδίας πρῶτον δρᾶμα (first drama of tragedy) according to Solon's testimony in Johannes Diakonos. Linguistic usage does not allow for an answer removed from all doubt. Patzer emphasizes that classical Greek only knows τραγικός in the sense of "tragic." But the evidence is scanty, and later passages up to Longus's τραγικὴ δυσωδία (goat stench, 4. 17. 2) show that "goat" could always be heard in the word.[114] And we must not exclude the possibility discussed by Webster (Pickard-Cambridge, Dith., 103), that Herodotos took the word from an older source, in which the goat meaning was still intact.

To look for the goat in the word is tempting, since then we could make the connection to the satyrs that sang for Arion, and to the explanation of the word tragedy offered here. But an argument vigorously advanced by Patzer (59 f.) speaks rather for the other interpretation. Herodotos is the contemporary of classical tragedy, and it is quite natural to think of a concept taken from that genre in his use of the word. But it would be incorrect to consider the problem solved.[115]

We ask now where we can fit into our picture of tragedy's development the process described by Aristotle with the words ἐκ μικρῶν μύθων καὶ λέξεως γελοίας διὰ τὸ ἐκ σατυρικοῦ μεταβαλεῖν ὀψὲ ἀπεσεμνύνθη. We cannot dismiss this statement with Peretti (77, 103, 253), who believes that it refers to the primitive nature of archaic tragedies in comparison with classical examples. Aristotle thought of a process that led from burlesque to seriousness and dignity. Ziegler (1939) wanted to understand this as a part of the cultural and stylistic development in the transition from the sixth to the fifth century. This is certainly a substantial observation. Yet if we allot such special significance to the institutions in Korinth and Sikyon, as is the case here, then we must assume that a serious character for choruses was already traditional, especially in Sikyon. In any case the decisive factor for the process described by Aristotle was the unification of the Dionysian, along with its burlesque and satyrical elements, with the song and dance practiced in the hero cults.

Our analysis recognizes a certain right of the Dorians to tragedy; the words of Themistios (Or. 27. 406) contain some truth and in fact are in the end Aristotelian: καὶ τραγῳδίας εὑρεταὶ μὲν Σικυώνιοι, τελεσιουργοὶ δὲ ᾿Αττικοὶ ποιηταὶ (The originators of tragedy were Sikyonians, but it was perfected by the Attic poets). In our opinion, however, the Peloponnesian stages of development are concerned solely with choral presentations. The attempt of E. Bickel to derive from the Arion story a hero-cult play as an early Doric dramatic form, with spoken verse and several actors, lacks any solid foundation.[116] Even the ᾱ in the trimeter of Attic tragedy cannot help. In a book that is extremely important for this question, Björck has examined the older theories and has convincingly explained the "alpha impurum" forms in tragic dialogue as being borrowings. Their genesis is different from that of the comparable forms of choral song in that, in Björck's striking image, the Doric element is placed from without like a transparent veil around the body of the Attic language. Both have in common a certain stylistic tendency toward Doric, that is, a formal element determined by the nature of the artistic language. But there is no evidence here for an early Doric stage of tragic dialogue.

We would be misunderstood if it were thought that we claim conclusive certainty for the interpretations developed here. On the contrary, we are well aware of the paucity of our sources and the hypothetical character of the individual steps, but we believe that we offer the most probable solution, given the range of possibilities. Nonetheless, for the sake of completeness, we must discuss three different recent attempts that explain the origin of tragedy in very diverse ways. We may spare ourselves much in the line of individual argumentation, since this already has been taken care of in the previous statements.

Patzer's approach differs methodically from our own in essential points, but does not differ completely in the basics. He considers the evidence of Aristotle at least partially correct, and assigns great significance to the tradition about Arion. But the sentences of the Poetics contain for him merely hypotheses, of which those concerning the dithyramb are correct, while the testimony regarding the satyr play is false. According to Patzer the satyr play must be banished from the early history of the tragic play. And while we and others believe to have found, in the notes on Arion in Korinth, the satyr dithyramb that is the point of intersection between the two lines drawn by Aristotle, Patzer relates this account to three distinct achievements: Arion created the (artistic) dithyramb, the satyr choruses, and tragedy in its original form, although the picture of this last remains necessarily quite vague. Patzer's interpretation is determined by the wish to find the nature of tragedy already realized in the preliminary stage. Hence the elimination of the satyrs, hence the claim that the process described by ἀποσεμνύνεσθαι (transformation to sublimity) could not have taken place. Yet when Patzer (121 f.) concludes that the original tragedy arose from a mimetic transformation of the dithyramb under the influence of the satyr choruses, this shows in fact a certain approximation to our own interpretation. His statements about the reception of the hero mythos in the Dionysian dithyramb also coincide well with our picture. The most radical opposition to all that has been said of the origin of tragedy up to now is offered by Else.[117] He goes so far in his rejection of Aristotle that he explains as an error the remark in the *Poetics* that the development of tragedy was a result of numerous μεταβολαί (changes, transformations). According to him, tragedy arose from rhapsodic recitations of Homer through a single act of creation. This was what Thespis achieved by the simultaneous creation of the part of the actor and the tragic choral song, elements that never would have existed independently of one another. It is hardly necessary to add that this hypothesis cannot be reconciled with the developmental picture described here.

Fundamentally different from the two interpretations just discussed is that of Burkert. He does agree with Patzer in the rejection of Aristotle's statement concerning the satyrikon as one of the preliminary forms of tragedy. Our explanation makes it clear enough that we cannot consider his argument sound: he cites Pratinos as the originator of the satyr play and supports the impossibility of ἀποσεμνύνεσθαι (transformation to sublimity). He has examined the word τραγῳδία with extraordinary care, without being able to exclude once and for all the meaning "goat song." Patzer too (131 f.) disagrees with him here. Burkert comes to the conclusion that the τραγῳδοί were originally masked men who offered the goat sacrifice in the spring and accompanied the sacrifice with their songs. Thus he comes rather close to the interpretation of the Alexandrians. With great care he has collected everything that indicates a connection of the goat with the realm of Dionysos, but this does not suffice as a basis for his theory: In the calendar frieze of Athens it is in fact the comic actor who offers the goat as sacrifice.[118]

The ancients had another theory regarding the development of tragedy that we have not yet discussed. They made Homer the father of tragedy, even occasionally its first poet. In the *Poetics* (1448b 38) Aristotle speaks of an analogy between the epics, *Iliad* and *Odyssey*, and tragedy,[119] while other authors, for whom Gudeman has collected the evidence (on *Poetics* 1448a 26), expressed themselves even more decisively. In doing this the ancients placed the mimetic element in the foreground, which they saw realized in dialogue. Besides the dialogical element, the structural plan of the *Iliad* appears especially important to us. Thank heavens we may believe in this again. Whoever proceeds from the excellent presentation of the characteristic features of epic in E. Staiger's *Grundbegriffen der Poetik* quickly perceives how the epic dimensions of Homer's portrayal lend poetry a new dimension and how the magnificent realization of Achilles' fate, suspenseful throughout despite its length, points beyond the possibilities of epic to those later fulfilled in tragedy. It makes sense that on the lower band of the late Hellenistic relief that shows the apotheosis of Homer, personified Tragedy also pays homage to the poet.

2

THESPIS

It is a strange coincidence that the word θέσπις occurs three times in the *Odyssey* together with words for song or singer, and that once the name Ikarios follows it directly.[1] Nonetheless, we should hesitate to reduce Thespis' name to a fiction for that reason and, if possible, to dispatch the person after it. To be sure, we know little enough about that person.[2] Only the article in the *Suda* expressly names the Attic deme Ikaria (the modern Dionyso) as the homeland of Thespis: Ἰκαρίου πόλεως Ἀττικῆς. But if we see Thespis as the founder of tragedy connected with rural entertainment and the song for the goat prize in a series of passages, and if further, according to Athenaios (2. 11; 40a), tragedy originated ἐν Ἰκαρίῳ τῆς Ἀττικῆς (in Attic Ikaria); and, according to the verse of Eratosthenes, the Ikarians were the first to dance around the goat, all this leads collectively to the same place.[3] This is contrasted to the herm-inscription of Aquae Albulae with Θέσπις Θέμωνος Ἀθηναῖος (Thespis, son of Themon, an Athenian), and Thespis is also an Athenian in Clem. Alex. *Strom*. 1. 79.

One might think that the designation "Athens" is inexact and offers no real variation from Ikaria, but another consideration demands attention. Ikaria and its eponym Ikarios belong, as the *Erigone* of Eratosthenes shows, to that Alexandrian bucolic realm out of which the goat-prize theory for the origins of tragedy arose. Thespis could here have been linked with the place whose sagas and customs in connection with ancient peasant festivals awakened scholarly interest. If Thespis became an Ikarian in this way, then Athens could justifiably lay claim to the other Thespis who stands in the Peripatetic picture of tragedy's development, and about whose achievements we can in fact make some comment.

In the discussion of the theory that finds the goat prize in the word *tragedy*, we encountered the invaluable evidence of the *Marmor Parium* ep. 43 (*FGrH* 2. 239A 43) concerning the first performance of Thespis. It is generally agreed that the date refers to the admission of tragedy into the state festival of the Dionysia, originated or elaborated by Peisistratos. The precision with which the year 534 has often been given for this performance is unjustified.[4] Jacoby may be credited with having pointed out that we must also consider three years of the Olympiad which the *Suda* (s.v.

Thespis) also mentions. Of the archon's name, only]ναιου τοῦ προτέρου is preserved, which excludes the final year of this Olympiad, since its archon was Therikles. The word for Thespis's achievement is also damaged. Jacoby accepted the supplement ὑπεκρίνα]το, while Patzer (22. 1), with reference to *Marm. Par.* ep. 46, prefers the ἠγωνίσα]το suggested by Else.[5] The connection of the institution with Peisistratos' politics, which favored Dionysos in religious matters, is obvious. Thespis will have played a role there similar to that of Arion in the Korinth of Periander and perhaps also of Epigenes in the Sikyon of Kleisthenes.

Of course the year of this performance cannot be equated with the beginning of Thespis's poetic activity. When we were concerned in the previous chapter with the question of whether Solon could have expressed views on the very beginnings of the tragic play, we encountered the anecdote in Plutarch's biography of the statesman in which Solon attacked Thespis for the lies in his play. We were of the opinion that the story was chronologically possible, but in no way authenticated. Tièche (10. 12) has cited Plato's criticism of art and attributed the anecdote to Herakleides Pontikos. The latter worked especially on Thespis, if we may believe Aristoxenos (Diog. Laert. 5. 92; fr. 114W), who reports that he wrote tragedies and ascribed them to Thespis. But Wehrli in his commentary on the fragment has pointed out with good evidence that Aristoxenos treated such questions rather irresponsibly. Thus it is not very easy to judge what has been transmitted under the name Thespis in all its parts with any certainty. We possess the four titles Ἆθλα Πελίου ἢ Φόρβας, Ἱερεῖς, Ἤιθεοι, Πενθεύς and four untitled fragments (nos. 1–4). Lloyd-Jones (13) has recently examined the fragments and titles with a view to separating the obviously false from the rest, whose rejection does not appear absolutely necessary.[6] He rightly excludes fr. 4N from the start and considers it improbable that fr. 3N could stem from the sixth century. Tièche (11) has fittingly said of these three verses about the greatness of Zeus, who transcends all deception and sensual pleasure, that they point to the Platonist Herakleides. For the titles and the two remaining fragments (frr. 1–2N), Lloyd-Jones, fully aware of our uncertainty, would not exclude Thespis as author. The two individual verses would then indicate dialogue. If the interpretation of Thespis's activity that we are about to develop is correct, then precisely this fact is no recommendation for their authenticity. Wehrli considers it most cautious to assume that Aristoxenos was imputing to Herakleides the authorship of certain Thespis forgeries in circulation at that time.[7] It is also possible that Herakleides could have placed his own plays as a literary game under the name of Thespis (as the oldest known composer of tragedy) without any intent of forgery. The wording of the Aristoxenos fragment does not exclude such an interpretation.

Numerous ancient sources designate Thespis as the creator of tragedy. The earliest author would be Charon of Lampsakos, if we follow the correction of Wilamowitz in the commentary of Johannes Diakonos on Hermogenes (see above). Aristophanes *Vesp.* 1479 points at least in the same direction, as do *Marm. Par.* ep. 43; Dioskorides *Anth. Pal.* 7. 410 f. (cf. M. Gabathuler, *Hellenistische Epigramme auf Dichter*, St. Gall 1937, 82 f.); Horace, *Ars Poet.* 275; Clem. Alex. *Strom.* 1. 79; Euanthius, *De Com.* 1 (Kaibel, *FCG* 1. 62); Donat. *De Com.* 5 (ibid., 68); *Suda* s.v. Θέσπις.

We will have to deal at once with the statements that ascribe specific achievements to Thespis.

Where Thespis is named as the first tragedian, the preceding development inferred for the Peloponnese has been passed over probably under the influence of Attic local patriotism; in any event Solon (in Johannes Diakonos) mentions Arion as Thespis's predecessor and the *Suda* (s.v. Θέσπις) offers Epigenes. But tragedy before Thespis was also considered by the Athenian tradition. This is clearly expressed in the pseudo-Platonic *Minos* 321a. The puzzling report in Pollux 4. 123 on ἐλεός (a sort of kitchen table on which meat was cut) also refers back before Thespis. According to Pollux an individual climbed up on the table and there responded to the chorus. Related information can be found about the θυμέλη in the *Etym. Magn.* (s.v.) and about the thymelici in Isidorus, *Orig.* 18. 47. These late sources are rather difficult to evaluate. Peretti (282) assigned them great significance, and Webster too (in Pickard-Cambridge, *Dith.*, 86) considers whether we grasp here an important phase of the development. This single person who uses the table as a podium to answer the chorus (in song of course) could have been the exarchon of the chorus. Aristotle could then have seen in him the precursor of the actor who worked with the chorus, spoke, and incorporated a specific character. It seems very probable that we can recognize here a section of the path that Aristotle followed, although the particular reference to the ἐλεός remains, of course, very uncertain.

The Peripatetics were interested in Thespis; we know of a work by Chamaileon about him (fr. 38 W). In this area also belongs an important note that leads us to the problem of the origin of spoken verse in tragedy. Theoretically, there could be two possibilities here: transition from sung dialogue, i.e. an internal development from choral song, or the entrance of spoken verse from without. Kranz chose the first alternative in his influential study.[8] Since the early dating of Aischylos's *Suppliants* was assumed at the time to be certain, he proceeded on the basis of three scenes of epirrhematic composition, in which parts spoken by an actor follow a song of the chorus. Beforehand he locates in the development of the song dialogue as the "final attainable tragic form." From the epirrhematikon he derives the fixed rhesis somewhat mechanically through the loss of the choral parts, and conversely the stasimon through the omission of the actor's verses. But this is a misunderstanding of the significance of the chorus as the basis for the development, and it is also unthinkable to assume that the great fixed choral songs of Aischylos were secondary formations from the epirrhematikon.[9] Kranz changed his position slightly in *Stasimon*. The final attainable form, assumed as being without actors, was now considered to be the antiphony of a chorus which was somehow split.[10] It is quite possible that double choruses, as they sometimes appear in the preserved dramas, played a role in the earliest beginnings of tragedy. But there is no discernible path which leads from the double chorus to spoken verse.

In favor of the other possibility, the entry of spoken verse from the outside, we can adduce first of all, the differences in language and dialect between sung and spoken parts and also the differences of style, which Peretti (78) correctly emphasizes.[11] A passage in Themistios, *Or.* 26, 316d, brings us beyond this rather general consideration: καὶ οὐ προσέχομεν Ἀριστοτέλει, ὅτι τὸ μὲν πρῶτον ὁ χορὸς εἰσιὼν ᾖδεν εἰς τοὺς θεούς, Θέσπις δὲ πρόλογόν τε καὶ ῥῆσιν ἐξεῦρεν, Αἰσχύλος δὲ τρίτον ὑποκριτὴν (ὑποκριτάς Med.) καὶ ὀκρίβαντας, τὰ δὲ πλείω τούτων Σοφοκλέους ἀπελαύσαμεν καὶ Εὐριπίδου.[12] Formerly, rash judgments such as that of Hiller (*Rhein. Mus.* 39 [1884], 321) were accepted: Themistios had simply paraphrased the *Poetics* and added on Thespis. It has since been taken into consideration that Themistios was far better educated than most persons of his time and that he himself composed Aristotelian paraphrases. Scholars have also considered how well the additions of this passage to the *Poetics* coincide with the fact that Aristotle himself hints at a wider knowledge than is included in his treatise (1449a 29, 37; b 4). The character of the *Poetics* forbids our drawing conclusions regarding the credibility of the Themistios passage from the circumstance that Aristotle does not name Thespis.[13] In more recent studies scholars have generally accorded the passage the credibility it deserves.[14] It is supported by Diog. Laert. 3. 56, according to which Thespis added the actor to choral tragedy, and indirectly by all the passages cited above that name Thespis as the true creator of tragedy.

Besides the speech, the Themistios passage names the prologue as the invention of Thespis. Here we see a place in the tragic play well suited for the introduction of spoken verse.[15] When the choral song of older tragedy seized upon richer myths that presumed more knowledge on the part of the audience, it was a short step to a prologue which clarified the material background of the following song. Such a prologue could also be found within the choral structure whenever the chorus was to be told of a new event or when a different mood was to be created. Thus the Danaids in the *Suppliants* of Aischylos (524–599) have sung a song that revolves around Zeus and Io in fearful anticipation of what is to come. Then Danaos appears and gives in twenty-one trimeters a short report about the granting of the request in the Argive assembly. This is not an "act" or an episode in the later sense; the short speech has only the task of making possible the following free-flowing choral song of benediction for Argos.

It is no refutation of our argument that *Suppl.* and *Pers.* begin with the chorus and not a prologue-speech. Apart from the fact that the early dating of the *Suppl.* has become untenable (see below), it would be wrong to underestimate the freedom of this development and to demand unity of form.[16] What we are searching for is offered by the *Phoinissai* of Phrynichos, which, according to the statement of Glaukos of Rhegion in the hypothesis of the *Persians*, preceded this play of Aischylos; it was probably produced in 476.[17] The play is opened by a eunuch, who sets up the chairs of state for the council meeting. His real task is to report Xerxes' defeat and thus, in a primitive way, to supply the prerequisites for the following laments. Aischylos has prologue-speeches in *Seven Against Thebes* and in the plays of the *Oresteia*; the *Laios*, the first part of the Theban trilogy of 467, also began with a prologue-speech of the actor in the title role (fr. 169M). Occasionally, as in *Ag.* and *Eum.*, an additional figure (πρόσωπον προτατικόν) delivers the prologue, like the eunuch of the *Phoinissai*. But the prologue-speeches of Aischylos, far beyond their material function, set the mood beautifully for the whole work. In sharp contrast to this stand the "playbill prologues" of Euripides, usually attached emphatically as informative prefaces. They can be meaningfully fit into our picture if we count them among the archaisms found so often in this poet.[18]

The question of the original function of the *hypokrites* leads necessarily to that of the word's meaning. Scholars are today further than ever from reaching agreement. Ὑποκρίνεσθαι is already used in Homer for "answer" (*Il.* 7. 407; *Od.* 2. 111), but the meaning "expound," "explain," is likewise present (*Il.* 12. 228; *Od.* 19. 535). Schwyzer-Debrunner (*Griech. Gramm.* 2. 525) offer as the basic meaning: "to give forth one's opinion from the depths of the heart, from concealment."[19] A passage like *Od.* 15. 170 can well illustrate the conceptual development to the meaning "answer." In Attic Greek this meaning is attested quite early by the pre-Euklidian epigram *IG* I² 410 (although epic influence must be reckoned with here), but Plato *Tim.* 72 b, τῆς δι᾽ αἰνιγμῶν οὗτοι φήμης καὶ φαντάσεως ὑποκριταί (interpreters of puzzling voices and apparitions), shows that the use closer to the original meaning was still very much alive. Even when ὑποκριτής was in general use for "actor," one could still refer back to the other meaning, as Lukian, *Somn.* 17, *Ver. Hist.* 2. 33, and Philostratos *Vita Ap.* 2. 37, show. In this context Pindar fr. 140b, with ἁλίου δελφῖνος ὑπόκρισιν ("hypokrisis" of the dolphin in the sea), deserves special attention. Wilamowitz remarks in his book on Pindar (502): "Here ὑποκριτής as 'answerer' seems questionable." The word first appears in the meaning "actor" in Aristophanes *Vesp.* 1279; we could go back a little further if we could assume what Pickard-Cambridge (*Festivals*, 126) considers as a possibility that the play inscription *IG* II² 2318 from the middle of the fourth century faithfully reproduces the language of the acts of the archons. This would make 449 the year of the first actor-agon. In any event the word appears so late that a definitive choice between "answerer" and "interpreter" is impossible, and thus the schools are as sharply opposed as ever. But a remark like that of Reinhardt[20] shows that the second meaning has gained some ground in recent years: "Up to the chorus steps the actor, 'the answerer' or the 'interpreter' (a newly discovered Pindar fragment has made the meaning 'answerer' questionable)." And so Bywater's protest against the then customary interpretation of the word as "answerer" (on *Poet.* 1449a 15) comes into its own once again. What is meant here of course is not the interpreter of the poet's words, but the expositor who prepares the play and offers transitions. This fits well with the crucial Themistios passage, while we have no evidence that the "answering" of the actor stood out as his significant activity. Euripidean prologue speakers are really ὑποκριταί in the sense as a possibility we prefer here.

The *Suda* reports that Thespis first painted himself with white lead, then covered his face with purslane, and finally invented the pure linen mask (ἐν μόνῃ ὀθόνῃ). This last could refer to unpainted linen masks, such as the simple female mask done in white on an oinochoe from the Athenian agora (Pickard-Cambridge, *Festivals*, fig. 32).[21] But this passage cannot support the assumption that Thespis invented the mask, which is in fact a very ancient discovery. Webster (in Pickard-Cambridge, *Dith.*,² 80) makes the attractive conjecture that the *Suda* or its sources might have forced different ancient forms of masking in dances and dramatic performances into a chronological schema.[22]

We cannot be certain that Thespis had already made the transition from trochaic tetrameter to iambic trimeter, since the authenticity of the fragments is suspect. The well-known passage in Horace, *Ars Poet.* 276, that made famous the wagon
of Thespis, cannot seriously be construed as describing a traveling stage on wheels, as
Flickinger (19), for example, thought. Horace's source here was confused by a misunderstood ancient custom during spring festivals, referred to in the *Suda*: τὰ ἐκ τῶν
ἁμαξῶν σκώμματα (gibes from the wagons).

3

CHOIRILOS, PHRYNICHOS, AND PRATINAS

A group of inscriptions that contain important information concerning the dating of dramas in Athens stems probably from a temple-like building erected in the third century B.C. by a prosperous citizen interested in the cultural past of his city. The texts, which originate in documentary records, have been beautifully arranged from a multitude of fragments by Adolf Wilhelm in his book *Urkunden dramatischer Aufführungen in Athen* (1906).[1] After their reproduction in *IG* II² they were edited again by Pickard-Cambridge (*Festivals*, 101), probably definitively, unless new discoveries bring restorations. The so-called Fasti catalogue lists beneath the names of the archons the victorious phylai and the choregoi for the dithyrambic agon of men's and boys' choruses, and the names of the victorious choregoi and poet for comedy and tragedy. Any attempt to determine the beginning of this state festival, an institution that survived for centuries despite many changes, depends on the uncertain restoration of either two or three columns for the lost first part of the inscription. The year 502/501, which would set us in the first period of the young democracy, has much to recommend it but cannot be maintained with certainty. The so-called Didaskaliai (*IG* II² 2319–23) give the dramatic performances for the Dionysia and the Lenaia. If we are supposed to imagine these inscriptions on the inner walls of the small structure, then the victory lists found their place on the epistyle or the architrave above, so that the observer could conveniently view both lists at once. These victory records (the remains were collected from forty-one fragments, mostly from the southern slope of the Akropolis) listed for both festivals the poets and actors of tragedy and comedy, in the order of their first victories, followed by the total number of their successes. The list of the tragedians for the Dionysia begins with Aischylos, who won in 484 for the first time. Before that about ten lines are missing, corresponding to the same number of poets' names. Of these, we know only a few well enough to be able to make some comment on them.

The *Vita* of Aischylos (16) names among the predecessors of the master, besides Thespis, also Choirilos and Phrynichos. The first of these two remains for us a shadowy figure. References in Hesychios and the *Suda* (s.v. Choirilos and Pratinas) attach considerable importance to him. According to these sources he first participated in a dramatic agon during the sixty-fourth Olympiad (524/523–521/520) and was the rival of Aischylos and Pratinas in such an agon during the seventieth Olympiad (500/499–497/496). At this time the wooden stands (ἴϰρια) for the spectators supposedly collapsed, which may be historical fact. The first of these remarks is inconsistent with the setting of Choirilos's floruit at 482 found in Eusebios. Could someone have calculated this using the time of his first professional appearance, since his exact date of birth was unknown? Since the *Vita* of Sophokles (19) also names Choirilos among the rivals of this poet, this presumes an extraordinarily long period of productivity. We could of course, with Schmid (2. 170. 1) construe the *Vita*'s συνηγωνίσατο (competed at the same time with him for the victory prize) as a misinterpretation of a note that has been preserved in the *Suda* (s.v. Sophokles), which claims that he wrote his treatise on the chorus πρὸς Θέσπιν ϰαὶ Χοιρίλον ἀγωνιζόμενος (contending against Thespis and Choirilos). In the account of the lexicographers, who claimed that Choirilos had written 160 plays and won 13 victories, only the second figure may be trusted, since it may go back to the Didaskaliai. Neither the only known tragedy title *Alope* nor the two single fragments with the expressions "bones of the earth" and "veins of the earth" yield much specific information. The report that he remodeled the mask and costumes of the actors remains quite uncertain. And the suspicion also continues, despite Schmid (2. 170. 1), that the comic verse ἡνίϰα μὲν βασιλεὺς ἦν Χοιρίλος ἐν σατύροις (when Choirilos was king in the satyr play) refers to a different Choirilos.[2]

The evidence yields more of a profile for Phrynichos, the son of Polyphrasmon.[3] According to the *Suda* he was victorious in the sixty-seventh Olympiad (512/511–509/508), most probably for the first time. Plutarch (*Them.* 5) testifies to a victory under the choregeia of Themistokles and the archonship of Adeimantos (476). The *Suda* article introduces its list of his works with the sentence τραγῳδίαι δὲ αὐτοῦ εἰσιν ἐννέα αὗται (these are his nine tragedies) followed by the titles: Πλευρώνιαι, Αἰγύπτιοι, Ἀϰταίων, Ἄλϰηστις, Ἀνταῖος ἢ Λίβυες, Δίϰαιοι ἢ Πέρσαι ἢ Σύνθωϰοι, Δαναΐδες.[4] Several points are uncertain in this catalogue. The first title is out of alphabetical order. The restoration of F. Marx, ⟨Ἀλθαία ἢ⟩, consistent with the context, can help here.[5] The inexact alphabetical arrangement would be supported by the two last titles. Since the play, if the restoration is correct, can hardly have been set in Pleuron, the title would probably be a reference to captive women from that city.

It is especially difficult to evaluate the three titles (second to last in the series) referring to one work. There is little point in attacking the problem with blind conjecture, postulating Δίϰτυς ἢ Περσεύς and then claiming to see in the Σύνθωϰοι the petrified companions of the king.[6] It is also a radical measure to delete, with Schmid (2. 171. 9), the two ἢ's between the three names. One could still bring to bear the possibility of a displacement from the double title immediately preceding, which would then have the advantage of producing the nine titles promised by the introductory phrase of the *Suda*. But what about alphabetical order?

The problem is further complicated by the fact that every theory must take into account what we know of the *Phoinissai*, which may be dated most probably to 476, the year of Themistokles' choregeia. In our chapter on Thespis we examined the prologue of the eunuch preparing the seats for the council of the king, as reported in the hypothesis to Aischylos' *Persians* as the note of Glaukos of Rhegion.[7] The eunuch announced at the very start the defeat of Xerxes. If we connect this with the observation of Glaukos that Aischylos composed his *Persians* after the play by Phrynichos, then the essential theme of the latter seems to have been the defeat at Salamis. Since this was announced right at the beginning of the earlier drama, an opportunity for dramatic tension was lost. Lament must have formed the main content of the *Phoinissai*. An Ammonios scholium on Hom. *Il.* 21. 111 (*P. Oxy.* 2, 221) offered the remains of two trochaic tetrameters from the play, which were read: $-\smile$ πϱ]ωῒην δεείλην πλείο[νες $--$]ίων/ἄνδϱες ἐκτείνοντο[$-\smile$ ὀψί]ην ἐς δειέλην.[8] F. Marx, in a rather unsuccessful essay, wished to refer the verses to the battle of Mykale, basing his argument on a false evaluation of the prologue technique that entailed dating the *Persians* before the *Phoinissai*, contrary to Glaukos.[9] He claimed support from Herod. 9. 101: τὸν δὲ ἐν Μυκάλῃ πεϱὶ δείλην (the battle at Mykale in the afternoon). Pohlenz (2. 25) has rightly called attention to the passages that testify to the continuation of the battle at Salamis until the late hours of the day. With this, the reconstruction attempts of F. Marx and F. Stoessl, who took over the Mykale-hypothesis, largely collapse. But the two verse fragments are valuable because they show that a complete report of the defeat at Salamis followed the evidently short reference to it in the eunuch's prologue.

Women from Sidon (frr. 9, 10N) formed the main chorus, which is not difficult to understand considering the role of the Phoinikians in the Persian fleet. For the councillors we may imagine either supernumerary extras like the judges in the *Eumenides* or a second chorus such as that of the hunters in the *Hippolytos*.[10]

We return to the question of whether there is a relationship between the *Phoinissai* and the Δίϰαιοι ἢ Πέϱσαι ἢ Σύνθωϰοι. Lloyd-Jones (24) tries to solve the problem by assuming confusion with the plays of a trilogy. According to him, Glaukos was in error; the play with the eunuch's prologue was the one with three titles in the *Suda*, while the *Phoinissai* was another drama in the same trilogy, whose content is wholly unknown. The necessity of correcting Glaukos's data is rather awkward, and thus we would like to retain the possibility (along with F. Marx, op. cit., 348 and F. Stoessl, op. cit., 159) which Lloyd-Jones himself does not exclude: that all three titles in the *Suda* refer to the *Phoinissai*. This can be supported by the probable assumptions that the *Persians* and the *Phoinissai* are identical, and that the Σύνθωϰοι might refer to the council meeting reported by Glaukos. The Δίϰαιοι remains a puzzle.

The *Phoinissai* represents for us, together with the Μιλήτου ἅλωσις (the *Capture of Miletos*) and the *Persians* of Aischylos, an attempt in the first decades of the fifth century to deal with the great events of contemporary history in tragedy. This was possible, since myth itself was looked upon as history, but we must not overlook the importance of political factors that could have become critical for the further development of tragedy. H. T. Wade-Gery dated the performance of the Μιλήτου ἅλωσις to the Dionysia of 493,[11] thus placing it as close as possible to the fall of Miletos in the autumn of 494.[12] But 492 seems more probable. Then the piece falls in the year of

Themistokles' archonship, so that we may reckon with the direct influence of the statesman on the play's creation and performance.[13] This seems even more likely because in all probability the play performed in 476 under the choregeia of Themistokles was the *Phoinissai*, as Bentley first conjectured. Herodotos (6. 21) reports that the Athenians fined the poet a hundred drachmas, no very large sum, for this play. It seems best to believe what the historian says: that they reacted in this way to the painful memory of the οἰκήϊα κακά. And of course we cannot dismiss the possibility that political opposition to Themistokles also may have been involved.[14]

It would be a great help to be able to determine more closely the relationship of the *Egyptians* and *Danaids* to the trilogy of Aischylos. The scholium on Eur. *Or.* 872 reports that in the first of these dramas Aigyptos came with his sons to Argos. This can refer only to the persecution of the Danaids and indicates subject matter similar to that of Aischylos. Since both plays belong to the same myth, the question arises whether they were parts of a trilogy. We just encountered Lloyd-Jones's suggestion of a Persian War trilogy, and the same scholar also considers assigning the *Gyges* drama to a trilogy (29). Both conjectures seem doubtful, but the *Aigyptioi* and *Danaides* certainly suggest the possibility of a trilogy based on content. It is painful for us not to be able to determine the originator of this magnificent dramatic structure. Now that we must date the *Suppliants* later, the form first appears for us in the Theban trilogy of 467, while all attempts to assign Aischylos's *Persians* to such a structure have failed. If Phrynichos really composed trilogies of this type, the possibility remains that he took over this form from Aischylos, who was his rival for quite some time.[15]

For the *Alkestis* I have concluded from schol. Dan. on Verg. *Aen.* 4. 694: "alii dicunt Euripidem Orcum in scaenam inducere gladium ferentem, quo crinem Alcestidi abscindat, et Euripidem hoc a Phrynicho [convincingly restored by O. Jahn from phenico T, poenia F] antiquo tragico mutuatum" (others say that Euripides brought Orcus onto the stage bearing a sword with which he cut a lock of Alcestis's hair, and that Euripides borrowed the motif from the ancient tragedian Phrynichus), from fr. 2N, and from the appearance of Thanatos as a character and name only at the opening and closing of the Euripidean play, that this drama was based to a considerable extent on the play of Phrynichos.[16] At the beginning of the play Thanatos came to fetch Alkestis and gained possession of her by cutting off a lock of her hair. The resolution was provided by Herakles, who overcame Thanatos. The outwitting of the drunken Fates by Apollo, mentioned in Aisch. *Eum.* 723 and Eur. *Alk.* 12, 32, could also have happened in the Phrynichos version.

The list of the dramas of Phrynichos breaks off at the letter Δ and so must have originally contained much more. Besides the two historical pieces, we know of a *Tantalos*, thanks to Hesychios, s.v. ἐφέδρανα, but the assumption of a *Troilos* on the basis of fr. 13N is quite uncertain. We cannot say whether any of the titles handed down to us refers to a satyr play, but this assumption is tempting for the *Antaios*. It would be rash to suggest this for the *Alkestis* because of features that appear burlesque to us.

For the *Gyges* drama, from which sixteen verses survive, Lloyd-Jones (24) accepts the conjecture of Lobel and Page that Phrynichos was the author. It is a distressing sign of our uncertainty that this suggestion is opposed by another that sets the play either in the fourth century or in the Hellenistic age. We prefer the latter date and will accordingly deal with this problem in a later chapter.

So long as the *Suppliants* of Aischylos was dated around the time of Salamis or even Marathon, it was thought possible to obtain on the basis of this work a picture of archaic tragedy. But that is no longer possible and we must for the most part admit our ignorance of this epoch of tragic poetry. Were Phrynichos's works mainly chorus plays or was the dramatic element already more richly developed in them? There is much to be said for the latter theory, supported by Lloyd-Jones. We can hardly imagine that Phrynichos composed completely archaic works during the time when he and the innovator Aischylos were both active. We know slightly more about the character of Phrynichos's art, in which his true nature was expressed. In Aristophanes (*Thesm.* 164) he appears as a handsome man who took care of his appearance and showed Ionian influences. There are also *Ran.* 1298 and the passages (*Vesp.* 220, *Av.* 750, both with scholia) that emphasize the special sweetness of his songs. He also composed asklepiads (fr. 6N) as we know them from Lesbian lyric poetry. Artful dances were added to text and song. An anonymous epigram in Plutarch (*Quaest. Conv.* 8; 732 f.) maintains that Phrynichos invented as many dance movements as the sea has waves on a stormy night. Wilamowitz (*Gr. Versk.* 465. 1) thought that the originator of this image was a poet like Dioskorides or Sositheos.

According to the *Suda* article Phrynichos introduced female masks and the tetrameter. The first would be possible, since feminine names are first attested for him, but precisely this could be the explanation for the note. In the same way he will have been credited with the tetrameter because the oldest examples were found under his name.

From the characteristics that can be approximately derived for Phrynichos we can judge the contrast that this poet of the Ionian style presented to Pratinas of Phleios, who exultingly closes his satyr dance with ἄκουε τὰν ἐμὰν Δώριον χορείαν (hear my Doric dance music). We have already discussed (in chapter 1) the questions involved with this hyporchema, and we consider it a tenable conjecture that a line of this song refers polemically to Phrynichos. The most significant achievement of Pratinas, the reestablishment of the satyr play, was also discussed at length in the first chapter. According to the *Suda* article he wrote thirty-two satyr plays and eighteen tragedies. The transmission of such numbers is unreliable, and they seem strange when set against the common tetralogy arrangement. But it is possible that the poet who revived the satyrikon from the Doric tradition into a new play form also devoted more attention to this form than to tragedy. The later tetralogy order resulted from the battles initiated by his reaction, although we cannot determine the exact date of this extraordinarily significant arrangement. (Cf. Ziegler, 1939.)

Cantarella connects the triumph of the newly formed satyr play rather arbitrarily with the agon of the seventieth Olympiad, in which Pratinas competed against Choirilos and Aischylos.[17] Flickinger (24) dates the innovation of Pratinas at about 515, which seems correct, for Buschor (83) has shown how after 520 satyr play paintings appear that are clearly impressed by the orchestra. In exemplary fashion he has also reclaimed from the vases an impressive series of these old satyr plays in their general outlines; much of this may belong to Pratinas.[18] Only one title of a satyr play is attested for him: the Παλαισταί (Wrestlers), produced in 467 by his son Aristias, which gives us the terminus ante for his death. We add the remark in the hypothesis to Aischylos's Seven: δεύτερος Ἀριστίας Περσεῖ, Ταντάλῳ,[19] Παλαισταῖς σατύροις τοῖς Πρατίνου πατρός. (Second was Aristias with the Perseus, the Tantalos, and the Wrestlers, the satyr play of his father Pratinas.) Then the fragment of a didaskalia, P. Oxy. 2256 fr. 2: δεύτερος Ἀριστίας ταῖς τοῦ πα[τρὸς αὐτοῦ Πρατίνο]υ τραγῳδίαις (Aristias was second with the tragedies of his father, Pratinas). According to this the plays mentioned in the hypothesis, the Perseus and Tantalos, must also be attributed to Pratinas. Aristias himself composed tragedies and satyr plays and had a memorial in the marketplace of Phleios, on the evidence of Paus. 2. 13. 6. In this passage he appears next to his father and Aischylos as an outstanding author of satyr plays. We know nothing of the content of the Palaistai; it is tempting to suggest a similarity of theme with the Isthmiastai of Aischylos, but there is really nothing to support this. Beyond this we know only one drama title: Δύμαιναι[20] ἢ Καρυάτιδες, possibly a tragedy. In any case Δύμαιναι refers to Dionysiac ecstasy, according to the Hesychios lemma.

Thus far it seems that the few statements about Pratinas contain no difficulty, but a special problem arises in further passages, collected now by D. L. Page, Poetae Melici Graeci (pp. 368 f.). Several of them contain statements from the history of music and poetry that suggest a choral lyricist rather than a dramatic poet. Was Pratinas also a lyric poet? Did he comment on such difficult questions as who originated the πολυκέφαλος νόμος (the many-headed melody), and whether Xenodamos was a composer of hyporchemata or paeans? It is understandable that Lloyd-Jones (18) carefully suggests separating the satyr play author of the drama's early period from a lyric poet of the late fifth century, and he includes in these doubts the hyporchema transmitted by Athenaios. In any event two fragments could indicate something like a gap between the two images of Pratinas: fr. 2P with the praise of Laconic choral poetry and fr. 5P with the rejection of Ionian music in favor of Aeolian harmony.

In Phrynichos and Pratinas the Ionic character and powerful Doricism are contrasted. This contrast between the two has paradigmatic significance. It points to the processes through which, in a unique synthesis, the Attic nature arose and reached a culmination in the Parthenon and in Sophokles.

4

AISCHYLOS

BIOGRAPHICAL NOTES

Several manuscripts offer a vita whose nature is probably best explained by the assumption that the material contained in it has been passed on from various sources. Much of this may go back to Chamaileon, who wrote *On Aischylos* (frr. 39–42W) around 300 B.C., but an exact demarcation is not possible. Chamaileon's treatise contains, besides anecdotal material, some excellent judgments on the art of the poet. The remaining evidence of ancient authors concerning the life of Aischylos has been collected by F. Schöll in Ritschl's edition of the *Seven* (Leipzig 1875); the essentials may be found in the ed. maior of Wilamowitz (Berlin 1914). In addition to this material of varying worth, we must not forget the grandiose portrait of Aischylos drawn by Aristophanes in the *Frogs*.[1] While the various passages offer at best tiny mosaic tiles to fill in an incomplete surface, the picture offered by the congenial Aristophanes fifty years after the tragedian's death portrays, for all its burlesque elements, a great personality deeply affected by the gravity of his poetic mission, separated from the world by the distance of solitary greatness.

The year 525/524 is confirmed for the tragedian's birth by the information on the *Marmor Parium* (*FGrH*. 239, ep. 48) that Aischylos was thirty-five years old at the time of the battle of Marathon and sixty-nine when he died. Since the *Vita* (see also schol. Aristoph. *Ran.* 886) names Eleusis as his place of birth, it has been repeatedly conjectured that the Eleusinian cult exercised a special influence on the poet. Méautis (29) would even like to interpret the report (Epitome of Athenaios 1. 21d) that the hierophants and torch bearers imitated the stage costumes invented by Aischylos as evidence for a counter-effect of the poet upon the cult site. But when in *Ran.* 886 f. Aischylos invokes Demeter, who nurtured his spirit, before the agon and requests that he be worthy of her mysteries, this can really only be construed with Radermacher as an appeal to the goddess of the poet's own deme.

In antiquity it was said that the poet had been put on trial for impiety; that he had been charged with violating the secrecy of the mysteries. Herakleides Pontikos dramatized this wildly in *On Homer* (fr. 170W, slightly varied in Ailian, *Var. Hist.* 5. 19): Aischylos was in danger of being murdered ἐπὶ σκηνῆς (on stage; he was thus believed to be his own actor); he fled to the altar of Dionysos and was acquitted in the trial before the Areopagos because of his conduct at Marathon. This is quoted in the anonymous commentary on *Eth. Nikom.* III. 2; 1111a 10, where Aristotle says that a man can be ignorant of what he does; he may not know, for example, that something may not be uttered, as was the case with Aischylos and the mysteries. J. Bernays has compared this passage with Clem. Alex. *Strom.*, II. 14, p. 145 St., according to which Aischylos proved he had never even been initiated, and this remains the most probable conclusion, given our sketchy source materials.[2] The indictment may be historical, which would also explain the zeal with which later scholars pored over the poet's works searching for passages relating to the mysteries. The Aristotle commentary just mentioned lists, before the report from Herakleides (fr. 170W), a whole series of plays in which this sort of reference supposedly appeared (fr. 116 Mette).

Here we would like to recall that the attempt has been made, independently of any trial stories, to connect early tragedy with the dromena of Eleusis as a sort of model.[3] The influence of the mysteries has always been sought in Attic tragedy—not least in that of Aischylos. However, this orientation overlooks the fact that tragedy and the mystery cults are two separate realms. The former concerns a λόγον διδόναι, an accounting for the position of man in the world, while the mysteries, according to a profound phrase of Aristotle (fr. 15), demand not learning, but submission.

The father of the poet was Euphorion, from a noble family, on the evidence of the *Vita*. From Aischylos's service as a hoplite we must conclude with Aylen (35) that his was in fact a middle-class family. It is assumed that the Aischylos of Eleusis who held the high office of *Hellenotamias* in 440/439 also issued from this line. The universal legend of the early calling of the artist is prettily told for Aischylos by Pausanias (1. 21. 2): as a boy he had fallen asleep in a vineyard when Dionysos appeared to him and told him to write tragedies.

Politics were decisive for the inner development of the poet. In his youth he experienced the replacement of tyranny by the citizen-state of Kleisthenes (to which the future was to belong) and the salvation of the young government from a threatening coalition of its neighbors. As an adult he was a fighter during the years of the Persian invasion when both freedom and the spiritual future of Greece hung in the balance. He fought at Marathon and Salamis. It was not forgotten that his brother Kynegeiros lost his life in the first of these battles, when he seized the stern of an enemy ship and his hand was cut off. It has been rightly emphasized that the epitaph (which may come from Aischylos himself but was probably composed in Athens soon after his death) names only the soldier at Marathon, not the poet. Salamis is attested to by Ion in his *Epidemiai* (fr. 5a Blumenthal). The *Vita* (4) also names Plataiai; Pausanias 1. 14. 5 adds Artemision, Schmid (2. 187n.) Mykale. This is all uncertain, and the suspicion is strong that other names of famous battles were added to Marathon and Salamis in the course of tradition, while Mykale was suggested only by modern conjecture. According to the *Vita*, Ameinias, the youngest brother of the poet, fought by his side at Salamis. Diodoros 11. 27, who probably used Ephoros as his source, claims that the Ameinias who distinguished himself at Salamis according to Herodotos (8. 84. 93) was in fact the same brother of Aischylos. There is some confusion here, for according to Herodotos this Ameinias came from Pallene. The confusion borders on the grotesque when Ailian (*Var. Hist.* 5. 19) tells how Ameinias effected the acquittal of Aischylos at a trial by showing his arm stumps to the judges. Here Kynegeiros enters, who according to the anonymous commentary on *Eth. Nikom.* mentioned earlier (Herakleides fr. 170W) was named as being influential in the poet's acquittal at the mystery trial. This is the same sort of dramatically inflated information that we encounter in the report of the same author, to the effect that Aischylos received multiple wounds at Marathon and was carried from the field. The whole account is equally instructive for motif variation and the pseudo-biographical style.

That Aischylos was a contemporary of Pindar was asserted by the *Vita* (3); that he was acquainted with the choral poet, as Eustathios reports (*Commentary on Pindar* 25), is quite possible, as is his meeting with Ion of Chios at the Isthmian games, where he praised the discipline of a fighter (fr. 5 Blumenthal). A. von Blumenthal dates this meeting very plausibly at 462, 460, or 458.[4]

The *Vita* says that he began composing tragedies at a very early age. This agrees with the *Suda* article on Pratinas, who supposedly competed with Aischylos and Choirilos at the seventieth Olympiad (500/499–497/496); it also agrees with the chronicle of Eusebios on the first year of the seventy-first Olympiad (496/495), according to which Aischylos became well known at this time.[5] The *Marmor Parium* (ep. 50) lists his first victory already in 484. In all, he was victorious thirteen times; we can date the victory with the *Persians* at 472. The *Suda* reports twenty-eight victories, but this may include repeat performances after his death.

For Aischylos's travels to Sicily we have the following data: the *Vita* reports that the poet came when Hieron founded the city of Aitnai (476/475), and that at this time he composed the festival play *Aitnaiai* with blessings for the new settlement.[6] Further, we have the note of Eratosthenes in the third book of *On Comedies* (preserved in the scholium to Aristoph. *Ran.* 1028), which states that Aischylos produced the *Persians* (whose performance in Athens took place in 472) in Syracuse at the request of Hieron. This is also found in the *Vita* (18), which speaks of an ἀναδιδάξαι (repeat performance) and a significant success.[7] Finally both the *Marmor Parium* (ep. 59) and the epitaph quoted in the *Vita* record the poet's death in Gela (456/455). Thus he must have returned once more to Sicily in his last years. Confusion reigns in the *Vita* (10), which informs us, after mentioning the *Aitnaiai*, that Aischylos was highly honored by Hieron and the people of Gela and lived for three (!) years afterward. It remains very uncertain whether these three years represent the duration of his final stay in Sicily.

If we believe these three reports (about the *Aitnaiai* on the occasion of the city's founding, a repeat performance of the *Persians* after 472, and his death in Sicily), then the poet made three journeys to the west. This is certainly possible, but we should not overlook the hypothesis of Mazon, developed in the introduction to his edition, which reduces the number of journeys to two. Hieron was involved in serious fighting with the Etruscans and Thrasydaios between 476 and 471. In 470 he set up his son Deinomenes as ruler in Aitna; Pindar celebrated the young city in

Pyth. 1. No doubt this would have been an appropriate occasion for the festival play of Aischylos, who also could have produced the *Persians* again about this time. Podlecki (155. 22) has objected that the wording of the *Vita* ʿΙέρωνος τότε τὴν Αἴτνην κτίζοντος (at the time when Hieron founded Aitna) points rather to the year of foundation, 476/475. It is correct for Mazon to oppose this, but the assumption of an error in the *Vita* is not at all difficult in view of its other achievements. Our sources are insufficient to decide the question.

For the question why Aischylos came to Hieron's court, the *Vita* (8) has collected all sorts of idle stories: he could not endure a defeat at the hands of Sophokles or Simonides (with an elegy to the fallen at Marathon). The story of the shock effect supposedly caused by the Eumenides rushing into the orchestra also surfaces in this context.

In 468 the poet lost in the agon that brought Sophokles his first victory, but a year later he was victorious with the *Theban Trilogy*, and in 458 with the *Oresteia*. It is difficult to say why he returned again to Sicily. Politics may have been a factor, and Aristophanes intimates (*Ran.* 807) a certain alienation between poet and public. The mystery trial has no connection with this, for the sources all record his acquittal.

Aischylos died in 456/455 in Gela, far from his homeland, in this regard like Euripides and unlike Sophokles, who was a more fortunate man in many things. The story of the eagle who dropped a tortoise on his head (*Vita* 10, testim. 32 Wil.) is an unimportant anecdote from the world of fantasy. But we are ready to believe that his grave in Gela was highly honored and sought out as a hallowed place by disciples of the tragic art.[8] Quintilian, *Inst. Or.* 10. 1. 66, evaluates the great but also unwieldy art of Aischylos. He goes on: "Propter quod correctas eius fabulas in certamen deferre posterioribus poetis Athenienses permisere. suntque eo modo multi coronati" (For this reason the Athenians allowed later poets to enter revised versions of his plays in the contests; and many were crowned in this way). The *Vita* (13) also cites numerous posthumous victories.[9] Aristophanes and late works of Euripides give evidence that the plays remained enormously popular after Aischylos's death. This popularity ended with the fall of Athens. When in 386 the performance of a παλαιά was generally permitted, this measure benefited Euripides above all and Aischylos very little.

It is characteristic of the genealogical tradition of Greek art that Aischylos founded a school of tragedians within his own family. Both his sons, Euphorion and Euaion, were poets; the former won in 431 over Sophokles and the *Medeia* of Euripides (hypothesis to *Medeia*). To Aischylos's sister and her husband Philopeithes was born the tragedian Philokles, who was victorious over the *Oid. Tyr.* according to Dikaiarchos (second hypothesis to *Oid. Tyr.*; fr. 80W); he sired Morsimos, whose son Astydamas, a pupil of Isokrates (*Suda*; chronologically difficult), brings us into the fourth century. His two sons, Astydamas II and Philokles II, composed tragedies, as did all the others mentioned. For the difficult assignment of dates for the two Astydamases we can thank Bruno Snell.[10] Greater fame came to Astydamas II. His first victory at the Dionysia came in 372, further victories in 341 and 340; in all he won fifteen times.

For a portrait of the poet one is often referred to the well-known head from the

Capitoline Museum, whose designation as Aischylos is nonetheless arbitrary. The sculpture's baldness does not assure the attribution. That he was bald is maintained by Ail. *De Nat. An.* 7. 16 and Val. Max. 9. 12 in connection with the silly story of the eagle who thought the poet's bald head was a stone on which he could crack open a captured tortoise. On the other hand, it has been conjectured with relative confidence that the poet's torso in the Vatican's Braccio Nuovo is a copy of the Aischylos statue in the Theater of Dionysos in Athens (Paus. 1. 21. 2; [Plut] *Vita Dec. Or.* 7. 841). It is thought that the missing head can be basically determined from a poet's portrait extant in many replicas.[11] The piece in Naples shows a fillet in the hair, the attribute of the poet; the replica in the Giardino Colonna is connected to the Farnese Sophokles in a double herm. In the find from Livorno the head is united with the Lateran Sophokles, Homer, and an unknown poet; moreover, there is a marked stylistic relationship with the head of Sophokles just mentioned. Therefore the conclusion is rather likely. We have not, however, identified the historical Aischylos, but merely a reflection of the statue that the orator Lykourgos had erected. At that, it is a portrait that is sadly disappointing in its lack of expression and depth.

MANUSCRIPT TRANSMISSION AND EDITIONS

The path leading from the autograph manuscript of Aischylos to our present editions is long and filled with straits and danger zones; it must be illuminated by the history of the textual tradition as laid down by Wilamowitz and described for the tragedians in his *Herakles*. The short presentations in D. L. Page's *Actors' Interpolations* and in the appendix of my book *Greek Tragedy* agree on the basics. The same may be said for Ziegler (2067), the introductions to the editions of P. Major (5th ed., 1949), and Murray (2d ed., 1955). The relevant chapters in Headlam-Thomson's *Oresteia* (1938) are still worth reading; many revisions and a more strongly polemical character have been added in the new edition (Prague 1966), especially in the chapter directed against the dogmatic certainty of the principles of textual criticism represented by P. Maas (p. 64).

Wilamowitz characterizes the manuscripts in detail in his edition (1914); cf. H. W. Smyth "Catalogue of the Manuscripts of Aesch.," *Harv. Stud. Class. Phil.* 44 (1933); and E. Fraenkel in "On the MS E of Aesch.," *Class. Rev.* 53 (1939), 59, and in the Prolegomena to his edition of the *Ag.*, Oxf. 1950. An important stage of research is reached here and for the other tragedians as well in the work of A. Turyn: *The Manuscript Tradition of the Trag. of Aesch.*, New York 1943. There are two tasks, both the focus today of lively discussion: the construction of a stemma, in which the relation of dependency of the manuscripts can be determined, and the separation of original and secondary (Byzantine) tradition. We shall discuss both questions as well as Dawe's book in the following outline, which also addresses problems significant not only for Aischylos but for the whole MS tradition of the tragedians.

The Mediceus and the Ven. Marc. 468 offer a catalogue with seventy-three titles of Aischylean works, from which we exclude the Αἰτναῖαι νόθοι. Besides this catalogue the following titles are also associated with the name Aischylos: *Alkmene,*

Glaukos Potnieus, Thalamopoioi, Hiereiai, Kyknos, Palamedes, Prometheus Pyr-
kaeus, Sisyphos Petrokylistes, Phineus, Oreithyia. Much of this, like the *Kyknos*, is
doubtful; for the works mentioned here that concern Prometheus and Sisyphos, the
question arises whether they are identical with other titles (more on this later). The
Suda article states that the works of Aischylos totalled ninety. Various emendations
have been proposed for the badly corrupted line of the *Vita* (13): δράματα ό καὶ ἐπὶ
τούτοις σατυρικὰ ἀμφὶ τὰ έ (seventy dramas and besides these, about five satyr plays).
The suggestion of Steffen,[1] ἐποίησεν δράματα ό,σατυρικὰ ⟨ιε⟩, ἀμφίβολα έ (he composed seventy dramas, fifteen satyr plays, five are contested), is tempting in that it
agrees with the *Suda*, but certainty is unattainable in such a tradition. Steffen and
others rightly reject the attempt of A. Dieterich to restore a fifth column in the catalogue.[2] If the catalogue's numbers remain lower than those of the *Vita*, it is simply
because its author could not find more titles.

Regarding the ultimate source of the tradition, the autograph MS of Aischylos,
we are able to state on the basis of inscriptions and papyri that it was written without
word separation and punctuation, and also without designation of crasis or elision;
the lyric sections were not subdivided and change of speaker was marked only by the
paragraphos, a horizontal line. Even if Mazon (in his edition, p. ix) were correct, and
it were necessary to take the Ionian alphabet into account, there would still remain
uncertainties in vowel designation, at least in the "spurious" diphthongs. All of these
conventions represent as many sources of error, which are found necessarily in the
early book editions as well. That such editions existed even at the time of the great
tragedians should not be doubted.[3] Paratragodia, so frequent in Old Comedy, presumes on the part of the public a familiarity with the texts that cannot be explained
by repeat performances alone. Of course it is difficult to date accurately when tragedies began to circulate in book form. The only real clue, Aristoph. *Ran.* 52, is late,
but one can always point in this context to the fact that Euripides had a library
(Athen. 1. 3a).[4] Since it must be assumed that the poets submitted titled works to the
archons in charge of directing the plays, titles must also be presumed for the book
editions.[5]

A special source of error, and one whose consequences are difficult to evaluate,
arose from the capriciousness of the actors during repeat performances.[6] Undoubtedly
they introduced errors in the text. This explains the passage in pseudo-Plutarch *Vit.*
Dec. Orat. 7. 841 about the law of Lykourgos, who had an official text of the tragedies
prepared for the state and forbade any deviation from it on the part of the actors. This
procedure presumably did not succeed in putting an end to such liberties, but we do
not regard the existence of this state text as insignificant, as Wilamowitz does
(*Einleitung*, 132).

It is difficult to discern the extent of actors' interpolations in our texts of the
tragedians, and how these interpolations crept into the book editions. Page makes
considerable progress, but his basic view, that the texts of actors and prompters were
what booksellers wanted, above all in the fourth and third centuries, cannot be
proved; neither, incidentally, can the existence of prompters at this time. In the
works of Aischylos this period could not have introduced extensive changes, since

Sophokles was then preferred to him for repeat performances, and Euripides was more popular than both.

Alexandria was the key station for the texts of the tragedians. What Galen says of Ptolemaios Euergetes in his commentary on the *Epidemiai*, we would rather refer to Philadelphos: that by wealth and stealth the king wrested a valuable edition of the tragedians from the Athenians—most likely the official text of Lykourgos.[7] We read in Tzetzes (*CGF* p. 19K) that the Aitolian Alexander was entrusted with the classification of tragic literature. Wilamowitz (*Einl.*, 146) disputed the assertion that Alexandrians were concerned with tragedy before Aristophanes of Byzantium. This remains a deduction ex silentio, but it is correct that Aristophanes, whose work is attested only for Euripides, certainly examined all three great tragedians, and that his edition became the basis for all following texts. It presented the extant dramas in alphabetical order.[8] He certainly composed a commentary on the works and very probably subdivided the lyric sections into cola. For tragedy, just as for Homer, we have only the scantiest evidence for forming a picture of the pre-Alexandrian condition of the texts. However, some papyri, notably the tragic-song papyrus from Strasbourg, give us an idea of the condition of the tradition before the work of the Alexandrians. The division of the lyric sections into cola is lacking, and the confusion is so great that Bruno Snell could say "if we had to rely on texts like the one on this papyrus, it would be senseless to try to restore the words of the poet."[9]

We come to the next stage with Didymos, contemporary with Cicero and Augustus. Not an independent researcher, he compiled his commentaries on the tragedians from older works. Even Chalkenteros (brazen-boweled, Didymos's nickname in the *Suda*) could not have written a commentary on all the tragedies available at the time. His edition probably exercised little influence on the tradition.[10] Lexicography was another of his interests; his τραγικὴ λέξις comprised at least twenty-eight books. And just as Didymos utilized the works of the great Alexandrians, so too the threads led from him to the extant scholia on the tragedians. Much of the lexicographical work of the time came, partly through Diogenian, into the lexicon of Hesychios. His glosses are especially useful for the textual criticism of tragedy.

Our manuscript tradition offers us seven tragedies each for Aischylos and Sophokles, and nine dramas with scholia for Euripides, with the *Bakchai* to be reckoned tenth. For Euripides, part of an alphabetical complete edition has also been preserved. The numbers 7–7–10 are not the result of chance; they can probably be traced back to a selection from the complete works of these poets, of which the Alexandrians still possessed the greater part. Wilamowitz (*Einl.*, 196) confidently proposed the theory that it was a single man, a schoolmaster of the second century A.D., who ultimately decided what would be lost and what preserved by his selection. Ziegler (2047) cast doubt on this conviction, which has all but vanished today.[11] For this field too papyri have been a major factor in altering interpretations. Other sources, quotations in various authors, can be adduced to prove the existence far beyond the Antonine period of dramas not contained in the aforementioned selection. Since, on the other hand, a special preference for the works in the selection is discernible from the Hellenistic age onward, we can see in our tradition the result of a long development

during which the canon of what was read constantly shrank. Wilamowitz was right
that the influence of the schools must have been very strong. This influence could
also help explain the thematic agreement of the plays preserved from the different
tragedians. In schools, the canon reflected in the numbers given above must finally
have become dominant. The transition from the papyrus roll to the parchment codex
no doubt also played a significant role. If we date the breakthrough of the new book
form in the fourth century A.D., this identifies only one important stage in a quite
complicated development.[12]

The question of how the texts of the tragedies survived the Dark Ages from
the decline of ancient culture until the Byzantine renaissance is connected with the
further question of what the medieval tradition took as its point of departure. For a
long time it was believed that Wilamowitz provided the answer—and not only for
Aischylos—in the Praefatio of his edition: "Unum esse librum, e quo omnis Aeschyli
memoria per omnes hos quos enumeravi codices repetenda est, nemo poterat non
videre, qui in fundamenta recensionis inquireret" (No one who has done research
into the basics of recension can fail to see that there was one text which must have
been the source of the whole tradition of Aischylos in all the codices I enumerated).
This belief in a codex unicus, which alone had survived the dark centuries to be the
exclusive source for the Byzantines, has been subjected more recently to strong doubt
or at least to modification. We will return to this point in connection with Euripides;
here let us first consider some points that apply to all three poets. Any theory must
account for the extensive agreement of our manuscripts as well as for the numerous
deviations. This is possible under the assumption of several uncial manuscripts that
survived into the ninth century and were used by the Byzantines. Here is the most
radically skeptical position regarding the postulate of a common archetype as taken
up by Dawe (160): "But when this archetype existed it is impossible to say: it could
be the Alexandrian edition itself, or it could . . . belong to the second century A.D.,
the time of our papyrus evidence. But there are many other possibilities open, and
our wisest course is to suspend judgement." However, instead of abandoning the
problem, we prefer the consideration offered by Zuntz (*Inquiry*, 261) for the plays
selected from Euripides. Zuntz properly evaluates the act crucial to the history of
manuscript tradition, the transcription of the uncial texts into Byzantine minuscules.[13] This transcription was a tedious process, and of course also a new source of
error. It is quite conceivable that such pains were taken only with an ancient manuscript. The wide range of variations found in our medieval tradition could be satisfactorily explained if this one transcription were accompanied by numerous variant
readings that had been gleaned from the collation of other available uncial codices.
Of course ancient manuscripts could also have included variations of their own, as
the Menander papyrus from Cairo illustrates. This theory rids us of that peculiar
codex unicus so miraculously rescued from shipwreck. The uncertainty that remains
is at least an advance over the dogmatic statement of Wilamowitz.

The unquestioned goal of recensio until recently was to establish a stemma
that would portray the interrelationship of the individual manuscripts. This was still
the object of Turyn's work on the tradition. A rebellious objection to this method has

recently been raised by Dawe for Aischylos and by di Benedetto for Euripides. It is argued that we can never obtain a secure vertical description of our tradition, in the sense of fixed lines of succession, because we must also reckon with reciprocal horizontal effects, contamination of the most various manuscripts caused by industrious collation. For Aischylos, Dawe has supported his conviction by careful examination of individual passages and comes to the conclusion (27): "even well-behaved manuscripts habitually desert their group, often correcting inherited errors by means of collation with exemplars belonging to other groups." This interpretation ends with the radical denial of the possibility of establishing stemmata. At best, Dawe claims, we can separate individual manuscript groups. This could be achieved for, say, BHΓΔ (notation according to Turyn).

These recent investigations amount to something like a revolution in the scholarship of tragedy. M. L. West, in his edition of the *Theogony*, also finds the manuscript tradition to a great extent characterized by contamination. But to reject every stemma, however fragmentary, is ill-advised. In the future, scholars will have to be more cautious than before in assuming dependencies, and they will probably reject any claim of completeness on the part of such stemmata, but we should never abandon any and all vertical considerations of our tradition in favor of one exclusively horizontal.

The oldest and most valuable of our Aischylos manuscripts is the Mediceus (Laurentianus 32. 9). It originally contained only the seven Aischylos tragedies (the only one with all seven and with the best scholia) and the *Argonautika* of Apollonios. Later the seven plays of Sophokles were bound together with these. Written about 1000, it was brought from Constantinople to Italy by G. Aurispa in 1423, and in the second half of the fifteenth century it came into the possession of the Laurentian Library. The entire eighteenth quaternio is missing, as well as the greater part of the nineteenth, which affects the *Ag.* 311–1066 and 1160–end, and also the beginning of the *Libation Bearers*. One hand can be distinguished for *Pers.* 1–702 and a second for the rest. Then everything was checked by a corrector, who altered a great deal, but we have not yet been able to determine if he used an independent source for the corrections. Dawe has gone too far in his depreciation of the Mediceus: the fifth chapter of his own book speaks rather for its worth.

The Byzantines made a later selection when they joined *Prom.*, *Seven*, and *Pers.* in a triad. The confidence with which Wilamowitz and Murray placed the majority of the manuscripts of this triad under a common archetype independent of M has been questioned by Dawe, who is content to arrange the manuscripts into tight groups that are not, however, inextricably bound together. Both aforementioned editors have already called attention to the special position of Q (Paris. gr. 2884; written 1299).

A Byzantine grammarian added *Ag.* and *Eum.* to the triad. This pentad, our only source for large sections of the *Ag.*, is preserved, among other places, in the Farnesinus (now Naples, II F 31), written by Triklinios himself in 1320. Zuntz has shown that we are dealing here with the end result of Triklinios's rather lengthy preoccupation with the texts, for which the manuscripts F (Laur. 31. 8) and G (Ven. Marc. 616) are preliminary stages that bear witness to his earlier work on Aischylos.[14] This yields an interesting parallel to Zuntz's observations concerning the work of Triklinios on Euripides.

Turyn, in his monumental studies, has placed great emphasis on the question of distinguishing the ancient tradition from Byzantine conjectures. His goal was to separate everything traceable to the Byzantines as a later addition and to rid our recensio of it. His work was continued by E. A. E. Bryson, with special emphasis on Thomas Magister.[15] Paul Maas has called attention to the difficulty of drawing definite lines of demarcation,[16] and Dawe has now described all the factors of uncertainty that will always be involved in an investigation of this sort.[17]

The strong emphasis of recent times on the horizontal components of our tradition corroborates Mazon's statement (in his edition, p. xxiv) that our evaluation of the manuscripts must necessarily be eclectic, within certain limits.

Schmid (2. 309) lists earlier editions, but we must gratefully mention here the textual achievements of men like G. Hermann (Leipzig 1852, 2d ed., 1859) and H. Weil (Giessen 1858/1867, Leipzig 1884; ed. ster., 1903). Newer editions are Wilamowitz (Berlin 1914, second printing 1958; ed. min., 1915); P. Mazon (2 volumes with French translation, Paris 1920/1925, new editions up to 1965); G. Murray (Oxford 1937, revised 1955) and M. Untersteiner (Ed. critica con trad. e note italiane, 2 vols. Milan 1946/1947). The first three of these editions were subjected to sharp criticism by Dawe (7), who contested the principle of their apparatus: ". . . necessity of having either a fairly full apparatus or none at all." This demand, with its standard of absolute perfection, naturally has its ideal justification. How the demand can be met is another question. The eclectic apparatus, which implies of course the rejection of the attempt to account for the tradition, can still be of use, even though this involves considerable latitude for subjective decisions in the choice of readings. Further, Dawe has shown that these editions contain in their apparatus much erroneous data regarding readings, corrections, glosses, and the source of conjectures. He maintains, quite fairly, that this is the result of a quite old tradition of errors that none of the editions could successfully deal with. Dawe offers in the second part of his book the specimen of an apparatus for the Byzantine triad (Prom., Seven, Pers.), based on careful collations of seventeen manuscripts. Precisely the narrow limits of this admirable achievement show how much work would be involved in reaching the goal set by Dawe. It is somewhat comforting to know that the demonstrated inadequacy of the apparatus has almost never led to a distortion of the text itself. Dawe's book, as well as his "Repertory of Conjectures of Aeschylus" (see Bibliography) presents an extraordinarily valuable preliminary study for a new edition of Aischylos, which D. L. Page has now provided, Oxford 1972.

The edition of the scholia in the third volume of the Oxford Aischylos edition of W. Dindorf is unsatisfactory;[18] O. Dähnhardt, Leipzig 1894, has edited the scholia on the Persians; Lidia Massa-Positano, Naples 1948, 2d ed. 1963, has edited the scholia of Triklinios for this play. See also C. J. Herington, The Older Scholia on Prom. Bound, Leyden 1972.

The first complete commentary on Aischylos in English since Paley (1897) was composed by H. J. Rose, *A Commentary on the Surviving Plays of Aeschylus*, Verh. Kon. Nederl. Akad. Afd. Letterkunde n.s. 64, nos. 1 and 2, Amsterdam 1957/1958. The commentary is primarily concerned with textual criticism and verbal explanation, and it excludes wide areas of exegesis. There are Dutch commentaries on all the plays and we shall cite these for the individual dramas. W. Kraus, *Strophengestaltung in der gr. Tragödie*, I: *Aischylos und Sophokles*, Sitzb. Oest. Ak. Phil.-Hist. Kl. 231/4, 1957 is helpful not only for metrical structure but also for interpretation.

The bibliography for the fragments of Aischylean dramas will be found at the beginning of the section on this topic. An indispensable aid is G. Italie's *Index Aeschyleus*, 2d ed., Leyden 1964 (with ten pages of addenda by Stefan Radt).

Finally, a few translations or new editions of older ones: Lewis Campbell, *The Seven Plays in English Verse*, World's Classics, no. 117, Oxford; L. Wolde, Samml. Dieterich 17, Leipzig 1938; J. G. Droysen-Walter Nestle, Kröners Taschenausg. 152, 2d ed., Stuttgart 1957, with valuable introductions. F. Stoessl also revised Droysen's translation, Bibl. d. Alten Welt, Zurich 1952 and offers besides introductions to some of the fragments. These pieces were recently published by W. Steffen, Berlin 1968. The translation of H. F. Waser, Zurich 1952, is composed in a grotesquely exaggerated verbal style. A dual-language edition with many aids was carefully prepared by O. Werner, Munich 1959; it is a fine Tusculum volume on thin paper. For the Fischer Bibliothek der Hundert Bücher, W. H. Friedrich, Frankfurt am Main 1961, compiled and edited an impressive collection of older Aischylos translations and added a noteworthy afterword. Included are H. Voss (*Persians* 1826), J. J. C. Donner (*Seven* 1854), G. Droysen (*Hik., Choe.* 1832, 1842), W. Humboldt (*Ag.* 1816), K. O. Müller (*Eum.* 1833), Leopold Graf Stolberg (*Prom.* 1802). A complete Italian translation by C. Carena appeared in Einaudi in 1956. The Spanish translation of Brieva y Salvatierra, first published in 1880, has been superseded by F. Rodríguez Adrados, *Esquilo Tragedias*, Traducción nueva, 2 vols., Madrid 1966. In the *Complete Greek Tragedies*, the translations of Aischylos were done by Richmond Lattimore, S. G. Benardete, and David Grene, Chicago 1959. We should not forget here the powerful influence exercised for so long by Gilbert Murray's translations of the tragedies (including the complete Aischylos).[19]

THE EXTANT TRAGEDIES

A tiny scrap of papyrus has radically changed our picture of the development of Aischylean tragedy. The twentieth volume of *The Oxyrynchus Papyri* (1952) offers under no. 2256 as fr. 3 the scanty remains of a didaskalia that poses some difficult questions for the names of the plays specified and for the succession in which they are listed. But the following facts are certain: at the performance referred to by our didaskalia, Aischylos won first prize with his *Danaid Trilogy* and the satyr play *Amymone*. Sophokles came in second; third was a Mesatos, whose existence was first postulated but later challenged. Whoever connects these facts with the first performance of the trilogy that began with the *Hiketides* (*Suppliants*)—which we consider necessary— arrives at a date that differs considerably from the early estimate proposed by so many scholars.[1] Since we have confirmed the year 468 for the first performance of Sophokles, which also marked his first victory, (*Marm. Par.* 56 with Plutarch, *Kimon* 8), we now have a terminus post for the *Danaid Trilogy* of Aischylos. The year 468 is excluded by the victory of Sophokles; 467 was the year of Aischylos's *Theban Trilogy*. Thus this year and 458 (the performance of the *Oresteia*) are established as the chronological boundaries within which we now must place the *Suppliants*.[2]

A more exact dating seems possible. Lobel was able to connect a tiny piece to our fragment, which contains the letters ἐπια[; and the remnant of the following letter suggests a ϱ. In the Loeb Classical Library edition of Aischylos, Lloyd-Jones gives ἐπὶ ἀϱ[, on the basis of his own comparison. The possibilities exist for restoring it to ἐπὶ ἄϱχοντος, or with the name of the archon for the year 463 to ἐπὶ Ἀϱχεδημίδου. For the second variant, there may be adduced the form of the synopses for the *Persians* and *Seven*, as well as to Sophokles' *Philoctetes*, which by the conciseness of their composition suggest proximity to the Alexandrian original. There is another important point: there was discovered at the same time a fragment of a didaskalia on the *Theban Trilogy* (*P. Oxy.* 2256 fr. 2), probably written by the same hand, which gives the dating with ἐπὶ Θεαγ]ενίδου.[3] With the year 463 we come very close to the estimate "around 462" that Walter Nestle had defended against general opposition long before the didaskalia came to light.[4]

There has been no lack of attempts to avoid the conclusions just drawn. A posthumous performance was considered; and in fact the *Suda* article on Aischylos reports that his son Euphorion was victorious four times with plays of his father that had never been produced. But these dramas, just as in comparable instances with Sophokles and Euripides, would have been plays from the last years of the poet, and therefore would not include the *Suppliants*. But the decisive factor is that, according to the *Suda*, Euphorion himself was awarded the victory, which fits very well with the didaskalia on the *Theban Trilogy*, where it is reported of Aristias that he won second prize with tragedies of his father Pratinas. In our didaskalia, however, Aischylos and no one else appears as victor, thus excluding the possibility of the fragment's referring to a posthumous performance.

As a final escape, the hypothesis remains open that Aischylos did in fact compose the *Danaid Trilogy* at an early stage of his career but produced it on stage much later. The idea of "writing for the drawer" was also suggested for the dating of the *Elektra* of Euripides in a similar argument by Theiler. Of course no one would postulate that all the plays of the ancient tragedians were written in the year of their first performance, but we have not the slightest evidence that any of these poets ever put a play aside in order to resurrect it again after some period of time. Therefore it seems misguided to use an assumption that applies much more to modern circumstances in order to confirm a date that is supported only by the conception of a continuous process of Aischylos's artistic development. Whoever reflects on the deeply archaic character of the *Seven* (467 B.C.), still far from the perfection of the *Oresteia*, will have no difficulty in assigning the *Suppliants* to a year close to that of the *Seven*.

As a result, we are in the same position regarding Aischylos as we are regarding the two other great tragedians: early works are denied to us; we become acquainted with these poets only at the height of their creative power.

In 472 Aischylos was victorious with a tetralogy that consisted of *Phineus, Persians,*[5] *Glaukos Potnieus,* and the satyr play *Prometheus Pyrkaeus.* The choragos was Perikles.

The *Persians* begins with anapests of the chorus of the elders who have remained at home (1–64); they introduce themselves in the opening verses. Immediately they introduce the motif that dominates most of the exposition, that of concern for the army abroad; here Xerxes appears imprudent and rash, a νέος ἀνήρ (young man), in anticipation of his later characterization. A motif follows that constantly joins and meshes with the concern motif: the broad portrayal of the Persians' power, a portrayal heightened by an abundance of foreign names. The succession of geographical designations, names of the commanders and the naming of the weapon types divide the section. The composition is circular; the conclusion repeats and intensifies the concern motif.

Both basic themes of the anapests also dominate the following ode (65–139). The first three pairs of strophes are composed in ionics, "the barbarian motif of tragic meter" (Kraus). These strophes bring movement into a heretofore static picture of Persian power, describing the crossing of the Hellespont, and they introduce the hubris motif, important in the Dareios section, with "the yoke on the neck of the sea." The Lord of Asia appears in the first antistrophe as the driving force of the expedition, whose irresistible dynamism, destined for Persia by divine decree, is broadly developed. The next section (93–100), still in ionics (to be placed after v. 114; O. Müller), is revealed by the change in motifs it contains to be the central portion of the entire ode. In shrill dissonance the anxious question follows the portrayal of power: "But the crafty deceit of god, what mortal man will escape it . . . ?" Ate sets inescapable traps. And the two last strophe pairs, beginning with lekythia, are wholly characterized by the fear and grief of those at home. The suffering of the women dominates at the end and thus points forward to the coming of Atossa.

Curious anapests of the chorus leader follow (140–154), with the exhortation to hold a council meeting on the fortunes of Xerxes by a στέγος ἀρχαῖον (old building). But this meeting does not take place; the final section of the anapests announces the coming of the queen-mother Atossa. That she enters in her chariot with full pomp is attested by verses 607 ff.

The large section before the first fixed stasimon (155–531) is divided into two parts: the disquieting dreams related by Atossa are followed by the lightning stroke of catastrophe. The path from premonition to terrible fulfillment is the same one that Aischylos describes in the *Agamemnon,* when he is at the peak of his artistic skill.

The Atossa section (we will not speak of "acts" here) is composed as a triptych: trochaic passages frame the narration of the queen's dream.

The chorus leader, declaiming in trochaics, greets Atossa as the consort of a Persian god, the mother of a god. But this exaltation is followed immediately by the fear that the ancient daimon who assured their power might have abandoned the army. With this, the cue is given for Atossa's reply, wholly determined by anxiety for her house. This anxiety still remains vague; not until the start of the trimeters do we learn that a dream has deeply upset the queen. In this dream, Xerxes wished to yoke two women to his chariot, one dressed in the Persian style, the other in the Doric (here synonymous with Greek). The Greek shattered the yoke and caused the king to fall. Significantly, Dareios sorrowfully approaches his fallen son. Over and over, the mention of the dead king's name prepares for his appearance. During a sacrifice intended to dispel her anxiety, Atossa saw a fearful omen: an eagle torn to pieces by a falcon. In the trochaics that close this section, the chorus leader advises the queen to pray to the gods and to make sacrifice to the chthonic powers, which leads to another mention of Dareios (221). Atossa inquires about the situation, power, and government of Athens in the following conversation, which turns into a stichomythy. The poet makes use here of the freedom granted him to allow information that must have been common knowledge for some time to be presented anew to us in a question-and-answer exchange. Here all light is focused on Athens, which appears (234; cf. 348, 824, 975; but 817, the Doric spear in connection with Plataiai!) as Ἑλλάδος Ἑλλάς (the Hellas of Hellas, i.e. the essence of Hellas; *Anth. Pal.* 7. 45). From her freedom Athens creates the power that already had conquered the army of Dareios.

This recollection of the past defeat provides a direct link to the present catastrophe, for now at 246 the chorus leader announces that the messenger is rapidly approaching.

The messenger section is divided up as a triad of speeches, each with its own exposition. It begins fortissimo with the first trimeters of the messenger: with one blow the entire Persian force was destroyed. The recapitulation of the total disaster in a few words triggers the lament of the chorus in an epirrhematic structure (256–289), where short lyric laments answer the trimeters of the messenger, who piles grief upon grief. The first and most comprehensive report of the battle has a prelude composed with great skill and psychological insight (290–352). The messenger understands at once Atossa's question about the fallen leaders as being the question of a mother: Xerxes lives. A list of losses follows (302–330), intimating the extent of the disaster by the plethora of names, structurally an artfully composed catalogue. First, three sets of two trimeters each name one victim, then two sets of three verses each name three more. After this, architecture of this sort is abandoned, but verses 320–325 (with five names) clearly show an escalation in the final section, ending in the broad utterance of the name Syennesis.

Atossa's question about the start of the sea battle leads to the great report on Salamis (353–432), the finest monument that the decisive hours of a people have ever received. A short exchange with Atossa results in the second report of the messenger, which tells of the catastrophe of the Persian elite on Psyttaleia and the flight of Xerxes. The lament of the queen and her question about the survivors then divide the third report from the second. Now we hear of the suffering of the retreat, which brought only a very few in deepest misery back to Susa. Following the two typical trimeters of the chorus (515 f.), Atossa concludes the messenger section with laments and the announcement of sacrifices (517–531). At the end she warns the chorus to give Xerxes a friendly welcome should he come before she returns.

Anapests of lament, primarily descriptive of the suffering of the women, form the transition to the stasimon (548–597), although in view of the atypical construction of this play it is difficult to speak of a first stasimon. A litany of lamentation over the catastrophe (first pair of strophes) leads to the fate of the corpses (second pair of strophes) and to concern for the stability of Persian hegemony (third pair of strophes), an obvious presage of the Dareios section.

This second great segment of the drama (598–851) likewise contains a broad prelude (containing the conjuration) followed by three speeches of great dramatic weight.

Atossa enters without royal pomp, minutely describing her offerings to the dead (598–622; who could speak here of an epeisodion!); the chorus bids her in anapests (623–632) to make sacrifice and prepares for the following song of conjuration (633–680; three short pairs of strophes with a closing epode) with its appeal to the chthonic deities. Here already the portrayal of Dareios receives its clear features: the great king, the beloved symbol of a magnificent past.

In a short speech of trimeters Dareios, arisen from Hades, asks why he has been summoned. The chorus, remaining in obeisance, confesses in a short ionic strophe that it does not dare confront the king with word or look. Dareios perseveres in three tetrameters that clearly express his increasing emotion, and again the chorus affirms its inability to answer. The king then (trochaic tetrameters remain the rhythm until v. 758) turns to his wife, who, like the messenger, epitomizes the catastrophe in a single sentence. In the following stichomythy (715–738), Dareios asks for the details; then in his first speech, he interprets the event: the hubris of Xerxes, who made the sea into land and bound the Bosporos with chains, who blasphemously encroached upon the divine realm of nature and brought on the disaster long foretold by oracle. For when a man is himself full of blind passion, the god also joins in leading him to his ruin. We recall the "crafty deceit of the god" sung of by the chorus at the beginning of the play. But it is not yet made clear that this involvement of the divinity is a part of the poet's theodicy. The tetrameters of Atossa immediately thereafter (753–758) attempt to vindicate Xerxes: bad advisers goaded him on, he had to increase the power amassed by Dareios. The second speech of Dareios follows; its trimeters represent the transition to a calm report. Atossa's recollection of former power is taken up in a retrospective passage that spans many generations of rulers. A conversational interlude (787–799) leads via the chorus leader's question "What now?" to the king's warning against any further undertaking against Hellas and then, with a skillful transition, to the announcement of what is to come in the third and longest speech of this trikolon, whose parts increase in length (14:28?:43). That the same Dareios who had to ask about past events now knows so much about the future is partly justified by the reference to oracles at the beginning of this speech. The heart of the prophecy is the defeat at Plataiai, which also acknowledges the Spartans with the mention of the "Doric spear." This Persian catastrophe is also a result of hubris: the destruction of Greek sanctuaries aroused divine wrath. The speech closes with the admonition to Atossa to meet their son and to bring him royal robes to replace his tattered garments.

After short lamentations of the chorus leader and Atossa, who is ready to rush to her son with new vestments, there follows a choral song in three strophes with a final epode praising the power and accomplishments of Dareios; this ode reflects on the previous passage and provides an effective contrast to the appearance of Xerxes.

The final section, whose central figure is the defeated king, begins with an-apestic lamentation, to which the chorus leader responds in the same meter. Then the chorus takes up the tones of mourning in lyric anapests and thus offers a transi-tion to the great threnos with its seven pairs of strophes and closing epode (931–1077). Although the meter at first is predominantly anapestic, this gives way in the course of the ode to agitated iambics. The grammatically closed statements of the king and chorus are followed by a succession of very short laments and wails in a sort of lyric stichomythy, from 1002 on. The play ends in a furioso of grief.

Wilamowitz is correct in rejecting the use of concepts like epeisodion and stas-imon for the *Persians*, but we cannot follow him when he criticizes its structure as consisting of three disjointed acts that are insufficiently connected.[6] Of course the architecture of the piece still appears archaic in comparison with the dramas in the high classical style, but this in no way implies that architecture is not there. Prepa-ration and final lament enclose two large sections separated by the ode (532–597), and they are fairly balanced in size: the messenger section (249–531) and the Dareios section (598–851). Between these two sections we can determine a formal responsion in that each of them contains three speeches, of which the last has for its subject the battle of Salamis. A further obvious correspondence between the frame sections re-sides in the abundance of foreign names. That the exposition, which we mark off from 1–248, is especially long, and the final threnos section conversely quite short, corresponds to an Aischylean mode of composition also demonstrable elsewhere. The preceding analysis should, however, make clear that a magnificent crescendo runs through the whole piece: from fearful premonition to one heightened by dreams; from the announcement of the catastrophe to the ascent of the interpreter from the realm of the dead and the final outpouring of grief.

The hypothesis of the *Persians* informs us that Glaukos (of Rhegion) termed our drama a recasting of the *Phoinissai* of Phrynichos. But there is much that speaks for a considerable difference between the two plays. Phrynichos opens with the pro-logizing eunuch, Aischylos with the chorus; the chorus of Phoinikian women differs from that of the Persian elders, and the announcement of Xerxes' defeat made at the beginning from the suspenseful preparation of the report by the younger poet. That the interpretive Dareios section belongs in its totality to Aischylos is very probable.

The question of the influence of the older play becomes urgent at the sugges-tion of a council meeting by the chorus leader (140). This meeting does not take place, nor is the question how Xerxes is doing a fitting subject for such. The words τόδ' ἐνεζόμενοι στέγος ἀρχαῖον (sitting on [in] this old building) remain completely mysterious. This invitation to a meeting that comes to nothing certainly does have a scenic function: the chorus has just sung its song in the orchestra, and now it must make room for Atossa's entry in her chariot. But if a motive for this is introduced that is never realized, it remains the most probable assumption that the poet took this over from the *Phoinissai* of Phrynichos, for whose beginning the hypothesis to the *Persians* expressly attests such a council meeting.[7]

With the question of the στέγος (στέος MA) ἀρχαῖον which, judging by the pronoun τόδε, was visible in some form or other, we come to the problem of the Aischylean stage before 458, the year of the performance of the *Oresteia*, which presumes a wooden skene as a fixed stage backdrop. For the *Persians* this is connected with the other question, where the στέγος ἀρχαῖον stood with reference to the tomb of Dareios, which likewise must have been visible.[8] In itself, the presumption of fixed backdrop for the *Persians* cannot be excluded a priori, but both the *Seven* and the *Suppliants* present another picture. It would be strange if this fixed wall appeared only in the fleeting mention of the στέγος ἀρχαῖον, while the palace from which Atossa rides in her chariot must be thought of as outside the stage area. For the *Persians* too we come to the assumption of a simple, perhaps tentlike wooden construction in the section of the orchestra separated from the audience. We may speculate that this is the same structure that serves as Dareios's tomb in the second half, on top of which the ghost of Dareios appears, while the elders, in the scene in question, sit on the slope or the steps of this structure.[9] Its completely vague description could thus be easily understood.

In our biographical section we spoke of the repeat performance of the *Persians* in Syrakuse. The question arises as to whether this involved a revision of the drama and whether traces of such a revision are still recognizable. In the *Frogs* of Aristophanes, Dionysos speaks (1028 f.), in a corrupt verse, of the joy he experienced at the play in connection (but how so?) with the dead king Dareios; he then adds that the chorus applauded and called ἰαυοῖ. With difficulty this could be reconciled with our play, if we join Radermacher in his commentary on the *Frogs* in seeking an emendation along the lines of ἀκούοντες τὰ πρὸ Δαρείου τεθνεῶτος. The ancient commentators thought otherwise, according to the scholium on *Ran.* 1028:[10] Herodikos (if the passage has been correctly restored by Dobree) and Didymos assumed two versions. In addition there are two phrases attested for the *Persians* that are not in fact preserved in our piece: νηριτότροφος in Athen. 3. 86B and ὑπόξυλος in schol. Hermogenes *Rhet. Gr.* 5. 486. Confusion with the *Perraibides* has been suggested here. We can draw no convincing conclusion regarding a second version for Syrakuse based on linguistic and dramatic anomalies in the preserved text, as Broadhead shows in his introduction. We follow him in admitting this as a possibility that cannot be proved.

Scholars have often been troubled by the passages in which Atossa speaks of her son's arrival.[11] She instructs the chorus to meet Xerxes graciously, should he come before her (529–531). However, after the choral song it is not Xerxes who appears, but Atossa, with the offerings for the dead. At 849–851 she announces, following the counsel of Dareios (832), that she will bring royal robes from the palace and attempt to meet her son.[12] But this meeting does not take place; Atossa never returns to the stage. There is no justification here for placing the first statement of Atossa after the

second (H. Weil), nor for any hypotheses about a version in which the plot ran differently. Dawe (30) correctly understood both passages as clasps that prepare the entrance of Xerxes but at the same time also arouse suspense concerning what is to
come. Further, we can see in them the attempt to portray the emotional bond between mother and son in a play that does not have a meeting between the two.

The *Persians* is a historical drama, but it transcends this level through the interpretation that the event receives. The victory of the Greeks is as much their work
as that of the gods who punish excess and sacrilege. No word of scorn for the opponent is uttered; his power is taken quite as seriously as the tragedy of his fall. The
figure of Dareios appears so magnified as to be entrusted with the revelation of the
meaning of the event. Of course the play remains a historical document, and it will
not be forgotten that the great report of the battle was written by one who fought in
it.[13] Beyond this we may ask whether we can perceive connections between the *Persians* and the situation in Athens about 472. The play was performed on the eve of
Themistokles' ostracism, and it is tempting to suggest, as Podlecki (12) has recently
done, that it was produced on behalf of the statesman whose position was at the time
already badly shaken.[14] Of course Aischylos did not write the play merely for a political purpose; we can also ask whether the play, centered as it was around Salamis, was
not obliged to include praise of the man who was the soul of the defense. In any event
it must be considered that the long report of the messenger (353) begins with the
decisive ruse of Themistokles, and at the mention of the silver mines of Laurion,
every Athenian probably thought of Themistokles' use of increased revenue for the
construction of the fleet.[15]

The *Persians* was preceded by the *Phineus*, which probably contained the adventure of the Argonauts concerning the blind man freed from the harpies. The attempt of Andresen to ascribe *P. Oxy.* 20, 2256 fr. 10 = fr. 538M to this play is not
persuasive.[16]

We know somewhat more about the play that followed the *Persians*.[17] Although the Mediceus lists it in the hypothesis merely as *Glaukos*, we have no reason
to doubt the full title *Glaukos Potnieus* in the manuscripts PVR. *P. Oxy.* 2160 = frr.
442–444; 447–449M, and *PSI* 1210 = frr. 441 f.M), with schol. Aristoph. *Ran.* 1528,
confirms for the content of the piece the fate of Glaukos, who was torn apart by his
own mares. This is probably connected with Servius on Verg. *Georg.* 3. 268, according
to which Glaukos, hoping to increase the speed of the animals, did not allow them to
mate, so that the wrath of Aphrodite struck him. The fatal chariot race probably took
place at the funeral games of Pelias.

As satyr play, the hypothesis to the *Persians* names a *Prometheus* without amplification, but individual fragments make clear this can only refer to the *Prometheus Pyrkaeus*. One of our finest papyrus texts can most probably be ascribed to this
drama.[18] In it the satyrs praise in song the miraculous gift brought by Prometheus and
its effect on nymphs and naiads. A magnificent kalyx-krater in the Ashmolean Museum from ca. 425–420 shows Prometheus, who has joined the satyrs, with the flame
on a narthex stalk, without doubt an illustration of the play.[19] N. Terzaghi considered
ascribing the papyrus in question to the *Prometheus Pyrphoros*; he wishes to see

here the rejoicing of divine beings over the reconciliation of the Olympians with Prometheus, but the attempt is not convincing.[20] A similar course was chosen by Mette, who inserts in his fr. 343 as verses 14–16 an Aischylos fragment preserved in Homer scholia, in which a female chorus is bidden to walk around a fire altar and pray.[21] On the basis of this necessarily hypothetical combination, he considers assigning our papyrus to a chorus of Okeanids that he assumes for the *Pyrphoros*.

The attempt has been made to connect these three tragedies in a thematic trilogy. Murray (113) thought of a prophecy of the Persian invasion by the blind Phineus and tried to obtain a link with the *Persians* through Potniai as the scene of the death of the Persian general Masistios. But even links as loose as this are improbable.[22] And even if the *Suda* reports that Sophokles was the first to compete in an agon with individual dramas, we must still realize that unity through content was not the rule for Aischylos. In this context the late dating of the *Suppliants* acquires special weight. The oldest preserved and reliably dated play is now the *Persians*, which stands outside any trilogical structure. It seems a reasonable conclusion that the content trilogy, perhaps Aischylos's most personal and splendid creation, had not yet become the norm at the time of the *Persians*.

The year of performance, 467, is confirmed also for the *Seven Against Thebes*.[23] The surviving play concluded a trilogy that began with the *Laios* and *Oidipous*; the satyr play was the *Sphinx*.

In a development that Schweitzer has well described, certain mythic materials, above all the legends of Troy and Thebes, grow henceforth into splendid form and are fitted into a profound, religious world view, thus achieving monumentality.[24] For the content of the Theban trilogy we may assume some historical background relating to the antagonism between Thebes and Argos in Mycenaean times, provided that we remember that a saga may contain history, but shapes it according to its own laws.[25]

Of the lost plays we know very little more than what their titles say. Stoessl has gone far in his utilization of methods developed by Zielinski in order to reconstruct lost plays from their influence in transmitted ones.[26] But no detailed scenario for the Aischylean *Laios* can be gleaned from the *Oid. Tyr.* of Sophokles, nor from his *Oid. Kol.* for the second drama of the Theban trilogy. The attempt of Deubner to postulate an Aischylean *Oidipous* play related to the *Kolonos* on the basis of schol. Hom. *Od.* 11. 271 (according to the atthidographer Androtion) also fails to convince.[27] The only real clue is offered by the remnants of the hypothesis to the tetralogy in *P. Oxy.* 20, 2256 fr. 2.4.1. = fr. 169M: Laios spoke the prologue in the first play; the chorus consisted of old men of the city. Three trimeters from the messenger's report of Laios's murder are probably preserved in fr. 172M. For the *Oidipous* the most probable assumption is that this report brought the discovery of the outrage. If fr. 169M is to be ascribed to this drama, then Aischylos anticipated the motif of the plague in Thebes.

The prologue of the *Seven*, in the ancient sense of the section before the parodos of the chorus (1–77), offers a short prelude, in which basic motifs of the drama are prefigured. It begins with a speech of Eteokles, who presents himself as the man responsible for the defense of Thebes. Here, as later, we are told nothing of the events

involving the division of power that preceded the battle. In this way the poet preserved his freedom to portray Eteokles as the responsible king, but at the same time
he could show both brothers as the victims of the family curse. The emphasis on the
gates (30, 33; cf. 56–58) prepares the way for the large, central section with its seven
pairs of speeches. A prophecy about the impending battle brings the first surge of
excitement, which is picked up by the messenger's report. When Aischylos has him
say that he left the enemy leaders casting lots for the gates they will attack, and in
the same breath describe the Argives marching against the city, he is treating chronological relations with the same high-handedness he displays elsewhere (*Ag.*!). In all
cases of this type, attempts at rational adjustment are misguided. A prayer by Eteokles concludes the prologue. In this, the curse and the Erinyes appear next to the
defending gods of the city, an extremely succinct anticipation of the two images of
Eteokles, whose development in the two parts of the play forms its subject matter.
Eteokles entreats the gods to spare a city that speaks the Greek language. In addition
the chorus prays (170) that Thebes not be handed over to ἑτεϱοφώνῳ στϱατῷ (a foreign-
speaking army). Is this merely a reference to differences of dialect? Or are reminiscences from the Persian Wars still at work here?

      Now the chorus of Theban girls (probably not in an orderly entrance march)
occupies the raised community altar. They sing (219) of θεῶν ἅδε πανάγυϱις (this assembly of gods), which must be a κοινοβωμία (community altar), such as we shall see
later in the *Suppliants.* The parodos (78–180) elaborates the image of an uncontrolled
panic, mostly in the form of desperate appeals to individual gods. Dochmiacs are
heavily represented, especially in the opening lines. A non-strophic section with individual responsive elements (78–150) is followed by two pairs of short responsive
strophes (Kraus, 58). The image of an on-marching army fades into the image of an
attack already in progress. Optical impressions give way to acoustic ones. Whirling
dust climbs high in the air (81), the clash of shields (100; 160, already at the gates),
the striking of spears (103; violently increased, 155) and the rattling of the chariots
(151) produce a symphony of horror. The confusion of perceptual spheres in κτύπον
δέδοϱκα (I saw the noise; 103, to be retained of course) works as a symptom of frightened confusion.

      Two domains of a most contradictory nature are set before us: on one side the
judicious helmsman of the state, praying calmly, and on the other side the terrified
chorus, in the grip of panic. This contrast is maintained with slightly varying intensity throughout the following section (181–286), in which two speeches of Eteokles,
balanced in length, surround an epirrhematic passage followed by stichomythy. In his
first speech (181–202) the king sharply chides the frightened girls as insufferable
womenfolk; in the following epirrhematic section (203–244), although the chorus
sings in agitated dochmiacs, the two parties agree on the point that prayer is now a
matter for the women, but only such prayer, Eteokles demands, as does not create
confusion. Again the contrast between calmness and fear is sharpened in the stichomythy (245–263), but the chorus leader ends it with a word of clearer judgment,
to which the king can add a more friendly admonition in his concluding speech (264–
286). He himself then appeals to the gods, thus taking up and amplifying the prayer

at the close of the prologue scene. Of scenic importance is v. 265, since the request that the chorus sing its prayer ἐκτὸς οὖσ' ἀγαλμάτων (away from the divine statues) is clearly intended to direct the chorus from the community altar into the orchestra. At the end of his speech Eteokles announces that he will now post suitable defenders against the attackers at the seven gates. Whether this action does not come rather late, given the situation previously described, is, again, a misguided question. The statement is significant, however, that the posting should occur before hasty messengers spread panic in the city. Such a messenger appears immediately after the following choral song; we understand that we have been prepared for the possibility that Eteokles might not have been able to conclude the tactical instructions by the time of his next entrance.

A word of submission (μέλει) connects the following choral ode (three pairs of strophes; 287–368) with the admonition of the ruler. But once again fear breaks out immediately. The real prayer is contained only in 301–320; the rest is a description, characterized by fear, of the horrible misery threatening Thebes.

If the chorus has up to now dominated the stage as the antagonist of the king, the long central portion of the drama is dominated by the archaic structure of the seven paired speeches, unique in all of Greek tragedy. The semi-chorus leaders announce the arrival of the messenger and king in three verses each; their haste is especially emphasized. In the following pairs of speeches (375–676), the messenger names and characterizes one of the attackers each time; in the process, the heraldic devices on their shields serve the purpose of characterization in ingenious variations. In his answer, Eteokles designates the Theban champion appointed to oppose the enemy, gate by gate. Here the characterization of his men throws the hubris of the opponent into higher relief; and he proceeds in all the speeches until the sixth with the same intention of upbraiding and scorning the enemy's blazonry. Each of these pairs of speeches except the seventh is followed by a short choral section, resulting in a system of three strophic pairs distributed throughout the scene. These strophic pairs maintain fear and distress as the lively background to the whole powerful passage.

If the first five paired speeches with all their variations are unified by their opposing stolid and determined manliness on the part of the Thebans to the blind arrogance of the Argive leaders, the sixth speech involves a significant change. Here the assailant is Amphiaraos, who against his better judgment participates in the battle. This pure and pious man carries his blank shield calmly (590); it bears no boastful heraldry. With this figure of a man forced into blasphemy and marked for death, a note is struck that anticipates the terrible tragedy to come. The section also has the important function of bringing Polyneikes to the foreground. The harsh reprimands that Amphiaraos forcefully utters against him characterize the criminal nature of the attack on his own native city. The response of Eteokles recognizes the tragedy in the situation of this opponent.

In the final pair of speeches, the coming catastrophe is etched as if in the light of a plunging lightning bolt. At the seventh gate stands Eteokles' own brother, cursing the city and eager for a life-and-death struggle. His shield's emblem, depicting

Dike as she leads the armed Polyneikes back to his homeland, shows us once again that we must not inquire too closely into the question of where justice lies. The assault on one's homeland remains a crime, but the power that impels the horrible event comes immediately and clearly to the fore. Eteokles' answer begins with an outburst of wild despair, and we reach a new stage in the plot's development: Eteokles, who complains of his family, so hated by the gods, no longer appears as the prudent defender of his city, but rather as the accursed son of Oidipous. What had been the fearful premonition of obscure dreams (710) will be consummated now in the atrocity of the fratricidal struggle. Then he collects himself, is again the king who will withstand even this opponent. His criticism of the boastful shield harks back to the attitude of his previous speeches, but at the end the juxtaposition ἄρχοντί τ' ἄρχων καὶ κασιγνήτῳ κάσις (ruler against ruler, brother against brother) sums up his tragic double role in what is almost an epigram. In this speech of Eteokles the lines converge: the duel at the seventh gate is the destiny of Eteokles, the final consequence of the curse on his house. At the same time, however, by a truly Aischylean diversity of motifs, we are witnesses to the decision to fight with his brother, which Eteokles makes before our eyes: εἶμι καὶ ξυστήσομαι (I will go and face him; 672). In this context we notice an unusual feature: through the variation of the tenses of those verbs in which Eteokles speaks of his instructions, it remains unclear how much the king has already determined by the time of the messenger's arrival and to what extent he is, in this scene, making fresh decisions. Eteokles does not enter at v. 372 with a fixed order of battle; the terrible destiny takes shape in the progress of the scene with a fateful inevitability that Eteokles embraces by reaching his own decision.

For the manner in which he does this, the next scene (677–719) brings an essential revelation. First, in the trimeters 677–682, the chorus leader begs Eteokles not to engage in a battle in which inexpiable blood will be shed. An epirrhematic section follows in which Eteokles is besieged by verses of the chorus, but remains resolute in his purpose. How the role of the young women has changed! Now they address the king as τέκνον (child; 686), point out to him the impiety of his action and tell him to his face that he himself desires the death of his brother (686–692). Whoever believes that the chorus is making a mistake (nowhere described as such or even contradicted) in failing to recognize the heroism of Eteokles, has missed a basic element of the tragic art of Aischylos: the intertwining of destiny's call with the free will that accepts this call and transforms an inescapable fate into a personal deed. In a short stichomythy (712–719), the renewed efforts of the pleading chorus fail to crack the determination of Eteokles. With a word about the inevitability of a disaster ordained by the gods, he strides majestically from the scene.

An ode with five strophic pairs follows, at the beginning and end of which the chorus expresses its fear of the coming disaster. However, in the central sections the song is retrospective; it throws light on the fateful course of the family curse, spanning generations, and thus looks back to the earlier parts of the trilogy: Laios, who fathered a child against the wish of Apollo; Oidipous, who murdered his father and sowed his seed in that sacred field, the womb of his mother. The curse extends into

the third generation (744). In the third antistrophe, the chorus expresses the important anxiety that the fate of the city could be sealed with that of the princes. Here we
see unified the two lines whose radical separation is presented in the following messenger scene (792–820; some individual transpositions are necessary). With remarkable brevity, eschewing all detail, the messenger proclaims the rescue of the city, and
ends with an intimation of the disaster at the seventh gate. In an excited stichomythy (the arrangement of the individual verses is problematical), the chorus inquires
about the double murder of the brothers; the messenger concludes the tripartite
structure with eight trimeters devoted to the lot of the brothers, again contrasting
their fate with the salvation of the city.

The organic conclusion of the play is formed by the broadly constructed lament of the chorus. A later author, whose hand may well reveal the intense interest
in Aischylos in the last third of the fifth century, has most unhappily expanded the
finale under the influence of the *Antigone* of Sophokles, adding the sisters Antigone
and Ismene, the prohibition of burial, and the opposition to that prohibition.

We shall first summarize the passage that may be considered genuine. In the
choral anapests (822–831), the two aspects of the event are once more separated: rejoicing over the deliverance of the city, mourning for the fate of the sons of Oidipous.
The following pair of strophes is entirely devoted to the lament for the brothers; once
again the family curse and the guilt of Laios are recalled. As if summoned by these
words, the funeral procession, with both bodies, now appears. The next choral passage (848–860) is poorly transmitted, but it seems to consist of a predominantly iambic pair of strophes, in which the rising lament takes on ritual forms. The intensity
of wild grief grows in the following kommos (875–1004), climaxing in the ecstasy of
the conclusion: at first the semi-choruses sing four pairs of strophes, alternating
within the individual stanzas. Then follows a structure consisting of a short proodos,
a strophic pair with an ephymnion sung by the entire chorus, and an epode. Very
short cola alternate within this section. The parallel to the conclusion of the *Persians*
is obvious. Throughout this great passage of lamentation, the defender of the city is
no longer contrasted with the impious attacker; both brothers are now united in an
unhappy partnership of fate and deed, united by the final fulfillment of the curse that
brought on the extinction of their line.

The later author could comfortably make use of the section sung by the semi-
choruses, in order to ascribe it to Antigone and Ismene. For the introduction of the
sisters he inserted the anapests 861–874; in the epode, at least verses 996 f. must be
his. At v. 1005 he introduces a herald from the council who proclaims the decree
against burying Polyneikes. Antigone sets her will against this; she will herself bestow the honors of burial on her brother. In an unsuccessful stichomythy that breaks
off abruptly, the decree and Antigone's intention collide once more. The anapests of
the departing chorus contain references to the decree and probably all belong to the
reviser, who did not comprehend the meaning of the authentic lamentation, so that
he again separates the dead brothers on their final path.

The structure of the play is in its larger features similar to that of the *Persians*.
Lengthy choral sections surround a central passage in which spoken verse predomi-

nates. There is no trochaic tetrameter in this play. All the events are communicated through reports, but the tragedy in the figure of Eteokles is formed with a dynamism foreign to the *Persians*.

We have no evidence regarding the stage other than the play itself. From the choral section at the beginning, it is clear that there is a large altar with images of several gods, to which the chorus appeals. It is also beyond doubt that v. 265 contains a stage direction: the chorus is supposed to leave the statues because it must sing and dance in the orchestra. All this is exactly repeated in the *Suppliants*, where we must also imagine an elevated κοινοβωμία (community altar; here θεῶν πανάγυρις, assembly of gods; 219). There must have been a simple podium-like structure that allowed passage into the orchestra; we cannot agree with those scholars who assume a fixed backdrop or even constructions of walls, towers, altars, or statues on the skene roof.[28]

Eduard Fraenkel has produced an outstanding interpretation of the seven paired speeches; he has, with proper emphasis, disputed the interpretation that the champions came on stage with Eteokles at the beginning of this scene and left for their respective gates after the characterization.[29] This theory originated in the use (twice) of ὅδε for one of the champions (408, 472). For the first of these verses, Grotius's τῶνδε seems plausible, and the second was first challenged by Murray and then athetized by Fraenkel (op. cit., 31). But even if the tradition were correct, it would never force upon us such a monstrous arrangement of the scene. The use of ὅδε for something directly visible is a rule with numerous exceptions; our section alone offers examples enough (395, 424, 470, 553, 631) for such a designation for persons absent from the scene.[30] The question is of some importance, for if Eteokles came on stage with the champions already at his side, this would solve the much-discussed problem of whether or not he had completed his dispositions before his second appearance. We do not believe that Wolff (op. cit.; Patzer follows him) and Erbse (op. cit.) were successful in denying the future force of the words ἀντιτάξω (408) and ἀντιτάξομεν (621), thereby assuming for the whole section an allotment that had already been decided. The futures in question have next to them in the corresponding passages of Eteokles' speeches both past and present forms. Nor can we agree with von Fritz's (op. cit., 202) evaluation of this material; he believes that all future, perfect, aorist, and present verbs must refer essentially to the same situation, viz., a distribution of the champions to the gates that was not determined before this scene. We grant full weight to the juxtaposition of the tenses and come to the conclusion, with others, that Eteokles has, at the beginning of the scene, only partly decided on the distribution.[31] We recognize here the intention of Aischylos to leave the audience uncertain as to how much is already determined and how much remains open. Only in this way could he reveal both aspects of Eteokles' decision: the fulfillment of the family curse that fate has foreordained, and the moment of decision toward which events develop before our eyes.

No one today would still wish, with Ritschl, to find numerical symmetry in the paired speeches,[32] but this does not dismiss the question of their structure. In the first pair (vv. 375 f. are the introduction for the whole) numerical equality is evident (twenty verses each), and in the second also, whether we athetize 426 and 446 or not;

the following three pairs show large differences in their length, while the sixth possesses either complete or approximate symmetry, depending on one's view of verses 579, 601, and 619. We can see then a carefully considered variation within the large structure. The seventh pair of course stands by itself.

Our evaluation of the figure of Eteokles is inextricably bound up with the question of his situation and behavior. Here we must thank E. Wolff and H. Patzer for refuting the widely held theory that the death of Eteokles should be understood as a sacrifice that brings about the salvation of the city. The play offers no evidence for this kind of bond between the destinies of Thebes and of Eteokles.[33] The two fates are of course variously interwoven, but are completely separate in the final odes. However, we cannot agree with Patzer's assumption that the poet had Eteokles erroneously believe that the paternal curse referred to the attack of the Seven in the first part of the drama, only to recognize his error in the final pair of speeches and see that the curse was to be fulfilled in the fratricidal duel. In this interpretation, Eteokles is also driven by his realization of the curse's fulfillment in the first half of the tragedy, although he still does not comprehend the final meaning of the curse. We for our part hold that in the sequence of both parts of the drama Eteokles is shown first as the responsible defender of Thebes, and then as the son struck by Oidipous's curse. This does not signify any disintegration of the play or character, but rather the way in which the two aspects are inseparably linked is shown by the shifting accents. In this analysis, too, verses 653 ff. remain the tragic climax of the play, but we regard them as the transition not from a false interpretation of the curse to the true one, but rather from premonition to knowledge (710).

Of decisive importance for our evaluation of Eteokles and, beyond his character, of Aischylean tragic art in general is the interpretation of his dispute with the chorus after his decision has been made (677–719). The theory has often been proposed that maidens who speak in the role of concerned advisers (they call him τέκνον, 686) and speak and sing of the evil ὀργή (passionate rage) of the king (678), of his δορίμαργος ἄτα (spear-crazed madness; 687) and his ὠμοδακὴς ἵμερος (fiercely gnawing desire; 692), appear helpless opposite the heroic warrior and misunderstand him completely.[34] This theory would ensure unity of character in a way different from Patzer's interpretation; Eteokles would be seen from beginning to end only as the heroic soldier who fights and dies for his city. This analysis burdens the poet with the reproach that he has included an error on the part of the chorus that is important to our understanding of the play, without a word to indicate it as an error.[35] Even Eteokles does not contradict the chorus; the γάρ in v. 695 signifies a continuation of what had been said before about his passion. In this pregnant scene—just as with Agamemnon and Orestes—the dual face of a fated action is revealed: it must be accomplished, but, borne by the will of the agent, it is also a terrible infraction against universal order. Otto Regenbogen (op. cit.) coined an apt phrase before the scene ever came to be misunderstood: Eteokles goes forth to mortal combat with his brother because he wants to and because he has to.

The question of the authenticity of the conclusion has not been settled since Snell supported it in his book on Aischylos. Lloyd-Jones (op. cit.) has recently sifted anew through all the evidence against it and has overturned a few points, but we still believe with Fraenkel (op. cit.) and R. D. Dawe (op. cit.), despite E. R. Schwinge (op. cit.), that the passage cannot be retained. The exact line of separation cannot be drawn with certainty in the epode 989–1004, since at least verses 996 f. belong to the later revision. It is also highly questionable whether genuine lines can be rescued from the final anapests.

If we cannot escape the assumption that the play has been revised, the question arises whether other sections too were tampered with in the course of repeat performances. The report of the messenger is remarkably short: we learn no details of the duel itself. Croiset already thought it necessary to oppose the theory that a detailed report has fallen out here;[36] von der Mühll has recently supported this position. But this short report, which triggers the lengthy songs of the chorus, offers an excellent comparison with the verses of Danaos (*Suppl.* 605–624) before the benedictory song of the chorus for Argos. Also, the triptych report-stichomythy-report (792–820) is such a formal and compact structure that we would not like to regard it as the result of an abridgment.

Eteokles leaves the stage with the magnificent verse 719, fully armed of course, yet at 675 f. he requested only his greaves. Two explanations are possible; the decision between them is not easy. In the first case we would have to imagine Eteokles coming on stage at v. 372 in full armor, but without greaves. This is not inconceivable, especially since greaves do not exactly facilitate quick walking. For the second possibility we could, with Schadewaldt, insert a lacuna after v. 676, which he fills with two trimeters by way of example.[37] In his translation he sets the donning of the individual pieces of armor in the pauses during the dispute with the chorus (677–719).

The desire to find contemporary historical references everywhere, which first caused so much damage in interpreting tragedy, and later gave way to extreme asceticism, has also had its effect on the criticism of the *Seven*. Neither is Eteokles a Perikles, as Post thought, nor was it Aischylos's intention to portray Aristides in Amphiaraos, whether the story related in Plutarch (*Arist.* 3) that the audience looked at Aristides on hearing v. 592–594 is pure invention or not. And least of all can we agree with Tucker who believes that the play was propaganda for fortifying Athens.[38] Gorgias (in Plut. *Quaest. Conv.* 715e; cf. Aristoph. *Ran.* 1021) termed the *Seven* a δρᾶμα Ἄρεως μεστόν (drama filled with Ares). This is only partly correct; Aischylos was personally acquainted with the misery of war as well.

Fraenkel's study of the seven paired speeches must be mentioned because it athetizes many passages and thus serves as a prelude to his vehement attack on conservative textual criticism in his study of the *Phoinissai* of Euripides. For a criticism of some of these deletions the essay of Erbse (op. cit.) is important.

For the first performance of the *Suppliants* we were able to isolate the time period between 467 and 458, and 463 seemed a probable guess.[39] The play represents the first part of a tightly bound content trilogy. The *Aigyptioi* and the *Danaides* followed; the entire trilogy was occasionally designated by the latter title. The satyr play *Amymone* was closely connected to the preceding dramas.

The *Suppliants* begins with the entrance-procession of the chorus, twelve maidens in foreign costume, that is, Egyptian linen garments with veils shading their suntanned faces; they hold the wool-tufted branches of suppliants. The maidens are accompanied by their father, who likewise has a foreign appearance (496). The introductory anapests of the chorus leader offer a compact exposition: as suppliants they have come from the Nile to Argos, their ancestral homeland, from which their ancestral mother Io was once driven by the gadfly until Zeus healed her in Egypt and made her the mother of Epaphos. What the chorus has to say about the reasons for their flight from the sons of Aigyptos is badly obscured by textual difficulties. Bamberger's αὐτογενεῖ φυξανορίᾳ (self-produced flight from man) remains the most probable emendation, but it is by no means certain. In this case the maidens were not banished from the land because of any blood guilt; the decision to escape from their marriage with Aigyptos's sons springs from their own will. The intentions or the actions (v. 10 is incomplete) of the Egyptians are called ἀσεβής (impious). We learn nothing more of the chorus's motivation in the course of the play.

An expansive choral lyric structure of eight pairs of strophes follows (40–175), whose first and last three strophic pairs are related in content. The opening consists of the Epaphos motif, already introduced in the anapests; in the second pair the chorus compares itself to the wife of Tereus, the archetypal woman of sorrow; in the third, the appeal for help from the gods arises from this grief. In the last three pairs, lament and appeal appear again, heightened by passion. Each strophe here has an ephymnion except the last antistrophe, where it would be incorrect to restore one. The chorus members anticipate the decisive motif in the dispute with the king when they significantly announce (160) that without help they will die in the noose.

These two triads frame a central prayer of two strophic pairs; this prayer stands next to the hymn to Zeus of the *Agamemnon* as an expression of Aischylean piety and praise for the god's omnipotence. In both hymns the transition to the direct occasion (here the distress of the Danaids) is already contained in the second antistrophe.

Now follows a long scene in trimeters (176–343) that despite its elaborately formal internal structure moves smoothly into the subsequent epirrhematic section. We must imagine, in the area of the orchestra set off from the spectators, the same mountable and fairly high structure as was discussed in connection with the *Seven*. Here too it represents a κοινοβωμία on which the statues of the gods with their symbols are located, but it also serves the function of a lookout from which Danaos can observe the proceedings in the plain and on the shore. His role in the play is to advise and admonish his daughters, but he fades into the background in the decisive scenes. In his speech (176–203) he reports the approach of a procession of wagons and horsemen (the king comes riding into the orchestra with his entourage) and warns the maidens for their safety to seek refuge at the community altar, but to address the newcomers courteously.

During a scene beginning with a short prologue by the chorus leader and continuing as a stichomythy between her and Danaos (204–221), the maidens ascend the great altar, praying to individual divinities. Then Danaos, with a renewed warning,

but also with an accusation against the violent sons of Aigyptos, rounds off this triptych section that precedes the entrance of the king. After his arrival, the Danaids, on
their way to the city that can offer them refuge, must overcome the first serious obstacle, the distrust and resistance of its ruler. A lengthy complex of scenes extends to
v. 523 and unfolds the dispute between the king and the Danaids, which leads in a
wide arc from distrustful probing to the tragic conflict of decision and finally to complete acceptance of the suppliants' cause.

The first section, a conversation between the chorus leader and Pelasgos (234–
343) during which Danaos remains silent, at first presents the opposing positions.
The astonished king asks about the homeland of the strange group; the chorus answers with a question: What authority does this man have? Pelasgos replies with a
description of his "Pelasgian" power, a power extending over all of Greece. After a
short declaration and an astonished reply by the king, the chorus reveals its ultimately Argive heritage in the form of a stichomythy that breaks off at one point (319;
322 in Murray) and then in the same conversational form develops the crux of the
plot: the appeal of the maidens for protection and the king's immediate scruple that
to guarantee it would mean war. It is noteworthy that in the concluding stichomythy
the chorus leader evades every question about the legality of her petition with very
general remarks.

In this stichomythy all the requirements for the following lengthy dispute between chorus and king are already fully developed. Already at this point the king sees
himself caught between the religious claim of hikesia and the dangers of war. How
can he decide, when every path leads to destruction? This aporia is further developed
and expanded in the following epirrhematic scene (344–417) between the chorus,
who press him in passionate song, and the king, who responds in trimeters; but at
the end of the scene it appears that no progress has been made at all. Three strophic
pairs by the chorus, with their insistent dochmiac rhythms, are dispersed throughout
the epirrhematic syzygy; to each choral utterance, the king replies with five trimeters, except in the case of the last antistrophe, to which he replies in a speech of
eleven lines, expanding upon the ἀμηχανῶ (I am at a loss) of v. 379. The only substantial addition is the remark (365, 398) that he can act only on the basis of a plebiscite.
This projection of a mature democracy into the heroic age may speak for the convic-
tions of the poet; in the play its main purpose is to set up the scenic structure of the
second part, but it is not so heavily stressed as to lessen the king's tragic moment of
decision. The chorus evades the king's very specific question of what just claim the
maidens can bring against their kinfolk; their evasiveness is not new, but here (392),
it is especially crass. A passionate eruption, without motivation in the matter at
hand, is their answer.

The change of form now is extraordinarily meaningful. The speech with which
Pelasgos concludes the epirrhematic section begins and ends with the assurance that
the situation demands thorough deliberation. We are still far from any decision. So
the chorus with heightened intensity begins its heated entreaty, based on the rights
of suppliants, in a formal ode consisting of two strophic pairs (418–437). The cretics
of the first strophe are like uncontrolled pounding on a locked door, escalated in the

dochmiacs of the second. But all is in vain, the demand of the chorus φράσαι (consider!) is met by the πέφρασμαι (I have considered) of the king at the beginning of the following speech (438–454). But his deliberation has only led him again to see that there is no escape from his dilemma.[40] The situation is controlled by the ἀνάγκη (necessity; 440) that the acceptance or rejection of the suppliants alike must bring on disaster. In his concluding words γένοιτο δ' εὖ παρὰ γνώμην ἐμήν (May it turn out well, against my expectation!) we hear a man who lowers his hands in desperation. Now the chorus leader precipitates the decision, and again it is significant that this occurs in the form of a short, agitated stichomythy (455–467). The decision is forced by the maidens' threat to hang themselves from the statues, thus bringing the foulest pollution upon the city. Once more the king looks at the harborless sea of threatening doom (468–489), but then he takes it upon himself to protect the maidens. The father—not until now does he again take part—must go into the city and lay branches on the altars as a token of the appeal for help. The excitement abates in the rest of the scene (490–523), which again displays the character of a triptych in the succession speech-stichomythy-speech. Danaos offers thanks and asks for guides. Stage directions are implicit in the stichomythy between the king and the Danaids. The maidens remain alone, and it would be understandable for them not to abandon the protecting gods. But they must go into the orchestra for their dance and song, so the king convinces them to go to the "level grove," which means nothing else than climbing down from the altar into the orchestra.

Looking back on this large section (234–523), we see a passage extraordinarily rich in formal technique, but more or less stationary in theme. The passage portrays a man inescapably trapped between two alternatives, and his struggle to make a decision; his *internal* processes are depicted for us with a breadth unheard of in the later tragedians. The decision itself is no escape from the difficulty, and Pelasgos does not decide with full freedom of his will; the pressure of necessity is brought to bear by the threat of the maidens.

The following choral ode (524–599), in which lyric iambics predominate, is framed by the first and fifth strophic pairs praising Zeus and appealing to him. With the mention of Io, the first antistrophe forms a transition to the central portion, which contains her story. It concludes with her salvation by Zeus, thus smoothly preparing for the prayer to him in the final pair of strophes.

In one of those short scenes (600–624) that reveal to us the original function of the speaker who introduced the choral songs, Danaos brings the news of the assembly's joyful decision to receive the suppliants. His report gives rise to the request (in anapests) by the chorus leader for a benedictory song for Argos. The chorus prays that peace at home and abroad and all the blessings of growth and prosperity may visit the city (630–709). When Aphrodite and Artemis appear at the end of the second strophe and antistrophe, it is because they are the goddesses who shape the antithesis at the play's conclusion. The fourth and last strophe invokes the three great commandments: respect for the rights of strangers (placed first for thematic reasons), respect for the gods, and respect for one's parents.

The action of the plot now accelerates; before now we could not really speak of a plot in the sense of dramatic action. Again we encounter a tripartite structure in which speeches frame a lively conversation interspersed with lyric. Danaos, whom we must imagine on the altar during the ode, reports (710–733) the approach of the Egyptian fleet; the chorus leader and he exchange fear and reassurance in a dialogue (734–763) in which the elements of two strophic pairs are inserted at regular intervals. Danaos ends the dialogue confidently and goes for help (764–775). Here there is another implied stage direction. Danaos must exit because the poet will soon need his two actors for different roles. The chorus is told to resort to the gods' statues only if help is delayed; meanwhile, the maidens are to remain below, which is to say, dance in the orchestra.

The chorus pours out its fears in the following iambic ode (776–824; three pairs of strophes), expressing the wish for death or escape and ending with a call to Zeus.

In a scene full of commotion (825–910), the maidens flee to the altar; and the Egyptian herald enters with his guards, dark-skinned men in white garments (719), threatening to drag the maidens, who moan and abuse him, from their asylum. Foreign phrases and intentionally simple sentence structure have led to severe corruption in this passage. It is composed lyrically, but the herald changes over to spoken verse from v. 873. Finally, in a section that soon escalates to stichomythy and ends with longer speeches (911–953), Pelasgos enters with his warriors and drives the herald from the scene. The threat of the retreating herald foreshadows coming battle. Then the king turns to the maidens (954–965) and instructs them to take up quarters in the city. Verse 954 mentions the attendants of the Danaids; this prepares us for the second chorus at the conclusion. The maidservants must have been on stage with their mistresses from the very beginning. Further, it is strange that the Danaids are given the choice of communal or individual housing. This is probably best construed as a foreshadowing of the murder of their husbands. In anapests the maidens thank the king and ask for Danaos, to whose counsel they feel bound, and order the maidservants to attend them.

Pelasgos has left during the anapests, and now Danaos enters. The actor who had just played the herald had to change costumes quickly. The father enjoins the maidens to be grateful to Argos and warns them of the dangers which await young beauty in a foreign land; this remarkably detailed speech should prevent one-sided interpretations of the maidens as being Amazons of some sort. Again Kypris is mentioned, a prelude to the final odes, and when it is said of her (1000) that her call reaches every living creature, this is clear presage of her splendid self-portrayal in the final play of the trilogy. The chorus leader replies with a word of comfort, then the chorus of Danaids and that of the handmaidens take their places for the concluding ode. The details are unclear, but it must have been an arrangement allowing each servant to be near her mistress (977) and at the same time assuring some sort of independent grouping of each chorus for the sake of the antithesis, which is so important to the theme. In this final section (1018–1074) new points are raised that prepare for the second part of the trilogy and confront the exceptional case of the Danaids with the great powers of the world order. In a pair of strophes the maidens profess their gratitude to Argos as their new homeland and invoke Artemis as their goddess. Never may Aphrodite force them into marriage! The chorus of maidservants answers this in a strophic pair in which the power of the thereby slighted goddess is praised: she accomplishes much in conjunction with Hera (the goddess of wedlock). Hard struggles are in store for the refugees. But all shall come as Zeus disposes. If it comes to marriage, this is the usual lot of women. In a following pair of strophes both choruses sing against each other in short phrases, whose exact assignment presents problems. The Danaids remain defensive; the final words of the maidservants advise moderation in conduct. The last short pair of strophes belongs again entirely to the Danaids. As in the opening lines of the play, they call on Zeus to protect them from despised marriage. Once more the Io motif appears; once again we see the steadfast resistance of the maidens, but also the power of the opposition which leaves the outcome in doubt.

The structure of the play is determined by three factors. The first is the large role of the chorus which is not, however, a relic of high archaism, but results from the chorus's role as the actual protagonist. Second, the exceptional length of the exposition is connected with the position of the play in the trilogy; the *Agamemnon* will display similar features. And finally, for the first time that we can see, action comes on stage not merely in the form of a report; instead, it is for the most part portrayed directly in the most vivid movement. Balance among the various elements is not yet the poet's goal. The dispute between the chorus and Pelasgos is played out in the broadest possible manner; when the decision is made in v. 478 we are already near the middle of the play, but then stroke follows upon stroke: the approach of the fleet, the attempted abduction, the intervention of the king, the procession to the city in total uncertainty as to the future. The play closes like the *Libation Bearers*, open for what is to follow.

The content of the play is drawn from epic poems of which we can still identify one as a *Danaides* or *Danais*, but we cannot be certain of its content.[41] Various speculations have been offered for the original meaning of the saga. Even if J. E. Harrison's explanation for the punishment of the Danaids in Hades as deriving from ancient rain-magic were correct, that explanation still would have nothing to do with Aischylos, since this feature has no place in his trilogy.[42] The sociological interpretation of the myth, based on the antithesis between exogamous and endogamous marriage laws, also remains without importance for the analysis of the drama.[43] On the other hand it is important to know that in the non-Aischylean tradition, the source of the conflict was a quarrel between the brothers Aigyptos and Danaos.[44] The poet's rejection of this motif has far-reaching consequences: For now the Danaids are not obedient daughters; their action springs from their own impulse. The result is the curious role of Danaos, who mostly stands next to the chorus but appears occasionally in the role of the admonishing and directing κύριος. In order to understand his dual position we must recall the end of the play: the problem of the spurned marriage could only become effective on condition that the Danaids reject of their own free will what according to the handmaidens will nonetheless be their fate.

At this point the question of the motive for the Danaids' flight becomes crucial: is it because of these suitors, whom they so passionately reject, or do they act out of some fundamental, deep-seated aversion to all men? We must first recall that crucial v. 9 with the impossible αὐτογένητον φυλαξάνοραν (λα in rasura). Despite the attempt of Elisei[45] with Hermann to read αὐτογενῆ φυξανορίᾳ γάμον, interpreting the phrase to mean "perfuggire uomini della medesima stirpe" (fleeing from men of the same race), as well as the suggestion of Maria Luisa Rosenkranz,[46] ἀλλ᾽ αὐτογενῆ τοι φυξάνορα γάμον, we believe Bamberger's αὐτογενεῖ φυξανορίᾳ (self-produced flight from men) to be the most plausible emendation, and in fact it is accepted by most scholars. But it is incorrect to translate, with Wilamowitz "aus angeborener Männerscheu" (from an inborn aversion to men), thus defining the meaning of the entire event in a way not intended by the poet.[47] Nor can we agree with Hiltbrunner's explanation (op. cit., 8) that the Danaids have rejected γάμος because Zeus created their ancestor Epaphos in a miraculous manner without it. Rather, we believe with von Fritz (op. cit., 123 = 161) that the decisive factors are the parallel with αὐτοφυής (grown of itself) and the antithesis of the doubtful words to those which preceded them: the maidens say simply that their flight was their own decision and did not involve blood guilt. Now we can inquire into their personal motive. A series of passages accuses the Egyptians of hubris (e.g. 31, 103, 487, 528) without elaboration, and again their action is termed illegal (39; 37 in Murray: λέκτρων, ὧν θέμις εἴργει: marriages which Right forbids), but it is highly significant that the Danaids immediately resort to generalities when Pelasgos expressly asks for the legal justification of their flight (333 [337 in Murray], 392). The assumption of lacunae, suggested by Wilamowitz, is unwarranted and has not been well received. Another passage (225), in conjunction with a verse from the narration of Prometheus (*Prom.* 855), could be understood to suggest that the maidens were fleeing from a marriage with their own kin. This explanation, however, does not correspond to Greek nomos, which under certain circumstances even encouraged such a union. Our only concrete evidence is Danaos's description of the Egyptians' undertaking (227): γαμῶν ἄκουσαν ἄκοντος πάρα (taking to wife an unwilling bride from an unwilling father; further, ἀεκόντων at the close of the entrance-march anapests). We understand that the poet is portraying for us in a drastic scene the barbaric coarseness of the Egyptians. Their courting is rude and marriage with them is slavery. The maidens flee from this in terror, but we need not therefore regard them as Amazons.[48] Our interpretation so far is surely vague, but at least unified; we now must deal with those passages that might be understood as expressing a general aversion to men. This is especially true of the ephymnion (141–151), in which εὐνὰς ἀνδρῶν (beds of men) can be taken generally or as a specific reference to the Egyptians. Linguistic support for the second interpretation is offered by passages like 393 and 426, in which the concrete reference is clear; in content it is supported by the circumstance that both previous strophes mention the flight from the persecutors. Verse 328 (322 in Murray) could also be understood in a general way, but here too the preceding passage leaves open the interpretation for the specific case.

The resulting picture of the character, legal status, and motives of the Danaids is not simple. Whoever rejects the proposition of Wilamowitz (*Aisch. Int.* 13) or Vürtheim (in his edition, 119) that Aischylos's capacity for unified characterization here reached its limits, will want to join von Fritz (op. cit.) in the conviction that the poet left suspended, for his own good reasons, that which he wished to leave undetermined. Thus he was assured of the possibility of dramatically exploiting the case of the Danaids in its concrete aspects determined by the courtship of the Egyptians, but at the same time he could give it a more general validity and portray in it the rule of the great divine powers. The passionate desire of the Danaids is contrasted to the valid institutions that ensure the continued existence of the living.

As long as the *Suppliants* was still dated very early, one could utilize the remark in Pollux (4. 110) that the original number of the chorus was fifty and reckon with fifty chorus members for our play. Since the new dating we are restricted to twelve, which is confirmed beyond doubt for Aischylos by *Ag.* 1348–1371. The larger number appears only once in the text (317; 321 Murray), where the fifty sons of Aigyptos are mentioned. If we assign every Danaid a maidservant, and think of the Egyptians in sufficient number to render their attack convincing, and then add Pelasgos with a corresponding number of soldiers, we must imagine an extraordinarily lively stage! In dealing with the two earlier plays, we have already discussed the construction of the common altar as a podium-like structure that could certainly be mounted.[49]

The *Suppliants* may be connected in two ways with the political situation at the time of its composition. With F. Schachermeyr[50] we see Aischylos as a moderate democrat and so understand his transposition of Athenian circumstances into the heroic age when Pelasgos refers the final decision to an assembly of the people. Euripides did much the same in his own *Suppliants*. Further, one might connect the image of Argos in the play, and especially the song of benediction, with the pro-Argive sentiments of the Athenian democrats.[51] But this is the last of the tenable theses. If we try to make the *Suppliants* into a political play by seeing reflected in it the reception of the fleeing Themistokles in Argos, then we are again the victims of those fatal methods that produce literary facts from speculative associations.[52] We cannot exclude the possibility that an interest in Egypt is evident in the foreign elements of the play; it was after all the land where the Persian hegemony had encountered stiff resistance and the Athenians later unsuccessfully supported the rebellious Inaros. But it is incorrect to make use of the *Suppliants* for dating this Athenian undertaking or to look for the pro- and anti-Persian factions of Egypt behind the Egyptians and the Danaids (C. Gülke, op. cit., 65, 71).

For the reconstruction of the two plays that followed in the trilogy, the most important studies are those of K. von Fritz, W. Kraus, and R. P. Winnington-Ingram. The fragments can be found in Mette, nos. 120–133, a discussion of them in his *Verl. Aisch.* 49.

We know so little of the second play, the *Aigyptioi*, that Mette dared to speculate that it could have been the first part of the trilogy and have been set still in Egypt. The title presents difficulties, since it seems to indicate that the sons of Aigyptos form the chorus. This would preclude not only their death but also the plotting of their murder in the course of the play. Likewise impossible is a fight on the stage. But a violent struggle has been set up in the *Suppliants*, and the old theory that Pelasgos was killed in the battle and that Danaos took over his command could be supported by the allotment of *P. Oxy.* 2251 with the complaint of a ξενοδόχος (host).[53] Under the assumption that the *Aigyptioi* formed the chorus that dominated the play, we are left with the slight possibility that the play contained a peace treaty after the battle and negotiations that led to marriage. Thus it is understandable that various scholars believe the title *Aigyptioi* refers to a second chorus, leaving the Danaids in the same role as in the first play.[54] This allows room in the play to develop the murder plot with the aid of Danaos. The plotting undoubtedly followed the decisive battle but preceded the murder of the grooms on their wedding night, which must be imagined to fall between the second play and the third. Occasionally the sporadically transmitted title *Thalamopoioi* (fr. 114M) has been taken as a second title for the play, but this attribution remains uncertain.[55]

For the third play, the *Danaids*, every reconstruction attempt must accommodate the splendid fragment (125M) in which Aphrodite proclaims her cosmic power. Two motifs can be adduced. According to one tradition (the earliest source is Pindar *Pyth.* 9. 112[56]) Danaos marries off his daughters on the basis of a race among the suitors. This version presumes the absolution of the maidens and offers a conciliatory conclusion to the trilogy. On the other hand, in the short report of Prometheus about the fifty daughters of Danaos (*Prom.* 853), the character of Hypermestra (although she is not named) receives special emphasis as being the one Danaid with feminine sensibilities, who spared her husband, Lynkeus. Pausanias (2. 19. 6) reports that Danaos brought her before an Argive court, where she was acquitted. She dedicated a xoanon to Aphrodite in thanksgiving. It is understandable that a trial was long ascribed to the third play of the trilogy, in which Aphrodite appeared for the defense. Here von Fritz (op. cit., 251 = 175) seems to reject too categorically the successful combination of both versions, only recognizing the marriage as the subject of the third play. Consequently he believes that the speech of Aphrodite was connected with this theme. We prefer Kraus's solution (op. cit., 157 = 65), which combines the motif of the marriage with that of Hypermestra's defense. One must not think of a trial in the style of the *Eumenides*; this would be impossible with only two actors. Hypermestra did not have to be present; Danaos's condemnation of her disobedience would have been sufficient. Aphrodite then intervened to vindicate and protect Hypermestra. She was also able to effect the conciliatory conclusion by the absolution and marriage of the maidens. Divine power, much like that of Athena at the close of the *Oresteia*, leads from suffering and confusion to a valid order.

The great questions discernible in the trilogy were lightly reflected in the satyr play *Amymone*.[57] This daughter of Danaos was assailed by a satyr as she was fetching water, freed by Poseidon, and then led by the god to love and motherhood. Zerbinetta at the end of Hofmannsthal's *Ariadne* understands: "When the new god comes along,/We surrender without a word."

The only preserved trilogy of content, the *Oresteia* (produced in 458), represents for us the peak of Aischylos's creative power.[58] Since according to the new dating it follows the *Suppliants* by hardly more than a half-decade, we have one more contradiction to those theories that assume a linear and steady development of great art. New dramatic and technical possibilities were opened to Aischylos by the use of the third actor, who was the contribution of Sophokles to the stage.[59] In the *Frogs* (1126) Aischylos quotes the introductory verses of the *Libation Bearers* as part of the prologue of the *Oresteia*. Radermacher has correctly concluded in his commentary that the second play was once also known under the name of *Oresteia*, referring to the return of Orestes, and that this title was later transferred to the trilogy.

The background material for the trilogy may be explained to the extent that the basic features of the plot were almost all predetermined for the poet.[60] An important link must have been the *Oresteia* of Stesichoros. We know that he presented Klytaimestra as the most guilty character, for this can be the only meaning of fr. 42 Page (15D, 42B), in which the dream motif of the *Libation Bearers* is foreshadowed: a δράϰων (snake) with bloody head appears to her.[61] The schol. on Eur. *Or.* 268 points in the same direction when it reports that in the Stesichoros version, Apollo gave a bow to Orestes so that he could defend himself against the Erinyes. This feature is confirmed now by a papyrus with remnants of a commentary on the lyric poets (*P. Oxy.* 29 [1963], fr. 26 col. ii = Stesich. fr. 40 Page). There we also learn that Aischylos borrowed the lock of hair as a mark of recognition from the choral lyricist. Pictorial representations, above all Melic reliefs, complete our knowledge of what was handed down to Aischylos.[62] The major role of Apollo, already confirmed for Stesichoros, appears as part of the Delphic overlay on Greek myth frequently seen elsewhere. Yet we need not imagine a Delphic *Oresteia* poem, as Wilamowitz suggested.[63]

For the third play of the trilogy, the poet assured himself great freedom vis-à-vis tradition, which offered him little more than Attic cult legends about the reception of Orestes into Athens and his trial before the twelve gods. The foundation of the Areopagos by Athena and the link between this court and the dissolution of the curse belong as much to Aischylos as does the entire inner formation of the myth, which, transcending the bounds of all tradition, springs from his own religion of Zeus.

The three plays of the *Oresteia* begin with prologue speeches which, beyond their significance for the exposition, strike the basic chords of the symphony. The stage of the *Agamemnon* shows us for the first time we may be sure of, the skene (whose front wall represents the palace facade) being utilized as a background for the play.[64] On the roof lies the watchman, propped on his elbows, who speaks the prologue (1–39). His complaints about the hardships of the year-long watch for the signal fire from Troy change quickly to joy when he spots the beacon. But his happiness is immediately stifled in the fearful knowledge of the incurable corruption of the house. The atmospheric movement of the entire play, concluding in catastrophe, is masterfully described in these few verses: victory celebration under the dark storm clouds from which the lightning bolt will flash down.

The chorus of Argive elders enters. A long anapestic section (40–103) evokes the image of the expedition of the Atridai against Troy. The remark (61) that it was caused by ξένιος Ζεὺς πολυάνορος ἀμφὶ γυναιϰός (the Zeus of Hospitality for the sake of a promiscuous wife) presents the entire undertaking for the first time under the aspect of the ambiguity of human affairs so characteristic of Aischylos.

The chorus asks Klytaimestra why she has ignited so many sacrificial fires, and remains torn between worry and hope at the conclusion of the anapests.

The powerful lyric section of six strophic pairs (104–257) that follows is to be understood as exposition for the entire trilogy. We have seen something similar in the *Suppliants*. The first strophic pair, the only one expanded by an epode, is lyric-epic narration with series of dactyls: in Aulis the army saw two eagles eat a pregnant rabbit and its unborn. Kalchas refers this to the conquest of Troy, but is at the same time—again the double vision of Aischylos—deeply concerned that Artemis, here so appropriately πότνια θηρῶν (mistress of wild beasts), angered by the destruction of the poor creature, could demand another sacrifice certain to arouse terrible hatred. Here the chorus, troubled by recollections and premonitions, offers up the greatest of all Greek prayers, the hymn to Zeus, in the two next pairs of strophes. The ancient form of the hymn of appeal reaches its climax here, where the name Zeus hardly suffices for Aischylos's image of the relentlessly just ruler of the world. Nonetheless, tradition is not abandoned, as the antistrophe shows, for it celebrates Zeus as the victor over his predecessors. In the third strophe we hear the law under which the god has placed the world: knowledge through suffering. As is also often the case with Sophokles, the final section of a two-strophe structure leads back to the narration, which is continued until the sixth antistrophe. The prophet reveals the sacrifice of Iphigeneia as the means of appeasing the goddess and of securing the departure of the fleet. Agamemnon struggles to make a decision fraught with guilt in either case: to sacrifice his daughter or abandon the mission of vengeance. That the name λιπόναυς (deserter of the fleet) would then adhere to him places him under the burden of necessity. But because he has come to the conclusion that he must sacrifice his child, he in fact wills it as well; he longs for the deed and so makes it completely his own. With the vividness of a vision, the chorus describes the image of the girl lifted like an animal onto the altar where she must bleed to death. This concludes the narration; Iphigeneia's rescue by Artemis has no function here. In the final antistrophe the important theme of παθοῦσιν μαθεῖν (knowledge through suffering) is emphasized again (250), then the chorus turns to the entering Klytaimestra, who also is the subject of the trimeters 258–263, with greetings and questions.

The queen opens the following scene (264–354) effectively with the news of Troy's fall, and continues, after a short stichomythy with the surprised chorus, with the report of the course of the signal fires from Troy to Mykenai, verses that are a verbal masterpiece in their wealth of nominal and verbal variations. After a brief interruption by the chorus, Klytaimestra delivers her second speech with a strangely penetrating account of the grief and confusion in the defeated city on this day (τῇδ' ἐν ἡμέρα 320). But disaster awaits the victors as well. Only if they do not offend the gods (as Aias of Lokris offended Athena) will they be granted a safe return home. This speech looks forward to the storm description of the messenger; coming from Klytaimestra it sounds like a suppressed wish. The chorus professes its belief in the queen's words: πιστὰ τεκμήρια (reliable signs; 352).

After a series of anapests that celebrate Zeus as the righteous judge of Troy, the first stasimon follows (367–487) with three pairs of strophes and an epode after the last. Its development is extraordinarily characteristic of this section's basic mood. With the mention of Paris's crime, the first pair of strophes frames in ring-composition the thought of the relentlessness with which the gods demand that expiation follow guilt. The second pair of strophes then shows the guilt on the side of Helen, who abandoned her house and left behind suffering and unfulfilled longing. But the turning point comes in the middle of the second antistrophe: all of Greece is in mourning as well, and the third pair of strophes relates at length how the land groans for those sacrificed for the sake of another man's wife (447; cf. 62). The gods look down on this act of genocide and the Erinyes bring about the collapse of a happiness based on injustice. Guilt is also connected with the victory of the Atreidai, and again the ambivalence of human action is revealed: even the just vengeance upon Paris is laden with guilt. Human lives were sacrificed for a promiscuous woman.

The epode brings us back to the plot in a curious manner: the chorus, which earlier claimed to be convinced by Klytaimestra's πιστὰ τεκμήρια (trustworthy signs; 352), now sings of its doubts and of the gullibility of women.

The following epeisodion (486–680), containing a triptych of herald-speeches, begins with verses of the chorus leader announcing the approach of the messenger who will put an end to their uncertainty. It would be incorrect to demand a rational explanation for the inconsistency of the chorus. With the doubts expressed at the end of the ode the poet was merely preparing for the report of the herald. We can observe a much more impressive example of his poetic high-handedness when he has the fleet sail in only a few hours after the signal fire. The excuse that the choral ode encompassed an arbitrary period of time has no weight here, for the chorus links its doubts clearly with the section before the stasimon when it sings of the beacon's message rushing through the city (475).

The herald's first speech is entirely devoted to a joyful greeting of his homeland and its gods. Like the nurse in the *Lib. Bearers*, this character maintains an unproblematic, naive attitude in a world of horror. This speech of jubilant return offers an effective foil for the suppressed gloom of the scene in which Agamemnon greets Argos and the gods. In the second speech of the herald, if anywhere, we can hear Aischylos the soldier, who lends to the report of the messenger his own recollections of the suffering and torment of war.

Four trimeters of the chorus leader provide the transition to Klytaimestra's entrance. Her speech (587–614) is first a triumph over the doubts of the chorus, but then a preview of the hypocritical subservience with which she will later receive her husband; δωμάτων κύνα (dog of the house; 607) anticipates the abundance of metaphor we will encounter there. She knows that by asserting her fidelity she can defy the chorus of elders without having to expect a rejoinder.

A short exchange between chorus and herald about the fate of Menelaos leads to the herald's third speech with its description of the storm. The hope expressed at the conclusion that Menelaos might still be alive prepares the audience for the satyr play *Proteus*.

The second stasimon (681–781), whose four pairs of strophes Kraus rightly calls one of the most powerful structures ever composed, shows the path from the specific event to general knowledge. The first two strophes, boldly deriving her name from ἑλεῖν, sing of Helen as the ruin of Troy; the second pair describes her with the metaphor of the young lion raised with tender care that grows into a murderous beast. The third strophe still refers to Helen's coming, but the very first words of the antistrophe strike up a new tone, which the fourth pair continues. Pursuing a solitary course of thought, the poet rejects the belief (retained by Herodotos) that excessive happiness brings down disaster. It is the wickedness of men which proliferates, bears hubris from hubris, and continually produces new destruction from new guilt. Again the poet has begun with Troy only to end with verses that refer darkly but unmistakably to the House of the Atreidai. The scene with Kassandra will fill the words of the ode with concrete substance.

Now Agamemnon enters the orchestra in his chariot; behind him crouches Kassandra, covered by her veil.[65] In anapests (782–809) the chorus greets the king with restrained loyalty, not concealing its former criticism of the expedition launched for that promiscuous woman, Helen. Agamemnon's speech (810–854) is conditioned by the self-control of a man who knows much of the world's false pretenses. His thanks to the gods are mingled with insight into the monstrousness of the victory: a whole city lies smoking in ruins, and all for a woman! But now he must see to justice in Argos. Here Klytaimestra enters from the palace, and her speech (855–913), with its baroque, exaggerated hypocrisy, is sharply contrasted from first word to last with the icy isolation in which Agamemnon remains. It is a master stroke that Klytaimestra, professing her ever faithful love, does not directly address her long estranged and bitterly hated husband, but the chorus. Only when she artfully excuses Orestes' absence, claiming fear of revolution in Argos, does she turn to Agamemnon. She greets him then with an abundance of metaphor in which the hypocrisy wrung from her pride literally runs riot. It is one of the most ingenious features of this drama that the poet prepares the act of murder with a symbolic battle in which the man succumbs to the woman. Klytaimestra orders Agamemnon's path into the palace spread with purple carpets. In his deathly cold reply to her long speech Agamemnon rejects this honor that would mean hubris, but in the following stichomythy he is maneuvered into agreement. He commends Kassandra, a gift from the army, to good treatment and strides into the palace, accompanied by a speech in which Klytaimestra's hypocrisy spirals to dizzying heights. Once he is inside, the queen (973 f.) cries out, almost screaming, for Zeus to grant the fulfillment of her wishes.

The third stasimon (975–1034) captures in two strophic pairs the atmosphere of fear and concern, the sense of imminent disaster, with which the previous scene left us.

Klytaimestra comes to bring Kassandra into the palace. Aischylos employs here the technique of silence ancient critics allocated for figures like Niobe or Achilleus.[66] Kassandra does not reply to the increasingly sharp commands of the queen or to the advice of the chorus leader. Only when Klytaimestra has left the stage does she break her silence with a scream. A scene follows in which πάθος and λόγος (passionate suffering and rational discourse) are so masterfully interwoven that we can well understand why the hypothesis here emphasizes the perfect presentation of ἔκπληξις and οἶκτος (violent emotion and pity). Within the whole of the trilogy this section has the function of revealing the chain of guilt and expiation to which the House of Atreus is bound.

Kassandra sings seven pairs of strophes in the lyric section of the scene (1072–1177); after each of the first four, the chorus leader replies with two lines of trimeter, then the chorus is drawn into the excitement of the vision and follows the spoken lines of the chorus leader with song, while in the final part of this section only the chorus's heavily dochmiac verses answer the prophetess. Kassandra begins with a wail of lament to Apollo, whose symbol she sees before the palace gate. Her clairvoyance reveals the intended murder with uncanny accuracy: the bath, the net, the fatal blow. Then she weeps for Troy and her own death. Not understanding or only half comprehending her words, the chorus resists the impending disaster. But Kassandra changes her tone and rends the veil concealing her fate and that of the House of Atreus in a lengthy spoken scene (1178–1330); the transition was prepared by pairs of trimeters in her last two speeches. She begins clearly enough but is again and again overwhelmed by prophetic ecstasy. The walls of the palace now open to her view: there Thyestes dishonored his brother's bed; it was there his brother served him the flesh of his own children for revenge, and there that the swarm of Erinyes, drunk with blood, settled, never to be appeased. In this same palace the vanquisher of Ilion will fall by the hand of his wife, and Kassandra herself will fall in the slaughter. In despair she breaks her scepter and throws her fillet from her head. But then she composes herself and, after one final shudder, for which we thank the humanity of the poet, enters the house of her death. The motif often connected with Kassandra, that her prophecies were never believed, is occasionally referred to in this long scene (e.g. 1212) but hardly insisted upon (1093, 1194).

A short anapestic recitative of the chorus (1331–1342) echoes the words of Kassandra, but immediately from inside the palace the two death shrieks of Agamemnon are heard, answered by the chorus in tetrameters. The next section (1348–1371) clearly divides up the twelve voices of the chorus with two trimeter lines each. The poet gives a noteworthy demonstration here of the inability of a group to make a decision. With increasing intensity the voices of those calling for action are drowned out by the more hesitant members, until the palace gate opens revealing Klytaimestra with the corpses of her two victims. In a speech that has no equal, she triumphantly discards the mask of hypocrisy. As if crazed with blood, she savors her deed once more in every detail. The metaphors of her earlier hypocritical speeches find a terrible resonance when she compares the blood splattered onto her forehead by her dying husband with the rain that refreshes the fields of grain.

There follows, introduced by two verses of the chorus leader and a second admission of guilt by Klytaimestra, a long epirrhematic scene (1407–1576) that portrays in a way unique in Attic tragedy the course of psychological processes, the change in the relationship of the agent to his act. Here only a verse by verse analysis could show how, step for step, Klytaimestra is forced to the defensive by the horrified chorus, then of a sudden speaks of Aigisthos as her protector, and slowly begins to realize that her deed is only one link in the chain which binds the House of Atreus. Suddenly she wants to appease the daimon of the house, and is ready to make sacrifice. It is not a repentant but perhaps a clairvoyant Klytaimestra who calls now μανίαι ἀλληλοφόνοι (the madness of mutual slaughter) a deed she had earlier so proudly acknowledged.

Formally this conflict is so structured that Klytaimestra first replies to a strophe and antistrophe of the chorus in trimeters. This is followed by three pairs of strophes by the chorus to which Klytaimestra responds in anapests, her confidence increasingly shaken. The first strophe of each pair is followed by an ephymnion that probably should be repeated, following our tradition, only after the second antistrophe.[67]

As if in answer to Klytaimestra's attempt to avoid her oncoming doom through a pact with the daimon, Aigisthos now enters the stage. He justifies the murder in his own way as the son of Thyestes. Having held himself in the background, he is treated by the chorus differently from the heroic wife. In a scene of conflict (1612–1673) that ends in excited tetrameters, Aigisthos calls for his men-at-arms, and already a battle seems inevitable. But Klytaimestra intervenes, no longer the same woman who exulted in the bloodstains on her brow: μηδαμῶς . . . ἄλλα δράσωμεν κακά (No, let us not work new evils! 1654). The chorus has already named Orestes as the coming avenger (1646, 1667), thus preparing for the second play, and it is of deep import that the poet has Klytaimestra say παθεῖν ἔρξαντας (whoever acts must suffer; 1658), foreshadowing her own undoing.

Despite the progress of dramatic technique in the development and unraveling of plot, the play exhibits a structure similar to that of the *Suppliants*. Here too the intensity of the action is greatly increased compared with the two earlier plays, but here as well an extraordinarily long exposition, important to the trilogy as a whole and composed for the most part as lyric, is followed by the dramatic events in accelerated tempo. But the Kassandra section as well as the splendid confrontation between Klytaimestra and the chorus serves to balance the lyric fullness of the first part of the drama with its ethical and reflective character.

A series of interpretational problems is connected with the parodos. We interpret, with Eduard Fraenkel, the hymn to Zeus as an appeal which has its source in the innermost center of the action.[68] Superficially it is inserted without connection into the narration, which is again resumed with καὶ τότε (184), in that the full weight of the facts replaces the predictions of Kalchas. The attempt to restore a better train of thought by placing the hymn after v. 217 has not been successful.[69]

Why is Artemis angry?[70] None of the motivations attested elsewhere—the killing of a sacred animal, the boastful hubris of Agamemnon, or an unfulfilled sacrificial vow—is even mentioned. Nor is there any word of a special preference of the goddess for Troy.[71] Aischylos has intentionally relieved Agamemnon of all guilt, for only in this way does the conflict situation of the king gain its full weight. The anger of the goddess has no origin other than the eagle-omen that destroys the pregnant hare. It is characteristic of the Aischylean world view that the same sign that proclaims victory over Troy simultaneously portends terrible misfortune.

The conflict forced on Agamemnon by the demand for sacrifice is already familiar to us from the *Seven* and the *Suppliants*. Again the necessity to make a decision is imposed by fate, and again every decision is tainted with guilt. The chorus describes clearly for us the distress of the king (205), but his obligations to the army and fleet (212: πῶς λιπόναυς γένωμαι ξυμμαχίας ἁμαρτών; How can I desert the fleet, failing my allies?) place upon him the yoke of ananke.[72] Agamemnon makes a decision that is his own, and for which he is responsible; nonetheless he makes it under the pressure of circumstances into which his fate has placed him. And now we see repeated what we observed in Eteokles in the *Seven*: once the fatal decision is made it is also affirmed, and what had been forced is now willed: βροτοὺς θρασύνει γὰρ αἰσχρόμητις τάλαινα παρακοπὰ πρωτοπήμων (For men are made bold by wretched evil-plotting madness, the source of all suffering).

At v. 83 the chorus addresses Klytaimestra and asks why she has ordered sacrifices on all the altars. But not until v. 264 do we hear the queen announce the victory. Hermann first suggested the interpretation that Klytaimestra had already come on stage during the anapests. This presumes that she leaves the chorus without a reply and remains mute on stage during the entire parodos, perhaps occupied with sacrifice, or else she leaves the scene to reappear before her speech. The debate between this solution and the other, that the chorus addresses in v. 83 a still absent Klytaimestra, remains unresolved even in the latest commentaries. E. Fraenkel's view seems to us the most convincing: the queen is not yet on the scene when the chorus makes its appeal. For the opposing view, represented by Denniston-Page,[73] could be adduced the echoing of θυοσκεῖς (87) in line 262 (θυηπολεῖς), but even then the silence of Klytaimestra, when she is addressed in v. 83, would remain incomprehensible.

The stichomythy between Agamemnon and Klytaimestra before his entrance into the palace has been given a new interpretation by H. Gundert (op. cit.) in which he takes issue with the commentaries of E. Fraenkel and J. D. Denniston–D. L. Page, who see in the submission of the king courtesy, resignation, or the fulfillment of a secret ambition; in Gundert's view it is the failure of a man as a prelude to his downfall. This is probably the real meaning of the scene, but we would not for that reason exclude the other motives just mentioned.

How is Klytaimestra revealed with her two victims? This is a question about stage technique. A broad central gate may have opened, or perhaps the ekkyklema was already in existence, a movable podium on which a set scene could be rolled out. K. O. Müller already suggested this for the *Oresteia* in his commentary on the *Eumenides* and the theory has received much support. But Bethe wished to rule out the ekkyklema for the entire fifth century,[74] and Pickard-Cambridge (*Theater of Dion.*, 106) does not exclude "some kind of ἐκκύκλημα," but considers it quite possible that a wide gate that opened sufficed for the presentation. This would have been a sliding door of some sort. Since there is no real evidence for the *Oresteia* beyond the text itself, the reticence of the two recent commentaries is thoroughly justified. Reinhardt (106, 163) emphatically supports the ekkyklema on the grounds that the lighting conditions in the Theater of Dionysos would have otherwise left the scene in the dark. The argument loses some of its force if we assume that the group was near the gate; moreover we will encounter a scene in the *Eumenides* that cannot be explained by the use of the ekkyklema.[75]

The poet's nonchalance in matters of detail is responsible for the uncertainty surrounding Klytaimestra's weapon. E. Fraenkel devoted a special appendix to this question. It is a subtle observation that the poet does not specify the weapon more precisely at the crucial points because he wants to focus our attention on the cloth thrown around Agamemnon as a net. *Ag.* 1262, 1528 and *Lib. Bearers* 1011 point to a sword as the fatal weapon. In the last passage, Orestes' reference to the sword of Aigisthos could best be explained if Klytaimestra used the weapon of her consort.[76] On the other hand we should not make too much of *Lib. Bearers* 889, in which Klytaimestra demands the ἀνδροκμῆτα πέλεκυν (the man-slaying axe) as the weapon closest to hand, or of the vase-paintings and passages in the later tragedians in which the axe appears as the murder weapon.[77]

Only the end of the prologue of the *Choephoroi* (*Libation Bearers*) has been preserved;[78] the rest was lost in the lacuna of the Mediceus that begins after *Ag.* 1159. But a few quotations supply enough to indicate the content and character of the section.[79] Here, as in the *Eumenides*, Aischylos has composed the prologue as an effective contrast to the conclusion of the previous play. The *Agamemnon* ended with the entry of Klytaimestra and Aigisthos, caught up in their guilt and destiny, into the palace of the Atreidai; here we find the innocent youth praying over his father's grave. Until now he was able to remain far from the morass of murder; now, however, he undertakes the weighty office of blood revenge. Like the striking of a muffled chord, the play opens with the call to Hermes, ruler of the underworld. The chthonic realm and its powers are fundamental to this play and the surely central position of Agamemnon's tomb on the stage is a powerful symbol for these forces.

The final verses of the prologue announce the approach of a band of women clad in black, and Orestes retreats with his companion Pylades in the parodos, opposite the oncoming women, in the first known eavesdropping scene, a device of which comedy was later to make all too abundant use.

The parodos (22–83) leads Elektra with the chorus of handmaidens onto the stage. Only briefly (75) does the poet mention that these servants are slaves captured in war, probably from Troy. They are, however, treated as part of the house; they feel fully its disgrace and await justice. Without introductory anapests they begin their song, which comprises three strophic pairs and a final epode. Through the ode runs a chain of tightly dovetailed thoughts closely connected with the plot. The chorus comes with offerings for the dead; thus the first strophe speaks of the relevant ritual gestures. The antistrophe interprets a dream of Klytaimestra as the occasion for their mission. The chorus already reveals its position in the second strophe when the mourners sing of the δύσθεος γυνά (godless woman) and the collapse of the house disgraced by murder. Significantly, the antistrophe mentions Dike, who finds her way sooner or later. The blood of murder drunk by the earth cannot be expiated; this is proclaimed in the third pair of strophes, while the epode reports briefly on the fate of the chorus women themselves, but also mentions their hatred for the instigators of violence.

Elektra has heard enough to ask the chorus in a rather lengthy speech at the beginning of the following scene (84–151; it is hardly worthwhile to separate epeisodion and stasima) what attitude she should assume with regard to this offering. In a short stichomythy with the chorus leader, she hears what she wants to hear: the offering should be made on behalf of Agamemnon's loyal followers and his avengers. With words to this effect (165 must be inserted here, then 124–151) she participates in the sacrifice, beginning with an appeal to Hermes Chthonios in clear parallel to the prayer of Orestes. The chorus accompanies the act with a short iambic-dochmiac song of conjuration. Then follows a lively scene (164–305), at first very closely connected with the grave mound. There Elektra has discovered a lock of hair, closely resembling her own, which must have come from Orestes. In the stichomythy (164–182) her sudden joy is cooled somewhat: Orestes may have sent the offering from afar. Her speech (183–211) shows her vacillation between doubt and hope, until she sees a new token: footprints that match the outlines of her feet. She is already about to faint when Orestes steps forward and in a scene that moves from stichomythy into expansive speeches, brother and sister unite, Elektra rejoices, and Orestes prays to Zeus. The chorus leader recommends caution, and now Orestes reveals why he came. The god of Delphi has charged him, under threat of fearful punishment (which he describes at length), to wreak vengeance on the murderers of his father.

In a long lyric section (306–478) Orestes and Elektra join the chorus in the great kommos, the most artful construction preserved in tragedy. Four triads follow an anapestic prologue of the chorus; in each, strophes of Orestes and Elektra surround one of the chorus. Also, the verses of brother and sister respond to one another in each triad, while in the middle sections, which belong to the chorus, there is response between the first and second and then again between the third and fourth triads. Between the individual triads are placed anapestic sections of the chorus leader, except after the fourth. This structure is followed by three strophic pairs that have been transmitted in the order A B C C A B (423–455). Two strophic pairs conclude the kommos.

This extensive section contains the lament for the dead king and summons him with a powerful conjuration to aid in the deed of revenge. The language and meaning of ancient rites are influential here, but this does not exhaust the function of the kommos. Orestes came on stage as the envoy of Apollo, under his strict orders. The command spoke of revenge on the killers of Agamemnon without mentioning specifically the most terrible side of the order, the murder of Orestes' own mother. The case is quite different in the kommos. Here there is not a word about Apollo's commandment. From the description of the distress of the house rises a picture of the crime in which Klytaimestra stands as the central figure. With the question of what they should say to attain their goal (418), Elektra introduces a series of strophes in which she and the chorus bombard Orestes with the facts that Agamemnon was buried in haste and without retinue, that his corpse was mutilated, that Elektra was bound in a corner like a dog; τοιαῦτ᾽ ἀκούων ⟨τάδ᾽⟩ ἐν φρεσὶν γράφου (hearing such things, inscribe them in your mind! 451; cf. 439, 442 f.). And when Orestes cries out: "She shall pay for my father's outrage!" his own will, inflamed, joins with the command of Apollo, divine and human motivation unite, and Orestes becomes like Eteo-kles and Agamemnon: he wants to do what he must.[80] The transposition of the strophe beginning at 434 to follow 455 must be considered, on the one hand because it mean-ingfully places the cry of Orestes at the climax of the intensity building in the scene, and on the other hand because it replaces the curious strophic sequence of the tradi-tion with parallelism.

After the kommos, brother and sister unite in a trimetric conjuration of their dead father (479–509), in which a central passage is bracketed by stichomythy of roughly balanced sections in two or three verses. A conversation between the chorus leader and Orestes (510–584) supplements the intimations of the parodos by the nar-ration of Klytaimestra's dream, which magnificently develops the δράκων motif in Stesichoros. Orestes interprets the vision and reveals his plan to ask admittance to the house as a stranger and, should he find Aigisthos on Agamemnon's throne, to kill the usurper immediately. A moment of dramatic tension is produced when events develop differently, due to Aigisthos's absence. Orestes sends Elektra into the house, and she disappears completely from the play, very much in contrast to the later Elek-tra plays.

The following ode with its four strophic pairs binds loosely connected mythi-cal examples with reflections relevant to the plot. Πολλὰ μὲν γᾶ τρέφει δεινά (The earth nourishes much that is fearful); this will be echoed later in Sophokles. Althaia, who surrendered Meleager to his death, and Skylla, who betrayed Nisos, are the ex-amples of the second strophic pair. The third strophe, with a bold turn, directs atten-tion to the outrage in the House of Atreus that Orestes now must avenge, while the antistrophe brings in the outrage of the Lemnian women, a crime especially close to Klytaimestra's deed, only to turn at once to more general concerns in preparation for the fourth strophic pair, which sings of Dike, who now accompanies Orestes.[81]

The scene from 652 to 718 gets Orestes into the palace. A servant answers his call. It is remarkable how particularly Orestes asks for someone who can give him information: he would rather it were a man than a woman. This can certainly fit in with his plan to kill Aigisthos first, but is it not also possible to ask if Aischylos here has his Orestes hesitate before the dreaded confrontation with his mother, and then achieves a special effect when Klytaimestra herself emerges from the house? Orestes relates to her the fictional report of his death, to which she replies with words of lament about the collapse of the house. In this passage, we seem to hear the Klytai-mestra we have seen in the conclusion of the Ag.

Following the anapests of the chorus with their appeal to the chthonic powers, the nurse of Orestes, Kilissa, appears, announced by the chorus leader, in a scene (734–782) fitted into the drama with extraordinary skill. She must summon the ab-sent Aigisthos, and now everything depends on whether the usurper will come with or without his attendants. Cleverly and without revealing too much, the chorus leader persuades the nurse, against her orders, to report to Aigisthos that he should come alone. But what makes the scene a jewel of Aischylean art is the simple heart-felt tone with which Kilissa laments the child she reared. Again—we think of the herald in *Agamemnon*—it is extremely effective to hear in a world of horror the sounds of pure, sensitive humanity.

To encourage Orestes there follows an ode closely connected with the plot; it contains three pairs of strophes (783–837), each of which encloses a mesodic section. Kraus (105) has with good reason sided with those who reject a repetition of this middle section after the antistrophe. Blessings for Orestes are offered in the first pair of strophes, appeals to the gods in the second, while the third spurs on the avenger with a preview of the successful outcome. A motif later used to great effect is sounded in the middle section: When you hear her call, *Child!* answer with the word *Father!*

Aigisthos comes; he does not rejoice over the report of Orestes' death either, rather he seems horrified and wants to make sure. Anapests of hope and fear from the chorus raise the suspense to its peak, until we hear Aigisthos's death cry, which is echoed when the chorus asks what has happened (870 f.). Then the chorus leader, enjoining the women not to become involved in what is to follow, introduces one of the most stirring scenes of the Aischylean stage (872–934). A servant bursts from the central gate and pounds on the door of the women's chamber (most probably one of the paraskenai), calling wildly until Klytaimestra comes. She immediately understands the full import of his phrase "the dead are killing the living" and calls for a man-slaying axe, but Orestes and Pylades already stand before her. Klytaimestra now seeks salvation through means stronger than any axe: she shows Orestes the breast from which he once drew life, horribly recalling the vision of her dream. Orestes is about to drop his weapon before his mother. At this point the god must intervene, which he does in the only three verses that Pylades speaks in the play. His command wins out and Orestes determines to kill his mother. Still she seeks with excuses and pleas (seldom is the effect of a stichomythy so powerful) to escape her fate. As the chorus foresaw (829), she clings to the word τέκνον (child), while Orestes, avoiding the word "mother," counters by mentioning his father. He kills her, laying her corpse next to that of her lover. But in the four verses of the chorus leader with which the scene closes, a significant and threatening note is sounded: Orestes has now reached the pinnacle of bloodshed in the House of Atreus.

But the following choral ode (two strophic pairs with ephymnia also after the antistrophe; 935–972) is still pure rejoicing. The chorus praises the victory of Dike and looks toward a radiant future for the house.

The contrast with the next scene is all the stronger. Again the gate of the palace opens (ekkyklema?) and shows Orestes over the corpses of his two victims. Now is revealed what we had already heard briefly intimated: the vengeful deed of Orestes, his loyalty to the command of the god and to his father, bears another countenance: as matricide it is a crime of unimaginable horror. Kassandra has already (*Ag.* 1283) named the avenging Orestes as the one who would crown the outrages of the house. This is now picked up quite exactly by the πολλῶν αἱμάτων ἐπήκρισε (he has reached the peak of much bloodshed; 932) of the chorus. But even at the end of the kommos the women of the chorus, who so passionately desired revenge, sang of the misery and guilt inextricably bound to the house, and with a telling oxymoron (830) urged Orestes to conclude the ἀνεπίμομφος ἄτα (blameless outrage).[82]

The closing scene of the *Libation Bearers* is a single desperate struggle to justify Orestes' deed, which he termed μὴ χρεών (what must not be; 930) immediately before performing it. He has the cloth in which Agamemnon died brought on stage, and in the confused series of metaphors concerning this object, his increasing madness becomes manifest. The chorus responds in gloomy anapests (1007–1018). In images of unsurpassed power Orestes describes the growing derangement of his senses; still he clings to the command of the god who alone can save him. But the friendly consolation of the chorus leader remains without effect; before his eyes, unseen by the others, the Erinyes arise from the earth; tormented by the Furies of madness he rushes from the stage.

Thematically significant anapests of the chorus conclude the play (1065–1076). They count Orestes' deed as the third storm in the destiny of the house. The banquet of Thyestes, the murder of the king, and now this: Salvation or a new blow of destiny? The poet leaves us with the apprehensive question: Where will the raging of disaster find its end?

The structure of the *Libation Bearers* is archaic insofar as its dramatic weight is concentrated toward the end. We are already considerably beyond the middle of the play when Orestes comes before the palace gate (652) and the action so elaborately prepared begins. The great kommos gives the first half of the drama a predominantly lyric character. To a large extent the play is still a choral piece. Aristotle (*Poet.* 18, 1456a 25) found his demand that the chorus should be a part of the whole and a co-actor realized in Sophokles, but this could be said even more strongly for Aischylos.

Especially deserving of emphasis in speaking of the play's structure is its extensive correspondence with that of the *Agamemnon*. In both works the catastrophe is brought on by a character who comes from afar, in one case as victim, in the other as avenger. In both plays the path leading up to the catastrophe follows four steps. In the *Agamemnon* the beacon reaches the watchman, Klytaimestra proclaims the news, the herald hurries with his report in advance of the king, who enters the palace after the great confrontation scene with Klytaimestra. In the *Libation Bearers* Orestes stands at the grave of his father, Elektra discovers the lock and footprints, a third step is the recognition scene, and finally Orestes goes into the house of the Atreidai, he too after a confrontation scene with Klytaimestra. The parallel construction of the two dramas was so important to the poet that it becomes almost obtrusive when each time after the decisive deed the gate of the palace opens and the murderer stands by the corpses of his victims. And in both plays this revelation is followed by a struggle for justification that inevitably fails and ends in the one case with the collapse of self-confidence and in the other with madness.

What the poet wished to show is clear: that in the course of destiny guilt and sin follow each other, forming a chain without foreseeable end. The concluding anapests of the *Libation Bearers* express this most emphatically.

The correspondence shown here follows from the content of the *Oresteia*; we cannot derive from it any sort of rule applying to the first two plays of an Aischylean content trilogy.

Considerable difficulties have been caused by the motif of the footprints that Elektra compares with her own and from which she concludes that her brother is present. These lines were first struck out by C. G. Schütz in his Aeschylus (London 1823); R. Böhme, following L. Radermacher,[83] wanted to exclude verses 205–210 and 228, while E. Fraenkel in an appendix of his *Ag.* commentary supports the athetesis of 205–211 and 228 f. This suggestion was not followed in the texts. Recently, too, a number of voices have been raised in defense of the passage.[84] To begin with we should not be too startled by the curious comparison of the footprints. The high-handedness with which Aischylos treats detail also obviates the necessity of justifying the passage by rational considerations (Wilamowitz), or folkloristic parallels (G. Thomson in his commentary). A strong support for the passage is further offered by the criticism of the recognition motifs of Aischylos in Euripides' *Elektra* 520–544, including that of the footprints. Consequently, E. Fraenkel and his predecessors had to refer back to the rejection of this passage by A. Mau.[85] The assumption of such a double interpolation remains improbable. But we must not consider the matter concluded beyond all doubt, for one argument is still disturbing: after the removal of vv. 205–211, the powerful exclamation of Orestes εὔχου τὰ λοιπά . . . (pray for the future!) connects better with Elektra's appeal to the gods (201–204) than it does now with v. 211.[86]

The problem of the kommos, important for the entire trilogy, is best stated by the question whether it is to be interpreted statically as a portrayal of the fate of the final Atreidai, constructed with elements of the threnos, or rather dynamically as a passage significant for interpreting the position of Orestes vis-à-vis matricide. The modern debate was ignited by an untenable interpretation of Wilamowitz, according to which the kommos first shows us Orestes rather cool toward the deed, so that the penetrating reports of the kommos are necessary before he can come to a final decision.[87] But in fact Orestes comes on stage with the decision already made, and he justifies it at length by the awful threats of the god. Thus W. Schadewaldt said in his interpretation of the kommos (op. cit., 350 = 137), in clear opposition to Wilamowitz: "The determination of Orestes to act is not a variable in the *Libation Bearers* that would have occupied the imagination of the poet, nor should it occupy his audience." Without wishing to dispute that the determination of Orestes remains constant from his first appearance on, I have proposed another interpretation (op. cit.), on which our analysis here is based: the kommos is the section in which Orestes assumes into his own will the murder commanded by Apollo, in which he comes to desire passionately what was formerly a mandate requiring blind obedience. In the kommos Orestes changes from a tool of the god into a man of action responsible for his deed. Independently K. von Fritz has characterized the function of the passage in a way consistent with our own view: "Thus a third element must be added to the command of the god and the objective reasons: the emotional preparation for the deed that is a prerequisite to its accomplishment."[88]

As we intimated above, the transposition of verses 434–438 to follow 455 would square well with this interpretation of the kommos and would also lessen the difficulties in the order of the strophes, but this strongly contested change is in no way an essential condition of the analysis proposed here.[89]

Modern scholars should not pass over the problems associated with the verses that Wilamowitz left in his edition of 1914, after wishing to delete them in his earlier edition of 1896 (see above) and in his translation. Orestes asks (297): Must one put one's faith in oracles like those of Apollo? The question has the strongest affirmative significance. Then follows (297–305): Even if I were not to trust them, the deed must be done. Many ἵμεροι (desires) coincide: the command of the god, the suffering of the father, the pressing need to free the citizens who conquered Troy from the power of two women. The very efforts of W. Schadewaldt (op. cit., 315. 2 = 109. 2; cf. Lesky, op. cit., 20) to explain this passage as a whole illustrate that this can only be accomplished by force. The worst problem remains that Orestes, directly after postulating the case that he not believe in the oracles of the god, names among the motives for still performing the deed the ϑεοῦ ἐφετμαί (orders of the god) first! Much would be accomplished simply by deleting verses 299–301 (as Wilamowitz did in his translation). Whoever retains them must construe the lines as a sort of statement of theme for the following kommos and burden the poet with very unsatisfactory continuity. The conjecture that in a later performance the lengthy kommos was omitted and the main motifs of the deleted passage replaced by a few interpolated verses, remains speculative. It cannot be proved, but it should not be ruled out of the realm of possibilities either.

The tone of the words spoken by Klytaimestra (691–699) after she receives the fictitious report of Orestes' death seems curious. We can only hope that no one today will still wish to assign them to Elektra.[90] The speech expresses the horror instilled by a power that strikes members of the house, even when they remain far away. Lamentation for Orestes is expressed only in restrained form (695, 698). Is Klytaimestra dissembling here? This has often been assumed by scholars who claim for support the words of the nurse (737) to the effect that the queen displayed a troubled countenance before the servants but with a hidden laughter in her eyes. R. D. Dawe (op. cit., 53) takes 691–699 correctly not as hypocrisy, but sees in the confrontation of both passages, following Tycho von Wilamowitz, a complete breakdown in the characterization of Klytaimestra. We would like to ask whether two aspects could not coexist side by side: first the genuine concern about the inevitability with which the daimon of the house strikes, and then the thinly disguised relief over the death of the avenger. From such considerations I would choose not even to interpret the entrance speech of Aigisthos (838) as hypocritical.

The prologue speech of the Delphic priestess in the *Eumenides* is divided by a sharp caesura into two sections of almost equal length.[91] The first contains the morning prayer of the prophetess before the temple of Apollo at Delphi. Again the contrast to the closing of the *Libation Bearers* with the madness of Orestes is most effective. The prayer offers a history of the Delphic sanctuary. The story is purged of possible motifs of violence in the changes of ownership of the oracle and contains the significant detail that Apollo, unlike in the *Homeric Hymn*, makes his way from Delos to Delphi via Athens.[92] Apollo will later direct Orestes to this city.

Hardly has the prophetess entered the temple when she stumbles onto the stage again, in evident horror. She must use her hands to drag herself on as she reports the terrible sight that drove her from the house of the god: A suppliant, his hands and sword stained with blood, sits on the omphalos; around him are gorgonlike women sleeping on stools.

After her speech the temple door opens and we see the group just described. Apollo stands by Orestes and the first words of his speech are the promise: οὔτοι προδώσω (I shall not forsake you). But at first he can do no more than advise Orestes to endure in his long flight over land and sea. When he comes to Athens, however, he must sit by the image of Athena; there he will find judges and also Apollo's help. He replies to Orestes' renewed appeal for aid by summoning Hermes to accompany his charge; then he withdraws. From the ground rises the ghost of Klytaimestra, who wakes the Furies with bitter reproaches. Sleepy groans and sighs answer her, increasing to cries for Orestes' capture, until the chorus leader wakes the group. Three pairs of strophes follow (144–178), in which lyric meters, often dochmiacs, and then trimeters again appear, indicating a lively exchange of vocal parts. We can hardly speak of a parodos here. In wild tones the Erinyes reproach the god who stole their victim from them and polluted his own sanctuary. A basic theme of the play is struck: a newer world of the Olympian gods slights the aged and honorable chthonic powers, wants to overthrow the ancient right of blood justice. Then the god himself takes his stand opposite them. In a scene (179–234) that contains two speeches of Apollo, each followed by a short stichomythy, Aischylos contrasts two divine realms so sharply that the reconciliation at the play's end only gains its full weight and depth by reference to this passage. While the god in his first speech orders the Erinyes, horrible offspring of the primeval world, to leave his shrine, the second contains an adumbration of the defense that Apollo will enter before the Athenian court on Orestes' behalf.

Now the scene changes: a time of unspecified length passes. We find ourselves in Athens, where the altar and image of the city's goddess indicate the sanctity of the place. Here Orestes settles as a suppliant; here he hopes to find the salvation promised at Delphi. But already the chorus of Furies enters like a pack of hunting dogs, its leader speaking of the travails of the endless hunt (244–253); four dochmiacs (255 f.) describe the final phase of scouting and searching. Finally they discover the fugitive, and in verses that now represent their real parodos, they fly at Orestes, who embraces the goddess' statue, and assert their right to avenge matricide. He too must be sent below, where he will find the others who have transgressed the triple commandment: Honor god, guest, and parents. In words not directly addressed to his pursuers, Orestes cites his ritual purification by Apollo (the question when this supposedly took place will concern us later) and directs his appeal for help to Athena. The Erinyes, through the chorus leader, stand by their right and, during anapests (307–320) in which they refer to the justice of their avenging duty, take their places for the great binding song, the ὕμνος δέσμιος, with which they tether their victim. These anapests powerfully strike the basic chords of the following ode (321–397), which contains four strophic pairs, with ephymnia after the first three. Their repetition after the antistrophe is attested only in the first pair, but may confidently be assumed for the following two as well. The ode follows a line of movement that anticipates the outcome of the play. In the first strophe the children of Night complain of the Delphic god—again two worlds separate—while in the next strophes until the end of the ode they sing of the relentlessness of their vengeance, representing themselves as strictly separate from the shining gods of Olympos. The severity of this contrast is maintained throughout the ode, but the final strophic pair strikes another note as well. When the pitiless Furies call themselves σεμναί (sublime, awesome), every Athenian must have thought of the cult of the sublime goddesses maintained for the city by the family of the Hesychides, and in the finale of the song they sing of the ancient honor that accrues to them, even though they live in sunless darkness. The daimons that Apollo drove from his temple as blood-hungry monsters display characteristics that include dignity and greatness.

Orestes is confined to his asylum at the statue; only the goddess invoked by him earlier can help him now. And she comes as the envoy of a great, order-establishing power, but at the same time as the wonderful embodiment of the Attic spirit that brings light to the darkness and reaches its pinnacle in the harmony of the Parthenon. Calmly she inquires about the meaning of the strange group at her altar (here we must accept the fact that the goddess, unlike her Delphic brother, knows nothing of the nature and duty of the Erinyes). They respond in a stichomythy, following three introductory verses by the chorus leader. Questions and answers concerning Orestes' case are quickly introduced, and it is an indication of new conceptions of justice that a settlement of the trial by oath is rejected, and an investigation expressly demanded (433). Athena's arbitration will decide. Now she summons Orestes to speak to the accusation, which he does in a set speech (443–469), a variation well calculated by the poet. He emphasizes first that he has been ritually purified, and has not therefore polluted the goddess's statue, then he speaks of his deed and the command of the god, whom he calls μεταίτιος (co-responsible), reflecting Aischylean thought.

Athena now finds herself in a situation similar to that of the king in the *Suppliants*: the suppliant cannot be dismissed, any more than the avengers who, if angered, can bring upon the land the poisonous breath of plague. But ἀμηχανία (helplessness), of which she also speaks (481), cannot place a goddess in the dead end of the tragic predicament. If, at the opening of her speech, she still found the case too difficult to be decided by any man or herself, she is now determined to form a sworn tribunal of the best citizens, who must decide.

The first three stanzas of the following stasimon (490–565; four strophic pairs) are filled with the fear that Orestes could go free and that in the future such a murder could remain unatoned. However, the second antistrophe continues a line whose starting point we have already seen at the beginning of the previous ode: the chorus members sing of the enormous import of their actions, and it is deeply significant that words are used here which we later hear spoken by Athena. What was evidently irreconcilable appears here in a new light, and sharp separations begin to converge. When the Furies sing (517) ἔσθ᾽ ὅπου τὸ δεινὸν εὖ (even the fearful has its good), this coincides with the words in the founding speech of Athena (698 f.); and the warning of the chorus, which applies equally to the life of anarchy and that of servitude (525), also finds numerous echoes there (696), some verbatim. In this ode the features emerge, even more powerfully, that now show us the bloodhounds at the Delphic omphalos as the strict but just servants of Dike.

An immense block of spoken verse (566–777), constructed with lively variation, depicts the course of the first murder trial before the Areopagos. Athena enters with a herald, the chosen judges, and a group of citizens. She opens the proceedings, summons Apollo, and asks the Erinyes to speak first. With outstanding effectiveness Aischylos has again constructed the sequence of a series of connected speeches after a passage composed as stichomyth. After two introductory verses, the chorus leader conducts the spirited examination of Orestes, dealing stroke upon stroke, and concluding in two triumphant verses (587–608). Orestes does not deny the deed, appeals briefly to Apollo's command and then confronts the question that becomes more and more the central issue of the trial: how are the deed of Klytaimestra and that of her son to be evaluated with respect to each other? The Furies deny, not without considerably limiting their sphere of authority, that they had to avenge the murder of Agamemnon, on the grounds that he was not a blood relative. When they indignantly reject Orestes' question whether he shares the blood of his mother, claiming that this is doubting the self-evident, he concludes his defense; now the god must help. Apollo states Orestes' case in a set speech (614–673) interrupted only twice by the chorus leader. He cites the dignity of his prophetic office, in which he is the voice of Zeus. Then he describes the crime of the woman who treacherously slew the army commander. Noteworthy here is the chorus leader's question whether Zeus could really value the death of a father so much higher, he who had chained his own father, Kronos. This exemplifies the kind of legalistic-argumentative evaluation of the myths, so frequent in Euripides and even more so later on, which plays off against each other themes that were originally quite disparate. The shot has not missed the mark, as is shown by Apollo's enraged reply as well as by his rather lame argument that bonds can after all be loosed again.[93] To the chorus leader's next question—what community would accept someone guilty of matricide—the god replies not with a reference to a purification carried out under his auspices (another proof of the uncertain position of the motif), but with an argument already mentioned at the close of the stichomyth with Orestes. The father means for the child something quite different from the mother. He is the begetter whereas the mother only preserves the seed; she is the field in which it grows.[94] Apollo closes with a political argument: he intends to be a protector of Athens and, through Orestes, will join Argos to the city as her constant ally.

The arguments are over with; now we await the vote. The following section (674–753) is in ring-composition, though quite asymmetrical. Athena introduces the vote briefly, then moves quickly into her long founding speech. For all time the high court on the Hill of Ares, which now for the first time passes judgment on spilled blood, will remain as the protector of justice for Athens. We have already mentioned that the warning never to ban all fear from the city but to find a middle path between anarchy and servitude teaches wisdom uttered earlier by the Furies.

At the close of her speech Athena instructs the judges to vote. We must picture this process as played out at some length, for it is accompanied by a rather long dispute (711–733) between the chorus leader and Apollo. In this distichomythy the Erinyes intone mighty threats of vengeance, should they lose their case, thus preparing us for the finale of the play. Athena, as presiding authority, votes last—her vote belongs to Orestes, since she herself is daughter only to her father. At the same time she establishes the rule that a tie vote should mean acquittal. That turns out to be the case when the votes are counted; the tie vote is accompanied by outcries on both sides, after which the goddess proclaims Orestes' acquittal.[95]

No one will misconstrue the meaning of the path along which the god of Delphi, recognizing an authority higher than himself, points the way to the tribunal in Athens. The ancient commandment of endless vendetta yields to the judgment of the polis in its highest court. We must not, however, as has been done, see in this a glorification of the state per se. The deadlocked vote is a symbolic expression of the utter impossibility of deciding Orestes' case through human agency. What saves Orestes and breaks the vicious circle of guilt and suffering in the House of Atreus is the charis (grace) of the goddess, made manifest in her ordinance, a charis that derives ultimately from her father, Zeus.

In a freely flowing speech Orestes gives thanks and takes a solemn vow that his Argos will prove a true ally to the city of Pallas for all time.

Here the tragedy of the Atreidai reaches its conclusion; but the stage is still held by the Erinyes, the spirits of vengeance, defeated and enraged, who threaten the land with poison and pestilence. It will be Athena's most difficult task to try to reconcile them. This is accomplished in a long composition, complete in itself, which consists of two epirrhematic sections (778–891 and 916–1020) separated by a spoken scene marking the turning point. The first epirrhematic passage shows the Erinyes in wild pain and boundless rage. This is further expressed by the exact repetition of the strophe in the antistrophe of both strophic pairs. Athena answers in a speech of trimeters, entreats and pacifies with endless patience, and displays Attic charis even when she mildly hints that the daughter of Zeus also has weapons and knows where the supreme god keeps his lightning bolts in a sealed chamber.[96] However, it is not a threat but a friendly promise that wins the day. High honors accrue to the Furies: what they represent for the rights and community of mankind will be included in the construction of the polis as the irrevocable prerequisite to its continued existence as a whole. Athena, the child of Olympian Zeus, the shining goddess, also knows the blessing of the powers that have their source deep beneath the earth. The change occurs in a short stichomythy: the avengers of guilt, who by no means are to lay down their office, shall become benedictory powers for the land of Attica and its people. And now, in the second epirrhematic section flow the blessings of the Eumenides for the city of Athena, reminiscent of the ode of the *Suppliants* for Argos. The goddess replies in anapests, praising these propitious promises for tree and hearth, for the people and the peace of the community. In solemn procession with the judges and townspeople, Athena herself leads the Erinyes to their new abode, from which they will rule as benedictory powers. Two brief strophes of the chorus close with the important statement that Zeus and fate (Moira) have united to a common end.

Varying from the close parallel construction of the first two plays, which pushed on toward the climax of the plot in energetic thrusts after lengthy, predominantly lyric exposition, the *Eumenides* shows a structure of four approximately equal blocks, the first two of which depict the outbreak of the conflict occasioned by Orestes' deed, while the final two contain the solution of this conflict for men and gods. The prelude in Delphi allows the two divine factions to set themselves off against each other, and also points the way to Athens. There the preparation for the trial is staged, which serves to reveal at some length the nature of the Erinyes in two long choral odes and also contains the intervention of Athena. Orestes' trial forms the third section, while the final block extends the conciliatory conclusion to the divine realm and incorporates the resentful avengers into the Athenian polis as benedictory powers.

In constructing the *Eumenides* Aischylos was faced with a problem of composition that arose from the combination of fixed tradition with individual creativity. Apollo was given both as the instigator of the matricide, and as the protector of Orestes, whether he equipped him with a bow to ward off the Erinyes, as Stesichoros relates, or cleansed his guilt with pig's blood, as shown on the krater in the Louvre. These motifs did not suffice for Aischylos; he tied the great reconciliation, encompassing god and man, to his own city of Athens, without, however, rejecting Delphi or its god. This synthesis was accomplished only with great difficulty. First there is the juxtaposition of a god on the one hand, who assures Orestes' salvation with his first line in the play and a freely deciding tribunal on the other, before which the god submits himself to the uncertainty of the outcome. Another unsolved problem is involved in the information provided by Orestes in Athens concerning previous purifications. Once (238) he refers to the lessening of his pollution on his long journey, then again (283) to the expiation through pig's blood. These two statements cannot be perfectly reconciled. To be sure, Apollo in the temple scene (75) speaks of the long wanderings of Orestes, but then gives him his brother Hermes (89), the surest guide on the way to Athens.[97] Completely irreconcilable is the ritual expiation through Apollo, for the prophetess spoke (41) of the suppliant sitting on the omphalos with bloody hands, and between the appearance of Apollo and his dismissal of Orestes there is no word of such an expiation.

In another way, too, Aischylos has made use of the license that is the privilege of genius. The Furies appear in various passages as the avengers of every heavy guilt, primarily blood guilt. Thus Kassandra (*Ag.* 1186) already hears the chorus making an uproar in the House of Atreus; verses like *Eum.* 336 and 421 point in the same direction; in the binding ode they are represented as the relentless executors of justice, and in *Eum.* 513 they lament that mothers and fathers will invoke Dike and the Furies in vain if their rights are scorned. Especially problematic in this context is *Libation Bearers* 283, in which Apollo promises Orestes that he will be persecuted by the

Erinyes of his father if he does not obey. To all this is contrasted the limitation of their avenging duties to the murder of blood relatives alone, clearly emphasized by the Erinyes: *Eum.* 210–212 and 605, where they disclaim any responsibility for Klytaimestra's deed for just this reason. We understand that the poet needed this optional limitation for the direction of the plot; it also provided the starting point for the dispute over the relative importance of father and mother for a child.

The trial itself is probably the section in which we least perceive the power of the Titan among Attic tragedians.[98] The scene surely meant more to the litigation-loving Athenians. In passing it should not be overlooked that something very substantial is expressed in the vulnerability of both sides of the argumentation: the shadow of doom over the House of Atreus cannot be dispelled in this way; only the charis of Athena breaks the curse.

In designating the locale, too, the poet proceeds without anxious narrow-mindedness. Orestes comes to Athens and seeks refuge at the statue of the city's goddess. We would naturally think here of the Akropolis, but the goddess in her founding speech (685 ff.) specifically describes the Areopagos as the scene of events.[99]

The question of references in a tragedy to the time of the poet may be delicate in many cases, but there is no doubt here that examples of such may be found in the scene of the founding of the Areopagos and in the assurance of the Argive alliance. To be sure, the conclusions that have been drawn concerning the political position of the poet show considerable variation.[100] As we remarked for the *Suppliants*, the special emphasis placed on the alliance with Argos shows how strongly the hopes of the democrats who had now attained power were placed in this city after the collapse of Kimon's pro-Spartan policies. The *Eumenides* also points in this direction.

Furthermore there can be no doubt that the glorification of the Areopagos by Aischylos is connected with the events that divested the ancient council of all its political rights in 462 B.C. We do not wish to recognize in the *Eumenides* a protest against the reforms of Ephialtes, because Athena, in founding the tribunal, grants it exactly the power left to the Areopagos by the democrats: jurisdiction over crimes of violence. And it is this right that the poet defends with all the force of his conviction. This is further confirmation for the interpretation of F. Schachermeyr introduced in our discussion of the *Suppliants*, which considered Aischylos to be a moderate democrat. Interesting also is his conjecture that the question that plays such an important role in the trial scene, namely whether father or mother is the true parent of the child, could be connected with the dispute over the civic rights of those who had Athenian fathers but foreign mothers.[101]

The satyr play *Proteus* may be imagined basically as a dramatization of the tale narrated by Menelaos in the fourth book of the *Odyssey*. The messenger in the *Agamemnon* (620 ff.) prepares us briefly for the subject of the play.

In the *Theogony*, Hesiod tells the story of Prometheus, Zeus's clever opponent, who tricked the father of the gods in the allotment of sacrificial offerings and stole fire to give it to men; he tells also of the cruel punishment by the eagle that ate the liver of the bound Titan daily, since it grew back during the night, until Herakles, with the consent of Zeus, shot the tormentor. The Attic cult also knew of a fire-daimon Prometheus, who with Hephaistos was the patron of potters and smiths and possessed a sanctuary near Kolonos.[102] Aischylos picked up on the story of the theft of fire but gave it dramatic complexity by combining it with a theme from another source. His drama takes place in the primeval age when Zeus had won world domination but had not yet secured it against all danger. He is the third in a succession in which his two predecessors had had to yield to brute force.[103] Who could guarantee that his fate, too, would not reverse? Prometheus, seemingly helpless in his bonds, becomes the dangerous opponent of the new lord of the world through his knowledge of the secret divulged to him by his mother (here Themis and Gaia united into one figure), a secret that threatens the power of Zeus.

Aischylos probably treated this struggle in a complete trilogy, whose satyr play is unknown to us. The *Prometheus Desmotes* (*Prometheus Bound*) alone has been preserved.[104]

The play begins with a vivid prologue scene. In the rocky wilderness at the end of the world Kratos and Bia, the henchmen of Zeus, led by Hephaistos carrying his hammer, conduct Prometheus to the site of his bondage. The smith-god fastens the Titan to the rock with bonds around his hands and feet and an iron wedge through his breast, but in the course of the action a sharp contrast is revealed in his uninterrupted dialogue with Kratos. The latter is merely the crude servant of Zeus, scornful of his defenseless victim, while Hephaistos displays deep sympathy and performs his cruel assignment only with complaints and reluctance.

Two observations must be made here. Immediately in v. 7 Kratos designates the theft of fire for man's benefit as Prometheus's transgression. This is referred to three more times in the scene (30, 38, 82), twice by Kratos; and near the end of the play (946) Hermes, another lackey of Zeus, abuses Prometheus as the thief of fire. But it is most significant that Kratos in the first two passages speaks of the παντέχνου πυρὸς σέλας (blaze of fire, skilled in all arts). Through this attribute the cue is already given for the steady deemphasis of fire per se as the object of the deed; it prepares us early on for the great speech of the Titan, in which he reveals himself to be the bestower of human culture itself.[105]

Hephaistos offers a key phrase for the entire tragedy when he closes his compassionate yet reproachful speech to Prometheus with the sentence: all are harsh whose rule is new. We are constantly reminded that this is the beginning of a new world age, a new regime, which resulted from a struggle that is not yet ultimately settled.[106]

We must imagine before us Prometheus bound to the rock and maintaining a long silence until he begins his lament with the magnificent appeal to the elements. The scene begins with lyric iambics marked by heavy alliteration, which give way to anapests without any thematic break. The return to iambics (101) signals a calmer reflection on his situation; a new, animated transition (114; anapests again after bacchiacs and iambics) announces the unexpected entrance of the chorus.

In none of the tragedies that have come down to us does the chorus approach the action so completely from without as is here the case with the Okeanids, who enter in their parodos (128–192) on a winged vehicle. This parodos is constructed in two strophic pairs, each followed by anapestic epirrhemata of the Titan. The maidens, who inhabit the river encircling the globe, have heard the hammering, have overcome their timidity, and have asked their father for permission to take a look at what has happened. Sympathy causes them to weep, and we hear the catchword for the new regime, in which Zeus rules lawlessly (ἀθέτως) in accordance with a new self-serving justice. The epirrhemata of the first pair of strophes take their tone from a painful, Look here! Prometheus expresses the genuinely Hellenic wish rather to be in the depths of Hades than to present a welcome spectacle to his enemies. In the second strophe the chorus gives the suffering hero his cue when it sings that Zeus will not end his severity before his heart has been appeased or until some other wrest his rule from him. Prometheus knows the secret on which depends a new change in the world order, and this knowledge is his great weapon. The chorus shudders to hear such bold words, but Prometheus remains steadfast in his last epirrhema: Zeus may have justice in his power (the phrase παρ' ἑαυτῷ τὸ δίκαιον ἔχων, having justice at his side, is strange), but he will learn mildness. It is an important indication of the fact that the Prometheus trilogy also ends with a reconciliation of opposites, when the Titan concludes (191): εἰς ἀρθμὸν ἐμοὶ καὶ φιλότητα σπεύδων σπεύδοντί ποθ' ἥξει (He will yet come to alliance and friendship, eagerly, with one likewise eager).

This drama, with its immobile protagonist, can be kept in motion only by visiting and questioning characters. The Okeanids duly ask their questions. In a tripartite spoken scene between Prometheus and the chorus leader (193–276), the latter asks the cause of this harsh punishment. In a long speech Prometheus takes his story back to the distant past. During the revolt of the Titans against Kronos, Prometheus followed the advice of his mother Themis (also called Gaia), who unites many names within a single figure,[107] and took the part of Zeus, aiding him to victory over his opponents, who are now confined to Tartaros. The new ruler has ill repaid the favor, for tyrants put no trust in friends.[108] When Zeus decided to annihilate mankind and create a new race, Prometheus saved the mortals. In the following stichomythy, framed by four verses of the chorus leader, Prometheus names as his aid to man, blind hope and fire as the basis of all technical achievements. This is identical with the meaning of ἔντεχνος σοφία σὺν πυρί (technical ability with the aid of fire) in the story of Protagoras (Plat. *Prot.* 321D). In a further speech Prometheus acknowledges his actions, where ἑκὼν ἥμαρτον (willingly I erred; 266) does not signify the confession of a sin, but is rather spoken from Zeus's viewpoint. Then he bids the Okeanids to dismount from their vehicle, so that he might finish his story. The anapests 277–283 accompany the maidens' movement. Now comes a new visitor, their father, Okeanos; anapests again accompany his approach; he rides on a griffin. A long conversation between the two matches up fixed speeches, then ends in a short stichomythy. The entire scene is drawn with subtle characterization, and in interpreting this section it is not always easy to decide where the poet intended us to perceive what undertones. To what extent is Okeanos truly determined to help, and to what extent does he wish, by this visit to the suffering god, merely to discharge a familial obligation? And when, dismissed by Prometheus, he says that his winged beast is already looking forward to returning to its stall, do we not hear his own relief at leaving this unpleasant conversation? In Prometheus, the hero of unbending defiance is contrasted with Okeanos, the counsellor of prudent submission. Thus he responds to the good intentions of Okeanos with a lightly ironic superiority and rejects out of hand his attempt at mediation. He warns him of the danger, hardly suited to Okeanos's nature, of coming into conflict with Zeus. What might be expected from such a conflict is shown by the fates of Atlas and Typhoeus. When Prometheus speaks of the latter's imprisonment beneath Aitna and the rivers of fire destined to burst forth, it is permissible to imagine the poet's recollections of his stay in Sicily furnishing the background for this passage.

The first stasimon (397–435), two short strophic pairs with following epode, is a single lament for Prometheus meant to resound through all the races of Asia, in the depths of Hades, and through all the waters of the sea and its rivers.

The second epeisodion (436–525), in a long speech divided into two approximately equal halves by four trimeters of the chorus leader, picks up the story of Prometheus at the point where Okeanos had interrupted it. Now Prometheus reports how he saved mankind from destruction. Here the line relegating his theft of fire more and more to the background is brought to its end. Fire is mentioned only once more, among the means used to recognize omens; what Prometheus gives here is an account of the origins of culture that places him in the center as its great originator. It was he who first made men intellectual beings, able to overcome their material obstacles and interpret omens. This noteworthy speech has its place within the broad cultural-historical contexts. The Greek tendency of naming an originator for every institution is here united with the transition that leads from Hesiod's pessimistic doctrine of civilization in decline to the image of an upward-moving development of mankind.[109] It is astonishing to find such a theory as early as Aischylos, and the uncertainty of the play's date is especially regrettable in this context. In any case, the Xenophanes fragment that seems related in thought (DK 21B 18) can attest to a positive theory of development at an early date.[110] Worthy of note also is the general agreement with parts of the first stasimon of the *Antigone*, where building, the yoking of oxen, plowing, sailing, and healing appear again, to be sure, not as the gifts of a god, but as man's achievements in the sense of the Xenophanes fragment. Moreover, one thinks immediately of the doctrine of cultural origins proposed by Protagoras in Plato, but here two things must be borne in mind. First, the Sophist bases his idea of progress on the opinion that "political capabilities" alone make possible community life, and second, our speech of Prometheus may be termed pre-Sophistic in that it gives an important place to prophecy and the prediction of the future by signs.

This speech is followed by a short conversation with the chorus leader, in which the thought is expressed that there are still ineluctable forces untouched by the despotism of the new ruler of the world: the Moirai and the Erinyes. Prometheus refuses to say more.

In the two strophic pairs, again short, of the second stasimon (526–560), the chorus retreats to a certain distance from the Titan. Significant new tones are heard when it sings of Zeus; we no longer hear complaints, but words of pious submission: never may the chorus have Zeus's omnipotence as opponent, never may it neglect sacrifice, or dare a presumptuous word. In sharp contrast stands the helpless Prometheus, abandoned by all. His great opponent appears now in a different light; from the role of the tyrant the ruler emerges who ordains a system of order (550 f.): οὔποτε . . . τὰν Διὸς ἁρμονίαν θνατῶν παρεξίασι βουλαί (the plans of man will never escape the order of Zeus). We cannot be far wrong in perceiving here a preview of the reconciliation at the close of the trilogy that follows in the sign of this ἁρμονία.

If such a compromise is intimated in the verses of the chorus it is quickly dropped with the appearance of Io. With anapests—Where am I? Who are you?—she rushes onto the stage, pursued by the ghost of Argos who once held watch over her (566–573; non-strophic). Then comes a strophic pair followed in each of its elements by four trimeters of Prometheus. In the strophe the fearful ecstasy of Io continues: she hears flute sounds; as the victim of Zeus she wishes only to die. When Prometheus calls her by name and reveals knowledge of her fate, she asks him to predict her future. With the trimeters following the antistrophe Prometheus prepares for the lengthy spoken scene with Io (613–876) that is interrupted only once by anapests of the deeply shaken chorus. The poet avoids repetition in the introductory stichomythy by having Prometheus respond tersely to Io's question about his distress.[111] Still the Titan hesitates, then he is persuaded by the girl's renewed request to foretell her future suffering. The effect is odd when (631) the chorus leader also requests for her side a portion of the pleasure (μοῖραν ἡδονῆς). The curious maidens first wish to know what drove Io to her unfortunate fate. This opens the way for her detailed story of Zeus's love, which drove her from the house of her father, and the raging torment caused by Hera's resentment. Only after the pause during the choral anapests does Prometheus redeem his promise to reveal her future. He does this in three long speeches, with a stichomythy between the first two, while the second and third are separated by four verses of the chorus leader (819–822) that determine in almost pedantic fashion the direction of the narrative.

In his first speech Prometheus describes the beginning of Io's wandering. The poet fully indulges his delight in exotic geography: Skythia, Chalybes, the Caucasus, the Amazons, the Cimmerian Isthmus, the Channel of Maiotis, where men will henceforth speak of the Bosporos. In five verses Io expresses her death-wish; Prometheus replies in five verses about his knowledge that he is immortal and that only the fall of Zeus can end his suffering. This gives the cue for the following stichomythy, in which the revelation of the secret proceeds another step: the son of a woman can overthrow Zeus. And here the destinies of the two are joined: Zeus can escape his fall if he frees Prometheus (thus learning the secret). But the Titan can be freed only by a descendant of Io in the thirteenth generation. In the meantime much suffering lies in store for the tormented Io. Prometheus wishes to remain silent, but at the insistence of Io, he offers a choice between learning about the rest of her toils or about his deliverer. The chorus, not to be denied, again joins in this curious bargaining (782): Prometheus should reveal both secrets, to Io her future wandering and to the chorus his savior. This determines the bipartite structure of the following speech. Prometheus first describes Io's continuing flight, which involves a host of mythical beings: Phorkyads, Gorgons, griffins, arimasps. Beyond the Aithiopians at the source of the sun she will come to Egypt and the Nile, where the end of her suffering has been preordained.[112] Now the chorus requests its portion of the prediction, and in his third speech Prometheus first establishes his absolute credibility by the certainty with which he reminds Io that the talking oaks of Dodona greeted her as the future spouse of Zeus. This is a curious feature of this puzzling tale, in which Zeus is intended to appear as the bringer of suffering. Also, the aition for the naming of the Ionian Sea is connected with this section of the narrative. Prometheus quickly summarizes Io's salvation in Egypt. In Kanobos at the mouth of the Nile Zeus will heal her of her madness by the touch of his hand, and make her the mother of Epaphos. In the fifth generation after him, the fifty Danaids will flee from their cousins to Argos. There a bloody marriage will take place; only one of the sisters will spare her husband and found a line of Argive kings. From her descendants will arise the great bowman who will liberate Prometheus. The Titan will say no more, and Io immediately rushes from the scene in a renewed fit of madness.

In the third stasimon (887–906), a short strophic pair with an epode, the chorus of divine maidens projects the experience of Io into the human sphere: A marriage above one's station brings calamity and they themselves would never wish to be the consort of Zeus or any other divinity. We must forget here that one of the Okeanids, Klymene, was the lover of Helios, and according to another version was even the mother of Prometheus by Iapetos.

Somewhat abruptly Prometheus begins the fourth epeisodion (907–1039) with a speech that powerfully emphasizes the basic motif, his knowledge of the secret that threatens Zeus. Without lifting the final veil, he proceeds one step further in his revelations: a monster armed with fearful flames can destroy the lord of the thunderbolt. In the following stichomythy the chorus construes these words as a dangerous challenge to the ruler of heaven, but Prometheus exults: You submit! To me Zeus is less than nothing, the days of his rule are numbered. Such defiance is immediately heard on high, and onto the scene comes Hermes, whom Prometheus contemptuously calls the underling of Zeus and his attitude is also defiant in the following dispute (944–1035) composed in the familiar schema of a long speech followed by doublets that become stichomythy, then opening again into a long speech and reply.

Hermes is a finely drawn character. As the servant of a mighty lord he at first rails against Prometheus, then resorts to persuasion. But since Prometheus, aware of the power of his knowledge, shows only contempt and scorn, Hermes ends by announcing what Zeus holds in store for the rebellious Titan: the descent of the prisoner into the abyss and his constant torment by the eagle which will devour his liver daily. This introduces a new theme that hints at the following play. The torture will end only when a god is ready to descend into the darkness of Hades to take Prometheus's place.

The chorus leader tries in vain to move Prometheus to yield; in the finale with its anapestic recitatives (1040–1093) the contrast is sharpened between the Titan, magnificently defying the god who upset the cosmos, and Hermes, who instructs the chorus to flee from this place of destruction. But the poet felt that an orderly exit of the chorus would be intolerable, and has the group assume an attitude hardly prepared in its odes: they decide to share the fate of Prometheus. In the final words of the play the Titan describes the outbreak of chaos and he descends with the chorus into Tartaros.

In the structure of the play, the prelude with the chaining of Prometheus clearly stands separate; it contains action such as does not occur again until the end of the piece.

From the behavior of Hephaistos and Kratos we learn that complete harmony does not exist even among the servants of the new master. A many-faceted picture of the ruling powers is revealed; only by achieving their balance can an orderly condition of world order come about. Between the action of the beginning and end, the structure of the play is determined by a series of visits to the Titan chained to the rock. Possibly a similar situation was presented in the *Niobe*, with the grieving mother sitting on the grave of her children. In the *Prometheus*, a powerful crescendo runs through the elucidation of the future, increasing from conversation to conversation: it involves Zeus as well as Prometheus and Io, whose appearance brings livelier movement to the play and whose long scene presents a drama within the drama. Like the first two parts of the *Oresteia* this play also ends with an unresolved situation.

Although no ancient source raises doubts about the authenticity of the play, this has become a much discussed problem among modern scholars. When R. Westphal (1856) pointed out peculiarities in the choral lyrics, he did not suggest deletion, and later too (1869) merely assumed that the passages had been revised by various hands. Later scholars became increasingly concerned with discovering further peculiarities and denied that Aischylos was the author. Alfred Körte gives an excellent overview of the state of the problem as of 1920, at the same time defending the authenticity of the play so energetically that it seemed for a time as if the question had been decided.[113] But soon afterward W. Schmid supported athetesis, basing his arguments especially on linguistic detail.[114] He finally went so far as to treat the play in the third volume of his literary history as a closet drama composed under Sophistic influence. This radical stance has not been widely accepted, but supporters of athetesis continue into the present day. Even such an excellent philologist as Walter Nestle, while first, albeit doubtfully, assigning the play to Aischylos (1934), deprived him of it a few years later in his revision of Droysen's translation.[115] His pupil Walter Jens claimed to find in the stichomythies of the play much that contradicted the technique of the poet.[116] Recently Ole Smith and Gerhard Müller have denied the authenticity of the piece; the argumentation of the latter is representative.[117] He asserts that the dialogue form of the tragic prologue was apparently invented by Sophokles, and thus the dialogue in the opening of *Prometheus* would be one cogent argument, among others, for dependence on Sophoklean technique and non-Aischylean origin.

While Bernard Knox also thought he noticed relationships to the art of Sophokles, he did not evaluate them with respect to the problem of authorship, but to that of date.[118] The assumption that we possess in the *Prometheus* a heavily revised Aischylean play has not found much support, but R. D. Dawe, in his valuable study, has excluded the *Prometheus* from the Aischylean canon on the suspicion that the play has undergone extensive alterations.[119]

It is characteristic of the state of this problem that the most thorough case made for athetesis, that of W. Schmid, contains a detailed chapter entitled "Aischylean Elements in *Prometheus Bound*." And in fact, besides the numerous points in which this play differs from the others,[120] an equal number can be found that indicate Aischylean authorship.[121] It is all too easily forgotten on what a narrow basis our comparisons are made. Repeatedly, scholars have pointed to the simpler language of the *Prometheus*.[122] Then came the *Niobe* papyrus, and Pohlenz (1. 84, 2. 42) was able with strong justification to show the linguistic simplicity of this fragment. A decisive argument against Aischylean authorship has never been adduced, and we should always bear in mind the phrase that a few dozen weak arguments can never add up to one strong one.

To be sure, the image of Zeus as a new and despotic ruler is difficult to reconcile with the praise for the just disposer of the world in the *Suppliants* and the *Oresteia*.[123] Jakob Burckhardt has written in his *Griechischen Kulturgeschichte* (1. 319 in the Kröner edition): "No settlement in the trilogy's lost tragedy *Prometheus Unbound* could erase this fearful impression and change it into a special glorification of Zeus." And yet there is every indication that the trilogy concluded with a reconciliation that resulted in the foundation of a new world order. We recall the future φιλότης (friendship) with Zeus mentioned once by Prometheus (191) and Διὸς ἁρμονία (order of Zeus) in the ode of the Okeanids (551). We said with those who see in *Prometheus* a preparation for the path to a solution in which violence and justice, power and spiritually based order were united, and with the conclusion of ancient battles for domination in heaven a new period in world history began.[124] This is not merely reverting to Wilamowitz, who in his *Aisch. Interpretationen* assumed a development in Zeus[125] and cited F. T. Vischer's phrase about the harshness of the Old Testament conception of god: The Good Lord himself was still young then." Our theory of the synthesis of the great, world-dominating powers does not agree either with the assumption that an erring Prometheus is brought to his senses[126] or that there was a development in the religious thought of Aischylos.[127]

The manuscript index contains besides the *Desmotes* also a *Prometheus Lyomenos* (*Prometheus Unbound*) and *Prometheus Pyrphoros* (*Prometheus Firebringer*). As we saw in our discussion of the *Persians*, the trilogy to which this play belonged closed with a satyr play, *Prometheus*. This is probably identical with the *Prom. Pyrkaeus* (*Prom. Firekindler*) mentioned in Pollux X 64 (fr. 457M). To this play we have also assigned the beautiful verses saluting fire from *P. Oxy.* 2245 (fr. 343M); those who assign them to *Prom. Pyrph.* are cited there.

It remains beyond doubt that the *Desmotes* was followed by the *Lyomenos*. We are aided in reconstructing this play by the fact that the index of dramatis personae for the preserved play mistakenly still lists Ge and Herakles. Ge, as Prometheus's mother, most probably persuaded him to reconciliation when after endless time he was lifted up on his rock to the Caucasus. Herakles shot the eagle that had been devouring the Titan's liver. As a reward he obtained from Prometheus the details of his journey to the apples of the Hesperides in the far west. A series of fragments with mythic-geographical references (326 ff. M) parallels Io's journey to the east and points to further correspondences.[128] The liberated Titans formed the chorus, impressive evidence of a new world order striving for reconciliation. Small portions of their entrance anapests are preserved (fr. 322 f. M), and Cicero composed a Latin translation of the hero's speech to his brothers (fr. 324M). Herakles freed Prometheus from the eagle, but did not loose his bonds. How this eventually happened is unknown—we can guess that either Hermes or Hephaistos came to him. The condition laid down at the end of the *Desmotes*, that a god must voluntarily go into the underworld for Prometheus, must also have been fulfilled. A remark by Apollodoros hints at the centaur Cheiron, who was incurably wounded by a poisoned arrow of Herakles.[129] There was also a mention in the *Lyomenos* of the custom that men should crown themselves with garlands in remembrance of the bonds of Prometheus. The motif also appears in the *Sphinx* (fr. 181M), the satyr play of the Theban trilogy.

Thus we can make something at least of the *Lyomenos*; for the content of the *Prometheus Pyrphoros* we have hardly a clue. J. G. Herder and F. G. Welcker founded the theory that the *Pyrphoros* was the first play of the trilogy and presented the theft of fire.[130] Pohlenz (1. 78) followed them, but this sequence takes so little account of the preparatory character of the *Desmotes* that the arrangement of R. Westphal has found widespread acceptance;[131] he places the *Pyrphoros* third in a tetralogy whose satyr play remains unknown. The single specific reference in the schol. *Prom.* 94 (fr. 341M), that according to the *Pyrphoros* Prometheus was bound for 30,000 years, presents only difficulties through its discrepancy with the thirteenth generation after Io, at which time Herakles comes. Reinhardt has rightly rejected the attempt to postulate from this a prophecy in the *Pyrphoros* as the opening play. And when we hear Prometheus in the *Desmotes* (94) speak of a torment that lasts for 10,000 years, we need not make unnecessary computations with such figures, which merely indicate immeasurable periods of time. The assumption that *Pyrphoros* contained the founding of the Prometheia and the inclusion of the Titan into the Attic cult, has much to be said for it, and seems tempting because of the parallel to the *Eumenides*. But all this is uncertain.[132]

Just as uncertain is the attempt to cut through the Gordian knot by equating the *Pyrphoros* with the satyr play *Pyrkaeus* and uniting the preserved *Desmotes* with the *Lyomenos* in a dilogy that somehow resulted from peculiar circumstances in Sicily.[133]

The dating, like everything else in the *Desmotes*, is difficult.[134] We would have a reliable terminus ante quem in the year 467, if fr. 181M from the *Sphinx*, with the reference to the garlands that according to Prometheus were the best of bonds, represents a self-quotation of the poet from the *Lyomenos*, but an older tradition cannot be ruled out. Another consideration may be more profitable. That Aischylos spent some time in Sicily around 470 is very probable. A few years earlier the eruption of Aitna had occurred, also referred to by Pindar in the *Pythian* 1 from the year 470. For the linguistic correspondences between his verses and *Prom.* 351 ff. the juxtaposition offered by Podlecki is very instructive, but does not prove the dependence of one from the other. In any event we may recognize a reminiscence of the catastrophe in the verses of Aischylos. Such an occurrence remained long in human memory, so that we are not obliged to set the date of *Prometheus* near 470. There are also quite a number of stylistic observations already mentioned here that indicate a certain similarity to the *Oresteia*. We can hardly offer anything more than was proposed by Croiset and Mazon, who set the play between the *Seven* and the *Oresteia*.

Such a date is also recommended by the scenic problems of the work.[135] If it is correct that the plays known to us that preceded the *Oresteia* did not yet utilize a fixed skene, but used only temporary constructions, the descent of Prometheus's rock could have been accomplished by exploiting the terrain. Modern performances of the play at Delphi (cf. Bieber, *History*, pl. 846) are instructive on many points. To assume a skene equipped with a paraskene, as does R. Unterberger (op. cit., 11) following Schadewaldt, seems to us to present even greater difficulties (ekkyklema?).

It is difficult to answer the question whether Prometheus was represented by an actor or a gigantic puppet behind which the protagonist spoke. Since masks were used in any case the difference would not have been all that great. Murray (39) and Wilamowitz (*Aisch. Int.*, 114) took over this idea from Welcker and Herrmann, and many recent interpretations follow them. But according to schol. *Prom.* 511, the *Lyomenos* contained the liberation of the bound Titan, and we can hardly imagine that this could have been shown by manipulating a puppet.[136] The conclusion of Unterberger (op. cit., 10. 132) that we should assume there was a puppet in the *Desmotes* and an actor in the *Lyomenos* is not very satisfactory.

That Aischylos introduced a third actor at the beginning of the *Desmotes* but did not make further use of him, would agree with a date not too long before the *Oresteia*.

The question of the Okeanids' entrance seems hopeless. A winged wagon was long imagined until E. Fraenkel ridiculed the Okeanids' "omnibus" and theorized, with the support of vase paintings, that the maidens entered individually in small winged carts.[137] A very simple solution is assumed by W. Buchwald in his edition: The maidens rolled into the orchestra on small carts whose wings concealed the movement of their hands. Schadewaldt's reconstruction of the stage in Unterberger (op. cit., 11) presumes a roller contrivance by means of which the small carts were pulled along tracks. It is understandable that Kraus in his study returned to the good old winged wagon. The assumption that the chorus, like Okeanos on his griffin, was carried along through the air by a machine, at least conforms best to the text.

We should be still more cautious here than in the other plays when searching for political references. Podlecki is discreet, but we cannot accept even his consideration that Themistokles, much admired by the poet, might have been responsible for his views against tyrants.[138]

FRAGMENTS

Since the monumental collection of A. Nauck, *Tragicorum Graecorum Fragmenta*, 2d ed., 1889, reprinted with a supplement for Euripides by Bruno Snell, Hildesheim 1964, a large number of fragments have been added. These have been the subject of intensive work by H. J. Mette. His *Suppl. Aesch.*, Kleine Texte 169, Berlin 1939, with a supplement (1949) and a summary in *Gymn*. 62 (1955), 393, was followed by *Die Fragmente der Tragödien des Aischylos*, Berlin 1959. The volume was complemented by a second, *Der Verlorene Aischylos*, Berlin 1963, which, along with the previous study, Mette termed a workbook. A comfortable overview may be found in the supplement to "Aischylos" by F. Stoessl, *RE* Suppl. 11. 1.

Wilamowitz was able to write in 1914: "Up to now Egypt has preserved not even one scrap," but this sentence was soon to be contradicted. The finds of 1932 are due to the energy of E. Breccia. He was successful in opening up the final unexplored kôm (rubbish heap) of Oxyrhynchos, after the tomb of the Arabic saint Ali Ghamman had been removed from the site. Grenfell and Hunt were able to dig up a series of papyri from this kôm in their exploratory excavation as early as 1902/1903. As investigation has shown, these papyri contained numerous fragments of Aischylos, most of them quite small, to be sure. A large portion of these has been made accessible by Edgar Lobel, with his usual consummate skill, in volumes 18 (1941) and 20 (1952) of *The Oxyrynchus Papyri*. They stem mostly from the same edition as the fragments discovered by the Italians and published in *PSI* 11 (1935). The fact that this edition was written in the second century A.D. demands a considerable adjustment of our conceptions about the survival of Aischylean tragedy.

An outstanding bibliographical aid (and not only for Aischylos) was compiled by R. A. Pack, *Greek and Latin Literary Texts from Greco-Roman Egypt*, 2d ed., Ann Arbor 1965. After the older compilations of P. Collart, "Les fragm. des trag. gr. sur papyrus," *Rev. phil.* 17 (1943), 5 and V. Martin, "La poésie lyr. et la poésie dram. dans les decouvertes papyr. des trentes dernières années, "*Mus. Helv.* 4 (1947), 74, we can especially recommend M. F. Galiano, "Les papyrus d'Eschyle," *Proc. of the IX. Int. Congress of Papyrology*, Norwegian University Press 1961, 81. An edition with commentary on the new finds was published by R. Cantarella, *I nuovi frammenti Eschilei di Ossirinco*, Naples 1948. H. Lloyd-Jones has offered the new texts with critical apparatus and extensive bibliography in the second edition of the Loeb Classical Library Aischylos, Cambridge, Mass. 1957. Several of them are also to be found in D. L. Page, *Select Papyri III: Literary Papyri*, London 1941 (revised 1950); the fragments from the satyr plays also are in V. Steffen, *Satyrographorum Graecorum Fragmenta*, 2d ed., Poznan 1952.

Of the Aischylos papyri found in Oxyrhynchos in 1932, twenty-one verses of the *Niobe* and a few shreds of the *Diktyoulkoi* were published in the same year by G. Vitelli and M. Norsa in the *Bull. de la Soc. Arch. d'Alex.* 28. 107. The first publication of the *Myrmidons* fragment followed two years later (*Mél. Bidez*, Brussels 1934, 965).[1]

The *Niobe* papyrus poses two difficult questions. Although the majority of the verses have been well preserved and letters have been lost only at the beginning of the lines, we still cannot be sure whether Niobe, sitting on the grave of her children, speaks here after she has broken her long silence (Aristoph. *Ran.* 912 = fr. 212M; *Vita* 6 = fr. 243M) or whether another person is referring to the long-silent mother. Vitelli maintained in the *PSI* edition that Niobe was the speaker, which I and others

have supported (*Wien. Stud.* 52, [1934], 1). H. Lloyd-Jones (see above) rightly emphasizes that a clear decision is impossible, but leans toward the assumption of another
speaker. This view has steadily won over more and more followers, who naturally
provide varying answers. We may probably rule out the conjecture of K. Reinhardt
(*Herm.* 69 [1934], 249 = *Tradition und Geist*, 153; *Soph.*, 2d ed., 21. 245) that the
fragment comes from the prologue, in which Leto explained the silent Niobe like a
picture, requiring extras to address in v. 14.[2] R. Pfeiffer (*Phil.* 89 [1934], 1) and Schadewaldt (*Sitzb. Heidelb.* 1933/4, third appendix) thought of a person close to Niobe,
perhaps Antiope, the mother of Amphion. If we exclude Niobe as the speaker, then K.
Latte's assignment of the lines to her nurse (*GGN* 1933, 22) seems most probable, and
this solution is also preferred by Mette (*Verl. Aisch.*, 44).

The most difficult problem of interpretation arises between verses 9/10 and 13/
14, where there is a gap in the continuity of the speech. Pfeiffer, Schadewaldt (but
with a different view in *Hellas und Hesperien*, 174. O), and Mette assign verses 10–
13 to the chorus leader, but then the persons of this dialogue seem curiously to talk
past one another. Lloyd-Jones (see above) emphasizes the difficulty of deciding here as
well, but favors, as does Vitelli in the *Pap. Soc. It.*, the assumption of a continuous
speech. I have attempted (*Wien. Stud.* 52, [1934], 15) to explain the gaps as pauses in
the mother's tormented, brooding, broken speech.[3]

Three verses (fr. 274), in which according to Plutarch a nurse in tragedy speaks
of her troubles with the children of Niobe, may belong to the play and recall the
speech of Kilissa in the *Libation Bearers*.

With reasonable confidence we can assign thirty-six verses from the Italian discoveries to the *Myrmidons* of Aischylos. Again Lloyd-Jones offers the most complete
bibliography in the *Aischylos* of the Loeb Class. Libr. D. L. Page has questioned their
assignment to this play in his *Lit. Papyri* (136), and has been followed by Lloyd-Jones
(cf. also *Gnom.* 38 [1966], 13). But after W. Schadewaldt's discussion of these verses
(*Herm.* 71 [1936], 25 = *Hellas und Hesperien*, 166), it hardly seems possible to deny
that they belong to the first play of the Achilleus trilogy of Aischylos (satyr play unknown). Bruno Snell also agrees with this conclusion; he has discussed the Aischylean *Achilleis* on the basis of the papyrus in his *Scenes from Greek Drama*, and in
the appendix has newly edited the text with a critical apparatus. Mette also includes
the Florentine fragment in this context. Snell (*Gnom.* 25 [1953], 437) has made substantial contributions to the arrangement of further fragments, which is often necessarily problematical. Lloyd-Jones (above, 583) and Mette (*Verl. Aisch.*, 114) consider
the possibility that in *P. Oxy.* 2253, in which there is mention of a reconciliation, we
could possess a piece from the prologue of the *Myrmidons*.[4] For the direction of the
plot—Schadewaldt speaks of a plot of defiance—verses from the *Myrmidons* of Ac-
cius are also instructive (fr. 225bM). We believe that the Florentine papyrus represents a scene between Achilleus and Antilochos, in which there is mention of the
danger of stoning the wrathful hero, whose resentment is not in the least influenced
by the threat. There follows the desperate dispatching of Patroklos, the report of his
death, and the lament of Achilleus over his corpse. Snell has now convincingly in-

cluded *P. Oxy.* 2256 fr. 55 (fr. 229M) in the lament scene. Together with frr. 228 and 230M, the erotic interpretation of Achilleus's relationship with his friend finds here its strongest possible expression.

The second play of this trilogy, to which the statement of Aischylos transmitted by Athenaios 8. 347c, 143 that his plays were τεμάχη[5] ἀπὸ τῶν μεγάλων Ὁμήρου δείπνων (slices from the great feasts of Homer) especially applies, was the *Nereids*, named after the chorus of sea maidens who brought the new weapons to Achilleus. But the reconciliation with Agamemnon, Hektor's fall, and the burial of Patroklos must also have had their place in the play—most probably in the form of report or allusion. The *Phrygians* or *Release of Hektor* reveals chorus and plot by its two titles. From the opening dialogue, we can recognize a conversation between Hermes and Achilleus, in which the god reproaches the hero for desecrating Hektor's corpse and probably commands its release in the name of Zeus. Achilleus speaks but little here and then waits in long silence (Aristoph. *Ran.* 912 with schol. = fr. 212M). The approach of Priamos is still discernible.

In her fine interpretation of the fragments of a red-figured krater in the archaeological collection of the University of Vienna, Hedwig Kenner, *Österr. Jahresh.* 33 (1941), 1, has shown that an important Attic vase painter ca. 435 chose the *Achilleis* of Aischylos as his model. This coincides well with the powerful influence that we know the tragedies of Aischylos exerted in the second half of the fifth century.

The most valuable gain from all these discoveries has been our chance to become acquainted with the Aischylos who was granted first place in antiquity among the authors of satyr plays (Diog. Laert. 2. 133; Paus. 2. 13. 6).[6] We can follow enough of the satyr play *Diktyoulkoi*, which followed the trilogy with the Perseus dramas *Phorkides* and *Polydektes*, to form some idea of the charm of this play.[7] Bibliography for these, too, is in H. Lloyd-Jones (see above, 531) and on frr. 464 and 474M. A comprehensive treatment is offered by M. Werre-de Haas, "Aeschylus Dictyulci," *Papyrologica Lugduno-Batava* x (1961); further Mette (*Verl. Aisch.* 155).

First, two columns from the Italian find (*PSI.* 1209; frr. 464, 467M) were published, which R. Pfeiffer, "Die *Netzfischer* des Aischylos und der *Inachos* des Sophokles" (*Sitzb. Münch.* 1938/2) magnificently interpreted and identified as a satyr play on the basis of metrics. The verses begin with a stichomythy that follows a connected speech in the prologue scene. One of the speakers is an old fisherman, the other in all probability Diktys, the brother or half-brother of Polydektes, king of the island Seriphos. The two are unable to draw up a heavy object with their net and call for help in a way closely paralleled by the call of Apollo in the opening of the *Ichneutai* of Sophokles. Of course the satyrs arrive, led by Silenos, and as net-pullers (giving the play its name) drag onto the shore a chest holding Danae and the young Perseus. Part of a later scene is offered by *P. Oxy.* 2161 (fr. 474M), which belongs to the same manuscript as the Italian discovery. E. Siegmann helps greatly in the interpretation: "Die neuen Aischylos-Bruchstücke," *Phil.* 97 (1948), 71. We can discern the courtship of the good-for-nothing Silenos, who pretends to be Danae's savior, but arouses in the unhappy girl only fear and loathing for the wood daimons. Craftily the lecherous satyr approaches the infant in order to win Danae by describing future familial bliss.

The whole is topped off by the satyr chorus, which misinterprets Danae's behavior as the expectation of pleasures to come, and calls for a marriage in swift anapests. The stichometric note Θ (= 800) at the second verse of the second column places the fragment in the final section of the play, which leads to the difficult question of what the previous sections contained. Knowing the *Ichneutai*, we may think of a fright scene when the satyrs hear strange noises from the chest, but this does not get us very far.

The *Theoroi* or *Isthmiastai* was likewise full of the splendid humor which is only imaginable in the world of the good-for-nothing satyrs, who are eternally curious and just as cowardly. H. Lloyd-Jones, in the appendix to the Loeb Class. Libr. *Aischylos* (541) has not only supplied an extensive bibliography, but also discussed the problems of arranging the four columns of *P. Oxy.* 2162. Bibliography for this is under fr. 17M.[8] Important in this context are B. Snell, "Aischylos's *Isthmiastai*" (*Herm.* 84 [1956], 1 = *Ges. Schr.* 164, with a few alterations) and K. Reinhardt, "Zu den *Isthmiastai*" (*Herm.* 85 [1957], 1. 123 = *Tradition und Geist*, 167).

The plot is recognizable in its broad outlines. The common motif of dependence and freedom of the satyrs is utilized here in an especially charming manner. They have run away from their master Dionysos and his festivals and want to compete as athletes in the Isthmian games. They find a sponsor; it may have been Sisyphos of Korinth. With his permission they nail satyr masks to the Temple of Poseidon, an aition for such ornamental masks on sacred buildings. The fixed skene wall, here used as the temple, would indicate a later period of Aischylos's work if our theory was correct in asserting that he employed the skene as background only after the *Suppliants*. Sections are well preserved that contain portions of a dispute between Dionysos and Silenos, who defies the reproaches of his master with the greatest insolence. The satyrs want Poseidon and his spruce garland instead of the effeminate god and his ivy, and Isthmian sport instead of Dionysian festivals. But that this is not the right way for them after all comes to light in the scene in which their Korinthian sponsor brings them a newly prepared sporting apparatus (racing cart?), but fails to arouse their enthusiasm. The finale is not difficult to supply: the satyrs return to their real master and become again the merry retinue of Dionysos.

Several satyr plays were mentioned in the discussion of the extant tragedies. We add to these the Τροφοί (*Nurses*; frr. 425–429M), probably concerned with the care of Dionysos. From the hypothesis to the *Medeia* of Euripides we know that in the play Medeia rejuvenated the nurses of the god together with their husbands by boiling them.[9] Also among the satyr plays belongs the Σίσυφος Δραπέτης (*Sisyphos the Runaway*; frr. 373–382M), which had for its subject the triple outwitting of Death by his clever opponent. That besides this the title Σίσυφος Πετροκυλιστής (*Sisyphos the Rock-roller*; frr. 383–386M) has been preserved, puts us at a loss. The possibility of different titles for the same play cannot be excluded.[10]

The *Glaukos Potnieus* was mentioned in connection with the *Persians*. This should not be confused with the *Glaukos Pontios* (frr. 53–65M). According to Pausanias 9. 22. 6 (fr. 54aM) Aischylos composed a complete drama from a story told in Anthedon about a fisherman named Glaukos who became a sea-god with prophetic

powers after eating a certain herb. Strabo 10. 1. 9 confirms *P. Oxy.* 2159 for this play
(fr. 55M).[11] An old shepherd seems to be telling a younger companion about the appearance of the sea creature. After Murray (113. 3), Mette (fr. 56; *Verl. Aisch.*, 179)
also thought of a satyr play. However, E. Siegmann has rightly emphasized the complete uncertainty of the conjecture.

    One of the most interesting discoveries, *P. Oxy.* 2257 fr. 1 (fr. 26M), contains in
all probability the end of a hypothesis to the *Aitnaiai*, the festival play written by
Aischylos ca. 470 for the city of Aitna founded by Hieron.[12] To our surprise we learn
that the play consisted of five parts; each was performed in a different location. This
was so unconventional that the author of the hypothesis tried to offer something at
least by way of parallel, citing the scene change in the *Eumenides* and in the Sophoklean satyr play Ἀχιλλέως ἐρασταί (*The Lovers of Achilleus*). It cannot be assumed
that the papyrus text referred to the Αἰτναῖαι νόθοι (the false *Aitnaians*) that is listed
next to the Αἰτναῖαι γνήσιοι (the genuine *Aitnaians*) in the manuscript catalogue.
Not much can be made of this festival play. Eduard Fraenkel, "Vermutungen zum
Aetna-Festspiel des Aeschylus" (*Eranos* 52 [1954], 61) has made the best attempt.
Fragment 27M (about the Palikoi and the explanation of their name) he assigned to
the fourth part of the play, which took place in or near Leontinoi, the location of the
pond and sanctuary of the Palikoi. *P. Oxy.* 2256 fr. 9a (fr. 530M) contains considerable
portions of a scene in which the goddess Dike speaks of the power and honor granted
her by Zeus, at whose side she stood in his righteous struggle against his father,
Kronos (a different view in *Eum.* 641 ff.). A stichomythy with the chorus leader follows, in which Dike proclaims herself the preserver of justice who makes note of the
transgressions of mankind on the tablets of Zeus (criticism of such a conception in
Eur. fr. 506N). The chorus leader assures Dike of a joyous reception, and she in turn,
as an example of her influence, tells how she tamed a wayward child of Zeus and
Hera, a wicked fellow who shamelessly shot at wanderers with his bow. Since fr.
377N recurs at v. 28, the papyrus text is confirmed for Aischylos. The attempt of E.
Fraenkel to assign it to the *Aitnaiai* has much to recommend it. H. Lloyd-Jones (see
above, 576 with bibliography) does not exclude this theory, but remains cautious.
Mette (*Verl. Aisch.* 187) picks up, on the basis of the conjunction ὅτιή in v. 9, the
conjecture of Lobel that the fragment came from a satyr play. The content does not
point in this direction; the theory is rightly contradicted by Q. Cataudella, *Saggi
sulla tragedia Greca*, Messina 1969, 95. We still have no clear idea who the villain
was whom Dike overcame. Ares, a common suggestion, seems unlikely because of
the type of weapon used by the miscreant. Phanis J. Kakridis (*Eranos* 60 [1962], 111)
calls our attention to a Roman inscription of the Imperial period (Kaibel 831) in
which Herakles appears as the adopted son of Dike, and has further shown the possibility of a version that made Herakles Hera's son. The reference is interesting, but
the solution far from certain.[13]

    We consider it probable that Aischylos was the creator of the tetralogy united
in content, and we attempted to keep this possibility open in our discussion of
Phrynichos. We have met examples of this great structural form in the *Thebais*, the
Danaids, the *Oresteia*, the *Prometheia*, and the *Achilleis*. In the last two cases the

satyr play is unknown; fragments and titles reveal a series of other tetralogies;[14] the most important are those in which Aischylos preserved the connection with the Dionysian origins of tragedy. For the *Lykourgeia*, K. Deichgräber has undertaken an extensive attempt at reconstruction.[15] The *Lycurgus* of Naevius is of some help for the first play, the *Edonoi*. Dionysos was captured at the command of Lykourgos, who already appears as his persecutor in the *Iliad* (6. 130) but is miraculously set free again. The *Bassarides* contained the dismemberment of Orpheus, the apostle of Apollonian sun worship, at the hands of the Mainads. The thematic connection with the Lykourgos story presents difficulties; Deichgräber thought that the killing of Dryas by his father, who had been blinded by the god, belonged to the content of the play. Little can be made of the *Neaniskoi*. That a reconciliation followed the punishment of Lykourgos would coincide well with the conclusions of better known trilogies. In the satyr play *Lykourgos* (fr. 97M) beer drinkers were taken to task; perhaps the conversion of Lykourgos to the gift of Bacchos was the point of this play.

P. Oxy. 2164 (fr. 355M) has preserved for us a considerable fragment from a scene in which Hera, in the form of a priestess of Argive nymphs, comes to a chorus of Theban maidens. In her recitative in lyric hexameters there occurs a passage that Asklepiades (schol. *Ran.* 1344; fr. 168N) attests for the *Xantriai*. K. Latte, *Phil.* 97 (1948), 47 = *Kl. Schr.* 477, argues very plausibly that the grammarian made an error; he sees in the passage the intrigue of Hera against the mother of Dionysos, and assigns the fragment to the tragedy Σεμέλη ἤ ʿΥδροφόροι (*Semele, or the Water Bearers*). Following similar cases of confusion of titles, he has assigned, probably correctly, the *Xantriai* to the same trilogy. According to fr. 367M, the poet transposed the dismemberment of Pentheus to Mt. Kithairon; from fr. 368 we know that Lyssa spoke to the Bakchai. Mette (*Verl. Aisch.*, 147) considers the possibility that the "wool carders" could refer to women in the company of the daughters of Minyas who rejected the Dionysian cult and were overtaken by bacchic frenzy. *Pentheus* and the *Bakchai* could possibly have completed the trilogy. Here all is open to question. If the *Pentheus*, as is reported in the hypothesis to the *Bakchai* of Euripides, treated the same subject matter as this play, then the *Xantriai* must have had a different subject from what Latte believed, or else it does not belong in the same trilogy as the *Pentheus*. If the *Bakchai* is not merely a double title for one of the plays, one of the four drama titles is still superfluous. The satyr play could have been the *Nurses* (of Dionysos).

The content trilogy Ὅπλων κρίσις (*The Trial of Arms*), Θρῆσσαι, and Σαλαμίνιαι, revolved around the fate of Aias. Its satyr play is unknown. Besides clear cases like an Argonauts or Odysseus trilogy all else remains hypothetical. The suggestion of Mette (*Verl. Aisch.*, 77) that the *Mysians*, *Telephos*, and *Iphigeneia* formed a trilogy has much to recommend it.

The *Philoktetes* of Aischylos will be mentioned in our discussion of Sophokles' play of the same name.

Much work has been devoted to the scanty fragments of the *Herakleidai*, but it has not been ascertained whether the subject matter corresponded to Euripides' play of the same name or to Sophokles' *Trachiniai*.[16] Two heavily damaged columns in P. Oxy. 27, 2454 containing a monologue of Herakles, who compares his present misery with his glorious past, pose a new question. The editor E. G. Turner favors the assumption that the play is a Hellenistic tragedy; this is supported by linguistic evidence, so that the fragments are perhaps best not associated with the play of Aischylos, despite Q. Cataudella, who himself leaves all doubts open.[17]

DRAMATIC FORM AND LANGUAGE

The goal of these summary paragraphs can only be to emphasize a few of the important points of view.[1]

When Aristotle says of tragedy (*Poet.* 4, 1449a): ὀψὲ ἀπεσεμνύνϑη (it achieved sublimity late), we may certainly assume, despite our scanty evidence, that this process was consummated in the work of Aischylos. The great structural form of the content trilogy, which we suggested may have been his own creation, opened up new possibilities for dramatic composition.[2] Of course even within the individual plays, Aischylos disregarded time relations with the boldness of genius (*Ag.*, *Eum.*!), but within the trilogy he was able to tie widely separated actions into the unity of large conceptions. As sparse as the surviving material is, it seems that we can still recognize a special side of this development. The oratorio-like character of the *Persians* has often been emphasized, and it is not difficult to draw a line from this play back to early tragedy and to imagine the succession of appearances of the *hypokrites* in continually changing characters, as well as the resulting change in the choral odes. In the *Persians* there is still no concentration of plot around a central figure. This is not the case in the later plays. In Eteokles we meet the first bearer of a great tragic destiny; in the *Suppliants* the chorus forms the center of the drama and apparently of the whole trilogy; the *Prometheus* requires no further comment; and even the *Oresteia*, in spite of its broader development of action, may be seen in this light. The central character of the *Agamemnon* is not the title figure. The king once had to act in his moment of decision, but the action of the play belongs to Klytaimestra: in her deed and her belated realization, the doom of the House of Atreus advances. It is instructive to compare the *Libation Bearers* with the two later *Elektra* plays. In Aischylos, Elektra exists only for the plot line involving Orestes: she is necessary for the recognition scene, prays with her brother and the chorus, and is then dropped from the play.

If the drama of Aischylos after the *Persians* is thus characterized by a new concentration on the action and sufferings of a single person, it does not follow that the poet created unique figures whose individuality confers on them an unmistakable existence. It is significant in this respect that none of his personae has been accepted into world literature as one of those fixed forms that seem to engender countless variations as do Antigone and Oidipous or Medeia and Phaidra, for example. The influence of Prometheus is a different case, since here it was not the figure as such, but its interpretation by later authors that was productive. The explanation for this lies in the fact that the personages of Aischylean drama are, to such a great extent, partners of a divinity that reveals its power and laws through them; they neither appear in complete autonomy with regard to this divinity, as do many Sophoklean figures, nor do they achieve outside of this bond the individual existence of characters in Euripides.

Of course this does not mean that Aischylos shows us mere puppets controlled by the gods. More so than the others, it is he who places his characters in fearful situations in which decisions must be made. The question of how free they are in making these decisions will occupy us shortly.

If we have just suggested a development after Aischylos that steadily releases the individual from the bonds of a sphere of action determined only by the divine element, we can nonetheless observe a particularly Aischylean manner of presenting characters that is not to be seen in his followers. Tragedy, primarily Euripidean tragedy, occasionally shows the succession of different psychological attitudes, without revealing the intermediary steps in these processes within the soul. More will be said about this when we come to Euripides. But it is the earliest of the great tragedians who depicts psychological change with a penetration that was never equalled after him. We recall the final section of the *Agamemnon*, in which the poet masterfully brings us step by step along the path from the Klytaimestra who, drunk with blood, extols her deed, to the woman who finally recognizes her fate as a link in a chain of horror. We further recall the great kommos of the *Libation Bearers*, which we believed to be decisive for the internal attitude of Orestes toward his deed, and the finale, in which madness does not strike him like a bolt of lightning, but rather his disintegration occurs before our very eyes. How long the poet allows us to observe the inner struggle of the king in the *Suppliants* before necessity forces his decision! Thus the characterization of man in the drama of Aischylos is determined by a remarkable antinomy. Though the principals stand completely in the power of divine forces, yet we still can see deep inside them, inside the crises that shake them, and inside the horror with which they, like Eteokles, confront the full realization of their situation. At work here is still a trace of that dual motivation on the divine and human levels that is occasionally to be seen in a completely unreflective manner in Homeric epic.

What we possess of the Aischylean canon allows us to observe the development described by Aristotle: Aischylos was the first to employ two actors, diminish the role of the chorus, and make spoken verse predominant. In the earlier dramas it is clear how restricted the use of the two actors was, since the second dialogue partner is often the chorus leader.[3] In contrast to this, the *Oresteia* shows that Aischylos made confident though not abundant use of the third actor, according to Aristotle an innovation of Sophokles. Whether a third actor should also be assumed for the opening of the *Prometheus* depends on the question discussed above, whether Prometheus was represented by a puppet.[4]

The antagonism inherent in the generic difference between choral lyric and actors' parts is clearly expressed in the construction of Aischylean tragedy. In this respect the *Oresteia*, especially in the first two plays, is still similar to the older dramas. The first part is primarily composed as lyric, while the second brings the action to a fitful conclusion. The exceptional case of the *Seven*, in which the composition revolves around the great central piece of the seven paired speeches, shows how Aischylos's technique was still in state of flux. Division into acts and the formation of typical sections are nowhere to be seen. The *Suppliants* and *Agamemnon* show us what a broad lyrical foundation Aischylos provided for the structure of the content trilogy.

For Aischylean dialogue sections, the desire for symmetry is occasionally evident, but we hope the day is past when total responsion was arbitrarily restored by assuming lacunae or interpolations.[5]

The character of Aischylean language is best discussed by starting with the address of the chorus to the poet in the *Frogs* of Aristophanes (1004): ἀλλ' ὦ πρῶτος τῶν Ἑλλήνων πυργώσας ῥήματα σεμνὰ / καὶ κοσμήσας τραγικὸν λῆρον ... (O thou first of the Greeks to heap up sublime words and form tragic babble!). L. Radermacher in his commentary argues for ληρός, attested in Hesychios and others, which designated a golden ornament for a woman's garment. But Aristophanes is at his best here, uniting in the speech two points of view: the respect for the magnificent and solemn language of the poet and the inclination to switch from the sublime to the ridiculous. The scorn of Aischylos's opponent includes the phrase (929): ῥήμαθ' ἱππόκρημνα, ἃ ξυμβαλεῖν οὐ ῥᾴδι' ἦν (breakneck words not easy to understand). Many may have judged Aischylos in this way in antiquity, even if the voices of admiration predominate, like Dion. Hal. περὶ μιμήσεως 2. 2; p. 206 in H. Usener-L. Radermacher's Teubner edition; Horace *Ars Poet.* 278.[6] But in Quintilian 10. 1. 66 we read praise for the Aischylean σεμνότης (solemnity) that is sourly half revoked: sublimis et gravis et grandilocus saepe usque ad vitium (sublime and solemn and magniloquent even to a fault), while Aristophanes was really just joking with fond respect. To understand the language of Aischylos we must avoid completely the notion of "language ornamentation."[7] Aristophanes, with sympathetic understanding, has his Aischylos say (*Ran.* 1058) that great thoughts necessarily beget words of the same type. In the verb τίκτειν lies a deeper and more original perception than the later doctrine of style can express with its πρέπον (fitting). In Aischylos, words convey not only meaning but also essence.[8] This language does not speak with detachment about things, it comes directly from their being. For this reason there is present here the still unbroken magic of words that can curse and bless. Related to this are the frequent etymologies, which are no idle puns but instead seek in a word the essence of the thing itself, and in a name the destiny of its bearer.[9] It has further been observed that Aischylos has more neologisms than the other tragedians.[10] This, as well as the dark riddles of many passages and that boldness of diction that was termed katachrese (misuse) in antiquity: all this is not the result of an attempt to raise the level of language, but a spontaneous expression of a mind that takes a large view of the world and goes at it with penetrating questions.[11] Even those phrases that the later doctrine of style called "figures" are not external trimmings of speech: word and sound struggle to achieve essentiality in the message with methods that can be grasped by the senses.[12]

For the assumption of Doricisms linked to the Sicilian journeys of the poet, the reservations of E. Fraenkel in his commentary on *Ag.* 1507 are worthy of consideration.

Individual words appear in a special and thematic way scattered throughout widely separated passages in the manner of a leitmotif. So Ζηνὸς (ἱκεσίου) κότος (wrath of the Zeus [of suppliants]), four times in the *Suppliants* (347, 385, 478, 616; numbers from Murray) and four times also ἀγώνιοι θεοί (gods of the contests), forms the conclusion of a line (189, 242, 333, 355). Sometimes an expression important for the sense is repeated only once as, for example, *Persians* 116, 161.[13] Individual metaphors also occur as leitmotifs. J. Dumortier has constructed his book about Aischylean imagery (see above) on this idea, not without occasional exaggeration. But since the *Seven* takes up the image of the state as ship immediately in the second verse and continues it right into the final messenger-speech, we cannot avoid speaking of a leitmotif.[14]

Aischylean images only seldom recall the expansive Homeric similes, e.g. *Libation Bearers* 506. Much more often the poet uses a method of comparison for which we read an impressive example directly before this (501): Agamemnon should take pity ἰδὼν νεοσσοὺς τούσδ' ἐφημένους τάφῳ (seeing the young birds sitting on his grave). He does not say that the children in their distress are *like* helpless young birds. No, they *are* νεοσσοί. This does not introduce a tertium comparationis but, much more, it is a total identification that reveals the essence of the situation of Agamemnon's children. The metaphor echoes an elaborately composed series of images earlier in the play (247): the orphaned brood of the eagle that died in the coils of the adder, the starving nestlings, incapable of flight and not yet able to drag prey to the nest. Incidentally, this is not the only passage in which the poet expresses his deep feeling for suffering creatures (cf. *Ag.* 49, 135). The boldness of many images borders on the bizarre: in v. 371 of the *Seven* the hastily approaching messenger twirls the hubs of his feet.

The language of Aischylos covers a wide range. In spoken verse the simplest statement sometimes produces a striking effect, as for example *Lib. Bearers* 1061, while in other passages the speeches move with ponderous steps. Something else again is the polyphony that results from the fact that the heterogeneous elements that produced Greek tragedy are closer to their origin here than later. Much good work remains to be done on stylistic analysis.[15] Most importantly we must separate the style of spoken verse, with its clear constructions, its propensity for antithesis, and the relatively restrained use of adjectives, from the fullness of choral lyric and flowing sentence structure. For the archaic rhesis, Peretti (*Epirrema*, chap. 11) has made significant advances in his analysis of the *Suppliants*. Two forms appear in the spoken scenes of this play: the stichomythy, in which the actor and chorus leader converse with one another, and the rhesis, by which new information is brought into the play. This archaic rhesis displays a strongly impersonal character that was continued for the most part until the creation of the pathos speech by Euripides. Even intense personal emotion is described objectively, as is well exemplified by the king's speeches in the *Suppliants*. Thus in the archaic rhesis, the motivation for requests, commands, and advice always comes from the realities of the external world. Using the *Suppliants* Peretti has also demonstrated how often a speech returns to its departure point in a type of ring composition familiar from choral lyric.[16] This technique is quite typical in the older plays but declined as time went on.

In analyzing the choral odes we owe much to the excellent contributions of Kraus, who examined the structural form of the strophes. He finds in the structure of the individual strophe the choral lyric triad of strophe-antistrophe-epode repeated in numerous variations. For a linguistic analysis of Aischylean choral odes with their heavy ornamentation and richness of adjectives and participial expressions often obscuring or even violating the clear forms of Greek speech patterns, Kranz's *Stasimon* and F. Dornseiff's book on Pindar's style still provide useful starting points. Recently J. Rode has examined the Aischylean ode in his Tübingen dissertation.[17] The distinction between an ode type that participates in the dramatic process and one that is complete in itself is useful for interpretation, but the surviving material does not suffice to establish a development toward more closely integrated odes.

If the literary critics of antiquity were correct in designating ἔκπληξις (astonishment) as the goal of tragedy, then there can be no doubt that Aischylos was the most powerful of the ancient tragedians.[18] The ancients perceived this primitive force as the Dionysian impulse, and so it was said (Athen. 1. 22, 10. 428) that Aischylos composed while drunk,[19] and the reproach of Sophokles reported in the same passage that Aischylos composed what was right but did it unconsciously can be turned into the highest praise for the elemental power of his art. Plutarch (*Mor.* 715e) pointedly corrects the phrase of Gorgias about the *Seven* as being a drama full of Ares: all the tragedies of Aischylos are full of Dionysos. And the chorus of Aristophanes (*Ran.* 1259) names him βακχεῖος ἄναξ (bakchic king), a judgment in which we concur in awe.

DESTINY AND GUILT

Today Aischylos's reputation as a religious thinker has been subjected to some doubts, most notably by H. Lloyd-Jones[1] and D. L. Page.[2] It is certainly incorrect to look for a systematizing theologian in the poet while forgetting the dramatist. But it is just as incorrect to attempt to identify the religious thought of the man who has the chorus of the *Agamemnon* proudly proclaim δίχα δ' ἄλλων μονόφρων εἰμί (I am of one mind, apart from others; 757) with that of the average citizen of his time.[3] For the religious world view of Aischylos it is far less important that many of his basic principles were already present in his day than that the struggle for a synthesis is recognizable in his work, a synthesis that strives for a wide perspective on the working of the divine element. It is of course easy to point out contradictions that show now a just divinity, now a cruel one incomprehensible to man, but what human inquiry about the nature and workings of the divine has ever been able to escape such contradictions? The hymn to Zeus from the *Agamemnon* alone would suffice to appreciate correctly the deep earnestness of this struggle for a theodicy.[4]

Under no conditions should the basis for Aischylos's religiosity be sought in the realm of the mysteries. While sifting through the biographical evidence we noted the false conclusions drawn from the poet's birth in Eleusis. What is more, antiquity (Cic. *Tusc.* 2. 23) had already made a Pythagorean out of him, and more recent scholars persist in searching for references to the mysteries in his work.[5] But decisive elements did not come to Aischylos from Orphism or any other mystery religion. Longing for salvation and confident expectation of redemption are separated by a deep gulf from the relentless calculation by which man in a tragic work of art strives to recognize his position in the world. A phrase of Aristotle (fr. 15R) states that the initiates were not supposed to learn anything, but instead to be formed by suffering in some way. We contrast with this the key phrase of Aischylean tragedy: Learn through suffering!

Also misguided is the attempt to make Aischylos a rebel against traditional religion.[6] He developed beyond the beliefs of his time, but common ground always remained.

That Aischylos was subject to the influences of certain Presocratics is quite conceivable but a conclusive proof in detail is not to be found.[7]

Aischylos's religious thought too is kindled by the ancient problem of man's helplessness and the inscrutability of the divine. In the *Homeric Hymn to Pythian Apollo* (190) the Muses sing of the joys of the gods and the hardships of men who live out their lives under the rule of the gods, without reason or escape. The speech of Zeus at the beginning of the *Odyssey* strikes a different note: the wickedness of men who do not regard even a divine warning brings them pain and destruction ὑπὲρ μόρον (beyond measure, i.e. over and above the measure already predetermined for them). These two passages reveal a tension between the evil predestined by the gods and that which originates in human will, a tension that has its roots deep in Greek thought and that is still fundamental for the tragedy of Aischylos.

His religious thought too stands in an antinomy that cannot be comprehended by merely stating the logical contradictions. We possess two hymns to Zeus by Aischylos: *Suppl.* 86 and *Ag.* 160. By contrasting them we can form an idea of the poles between which the tragic essence of Aischylos unfolds.

The magnificence of the *Oresteia* rests on the passionate intensity with which Aischylos struggles to understand the power of God in the world. From his solitary thinking arose the protest *Ag.* 750) against the ancient belief that great happiness by its very existence brings on disaster and destruction. It is the guilty deed that further begets its own kind and topples noble houses. Δράσαντι παθεῖν (the doer must suffer) is proclaimed by the poet in the *Lib. Bearers* (313) as a "thrice-told tale" (τριγέρων μῦθος).[8]

But in the hymn to Zeus from the *Ag.* we hear the second phrase through which we come to an understanding of divine rule, and for which Aischylos finds that the name of Zeus barely suffices (Ζεύς, ὅστις ποτ' ἐστίν: Zeus, whoever he is): the deed is followed by suffering, but suffering is followed by an understanding: πάθει μάθος (learning through suffering).[9] God leads men to the knowledge of this binding law even against their will.

But Aischylean tragedy is not simply a game of guilt and reconciliation, an accounting completely balanced in the moral sphere. It becomes tragedy only through the elements of the irrational that are operative in it. We may contrast the hymn to Zeus from the *Ag.*, with its clear statement about the path from guilt through suffering to wisdom, to the ode in the *Suppliants*. Here too the poet praises the omnipotence of Zeus in words that come from the depths of his belief. But we are told of the ἵμερος (desire) of god: οὐκ εὐθήρατος ἐτύχθη (it is not easy to hunt down). And the pathways of his thoughts move in utter darkness, removed from human vision: κατιδεῖν ἄφραστοι (impossible to observe; 95). One word forms the bridge between the two poems: at *Ag.* 182 it is said of the divine beings that they direct man's fate βιαίως (violently) from the august steersman's seat.[10] But they also know χάρις (mercy) and here we could interpolate directly words from the prayer of the *Suppliants*: the ways of divine influence remain dark and concealed from man, even if he can give an account of the final goal, insight into inviolable laws.

The nature of guilt itself possesses irrational features in Aischylos. At *Lib. Bearers* 697 Klytaimestra speaks of the blood morass of the Atreidai, from which Orestes has kept his foot distant. This is a survival of the idea of the truly magical power with which human guilt poisons all around it. No modern writer has expressed this thought in a more Aischylean manner than Otto Ludwig in his novella *Zwischen Himmel und Erde*: "The nature of guilt is that it does not ensnare in new guilt its originator alone. It has a magical power that pulls all who surround him into its fermenting sphere of influence and to ripen the evil within him to new guilt. Happy is he who resists this power in his unblemished heart." We recall the binding song of the Erinyes, *Eum.* 313.

The conviction that guilt begets renewed guilt, bred in its own likeness (*Ag.* 758), also placed the ancient belief in the hereditary curse in a new light for Aischylos. Actually, Greek thought is well acquainted with the idea that the individual has no special existence of his own apart from his lineage and therefore bears responsibility for the guilt of his forefathers. Aischylos's wonderful simile of the corks that save the net from sinking (*Lib. Bearers* 506) and Plutarch's statements in his treatise *De sera numinis vindicta* (559d) are our most impressive evidence for this belief.[11] But Aischylos did not remain satisfied with the conception of a collective responsibility that permitted even innocent men to suffer. In the *Oresteia* the nature of the inherited curse is revealed as guilt that rises anew from generation to generation. This is seen not as a recurrent hereditary factor, but as daimonic power that progresses through the family's descendants.[12] Already here there appears that opposition, irreconcilable by rational thought, between the destiny of the individual member of a family marked by a curse and the guilty deed that he commits of his own will and on his own responsibility.

A curious position in Aischylos's struggle for a theodicy is assumed by the thought that god can himself lead men into guilt, or at least hasten them along such a path. Thus he creates the opportunity to reveal the inviolable law δράσαντι παθεῖν (the doer must suffer) in the course of πάθει μάθος (learning through suffering). In the *Niobe* papyrus (fr. 273M) we read the words (v. 15) that Plato (*Rep.* 380a) considered scandalous: when god wishes to destroy a house, he plants in men an αἰτία (responsibility). The word encompasses both the divine cause that brings on the fall and the human fault by which a man draws down his fate upon himself. Man does this in delusion, in ἄτη, and this word again approaches the meaning of ἁμαρτία (fault).[13]

Closely related to this is the conception of the deceitful guile of god from which man cannot escape and that leads him into delusion and suffering (*Pers.* 93).[14] In the great symbolic scene Dareios proclaims (742): when a mortal himself hastens toward destruction, then god also aids in his undoing.[15] The accents are placed differently, but this is still the tightly spun, inseparable web of human will and divinely predetermined destiny.

We select the brilliant formulation of Jacqueline de Romilly (*Ombres sacrées*) in order to understand how this question involves a whole series of interpretational problems: "Le théâtre, où les dieux interviennent plus fréquemment et plus souverainement que dans aucun autre est, en fait, celui où l'action de l'homme semble se détacher avec le plus de relief." Snell introduced a new phase of interpretation with his Aischylos book when he placed the importance of the personal responsible decision emphatically in the foreground. His view was challenged by A. Rivier, who sees the characters of Aischylos much more strongly under the constraint of an inescapable destiny.[16] The heated debate was concerned primarily with four situations involving crucial decisions. We focused our attention on them in the analysis of the respective plays: (1) Eteokles before his advance to the seventh gate and the combat with his brother; (2) the king in the *Suppliants* forced to choose between rejection of the suppliants and battle with their persecutors; (3) Agamemnon in Aulis before the command to sacrifice Iphigeneia, on which the expedition against Troy depends; (4) Orestes in the *Lib. Bearers*, where it is not a matter of decision, but of his own part in the action commanded by the god.

Certainly we agree with A. Rivier when he proposes that one not speak of "free will," a concept burdened with philosophical and theological problems, when interpreting Aischylos's work. Further, it has become clear that in the aforementioned decisive situations, the force of necessity, in accordance with fate, plays a significant role. It restricts considerably the freedom of the decision and severely limits the possibility of free choice. It is important to note how the king in the *Suppliants*, after lengthy deliberation, does not make his decision until the maidens' threat to hang themselves from the divine statues makes the rejection of their plea impossible.

The boundaries between fateful constraint and personal decision are not easily drawn in each case. Thus opinion is divided whether a real choice exists for Agamemnon in Aulis, or whether, with his πῶς λιπόναυς γένωμαι; (How can I desert the fleet?), the sacrifice of Iphigeneia has already become for him an inevitable necessity.[17] Differences of opinion remain in the details, but more and more the view of Fischer (see n. 16) has become accepted: "Freedom and Necessity, divine and human action become intertwined in a nexus that cannot be rationally dissolved." What we observe concerning the totally unreflected bond between divine and human motivation in the epic produces, on another level, tragic action. An important and, we believe, conclusive remark was made by A. Rivier in the final section of his "Remarques sur le nécessaire," *Rev. Et. Gr.* 81 (1968): "Certes, la décision du personnage eschyléen est aussi l'œuvre de sa volonté. . . . Mais c'est une volonté liée et une liberté sous conditions." Many quotes could be cited to prove that widespread agreement has been reached regarding the complex character of Aischylos's tragic art that we have emphasized so strongly; we will content ourselves with the concluding lines of E. Wolff's essay on the *Seven*: "Is the decision of Eteokles made . . . according to the will of the gods, or is it his personal choice? Or are both forces, divine destiny and human will, working together?—Only this last possibility is Aischylean."[18]

It seems to us that in these inescapable crises of decision, where all paths lead to disaster, Aischylos has objectified in his dramatic art man's helplessness and the doubtful nature of his actions: the harsh necessity of choice and the impossibility of escaping destruction.[19] Important in this context is an often misunderstood feature that Eteokles, Agamemnon, and Orestes all exhibit in the same way. After each submits to the fated necessity of decision, he also desires what he has been forced to do in the yoke of ananke: thus his ἵμεϱος (desire) drives Eteokles to the seventh gate, thus Agamemnon craves the sacrifice of Iphigeneia, thus Orestes accepts fully into his will his matricide. And they all bear the responsibility and must suffer. But while Eteokles and Agamemnon perish, Orestes, liberated from the curse, is permitted to return to his homeland.

The *Eumenides* is not the only play that concluded a trilogy with reconciliation. We know that this was also the case with the *Danaids*, the *Phrygians*, the *Eleusinians*,[20] the final drama of the *Prometheia*, and we may, with Deichgräber, assume the same for the *Neaniskoi* of the *Lykourgeia*. Aischylos leads his characters, who are subject to divine power, into tragic situations of fearful difficulty; but the world view of a man who experienced the salvation of his city from the hands of the Persians is not determined by a sense of a universal tragedy according to which destruction would necessarily be the end of all action.[21] The gods direct the helm with a stern hand, but χάϱις is with them as well.

5

SOPHOKLES

BIOGRAPHICAL NOTES

The biography preserved in several manuscripts is the abridged version of a description of the poet's life pieced together in the manner of a satyros from many sources rich in anecdotes.[1] The author Karystios cited in *Vita* 8 lived in the latter part of the second century B.C. The original of our version may be dated not much later, probably in the first century B.C. Our other sources (including a *Suda* article) are collected in O. Jahn's edition of the *Elektra* (3d ed. by A. Michaelis, Bonn 1882). It will be remembered that Lessing wrote a life of Sophokles.

The year of his death has been confirmed as 406/405. Jacoby has collected and examined the evidence under *FGrH* 244 (Apollodoros) F 35. Since there is no cause to doubt the touching tribute described in the *Vita* of Euripides (that Sophokles, after the younger tragedian's death, presented the chorus in mourning dress and without garlands for the proagon of the Dionysia in 406), and since, on the other hand, the *Frogs* was produced at the Lenaia of 405, we must place the poet's death somewhere between these two dates.

The year of his birth is more controversial, for we possess conflicting reports. They are (following Jacoby's probable conjecture, op. cit., and on 239 *Marm. Par.* ep. 56 and 64, with the source material) the result of synchronistic speculations. The *Marmor Parium* lists 469/468 for the first victory of the twenty-eight-year-old poet (ep. 56), and 406/405 for his death at age ninety-two (ep. 64). This gives us the year 497/496 if we count exclusively in the first case and inclusively in the second. The date could have been reached by counting backward from the battle of Salamis. It was known (*Vita* 3) that Sophokles as an ephebe had led the singing of the victory paean. Since we can easily believe this of the handsome youth (Athen. 1. 20e) from a noble family, the calculation is probably also correct. Apollodoros (244 F 35) comes close with 495/494 as the year of birth; he may have dated the poet's acme at 456/455, "the great synchronic year of tragedy" (death of Aischylos, first victory of Euripides). Less convincing is Jacoby's explanation for 500/499 in Lukian *Macrob.* 24 from an earlier synchronism in 480/479: Aischylos's prime, birth of Euripides, Sophokles' twentieth birthday.

Sophillos is well attested as the name of the poet's father. The various reports about a trade that this Sophillos is supposed to have practiced are reasonably traced back in the *Vita* (1 = Aristoxenos fr. 115W) to the fact that being wealthy, he possessed slaves who worked such a trade.

It is a curious coincidence that the purest expression of tragedy in Western civilization came from a life over which a clear, serene light seemed to shine. The poet who portrayed the terrible helplessness of man's existence so mercilessly in the *Oidipous Tyrannos*, was loved all during his lifetime in Athens for his charming nature (*Vita* 7) and admired for his good fortune (Ar. *Pax* 696, Phrynichos [Comicus] *Muses* fr. 31K). Aristophanes truly makes a virtue out of the necessity of excluding Sophokles from his play when he has Dionysos (82) refuse to summon the poet with this fine characterization: ὁ δ' εὔκολος μὲν ἐνθάδ', εὔκολος δ' ἐκεῖ (He was good-natured here, and is good-natured there as well).

Born in the district of Kolonos, Sophokles was called φιλαθηναιότατος (greatest lover of Athens; *Vita* 10) and was very closely bound to the way of life, poetry, public service, and cults of his city. As far as we know, he left Athens only for official purposes.[2]

We believe the tradition (*Vita* 3) that he received a thorough education and achieved early success in gymnastics and musical instruction. His music teacher was reportedly Lampros, who is associated with Pindar and Pratinas in Pseudo-Plutarch *De Mus.* 31, 1142b. Webster cleverly remarks that the contrast of Lampros to Philoxenos and Timotheos mentioned in *De Mus.* is repeated in the opposition of Sophoklean choruses to those of the late Euripides, which were influenced by the new dithyramb.[3] It was inevitable that the ancients made Aischylos his teacher in the composition of tragedy. There must have been personal contact. Sophokles himself admitted in retrospect that at one time his art was heavily influenced by his predecessor. Plutarch (*De Prof. in Virt.* 7, 79b) has preserved his remark that he first had to free himself from the ὄγκος (bombast) of Aischylos and then overcome a harsh and artificial style of his own before he could achieve perfection.[4]

It coincides well with our image of the poet that he quickly won over his public and maintained this hold throughout his lifetime. *Marm. Par.* ep. 56 and Plut. *Kim.* 81 list 468 as the year of his first production, which was also his first victory.[5] Lessing was the first to connect this with Pliny *N. H.* 18. 65 and assign the *Triptolemos* to the victorious tetralogy. Fr. 541N reveals the delight in geographical detail that we recognize as Aischylean. Brommer (*Phil.* 94 [1941], 336), assumes that the *Triptolemos* was a satyr play, but the vase-painting done a few decades later with Triptolemos on his winged wagon between two satyrs is too weak a support for this. The report of Plut. *Kim.* 8, that the prize was awarded by the council of the strategoi under Kimon instead of by judges chosen by lot, betrays the influence of partisan struggles that were undoubtedly quite heated among the audience of the time.

The epigraphical catalogue of victors in the City Dionysia (*IG* II[2] 2325) lists eighteen victories for Sophokles. Though the *Suda* article speaks of twenty-four and the *Vita* of twenty (according to Karystios), the difference can probably be attributed to the inclusion of the Lenaia. We may believe the remark in the *Vita* (8) that Sophokles never won third prize. In that case years like 415, for which we know the first and second prize winners, would be excluded for his productions. According to the *Vita* (18), Aristophanes possessed 130 of Sophokles' plays in Alexandria, of which seventeen (or seven) were considered spurious. If one reads ζ' in the *Vita*, this would agree with the *Suda* article, which mentions 123 plays.

Vita 5 reports that Sophokles himself made an appearance playing the kithara in his *Thamyris*. Athenaios 1. 20 says that he distinguished himself as a ball player in the *Nausikaa*.[6] However, he then supposedly was the first playwright to give up acting in person because his voice was too weak (*Vita* 4). All this is thoroughly plausible, except for the explanation, which strongly resembles anecdotal aetiology and recurs in a similar way for Livius Andronicus in Livy 7. 2. The report (*Vita* 5) that he was depicted with the lyre in the Stoa Poikile could have originated from an arbitrary interpretation of one of the Polygnotan paintings.

If we choose to believe two very problematic statements, then there must have developed some sort of independent artistic life in Sophokles' time, in which the poet assumed a special position. According to *Vita* 6 he established a thiasos dedicated to the Muses. We can easily imagine Sophokles founding such a cult. The expression θίασος ἐκ τῶν πεπαιδευμένων (a company of educated men) creates problems. Blumenthal (*RE* 1049) thought of the actors whom Sophokles had instructed, a conception that resembles the scribae histrionesque more than a prototype of the Platonic Academy. The *Vita* mentions earlier that the poet wrote plays with specific actors in mind, but in view of the summary nature of this compilation, we cannot assume any connection between the two notes. Webster (*Soph.*, 7) rightly contradicts this assumption, although his "society of educated Athenians which was founded by Sophokles to discuss problems of literature and drama" (similarly, H. Herter, *Platons Akademie*, Bonn 1944, 29 with bibl.) sounds somewhat modern. But the reference to the θίασος Μουσῶν in Aristophanes *Thesm.* 41 is supportive.

Another difficult passage occurs in the *Suda* article, which states that besides dramatic works, Sophokles also composed elegies, paeans, and a prose tract περὶ χοροῦ in which he opposed Thespis and Choirilos.[7] If this work reflects a literary dispute among contemporaries, we should have to date it improbably early. Actually it is quite possible that in later life Sophokles wrote such a technical treatise, perhaps justifying his expansion of the chorus from twelve to fifteen members.[8] It is reported that men like Iktinos, Polykleitos, and Parrhasios also wrote about their professions around this time. In any case the confession of our uncertainty remains preferable to an overly hasty suspicion of the note.[9]

The closeness of Athenian society must have brought Sophokles into contact with a number of important men. Government service introduced him to Perikles; at age fifty-five he composed an elegy for Herodotos;[10] in Plato, *Rep.* 1. 329, we read that Sokrates once heard the aged poet express gratitude for his liberation from erotic passion.

Sophokles, whose works contain considerably fewer political references than those of Aischylos and Euripides, differs from these two also in that he often held high office in the service of his city, and refused every summons to a foreign court

(*Vita* 10). In the year 443/442, at the time of an important revision of the tribute districts, he was Hellenotamias; *IG* I² 202. 36; cf. *Suppl. Ep. Gr.* 5, 1931, p. 15. It is well attested (above all by Ion fr. 8 Blumenthal) that Sophokles was strategos together with Perikles during the Samian War (441/439).[11] According to the hypothesis of the *Antigone*, the Athenians elected him general because of this play. They were certainly capable of such an act. In the summer of 440, while Perikles was defeating the Samians at Tragia, a section of the fleet was dispatched to Chios and Lesbos to bring help (Thuk. 1. 116). It was there that the poet attended a banquet with Ion, who reports the rather insignificant incident (*Epidemiai*, fr. 8 Blumenthal) that Sophokles stole a kiss from a handsome youth. But we are grateful for Ion's description of the poet: τὰ μέντοι πολιτικὰ οὔτε σοφὸς οὔτε ῥηκτήριος ἦν, ἀλλ' ὡς ἄν τις εἷς τῶν χρηστῶν Ἀθηναίων (In political matters he was neither clever nor effective, but like one of those Athenian gentlemen). This fits well with Sophokles' own statement there that Perikles called him a good poet but a bad general. Nevertheless, he seems to have held this office a second time. The *Vita* 9 reports that the Athenians elected him strategos in the war against the Anaians (428),[12] and in fact in this year, when Euripides won with the extant *Hippolytos*, Sophokles did not produce a play.

Sophokles was often employed as an ambassador by the state (*Vita* 1), which might explain the only known attack on him in comedy: in Aristoph. *Pax* 698 he is accused of avarice.

According to Aristotle *Rhet.* 3. 18, 1419a 26, a Sophokles was a member of the council of probouloi that was supposed to introduce an authoritarian tone into the democracy after the Sicilian catastrophe. After the oligarchic putsch of 411 this Sophokles, responding to Peisandros's question, supposedly said that he did not approve of what had happened but that after all, there was no better way. The speaker lends weight to this statement and there is no reason to doubt that our poet was the man involved.[13] It is understandable that troubled times sought out great names.

His interest in the state was matched by a close relationship to its cults. The *Vita* (11) attests for Sophokles the priesthood of a heroic savior, for whom the name Halon has been transmitted. Sophokles, as priest of this hero, received Asklepios in his house when the god came from Epidauros and did not yet possess his own sanctuary. For this pious act the poet was heroized as Dexion after his death (*Etym. Magn.* 256. 6). When in the course of the German excavations on the west slope of the Akropolis the shrine of a healing deity, Amynos, was found, and two honorary decrees from it (*IG* II² 1252 and 1253) listed Dexion next to Amynos and Asklepios, it was tempting to accept Körte's suggestion that Amynos be inserted also in the *Vita* in place of the Halon of the tradition. But Walter has shown that two different shrines were involved, one of Amynos and Asklepios, and the other of Dexion.[14] If the heroon of Sophokles-Dexion must be separated in this way from the Amyneion, there is still no reason to doubt that the poet really was a priest of a Halon. Walter suggests that Halirrhothios may be the basis of the transmitted name.

Amidst the gossip that was inevitably connected even with the life of this great man, we must mention the trial that Iophon, the son of Sophokles and his wife Nikostrate, supposedly conducted against his aged father for showing undue preference for a like-named grandson of lower birth. This was the son of Ariston, whom Sophokles had sired with the Sikyonian woman Theoris. The story is not worthy of the belief it has found in Schmid (2. 321) and Perrotta (48).[15] But a son of Sophokles named Ariston with further descendants is historical; cf. hypoth. 2 to *Oidipous at Kolonos* and the family tree drawn by von Blumenthal (*RE* 1042).

The *Vita* (14) offers an assortment of peculiar causes of death: choking on a grape, overexertion while reading (out loud, of course) a long uninterrupted section of the *Antigone*, joy over a victory. That he was buried in a family grave on the road to Dekeleia, eleven stadia from the city walls, may be believed; not so the touching story that Lysander, twice warned by Dionysos in a dream, permitted the funeral procession free passage through the blockade of the city.

Of the three extant types of Sophokles portraits,[16] the oldest is the least assured.[17] Several copies from a bronze work of the early fourth century have been preserved, of which we mention the head in Berlin, no. 296. It is a portrait of strong, introverted determination, which Wolters connected with Sophokles on the basis of its similarity to the Lateran type. Schefold suggests that the model could have been a statue dedicated by Iophon after his father's death. But the heavily damaged passage in *Vita* 11 cannot offer sufficient proof for the existence of such a statue.

The well known statue in the Lateran belongs to the second type and is still considered the best ancient portrait of Sophokles, even though it has long been known that the expressive head is the result of reworking by Tenerani.[18] A plaster cast in the Villa Medici, fortunately made before the restoration, shows even more intensely the painful earnestness and sorrowful understanding of the first type. Stylistic comparison supports the conjecture that the archetype could have been the statue of the poet erected by Lykourgos in the Theater of Dionysos ca. 330.

A third model is represented by the Farnese type, which shows the poet in advanced age.[19] Numerous reproductions attest its popularity in antiquity; we mention the head in the Museo Nazionale in Naples (no. 6413). The identification is confirmed by an inscribed herm in the Vatican and a portrait bust (now lost) with an inscription. Dating varies, but the type is probably later than the Lateran example. Schefold imagines a classical original.

To these three types may be added a fourth, less well attested (Richter, *Portraits*, plates 708–710). The best example is the bronze head in the British Museum.

MANUSCRIPT TRANSMISSION AND EDITIONS

Here we must first remind the reader of the various stages in the transmission of the tragedians that were distinguished in our discussion of the Aischylean tradition.

The definitive edition for Sophokles, too, was prepared by Aristophanes of Byzantium, traces of whose work (*Vita* 18; hypoth. 1 *Ant.*, schol. *Aios.* 746 et al.) are still discernible. For the scholia as we possess them today, Didymos was decisive. That he was not simply making a parasitic compilation is shown by the extant portions of his polemics against earlier Sophokles commentaries. Here too the development led to the selection of seven plays in explanatory editions. In the final years of the fourth century these editions were further edited by Sallustios, whose hypotheseis to the *Ant.* and *Oid. Kol.* and probably also to the *Aias* and *Oid. Tyr.* still exist. In the hypothesis to the *Oid. Kol.* he is called a Pythagorean, and would thus be the author of the treatise περὶ θεῶν καὶ κόσμου, but there is good reason for the caution exercised by Wilamowitz in his introduction to the *Herakles.*[1]

The evaluation of the manuscript tradition reached a new stage primarily through the work of A. Turyn, supplemented by the studies of V. de Marco and R. Aubreton, among others.[2] The first important step in this process was the most exact editing possible of the individual Byzantine recensions of the Sophoklean texts. Through careful interpretation of the scholia, Turyn attempted to ascertain to the greatest possible extent the influence of authors such as Planudes, Moschopoulos, Thomas Magister, and Triklinios on our manuscript tradition. Aubreton also made substantial contributions to our knowledge of Trinklinios's role, whose most important work involved the metrical supplementation of the commentaries of Moschopoulos and Thomas Magister on the basis of Hephaistion's teachings. The goal of all this painstaking effort was to free our Sophokles apparatus from an entire series of readings that were introduced by Byzantine grammarians and thus have nothing to do with the genuine tradition. But differences, particularly in the evaluation of the "Roman family" (see below), show that a clear decision remains uncertain in a number of individual cases.

From the material considered to represent ancient tradition, uncontested first place is held by the same Florentine MS that we mentioned as our leading source for Aischylos. There its general name was *Mediceus*; here however we call it *Laurentianus* because in fact the Sophokles text was bound to those of Aischylos and Apollonios as a later addition, though it was written approximately at the same time (between 960 and 980 according to Dain). It contains many scholia and corrections by several hands. In the important introduction to his edition, Dain argues convincingly that the Laurentianus 32. 9 was copied directly from an uncial codex, possibly of the fifth century A.D. The view proposed by Cobet that it was the archetype of the other manuscripts, has today generally been abandoned.[3] This manuscript is followed in importance by the palimpsest from Leyden 60A (P), which can be traced back to the same uncial manuscript.[4] It is occasionally valuable in determining the original reading of the Laurentianus where, as A. Turyn recognized, the writer of *Parisinus gr.* 2712 (see below) made erasures in L and restored them with readings from the Leyden manuscript.

In the studies mentioned above, V. de Marco was successful in proving the existence of a second line of the tradition. This "Roman family" contains the *Laur. Conv. Soppr.* 152 (G), which according to the subscription was completed on 15 July 1282 and contains *Aias, Oid. Tyr., El.,* and *Phil.*; the *Vat. gr.* 2291 (R) from the fifteenth century with all seven plays (*Trach.* to v. 372); *Estensis gr.* 41 (M) closely related to the previous MS and from the same period; and the *Paris Suppl. gr.* 109 (Q), the latest of the four (beginning of the sixteenth century). A series of more recent manuscripts (classified in Turyn) is heavily contaminated with readings of the first group and is thus one more example of the open tradition whose importance has lately been increasingly recognized.

The Roman family, beneath a layer of later mistakes, reveals a source that is closely related to that of the first group, but according to Dain (introd., xlii) the two can hardly be equated.[5] For the good readings of the Roman family the difficult question arises whether they represent ancient tradition or Byzantine conjecture.[6] P. E. Easterling emphasizes the uncertainty, but comes after all to the conclusion that this MS group contains authentic ancient readings.[7] The author manages to separate somewhat the close bond of GRQ by demonstrating cases when R and Q are opposed to G.

A third manuscript group is best represented by *Parisinus gr.* 2712 (A; second half of the thirteenth century). Turyn attempted to downplay the value of this codex, but was not entirely successful. He claimed to be able to prove the dependence of *Aias, El.,* and *Oid. Tyr.* on the recension of Manuel Moschopoulos. A. Dain (introd., xliv) concedes the influence of Byzantine philologists, but also appreciates the independent value of the manuscript, which alone has preserved several ancient readings. A similar verdict has been reached now by P. E. Easterling as well.[8]

The conclusion drawn by J. C. Kamerbeek well illustrates the state of flux that still exists regarding the tradition: after the publication of Turyn's studies, he postponed the compilation of a text for his commentary, since it seemed to him necessary first to examine these partly revolutionary theories.

Many of the other manuscripts (Turyn describes a total of 190) contain the Byzantine triad (*Aias, El., Oid. Tyr.*), a selection from the selection.

Ant. 1167 offers a striking example of the importance of the indirect tradition for Sophokles. The verse is missing in the manuscripts, has left only a trace in the scholia, and is preserved in Athen. 280b, 547c (Eusthathios 957, 17, following him).

For modern editions, the seven-volume set with commentary by Sir Richard Jebb, Cambridge 1883–1896 (1902–1908, reprinted without alteration) still deserves special mention. A valuable supplement to this is the three-volume edition of the fragments with commentary by A. C. Pearson, Cambridge 1917. An editio minor with Jebb's text was published in Cambridge 1897; and L. Campbell's *The Plays and Fragments* was published at Oxford 1879–1881 and reprinted at Hildesheim in 1965. A. C. Pearson employed an eclecticism in his Oxford text of 1924, which Radermacher opposed without fundamental justification.[9] In the Budé series, P. Masqueray first published the text with a translation (Paris 1922–1924, 2d rev. ed. 1929–1934, reprinted up to the 5th and 4th editions of the first and second volumes respectively). He largely recognizes the primacy of L. This edition has now been replaced in the same series by the dual-language text of A. Dain and P. Mazon: I. (*Trach., Ant.*) Paris 1955; II. (*Aias, Oid. Tyr., El.*) 1958; III. (*Phil., Oid. Kol.*) 1960. The text, probably the best in use today, and the apparatus, which is excellent but spare, are Dain's, whose evaluation of the tradition was mentioned above. The translation is the work of Mazon. The importance of the dual-language edition *Théâtre de Sophocle* by R. Pignarre in the Editions Garnier, 2 vols., Paris 1947, using the text of Dindorf-Mekler (1884) vanishes in comparison. The first volume (*Oid. Tyr., Oid. Kol.*) of a Spanish dual-language edition was prepared by J. Errandonea, Barcelona 1959. The apparatus leaves something to be desired. The tragedies and fragments in Greek and German appeared in the Tusculum-Bücherei, edited and translated by W. Willige, revised by K. Bayer with good explanatory appendixes, Munich 1966.

Of the editions with commentary besides Jebb's we should note E. Bruhn's revision of the old Schneidewin-Nauck texts (*Oid. Tyr.* 1910; *El.* 1912; *Ant.* 1913) and L. Radermacher (*Oid. Kol.* 1909; *Phil.* 1911; *Aias* 1913; *Trach.* 1914). To date J. C. Kamerbeek has published the following volumes of commentary: I. *Aias*, Leyden 1953. II. *Trach.* 1959. IV. (with temporary postponement of *Ant.*) *Oid. Tyr.* 1967.

Individual editions are cited under the respective plays.

Besides Pearson, E. Diehl, *Suppl. Soph.*, Bonn 1913, is still important for the increasing number of fragments. The new longer fragments are in C. E. Fritsch, "Neue Fragm. d. Aisch. u. Soph.," Diss. Hamburg 1936, and in the volume *Greek Lit. Pap.* 1, London 1950, prepared for the Loeb Class. Library by D. L. Page, a collection important for all three tragedians. R. Carden, *The Papyrus Fragments of Sophokles*, with a contribution by W. S. Barrett, Berlin and New York 1974. For the fragments from satyr plays, see V. Steffen, *Satyrographorum Graecorum fragmenta*, 2d ed., Poznan 1952. For the papyri, cf. our comments on the Aischylos tradition.

The editions of the scholia by W. Dindorf (Oxford 1852) and P. N. Papageorgios (Leipzig 1888) rely on the Laurentianus. V. de Marco recommends enlarging upon this narrow base in the works cited in note 2 of this section, which are important not only for the history and text of the scholia, but also for Sophokles himself. The *Sophokles-Lexikon* of F. Ellendt, 2d ed. by H. Genthe, Berlin 1872, has now been reprinted, Hildesheim 1958.

A survey of the older translations is offered by W. Schildknecht, "Deutscher Sophokles," Diss. Bonn 1935. Further, G. Luzzatto, "Traduzioni tedesche di Sofocle," *Dioniso* 12 (1949), 193, 267; id. 13 (1950), 52. H. Frey, *Deutsche Sophokles-übersetzungen*, Winterthur 1964.

In addition to the above mentioned dual-language editions the following translations are recommended: C. Bruch, Heidelberg (no date); J. R. Woerner, Inselverlag 1937; H. Weinstock (Kröners paperback ed. 163), 3d ed., Stuttgart 1957; E. Buschor, 2 vols., Munich 1954 and 1959; R. Schottlaender, *Bibl. d. Antike*, Berlin and Weimar 1966.

Two opposing theories of translation are paradigmatically represented in two important renditions, by E. Staiger, Zurich 1944 and W. Schadewaldt, *Griechisches Theater*, Frankfurt 1964 with *Ant., Oid. Tyr., El.*; Sophokles, *Tragödien*, Bibl. der Alten Welt Zurich 1968 with *Aias, Ant., Oid. Tyr., El.* in Schadewaldt's translation; *Trach., Phil., Oid. Kol.* in Buschor's. Schadewaldt has also newly edited the translations of Friedrich Hölderlin and added a penetrating introduction (Fischerbücherei 1957). Staiger and Schadewaldt have contrasted their theories in a discussion published by the Artemis-Verlag (*Das Problem der Übersetzung antiker Dichtung*, Zurich 1963). Schadewaldt distinguishes his own principle of documentary translation, which, stated epigrammatically, attempts to translate not Sophokles into German, but German into Sophokles, from a transposing translation that gives a new stylistic dress to the Greek thought. This valuable discussion determines the poles of an antinomy between which every translator must find his way anew.

The *Fischer-Bibliothek der 100 Bücher* offers in volume 81 (1963) a collection of representative translations: E. Staiger, *Aias, Trach.*; K. Reinhardt, *Ant.*; W. Schadewaldt, *Oid. Tyr., El.*; E. Buschor, *Phil., Oid. Kol.*

We remind the reader of the far-reaching influence of Gilbert Murray's translations, those of Sophokles included. The translation of L. Campbell, *The Seven Plays in English Verse*, was published as volume 116 of the World's Classics, Oxford. *Aias, El., Trach., Phil.* have been translated by E. F. Watling, Penguin Classics 28, London 1953. Also see L. R. Lind, *Ten Greek Plays in Contemporary Translation*, Cambridge, Mass. 1957. In *The Complete Greek Tragedies*, Sophokles was translated by D. Grene, R. Fitzgerald, E. Wyckoff, J. Moore, and M. Jameson, 2 vols., London and Chicago 1954, 1957. French: P. Mazon, 2 vols., Paris 1950, now in the Budé series (see above); a special edition with an outstanding introduction by J. de Romilly in Club du meilleur livre, Paris 1959. Italian: first place is held by the version of E. Bignone, *Le Trag. di Sof. trad. in versi ital. con saggi introduttivi*, 4 vols., Florence 1937/1938.

For the later influence of the poet we refer the reader to the books of Sheppard and Hamburger (see the Bibliography, under Tragedy [Gen.] and Aischylos).

We cannot be thankful enough for the aid of H. Friis Johansen, who presents the bibliography on Sophokles from 1939 to 1959 with excellent critical comments, *Lustrum* 1962/7 (1963). His work continues that of A. von Blumenthal, *Bursians Jahresber.* 277 (1942). Bibliography since 1960 appears in *Sophokles*, Wege der Forschung 95, Darmstadt 1967, 537.

THE EXTANT TRAGEDIES

Our understanding of Sophokles was considerably advanced by the particularly lively interest in his works that arose after the war. In no play, however, has the interpretation remained so difficult as in the *Aias*.[1] The fateful judgment of arms between Aias and Odysseus was described in the *Aithiopis* and the *Little Iliad*, and Aischylos presented the fate of the hero in the trilogy Ὅπλων κρίσις, Θρῆσσαι, Σαλαμίνιαι (Σαλαμίνιοι in the MS catalogue). Here too his sense of insult drove Aias to suicide, which was reported by a messenger in the second play. We may confidently assign fr. 110 adesp. N to Aischylos, according to which Aias called dishonor the greatest suffering of a free soul.

The structure of the play (as shown by Reinhardt in his book on Sophokles), the handling of the motifs, and the composition of dialogue all point to its position as the earliest of the extant dramas.[2] It may have been produced as early as the fifties.

In the *Aias*, the decisive event occurs prior to the beginning of the play. This places special demands on the exposition, which are met by Sophokles with consummate skill in a tightly structured prologue scene (1–133) that differs markedly from the beginnings of the Aischylean tragedies we know. Following a trail, Odysseus comes before the tent of Aias (the skene must have represented a sort of square hut) when Athena calls to him and announces that he is at the end of his search. Inside sits Aias with his murderous sword. Odysseus recognizes the voice of the goddess (although he cannot see her) and reveals in his reply indistinct outlines of the night's activity: a slaughter among the captured animals, a scout who saw Aias rush through the fields with bloody sword. The excited questions of Odysseus determine the following stichomythy, in which the attack and motive of Aias become clear. In a set speech, the aversion of danger by the madness with which Athena struck Aias, and his crazed butchering of cattle are depicted by the goddess as the work of her own power. That Odysseus might be absolutely certain, she will show him the demented Aias in person. Near the middle of the prologue scene (71) she summons Aias before his tent. Her first call is unsuccessful, but it terrifies Odysseus, who, in excited stichomythy, tries in vain to restrain the goddess; she promises him sweet laughter over the utter collapse of an enemy. At her second call Aias emerges and now, in a swift exchange of blows in single and double verses, the goddess cruelly toys with the insane warrior, whom she lures further and further into a crass self-portrayal of his madness. This Athena, unlike the great founder of the *Eumenides*, bears all the features of the Homeric divinities, who can be either helpful friends to man, or his savage destroyers. When Aias has left the scene, she reveals to Odysseus in a highly significant speech that what he has just seen is a great example of divine power. Throughout all this, one element is essential for the character of Aias. In the last word of his conversation with the goddess, he commands her to remain by his side. This expresses not only the depth of his insanity but also his real nature, for these words anticipate what we shall hear later about his hubris. Immediately the poet warns us against any one-sided judgment. For now the goddess asks Odysseus if he recognizes the power of the gods in the fate of this man, who surpassed all in circumspection (προνούστερος) and opportune action. Odysseus does see this, but the effect of the spectacle is different from what the goddess foretold. We hear no laughter; instead, man recognizes man in the frailty of his existence (121–126). Odysseus feels only profound sorrow for his fallen enemy, in whose lot he sees his own, the lot of man. Thus the poet presents here the same Odysseus who will bring the solution of humanity to the burial dispute in the play's second part; far beyond this, however, Odysseus, as if he were the ideal spectator of Sophoklean tragedy, speaks words that stand above the poet's work like the γνῶθι σαυτόν (know thyself) over the temple door at Delphi. With an admonition to be humble before the gods and to accept man's lot, Athena concludes the prologue that depicts for us the catastrophe of the hero in all its harshness, and at the same time introduces the significant themes of the play.

This tight exposition is followed by the broad unfolding of the situation in which Aias finds himself when he regains consciousness. With an increasing intensity that suffers only an apparent ritardando in the deception speech, his only escape from disgrace becomes clear.

The chorus of Salaminian sailors enters with anapests (134–171), deeply disturbed by the current rumors. In their words is expressed the concern of the small man for the great one who protects him: They reveal the distance that, especially for Sophokles, separates the hero, isolated in his tragic destiny, from the chorus as a group. A pair of strophes with epode (172–200) asks which divinity sent such destruction, offers some mistaken guesses, and calls for Aias. But Tekmessa comes out instead and confirms the rumors in a short anapestic conversation, characterizing Aias as he must have seemed to her, his wife: ὁ δεινὸς μέγας ὠμοκρατὴς Αἴας (strong-shouldered Aias, great and fearful). A short epirrhematic structure follows (221–262), in which anapests of Tekmessa respond to the strophe and antistrophe of the chorus. In the first half they exchange their knowledge of the event, which becomes ever clearer; then the chorus, in its fear of becoming involved in Aias's destruction, expresses a cowardly wish to flee, while Tekmessa worries about her husband, who has returned to his senses.

The beginning of the following dialogue, which leads into a report by Tekmessa, is important for the distance between the chorus and the individual directly involved in the tragic action. The chorus has heard that the madness of Aias has passed and now thinks all will be well. Tekmessa must first tell them that understanding is only the beginning of his suffering. Then she reports what happened, first adding to what we know from the prologue, but then portraying the awakening of her husband to terrible knowledge. He sits inside, gloomily brooding, plotting danger. She is preparing us to see Aias himself in his misery.

But he does not yet show himself; we hear his cries of pain, his calls for his child and his half-brother Teukros, which are alternately glossed by trimeters of Tekmessa and of the chorus leader. After such renewed preparation the door of the skene is opened (Tekmessa may take care of this) and we see Aias sitting amidst the slaughtered animals. It corresponds to the rhythm of tragedy, the succession of πάθος and λόγος, that his despair is first released in a kommos (348–429), after which the problematical side of his situation is developed in a lengthy trimeter scene (430–595). It corresponds further to the formal demands of Attic classicism that the kommos, for all its internal movement, is organized strictly according to the structural rules of an epirrhematic composition. In the first pair of strophes, the lyric sections are each followed by two trimeter lines of the chorus leader while the second strophe and antistrophe are both interrupted by three separate trimeter verses, the second of which is spoken by Aias in both cases and ends in a cry of pain. Each individual strophe is concluded here, as in the third strophic pair, by two trimeters. The lyric parts, expressing the deepest despair, are given to Aias throughout. In the third antistrophe he addresses his lament to the sea, to the grottoes and groves by the shore and near the neighboring Skamandros. This both foreshadows significantly his moving farewell monologue and testifies in a barely concealed manner to his determination to die. That decision is brutally explained in the following conversation with Tekmessa. Aias begins with a long speech (430–480) that divides into two approximately equal sections, with the break in thought occurring after 456. In the first of these, after a painful word about the suffering inherent in his own name (αἰαῖ!), he thinks of his distant father, who himself once had gained fame fighting before Troy, while undeserved and disgraceful wrong has befallen his son Aias. The second part begins with the question, What to do now? The possibilities of returning home or embracing death voluntarily in battle (to the delight of the Atreidai!) are rejected; only suicide remains. Here too the father motif continues as the hero's main concern. In disgrace, Aias cannot face his father; he must do something that will prove to him the worth of his phusis. Significantly Sophokles uses this word for "inborn nature" here and at v. 549: it will later play a key role in the *Philoktetes*. In verses 479 f., however, Aias expresses not only his thoughts but his whole being: ἀλλ' ἢ καλῶς ζῆν ἢ καλῶς τεθνηκέναι / τὸν εὐγενῆ χρή (the nobleman must either live honorably or die honorably).

The chorus leader adds four verses; he knows that Aias speaks sincerely but from his own viewpoint bids him put aside such thoughts.

Now Tekmessa, the antagonist, speaks, using all the arguments natural to her position (485–524). We scarcely perceive her as the loving wife; she is the war captive whose only security is with Aias. She begins with her own fate, imploring her unrelenting husband on behalf of his father, mother, and child, then ends again with her own lot. The chorus assists in two verses, then two more of Aias introduce a short stichomythy (527–543), which advances the plot after the speeches are over. It is an ingenious touch that the poet has Aias make no reply to Tekmessa's long speech. She must bring their son Eurysakes, whom in her fear she has hidden. But the speech (545–582) of Aias to the child is his real answer to the pleas of the mother. He leaves the boy with the proud wish that he be blessed with better fortune than his father but like him in all other respects. No one need be concerned about his future (this was a theme of Tekmessa). Teukros will bring the child to its grandparents for proper care and upbringing. For Tekmessa there is only the initial command to give him the child and another command at the end to stop crying and shut the door—unless we can detect a thought of consolation when Aias speaks of Eurysakes as his χαρμονή (joy): only one word, but one word in Sophokles can mean a great deal, as the ancients well knew (*Vita* 21).

After two unimportant verses of the chorus leader, the scene closes with a stichomythy (585–595), which, following a short pause of two double verses, bursts into lively antilabai. A final stormy plea by Tekmessa shatters against the unbending will of Aias.

The following choral ode (596–645) is wholly a lament, but in the predominantly glyconic meters it sounds softer, thus leading over to the following speech of Aias. The chorus thinks of Salamis in the first strophic pair; the distant homeland appears as an image of happiness in contrast to the present misery. The sailors sing of the suffering of their leader's mother and father in the second pair of strophes.

Then Aias emerges from the tent and speaks words (646–692) that apparently indicate a transformation. He who before had only commands for Tekmessa, now declares himself overcome by her word, filled with pity, and prepared for a reconciliation. He goes to bathe, to be purified by the shore, making his peace with the gods. The sword that he holds, once the fatal bequest of Hektor, he will hide someplace out of sight. He has, so he says, come to understand that everything in nature and human life is subject to change, so why should not he too learn moderation? He leaves the scene saying that he goes where he must and that soon they will hear he has been saved.

This speech of Aias is, despite all speculation, primarily to be understood in its dramatic function as a speech of deception. A man who has informed his friends so clearly of his resolve to die must escape these friends in order to carry out his purpose. To do this Aias must make them believe that he will return. With his incomparable irony Sophokles allows the veil of deception to part here and there so that the truth becomes clear. Aias will be reconciled with the goddess, but by his death. He will bury his sword, but in his body. His wife should pray that his wish be fulfilled; he walks the path that must be taken; soon he will be saved: everything points to suicide.

Beyond that, however, this speech is a magnificent monologue in which irony is used to reveal Aias's relationship to the ways of the world with a final, utter clarity. When he speaks of the constant change from which neither nature nor man can escape, when he wants to learn to respect the Atreidai, he speaks of things that lie beyond the possibilities of his nature. He holds the image of world up before him, with all the labors and delusions of the πολλοί, the many (682), in order to recognize that he has no place here, that only a withdrawal into death can satisfy his φύσις (inborn nature).

But at the point where Aias speaks of what is impossible for him, of hating an enemy only so far that he may become a friend again, an important connection is made to the end of the play. The possibility that does not exist for Aias is realized through the humanity of Odysseus.

Quite contrary to common practice, the chorus leader makes no statement following this speech of Aias. Immediately after the hero leaves, a short ode of joy (one pair of strophes) begins. The chorus rejoices over Aias's change of heart. This is that παρέκτασις tragica, *id est gaudiorum introductio ante funestissimum nuntium* (tragic lengthening, i.e., the introduction of cheer before the most dismal news; Donatus on Ter. *Ad.* 293) which we find again in *Ant.* as well as in *Trach.* and *Oid. Tyr.* It signifies much more than an effective method of contrast, and expresses man's tragic entanglement in error.[3]

This false hope means a considerable delay in the path toward catastrophe. This path must now be reassumed, a new line must be introduced, and so Sophokles stages the following messenger scene (719–814). The first section of the report, which begins without an introduction, tells of the humiliating taunts leveled at Teukros on his return to the Greek camp. Then the messenger asks for Aias, for whom he has information. In a short excited conversation with the chorus leader we hear the words "too late," shaking the hopes of all. We learn that a prophecy of Kalchas involves a life-and-death decision for Aias. In the second, longer part of the report, which continues after the dramatic interruption, we hear what Kalchas proclaimed: Aias has incurred the wrath of Athena, lasting only until this one day is out, for his hubristic speech at his departure and in a certain battle. If he survives this day he can be saved. The chorus leader grasps the new situation immediately and calls for Tekmessa. In the following highly dynamic dialogue between the messenger and Tekmessa, Sophokles has avoided all annoying repetition and placed the accent wholly on the danger of the moment. Tekmessa issues the commands to bring Teukros and, in separate groups, to search for Aias. The hero's tragedy also includes that of his wife; thus we hear the painful cry "Thus am I cast out from the favor of old" (808) and it is a stirring touch that in her panic she calls their child to her side (809).

As in the *Eumenides*, the *Alkestis*, and the *Helena*, the chorus leaves the stage, and as in the first of these dramas, a change of scene takes place. We find Aias in a remote spot, his sword stuck in the ground, pointing upward; we hear his farewell to the world. He prays first to Zeus but prays in his own way. That the god help him is only right and fair, and his request is modest: that Teukros might be the first to find him, and that he take care of the corpse. He summons Hermes, the guide of the dead, and the Erinyes, to whom, in a curse, he condemns the Atreidai and the entire army. Helios must report these events to Aias's parents in Salamis—not a word about Tekmessa. But then, in one of the most moving passages in Sophoklean tragedy, we perceive how this rough hero, having rejected mankind, still is bound with every fiber of his being to this world of light, of springs and rivers, the soil of his homeland, and even to the earth of Troy. He calls to them all before he falls on his sword.

Divided into semi-choruses (805!) the chorus returns to the stage with a lyric epiparodos, whose second part is composed of trimeters by the two choral groups, which are interrupted by short questions (bakchiacs). This search scene, presented with the same liveliness as in Sophokles' *Ichneutai*, is continued without a break in the following lengthy kommos (879–973), an excited passage in two parts in which the purely lyrical sections of the chorus alternate with short dialogues. Ten trimeters by Tekmessa follow the first section, thirteen more follow the second, which corresponds very strictly to the first. The discovery of the corpse by Tekmessa occurs in the beginning section of the kommos; then the lament is sounded by a swift exchange of voices. It is significant for the unified characterization of the chorus that its first thought is for its own return to home and safety (900). A well calculated contrast to the next scene is offered by the conclusion of the kommos, in which the chorus sings of the laugh Odysseus will surely have when he hears of his fallen enemy (remember the prologue scene!), while Tekmessa in her last speech begins and ends her lament with this theme.

The drama comprises 1420 verses; Aias ends his death-monologue at v. 865. A threnos could end the play, but what follows instead is a lengthy section, a dispute in three subtly differentiated scenes of argumentation, which secures for the dead man the honors of burial and returns to him the dignity of his heroism. In the center of this dispute now stands Teukros, who is emphasized at first as the man deeply stricken by the loss of his half-brother (974–1046). After a short exchange of laments with the chorus leader, and the command for Tekmessa to bring Eurysakes, Teukros speaks over the corpse of Aias. His trusty spirit lacks the great nobility of the dead hero. His place is between Aias and the small world of the chorus. Teukros expresses pain at his loss and then broadly develops the thought of what his return home will bring, since he must inform Telamon of the loss of his great son.[4] In the final section his speech returns to Aias and the fatal gifts exchanged with Hektor.[5]

As Teukros's first opponent, Menelaos enters. When he is announced by the chorus leader as "Menelaos, for whose sake we made this journey," he is immediately

placed in the position of a miserable egoist. And he then reveals himself as such in
the agon with Teukros (1047–1162). He rashly forbids anyone to touch the corpse.
Teukros's indignant reply is countered with a long speech, a masterpiece of characterization. His command to cast the corpse out on the beach to be eaten by birds is utter
hubris. In this dispute over the burial of the dead man, a problematical situation is
developed that will be the main theme in the *Antigone*. The baseness of a petty soul
is unmasked when Menelaos reveals a final reason for his hostility (1067 ff.): this
Aias would not bow to them; if they couldn't rule him while he was alive, they will
at least control his corpse. Then he adopts a rather lopsided preaching tone, exposed
as such by the chorus leader in his two concluding lines (1091 f.). What Athena in the
Eumenides said of the great wisdom and benefit of valuing fear, becomes here
through the obtrusive repetition of the thematic word δέος (1074, 1079, 1084) the
empty phrase of a vain and petty despot.

In his reply Teukros denies that Aias ever stood under the command of Menelaos and remains determined to bury the body, even against the will of the commander, thus preparing for the next dispute scene. The chorus leader—in another
stroke of characterization—finds Teukros's words too harsh. The struggle intensifies
to a heated exchange in the stichomythy, though no new arguments are raised. Both
men confront each other once more, then Menelaos leaves the scene with a threat of
violence.

The chorus, forever worried, foresees in its anapests a violent conflict and
counsels a quick burial. Then Tekmessa comes with the child, and Teukros instructs
the boy to sit by the corpse with the triple offering of hair from his mother, Teukros,
and himself. Thus Eurysakes, as the pledge that the dead man will live on in him, is
present on stage until the end of the play.

In two strophic pairs the following choral ode (1185–1222) depicts the war as
the broad context in which the sorrowful event stands. The Trojan War to be sure,
but beyond this we hear words that describe war as such as the death-bringing de-
stroyer of all life's joys. That the chorus applies all these statements to itself suits its
character.

After the ode, Teukros enters just before Agamemnon, his second and more
serious opponent, to begin another argument (1223–1315). The commander pits his
entire authority against this bastard, whom he treats as a rebellious slave. His demand that Teukros have a free man plead his case will soon be fulfilled by Odysseus.
In the stichomythy between Teukros and Menelaos we were briefly prepared for Agamemnon's reference to the judgment of weapons and its validity. After two vapid
verses from the conciliatory chorus leader, Teukros replies with much greater vehemence than in the first agon. He sharply criticizes Agamemnon's ingratitude toward
the hero who saved the burning ships and withstood hand-to-hand combat with Hektor. He counters the charge of ignoble birth by sharply rebuking Agamemnon, son of
the adulteress Aerope and the grandson of the barbarian Pelops. His threats of violence bring the situation near catastrophe, when Odysseus enters, greeted with relief
by the chorus (1316 f.). A new opposition now is presented on another level between
the two great men of the army (1318–1373). Odysseus's first words already make his

position clear. He heard the Atreidai shouting over the valiant corpse. When he is informed of the dispute, he asks Agamemnon with the utmost suavity to allow him to speak truly to a friend. With well calculated variation, Sophokles lets only one of the partners, Odysseus, speak here, only in a short set speech, while the real agon is conducted in a long stichomythy. The speech of Odysseus is a complete rejection of irreconcilable hatred. His statement that such action wrongs not the dead man, but the laws of the gods, anticipates the problematic situation of the *Antigone*. In the brilliant stichomythy, he blocks every step of Agamemnon, who wants to invoke authority, the hostility of Aias, the necessity of being consistent, the threat to his reputation; finally the commander, spiteful to the end, leaves the field to Odysseus. When Odysseus says (1365) that he too will walk the road of death, we should recall the prologue scene; when he speaks of the possibility (1359) that friendship and hostility exchange places, we think back to Aias in his deception speech, who could only say such a thing to describe what was, for him, impossible.

Odysseus reaps the just praise of the chorus leader (1374) and declares his willingness to aid in the burial, a final gesture of noble reconciliation. Teukros thanks him, but declines, saying that such an act of kindness might displease the dead man. Aias remains unrelenting, even in death, through the words of his brother. After Odysseus leaves, Teukros gives the command to prepare for the burial, and the chorus concludes the play with a very general gnomic statement about the utter uncertainty of man's future.

The structure of the *Aias* is distinct and clearly arranged. The short but dramatic prologue scene aids considerably in illuminating the catastrophe and presents the character of Aias as well as that of Odysseus. In the latter's conversation with Athena, the frailty of mankind is stressed from both the divine and human standpoints. The first and longer of the play's two main sections shows the path of Aias from black despair to his collapse on the sword. That line is interrupted by the deception speech, which retards the action; this requires a new start, with the impetus given by Kalchas's prophecy. A second shorter section (731. 544 verses) is concerned with the dead Aias. Search scene and lament are followed by a dispute in three sets of speeches that secure for him the honors of burial. Borrowing a happy coinage from T. B. L. Webster, scholars speak of diptych composition, which is characteristic of the earlier dramas. This does not mean, of course, that the play is split into two parts which the poet was unable to unify. The ancient literary critic in the scholium on v. 1123 simply exposes his own ignorance when he writes that Sophokles forcibly extended the drama beyond the death of Aias.[6] The κάτω ὁδός (descent) of the hero is followed by the ἄνω ὁδός (ascent), with the restoration of his honor, and these lines are then joined together in a παλίντονος ἁρμονίη (balanced harmony). Conversely it would be incorrect to ignore the fact that this method of composition differs from that of the *Oid. Tyr.* or *El.*, in which the poet ties all action with the utmost concentration to one character who dominates the play throughout.

Our most difficult problem involves the interpretation and extent of Aias's personal guilt.[7] The question arises immediately in our evaluation of the prologue. When Athena admonishes humility at the conclusion of that scene, a connecting line can be drawn to the report of Kalchas about the two occasions when Aias treated the goddess with hubris. But does this prove that the play's meaning is wholly contained in a game of guilt and expiation? Didn't the same Athena just before this speak of Aias's prudence? And for Kalchas's report we must first bear in mind that the motif was already present in the epic cycle.[8] Further we must consider its emphasis within the drama, since the wrath of Athena is by no means the driving force in the play. She struck Aias with insanity in order to save the Greeks. The motif of the goddess's anger is further weakened by the curious limitation of her resentment: if this one day passes well, Aias can be saved.[9] And finally we must understand the speech of Kalchas above all in terms of its dramatic function: Aias must be found, his men must be shocked out of their false security.

Thus we conclude that Aias's hubris is certainly an essential feature in the totality of the action, but that the meaning of the play is by no means exhausted in this motif. We repeat the profound statement of F. G. Welcker: "But it seems, too, that Aias fills the drama far more through what he is than through what he did wrong."[10] Divinity, however, is recognized not only as the power that punishes and teaches by punishing, but also as a force that is incalculable, neither responsible for, nor sparing of, humankind. This still echoes the ethical world of Aischylos, yet we can already look forward from here to the *Oidipous Tyrannos*.

Welcker, who could not bear the thought of a deceitful Aias, is responsible for the many unnecessary problems involved with the deception speech. In his view Aias is speaking the absolute truth, and it is the fault of Tekmessa and the chorus that they misunderstand him. He was followed by Ebeling (op. cit., 297), who even finds it tragic that Aias unintentionally deceives those around him; not far from this is the interpretation of I. M. Linforth,[11] and even B. M. W. Knox, who evaluates the speech well as Aias's great realization, and denies the intent to deceive.[12] Wolfgang Schadewaldt offers a different line of thought: the speech is of course the means of clearing Aias's path to death, but it signifies at the same time an inner transformation to an attitude of submission.[13] This was taken a step further by T. B. L. Webster (Introduction, 96), followed by Bowra (40): the unbending will of Aias is softened by Tekmessa; he drops the idea of suicide and only at the seashore does he return to his former rigidity. W. B. Stanford in his edition (282) also spoke of a "conversion." To these we contrast the interpretation presented above, which agrees in the main with that of K. von Fritz[14] and with Reinhardt's in his book on Sophokles: the speech is a dramatically necessary tool for deception, in which the truth is partially revealed through tragic irony; at the same time, however, it contains Aias's recognition of the true nature of things, not indeed in the sense that he might now yield, but as the confirmation of his resolve to leave this world (unable as he is to come to terms with it) and go to his death.

The *Aias* poses some difficult scenic problems. In the prologue Athena cannot be seen by Odysseus (15). J. C. Kamerbeek in his commentary on this line mentions that Hippolytos probably does not see Artemis in the death scene. It is then difficult to assume with Reinhardt that the goddess was visible to Aias, though she may have been to the audience; the scholiast also pictured the scene in this way.

Reinhardt (39. 1) calls for the use of the ekkyklema twice: for the first appearance of Aias and for his death scene. We would like to leave open the possibility that in the first case the opening of the skene door sufficed. The chorus's ἀνοίγετε (Open! 344) seems to point in this direction, with οὐ συνέρξεθ᾽ ὡς τάχος (Won't you quickly assist me? 593) as a corresponding command to the servants. But of course this also may have been the cue for the operation of the ekkyklema.

It remains totally uncertain how we are to imagine the staging of the death scene. It is difficult to assume here that a scene was rolled out, and completely impossible that the suicide was staged on the logeion.[15] With Flickinger (244) and Kenner (110) we would rather imagine the inclusion of a paraskenion. Shrubbery, indicated by νάπος (892), might have blocked the audience's view of the corpse and given the actor an opportunity to leave unseen in order to assume the role of Teukros.

The chronology of Sophocles' plays can generally be considered valid to the extent that an earlier group: Aias, Ant., Trach., and a later group: El., Phil., Oid. Kol., frame the Oid. Tyr. as midpoint.[16] The dating of the Trachiniai is the most problematical. In E. R. Schwinge's important study there is a table with an astonishing survey of the various dates proposed.[17] For a long time a late date was accepted, based on Wilamowitz's comparison of the sleeping scenes in the Trachiniai and the Herakles of Euripides.[18] The assumption of such a connection has long been recognized to be erroneous.[19] Nor has the supposed dependence of the play on Euripidean dramatic technique been accepted as an aid in the dating. This was convincingly proved by Kirkwood among others.[20] The decisive change in the dating problem first came when Webster (Intr., 4. 172) established that the diptych composition placed the play among the earlier tragedies, and then by Reinhardt's penetrating structural analysis, which he used to illuminate the development of Sophokles' dramatic art and thus confirmed the closeness of the Trach. to the Aias and Ant. Linguistic examination by F. R. Earp, The Style of Soph., Cambridge 1944, points in the same direction.[21]

The question of the play's chronological relationship to the Antigone remains as difficult as ever. Reinhardt has shown how close the Trachiniai stands to the Aias, both in structure and individual elements, and supported a date prior to the Antigone. He was followed primarily by E. R. Schwinge in the study cited above.[22] The question would be decided if those scholars were correct who believe that Bakchylides XVI is dependent on Sophokles, since the choral lyricist died not long after 450. F. Stoessl accepted this sequence.[23] Schwinge tried to support this view in his book (128) but in doing so was forced to abandon Bruno Snell's earlier theory[24] based on vase-paintings. But in fact the typically choral lyric style of narration in the short fragment does not permit us to conclude that the poem of Bakchylides was dependent on Sophokles.[25]

The problem cannot be solved in this way. Webster (167) dated the play after the Antigone, as did Bowra (377), who argues from a succession of different stages in the poet's religious thought, and Diller,[26] who carefully considers a development in the self-awareness of the dramatis personae. Such solutions remain speculative and we would undoubtedly have to follow Reinhardt, if the question were not dependent on the relationship between the farewell of Deianeira to her marriage bed and house and the corresponding scene in the *Alkestis*. Both cases involve the report of a maid-servant. Despite Reinhardt's and Kamerbeek's objections, it is probably best to assume, as numerous scholars have done, that dependency does exist here, and that Sophokles had the *Alkestis* of Euripides in mind, which gives us 438 as a terminus post for the *Trachiniai*.[27] This view was adopted by Weber in his commentary on the *Alkestis*, as well as by others;[28] it was supported by Johanna Heinz,[29] joined by Pohlenz (2. 86) and Schadewaldt,[30] who correctly allots special significance to the concern of the dying woman for her servants. I myself considered probable in earlier editions that Euripides' play preceded the *Trach.*[31] E. R. Schwinge, who speaks of "obviously parallel scenes" (op. cit., 44) believes Euripides was influenced by Sophokles' play and makes 438 the terminus ante for the *Trach*. He was followed by Chromik (24. 17). For Schwinge, the farewell scene did not fit so well into the structure of the *Alkestis* because he supports the radical depreciation of Admetos (this view will be opposed in our discussion of the play), which would render the sacrifice of Alkestis meaningless, and thus the whole scene at the marriage bed as well. In fact Alkestis has a home and a close circle of friends, while we hear from Deianeira herself (39) that since Herakles murdered Iphitos, she and her family have been living ξένῳ παρ' ἀνδρί (with a strange man). It is obvious that the conception of a home with servants and furniture as familiar surroundings fits the *Alkestis* better than Sophokles' play.

We were obliged to deal with this difficult set of problems in order to justify our arrangement of the plays, but we do not wish to create a false sense of certainty. We must add to our discussion J. C. Kamerbeek's resignation (in the introduction to his commentary, 29); he believes that it is impossible to go beyond dating the play near the *Aias* and *Antigone*, and gives this final statement on the question: "*Trachiniai* is roughly contemporary with *Antigone*—that is the best we can say."[32]

For few tragedies can we say as little about the origin of the subject matter as for the *Antigone*.[33] The *Thebais* is excluded as a source, because in it the body of Polyneikes was cremated. Contrary to Wilamowitz, G. Müller (op. cit., 22) has shown that a pre-Sophoklean version is not attested by Apollodoros (3. 78). Nonetheless, it seems more probable to assume the existence of some similar local legend rather than pure invention on the part of the poet. This is suggested by the Theban tradition of Ἀντιγόνης σύρμα (Paus. 9. 25. 2), the place where it was thought that traces were left by Polyneikes' body as Antigone dragged it to the pyre of Eteokles.

For the dating of the play we must start with the statement in the hypothesis that the Athenians elected Sophokles general for the Samian War (begun in 441) because of the success of *Antigone*. There may have been a connection or perhaps a post hoc later became a propter hoc. Even after G. Müller's careful examination of all factors involved (op. cit., 24), 442 remains the most probable date. The objection of Wilamowitz that in 443/442 Sophokles would have been too busy in his capacity as Hellenotamias at the time of a new tribute assessment to be able to complete a play for the Dionysia of 442, is unconvincing.

The hypothesis designates this play as the playwright's thirty-second. Similar numerical references are given for Euripides' *Alk.*, the *Birds*, the *Dionysalexandros* of Kratinos, and the *Imbrioi* of Menander. They are generally taken today as the remnants of a chronological enumeration.[34]

The play begins with a highly emotional dialogue between two magnificently drawn characters. In the first dim light before dawn Antigone leads her sister into a private conversation before the palace.[35] Antigone's first words to Ismene are an expression of the close sisterly bond between them, but the dialogue she begins in this way ends with the irreparable estrangement of the girls. Even at the start Antigone, well informed and feverishly excited, is contrasted to an Ismene who displays the calm of ignorance in her short speech, composed in ring-composition (11–17). Antigone's explanation strongly stresses the inhuman aspect of Kreon's decree—not only can there be no burial for Polyneikes, but his body must lie as carrion for scavenging birds. She ends with the summons to action. Ismene's incomprehension ignites a short stichomythy in which Antigone demands that her sister help with the burial. Ismene is taken aback; for her, Kreon's prohibition is spoken with the authority of the state (44, 79) and may not be overridden. She defends her refusal: Must all the disasters of the house be followed by our destruction as well? We are only women, not made to fight against men. In these few verses Sophokles has sketched a complete character. Ismene assents and accepts compromise readily; she would obey orders even more painful than this (64). But within her weak soul there is yet a consciousness of right. She will pray to the chthonic deities, against whose realm Kreon blasphemes, to forgive her for yielding to necessity. Antigone's reply likewise reveals her character; defiance, a basic element of her nature, gives its distinctive tone to her angry outburst: Even if you wanted, I wouldn't take your help now! This is the same Antigone who, in the following stichomythy (78–92; beginning with distichs) rejects with extreme harshness Ismene's humble promise to remain silent: Go! Scream it out! The prologue, however, also presents, in the epigrammatic ὅσια πανουργήσασα (holy blasphemy), the conflict of two positions which continues in the play until both are destroyed; further, it reveals Antigone's readiness to die—she realizes that she is bound to the world of the dead. Fully determined, she leaves the scene; Ismene, after declaring her love for her sister, returns to the house.

The parodos of the chorus of Theban elders (100–162) begins immediately with the first system of two strophic pairs, each of whose elements are followed by anapests. Their linguistic connection with the strophes is quite close; with their marching rhythm, they probably mark changes in the position of the chorus. The parodos opens like a trumpet blast with a cry of jubilation in high-pitched vowels, and maintains this tone of victory throughout the choral lyric account of the defeat of the Seven.

The prologue presented Antigone; now the first epeisodion (163–331) introduces her antagonist Kreon, who proclaims his edict against burial at the end of a long speech. For his previous lines, the phrase "throne speech" has been appropriately used. From recent events the new ruler develops the principle of his regime: the state is all, his speech and action will be ever in its service. From this attitude also arises his verdict. Here Kreon speaks neither as a hypocrite nor as an egotistical tyrant, but as a ruler for whom the omnipotence of the state is inviolable. When he says of the polis (189): ἥδ' ἐστὶν ἡ σῴζουσα (it is she who saves us), this signifies a secularization that no longer recognizes any absolute value higher than the state.[36] A short conversation with the chorus leader follows: the elders yield to the king's command, since only a fool would endanger his life by transgression. We heard something similar from Ismene. But these men stoop before a ruler whose gaze terrifies common men too much for them to say what they think, as Haimon will say (690).

Kreon cannot feel completely secure in the matter, for he knows many are seeking their own advantage. This remark prepares us for his uncertainty in the next scene; at the same time, there begins an atmosphere of mistrust that culminates in the Teiresias episode.

It is an ironic indication of the fragility of Kreon's position that his commandment, when he proclaims it, is already broken. The parodos covers a period that is not identical with real time. One of the guards posted by the corpse enters, an ordinary man characterized here with a degree of realism uncommon in Sophokles. He would very much like to escape in one piece from his deadly mission of reporting the burial that has since occurred. After considerable fussing, he blurts out that someone has buried the dead man. His extremely vivid description follows: how it was more a case of covering the corpse with dust than an actual burial, and how—always his speech revolves around his own safety—the bitter lot of reporting the fact fell to him. Here the scene takes a very significant turn: two choral verses, which often follow a speech with some unimportant generality, here ask Kreon whether this deed was worked by the gods (278 f.). The suggestion enrages Kreon to such an extent that he answers the chorus with a seething outburst: Would the gods honor one who marched against his homeland? And then, with an abrupt shift in thought (289): But that's just it, resentment and resistance *are* secretly at work in the city; the ones who broke the law must have been bribed (κέρδος motif). At the end of the speech he threatens the guard with severe punishment if the guilty party is not found. After a short stichomythy with Kreon, the guard, who has a ready tongue despite the threats, leaves the scene, relieved to escape and never to return.

The two strophic pairs of the first stasimon follow (332–375), an ode of incomparable magnificence whose interpretation has proved highly controversial. Difficulties arise in the very first line, with the meaning of δεινόν. These statements about man refer to the boundlessness of his ability, but testify as well to the uncanny, threatening, even terrible element bound to this monstrous, all-encompassing power. Man knows how to make use of every creature, he confronts the powers of nature, and he taught himself language; even his ability to establish community life is mentioned in this context. And yet, above all this stands something final, a constant: the laws of one's homeland and the sworn justice of the gods. How man acts with respect to these alone determines his worth or worthlessness. The ode is no "parabasis" standing outside the plot; if one must see a reference to a particular person, then this person is more likely Kreon than the unknown culprit. But its close connection to the whole lies in the fact that it defines the ethical norms that underlie the crux of the play: opposition under divine sanction to the absolute claims of the state.

The second epeisodion (376–581) is introduced by anapests of the shocked chorus leader, who sees the guard approaching with Antigone. She has been caught ἐν ἀφροσύνη (in folly). This is not an ethical judgment but rather, it characterizes an attitude expressed by the chorus in v. 220: Only a fool can wish for death.

It is a well calculated touch that Sophokles delays the direct confrontation between two opponents, each in a different world, by a conversation with the guard and his vividly realistic report.[37] This scene is skillfully interwoven with the following conflict, in that after the guard's speech, Kreon flies at Antigone (441), but when she tersely and proudly admits the deed, he turns back to the guard, ridding the stage of this prop whose presence is now only annoying. The confrontation follows; it marks the high point of the first half of the play and concludes the first stage in the ever tightening conflict with the pronouncement of the death sentence on Antigone.

The agon begins with two speeches that clearly define the positions of both contestants. Here Antigone declares the cause for which she is fighting and for which she is prepared to die: ἄγραπτα κἀσφαλῆ θεῶν νόμιμα (the unwritten and unfailing laws of the gods: 454). Next to these, the κηρύγματα (proclamations) of Kreon have no validity. Her great argument is already anticipated in the *Aias*, where (1343) Odysseus says of the burial prohibition that it offends not Aias, but the decrees of the gods. In its intermediate verses (471 f.) the chorus calls Antigone the "fierce daughter of a fierce father," but here, too (as in similar passages later on), the judgment carries no ethical emphasis. Kreon's wrath first explodes in metaphors that describe injured pride. Beyond the breaking of his law, he is incensed at Antigone's self-confident confession. Now he speaks no longer simply as ruler, but as a man whose will to dominate has been threatened. And because he feels that his opponent can be destroyed but not humbled, he demands another victim: Ismene, whose distress makes her suspect, shall die with her sister. The manner in which he speaks of Zeus ἑρκεῖος (Zeus, protector of the home) foreshadows his blasphemy in the Teiresias scene.

Once more (499–507) Antigone confesses and asserts that she acted out of sisterly love; she apostrophizes the chorus in a highly significant way: They would all approve my deed, if fear did not seal their mouths! Is Antigone mistaken here, or is this an indication that the chorus, with its evasive generalities and criticism of Antigone's folly, is acting strictly out of fear and really thinks otherwise? We would like to think so and thus see here a preparation for the completely different attitude of the chorus in the final sections of the play.

The battle of words now moves into stichomythy as its appropriate form. The gap between the opponents can no longer be widened, but only deepened, as each proclaims the justice of his side once more. Here occurs the phrase of Antigone (523) whose meaning has been constantly limited by scholars seeking to apply it only to the particular case. Of course Antigone's rejection of mutual hatred and her declaration of mutual love reveal her position regarding Polyneikes, but at the same time she expresses her very nature (ἔφυν!). In the *Aias* (1347), Odysseus had spoken of the limits that should be set to hatred. That Kreon concludes with an outburst of rage underlines the inferiority of his position.

Ismene is brought in, and a scene follows (531–581) that opens and closes with five verses by Kreon but is otherwise composed in stichomythy. From a heroic impulse such as is possible precisely for weak characters in exceptional situations, Ismene wishes to share the guilt of Antigone. But Antigone rejects her harshly (the exchange of double verses is heightened into that of single lines). Her speech is not determined by concern for her innocent sister, but by her defiant claim to the deed that belongs to her alone. A deeper level is revealed in her words, which separate her, long a member of the world of the dead, from Ismene, who should not now recant her decision to live. Then Kreon takes up the dialogue with Ismene and rejects every plea for mercy. When he speaks of evil women whom he does not want as wives for his sons, Antigone laments loudly: How your father dishonors you, dearest Haimon![38] Again, this is a foreshadowing of a scene to come. Despite protest from the chorus leader, Kreon remains firmly set in his purpose.

With a magnificent ocean simile, the second stasimon (also comprising two strophic pairs; 582–625) places the event within the history of the accursed House of the Labdakidai, a traditional motif that otherwise remains in the background of the poem. The blade of the gods below is now cutting down Antigone as well.[39] The means which they employ are λόγου τ' ἄνοια καὶ φρενῶν ἐρινύς (word's folly and fatal thoughts). This refers first to Antigone and coincides with the ἀφροσύνη (irrationality) for which the chorus reproaches her. But the second pair of strophes changes direction and renders these words ambiguous. For when the chorus now contrasts the aimless delusions of man to the inescapable power of Zeus, and says, strongly echoing Aischylean thought, that evil appears good to those whom god leads into Ate, then a specification of these general thoughts can only refer to Kreon. The change that we have described signifies the beginning of the κάτω ὁδός (descent) for his fate, and the following scene is the first stage.

Haimon enters, announced by choral anapests. His agon with his father (631–765) displays the usual form: after a short introductory dialogue, two long speeches (almost or, if we accept an admittedly doubtful conjecture of a lacuna after 690, exactly equal), followed in each case by two conciliatory verses of the chorus, then the transition to emotionally charged stichomythy. Kreon's speech is a single protrepti-kos urging obedience to one's father and the power of the state. That he sees the latter incorporated in himself is revealed by his crass self-exposure: he demands obedience in trifles, in justice, and in the opposite (667)! His scornful reference to Zeus as protector of families corresponds to his earlier phrase (487) and likewise prepares us for the Teiresias scene. Haimon's speech carefully works up to the main point. At first, he appears totally concerned with the well-being of his father, whom he, as his son, wishes to restrain from error. He is specific only at one point, when he makes the entire city a witness for Antigone's innocence, and even her glory (692; later 733). The antitheses are masterfully escalated to a complete break in the stichomythy. Here too Kreon's *l'état c'est moi* (736, 738) betrays the exaggerated claims of the state. But when the argument reaches its peak (743), there clash once more the two opposing worlds: Kreon stands for the honor of his sovereign office, while Haimon reproaches him for trampling on the honor of the gods. In their final exchange Kreon resorts to utter brutality; Haimon rushes from the scene with scarcely concealed threats of suicide.

Von Fritz has shown (op. cit.) that Haimon is here not simply driven by his love for Antigone to feign concern for his father's honor. He abruptly parries all Kreon's reproaches on this count (740, 746, 748). But if Haimon does not speak of his love (Attic classicism could hardly find words for it), if he does not bring love into his argumentation, this is not to say that he feels none. We can no longer follow von Fritz when he interprets the third stasimon (781–800), with its praise for the omnipotence of Eros, as a misunderstanding on the part of the chorus, which falsely construes Haimon's intervention on Antigone's behalf. Rather, we believe that the ode presents a motif that is as important to Haimon as is his concern for his relationship with his father, but which he cannot bring to expression on his own.

The stasimon is preceded by a short but significant scene between the chorus leader and Kreon, whose confidence is now seen to waver. It is true he disregards the warning that Haimon has left in a boundless rage but, as if as an afterthought, he pardons Ismene. The ritual pollution incurred by Antigone's entombment in a cave will be avoided by providing her with some food.

In an interweaving pattern that we have already recognized as part of Sophokles' technique, Kreon's κάτω ὁδός is at first not continued; instead the Antigone thread is brought to a conclusion with the portrayal of the path leading up to her death. In a kommos, which after its introductory anapests consists of two strophic systems (the first with anapests after strophe and antistrophe) and a short epode (806–883), Antigone comes on stage bitterly lamenting her lot. She rejects as mockery the words of consolation from the well-meaning chorus (839) and assents only to their mention of the fate of the Labdakidan house.[40] We condemn the pettiness of those who have been put off by the lamenting heroine. The full extent of her sacrifice becomes wholly visible only now, when we see the suffering of the woman who has offered it. It is precisely Antigone's knowledge of the fullness of the life she abandons that makes her into a character who transcends the rigid adherence to principle and becomes flesh and blood.

Kreon comes, demands swift action and assures himself once more of the formal cult purity involved in this sort of capital punishment. Again Antigone speaks of justice and her suffering. This scene (883–928) contains her notorious calculating rationale by which she justifies her sacrifice on the grounds that only a brother can never be replaced. Adapted from the story of Intaphernes' wife (Herod. 3. 119), this speech aroused Goethe's extreme displeasure (*Conversations with Eckermann*, March 28, 1827). If the lines are to be retained (see below), then they must be understood as an attempt, using sober, deliberate logic, to complete the process of λόγον διδόναι (giving reasons) for a deed that arose from the depths of her emotion and religious attachment.

In a short anapestic scene Antigone is led to death at Kreon's insistence. The final words of her lament (τὴν εὐσεβίαν σεβίσασα; holiness I have kept holy) significantly echo verse 872 of the chorus.

The fourth stasimon (944–987) offers mythical paradigms in its two strophic pairs. A similar fate was suffered by guilty (Lykourgos) and innocent (Danae and Kleopatra the Boread) alike.

Thus far Antigone has dominated the stage; now the Teiresias scene (988–1090) draws out the thread of Kreon's half of the plot, illuminating the king's position. After a short preliminary dialogue in which the prophet immediately asserts the full authority of his office, he reports the collapse of order brought on by Kreon's deed and the displeasure of the gods evident from the sacrifices. He ends mildly (τέχνον; 1023), counselling a change of heart. Kreon's short enraged reply shows how deeply he is caught in delusion. Ever mistrustful, he suspects bribery (κέϱδος motif) and betrayal, and resorts to utter blasphemy: Polyneikes shall not be buried, even if Zeus's eagles should bring his carrion to the throne of the god! He claims to fear no pollution: mortals are not capable of defiling the gods. The following stichomythy begins immediately with the full indignation of the prophet, to whom the king replies in equally embittered terms. Blindness such as Kreon's cannot be cured by advice; his obstinacy cannot be bent, only broken. Teiresias does just that: he warns Kreon that even now a terrible atonement for his sin stands ready and that he will pay with one of his own blood for defiling the dead.

Teiresias leaves; Kreon does not conceal his alarm from the chorus, whose leader needs few words to effect the king's decision to free Antigone and bury Polyneikes. This is the sequence he recommends; that Kreon reverses it will prove fatal. Already the speech of the chorus leader is freer than ever before, when he speaks of the κακόφϱονες (evil-minded; 1104) who are assailed by harmful spirits. However, Kreon leaves with a word indicating the depth of his new perception: It may be best after all to preserve τοὺς καθεστῶτας νόμους (the firmly established statutes). These are the laws Antigone dies for, and they are different from the πϱοκείμενοι νόμοι, the ordinances issued for the day, of which he had earlier (481) spoken so emphatically.

The fifth stasimon presents the παϱέκτασις τϱαγική (tragic lengthening) familiar to us from the *Aias*. In two strophic pairs (1115–1154) that are among Sophokles' most beautiful lyric creations, the hopeful chorus directs its exultation to Bakchos, summoning the god himself to come as savior and bringer of festive joy.

In sharpest contrast to this ode the messenger now comes on stage. His report of the terrible events is drawn out skillfully. After sixteen verses of general thoughts on human frailty, we first hear in a short stichomythy with the chorus leader the still quite indefinite τεθνᾶσιν (they are dead; 1173); then we learn little by little that Haimon is dead, killed by his own hand. Here Eurydike emerges from the palace, and only now does the messenger deliver his set report. First the corpse was buried, then the crypt was opened, and Kreon found his son by the body of Antigone, who had hanged herself.[41] Haimon rushed at his father with his sword, missed him, and killed himself αὐτῷ χολωθείς (angered at himself). In two words a complete psychic drama! To the messenger, it is clear who is responsible for all this. Kreon is guilty (1173) and the condemnation of ἀβουλία (folly; 1242) that concludes the report and anticipates the final lines of the play is aimed at the king. Mute, like Deianeira in the *Trach.*, Eurydike leaves the stage. A dialogue between chorus leader and messenger, both of whom are deeply concerned about the queen's intentions, is interrupted by the appearance of Kreon, announced by anapests of the chorus; he enters with the corpse of Haimon. The great final kommos follows (1261–1346), which combines Kreon's lament (rich in dochmiacs) with the intrusion of a new disaster: the messenger comes out of the palace and reports that Eurydike has killed herself with a sword.[42] Passionate and excited in content, the section is carefully structured in two strophic systems.[43] In the first system each strophe is interrupted by one trimeter of the chorus leader; the conclusion is formed by six (or five, depending on the MS) trimeters. Each strophe in the second system is interrupted by a five-line dialogue between Kreon and the messenger or the chorus. The constant variation of pathetic lament and spoken verse gives to the whole its restless movement. It is of decisive importance for our understanding of the play that everyone, Kreon himself, the chorus, even the dying Eurydike (through the mouth of the messenger), heaps all the blame on the one who himself laments his φρενῶν δυσφρόνων ἁμαρτήματα (errors of a foolish mind 1261). And so the chorus also proclaims in its concluding anapests: a prudent mind is the greatest of possessions. Awe of the gods permits no transgression. Terrible blows strike the haughty and teach them wisdom.

The form of the drama must be understood from its nature as a two-character play. All attempts to place the accent exclusively on one figure go astray.[44] The structure displays clear lines in the separate expositions of the two main figures and in their confrontation immediately afterward. Into this development the conduct of Ismene is woven for purposes of contrast; after her rise to heroism she is completely dropped from the play. Approximately in the middle of the piece the threads unravel to a certain degree. The Haimon scene introduces Kreon's κάτω ὁδός, after which the Antigone thread is concluded with the portrayal of the path leading up to her death. That this scene interrupts the course of Kreon's fate knits together the whole plot more tightly. In the rest of the play Kreon occupies the foreground.[45] But his collapse is both punishment for his hubris and the justification of Antigone, so that one can only speak of the tragedy's diptych character to a limited extent. But its structure is clearly to be distinguished from that of the *Oid. Tyr.* or *El.*

The interpretation of the *Antigone* was long determined by Hegel's analysis, which recognized in the play the conflict between two equally justified spheres of value.[46] The influence of this view can still be seen when scholars attempt to find fault with Antigone's conduct.[47] It may be confidently asserted that today an interpretation prevails that rejects Hegel totally and sees in the *Antigone* a personal struggle against the excessive authority of a state that recognizes no law as absolutely valid, beyond its grasp, or above its own omnipotence.[48] In this view the *Antigone* becomes world literature's classic drama of resistance. It must not be forgotten that K. O. Müller (*Gesch. d. gr. Lit.*, 3d ed., 1875, 2. 118) already interpreted the drama essentially in this way. That H. Funke (op. cit.), J. Goth in his valuable dissertation, and G. Müller in his commentary have all recently seen Antigone as the fighter who dies for the eternal laws of the gods, may strengthen our conviction. The statements of Antigone in which she herself speaks of guilt (74, 469, 923, 925) must be understood wholly as ironic assertions of the justice of her cause. Of course scholars who speak of Antigone's hubris have not developed their view out of thin air. She does display features of defiance, even of savagery, which run contrary to Attic σωφροσύνη (moderation and restraint). But the tragedy of the play is precisely that Kreon's blasphemy demands unconditional resistance of the harshest and most violent kind. How else could Antigone bear witness to the unwritten laws?[49]

Kreon errs. The various attempts to exonerate him as the loyal servant of the state have failed. To refuse a traitor burial in his homeland certainly corresponded to Greek custom. But Kreon does much more: he wishes to prevent the removal of the corpse by posting guards, thus feeding the body to birds of prey.[50] Consequently he is rejected by his son, the city, and the gods. It is nonetheless incorrect to make him into a straw villain. Kreon is also a tragic character trapped by circumstance, spreading disaster through his error and finally bringing doom down upon himself. He commits grievous impiety, not out of intentional evil, but out of a calamitous misunderstanding of the world order. When his eyes are opened, he admits this himself (1113).

We have treated Kreon and Antigone as sharply defined characters; this represents a rejection of Tycho von Wilamowitz's theory that the poet, concerned only with the effect of the individual scenes, did not make use of characterization at all. Among others, von Fritz (16. 228f.; see also G. H. Gellie, *AUMLA* 20 [1963], 241) has emphatically raised objections to this view. Knox (38) speaks of "sharply differentiated individuality." Even if this is going perhaps too far, still it is infinitely preferable to the reduction of Sophoklean characters into scenic effects. How else could these figures, drawn in broad strokes, incorruptible and above confusion, have endured for thousands of years to become great paradigms of Western man?

It is an altogether different question to what extent we may credit the chorus with individual characteristics and treat it as one of the dramatis personae.[51] For the *Antigone* especially this is connected with the further question (to be repeated in our discussion of the *Oid. Tyr.*) to what extent the chorus is capable of expressing thoughts which, though perfectly integrated into the structure of the drama, at the same time represent the opinion of the poet. The opposition to the feverish hunt for political allusions in the play, while salutary in itself, has recently led to an anathema against all who claim to see in the tragedy any contemporary references at all.[52] For Sophokles, support is claimed from the eighteenth chapter of the *Poetics*, in which Aristotle says that the poet must consider the chorus an actor and make it a part of the whole, not as in Euripides, but as in Sophokles. But the question cannot be solved by such a wholesale judgment. The integration of the chorus into the structure of the plot varies greatly in Euripides, and even if Aristotle with his richer knowledge rightly recognized Sophokles' superiority in this respect, that does not exclude the possibility that, although Sophoklean choral sections fit tightly into the play's structure, they simultaneously express the real thoughts of the poet. Although it is controversial, we claim just this for the first stasimon of the *Antigone*. We do not believe in the curious coincidence that a poet, at a time when Sophism was relativizing all tradition, could contrast immovable law to man's sinister drive for progress without connecting these two phenomena in the slightest way. Nor can we follow G. Müller, who understands the ode superficially as a condemnation of the transgressor of

Kreon's edict, but ultimately leaves open a possible reference to Kreon that the erring chorus does not realize. Here we can only briefly point out the resistance of the chorus to Kreon's decree, expressed in 211 (initial position of σοί!), 216, and quite clearly in the suggestion that upsets Kreon so much (278; πάλαι!): that the burial could be the work of the gods. Also we find it untenable that the series of great human inventions should conclude with the deed of covering Polyneikes with dust. Our opinion presented above in the analysis of the play coincides largely with that of P. Friedländer, according to whom we should not fret over finding a concrete referent for the ode (the best case might be made for Kreon) but see in it the ethical and religious background before which the entire action of the play is set.[53] This gives us the integration demanded by Aristotle, but should it then be forbidden to recognize thoughts here that aroused Sophokles in the time of a spiritual revolution of unparalleled scope? We agree fully with the evaluation of the ode by W. Schadewaldt (*Hellas und Hesperien*, 941) "And it is as if, at the end of the ode, two hands stand in space raised in aversion."

That our stasimon would be unthinkable without the influence of the theory of the origins of culture developed by Protagoras (author of *On the Original State of Being* and the "myth" preserved by Plato *Protag.* 320D), has often been noted.[54] But an important difference cannot be overlooked: in Protagoras, Zeus saves mankind, whose continued existence was not even assured by technical skill, by giving men "political virtues." In Sophokles, however, these skills (355: ἀστυνόμοι ὀργαί, city-directing impulses) are included in a list of achievements that man himself created. But above all else stands the binding law of one's homeland (the καθεστῶτες νόμοι, the firmly established statutes of v. 1113) and the justice that comes from the gods: these are the supreme authorities that ultimately decide the worth or worthlessness of a man.

Apart from the stasimon in question, the conduct of the chorus is problematical in itself.[55] But we cannot quite share the opinion represented recently by G. Müller in particular that the chorus, through development of character, shifts from its initially erroneous condemnation of Antigone to a correct judgment in the second part of the play. These Theban elders have just as little character as the sailors of Aias. But a certain change cannot be denied. To be sure, the chorus never completely sides with Kreon, but it submits so obediently that its internal resistance can only be noticed in hints (see above). And too, Antigone's harshness and contempt for death are foreign to the world of the chorus (220!) so that it cannot understand her when it is confronted with this side of her nature. However, at the point where Kreon falls, the chorus expresses without restraint what it had thought from the beginning but—Antigone says it to the chorus members' faces (509)—did not dare to speak to the king. All this is understandable in terms of human motivation, but it has a special function in the play. Only in this way does Sophokles place Antigone in that complete isolation in which his characters reveal the essence of their nature.

Why does Antigone go twice to the corpse of Polyneikes? This question has given rise to a flood of conjectures.[56] W. M. Calder III has eliminated all the misguided hypotheses that claimed Antigone forgot some part of the ritual, so that she had to return. It is pointless to search for rationalizations where the poet himself says nothing. Such speculations are also opposed by line 247. The double burial is simply dramatically necessary: the success of the burial and subsequent escape are prerequisites for the first scene with the guard, which in turn continues the exposition of Kreon, increasing the tension to a point where the confrontation of the opponents can follow with heightened intensity after Antigone is caught in her second attempt.

For verses 904–920 with Antigone's calculating logic which so offended Goethe that he called for the athetizing philologist (see above), authenticity was comfortably assumed for quite a while. Scholars as different as Reinhardt and Pohlenz considered the discussion closed. This hope proved vain, however, for recently H. Funke (op. cit., 41. 56) and G. Müller (in his commentary) have emphatically contested the authenticity of the lines, while J. Goth (op. cit., 149. 1 with bibl.) defends them just as emphatically.[57] It is difficult to decide. Authenticity is supported by the fact that Aristotle already refers to the passage (*Rhet.* 1417a 32; of course this does not exclude the possibility of an early interpolation), and further by its obvious dependency on Herodotos (3. 119). Such an imitation is paralleled by the borrowing of a motif from the dream of Mandane (Herod. 1. 108) for that of Klytaimestra (*El.* 417). On the other hand the verses are suspect because they limit Antigone's conduct with their one-sided emphasis upon the brother relationship. Another serious offense is βίᾳ πολιτῶν (against the will of the citizens; 907). Ismene could say this (79), but Antigone (509) is confident of the chorus's approval, even if it is silent, and Haimon (602, 733) strongly emphasizes the city's agreement with her.

It cannot be our purpose to increase the number of diametrically opposed but almost always apodictic judgments. We recognize the weight of the opposing arguments but still lean toward the preservation of the verses; our view is best summed up by A. Bonnard,[58] who finds in the lines "un sophisme du coeur," the rational attempt to justify an essentially emotional act.

For the *Antigone* it is even less advisable than for the other plays to establish connections with contemporary historical events.[59] Of course an entirely different question is to what extent the ethical and religious issues of the drama are determined by a tension that must have been felt in a time that saw both the completion of the Parthenon and the beginning of Sophism. Great credit is due V. Ehrenberg for showing us the historical reality behind the deceptive façade of noble simplicity and calm grandeur.[60]

The dating of the *Trachiniai* was already discussed in the context of the *Antigone*, as was its relationship to Bakchylides XVI.[61] Little is known of the legend's earlier history. The epic Οἰχαλίας ἅλωσις told of Herakles' love for Iole; a catalogue poem of Hesiod (fr. 4, 14 Merkelbach) mentions Deianeira's sending of the poisoned garment to Herakles. Dio Chrys. 60. 1 tells of the people who reproached Archilochos because of the excessive length of the speech he wrote for Deianeira when she was asking Herakles for help after the centaur had raped her. When these elements were joined into a cohesive story escapes our knowledge. That the Herakles epic of Panyassis, the close relative of Sophokles' friend Herodotos, played a role in the development is possible, but nothing more definite can be said.[62] I. Errandonea (op. cit.) has collected all the evidence indicating that Deianeira, corresponding to the etymology of her name, once knowingly murdered her husband.[63] However, it is impossible to conclude from this that such is the case in Sophokles' play, and that she deceives Lichas and the chorus. Just as unconvincing is the conclusion that Sophokles was the first to turn Deianeira into a tolerant and loving wife through a sort of Euripidean "vindication." As with the *Antigone*, we are denied any certain knowledge of the poet's contribution to the subject matter.

Of all Sophokles' plays, only this one begins with a monologue, although of course it is spoken to and heard by the servant (probably the nurse) who enters with Deianeira, the speaker. We learn something of the background: Deianeira recalls her dreadful courtship by the river monster Acheloos and her rescue by Herakles, who has been lingering in unknown lands for fifteen months since slaying Iphitos. She has found lodging with a guest-friend in Trachis and awaits news of her husband. This monologue is important not only for its presentation of the facts, but also for the poet's convincing portrayal of Deianeira through her own words. Her entire existence depends on Herakles, who saved her from outrage and whom her fearful and anxious thoughts now seek.

In this scene Sophokles demands that we abandon meticulous chronological reckoning, for what now follows must actually have already occurred long before. Nonetheless, the servant makes the excuse that although she has often seen her mistress in tears, she, as a slave, would not like to seem forward in counseling a free woman (52); only now does she dare to advise sending one of the sons, Hyllos in particular, to inquire after Herakles.[64] It corresponds to the somewhat sketchy arrangement of the prologue that Hyllos comes on stage at just this moment, and mother and son only now reveal to each other what they know in a stichomythy freely interspersed with pairs of lines. Hyllos tells of the hero's long bondage to the Lydian Omphale and how he then marched against the city of Eurytos on Euboia. This gives a cue to Deianeira: now she mentions the oracle that Herakles left with her, vaguely alluded to by τοιαύτη δέλτος (such a writing tablet) in v. 46. We learn that Euboia will be the land of destiny for Herakles, where his life will either come to an end or change to one of complete happiness. Hyllos starts off to seek his father.[65]

The following parodos (94–140) of the chorus of Trachinian maidens, whom Sophokles deliberately contrasts to Deianeira, whose bloom has faded, comprises two strophic pairs with concluding epode. The first set picks up the grief and concern of Deianeira, the second encourages her, and the epode consoles her with the thought that hope must be maintained throughout life's vicissitudes: Who ever knew Kronion to be forgetful of his children? These words have a double significance: they look forward to the news of Herakles, so joyous at first, that will soon be reported, but then, in sharp contrast, they are echoed much later in the reproachful words spoken by Hyllos (1264–1274) about the gods who are said to beget men and are called their fathers, and yet look indifferently on the most fearful human misery.

Deianeira appeals to the chorus in a rather lengthy speech (141–177) in which she first elegantly contrasts the carefree pleasure of youth to the sorrows of the mature woman, but then turns to the worries she suffers because of the oracle left behind by Herakles. In a third and final shift we learn more details about the prophecy. Herakles received it at Dodona.[66] Here again we hear of the fifteen months first mentioned by Deianeira in her introductory monologue. Herakles knows about this fateful time limit. Either he will die after this time or, if he survives it, begin an untroubled life. Now the time is up and the outcome must be decided. In fact it is brought about by the woman whose whole concern revolves around this allotted time; therein lies the tragedy of Deianeira.

The entrance of the messenger introduces a most carefully planned sequence of events. The plot leads Deianeira down a roundabout path that only intensifies the pain of her final realization when she is brought to the cruel truth. The messenger—he is designated as an old man (184) in order to assure him later of a certain superiority over Lichas—relates only good news in his conversation with Deianeira: the victory of Herakles and his approach with offerings for the gods of his homeland. The division of the report into two parts, beginning here with the still untroubled message of joy, is skillfully motivated by the delay that Lichas suffers at the hands of the curious crowd.

Deianeira's rejoicing is taken up by the chorus in a short ode (205–224) that ends in bakchic ecstasy. The misguided exclamation of joy is heard here earlier than in the two plays discussed above; it is heard at the hour when the catastrophe is imminent.

The following long epeisodion (225–496) begins with the entrance of Lichas. That Deianeira's first hasty question (232) concerns Herakles' life, a fine touch of Sophoklean characterization, shows her to be a quiet, loving woman. In a dialogue with Lichas she learns that her husband is still offering sacrifice to Zeus at Cape Kenaion on the northwest tip of Euboia. (The entire structure of the drama is determined by the retardation of the arrival of individual characters.) Then she catches sight of the captured women, and again we see her noble character: her first reaction is pity. In his report Lichas fills with content words heard in the prologue scene—service to a Lydian woman, Euboia, the city of Eurytos—but at the same time of course he conceals the essential truth from Deianeira. In his version Herakles, insulted by Eurytos, the king of Oichalia, killed the king's son Iphitos, and for this was commanded by Zeus to serve the Lydian Omphale. Afterward, however, he wreaked fearful revenge on Eurytos, destroyed his city, and abducted the women.

The two follow-up verses of the chorus leader seek to reflect the joy that they presume Deianeira to feel. With a brief word of assent she turns from the chorus toward the captured women who have aroused her deep pity. One in particular catches her eye, Iole, daughter of the king. She addresses her sympathetically, but receives no answer; we recall Kassandra's silence before Klytaimestra. Deianeira now asks Lichas about the foreigner, but he is clearly embarrassed, as is shown by his rough and evasive reply. Once more Deianeira turns to Iole; again she remains silent and Lichas begs indulgence for the girl, who can only weep for her fate. Deianeira answers with the same kindness she showed previously, and has Lichas bring the women into the house that she herself will now enter. But her path is blocked by the old messenger, who has overheard Lichas's whole story. After a brief exchange he tells what really happened, correcting Lichas's version with the painful truth: It was not because of a Lydian insult that Herakles destroyed the city, but solely for the sake of Iole, whom her father would not give him for his κρύφιον λέχος (secret bed; 360). We must accept the fact that in all this the position of the murdered Iphitos becomes very uncertain. But this is incidental to the main point of the scene: Deianeira must learn that Iole was the object of the expedition and that the woman who just entered her house is now the object of Herakles' love.

The reactions of those who hear the messenger's story differ subtly: Deianeira first breaks into a painful cry (375), but when the chorus has spoken harshly of those who do evil in secret (383 f.), she turns to them helpless, seeking advice. The chorus leader recommends that she interrogate Lichas. Up to this point Sophokles has been sparing in his use of stichomythy; now, at this crucial point, he employs it with great effectiveness. First Lichas and Deianeira confront each other; she demands that he, as her servant, tell the truth, but the conversation becomes increasingly intricate. Before too long the old messenger (410) demands his say and pins Lichas in a corner. The flow of dialogue is lively but it does not yet amount to a dialogue of three. Lichas makes excuses and finally calls the man crazy. His attempts to convince are so futile that Deianeira can no longer doubt, but Lichas himself must yet confirm her fear.

Deianeira's next speech (436–469) is not easy to interpret. The woman so painfully stricken at first now appears very much in control of herself; she speaks of the omnipotence of Eros, which excuses Herakles, as she herself has had to make allowances for him in the past. Iole has nothing to fear from her, for she won her sympathy immediately. Is this speech wholly sincere? One purpose seems clear enough: to reassure Lichas so that he will not fear for himself or the girl, and so that he will tell the whole truth. But surely we can also hear in these words a woman speaking to herself, as she struggles for control, summoning up all that might help her regain composure. The speech has the desired effect on Lichas. His relief is already evident in his address to Deianeira, ὦ φίλη δέσποινα (Oh, dear mistress; 472) compared to the rude γύναι (woman) at the beginning of this scene (393). From now on he will conceal nothing. With another word of reassurance, Deianeira accompanies him into the house to give him a gift for Herakles. It becomes clear from her words after the subsequent choral ode that she is already firmly intent on using the love charm.

After a brief mention of Kypris's power, the following choral ode (497–530: one triad) refers back to the battle between Acheloos and Herakles recalled by Deianeira in the prologue scene. Its horrible aspect is here even more strongly emphasized; we see a touching picture of Deianeira's helplessness. The allusion once more helps us to understand Deianeira in terms of her fate; at the same time it rounds off a complex of scenes before a new line begins with the sending of the fateful garment.

The second epeisodion (531–632) opens with a speech of Deianeira that is masterfully composed in its use of nuance. While Lichas is still occupied with the captives, she has slipped out of the house so that she can speak as a woman to her close friends. This sounds a bit different from her speech to Lichas. We see all the bitterness of her stricken heart; she can have no more illusions about the threat to her marriage. And yet the poet has taken pains that we not misinterpret her earlier display of self-control to Lichas as hypocrisy. Twice (543, 552) she expresses her understanding and willingness to forgive: she cannot be angry with Herakles, sick as he is with passion. Beset with the cares of an aging wife who must struggle for the love of her husband, she now unfolds her plan. She relates how the centaur Nessos once, while carrying her across the river, tried to violate her, and how, when struck by Herakles' poisoned arrow, he advised her in his dying words to preserve his blood as a potent love charm. She has now smeared this blood on a ceremonial robe that a servant has brought from the house in a presumably sealed box (χιτῶνα τόνδε cannot, after v. 606, refer to the chiton openly displayed). As she concludes, uncertainty creeps into her speech: If her plan is foolish, she will drop it immediately. This uncertainty is not dispelled in the short dialogue (588–597) with the chorus leader, who encourages Deianeira and can only advise her to remove all doubt by trying the charm. Deianeira acts without evil intent, but her last words to the chorus show that a considerable amount of moral uncertainty is involved in her decision: Quiet! For whoever acts shamefully in the dark does not succumb to shame.

The following scene presents the departure of Lichas with the fateful gift. Deianeira does not mention a word of her concern, but tells him instead that he should report the friendly reception of the foreign woman (we can judge his relief at hearing this from his answer in v. 629), but at the close of the scene the tenderness of her heart is revealed once more: Speak not of my longing, for I know not yet if I am loved in return.

In the first of its two strophic pairs, the second stasimon (633–662) sings of the rejoicing throughout the land and, in the second, expresses the wish that Herakles return quickly and that the love charm work. The tone of the ode provides contrast with the now imminent disaster. Somewhat unexpectedly we hear from the chorus that they have been hoping for the hero's return for twelve months. This cannot be readily reconciled with the fifteen month absence mentioned by Deianeira in vv. 44 and 164, with reference to Herakles' testament. But in v. 824 we learn of an oracle, which can only be the one delivered at Dodona, and also mentioned by Herakles in vv. 1164 ff.: according to this prophecy he will find release from troubles after twelve years have passed. It is conceivable that Herakles, when he set out, knew that this period of time would be up after fifteen months. He does expressly refer to Dodona at that point (171). A more exact reckoning is impossible; the twelve months of this choral passage (648) most likely refer to the last of the twelve years in the other prophecy.

In the third epeisodion (663–820), an eerie rumble of thunder first announces the oncoming blast of the lightning bolt. In a brief exchange with the chorus leader Deianeira speaks of her fearful anxiety and then reports in her speech how the tufts of wool that she used to smear the chiton decomposed in the sunlight and bubbled up in a sinister foam. She followed Nessos's instructions scrupulously, but now, realizing his intention too late, she is confronted with the enormity of her deed. She immediately decides to die, for a life in public disgrace would be unbearable. We recall her corresponding line (596) that shame cannot come from shamefulness that hides in darkness. In a short dialogue the chorus leader makes a futile attempt at consolation, and now it is she who advises silence, unless Deianeira should wish to speak with Hyllos, who has just returned. The scene is constructed as a triptych. Short dialogues frame the long detailed report of Deianeira.

This structure is repeated in the following scene, with a variation to be discussed later. After a brief dialogue between Deianeira and her son, in which the catastrophe is revealed almost immediately, Hyllos begins his dramatic report—the first messenger-speech of the play—which begins calmly but then, in a brilliant crescendo, recreates for us the torments and raging of a Herakles wracked with pain by the poison devouring him. His wild spasms reach their peak with the crushing of Lichas. Now Herakles, fallen victim to death, must be brought home. Hyllos concludes with a curse on his mother. Here again a short dialogue follows, but the principals are Hyllos and the chorus leader; Deianeira, mute, has left the stage, and neither the demand of the chorus that she defend herself nor the maledictions of her son can coax a word from her. In the *Antigone*, we recall, Eurydike too left the scene in total silence.

Sophokles plays with time relationships quite as freely as Aischylos. Lichas took his leave before the short second stasimon; now Hyllos appears, and look at all that has happened in the meantime! Yet Deianeira's fright at the crumbling of the woolen tufts is directly related chronologically to the section before the stasimon. Here we must not even attempt to reconcile the discrepancy.

The third stasimon (821–862) again comprises two strophic pairs that reflect on what has just transpired. The first speaks of the fulfillment of the oracle that promised a crucial decision for Herakles after twelve years. The outcome is now decided: he must die. The second strophe is devoted to Deianeira's grief, the antistrophe to the suffering of the hero brought about ultimately by Aphrodite.

Twice in this play important off-stage actions are brought on stage by means of a report. Thus it is in the fourth epeisodion with the death of Deianeira. An excited prelude precedes the report of the nurse. Two speakers from the chorus have heard wailing within the house and announce the entrance of the nurse.[67] The conversation containing her report of Deianeira's death is quickly broken into antilabai and then continues in a kommos. In three trimeters the dialogue calms down, giving way to the long speech of the nurse (899–946). We have already discussed the relationship of this report to the parallel speech in the *Alkestis*. Problems have arisen with the passage in which the nurse relates how Deianeira threw covers onto Herakles' bed, then jumped up on it and killed herself. We can hardly agree with the explanation that Deianeira, "like the good wife she is," prepared the bed for Herakles' return, then realized the futility of her act and committed suicide. The truth is much simpler. The δέμνια (bedstead; 915) of the long-absent Herakles is an empty rack, a frame with straps. We should not be surprised when a messenger-speech goes into such details.

In the final part of her narration the nurse depicts the grief of Hyllos, who recognizes the innocence of his mother and laments his precipitous anger as the cause of her death.

The fourth stasimon (947–970; two pairs of strophes) again short, is completely devoted to lamentation and announces at its end the approach of the sorrowful procession.

Herakles is brought on stage, sleeping on a bier; he is accompanied by an old man, probably the leader of the carriers, and Hyllos, whom the nurse saw earlier (901) preparing a stretcher for his father; the time interval is masked by a choral song.[68]

The first section of the exodos (971–1003) is formed by the anapests of the old man, Hyllos, and Herakles, who painfully awakens from his sleep. Total responsion is only to be assumed for the two escorts, not for Herakles himself. His attacks of pain and the helplessness of the others are presented in a lyric scene (1004–1043) that fits the wildest pathos into a complex and tightly structured framework. Two agonized outbursts of Herakles are separated by five hexameters divided between the old man and Hyllos (1018–1022). Each of these outbursts surrounds with one pair of strophes a central section that consists of a short strophe and five hexameters. Responsion exists between the middle passages of both sections, and again between the dactyls and those in the separate section with Hyllos and the old man.[69]

The horrified chorus leader marks a pause in her two verses, after which follows a long speech of Herakles; he continues the pathos of the lyric verses in his convulsive, almost gasping manner of speaking, and in the crowded tangle of clauses. His wish to wreak revenge on Deianeira is stressed repeatedly until, in the midst of the speech, he is overwhelmed in his suffering by renewed spasms of pain. Single lyric meters interrupt the trimeters, followed by bitter reflection on his own deeds and, once more at the end, the desire for revenge. Hyllos's task is now to stand up for his mother, who has been so terribly accused. Carefully probing, he begins a conversation that soon is condensed into stichomythy and ends with the revelation of Nessos's deceit. This dialogue continues without the customary caesura by verses of the chorus leader, until v. 1258. Its rhythm is determined by the alternation of Herakles' set speeches with the subsequent stichomythies, in which the dying hero commands obedience from Hyllos and crushes all his resistance in an authoritarian, even brutal manner.

The moment Herakles hears the name Nessos, Deianeira is forgotten and his fate becomes clear. Once again the oracles appear as superior forces. An older prophecy predicted death by a dead man, and the other from Dodona, already familiar to us, promised salvation at this time in his life. Now he realizes that his salvation is death. Herakles forces his son by solemn oath to fulfill his last desire. First he demands that Hyllos cremate him on Mt. Oeta. In the same stichomythy, he first brings his son painfully to compliance and then prepares him for his next wish: Hyllos must take Iole as his wife. The boy protests in horror, but must yield to the unbending will of his dying father. Now there is nothing left for Herakles but the road to his pyre. Chanting anapests, the procession leaves the stage. Herakles stifles his pain with grim determination. But in Hyllos's final lines, which are without parallel in Sophokles' extant plays, he rebels against the gods who are called the fathers and begetters of men, yet to their shame allow such things to occur. The concluding words of the chorus leader, however, immediately cancel such sentiments: terrible things have happened but there is nothing in all of this that is not of Zeus.

One can speak of the diptych structure of this play, if some important reservations are kept in mind. The Herakles section is by far the shorter of the two. Conversely it would be incorrect were we to conclude the tragedy of Deianeira with the report of her death and consider the Herakles scenes as an appendix. Here too the close internal unity of the play is beyond question. The tragic error of Herakles' loving wife does not culminate until his terrible suffering: it is present in each scream of pain. Certainly the *Trachiniai* is also a two-character play, but the dramatic weight of the two main figures is placed differently than in the *Antigone*. There the two opponents confront each other in an active struggle; here Herakles is the victim of a deed which he set into motion by acquiring Iole but which was not intentionally directed against him.

The play begins in an atmosphere of uncertainty and anxious expectation. The first step out of this situation occurs when Hyllos is sent away, removing him from a series of episodes in which he has no place. The fog is steadily lifted in scene after scene, whose agitated succession is made possible by the poet's technique: characters who really belong together are introduced at separate times. Thus the messenger arrives before Lichas, who is delayed by the crowd, and the whole truth is not revealed until the two confront one another; Herakles, however, still lingers in Euboia, where he prepares a sacrifice on Cape Kenaion. There he is met by Hyllos, who thus returns to the play. The clever disposition of chronology and locale, together with the poet's high-handed treatment of real time makes possible a compact dramatic structure that represents a clear advance over the *Aias*.

Oracles play a significant role in the play.[70] Unlike the situation in *Oid. Tyr.*, however, they do not cause any decisive action (the dispatching of Hyllos is of minor importance); rather, events run their course independently of them only to result in the confirmation of the dark and ancient prophecies. We took pains in our analysis to harmonize the various oracular messages in the play, but there remains one important discrepancy. At the point where Deianeira first speaks of the oracle (79, 166), the prediction concerns the alternatives facing Herakles after the destined time has elapsed: death or peaceful happiness. When the chorus mentions the oracle (825), they speak only of liberation from toil. That the alternatives were set at the beginning was a dramatic necessity which then makes possible the subsequent play of fear and hope, but the contradiction is in any case only apparent. Certainly, following Diller, we can see that man, construing the oracle in terms of alternatives as he does, is limited in his knowledge and misses the truth, which is with the gods alone; only after the catastrophe does he realize his error. Herakles was mistaken when he left Deianeira the message about a future decision. The gods had already made the decision long ago. But Herakles' error is quite understandable, because the oracular phrase in which τελεῖν (put an end to) governs ἀναδοχὰ πόνων (assumption of toil; 825) can actually mean either death or a peaceful life. A real contradiction occurs when the dying hero says (1171) that he understood the λύσις πόνων (release from toil) as the promise of a blissful existence. The poet employs this optimistic interpretation of an obviously ambivalent prophecy in order to provide an effective contrast to the final recognition of its true meaning. The will of the gods is unequivocal, but its proclamation through oracles is subject to human delusion and error.

For some time there was much ado about the supposedly Euripidean elements of the *Trachiniai*. It is of course the only preserved play of Sophokles that begins with a sort of prologue speech. But a thorough analysis has long been able to show that the differences from Euripidean prologues far outweigh the similarities.[71] The most telling divergence is that Euripides' prologues are insular, while Sophokles tightly integrates the speech into the dramatic structure. Moreover, as Reinhardt stated decisively, there is no comparison whatever between the love charm of Deianeira and the intrigues of Euripidean plays.[72]

Eros certainly plays a role in our drama, though a role completely different from the one found in the plays of passion by Euripides. The *Trachiniai* is not merely a psychological drama; such a designation mistakes the forces that bring about man's downfall here. These forces do not arise from the inner depths of the main characters, but rather, they confront them as fixed and unfathomable powers partly revealed through oracles. And yet no interpretation could do justice to the poet if it failed to recognize the subtle touches by which he draws the character of this woman whose love runs silent and deep. We hope we will hear no more about her lack of sense or her guilt.[73] The use of the love charm is convincingly motivated by the anxiety and concern of an aging woman who fears for the love of her husband. Moments of uncertainty only heighten the tragedy of her fate. It is precisely the expedient that is supposed to bring Herakles back to her that causes both his and her downfall. Imperfect human knowledge and blind delusion run aground on the predestined order of the gods. The *Trachiniai* is far closer to the *Oidipous Tyrannos* than to plays like the *Medeia* or the *Hippolytos*.

In view of our evaluation of Deianeira's character, we cannot agree with Reinhardt's attempt (34) to establish a parallel between her speech to Lichas (436) and Aias's deception speech.[74] As we see it, Deianeira wishes to deceive no one; the fact that she speaks to Lichas in a subtly different way from her manner when speaking to the chorus results from the discretion imposed on her by the situation and her own nature.

It is difficult to come to grips with the character of Herakles. He is hardly what we might call appealing. The savagery with which he destroys a city for the sake of Iole suggests the boundless erotic passion often attributed to him; he quite casually sends a concubine to live in his wife's house; his physical pain prompts him to shatter Lichas and goads his desire for revenge on Deianeira to the point of paroxysm. When he finally discovers the reasons for her act, he ignores her fate totally, very much in contrast to Hyllos (932, 1233). And yet we believe that Gilbert Murray has gone too far in his wish to portray this Herakles as a loathsome monster.[75] Certainly the poet, in presenting the hero's coarseness, contrasts him to Deianeira in the sharpest possible manner; but we are reminded again and again that his great deeds stand in the background, deeds which themselves transcend all bounds. Nor should we forget that this Herakles, who deals so severely with others, also turns this severity on himself in the hour of his death.

With Kamerbeek and others, we attribute to Hyllos the concluding words of the play, so crucial to the religiosity of Sophokles' drama. The MS tradition, of little relevance in such cases, wavers between Hyllos and the chorus. The reading ἀπ' οἴκων (from the house) should be retained as the direction of the chorus leader to the women of Trachis. We gratefully note that Rivier also gives the decisive words to the chorus.[76]

The *Oidipous Tyrannos* represents for us the midpoint and zenith of Sophokles' work.[77] The latest possible date, the year 425, is determined by verse 27 of the *Acharnians*. The upper limit hinges on the question of whether the pestilence depicted in the prologue reflects the plague of 429.[78] It is difficult to decide, since the plague in our play is not similar to the one described by Thukydides, but rather a withering of all life forces, of the sort the Furies of Aischylos threaten to visit on Attika. However, since the first half of the 20s (thus also recently Kamerbeek: "some years after Pericles' death") remains the most probable time of production for the play that occupies the central position among Sophokles' extant works, we cannot exclude the possibility that memories of the plague are involved.

Deubner (op. cit., 38) has, we hope, rid us for good of Oidipous as Year God and Iokaste as Mother Earth; F. Dirlmeier has convincingly demonstrated that the character of the legend is extremely ancient and probably non-Greek in origin.[79] We know so little of the epics in the Theban cycle (the *Oidipodeia* and the *Thebais*) that a more exact knowledge of this version of the tale is denied us.[80] That the story in all its essentials existed before Sophokles is shown by Pindar (*Ol.* 2. 38), who mentions the oracle given to Laios, his fatal meeting with his son, and the revenge of the Erinyes. In Aischylos's *Theban Trilogy*, Oidipous's blinding himself was either staged or reported (*Seven*, 783).

The incredibly swift and coherent action of the play is set in motion by a plague that threatens all life in and around Thebes. Apollo indicates the means to save the city, and initiates the search for the murderer of Laios, which ends with the fulfillment of ancient oracular prophecies, as the fearful truth is revealed in unbearable clarity. Just as each part of a great artwork can function on many different levels, here too Sophokles has used the opening situation to depict Oidipous as a king who has won the trust of his people and is sympathetic to all their concerns. He who earlier rescued the city from the Sphinx will help once again. Ὦ τέκνα (Oh, children) are his first words to the group of suppliants, young and old, in front of the palace. Once more (6) Oidipous uses this benevolent expression, and after he has allowed the priest to lament the general distress in a long speech, he begins again (58) ὦ παῖδες οἰκτροί (You poor children!). We must compare this to the final scene, in which the blinded Oidipous begs for exile, to appreciate the skill of the dramatist, who has us follow Oidipous's path between these two extremes with the utmost suspense and deepest horror.

Oidipous knows everything that has befallen the city but still permits the priest to unburden his heart in a long lament. He replies (59) that he knows all are

sick and yet none is sicker than himself: here is the first instance of words spoken
with the terrible ambiguity of tragic irony that reveals the discrepancy between appearance and reality.[81] Oidipous has already done what was necessary: Kreon, Iokaste's brother, has gone to Delphi to seek the god's counsel. Already Kreon is seen
approaching; when the king calls out to him as soon as he comes within earshot, we
note a characteristic example of his ever impatient eagerness to act.

Kreon's message, that the god demands the punishment of Laios's murderer, is
relayed in a dialogue with Oidipous in which questions and answers are reeled off in
rapid succession. It is instructive to consider how strict the form is that contains
such movement. After two exchanges of double verses follow four by Kreon, with the
gist of the oracle, then three exchanges of a question or statement of the king in one
verse and the answer in two. Finally there is a distichomythy of twelve verses.

We must understand that the inner laws of the drama require that Oidipous
only now learn more about Laios and his death (the prologue of *Philoktetes* is similar), and not content ourselves with the excuse that the murdered man was forgotten
because of the Sphinx.

Here (122) we first hear the version that Laios was slain by robbers; later this
will loom large as a final hope. The story was reported by the only servant to escape;
understandably, since it was hard to believe (and disgraceful as well) that one man
killed all the others. Again at v. 292 unknown travellers are mentioned.

Oidipous concludes the conversation with a speech expressing his firm resolve
to find the culprit (132–150). His opening words, in which he praises Apollo for de-
voting the proper care to the dead Laios, will stand in bitter contrast to his cry (1329):
Apollo, Apollo it was, friends, who finished me! His intellect—crystal clear, positing
connections, searching out pathways—falters with terrible irony when he imagines
he is protecting himself by punishing Laios's murder: the unknown assassin might
also make an attempt on his life!

The auxiliary chorus of suppliants leaves the scene with an appeal to Phoibos.
No anapests introduce the chorus of Theban elders as they enter the orchestra in a
parodos of three strophic pairs (151–215). The first strophe asks the meaning of the
response from Delphi, the antistrophe calls to Athena, Artemis, and Phoibos. In the
second pair we are once more presented with the grief and anxiety of the city. Later,
in the "Kreon act," this motif is held in the background (mentioned briefly in 515,
636, 665, 685 with the better tradition), then it fades out totally; the rest of the play
is concerned with Oidipous's personal fate to such an extent that the release of the
city from its distress is not mentioned at all. The third strophe contains an
ἀποπομπή (driving away) of Ares, the bringer of disaster, the antistrophe another
prayer, this to Apollo, Artemis, and Bakchos.

At the beginning of the first epeisodion (216–462) Oidipous comes out of the
palace and, in a long speech that bears the stamp of an authoritative edict, summons
the citizens to aid actively in the disclosure of the crime. If the criminal gives himself up, he will leave the land unmolested; whoever reveals a foreigner as the culprit
will be rewarded; but he who conceals information will be proscribed.[82] Oidipous's
speech is filled with unconscious self-accusation; significantly, he refers also (246) to

the question, later so important, whether the deed was done by one man or several.

This speech is followed by a dialogue with the chorus leader, who can offer no further help, and trusts that Teiresias alone, god's prophet, can clarify the matter. Oidipous has already summoned him on the advice of Kreon (an important point, as we shall see).

The confrontation with the prophet develops in a highly dynamic scene; comparison with the Teiresias scene in the *Antigone* is instructive. Both scenes conclude with the revelation of a terrible truth, but whereas the scene in the earlier play leads up to this in a linear progression, here an abrupt change occurs in the flow of the action. Here too, however, the movement proceeds within strict formal bounds. The lengthy scene is framed by speeches of Oidipous and Teiresias, each comprising sixteen verses.

In his speech, the king greets the seer with respect, for all hope of salvation is placed in him. A structure follows in which the emotion builds steadily in an only occasionally expanded or condensed distichomythy (316–344), climaxing in a central section where Oidipous and Teiresias hurl the most grievous accusations at one another. A stichomythy follows (354–379; interspersed with double verses) which, with its twenty-six verses, counterbalances the twenty-nine verses of the passage preceding the central section.

Oidipous quickly loses his temper when the prophet refuses to speak. The angry outburst (334) is part of his nature. His rage intensifies to the point that he accuses Teiresias himself of instigating the murder. This prompts the seer to reveal part of what he knows: it is Oidipous who pollutes the land. In the stichomythy he discloses the whole truth: the king is guilty of murder and incest. To place this revelation so early in the drama was a bold stroke of Sophokles' genius. Teiresias's words are so monstrous and seem to be so completely divorced from the facts, that we understand Oidipous when he refuses to consider them seriously even for a moment. His quick mind has already found the solution to the riddle: Kreon is behind all this, he put the seer up to it.

Next come set speeches by both dialogue partners (24:21), separated by four conciliatory verses of the chorus leader. Oidipous is swift in drawing conclusions and his suspicion of Kreon has already become certainty. He believes that he has seen through Teiresias. Led astray by his own cleverness, Oidipous can boast that he solved the riddle of the Sphinx when the prophet was silent. But now Teiresias, doubly insulted, flares up and proclaims to Oidipous that he will succumb to misery beyond all bounds. To these two speeches is added a short stichomythy (429–446; irregular at first) continuing the dispute. At one point (436) Teiresias mentions the parents who begot Oidipous. This strikes the king's soul like a lightning bolt; in vain he attempts to learn more, and after the prophet's final speech, in which he once again speaks of murder and incest (this time in more veiled terms), Oidipous goes into the palace without a word.

The first stasimon (463–512) seems strangely to contradict itself. The first strophic pair is wholly concerned with Oidipous's decree at the beginning of the epeisodion. The chorus imagines the criminal in endless flight from the oracles that pursue him. The second pair, on the other hand, is a somewhat perplexed reflection of the Teiresias scene. The chorus is disturbed, yet cannot believe in the guilt of a man who was never hostile to the house of Labdakos and rescued Thebes from the Sphinx. Again and again, until the final words, we are reminded that it is a man of the highest intelligence who is broken on the cliffs of divinely ordained destiny.

The second epeisodion (513–862) concentrates for the most part on the dispute between the king and Kreon, but then sets in motion a new, deeply disturbing chain of events, leading the way to catastrophe.

Kreon enters, upset about the charge against him; but the chorus merely adopts an evasive and conciliatory manner. After this retarding prelude the action resumes in a lengthy scene (532–633) developing the conflict with Oidipous. The king jumps to the attack immediately with a short, indignant speech followed by a rapid stichomythy. At its beginning (545) Oidipous characterizes himself with the statement μανθάνειν δ' ἐγὼ κακός (I am a poor learner) which, to be sure, is limited to the particular case by σοῦ (from you) following in enjambment. Trapped in his error, he concludes: You advised me to consult Teiresias. He was already in Thebes when Laios died. Did he then say I was guilty? And now suddenly I'm the killer! At the end of this stichomythy Kreon in turn introduces a line of argumentation based on probabilities, which he continues in a long set speech. Why should he, who stood secure and respected by the royal couple, want to seize greater power? He offers irrefutable proof: Go to Delphi and you will learn that I have faithfully relayed the god's message. The chorus leader praises this speech and tries to deter Oidipous with words that strike to the center of his being: The thoughts of hasty men lead them on uncertain paths! In the following short section (intensified to stichomythy and still further to antilabai; the relative lengths of passages surrounding a central rhesis are similar to those in the Teiresias scene) Oidipous picks up on the word "hasty" (ταχύς), for he must react immediately to foil the usurper. He sentences Kreon to death. The chorus is relieved to see Iokaste approaching; she must settle the quarrel.

After a short three-sided dialogue, in which Iokaste learns only generalities, pent-up emotions are released in a kommos (649–696). It is primarily composed in lyric iambics, with dochmiacs interspersed throughout. The two consecutive strophes are separated from the antistrophes by a short bit of dialogue containing Oidipous's decision. He yields to the chorus's insistence and pardons Kreon. The first antistrophe unites all three voices, but Iokaste's question about the origin of the dispute still remains unanswered. The second antistrophe concludes the kommos with the chorus's assertion of loyalty to Oidipous.

Now—we are at the center of the drama—comes the turning point, in the long dialogue between king and queen. The now familiar structure repeats itself: a long, excited dialogue, occasionally heightened to stichomythy, is followed by an uninterrupted report, then a shorter dialogue.

Iokaste asks once more, and now she learns that the prophet—obviously with Kreon's backing—has named Oidipous the killer of Laios. The word μάντις (seer) gives Iokaste the cue for a speech that is intended to calm her husband. Prophecy! Did not Delphi also predict that Laios would die at the hands of his son, when in fact he was slain by robbers at the crossroads, while his child was exposed to die in the mountains! But here another cue is given that transforms consolation into terrible anxiety: the crossroads! Hurried questions about the place and time, the appearance of Laios and his escorts force Oidipous deeper and deeper into his recollection of a violent deed that he now recounts at length. Because of an incident in Korinth he was confused about his parentage, went to Delphi, and received the awful response that he would kill his father and wed his mother. He decided thereupon to flee Korinth and in this way came to a certain crossroads, where, answering blows with blows he slew an old man with his attendants. Deeply distressed, Oidipous once again shows himself caught in error: if he is the murderer of Laios, then he has exiled himself from Thebes, but Apollo's oracle also prevents him from returning to Korinth, the home (as he thinks) of his parents. In the scene's final dialogue, the chorus leader kindles one final hope. The only man who escaped from the crossroads (and requested service as a shepherd far from the city, 758) has yet to testify. If he stands by his story that a number of robbers killed Laios, then Oidipous cannot be guilty. Iokaste must quickly summon the shepherd.

The second stasimon (863–910) begins in the first strophe with a hymn of praise for eternal laws, begotten in the aether, in which God does not age. The antistrophe depicts the man of hubris who falls swiftly into destruction. May god preserve the just struggle of the city! The second strophe calls down the chorus's curse on the blasphemer who seeks unjust profit and defiles by his touch what is holy. When such things are held in honor, why should they dance! In the antistrophe it becomes apparent that the chorus sees its world of faith sinking with the decline of the oracles' validity. May Zeus bring aid, for already the Delphic responses received by Laios are disregarded, Apollo remains without honor, and divinity is dwindling from sight.

We will discuss this much mistreated ode in our later section on interpretational problems. It is sung in response to Iokaste's skepticism about oracles, but beyond this the poem is addressed to the poet's own time.

The third epeisodion (911–1085) begins with Iokaste's sacrificial prayer to Apollo. The woman who claims to guide her life by the phrase εἰκῆ κράτιστον ζῆν (It's best to live without plans; 979) and wishes to dismiss inauspicious oracles, nonetheless retains belief in the gods.

Contrary to our expectation, the shepherd sent for by Iokaste does not now come on stage. He could only have clarified one part of the misfortune, the murder. In a masterly interweaving of motifs, Sophokles first has the messenger from Korinth arrive with the news of Polybos's death. He initiates a scene in which the drama's curve is repeated on a smaller scale: triumphant self-assurance, deep entanglement in mere appearances, until one word bursts open the gateway to the dark path of disaster. Long speeches have no place here; fast-moving dialogue dominates the action until shortly before the end of the episode.

The Korinthian first reports the news to Iokaste, who quickly sends for Oidipous. The king shares her triumph over the Delphic oracles. To be sure, his quick mind hits upon a rational explanation: perhaps Polybos died of longing for his son. But though he has just made light of the oracles with Iokaste, he still fears the part which threatens him with his mother's bed. The same man who is now rid of half his dread, still recoils from the other horrible prediction. At this point the messenger breaks in, and again consolation turns to utter disaster. Merope is not your mother at all, the Korinthian informs the king. The true story is revealed verse by verse in a flurry of questions: on Mount Kithairon the messenger once received Oidipous, a helpless infant with pierced ankles, from a shepherd of Laios's house. Immediately Oidipous asks about the man. The chorus leader suggests that it could be the same man he just summoned; Iokaste would know more about it. By this time, however, she knows the whole truth. But Iokaste is not Oidipous; she could now let the curtain raised so disastrously fall once more over everything, and live on with her knowledge. But Oidipous must search and question to the end. Iokaste will not prevent him; with a cry of woe she rushes from the scene.

Now Oidipous is alone with the chorus, and one final time the darkness of ignorance is deceptively illuminated by false conjecture. He responds to the chorus's anxious question with another hasty inference, explaining Iokaste's peculiar behavior on the grounds that she feared her husband would prove to be low born. Horribly confident, he calls himself the son of beneficent Tyche. He is determined to establish his parentage and hopes for the best. We join him in forgetting for the moment the question of Laios's murder.

Oidipous has infected the chorus with his blind confidence. The short third stasimon (1086–1109) is filled with rejoicing and rambling delusion. Kithairon will be celebrated, for there the king was begotten, most likely by some god, perhaps Pan, Apollo, or Hermes. To Oidipous the chorus now sings as proof of its devotion.

The fourth epeisodion (1110–1185) brings the sudden fall. Oidipous, who probably has remained on stage during the chorus's short ode, sees the man he sent for approaching. It is characteristic of the extraordinary compactness of the play's dramatic structure that he is announced only as the shepherd of Laios; that he was once Laios's escort at the crossroads is not mentioned. So, too, the revelation of Oidipous's parricide is completely dropped; it will coincide with the horrible discovery of incest.

Oidipous asks the shepherd about his family and occupation and permits the Korinthian to refresh the old man's memory. When in despair the old man refuses to speak further, Oidipous uses force. Utter ruin is united with the strongest confirmation of human greatness when the hurried exchange of question and answer reaches its zenith (1169 f.) The messenger: God help me! I am near to telling horror. Oidipous: And I to hearing. But hear it I must. With an appeal to the light which he sees now for the last time, he rushes into the palace.

The first strophic pair and the second strophe of the fourth stasimon (1186–1222) form a single lament for the frailty of human happiness exemplified by Oidipous. The second antistrophe however offers a touching acknowledgment of the fallen king: All-seeing Time has found and rejected you. Would I had never seen you! And yet: Because of you I (once) breathed new life and closed my eyes in peace.

The exodos begins with the appearance of a messenger who reports the horrors in the palace. Iokaste has hanged herself; Oidipous, standing over her corpse, put out his eyes with the brooches from her robe. When the chorus briefly asks about the wretched king's condition, the messenger announces his appearance. He enters accompanied by anapests of the chorus, followed by a kommos (1307–1368). The whole structure is reminiscent of *Antigone* 1257 ff. The choral sections are primarily iambic, the actor's parts dochmiac. In each of the two strophic pairs the individual strophes are followed by two trimeters of the chorus leader, expressions of sympathy, but also of utter perplexity in the face of boundless suffering. The blinded Oidipous's outburst in the kommos is followed by his speech of lamentation; this too is marked by the deepest pathos of suffering, but at the same time he justifies his deed as being a reaction to the excess of horrors he has heaped upon himself. The bitter cry to Kithairon (1391) is a terrible echo of the joyful praise with which the chorus had glorified the mountain (1089). The prophecy of Teiresias (421) has been fulfilled.

The concluding events are to a great extent determined by Kreon, who now comes on stage. His cool deliberation, which does not, however, exclude concessions of kindness, is sharply contrasted to Oidipous's fiery manner. Kreon counters the king's impetuous desire to be removed from the land with the necessity of asking Delphi first. Verses 1442 f. might be a final reference to the distress of the city. Kreon grants Oidipous's request to take leave of his two daughters—the detached manner in which he speaks of his sons foreshadows their future strife. The farewell scene is filled with such sounds of pain and of love as only Sophokles could render (similar tones are heard again in the *Elektra* and *Oidipous at Kolonos*). The scene's conclusion changes to excited trochaic tetrameter, broken by antilabai. Oidipous does not want to be separated from his children but must yield to Kreon's command.

The final words (in the same meter: better assigned to the chorus than to Oidipous) point to the fall of the riddle solver as an example of the fragility of human happiness and power.

In the first half of the play Oidipous is shown to be master of the situation. The turn comes through Iokaste, who tries to avoid trouble and comfort Oidipous, but her very attempt to calm his anxiety only increases it, leading him down the path that brings him, step by step, to ruin. In the finale, the suffering of the broken king is presented at some length to contrast with his security and power in the early part of the play. Sophokles achieved the extraordinary compactness of the drama's structure by an ingenious device. Four characters—the two shepherds who rescued the child on Kithairon, the one escort of Laios who escaped, the messenger from Korinth who reports Polybos's death—are combined into two, each with a double function. In this way the poet attained that compression of events that makes this "prototype of all tragically fatal consistency" (Staiger) a dramatic masterpiece without equal.[83]

Happily, a polemic against the assumption of Oidipous's moral guilt has today become superfluous. At one time Theodor Fontane had to point this out to classicists. When Aristotle (*Poet.* 1453a 10) names Oidipous as an example of those whose fall is brought about by a ἁμαρτία, this refers to a mistake that is not rooted in the moral sphere. The nature of such a mistake (far removed from modern day interpretations of tragic guilt), which nevertheless as an inexpiable pollution brings down destruction on man, is best described by von Fritz in the first chapter of his book.[84]

Nor does the term "tragedy of fate" do justice to the content of the play.[85] Certainly the fate destined by the gods for Oidipous is monstrous. But against this stands the tragic man whose active participation knows no bounds, who strides unfailingly toward his destiny and overcomes fate by assuming it into his will. Iokaste is added as a foil; right up to the final moment, she would have been capable of closing her eyes to the oncoming horror.

Oidipous, though caught in the depths of illusion, extracts himself from error by his own power, taking upon himself the truth and all its consequences: herein lies the cause of the puzzling pleasure in the tragic experience that Hölderlin spoke of in his famous epigram. To describe the nature and greatness of this Oidipous we can do no better than offer two passages from the *Antigone* of Jean Anouilh. Antigone: "Yes, like my father! We are the sort of people who never turn back with our questions before the end. We go so far, until there exists not even the smallest possibility of hope, not the tiniest hopeful spark to stamp out. We are the sort who leave behind with a single bound all your hope whenever we meet it, your precious hope, your dirty hope." And: "My father became beautiful only when he was finally quite certain that he had killed his father and gone to bed with his own mother, and that nothing, nothing more in the world could save him."[86]

The inherited curse portrayed by Aischylos as it moved through generations has receded completely into the background of the fate and struggle of Sophokles' Oidipous.[87]

Only very late, when Oidipous groans under the fullness of suffering, can we find any allusion to his accursed lineage (1184, 1360, 1383, 1397). But nowhere is a causal connection made between what happens to Oidipous and any guilt of his ancestors.

The second stasimon poses a difficult problem of interpretation.[88] Nonetheless, we believe that some assertions can be made with confidence. The ode is connected to the plot in that it responds to Iokaste's doubts about the Delphic oracle. To be sure, she evasively spares the god at first when she places the responsibility for the oracle given to Laios not directly on Phoibos, but on his attendants (712). But already at v. 720 we hear her say that Apollo did not fulfill his prophecy, and at v. 853 that Loxias "made a clear prediction" (διεῖπε). Thus he, too, is included in her disdain for the prophetic art (857). This disdain is continued and intensified after the ode (953); Oidipous readily agrees (964, 971). As so often in structures of two strophic pairs, the last antistrophe in this stasimon also contains a reference to the particular case. It is clear enough in the mention of the ancient oracles given to Laios.

Furthermore, it is wholly impossible to justify the skepticism that denies a connection between the first strophe, with its praise of eternal divine laws, and those unwritten principles for which Antigone dies, along with the justice sworn by the gods in the first stasimon of that play. The chorus, disturbed by Iokaste's criticism of the oracles, has a clear opportunity to profess its faith, during which we also hear the poet himself, as in the ode from the earlier play. And we believe as well that the chorus's question (895); When such actions are held in honor, why should I continue to dance?) should not be understood as a totally meaningless consideration on the part of these Theban elders of the myth (whose business after all did not include choral dancing), but rather as an alarmed protest of the Athenian citizen chorus, for whom Sophokles composed and through whom he speaks here.[89]

If this much can be clarified, a difficult question yet remains: Who is meant by the tyrant bred by hubris, whose path leads to the abyss? Here we cannot agree with the opinion often proposed (recently again in Kamerbeek's commentary) that Oidipous is meant,[90] and that the chorus fears that if he turns out to be the killer of Laios, he would set up a tyranny in the city and topple the divine laws. Our ode stands between the expressions of love and loyal dependency that the chorus offers its king (510, 689, 1086, 1220). Now we certainly do not support the thesis that the chorus must preserve an essential unity as a dramatic character, but the degree of inconsistency that would have to be ascribed to it in this case simply goes beyond all tolerable limits. We consider the search for a personal reference in our passage to be hopeless, and we refuse to indulge in political conjecture. The chorus is moved to this song by Iokaste's doubts. They seek support through belief in the absolute, and continue the thought further: If hubris invalidates the eternal laws, then it also begets the tyrant, who walks a path to destruction, for himself and for the city.

Another difficulty is presented by the chorus's statement (1089) that tomorrow's full moon will bring honors to Mount Kithairon. It has often been thought that the chorus is alluding to the Festival of Pandia that followed immediately after the Great Dionysia and was celebrated in the middle of the month Elaphebolion during the full moon. This would certainly be a leap outside the bounds of the tragedy without readily apparent meaning. The passage remains peculiar, and we can hardly find a better solution than that offered by Kamerbeek, who suggests a pannychis, like those held for Dionysos.

No less difficult is the allotment of the final trochees.[91] Athetesis is out of the question. They are simple, even shallow, but give a final impression of deep rest to the turbulent scene. The recurrence of the thought in Euripides' *Andromache* (100) does not speak against their authenticity; considering that they are, in part, repeated verbatim in the *Phoinissai* (1758), we are really obliged to ask who borrowed from whom.[92] I do, however, confess that I earlier overestimated the argument of Pohlenz (2. 92), who assigns the final lines to Oidipous on the basis of v. 8, and I now assign them, with J.C. Kamerbeek, in accordance with the MS tradition, and contrary to the scholium, to the chorus leader.

Today it is generally accepted that the *Elektra* belongs among Sophokles' later works.[93] We will postpone the question, still unsolved, of the play's relationship to Euripides' *Elektra* until our discussion of that drama. The exact date of Sophokles' play is difficult; of the most probable decade (419–410), the years 412 and 411 seem likeliest, but the uncertainty remains.[94]

As the play opens, Orestes, Pylades (who remains silent throughout the piece), and the aged pedagogue approach the palace in Mykenai. A speech by the pedagogue is followed by a longer one of Orestes. Animated dialogue is lacking; emotion is not brought into the prologue scene until Elektra begins her lament. Orestes is now entering his homeland for the first time with full consciousness, so the old servant points out to him the places that concern his destiny. In just a few verses the poet captures the atmosphere of a radiant morning, symbol of a new light for the House of the Pelopides. In his reply, together with praise for the loyal servant and a prayer to the gods (each comprising six verses), Orestes also reports the prophecy of Apollo and his own plan. The aged servant must reconnoitre the house and announce Orestes' death. Orestes will then come with Pylades and bring the urn (hidden for the moment in the bushes) as proof of his own death. As in the *Trach.*, *Phil.*, and *Oid. Kol.*, we must accept as a dramatic convention that details are now discussed that the partners would have to have worked out long ago. It is important to notice that Orestes speaks of the deed imposed upon him as an act of revenge that is fully justified and promises glory (37, 60, 70). No threatening god had to force this character, who thus differs from the Aischylean Orestes, to perform his duty.

A short scene (77–85) connects the previous action to the following. Elektra's cry of woe is heard from within the house. Orestes asks if they should stay and listen (echoing the eavesdropping scene in the *Choephoroi*) but the old man advises him to sacrifice to the dead Agamemnon, and thus take the first step toward his deed. Once again Sophokles differs from Aischylos: Here the king's grave is located off stage, which will be significant for the scenes with Chrysothemis.

Elektra enters with a recitative of lament composed in lyrically tinged anapests (86–120).[95] The character and situation of the play's central figure are here presented: The ceaseless grieving, the ever vivid recollection of her father's murder,[96] the fierce desire for revenge, the hope placed in her brother.

The parodos of the chorus of Mykenaian women[97] comprises three pairs of strophes with an epode (121–250). In each individual section, generally near the middle, the voice of the chorus yields to that of Elektra. The antagonism between them runs through the first two strophic pairs. The comfort offered by the women, the mention of Orestes, who is still alive, and of the justice of Zeus are offset by insatiable grief and a hopelessness no longer bearable. In the third strophe, however, the voices join in the lament for Agamemnon's death.[98] But immediately the voices separate again in the antistrophe and remain so until the end. As a prelude to the Chrysothemis scene the chorus warns Elektra about the excess of hate through which she antagonizes those in power. But Elektra herself knows about the excess of her ὀργά (passion; 222); it is her response to excess of suffering.

In the first epeisodion (251–471) Elektra, in a dialogue with the chorus leader, first justifies her unrestrained outbursts of pain in a speech that describes the disgrace of the house at some length: Aigisthos on Agamemnon's throne, her mother his bedmate who brazenly celebrates the day of the murder. The accusations of inhumanity against Klytaimestra are especially grave. But at the end Elektra herself expresses the fate of those Sophoklean characters who have been driven beyond all limits by the excess of the suffering and injustice they have experienced; they are granted neither σωφρονεῖν (moderation) nor εὐσεβεῖν (piety; and this they lack as a result of their own piety, which they possess to an extreme degree!); they are surrounded by an order so fearfully disjointed by evil that they themselves must do wrong. Through ring-composition words repeated from the beginning of the speech are intensified.

Elektra's speech is followed closely by a dialogue with the chorus leader, whose anxious questions bring to light the absence of Aigisthos, a fact (emphasized again at 517) of great significance later in the play. Once more we hear that Orestes remains Elektra's final hope.

The following scene with Chrysothemis (327–471) reverses a schema of composition rather common in Sophokles: two dialogue sections of equal length, each with a longer speech by Elektra, surround a stichomythy. The conversation between the two sisters displays a turbulence of argument and reaction unparalleled in the earlier plays. In her warning to her sister, whose loathing she inwardly shares, Chrysothemis characterizes herself as cautious and willing to acquiesce; she is similar to Ismene and also, to some extent, Iokaste. Thus she invites the following abusive speech of her sister. Elektra, whose hate is unmitigated, is unjust when she accuses Chrysothemis of saying only what their mother has told her. The chorus leader attempts to pacify her in banal phrases that are of no help.[99]

The next dialogue reveals something new: The king and queen intend to confine Elektra in an underground dungeon, where for all they care she can continue her lament. The agitation breaks into stichomythy: Elektra maintains her defiance against the advice and pleading of her sister; instead of reconciliation, they alienate each other even further. A turning point within the stichomythy occurs when Chrysothemis decides to abandon the fruitless argument and continue on her way. Where? Their mother, frightened by a dream, has sent her with offerings to the grave of Agamemnon. What dream is this? Chrysothemis relates how Klytaimestra saw her murdered husband return and plant his scepter in the hearth, and how a powerful young shoot, overshadowing all Mykenai, grew out of it. Here Sophokles again (cf. Antigone's notorious "rationalization speech") borrows a motif from his friend Herodotos—this time the dream of Mandane (l. 108)—which he has set in place of Klytaimestra's splendid account of her dream in the *Choephoroi*.

The conversation thus far has served only to widen the opposition between the sisters, but now Elektra's speech offers something of a compromise. She implores Chrysothemis to discard the offerings, and in their stead to present a lock of her own hair and one of Elektra's (who also dedicates her poor waistband) to their dead father, that he arise to lend mighty assistance in the revenge of his murder. Echoes are heard from the kommos of the *Choephoroi* (444, 454). The emphasis is placed squarely on Klytaimestra as the culprit. The chorus leader agrees with this plan and Chrysothemis, though frightened, gives in.

The first stasimon, one pair of strophes with an epode (472–515), again echoes the Aischylean kommos. The dream apparition has awakened the confident hope that vengeance is at hand. The epode connects the suffering of the house with the outrage of Pelops against Myrtilos, but we should not look for any causal significance in the Aischylean sense. The family curse has been pushed far into the background.

The second epeisodion, the lengthy centerpiece of the drama with its two countercurrent sections (516–822), first presents the confrontation between Elektra and Klytaimestra and begins immediately in fortissimo with the invective of the queen. Ferociously she attacks Elektra, who, in Aigisthos's absence, is on the loose again slandering her mother. But this fierce attack is also a defense. Yes, she did kill

Agamemnon, but her deed was only just retribution for the sacrifice of Iphigeneia. Her soul feels no burden. (How different is the speech of Klytaimestra in Euripides!) Sophokles lends a magnificent strength to Elektra's reply. Stifling her bitterness she replies with a cool calm that this time she did not initiate the attack and requests permission to speak openly; her politeness in this utterly tense situation is quite unsettling. When Klytaimestra grants this request, Elektra systematically destroys the lines of her mother's defense: After his unfortunate shot at the stag in the grove of the goddess, Agamemnon was placed under the inescapable yoke of necessity. The power of necessity is further stressed by the motif that, due to the calming of the winds imposed by Artemis, the army was unable either to sail for Troy or to return home. Near the middle of the speech Elektra ends the first section with an undisguised threat: If thus you demand blood for blood, see to it that your own life does not succumb to the same law as well. In a renewed onset she crushes her opponent completely: Even if you were justified in your revenge of Iphigeneia, were you then obliged to sleep with father's mortal enemy and reject his children? This section also ends with a threat, which now becomes more definite: Orestes's name is mentioned.

Elektra emerges the victor in this battle of words, but the price she must pay becomes clear in the following argument with her mother (612–633). In two verses the chorus leader speaks of Elektra's rage but doubts if she is justified. The chorus here reflects the same attitude as the Theban elders in the *Antigone*: they are quick to acquiesce before those in power. But in fact, Elektra has, though her arguments are quite correct, overstepped her limits. She knows this and says it herself. All appearances to the contrary, she feels shame at having exceeded the bounds set by morality (cf. 307). But this transgression is only her reaction to the shameless actions of her mother. The essence of this character lies in the prayer of Aischylos's Elektra (*Choe.* 140): Grant me a sounder mind than my mother's! This prayer has not quite been fulfilled in Sophokles' Elektra.

Klytaimestra ends the quarrel and prays to Apollo. In a sort of shameless intimacy she approaches the god: May the dream turn out to her advantage; for the rest, the god himself knows what she dares not express openly in front of her enemies!

The second part of this epeisodion, approximately balanced in length with the first, begins with the apparent fulfillment of Klytaimestra's hubristic request. The old pedagogue arrives. His report is surrounded by extraordinarily lively conversations among several participants. After brief questions addressed to the chorus leader, the old man turns to Klytaimestra with what he presumes to be welcome news: Orestes is dead. Elektra's painful cries are contrasted to the eagerness with which Klytaimestra demands more certain knowledge. The long report of Orestes' fatal accident at the Delphic chariot race is a marvel of direct observation, equalled only by the best efforts of Euripides. We can understand its effect on the characters in the play. Sophokles has presented Klytaimestra as a woman marked by her crime, but he has not deprived her of the last remnants of maternal instinct. When she hesitates a moment (766) between relief and pain, she is not being hypocritical. But when the messenger asks if he has come in vain, her joy breaks through as she sees the sword of Orestes' revenge broken at last. The first half of the episode ended with her moral defeat; the second presents her triumph over all possible threats. From now on she feels nothing but contempt for Elektra. Accompanied by the messenger she enters the palace.

The scene closes with a lament of Elektra in preparation for the following kommos. She begins with her indignation at Klytaimestra's heartlessness. Her every hope is extinguished; never again will she enter the palace (her continued presence on the stage is thus convincingly motivated). She wishes only to die.

In place of a stasimon, a kommos between Elektra and the chorus now follows (823–870). In a spirited exchange throughout the two strophic pairs the two voices unite in a tightly structured composition. The chorus's consolation gives way to Elektra's full expression of her suffering and finally to the women's approbation of her lament. There is a vague and curious reference to the story of Amphiaraos, which can offer Elektra no solace at all: Alkmeon avenged his father, but Orestes is dead.

The structure of the second scene with Chrysothemis (871–1057) is organized by stichomythies. An introductory distichomythy is followed by the report of Chrysothemis, then comes a central section composed for the most part in stichomythy, next Elektra's speech with her sister's reply, and finally the scene's movement ends in another rapid stichomythy.

In the first of these passages, Chrysothemis's radiant joy clashes with the grief of Elektra, who finally, with the weariness of one who has lost all hope, invites her sister to speak. Her speech is a single shout for joy: The offerings of milk, flowers, and locks of hair bespeak the arrival of their brother. The turning point comes in the central stichomythy; Chrysothemis abandons all hope when she hears of Orestes' death. Elektra, however, has formed a new plan, which she outlines in her speech: Now the sisters must help themselves; Aigisthos must fall by their hand. She employs every imaginable argument to win over her sister: their chance for marriage as well as the glory of bold action. But two verses of the chorus leader minimize the chances of persuading Chrysothemis. The word "forethought" is mentioned, giving her the cue to call Elektra's plan madness. The quarrel between the sisters heats up rapidly in the concluding stichomythy. Motifs are repeated from the *Antigone*. Antigone, hasty and unjust, dares Ismene to reveal her plan to all; in the same way Elektra suggests that her sister inform their mother of the plot.

The course of this second Chrysothemis scene is exactly the reverse of the first. Here the beginning joins the sisters in an ironic play of appearance and reality, but after the turning point they are separated by a quarrel that culminates in bitter animosity.

Concluding trimeters of the chorus leader are lacking at the end of this dispute, which is the subject of the following stasimon (1058–1097). In the first pair of strophes the chorus regrets the argument, but then immediately changes in the antistrophe to unrestrained praise for Elektra, which is further intensified in the second strophic pair. The dialectic of the main character is revealed when the same Elektra who complains (308) that it is impossible for her to εὐσεβεῖν (be pious), now receives high praise for her εὐσέβεια (piety).

After her plunge when Orestes' death is reported, Elektra's bold decision now represents the beginning of the upward path. In the fourth epeisodion (1098–1383), which includes a kommos, this path climbs swiftly to its zenith, after an impressive intervening retardation.

In the scene before the kommos, in which excited conversations surround the long speech of Elektra, Sophokles masterfully allows the tension to mount. In a calm dialogue with the chorus leader, Orestes asks for someone to report his arrival within the palace, and is directed to Elektra. He is unmoved by the emotion of his sister (whom he does not yet recognize) when she hears that the urn he has brought contains the ashes of Orestes, but he yields to her request to embrace the vessel. Now Elektra speaks to the urn that supposedly shelters the remains of her brother. Just as in the lament of Antigone the heroine's humanity is revealed, so here the poet completes Elektra's characterization for the first time in the play. The harsh, uncompromising woman possessed by the desire for vengeful justice shows more than sisterly affection here; maternal feelings are revealed. With great tenderness she thinks of the child that she cared for, and which was really hers. Her painful longing culminates in the wish to share the narrow abode of her brother, to be united with him as nothing with nothing.

Only after Elektra has spoken for a long time is she recognized by her brother. Scholars have occasionally objected to this as being rather improbable, but now we understand the scene better.[100] Elektra's miserable condition hinders a swift recognition, and besides, Orestes must move with the utmost caution. We can imagine him standing off to one side so that he understands little of what Elektra says, only pricking up his ears when the chorus leader addresses his sister. At this point a stichomythy is the only conceivable form of expression; at the decisive moment it is intensified to antilabai and finally ends in the kommos.

Sophokles has delayed the recognition with great skill. Now, however, Orestes knows who stands before him, but before he speaks the word that will gladden his sister's heart, he wishes to learn as much as he can about her fate and her life in the palace. Again he postpones the revelation by demanding that Elektra give back the urn. While Aischylos and Euripides draw out at some length the game with the recognition tokens, Sophokles is content with a fleeting reference to Agamemnon's signet ring, which convinces Elektra. The emphasis is placed entirely on evoking the psychological effect.

In the following kommos (1232–1287; one pair of strophes with epode) Elektra's rejoicing is met by Orestes' cool response, in trimeters, advising caution. A smooth transition joins the kommos to the next passage: Orestes: Enough talk! Now we must enter the house and do the deed. Elektra must not betray the plot by showing any sign of joy! In Elektra's reply two motifs testify to the power of her hatred and of her love. How could she possibly face such a mother with a joyful countenance! And she need not feign tears: they stream unceasingly down her cheeks from happiness at finding her long lost brother.

Verses 1319–1321 serve two related functions: we are reminded of Elektra's desperate decision to perform the deed alone; on the other hand we are prepared for the manner in which Sophokles has her participate in the plot's fulfillment. Someone is heard coming from the house, and immediately Elektra assumes her role, leading the guests inside. We must accept the fact that she takes no notice of Pylades, who has been at Orestes' side throughout the scene.

The old pedagogue comes out of the house and criticizes brother and sister sharply for their lack of caution. In the following stichomythy Orestes asks about the situation inside the palace, then Elektra leaps into the conversation, causing a second recognition scene with the man who once sheltered Orestes. The aged servant, however, once more calls for action. Orestes agrees (at 1373 he addresses Pylades once) and after a silent prayer to the gods at the gate, they enter the palace. Elektra, who now departs for a short time after a lengthy presence on stage, follows them after praying to the image of Apollo that protects the entrance.

The third stasimon consists of a single short pair of strophes (1384–1397). Ares and the Erinyes have entered the house. Vengeance is near; Hermes, who conceals guile in darkness, leads the way.

The finale, in which the reversal of the family's fate is consummated in the two murders, is merely 113 lines long. Steidle (93) was certainly somewhat justified in warning against the dismissal of this section as a sort of afterword. On the other hand, there is no question that the relative lengths of the various passages are of great importance for determining what the poet wished to emphasize.

The order of the two murders is the opposite of that in Aischylos and Euripides. Klytaimestra falls first; the punishment imposed on Aigisthos is our final impression.

The murder of Klytaimestra is composed as an amoibaion, with the elements of a strophic pair distributed among several characters (1398–1441).[101] As so often in Sophokles, rapid and excited action is enclosed within strict form. At the beginning of the strophe Elektra comes out of the house. This move, which enables the poet to employ her voice to accompany the deed and allows her to participate in it at the same time, is motivated by her task of ensuring that Orestes and Pylades are not surprised by the arrival of Aigisthos.[102] After a short dialogue with the chorus leader we hear the fearful cry of Klytaimestra, her call for help, her pleading, and two screams when she is struck, all accompanied by Elektra's encouragement.[103] The scene culminates in v. 1415: Strike a second time, if you have the strength!

At the beginning of the antistrophe Orestes and Pylades come out of the palace. Aigisthos is seen approaching and again Elektra steps forward, declaring her readiness to receive him. In the short dialogue of the Aigisthos scene (1442–1507), Sophokles has condensed a highly charged dramatic situation into a remarkably tight form. With pretended humility Elektra confirms Aigisthos's triumph, the death of Orestes, and, at his insistence, opens the gate. Orestes and Pylades are seen at the bier of Klytaimestra.[104] Orestes, in ambiguous terms, invites Aigisthos himself to raise the shroud from the corpse. The king recognizes his fate at once; he tries to begin a speech but is cut short by Elektra, and Orestes leads him inside the house to be killed where he murdered Agamemnon. Brief choral anapests conclude the drama.

The strictness of form expressed within the entire structure of the *Elektra* is extraordinary. Clearly separate from the rest is the bipartite central section with

Elektra's moral victory and her collapse at the report of Orestes' death. This is framed by the two Chrysothemis scenes, in which the contrasting movement within the central section is repeated. Moving further outward, we can recognize a symmetry between Elektra's grief and her speech of lament on the one side, and the anagnorisis and her rejoicing on the other. Finally, the preparation for the deed in the prologue is joined with its execution in the finale as a frame for the whole.[105]

Sophokles' *Elektra* differs from the plays of Aischylos and Euripides in that its main theme is not concerned with the problem of matricide. Pain and misery, endurance and liberation of a great soul are the poet's subjects. That Elektra rarely departs from the scene clearly establishes her as the center of the play. In this drama we see above all the extent to which the noble character, who towers over the average humans of the chorus, represents the focal point of Sophokles' compositions. The comparison with the great figures in the *Aias*, the *Antigone*, and *Oidipous Tyrannos* is evident, but we should not overlook the different, the new element in *Elektra*. The world of the gods is also unquestionably present in this play, but it has receded appreciably into the background. There is a corresponding new richness in the portrayal of the human soul, a deeper insight into the problems of human beings, who must unswervingly tread the path of righteousness in a chaotic world. In our analysis we have emphasized the moments when Elektra, in bitter self-recognition, explains how rampant injustice forces her to shatter the bonds that in an orderly world would have been given to her character by nature and morality. Noteworthy, too, is the paradox that Elektra, driven to impiety by her hatred, wins the highest praise for her εὐσέβεια. Such problems belong to all the great characters of Sophokles, yet they are rarely gathered so clearly into the consciousness of the human agent.

It is a widely held view that, in the light of the heavy emphasis placed on the central character, the question of justifying matricide has receded into the background, if not become totally irrelevant.[106] A reaction has set in against this interpretation; now some scholars allot great, though not central, significance to the question of matricide in Sophokles' play as well. A pioneer in this line is J. T. Sheppard;[107] further contributions were inspired by R. P. Winnington-Ingram (op. cit.), and H. F. Johansen (op. cit.) has thoroughly worked out the gloomier sides of the deed. In his view we are supposed to see at the play's end a confused young man and a woman whose soul has been shattered. This bears many similarities to C. P. Segal's treatment (op. cit.) of the play.

We do not believe that this interpretation forces us to reevaluate the drama as a whole. The central theme is Elektra's endurance and not the matricide. Nonetheless we should recognize that although Sophokles does not focus on the problematical nature of the deed, he is aware of it. There is only one expression of mild doubt on Orestes' part (1425): "If Apollo's prophecy was correct." We have just been discussing Elektra's awareness of the tragic nature of her action. Also noteworthy are the statements of the chorus revealing the dialectic involved in judging the deed. The chorus reacts to Klytaimestra's first cry with deep horror (1407), and when Elektra mocks her mother's pleas, they raise a lament for the city and the family (1413). But the same chorus (or one voice from it) will not find fault with the blood on the hands of the killers (1423) and in the final anapests praises the seed of Atreus that found the way to freedom after many sorrows.

When Sophokles won first place with the *Philoktetes* in 409, he was almost ninety, but there is not the slightest trace of a slackening in his skill of tight dramatic composition.[108]

In his fifty-second oration, Dio Chrysostom offers a comparison of the different treatments of the Philoktetes myth by the three great tragedians; the basic legend was already known to the epic poets.[109] More can be added, so that we can form some idea of the plays by Aischylos and Euripides. For the drama of the elder poet we now possess the fragment of a hypothesis: *P. Oxy.* 20, 2256 fr. 5 (fr. 392M). In it the name Neoptolemos appears. Stella G. Kossyphopulos has demonstrated the possibility of a restoration according to which it was actually the absence of this character that was being emphasized.[110] Aischylos's chorus, like that of Euripides, consisted of inhabitants of Lemnos, which thus was not the deserted island of Sophokles' play. Odysseus had to do his work alone in this early version. Unrecognized by Philoktetes, he won him over by concocting a story about the collapse of the Greek expedition, and deceitfully obtained the bow when Philoktetes succumbed to an attack of pain (frr. 391–404M).

Euripides produced his *Philoktetes* in 431, together with the *Medeia* (frr. 787–803N).[111] We know from Dio's oration that the prologue was spoken by Odysseus, and that he was disguised by Athena; he knew that the Trojans also sent an embassy to Philoktetes to win him for their side. Fragment 792N from Euripides' play, which repeats almost exactly fr. 397M of Aischylos, leads us to believe that the younger poet's Philoktetes also suffered an attack of pain on stage. How he finally decided to side with the Greeks cannot be determined. The fragment of a hypothesis edited by E. G. Turner (*P. Oxy.* 27, 2455 fr. 17, col. xviii) offers little help, but the final words indicate that someone forced Philoktetes to board the ship, which then, of course, brought him to Troy.

Sophokles' prologue scene (1–134) performs a number of functions. It not only provides information, but also reveals the character of two people who are assigned important roles in this unique contrast study of three different types of men; further, it allows us to share in Philoktetes' misery before he actually comes on stage.

Odysseus opens and directs the conversation. The purpose of these introductory statements is to explain to Neoptolemos how Odysseus came to abandon Philoktetes (he was commanded to do so by his superiors), but they are also tinged with the feeling: So this is the beach—after all these years. Now Neoptolemos must first scout out the cave of Philoktetes to determine if he is there. Odysseus remembers everything: the double entrance, the spring, if it still flows. Neoptolemos climbs up to the cave (we must assume some appropriate disguise of the skene wall) and reports his findings, partly in stichomythy, to Odysseus. The cave is empty; from the objects within—a rough-hewn drinking cup, some kindling, a few bloodstained rags left out to dry—a picture emerges of the suffering hero's life. A scout is dispatched for protection and now (we must accept that this has not yet taken place) Odysseus reveals the plan to his companion. Neoptolemos must deceive Philoktetes with the story that he is now returning home in anger following a dispute over the arms of his father Achilleus. In this way they will obtain the bow that alone can conquer Troy. He anticipates Neoptolemos's resistance, which ensues immediately. Odysseus is able to win him over in a lively stichomythy. This section is rich in subtle characterization. He puts himself in Neoptolemos's place: When I was your age, I too preferred action to words. He finally overcomes the youth's reluctance first by stating that it would be pointless to use force against the possessor of Herakles' bow, but principally by tempting his ambition with promises of glory. Now he can send the boy on his mission. Odysseus takes with him the scout who will be sent to Neoptolemos in the guise of a sailor, should the plan move too slowly, in order to back up his fabricated story.

Two things must be remarked about this scene. The question of whether the bow alone is necessary for the sack of Troy, or both man and bow, is not broached. The taking of the bow seems paramount (68, 78, 113), but Odysseus also speaks quite naturally as if his assignment were to capture Philoktetes (101, 107). Further, he emphatically dismisses the question (103) whether they might achieve their goal by persuasion.

Secondly, we note that the φύσις (inborn nature) of Neoptolemos appears from the very start (79, 88) as something to be taken for granted, an important factor that is simply there.

The lively dramatic movement that runs through the prologue also determines the form of the parodos. In the first strophe, the chorus of sailors (the hypothesis, strangely enough, calls them old men) asks Neoptolemos for directions; he tells them (in anapests) to look at the cave and then to stand ready. In the antistrophe the chorus asks about Philoktetes' living situation; this is followed by anapestic dialogue about the outcast's present whereabouts. The second pair of strophes laments the man's misery in smooth flowing glyconics, followed by Neoptolemos's significant reply (again in anapests); he speaks of the divine order that ordained such suffering but at the same time delays Troy's fall until its hour of destiny. Philoktetes must draw the divine bow against Ilium. The third strophic pair is composed as a dialogue: the chorus announces Philoktetes' arrival to Neoptolemos, who questions them anxiously.

The first epeisodion (219–675, with a pair of strophes placed at the crucial points of the scene) continues the line of intrigue, effectively enhanced by the emporos scene, until its near completion; success is thwarted only by an incident in the second epeisodion.

The introductory dialogue presents Neoptolemos, who, as his role demands, pretends to know nothing of Philoktetes. This slight to his reputation triggers a long lament by the outcast. Now at last he can speak to his own kind (how close the two men really are will be seen later) and describe his abandonment and sorrowful life. For him, Odysseus was not merely following orders, but was equally guilty as the Atreidai (264, 314). Only in light of this can we fully understand his boundless hatred, a motif that largely determines the events of the play.

After the chorus's noncommittal expressions of sympathy, Neoptolemos zeal-

ously sets about the performance of his task. Again a longer speech follows a preparatory dialogue, paralleling the previous section, although here the dimensions are
somewhat abbreviated. In the opening dialogue Neoptolemos speaks of his hatred for
the Atreidai and Odysseus and reports the death of Achilleus. In his speech he skillfully bases his deception on truth. Odysseus really did take him from Skyros and
promise him glory at Troy, and Odysseus also received the arms of Achilleus. But
Neoptolemos embroiders his tale with lies: he demanded his father's armor, which
was shamefully denied him, an ugly quarrel developed, and now, filled with indignation, he is returning home. He makes liberal use of Odysseus's permission to slander
him (64), but accuses the Atreidai in particular. The chorus dutifully backs up his
story: they claim that they appealed to Ge, the mother of Zeus, to witness the outrage done to Neoptolemos.

For the third time an introductory dialogue, here expanded somewhat, precedes a decisive speech; the emphasis of this complex of scenes is placed on three
such ῥήσεις. This dialogue offers something like a catalogue of heroes, since Philoktetes asks about the great figures of the Greek expedition. He must learn that the
best have died and the worst have survived. Even Thersites is still alive! This conversation increases Philoktetes' trust in Neoptolemos and binds the two more closely
than before; it also confirms the fears of the older man whose suffering has led to
serious doubt about the justice of the world order. Beyond this the dialogue acquires
a fascination of its own, through the manner in which falsehood is built up on a foundation of truth. That Diomedes is singled out for special abuse (416) is a result of his
role in the epic treatment of the Philoktetes story.[112] With the utmost cunning Neoptolemos concludes the dialogue by mentioning his imminent departure for Skyros
and adds a polite parting wish for the recovery of the invalid—as if he were formally
concluding a visit. Hereupon Philoktetes snatches at this final hope after so long; he
falls at the boy's feet and begs in his speech to be taken along. Again the chorus assists, and supports his request. Neoptolemos agrees, but only after a show of hesitation and careful consideration.

Odysseus, as he promised, tries to expedite matters by sending the spy disguised as a merchant. This emporos pretends to have chanced upon the island, but
wishes to greet Neoptolemos and inform him that the Argives have dispatched a ship
to bring him back. In skillful byplay with Neoptolemos he refuses to say more, but
then adds that Odysseus and Diomedes have set out with another ship to bring Philoktetes to Troy, by force or persuasion (594). For the captured Helenos has prophesied
that they would take Troy only if they persuaded Philoktetes (612) to lend them his
aid. Odysseus swore publicly to fetch the man; he claimed that he would succeed
with or without the agreement of Philoktetes (618). The attempt of certain scholars
to find the key to the play's meaning in the contradiction between these two lines
will be discussed in the critical section.

The emporos scene has introduced no new developments in the situation, but
it does considerably heighten the suspense. In any event it is important for the plot,
because later (769) Philoktetes will entrust Neoptolemos with his bow for fear of
being captured by his pursuers.

The following dialogue, primarily composed in a free exchange of single verses and distichs, offers first a short retardation in the plot by Neoptolemos (is his reference to an unfavorable wind, which he then drops immediately, an expression of a growing inner opposition?), then the final preparations for departure. Philoktetes must first collect a medicinal herb and search for any stray arrows. That gives Neoptolemos his cue: he asks permission to touch the miraculous bow and hold it in his hands. This is no longer part of the deception; he speaks with honest respect. The scene joins two men in kinship that springs from the nobility of their souls. It is a touching symbol of this awakening friendship that the youth supports Philoktetes as he enters his cave.

The content of the first stasimon (676–729) is arranged in a typically Sophoklean manner. The first strophic pair and the second strophe depict the suffering that Philoktetes had to endure. The second antistrophe, however, speaks of a happy release and a joyous return home. Thus the ode reflects the present situation, it is a lyrical summary of the course of the plot up to this point. The chorus has been deeply affected by the man's sorrows, but at the conclusion the fiction is maintained once more. Appearance and reality have not yet been separated.

As the short second epeisodion (730–826) begins, Neoptolemos and Philoktetes are approaching the ship when the latter is seized with a painful attack of his disease, forcing them to stop. His futile efforts to conceal his suffering so close to the goal, his breakdown from the searing pain, his screams, and finally his collapse into deep sleep are all presented with an immediacy born of keen observation, yet with no break in style. The dialogue is extraordinarily agitated: short speeches alternate with single verses, which are partly broken into antilabai; interjections are inserted. A strict stichomythy would be unthinkable here.

This scene advances the plot significantly, as Neoptolemos gains possession of the bow. However, the desperate courage with which he plunged into the intrigue against his better judgment now begins to forsake him. This is only intimated in the scene, once in the restrained prayer (ambiguous in this context) for a safe passage to the goal determined by the gods (779), but then, more insistently, in v. 806: "For some time now I have been pained, lamenting your woes." This is the first instance of πάλαι (for some time now), later to appear in a crucial passage, which places much of what has gone before under the aspect of pity and violent emotion.

The situation—Philoktetes fallen into a deep sleep, next to him Neoptolemos with the bow in his hand—is too highly charged with suspense to allow for the singing of a peaceful stasimon. Instead, the following triad (827–864, interrupted after the strophe by hexameters of Neoptolemos) is fully integrated into the dramatic flow. The strophe summons sleep to visit the sufferer, but then demands that Neoptolemos quickly take advantage of the opportunity for action. He responds, however, in solemn oracular style with four hexameters. The choice that up to now has been neither clearly defined nor even discussed—to take the bow alone or the archer with it—is now unequivocally decided by Neoptolemos: The god demands the man with his weapon; any other way would be useless. The tone of the lines is one of an immediate enlightenment, but we may ask to what extent Neoptolemos's own misgivings contribute to his decision.[113] The chorus backs off: Leave it to the gods to see what is right! From the antistrophe to the epode, their attempts at persuasion become more insistent: The opportunity is there, seize it! At this point Philoktetes awakes, putting an end to the discussion; this begins the third epeisodion (865–1080). His speech, an extravagant expression of thanks for the protectors of his sleep, is a new and now decisive burden for Neoptolemos. Philoktetes entrusts himself to him alone, will look only to him for support—now they must leave for the ship and thus reach the goal set by deception. But Neoptolemos can dissemble no longer. In a stichomythy often punctuated by double verses but also quickened by antilabai, he reveals the truth. The path taken by Neoptolemos to preserve his integrity is not depicted by the poet as a psychic process viewed step by step; instead, πάλαι becomes the key word in the scene (906b = 913b, 966); its force is retrospective and permits us to imagine the increasing internal resistance of the youth against his actions.

Philoktetes reacts in a speech filled with boundless disappointment, bitterness, and despair. Sophokles' unique ability to reveal the inner bond between the suffering man and his natural surroundings finds here its most gripping expression. Betrayed and abandoned by his fellow men, Philoktetes laments his sorrows to the inlets and cliffs, the creatures of the mountains, and the rugged crags. But his resentment is so deeply rooted that he would rather starve to death on the island than yield, despite Neoptolemos's promises of a cure and victory over Troy. His only hope is for the boy to change his mind. In his command (950) ἀλλὰ νῦν ἔτ ἐν σαυτοῦ γενοῦ (But now become yourself again!) he shows great insight into the temptation offered to Neoptolemos's nature.

The youth is deeply moved but still undecided. The chorus leader leaves the decision up to him (963). Philoktetes asks for the bow, offering, as it were, a chance to undo all that has been done: You are not evil. Go your way, give me the weapon. Neoptolemos is just about to relinquish the bow when Odysseus, who must have been observing them all this time, abruptly intervenes. Now Philoktetes confronts the man whom he hates as his archenemy. The emotional dialogue pits will against will. Odysseus tells Philoktetes that he must accompany him to Troy, repeating what the emporos had reported about him (618): if all else fails, he will use force to bring Philoktetes with him. But Odysseus speaks from the conviction that he is fulfilling a divine mission involving this man, whom he equates with the best of the warriors (997). In no way should we imagine that he is being hypocritical when, with a triple invocation of Zeus, he asserts that his mandate comes from god (989 f.). But Philoktetes threatens to throw himself from the cliff before yielding, and when Odysseus orders him to be seized, he breaks out in a torrent of abuse. He also speaks of Neoptolemos in a way that clearly shows how the allegiances have changed in the course of the play. Of the youth who accompanies Odysseus, he says (1009): His nature is too good for you—he belongs to me! He charges his enemies with more than he can know (1018): Both the Atreidai and Odysseus tried to pass to one another the responsibility for having betrayed him. Odysseus defends himself only briefly; he now tries another tack. Neoptolemos has the bow: it can be used by an archer like Teukros or even Odysseus himself. Stubborn Philoktetes can stay where he is! It is open to question (since the poet provides no clear answer) whether Odysseus intends this threat seriously or whether he is attempting one final time to break down Philoktetes' resistance by leaving with Neoptolemos. The barbed reference to others who would shoot the bow of Herakles seems to favor the second alternative.[114]

Neoptolemos leaves the stage with Odysseus. That this is difficult for him is shown by his parting words to the chorus of sailors near Philoktetes; he still hopes that the hero will change his mind.

Again the suspense of the situation does not permit a detached choral ode, so a long alternating song follows (1081–1217); it begins with two strophic pairs arranged in exact responsion such that a shorter passage of the chorus always follows a longer one by Philoktetes. Glyconics and related meters predominate. Joined to this is a large astrophic section with lively variation in voice and meter. In the two strophic pairs, the laments of Philoktetes stand without connection to the chorus's verses, in which the sailors defend their conduct and give good advice. In the astrophic section, however, the voices are tightly interwoven. Philoktetes rejects the chorus; then, tortured by a renewed attack of pain, he begs them to stay and adds to all this a final assertion of his unbending will. He is faced with annihilation: I am nothing.

In the sharpest contrast to this, the next scene brings his salvation. The chorus has tired of dealing with Philoktetes' stubbornness. The leader complains that they might have left for the ship long ago, when Odysseus and Neoptolemos approach. In a manner later quite common in comedy, Sophokles has the two appear on the scene in the middle of a spirited discussion composed as stichomythy. Odysseus follows the youth who, with incomprehensible haste, heads for the cave of Philoktetes. The Neoptolemos who now speaks has escaped from his commander's influence totally; he has become himself again. He announces that he will return the bow and stands up to the furious objections of Odysseus. In the heat of the dispute they draw their swords, but Odysseus breaks off abruptly, threatening to report the event to the army, and makes his exit. Now Neoptolemos calls Philoktetes from his cave and overcomes his bitterness by returning the bow. Once more Odysseus appears (in the parodos or among the decorative rocks of the scenery?) and commands him to stop. But now Philoktetes has his bow again. Odysseus must flee quickly, while Neoptolemos is barely able to prevent the release of a murderous arrow.

Neoptolemos has reconciled the solitary hero and won him as a friend once more. It is understandable that he now hopes, in a final assault, to persuade Philoktetes with earnest but kind arguments. He delivers a splendid λόγος προτρεπτικός (speech of persuasion), a masterpiece of eloquent rhetoric without a trace of verbosity (1314–1347); he offers friendly criticism and tempts Philoktetes with promises of glory and recovery from his wound. We must accept the fact that he knows much more about the prophecy of Helenos here than we presume after the prologue scene. No doubt Sophokles was confident that no one in the audience would object to this contradiction.[115]

We would have to deny Philoktetes our sympathy if he stubbornly rejected this appeal out of hand, as Sophokles well knew. Thus he has the hero begin his reply with an outburst of pain, showing us the man who—not unlike the Achilleus of the

Presbeia—is unable to overcome his resentment and must reject the advice of a friend. In his distress he even resorts to excuses, for so we interpret his statement that it is not the past (but never forgotten!) suffering that prevents him, but his fear of the mockery to come. Sophokles very subtly allows Neoptolemos's lies to be used once more as a weapon against himself, when Philoktetes mentions the outrage done to the boy by the Atreidai. And the poet displays an equally subtle understanding of his art by rejecting a laborious correction of the error.

The final attempt to salvage the expedition has failed, and in a brief stichomythy this minute spark of hope is completely extinguished. Again Neoptolemos is at a loss (969, 974; cf. 1393). He betrays a trace of fatigue when he threatens to break off the conversation and abandon Philoktetes to his fate. The hero needs but to give one final push: the recollection that Neoptolemos promised to bring him home, and that only keeping this promise could restore to him his untarnished honor. As he had earlier thrown aside the mask of deception, now the youth abandons every other plan: If you desire this, then let us go! In six tetrameters broken into swift exchanges, the play is completed, at least insofar as it is determined by the harsh temper of the sufferer and the generous soul of Achilleus's son. Philoktetes' arrows will defend Neoptolemos from the anger of the Greeks. The path to the ship is now the path homeward, but it represents at the same time the sacrifice of a young man, who leaves behind him all his hopes and obligations.

He need not tread this path, for Herakles appears on high and speaks to the man to whom he once gave his bow on Mount Oeta. After the anapests that accompany his appearance, he begins a speech, relatively short by the standards of the Euripidean deus ex machina, which sets before Philoktetes the example of Herakles' own life: through countless labors he was vouchsafed immortality. No different is the path that Philoktetes must take, for whom it has been ordained that he find his cure and subsequent glory at the walls of Troy. He and Neoptolemos shall fight together ὡς λέοντε συννόμω (like two lions side by side). With these words Herakles seals a friendship that has developed before our eyes amidst great pain. He closes with an exhortation to piety that never dies, thus showing himself to be a true creation of Sophokles.

Confronted with such words, Philoktetes' harsh obstinacy disappears. In anapests that are among the most beautiful verses of ancient tragedy, he bids farewell to the island of his suffering which, with its springs and pastures and thundering surf, had become a part of his life. With a short prayer to the sea nymphs, the chorus concludes the play.

The structure of the drama must be understood from its nature as a three-character play. The swift pace of the action, maintained without a moment's pause, results from the interaction of the three men whose characters are clearly drawn and sharply distinguished (the only extant tragedy without a feminine role!)—all this makes our play perhaps unique in world literature. The drama is titled *Philoktetes* and it is undoubtedly true that the fate of the suffering hero who, despite his bitter disappointments, still seeks trust, represents the focal point of the play. But the unfolding of this destiny is so closely interwoven with the actions of the two other characters that neither plays a secondary or peripheral role; this is especially true of

Neoptolemos.[116] He is stamped with the concept of φύσις (inborn nature) that recurs throughout the play.[117] Philoktetes' drama also includes a like one of Neoptolemos, who violates his nature against his better judgment and must follow a painful path to return to himself. It is this concept of the innate magnanimity of the nobleman, central to ancient aristocratic thought (in Pindar, φύσις is contrasted to all acquired knowledge) that is threatened and then it triumphs, played off against the unbending will of Philoktetes, who is stamped by his suffering.[118] It is this latter whose praise rewards Neoptolemos's victory (1310): "Now my child, you have preserved the φύσις from which you are sprung." Neoptolemos's way out of his entanglement encompasses three steps: confessing the deception, returning the bow, and deciding to leave everything behind and fulfill his promise to Philoktetes.

Scholars have gone astray in trying to make Odysseus into some sort of Mephisto. Of course he represents temptation for Neoptolemos, but his actions do not spring from any baseness within him. He is the loyal servant of the military assembly; measured against the great freedom that the two other characters enjoy, he appears limited in the manner of an executive agent. But within these limitations he displays a certain sense of mission. We were careful to emphasize vv. 989 f. To be sure, his character differs significantly from that of Neoptolemos or Philoktetes: for Odysseus, the end justifies every means. The movement of this splendid play is largely determined by Neoptolemos's painful change of allegiance, after his initial mistake, from Odysseus to the man whose nature more closely resembles his own (1009!).

In our analysis we paid special attention to the way in which the various characters speak of the prophecy regarding Philoktetes: must they take only the bow, or take the man along with it? By friendly persuasion alone or also by force? Differences crop up in testimony and attitude. While the prologue scene left the first question open but rejected the possibility of persuasion (103), there occurs later a restriction of the oracle on two points: in his prophetic words Neoptolemos rejects the theft of the bow, since the man himself must also come to Troy (839).[119] In the fabricated story of the emporos, the prophecy seems to indicate that Philoktetes must be persuaded, but in the same report the emissaries twice (594, 618) consider force as an alternative. And in his final attempt to overcome Philoktetes' animosity, Neoptolemos says (1332) that the hero will never be cured until he accompanies him to Troy of his own free will.

The different passages cannot be perfectly reconciled and these discrepancies have given rise to an interpretation founded by Bowra (261) and later made the basis for K. Alt's analysis (op. cit.); H. Erbse (op. cit., 184) also sees the problem along similar lines. In this version Sophokles was trying to show in this drama what he had shown in earlier plays: the mistaken hero who interprets a divine prophecy in his own way, tries to bend it to suit his purpose but runs aground on the will of the gods. Thus Odysseus had to fail, since he sought to obtain by trickery and force what was only to be achieved by friendly persuasion, according to the god's word. We have objected to this view elsewhere and note that recently also A. E. Hinds (op. cit.) and Steidle (169) oppose such an interpretation.[120] The attempt to make the misunderstanding of the oracle into the dominant motif of the drama fails simply through lack

of emphasis within the play, as Steidle has well pointed out. If such had been Sophokles' purpose, we would have no alternative but to object to his woefully inadequate
treatment of the antithesis on which the play supposedly depends. This motif, unjustly overestimated as it is, does have a certain validity, since Herakles really does
achieve Philoktetes' voluntary departure for Troy.

With our last statement we come to the evaluation of this deus ex machina
that differs considerably from its Euripidean counterparts.[121] Herakles is not only
closely bound to Philoktetes by mythical connections; he also speaks to the hero as
the great example of everlasting endurance that may be confident of its reward. His
appearance is truly the "solution to a human borderline situation" (Spira).

The attempt to project a certain complex of problems into Sophoklean choral
odes was also applied by G. Müller to the first stasimon of our play.[122] Here too we are
supposed to imagine the chorus caught in error, capable only of superficial judgments; it believes that the human understanding between the youth and the suffering
hero is so complete "that the wishes of both could be fulfilled simultaneously: Philoktetes could return home, Neoptolemos would win the bow and Philoktetes' aid in
conquering Troy." In our treatment of the ode above, we rejected a solution to the
problem based on stage direction (viz., that the last strophe is intended only for the
ears of Philoktetes), but we believe still less in a mistaken chorus; rather, we see in
the stasimon a picture of the situation as it exists at that moment: an expression of
pity for Philoktetes' sorrows and of the joyful hope that the intrigue (which the chorus actively supports: 391, 507) must have awakened in Philoktetes.[123]

According to the second hypothesis the last of the preserved plays, the *Oidipous at Kolonos*, was produced in 401 by Sophokles' grandson (also named Sophokles), the son of Ariston.[124] The chaos in Athens at the close of the war may have
been responsible for the delay in production.

We first encounter the local saga of Oidipous's grave in Kolonos Hippios
through the *Phoinissai* of Euripides (1703). We have no reason to assume that another
dramatic version of the story preceded Sophokles' play. It is very doubtful that the
impetus to compose the piece was provided by an unsuccessful attack of the Boio-
tians against Athens near Kolonos in 407.[125]

The prologue scene (1–116) is tripartite and already contains a decisive element
of the plot: the blind begger Oidipous, who enters accompanied by Antigone, has arrived at the grove of the Eumenides, where Apollo has promised him release from his
sufferings. Two long sections of nearly equal length surround a somewhat longer central section. The first of these passages presents a conversation between Oidipous and
Antigone that condenses into stichomythy: Oidipous asks where they are and Antigone replies that they have stopped at a holy place near Athens. The central passage
contains a dialogue between Oidipous and an inhabitant of the region who chances
upon them. In this section the structure of the prologue is repeated on a small scale:
passages of spirited conversation frame a central portion in which the stranger speaks
of the tutelary deities of the spot, Poseidon and Prometheus, and of the "bronze
threshold." Previously, however, he had already named the goddesses who rule in the
sacred grove that Oidipous has entered. Hearing of the Eumenides, the daughters of

earth and darkness, the blind man recognizes the goal of his wanderings, and, when he learns that Theseus is the king of the land, he wishes immediately to send him a message, for Oidipous's arrival will prove a boon for the king. No further details are given; the stranger leaves to inform his fellow citizens. They must decide whether the intruder may remain on the holy ground.

Now, in the third part of the prologue, Oidipous reveals the significance of these events in a prayer to the Eumenides. With them—so it was promised him by Phoibos—he will find peace, as a guardian spirit for the land that welcomes him, a curse for the enemies that persecuted him. He declares that an earthquake, thunder, or lightning will announce his end, thus foreshadowing the powerful finale of the play.

At this point we should assert, in contrast to all interpretations that attempt to separate Oidipous as a chthonic hero from the sphere of the gods, that he is led to peace by a prophecy of Apollo, and that the decisive sign is given by Zeus himself.

The parodos of the chorus of elders from Kolonos (117–253) is woven into the dramatic sequence even more tightly than in the *Philoktetes*. It consists of two strophic pairs with a lengthy epode; such broad expansion of individual sections is characteristic of this play and probably of Sophokles' late style in general. In the first strophe, the chorus comes to the grove, their voices certainly alternating in a lively manner as they search for the newcomers. While they recite the adjoining anapests, Antigone emerges from the grove with her blind father. Some sort of shrubbery would have sufficed to create the illusion. In the antistrophe the chorus demands that Oidipous abandon the sacred spot; he agrees in the following anapests (no responsion). The second pair of strophes, (interrupted by anapests of Oidipous, 188–191) a lively exchange between both actors and the chorus leader, accompanies Oidipous's movement to a boulder outside the grove, and ends with questions concerning the foreigner's name and family, thus determining the dramatic course of the epode.[126] After much hesitation (v. 210 with the horrified triple μή!) he reveals his identity to the chorus, who in horror try to send him away. Antigone's song of entreaty provides the transition to the first epeisodion (254–509). In the opening section the chorus yields and decides to wait for the king, thus repeating the attitude of the stranger in the prologue scene. In his speech, in which Oidipous appeals to pious Athens as the haven for the persecuted, there appears a new aspect of his past, already touched on by Antigone (240) and maintained throughout the play (521, 539, 547, 964, 966). The terrible deeds associated with his name were suffered rather than performed by him. In a manner completely foreign to the earlier Oidipous play, a distinction is made between subjective and objective guilt. This is not to deny the pollution incurred by Oidipous, which is especially emphasized when he refuses the thankful touch of Theseus's hand and cheek because of his stain (1132). No enlightened Theseus removes his misgivings, as is the case in the *Herakles* of Euripides.

With v. 310 Antigone introduces a shift in the action. The approach of a woman on a mule has aroused her excitement: It is Ismene! Their greeting (in highly stylized antilabai) shows us the group united in love that we will see once more before Oidipous's departure. His question about the women's brothers is answered only briefly by Ismene, but she intimates that all is not well. This reply cues Oidipous to vent his indignation at the perverse order of his world in which, as in Egypt (Sophokles knew his Herodotos), the women must bear all the burdens, while the men sit at home. Then, with a changeover soon into stichomythy, Ismene reports the quarrel between the brothers and the Delphic oracle that promised victory to those who bring Oidipous to their side. Of course he cannot return to Thebes nor be buried there, but Kreon has set out to take him back to his country's borders. This report touches on a basic theme, that of the exaltation of the fallen by the gods (394); at the same time it prepares us for the struggle to come. Of the two brothers, Polyneikes appears as the elder, who has been forcibly expelled (374, 1292), but his position is more ambivalent than in the *Phoinissai*. He cannot escape the stain he incurred when he drove out his father (1354).

Oidipous replies with a bitter curse on his sons. Here it is important to note Sophokles' efforts to unify thematically the two Oidipous dramas. Oidipous himself anticipates the possible objection that he passionately desired to be expelled from the city—as in fact was the case at the end of *Oid. Tyr.* But at that time he was consumed by the initial outburst of his terrible suffering. Later he realized that he had punished himself too severely for his sin (439: ἡμαρτημένα; the aspects change!). And so he wished to remain in Thebes, but the city banished him and neither son spoke a word on his behalf.

The chorus leader now speaks for a chorus whose attitude has softened somewhat; in a stichomythy that leads into a broader form of conversation, he advises the blind Oidipous how to appease the divinities of the grove by sacrifice. The libations for chthonic powers, the wineless mixture, must be offered to them. Oidipous charges one of his daughters with the sacred ritual (Ismene performs it) and then utters curious verses (498 f.) that seem doubly strange, because their connection with the dramatic situation, if indeed there is one, is extremely loose: "One soul, I believe, suffices to atone for thousands, if it is pure of heart." We are aware of the taboo that adheres to any form of Christian interpretation; but we still believe that this passage bespeaks Sophokles' own religious views.

In place of a stasimon (we noted a similar technique in the *Philoktetes*), a kommos with two strophic pairs now follows (510–548). The meter varies greatly and the lines are distributed with such variation between Oidipous and the chorus and the exchanges are at times limited to a single word. In this section of extreme agitation, the chorus, even haggling to satisfy its curiosity, brutally wrests from Oidipous the confession of the fearful deed he once committed without volition.

This highly charged, at times even repugnant passage can only be understood from the well calculated contrast it presents now to the Theseus act (second epeisodion: 549–667), the most splendid monument to Attic humanity.

The episode, concluded with two unimportant verses of the chorus leader, exhibits the familiar structure: speeches of the two dialogue partners surround a mostly stichic passage containing the essential information. Theseus approaches the blind beggar with kindness. He compares the fundamentally incomparable when he speaks of his own youth in foreign lands and the troubles he endured, but only so as to address Oidipous as an equal. He will not bring up the past—quite a contrast to the pulling and tearing of the chorus! Oidipous tells of his expulsion by his sons and of his significance for the outcome of the battle, as told by the oracle.[127] If Theseus will grant him protection and burial, he will ensure that the king will be victorious over Thebes, with his spirit as guardian. Theseus asks how Athens could come in conflict with that city, to which Oidipous replies with a speech on the transience and mutability of all things. Echoes of Aias's "deception speech" are unmistakable, but the speaker here is not the powerful hero who with grand resolve departs from such a world, but rather an old man, tired of living, who speaks from his knowledge of man's inevitable lot.

The last section of the epeisodion (631–667) repeats the form of the first and larger part. The stichomythy, framed by speeches, concludes with antilabai that divide the lines rather monotonously at the penthemimeral caesura.

Theseus assures Oidipous of his protection and leaves him the choice of accompanying him to Athens or remaining in the grove. Oidipous decides to stay, for he wishes to confront his enemies at this spot. Before he departs, Theseus once more reassures Oidipous of his assistance.

The following stasimon (668–719), a hymn of praise composed by Sophokles for his native Kolonos, seems almost a reflection of the open and kindly charity of the king. The first (primarily glyconic) pair of strophes beautifully unifies the image of pleasant and fertile abundance by the mention of the local divinities: Dionysos with his thiasos at the end of the first, Aphrodite with the Muses at the end of the second. The next pair of strophes (the meter is dominated by ionics) parallels the structure of the first; here the chorus praises the olive tree, protected by Athens and Zeus, as well as navigation and horsebreeding, the gifts of Poseidon.

The third epeisodion (720–1043), whose emotional content and form are determined by a kommos, depicts in the figure of one of the Theban antagonists the first assault from Thebes on Oidipous's journey to peace and exaltation. After a short preliminary dialogue in which Antigone announces his approach, Kreon begins immediately his expansive attempt at persuasion. His words drip with sympathy for Oidipous, whom he now wishes to bring home at the city's request. Not a word about the god's oracle! Oidipous's retort is just as extensive; he rips the mask from his opponent. Again Sophokles forges a link with the earlier play: When I desired banishment, you refused my request; later, when I wished to stay, you drove me out! Oidipous knows that Kreon wants only to bring him to the outskirts of the city, and he also knows why. His knowledge comes from Phoibos, who speaks for Zeus.

The two long agon speeches are followed by a heated discussion, a stichomythy with free substitution of double verses but concluding with antilabai. Here Kreon resorts to force. Ismene (who left for the sacrifice) has already been seized on his orders, and now he will lead Antigone away. The agitation expressed in the antilabai is continued in the strophe of a kommos with its predominantly dochmiac rhythms. The pace is speeded up, but the protests of the chorus have no effect. The next dialogue section (844–875) with its antilabai, single verses and longer verse groups, is, like the kommos, a formal reflection of the turbulent movement on stage. First Antigone is led away, then Kreon tries to overpower Oidipous himself. Here the antistrophe of the kommos begins; it ends with the call for aid by the helpless chorus.

With four trochaics (etymologically the "running" meter) Theseus makes his hurried entrance. The tension of the situation is now further developed in long expansive speeches. Theseus asserts the illegality of Kreon's actions, and twice, at the beginning and end of his indictment, he demands that the girls be returned.

Kreon submits with slightly ironic humility. How could he have guessed that the city of the Areopagos would welcome an incestuous parricide? Oidipous's passionate reply follows with no intervening verses. The poet uses this speech to impress upon us once more that we must now see the past in a different light. The deity ordained horror for Oidipous, but he himself is guiltless. In fact, Sophokles takes pains to mitigate our reaction to the violent deed at the crossroads, which appears more tolerable than in the earlier play. Here (993) the act has become self-defense against a murderous attack. The Kreon act is clearly delineated within the play; it now closes with a short dialogue dominated by Theseus. Kreon himself must lead him to the girls if they are still being held in the vicinity.

A stasimon follows (1044–1095) whose two strophic pairs are closely integrated into the plot. In the first three stanzas the chorus travels in imagination the possible avenues of pursuit; delight in local detail is evident. As so often, the second antistrophe assumes a separate position, with its appeal for divine assistance.

The fourth, considerably shorter epeisodion (1096–1210) concludes the action attempted by Kreon and then provides the transition to the Polyneikes act.

Theseus has brought back the girls, and again we see the loving family united in animated conversation.[128] The daughters cling to their father. Deeply moved, Oidipous offers thanks, but guiltless sinner that he is, he must refuse the touch of his benefactor. Theseus chooses not to relate how he rescued the girls. Such a report, before the magnificent messenger speech at the end, would be out of place here. A new disturbance threatens Oidipous. In a dialogue loose in form but compact in substance, the king tells of a man who sits at the alter of Poseidon and requests a conference with Oidipous. The name Argos reveals the man's identity: it is Polyneikes. Oidipous refuses the request, then Antigone intervenes with a speech. Theseus has just invoked the rights of a refugee at an altar; now we hear the Antigone who dies for the burial of this same brother in another Sophokles play. She warns her blind father, who must know the danger of passion, not to ἀντιδρᾶν (requite) evil for evil. Oidipous's fury abates, but, still mindful of Kreon's brutality, he seeks again the assurance of Theseus's protection.

A choral ode follows (1211–1248, composed as a triad), which in its two strophes sings of the bitter afflictions of old age from which only death can grant release. We hear the gloomy wisdom once offered to King Midas by Silenos: Best of all is never to be born. The epode applies this saying to Oidipous's fate.

Whoever subscribes to the recently proclaimed dogma that "no Sophoklean chorus speaks the mind of the poet" is prevented from perceiving here the voice of a man who, on the threshold of death at age ninety, created this play about the path from suffering to status as a hero—the very status Athens vouchsafed the poet after his death.

But before Oidipous treads this path, Sophokles gives us the darkest scene of the play: the confrontation with Polyneikes (1249–1446). Before Oidipous enters upon the life of a hero, blessing his friends from beneath the earth, we feel the terrible power of his curse, a power he will also possess once below.

Polyneikes stands deeply shaken by the misery in which he finds his father. Repentant, he directs his pleas to Antigone after Oidipous refuses to speak. She can only advise him to present his request, which he does in a long speech. In contrast to the rapid movement of the Kreon act, this entire scene is smothered by the gloomy silence of Oidipous. Polyneikes begins in the distant past, reports of his expulsion, inserts a catalogue of the Seven against Thebes and pleads with his father for assistance. Unlike Kreon, he does not conceal his knowledge of the oracle that makes the outcome dependent on Oidipous. Finally, at the chorus's insistence, Oidipous breaks his silence. He too speaks at great length in this scene of prolonged discourse. At the very start he rejects the plea of Polyneikes. This is the son who once drove him out of Thebes into a life as a beggar. Then he picks up a theme from his speech at the arrival of Ismene (337): his daughters do what should be the duty of his sons. The greater portion of the speech, however, is devoted to his curse on both sons who shall die at each other's hands—a fate to which older curses had already damned them.

Polyneikes laments his destiny without further addressing his enraged father. How can he face his comrades now? His request that his sisters take care of his burial links this section with the *Antigone*.

In a conversation that is emotional in form (antilabai) and content, Polyneikes takes leave of his sister. Antigone wishes to restrain him from the fateful battle, but he feels bound to the code of the warrior and knows that he goes to his death burdened by the curse. The situation bears extensive similarities to the attempt of the chorus in the *Seven* to hold Eteokles back from fratricidal combat;[129] but in the late Sophokles the dark grandeur of the Aischylean scene has given way to softer tones.

Now a sharp break in the plot occurs, as the deity intervenes. In an epirrhematic scene (1447–1499), the first three stanzas of two strophic pairs are followed by trimeters in exact responsion which are divided between Oidipous and Antigone (2–1–2). A powerful thunderclap frightens the chorus, but Oidipous realizes immediately that his hour has come. The thunder of Zeus will send him to Hades, for the god rules over his path, over his sufferings as over his exaltation. Twice more the god thunders, as if urging him to hasten. Oidipous now wishes to see Theseus at his side. However, the terrified chorus cannot understand the sign and fears that the supreme god is angry because the accursed stranger was granted refuge. In the last strophe the emotion climaxes in the urgent call for Theseus, who is summoned from his sacrifice of cattle for Poseidon; this establishes a link far back to v. 887, in which Theseus also interrupted a sacrifice for the sea god to respond to the chorus's appeal.

The short sixth epeisodion (1500–1555) contains a conversation with Theseus that develops into a longer speech of Oidipous. The king learns that Oidipous himself wishes to lead him to the place of his departure. The king must keep his knowledge of the spot strictly secret, and must hand it down only to his son; this will ensure for his land eternal protection from Thebes. Now the blind man becomes the leader, as Theseus and his daughters follow behind, Oidipous is safely guided by Hermes and the goddess below.

In the following strophic pair the chorus sings of an exaltation of the blind Oidipous, but can only imagine that he will tread the path determined for all men, the road to Hades.

What really happened is reported by the messenger in the exodos (1579–1779); his speech is not only the climax of this play, it is also one of the most stirring monuments to Greek piety ever composed.

Oidipous leads his companions to a place designated by sacred tokens, one familiar to his Athenian audience. There he directs his daughters to provide a lustral bath and suitable clothing, after which he bids them farewell.[130] For the third time we see the three bound closely together. Oidipous offers them a touching consolation: Hard was the toil you had with me—but one word sets it right: no one loved you as I did.

Then he is called by the god (whose identity is purposely left unspecified). Confronted with the brusque, familiar manner of the summons ὦ οὗτος οὗτος Οἰδίπους, τί μέλλομεν χωρεῖν; Ho, you there Oidipous! why do we delay our walk?) that establishes an intimate communion between god and man, we can only repeat Reinhardt's words: "The plural of this covenant . . . is wholly unique in the chorus of divine voices that have spoken through epochs and religions down from heaven to divinely favored mortals."

Now Oidipous entrusts his daughters to the care of Theseus and leaves with the king alone. When, after a time, the weeping girls look around them, they see only Theseus, who shields his eyes with his hand, as if he had seen something incomprehensible. The unprecedented and awe-inspiring manner in which Oidipous was taken away at the end of his suffering remains a secret to all except the king.

The messenger scene is followed by a kommos of two strophic pairs (1670–1750) between the chorus and the sisters, a single lament for the departed hero, into which is injected a note of anxiety about the future. The second pair of strophes, with an especially lively exchange of voices, presents a moment of agitation when Antigone desires, in vain, to hasten to her father's grave. Ismene, more prudent, holds her back—a reminder of the opening scene of the *Antigone*, where the accents are much sharper.

In the short anapestic finale, Theseus offers consolation, speaks of the secrecy of the place, and promises that he will fulfill the sisters' wish to go to Thebes to prevent the deaths of their brothers. Once more we see a triad of characters on stage, but now it is Theseus who stands between the girls.

Probably the most unfortunate hypothesis ever made concerning the composition of this play was Wilamowitz's conjecture (in his son Tycho's book on Sophokles; 335, 367) that the central section was a later addition designed to enhance the dramatic action. Reinhardt's protest that the play was "one of the most unified ever written" is understandable, but must be modified to some extent.

The unity of the piece is not to be found in the chorus, contrary to I. Errandonea's view (op. cit.), but appears clearly enough in the figure of Oidipous. His path to heroic exaltation is the object of his coming and of his mysterious departure. But his present and future existence is closely connected with the powers of blessing and cursing he now possesses in accordance with divine will. Therefore the unrest in the world clutches at this man who seeks peace and the bliss of death. This happens in two ways. Preparation for and completion of the path to heroism form the larger frame for the two middle acts of Kreon and of Polyneikes, both sharply separated and clearly distinguished in atmosphere and execution. But it would be wrong to overlook the fact that the structure of the aged Sophokles' last play, composed in large blocks, differs from that of the other plays written when the poet was at the height of his dramatic art. The compactness of the dramatic composition, the line of development that runs straight through the work without interruption or expansion, is present in the *Oid. Tyr.*, the *Elektra*, and even in the *Philoktetes*, but not here.

Of course, in interpreting the play, we must be wary of such concepts as redemption and retributive justice; the two Oidipous dramas do not together form a perfect whole with no loose ends. But it is just as incorrect to follow Linforth (op. cit.) who interprets the play on an entirely secular level, so that at the end the sanctuary of the Eumenides becomes meaningless scenery. Consequently he must reject Ismene's statement (394) "Now the gods uplift you; before, they destroyed you" as a misunderstanding on her part. The chorus's prayer (1565) that a just god should now exalt the man who has endured so much sorrow also refers to what is really happening. By emphasizing the relevant passages in our analysis we have shown that Oidipous's destiny is determined by divine power, that it is a confrontation between god and man. This confrontation is not a neat moral paradigm; rather, it results from the sphere of the irrational that for Sophokles is the sphere of the divine. We must not ask why the gods struck down Oidipous so terribly, but we must comprehend the great paradox that they made him the witness of their impenetrable power, by this very fact uplifting him above all others, and took him into their realm so that, when he came to the end of his sorrowful journey, they exalted him and made him a powerful, heroic being. Goethe understood the poet when he spoke of the boldness of this work, "where a half-guilty criminal . . . was exalted to kinship with the gods as a benedictory guardian power of the land and worthy to receive his own sacrificial offerings."[131]

A special problem is whether the play could be performed with three actors, or whether a fourth was demanded as a parachoregema. The question is difficult to answer since we possess no certain evidence regarding the distribution of one role among various actors. K. F. Hermann already attempted his own allotment of the roles;[132] an interesting diagram is offered by Flickinger (180), who manages to make do with three speaking parts and needs a mute assistant only for Ismene in the section 1098–1555, in which her silence is conspicuous. But the problem is solved by dividing the role of Theseus among all three actors. A solution that makes very sparing use of such division of roles is preferred by E. B. Ceadel, who also offers a survey of earlier attempts.[133]

FRAGMENTS

The most important editions have been listed together with those of the plays. A comprehensive list of drama titles which can still be ascribed to Sophokles with some certainty is offered by Blumenthal (*RE* 1051). They number 123. If we add the seven extant plays, we arrive at 130, the number given in the *Vita* (18). This is misleading however, since it is very uncertain how many spurious or duplicated titles are hidden in this collection. Nonetheless it seems fair to say that most of the plays that came to Alexandria are known to us, at least by title. Schmid's arrangement of the works according to legends (2. 422) confirms the remark in Ath. 7. 277e, that Sophokles preferred the epic cycle as the source for his material. Several lost plays are treated by Webster (Soph., 172), from a chronological point of view. A helpful overview may be found in F. Stoessl's supplement to Sophokles (*RE* S 11, 1247).

Among recent discoveries, the most significant is the papyrus that brought to light large sections of the *Ichneutai*.[1] These were first published in 1912 (*P. Oxy.* 9), a few restorations were added in *P. Oxy.* 17, 1927, 72 with the publication of six fragments that had been overlooked in the first edition. Also important are the results of E. Siegmann's examination of the papyrus, undertaken before the Second World War.

Wilamowitz supported an early dating on the basis of arguments that have been partially invalidated by Buchwald (48).[2] But the character of the play does seem to favor an early date, which is accepted by H. Diller, among others.[3] E. Bethe's later date was defended by Perrotta (291), but he is not convincing.

The plot of this satyr play concerns the theft of Apollo's cattle by Hermes, the child prodigy, as related in the *Homeric Hymn*.[4] But the play is set on Mount Kyllene, and the nurse of Zeus's infant is the local nymph of the same name, not his mother Maia. The prologue can be pieced together. Apollo opens the play with the demand that his stolen cattle be found. To Silenos, who hurries up to him, the god promises not only a reward of gold, but also freedom for his whole swarm of children. The satyrs begin the search, but are soon utterly confused by the jumbled footprints of the cattle, one of Hermes' tricks. A delightful scene in which the satyrs are presented in the full splendor of their cowardice, concupiscence, and curiosity is achieved by the poet by reversing the sequence of the legend in the hymn: here Hermes invents the lyre only *after* stealing the cattle. And so, suddenly, the depths of the earth resound with sounds never heard before, terrifying the satyrs who try to run away. Old Silenos boosts their courage by referring to his heroism in earlier years, but he too becomes noticeably pale when he hears the mysterious sounds. Now the stamping of the satyrs (some sort of wild sitcinnis) induces Kyllene to leave her cave. She demands to know what the group is about. The speech of the nymph, who is conscious of her rank as guardian of a child of Zeus's, is set off splendidly from the style of the satyrs, who try to raise the tone of their impertinence. In a charming display of wit, Kyllene reveals the secret of the lyre, but then it is discovered that Hermes used something from the cattle in constructing the new instrument (292, but the crucial detail must have come earlier in a lacuna). The chorus triumphantly proclaims that they have caught the cattle thief. Kyllene is indignant at the accusation; in the middle of her quarrel with the satyrs the text breaks off. Of course the play concluded with the reconciliation of the divine brothers. Apollo received the new instrument and Silenos and his children were given their freedom. We know that the satyrs of these plays always seem bound in someone's service; who their master was in this drama is impossible to say. E. Siegmann (op. cit., 54) has brought forward much to indicate that it was Pan.

This play, with its delightful good humor, its refreshing primitive quality, and its natural, fairy-tale atmosphere, has proved a fortunate addition to our image of the poet of the Oidipous dramas. The papyri have also contributed much to our picture of Aischylos as well; but on the other hand we can hardly say that it is necessary to read the *Kyklops* to know the real Euripides.

Two difficult texts—seventy-eight verses on a mummy wrapping and a papyrus edited by E. Lobel, *P. Oxy.* 23, 1956, 55—were assigned to the satyr play *Inachos* by R. Pfeiffer in his outstanding editions of this material.[5] The play is dated before 425, close to the time of *Oid. Tyr.* In the first of these texts, we can discern a scene between the cowardly satyrs and Hermes, wearing the Hades cap, who evidently comes in the service of Zeus to slay Argos. The second text seems to be part of a speech of Inachos, with a description of Io's wanderings. It should not be assumed that Zeus himself appeared on stage.

A special problem was posed by the inscription of Aixonai[6] with the mention of a *Telepheia*.[7] The *Aleadai* and the *Mysians* are assigned to this trilogy with relative certainty. In the first play Aleos of Tegea, warned by an oracle about a son of his daughter Auge, makes her a priestess of Athena. Herakles seduces her, the child is exposed on a mountain but survives miraculously. As a youth the unknown Telephos comes to the court of Aleos and kills his mother's brothers in a quarrel. B. Snell, *TrGF* 17, gives the *Telepheia* to a younger Sophokles. In agreement are Webster, *Gnom.* 45 (1973), 612, and Luppe, *Arch. f. Pap.* 22 (1973), 211, who newly edited the inscription: *Arch. f. Pap.* 19 (1969), 147.

For the *Mysians*, *Fab.* 100 of Hyginus has often been used as the basis of reconstruction attempts (so too Schmid, 2. 425). Hyginus's source was certainly greatly influenced by tragedy, but C. Robert, in his presentation of the legend, and others have gone much too far in their allotment of individual stories to the great poets. In this case also, we should not interpret the complicated story of how Telephos found his mother at the palace of King Teuthras as a reproduction of the Sophoklean play. We can do no more than conjecture that the purification of blood guilt and reunion of son and mother were possible motifs of the drama.

With its dramatic presentation of the cure of Telephos, Ἀχαιῶν σύλλογος may seem the likeliest candidate for the third play, but in no case may we equate it with the *Syndeipnoi*. A. Szantyr lists the literature (291); his hunch regarding an unattested *Auge* has not found favor. It remains very questionable whether a satyr play *Telephos*[8] was the fourth play.

From the inscription of Aixonai, it is clear that this Sophoklean trilogy was united in content. This assumption formed the basis for an interesting hypothesis of T. B. L. Webster.[9] He supposes a date before 450 for the *Telepheia* and picks up the idea of Oemichen that around 449 the dramatic festival was changed so that on each day each of the three competing poets would present one play. The familiar phrase δρᾶμα πρὸς δρᾶμα ἀγωνίζεσθαι (competition of play against play) in the *Suda* would thus acquire a more particular meaning. Later, however, the theory continues, the victorious actor of the previous year was assigned to each of the three poets for one of his plays, thus making possible a return to trilogy form. This cannot be proved, but the three later trilogies that are known to us (*Pandionis* of Philokles, *Trojan Trilogy* of Euripides, *Oidipodeia* of Meletos) are in fact dated after 420.

With the *Ichneutai*, verses of the *Eurypylos* also came to light (*P. Oxy.* 9, 1175. D. L. Page, *Lit. Pap.*, 1950, 16), to which other fragments can be added (*P. Oxy.* 17, 2081). These remnants were re-examined by Siegmann in connection with his MS comparison of the *Ichneutai*. We can discern a messenger speech about the lament of Priamos, who weeps for Eurypylos as if he were his own child; actually he was his sister Astyoche's son, who had been slain by Neoptolemos. Priamos had bribed Astyoche to send her son into battle. Reinhardt (235) considered an early date for the play based on this pathos scene.

We may reconstruct with reasonable confidence in the *Niobe* of Sophokles a messenger report that related the slaying of the sons on Mount Kithairon, while Artemis shot down the daughters in the palace.[10] It is possible that a papyrus text (D. L. Page, *Lit. Pap.*, 1950, 144) comes from a scene in which one of Niobe's daughters, struck by a fatal arrow, stumbles out of the palace. According to schol. T, *Il.* 24. 602, Niobe in Sophokles' play returned to Lydia; this probably refers to an announcement at the end of the drama. If *P. Oxy.* 2, 213 (Page, *Lit. Pap.*, 1950, 146) belongs to Sophokles, it most probably comes from a tragedy *Tantalos*.

The beginnings of seventeen trimeters in Milne (*Cat. of the Lit. Pap. in the Brit. Mus.*, London 1927, 79) were tentatively assigned by C. E. Fritsch to the *Iphigeneia* of Sophokles.[11] Some words seem to suggest the location as Aulis, but the "Lokrian leader" might refer to the delayed departure after the destruction of Troy.

The remains of about thirty tragic trimeters in *P. Oxy.* 17, 1927, 2077 (Page, *Lit. Pap.*, 1950, 20) were confirmed for the *Skyrioi* by R. Pfeiffer's brilliant identification of the scanty remains of the first three verses with the last verse endings of fr. 511N, 555P.[12] The emphasis was probably on the figure of Deidameia, who sent Neoptolemos to Troy only after resistance proved futile. Since Neoptolemos's departure turns up in vase painting after 450, the production of the play may have occurred around this time.

The *Polyxena* was also taken from the legends of Troy. W. M. Calder III offers a detailed attempt at reconstruction.[13] For the prologue he posits a dialogue between Agamemnon and Achilleus's ghost, but emphasizes correctly that the tomb of Achilleus was not represented on stage, since the sacrifice of Polyxena later had to occur on it. For the princes' quarrel, in which Agamemnon tries to save the maiden, he makes extensive use of Seneca's *Troades* 203–348. At this point, of course, as well as with the construction of a scenario, we enter the realm of pure conjecture. Calder would date the the play before Euripides' *Hekabe*.

E. G. Turner published (*P. Oxy.* 27, 1962, 2452) eighty-six fragments from the *Theseus*, of which only a few are really substantial. In one we can discern Ariadne and Eriboia as speakers. We must, with Turner, leave open the question whether one can conclude from fr. 4, 3 f. (δύστηνα τέχνα) that the chorus was composed of the children sent to be sacrificed. No. 2453 contains twenty-three tiny fragments from the *Polyeidos* with the subtitle *Manteis*.

We would gladly know more about the *Phaidra*, especially since there is a reasonable possibility that this work was composed between Euripides' two Hippolytos tragedies as a response to the first.[14] The fragments were recently assembled by W. S. Barrett,[15] who, aware of the caution necessary in such cases, hazards the view that much of Seneca's *Phaedra* could have been influenced by Sophokles. From the fragments we can discern that Theseus was in Hades and was thought to be dead, that Phaidra looked upon her love as a suffering sent from Zeus, and asked the chorus of women not to reveal her secret. Fr. 617N, 678P comes from a report about the rejection of the nurse by Hippolytos.

For the *Skythai*, whose subject was probably the murder of Apsyrtos during the pursuit of Medeia, Wilamowitz (*Hell. Dicht.* 2. 197) considered the possibility that the play was the model for the fourth book of Apollonios Rhodios.[16]

The *Tereus* dealt with Prokne's infanticide to avenge her husband Tereus's violation of her sister Philomele. Buchwald, who offers a commentary on the fragments, dates the play before 431, believing that Euripides borrowed the infanticide motif for his *Medeia*. Webster (*Soph.*, 4) also arrived at a date before 431 based on connections with the *Trachiniai*. Others support a later date, based partly on the assumption that Athens' relations with Sitalkes, the king of Thrace, an Athenian ally at the outbreak of the Peloponnesian War, influenced Sophokles' treatment of the material.[17] None of these dates can be accepted with confidence, and we must exclude the importation of dates from contemporary history, a practice that has been much abused in the criticism of tragedy.

DRAMATIC FORM AND LANGUAGE

Among the many books on Sophokles, Webster's *Introduction* is especially useful for questions of technique and style. The importance of Reinhardt's book will be discussed presently. It should not be forgotten that Bruhn's appendix to the edition of Schneidewin-Nauck (1899) offers a valuable treatment of numerous linguistic phenomena.[1]

Of the innovations that were ascribed to Sophokles, the most significant is that described rather vaguely in the *Suda*: καὶ πρῶτος ἦρξε τοῦ δρᾶμα πρὸς δρᾶμα ἀγωνίζεσθαι, ἀλλὰ μὴ τετραλογεῖσθαι (and he was the first to begin the competition of play against play, and to stop writing tetralogies). We mentioned above Webster's revival of Oemichen's idea, according to which the remark could refer to a new arrangement of the plays performed at the Dionysia, such that now each of the three poets produced just one play each on a given day. The abandonment of the thematic trilogy brought with it substantial structural changes; most important, dramatic composition was tightened considerably.[2] This development away from the monumental structure of the Aischylean trilogy is closely connected with the ever increasing emphasis on individual personality within the tragic play.

We may believe that Sophokles increased the number of chorus members from twelve to fifteen (*Vita* 4, *Suda*); his treatise *On the Chorus* may have been connected with this. He is also supposed to have introduced the third actor: Aristot. *Poet.* 4, 1449a 19; Dikaiarchos fr. 76W; Diog. Laert. 3. 56; *Vita* 4; *Suda*.[3] In this respect Aischylos was his imitator. In Sophokles' extant plays we can still perceive how slowly the freer use of the third actor within a dialogue was brought to perfection. It is instructive to compare the concluding scenes of the *Aias*, where the dialogues alternate between partners, with the scene of the *Oid. Tyr.* in which Iokaste intervenes in the dispute between Oidipous and Kreon.[4]

According to Aristot. *Poet.* 4, 1449a 19, Sophokles also introduced scene painting. This must be linked with the report of Vitruvius (7, pr. 11) that the inventor was Agatharchos of Samos, who is also said to have written a treatise on the subject and induced Anaxagoras (*VS* 59A 39) and Demokritos (*VS* 68B 15b) to study perspective. However, Vitruvius goes on to say that Agatharchos achieved prominence with his innovation, *Aeschylo docente*, which agrees neither with Aristotle nor with our other reports of the poet's life. The most probable solution to the problem was offered by A. Rumpf, who conjectures that Vitruvius's remark refers to a repeat performance of an Aischylean tragedy, and that Agatharchos should be dated not too early in the second half of the fifth century.[5]

The most significant advance for our understanding of Sophokles' work proceeds from the fact that the earlier plays, i.e., those preceding the *Oid. Tyr.*, are set off quite sharply from those that follow this work, the masterpiece of the poet's maturity. The decisive demonstration of these differences was primarily the work of Reinhardt, but Webster also deserves much credit.

Clearly discernible in the three earlier plays (in a distinctive way for each, to be sure) is the method of composition described by Webster's concept of the diptych form. This does not imply any lack of unity within these plays (we have rather tried to show in our analyses how the two parts unite to form a whole), but in the *Oid. Tyr.* Sophokles achieved a unity of structure that makes any such explanation superfluous. The way in which all the action in this play (and in the *Elektra* as well) is completely centered around one major character shows that, in the perfect unity of form and content, the pinnacle of classicism has been reached.[6] In a different but no less ingenious way, the unity of dramatic structure is preserved throughout the rich and complex design of the *Philoktetes*. In the *Oid. Kol.* we were again able to discern more distinctly the parts that were combined to a whole.

The structural development as a whole corresponds to a similar process in the formation of individual scenes. Using Reinhardt's apt terminology, we can distinguish an earlier dramatic technique of *contrast* from a later preference for *development*, which begins as early as the *Antigone*, while the *Aias* furnishes the most convincing evidence for the former method. Thus in the early play we find a rigid opposition of fixed characters; in the later plays there is a much stronger drive towards interaction. And while sorrow and despair are expressed in the *Aias* in a "stationary pathos form," such expressions are later imbued with a much deeper internal movement; if the changeover within a dramatic section is unknown in the oldest play, in the others Sophokles develops an increasingly rich interplay of smooth transitions and dramatic turning points. We must realize that much of the *Aias* is determined by the natural properties of the main character, and certainly the position of the *Trachiniai* within this development remains more problematical than it appears in Reinhardt; but in general we can discern a development that culminated in the rapid movement and rich humanity of *Philoktetes*.

According to the poet's own testimony in Plutarch, *De prof. in virt.* 7. 79b, which we mentioned in the biographical section, Sophokles distinguished three stages of creativity that led him from dependence on Aischylos, past the πικρὸν καὶ κατάτεχνον (the harsh and artificial), and finally to perfection in expressing ἦθος (natural character), the mastery that is especially praised in the *Vita* (21).[7] Although it seems that we possess no early work of Sophokles, nonetheless the seven extant plays cover such an extensive time period that we may well ask whether we can discern something of this three-stage development. The language and style of the earlier plays, especially the *Aias*, do in fact display features that allow us to characterize in them a technique corresponding to the poet's middle period and preceding the perfection of method in the later works.

For example, there is an unmistakable change in vocabulary.[8] Although Aischylean coloring does not dominate the earlier plays, expressions characteristic of him do occur. Borrowings from the language of Homer and the lyric poets are also more frequent than in the later dramas.[9] In general, the preference at this stage for colorful and ornamental language still betrays traces of the archaic; so too do the deviations from normal forms in word construction, the adverbs not derived from adjectives (e.g. ἐγερτί), and above all the preference for composite and privative adjectives. The occasional repetitiveness of language in the *Aias* also reveals that Sophokles had not yet perfected his medium. Thus at one point a fairly unimportant παρών concludes four verses within a short span (1131, 1156, 1288, 1384). Such repetition will be sought in vain in the later works. An impressive example of an overloaded style from the poet's early period may be found in fr. 554N, 611P from the *Triptolemos*, which belongs to the tetralogy with which Sophokles made his debut in 468. Demetrios, *De el.* 114, criticizes his ὄγκος (heavy ornamentation) in the wrong place.[10]

Of course similar occurrences are not wholly absent in the mature and late plays, but there is a considerable reduction in number. What Reinhardt (27) termed "the fullness of sound and image from the world of chivalry" (on *Aias* 17) is not to be found to this degree thereafter. And while this verse exhibits the characteristically

Aischylean manner of filling a trimeter with but a few ponderous words, it should be noted that such an ornamental mode of expression later occurs far less often. The language of Sophokles, as we see its development, strives for a quicker tempo and a simpler form. This means a heightened ability to express ἦθος but not a special inclination toward colloquial idioms.[11] Even though Sophokles' vocabulary has affinities with that of Euripides, as Webster (*Soph.*, 147) points out, and though the more frequent use in and after the *Oid Tyr.* of abstract nouns ending in -ις may reflect the popularity of that formation in prose,[12] nonetheless a question such as the one posed by the *P. Didot* (Euripides or Menander?) would be utterly inconceivable for Sophokles.

One cannot do justice to the noble solemnity of Sophokles' mature style by using words like "straightforward" or "natural"; it is best understood as the expression of Attic classicism. One could speak of a "Parthenon style." A fine description is offered in the passage of Quintilian (*Inst. or.* 10. 1. 68), in which he speaks of people who prefer Sophokles to Euripides: quibus gravitas et cothurnus et sonus Sophocli videtur esse sublimior (those to whom the weightiness, the buskin, and the sonorousness of Sophokles seem to be more exalted).

One of the secrets to the form of this language was explained by Reinhardt in the introduction to his translation of the *Antigone*, in which he speaks of the preference for "binomial" forms whose logical skeleton can be characterized by "both-and, not-but rather, neither-nor." Besides this double mode of expression, there is also a propensity for triple formations. Webster offered some examples in *Herm.* 71 (1936), 271 and referred to H. St. J. Thackeray for further material.[13]

The effectiveness of Sophoklean dialogue depends greatly on the relationship between clause and verse, which despite all harmonious arrangement nonetheless still maintains a certain tension. This is a manifestation of one of the basic principles of Attic classicism: freedom in restraint. It is significant that Sophokles permits a greater flexibility in enjambment than Euripides, who returns to the older limitations, just as he constructs a stricter form of stichomythy. Sophoklean dialogue also owes much of its suppleness to the close synapheia of the trimeters.[14] Another phrase for this is the σχῆμα Σοφόκλειον, in which syntactically proclitic words appear at the end of a verse, thus forming the closest possible connection to the following trimeter.

The style of Sophokles, the tragedian of high classicism (he deserves this title far more than Euripides) stands between the magnificent power of Aischylos and the pathos, alternating with passages of reflection, of his younger rival. Sophoklean style also expresses extreme horror in a form that remains within the restraints imposed by its nobility. But this taming of elemental forces must not be misconstrued as indifference. It is the essence of the poet's style that he does not seek to recapture the power of Aischylean imagery. The dark splendor of some maritime similes (*Ant.* 586; *Trach.* 112; *Oid Kol.* 1239) is of a different type. Here there is a greater desire to create a mood than for complete clarity of detail.[15] Further, it corresponds to the linguistic development noted above that the later plays are significantly poorer in images than those of the earlier period.

There remains much work to be done on the language and composition of the choral odes. Sophokles did not participate in the trend that began with the new dithyramb. Also, his odes are tightly set within the dramatic structure. He allowed only moderate space for the actor's song. Although kommoi between chorus and actor occur not infrequently, something comparable to Euripidean monodies can be found only at the beginning of the *Elektra*.

THE INTERPRETATION OF SOPHOKLES TODAY

Sophokles' reputation as the greatest of the three ancient tragedians, a position advocated by Voltaire, was also dominant in the New Humanism of Germany. From there its influence lasted quite some time, but the onset of historicism which shattered many of the old values left its mark here too.[1] The latter part of the nineteenth century then turned to Aischylos with a newly awakened delight in the archaic and focused special interest on Euripides, who seemed so close to the complexities of the modern world. But with the shock dealt Western culture by World War I, a new relationship to Sophokles was established. This coincided with the powerful impetus given to the scholarship of tragedy by Tycho von Wilamowitz's book on the dramatic technique of Sophokles (1917). To a great extent this book must be understood as a reaction against the then current treatment of the poet, which modernized the dramatic characters through the application of psychological interpretations. Supporters of this method were wont to piece together the most minute details spread over the course of the drama (often enough using material of a purely speculative nature) to form a sort of mosaic that could be roughly compared to the concept of character in a modern play. Such attempts at psychologizing could be found in G. Kaibel's great commentary on *Elektra* (1896) or again in Bruhn's analyses; even U. von Wilamowitz contributed much in this vein. Rebelling against such artificial interpretations, Tycho tried to reinstate the poet by showing the great variety of elements that were necessary for the composition of a Sophoklean tragedy.

Today his book in turn is out of date; its formal, technical manner of observation presents a challenge and something of a shock to modern readers. Above all, Tycho exaggerated greatly when he asserted that Sophokles was unfamiliar with the concept of unified characterization, but instead determined the behavior of his characters so as to achieve the maximum effect in each individual scene.

On the question raised by Tycho, modern views clash. Jones (*Aristotle*) rejects any "personalistic interpretation," while Knox (*Heroic Temper*, 38) sees in Sophokles' characters "sharply differentiated individuality." But von Fritz, too, in his book speaks of completely individual characters (448); this we consider correct, although not of course in the sense of modern psychology. Two concepts provide valuable assistance. The first is contained in ἦϑος (approximately: behavior appropriate to one's fundamental nature). Aristotle incorrectly subordinated this element to the μῦϑος (material; *Poet.* 1450a 38; *Vita* 21);[2] his comments provoked criticism even in antiquity. The word in question occurs when Aias speaks of the inflexibility that stamps his basic nature (595). The second term fundamental to Sophokles' portrayal of mankind is φύσις (inborn nature), the innate quality that is indestructible in a noble man.[3] The dissolution of this concept in the educational optimism founded by the Sophists and occasionally evident in Euripides is foreign to Sophokles. The essence of great men as portrayed by Sophokles may be described in the words of W. Humboldt (Akademieausg. 3. 150): "Everything too individual is scorned and scrupulously avoided. It is not a particular man, but Man himself who appears in the varied (to be sure) but simple lines of his character." These words deserve special emphasis: equally far removed from the merely typical as from the separate differentiation of individuals in the modern sense, the figures of Sophokles stand before us with their characteristics broadly conceived and executed by the poet, very images of human nature.

Sophoklean scholars of the last few decades, whose lively interest is well attested by the wealth of new books and essays, are no longer willing to concentrate on the dramatic technician at the expense of the poet.[4] There is now no reluctance to inquire into the conceptual content of the plays, but instead a conviction that great fundamental questions lie behind the dramatic action and its characters—in fact, that these underlying principles in Sophoklean tragedy are exactly what determine its significance for modern man. Some of these new lines can be traced back to Hegel's ethical analysis and the religious viewpoint of Hölderlin, but we must not forget that the new understanding of the poet does not rely on such interpretations.

Sophoklean tragedy is at once similar to and different from Aischylean drama in the way in which it sees human destiny against a divine background. In the *Oresteia* we met with the conviction that a divine will rules over the suffering of guilt-laden men, a will that can give meaning to this suffering as a path to knowledge and understanding, or else remove it from man with the hand of grace. If our reconstruction of the *Danaid Trilogy* is correct, the foundations for such a world view were set down there as well. Of course Aischylean tragedy cannot be reduced to a formula—the *Seven* and *Prometheus* forbid any such attempt—but there remains clear in the poet's work a burning desire to understand divinity, and the belief that godhead can be understood, if not along all its paths, then at least in the finality of the divine plan. Over Sophokles' work, however, we may inscribe in bold letters the words from fr. 833N, 919P: ἀλλ' οὐ γὰρ ἂν τὰ θεῖα κρυπτόντων θεῶν / μάθοις ἄν, οὐδ' εἰ πάντ' ὑπεξέλθοις σκοπῶν.[5] The differentiation in this passage between τὰ θεῖα (cf. the great role of τὸ θεῖον in Herodotos) and θεοί is curious. That this was truly an important difference in Sophoklean thought can be seen from Philoktetes' argument (452) that it is difficult to praise τὰ θεῖα (the divine) when he perceives τοὺς θεούς (the gods) as evil.

It need not always be the case that the gods remain hidden from men. In the *Aias* the poet tells us the reason for Athena's wrath, even though we clearly perceive that the annihilation of the great hero involves more than the simple balancing of accounts between guilt and expiation. The *Antigone* reveals most clearly how terribly the gods strike down mortals who break their commandments. But for Deianeira and Oidipous it is impossible to find even a trace of moral guilt. Nor, in Oidipous's case, can we resort to the excuse that, in the religious thought of Sophokles, unconsciously committed crimes carry with them the same guilt as any other kind.

At all events, it becomes quite clear in the *Oid. Kol.* that the problem of attributing guilt was central for Sophokles. Of course Oidipous is, by the fact of his deeds, an abomination to gods and men. But his deeds are his fate, which strikes a man of great and noble soul, a man with no apparent fault that might render such misery understandable as punishment. It is only natural that the *Oid. Tyr.* has always been considered the pinnacle of Sophokles' art, indeed, of all tragedy. For this play too, more than for all the others, tragic irony is an essential element that shows man in hopeless entanglement. The gods have thrown the net over him, and his every attempt to shake it off only pulls it tighter around him in his tragic struggle. "It was Apollo, Apollo, oh friends." In the *Elektra* and *Philoktetes* it seems as if the terrible superiority of the gods has withdrawn into the background. But the divine will is present here too in Apollo's command and Herakles' orders. The path to the goal leads past suffering and confusion, but the goal is still in the gods' will and is fixed.

The gods work in various ways; they may exact obvious punishment for obvious crimes, or else choose an innocent victim to sacrifice. But it is always the same great divine will to which man, recognizing his own limitations, must reverently submit. Sophokles' profound piety, which has impressed his audiences since antiquity, springs from the soil of traditional Greek religion and yet grows beyond it.[6] The poet ascends to the level of a piety that plumbs the greatest depths of all the misery in men's helplessness, yet despite these terrors and in their very midst, his piety still finds reverence for the gods. Nowhere is this so clearly expressed as in the concluding lines of the *Trachiniai*. A loving wife has innocently destroyed her husband and then committed suicide. The hero and divine son, man's great benefactor, suffers before our eyes the agonies of a terrible death. His son accuses the gods: It is a disgrace that they let noble men suffer! But the chorus immediately cancels such an accusation in their final words: There is nothing in all this that is not Zeus![7] This means something different from the oft-recurring formula at the end of Euripidean plays, e.g., the *Medeia*, and something else again from the chorus's words in the *Agamemnon* (1487): What is accomplished for mortals without Zeus? In the *Trachiniai* the world is affirmed as divine as it is and as it has been revealed in all its terrifying aspects. A similar effect may have been intended by fr. 531N, 590P as the conclusion to the *Tereus*.[8]

It would be a mistake to wish to derive some sort of Sophoklean theology from these last remarks.[9] Conversely, only a portion of his spiritual world is encompassed in E. R. Dodds's claim that the poet is "the last great exponent of the archaic worldview."[10] In a penetrating essay, R. P. Winnington-Ingram correctly protested against an image of Sophokles that pictures the poet simply as a man content within the tradition.[11] Without seeking the solution in a theodicy, he is aware that the acts of the gods can appear as punishment for human misdeeds but can also, as pre-moral expressions of power, be detached from any ethical considerations.[12]

In this context we must recall once more the prologue to the *Aias*, in which Athena exposes the misery of the hero, broken by the gods, with such sadistic pleasure that Odysseus, the mortal, turns away in horror. And yet this is the same goddess who concludes the fearful game in this scene with an admonition to piety! A

similar exhortation is delivered by Herakles at the close of the *Philoktetes* (1440).
Pohlenz (2. 138) has demonstrated the closeness of these words to fr. 734 from the
Temenidai of Euripides. It is highly significant that in describing what it is that lives
on after men, Sophokles names eusebeia but Euripides names arete. The verses of fr.
759N, 843P conceive this kind of piety that knows human limitations—even if their
context is lost to us:[13]

> τὰ μὲν διδακτὰ μανθάνω, τὰ δ' εὑρητὰ
> ζητῶ, τὰ δ' εὐκτὰ παρὰ θεῶν ἠτησάμην.[14]

The gods can also speak to men through prophecies and oracles. The large
role they play—the *Trachiniai* is totally dominated by them—is well known.[15] It
would be quite hazardous to assume that oracles meant nothing more to Sophokles,
the friend of Herodotos, than a convenient literary motif provided by the traditional
myths; such a view will certainly not suffice for the interpretation of the *Oidipous
Tyrannos*. Of course, that is not to say Sophokles accepted as gospel truth every
oracle circulating in Athens, but the possibility that divine revelation could take
such forms most likely occupied a place in his beliefs. However, the way in which
this revelation comes about is extremely significant for the poet's view of divine action. Only in rare cases, such as in the second *Oidipous*, is the gods' direction clear
and unequivocal. More commonly the transmission of divine order is a veiled utterance, a vague hint that leaves many paths open. The gods cannot be gotten at with
questions. Thus Oidipous, wishing to verify his parentage, receives no reply from the
gods, but a terrible prophecy instead, worded in such a way that it is actually responsible for setting him on the wrong track. The will and the course of divinity are unfathomable.

From all this it is clear that Sophokles did not embrace Sophism. Two choral
passages, *Ant.* 332 and *Oid. Tyr.* 863, express clearly what separated him from the
new movement. Fr. 97N, 101P could also be understood as a personal statement by
the poet. Ehrenberg (in *Sophocles and Pericles*) offers the best discussion of the intellectual tensions of Sophokles' time.

It is highly instructive to compare *Ant.* 1043, in which Kreon, in a statement
of extreme hubris, asserts that men are incapable of polluting the gods, with Eur.
Herakles 1232, in which such a view is presented under the aspect of enlightenment.

Twice, Sophokles firmly avows his faith in the law that is from the gods and
with the gods—once in the person of Antigone (454) and then through the chorus of
the *Oid. Tyr.* (863). In the *Antigone* it is evident that this law exists independent of
the temporary executors of power in the polis, yet it holds them under strict obligations. For the interplay between god and man the polis is no longer the fixed framework into which everything must fit.

In his valuable survey, H. F. Johansen (op. cit.) has separated the extremists of
recent Sophoklean studies into the radical "pietists" and the equally radical "hero
worshippers." Neither of these two directions encompasses the whole of Sophokles.
We too would succumb to the verdict of partiality, were we to view the poet's work
solely from the side of divinity and not give due respect to the second element in the

action, that of man.[16] He too achieves immense stature in Sophokles' compositions. In both spheres his tragedies reaffirm the words of Pindar (*Nem.* 6. 1): Men in their feebleness are far apart from the ever blessed gods, and yet they are similar in form and in nobility of spirit. We are to see in Aias and Oidipous not merely the limits of man, who is broken by divine will like a straw in a storm; we must also recognize the greatness with which these bearers of tragic destiny confront their daimon. To help us perceive this solitary greatness, the poet places Ismene beside Antigone, Iokaste beside Oidipous, and Chrysothemis beside Elektra. In the main characters, to whom weak and submissive figures are juxtaposed for contrast and to figure temptation, there is a tremendous determination and a colossal will to action. Destiny is not painfully accepted: the tragic character goes to meet it with the zeal of an Oidipous, helping the gods to accomplish what he perceives as their will. And in the terrible suffering which Sophokles unmercifully and horribly brings down on his characters as no other poet has ever done, the indestructible element in man, great and pure, rises up to the gods.[17] In Sophoklean tragedy, tragic man and the divinity are inextricably bound in the hate-love relationship sensed by Hölderlin in the first version of his *Death of Empedokles* (Act 1) when he has Panthea speak of the lovers' quarrel. It is just such a quarrel that the gods conduct with Oidipous, for his destiny at once destroys him and makes him one of their elect. That is why they exalt him at the end and call him to their peace. And how they call him! In the ὦ οὗτος οὗτος, Οἰδίπους, τί μέλλομεν χωρεῖν (Ho, you there Oidipous, why do we delay our walk? *Oid. Kol.* 1627) there is a closeness to the immortals that is alone the privilege of one marked by suffering.

Whenever one seeks to examine more closely Sophokles' view of the world, one is struck by its polarity. Thus, in R. P. Winnington-Ingram (op. cit.) and in E. R. Dodds's essay cited in n. 77 above, there is a clear emphasis on the tension between the divine order and man's freedom to act. For this opposition between a devout acceptance of the gods' power and its impenetrability (cf. above), Dodds (47) has formulated a statement that poses a new problem: "For him, as for Heraclitus, there is an objective world-order which man must respect, but which he cannot hope fully to understand." The convergence of Sophoklean thought with that of Herakleitos has been noticed by others,[18] and extends so far into particulars that, while nothing can be proved, it is probable that the poet was familiar with the philosophy of the Ephesian.

Yet another polarity is revealed in Sophokles' tragic characters. Many of these great sufferers, isolated in their sorrow, are at the same time capable of great love. How much effort has been spent in trying to downplay the significance of Antigone's assertion that she exists not for mutual hatred, but for mutual love![19] And yet in this great capacity for love there is expressed a basic characteristic of Sophoklean humanity. It is as if man hoped to confront the tragic helplessness of his existence by trusting in the powers of love that have been granted to him. Thus Elektra stands next to Antigone as an example of sisterly love. And what expressions this love is capable of! Consider how Oidipous stands among his people at the beginning of the first drama, how he speaks to his daughters in both plays, he who can curse so violently in the second one. Even inanimate nature is embraced by man's loving gesture, above all when, at the hour of parting, he casts his glance once more upon his world. We think of Aias before his death or Philoktetes at his departure.

Sophoklean tragedy does more than summon up the power of great courage in the storms of god-given destiny; it reveals as well all the wealth and depth of the human soul. And that is perhaps the ultimate source of the joyousness to be found in Sophokles' work. As Hölderlin put it in his oft-quoted epigram on our poet:

> Many attempted in vain with joy to say the most joyous;
> Finally it speaks to me here, brought to expression in
>   sorrow.[20]

6

EURIPIDES

BIOGRAPHICAL NOTES

Euripides' relationship to his state and public was different from that of his two predecessors. We know nothing of any military campaigns in which he might have participated, nothing of governmental positions he might have held.[1] His love for Athens was deep, but in no way unproblematic; his plays testify to that. As a result of the distance he maintained from the polis, we know even less about his life than about the lives of Aischylos and Sophokles.[2] Gossip about Euripides, for which comedy provided an excellent mouthpiece, was especially rich and colorful. It begins with his parents: his father was a shopkeeper, his mother a greengrocer. Dirty stories were told of the poet's wives, Melito and Choirine, and of another household member, Kephisophon, who purportedly did more than compose poetry with him. An animal fable was connected with the poet's death: he was torn to pieces by the offspring of a Molossian hound whose slayers King Archelaos had pardoned at Euripides' insistence. Most astounding of all is that in the accounts of the *Vita* and Satyros, both of which make use of the same sources for their anecdotes, we find the *Thesmophoriazusai* of Aristophanes recorded as factual history. And yet only two centuries separate Satyros from Euripides!

His alleged low birth was disputed even in antiquity by sensible men like Philochoros in the *Suda*, who may also be responsible for the reserve with which Pausanias (1. 2. 2) refers to the stories about the poet's death. It is of little benefit to rely on personal preference when deciding which interesting anecdotes deserve credence. Van Lennep (10) and Schmid (3. 320) think that the story of Euripides' adultery contains some truth; the latter sees traces of the poet's embarrassing experiences in the character of Helen in the *Orestes*. He also considers the hunting dogs of Archelaos to be historical (3. 327). Of course, some truth may be hidden in this or that story, but we feel it necessary to confess our total uncertainty in such matters.

In fact, we do not even know the exact date of the poet's birth. The spring of 406 is confirmed for his death by *Marm. Par.* 63 and the accounts of Sophokles' obsequies during the proagon of that year. Timaios lowered the date by a year in order to synchronize it with the beginning of the tyranny of Dionysios I. He was followed by Eratosthenes and Apollodoros.[3] The birth of the poet, whose parents kept an estate on Salamis, was assigned to the year of the famous sea battle; Jacoby (on *FGrH* 239A 50) believes Timaios was responsible for this date as well. As a consequence of Timaios's chronological skills, Euripides would have been born, produced his first play (456/455), and died in the archonship of a Kallias. The *Marm. Par.* 60 (cf. 50, 63) sets his birth at 485/484, a date which is plausible in itself, but perhaps is a synchronization with Aischylos's first victory.

The poet's father, a landowner named Mnesarchos or Mnesarchides, and his mother Kleito both belonged to the deme of Phyla, but Euripides was born at his parents' estate on Salamis. Ancient tradition (*Vita*; Gell. 15. 20) told of an oracle that promised Mnesarchos that his son would be victorious in competition. Thus the boy was trained for the pankration and boxing ring until he found his way to tragedy. The obvious point of this story is the mistaken interpretation of the oracle, which led at first in a direction opposite the one intended. But behind this lies the image of Euripides the intellectual, who sings of wisdom's gifts and of the Muses in his ode of praise for Athens (*Med.* 824), whom Aristophanes (*Ran.* 943, 1409) ridicules as a bookworm, and who is on occasion quite frank in expressing his aversion to mindless athletics.[4] He reportedly also tried his hand at painting, and we are told that some of his pictures could be seen in Megara. There may be some confusion with a painter of the same name, but pictorial elements, which, like much in Euripides, foreshadow the Hellenistic age, are unmistakable in his poetry. Of the few reports that seem to have no special point and are therefore fairly trustworthy, we mention that the young Euripides is said to have rendered cult service to Apollo Zosterios as a dancer and torch bearer and in other functions (*Vita*; Gell. 15. 20; Athen. 10, 424E).

Euripides is often carelessly referred to as a pupil of the Sophists, as if he had been educated in their circle. Our poet was born in the second decade of the fifth century, and Protagoras is almost his exact contemporary. When Sophism began its rise to supremacy around the middle of the century, Euripides was in the prime of life. These dates alone make it probable that although influenced by the new teachings he was not a strict disciple of the movement. The ancient biography quite simply lists Anaxagoras, Prodikos, and Protagoras as his teachers, Sokrates as his friend.[5] He may have known these men, and in many passages of his work we can discern familiarity with their ideas, which are sometimes imitated and sometimes contradicted. However, the extent of the poet's personal contact with the philosophers and Sophists is wholly unknown to us.

We possess fragments of an epinician ode that celebrates the chariot victory of Alkibiades in 416[6] and has been ascribed to Euripides (fr. 3D, *PMG* nos. 755 f.) According to Plutarch, *Demosth.* 1, this was a widespread but unconfirmed conjecture. It is quite conceivable that the eccentric Alkibiades and our poet, who likewise went his own way apart from the many, may have briefly become friends with one another. But the *Troades* certainly shows how Euripides felt about Athens' rash war policy, and Aristophanes (*Ran.* 1427) has him pass a harsh judgment on this politician who proved so destructive to his homeland.

It is understandable that the author of the *Troades* was also believed to have written the epitaph for the Athenians killed at Syracuse. Plutarch, *Nik.* 17, records the short and simple epigram. Its poetic value has been unjustly slighted by many, however, including the author.[7]

An indictment for impiety supposedly brought against the poet by Kleon might be considered genuine, were it not recorded only by Satyros (col. x) together with the *Thesmophoriazusai* story.[8] We also read in Aristotle, *Rhet.* 3, 15, 1416a 29, of a suit brought by a certain Hygiainon against Euripides challenging him to an antidosis for a liturgy, and this seems rather more plausible. It is possible that the alleged impiety of the poet was proved with references to verses like *Hipp.* 612, and likewise possible that such lines gave rise to the whole story of the charge of impiety.

That he was a longtime friend of the musical innovator Timotheos seems credible enough. But we may well doubt Satyros when he reports (col. xxii) that Euripides consoled the discouraged poet after one of his failures and wrote for him the prooimion of the *Persians*, which was composed, in Wilamowitz's estimation, about 398–396.

All these details are overshadowed by the fact that a series of harmonious reports (*Vita*; Satyros col. x; *Suda*; Gell. 15. 20) produces an image of the poet's nature that had probably remained alive for generations and may correspond largely to the truth: that he was not very sociable, indeed rather sullen, always lost in thought, and abrupt in his dealings with others. In this vein we note the account of the grotto on Salamis, still shown in Imperial times, in which Euripides, gazing out over the wide sea, far from the bustle of the crowd, pondered the mysteries of human existence.[9] True or not, the essence of the account fits nicely with our image of a poet detached as never before from the life of the community. What we glean from these reports is more than a personal characterization of the poet: it is the first expression of a concept of genius—later to play such an important role in Western civilization—that depicted the creative artist as a misunderstood personality tragically isolated from his environment.

The poet's antipathy to political affairs as they were normally conducted in his day may explain the tirades in the *Ion* (esp. 598). Though conscious of all the risks involved in arguments ex silentio, we note the lack of any evidence that connects the poet with Perikles.

We can imagine that Euripides was an avid reader; cf. the remark in Athen. 1. 3A that he possessed a library.

The poet's contact with his environment was provided by his audience. Even if the accounts about theatrical scandals collected by Nauck (on fr. 324) are fictitious, still the poet was denied the kind of relationship with his public we may assuredly assume for Sophokles. In 455 he obtained a chorus for the first time; he produced the *Peliades* and suffered his first defeat in the agon. According to the *Marm. Par.* 60, he did not win first prize until 441. Nike, to whom the chorus prays at the end of his *Iph. T.*, *Phoin.*, and *Or.*, bestowed this favor on him only four times in his career: not often, when we recall that he obtained a chorus twenty-two times.[10] Though the *Vita* (8. 23), the *Suda*, and Gellius (17. 4. 3), following Varro, speak of five victories, this includes the one awarded posthumously for a tetralogy produced by his like-named son (schol. *Ran.* 67) or nephew (*Suda*).

We can well imagine the poet's reasons for leaving his homeland in the last years of his life, but the exact details cannot be established. Vexation with Athens and his audience, as assumed by Satyros, seems the likeliest motive.[11] The decision would not have been easy for him, and we may believe that the poet is speaking from his heart when he calls exile the greatest of all evils (*El.* 1314 and *Phoin.* 388).[12]

According to the *Vita*, before he settled in Makedonia Euripides stayed awhile in Magnesia, where he was honored with proxenia and ateleia. We cannot substantiate the report and cannot even determine which Magnesia this was supposed to be. Schmid (3. 325) and Goossens (671. 18), among others, suggest the Thessalian peninsula; Murray (*Eur.*, 109), the city on the Meander. With Wilamowitz (*Einl. i. d. gr. Trag.*, 11) we must consider the possibility that a document concerning honors bestowed on the poet by Magnesia later gave rise to the report of his stay there.

Since we are familiar with some of Euripides' work from his Makedonian period, he must have gone to the court of Archelaos in Pella shortly after the production of his *Orestes* (408). This ruler attempted to emulate the splendor of older tyrannical courts in a world which was undoubtedly rather barbaric. He summoned to his court Agathon, Choirilos of Samos, the dithyrambic poet Timotheos, and Zeuxis the painter. It is possible that Thukydides also went there. That Euripides was honored by Archelaos, as Satyros relates, seems quite plausible; that he was active in the royal administration, as the *Vita* claims (26), is rather improbable. Euripides thanked his royal host by providing him with a heroic ancestor in his tragedy *Archelaos*. We will discuss the final great works of this period later. Euripides died and was buried far from his homeland in 406. In the *Suda* article (cf. *Anth. Pal.* 7. 44. 5) it is reported that Archelaos had him interred in Pella; others told of a grave near Arethusa, a rest stop for travellers (*Itiner. Hierosol. et al.*), still others of a cenotaph on the road to Peiraieus; its fine epigram is offered in the *Vita*.

Among the extant Euripides heads two types may be discerned.[13] The first is named after the most important replica, the Rieti-Copenhagen.[14] These copies, classical in style, depict a sullen, not overly expressive countenance. As Schefold rightly reminds us, the widely held opinion that the original was a bronze statue dedicated by the orator Lykourgos for the Theater of Dionysos in Athens cannot be verified.[15]

The second type, represented in twenty-five copies, is named the Naples or Farnese Euripides, after the best-known example. This magnificent head exhibits the features of creative genius and tragic torment. The original, of which this copy from the Claudian period derives, would be worthy of a Lysippos, to whom Schefold (op. cit., 94) tentatively ascribes it. Its relationship to the prototype of the Rieti is hotly contested. Laurenzi (op. cit., 108), who with others believes that the Rieti is the older of the two, offers a good overview. Schefold (op. cit., 94) dates the original of the Naples type to 330 and very shortly before the first Rieti exemplar. We may form some idea of the statue to which the Naples portrait belongs from a statuette in Paris (Lippold, *Porträtstatuen*, 49, fig. 5) and the beautiful relief in Istanbul (Schefold, op. cit., 162) that depicts Euripides presenting a mask of Herakles to the personified Skene.

Schefold's conjecture (op. cit., 78) that the melancholy head of a double herm in the Louvre is a likeness of Euripides based on the sculptor's personal recollection of the poet's appearance remains doubtful. It is also uncertain whether a statuette discussed by Studniczka (*Journ. Hell. Stud.* 43 (1923), 64, fig. 8) and a sarcophagus in Split (Dornseiff, *Arch. Anz.* 1932, 598) represent our poet.

MANUSCRIPT TRANSMISSION AND EDITIONS

In the *Vita* and *Suda* article we read that the corpus of Euripides' dramatic works comprised ninety-two plays. The *Suda* further reports that all in all Euripides produced plays in twenty-two years. This can be traced back to the information provided by the didaskaliai that he received a chorus for twenty-two tetralogies. We know that three plays, the *Peirithoos*, *Rhadamanthys*, and *Tennes* actually belonged to Kritias, to which we add the spurious *Rhesos*. Thus the account that lists eighty-eight genuine plays seems to tally perfectly. But it must not be forgotten that Wilamowitz (*Einl. i. d. gr. Trag.*, 40) raises some well-founded doubts about the total of ninety-two, which obviously derives from the research and conjecture of the Alexandrians. The *Archelaos* certainly was not included in the Attic didaskaliai; of the *Andromache* it is expressly stated (schol. 445) that it was not produced in Athens; at least it could not be found listed in the rolls, and the Lenaian festival also adds uncertainty to the calculation of the total.[1] Thus more plays may have been lost than the Alexandrians assumed.

Another source puts the total number of plays at seventy-five (Varro in Gell. 17. 4. 3. *Suda* as variant); this of course refers to the number of surviving plays. The extant number is expressly set at seventy-eight in the *Vita* and seventy-seven in the *Suda* article. The difference (78:75) may depend on the inclusion of the plays by Kritias. Of the dramas that found their way to Alexandria, eighteen are still extant (without the *Rhesos*); of the rest we have the titles and numerous fragments. It has often been noted that the Alexandrians possessed remarkably few of the poet's satyr plays. If we assume that they read the genuine *Sisyphos*, then the exact number was eight. Not infrequently Euripides may have concluded a tetralogy with a nonsatyrical play that had a happy ending, as with the *Alkestis* in 438; or else more satyr plays have been lost than tragedies. In either case it is pertinent to observe that the poet's forte did not lie exactly in the satyrical genre.

In general, the fate of Euripides' text in the pre-Christian era is similar to that of the Aischylos tradition described earlier. But here the problems of transmission are much more complicated, even in this early period, and they become still worse in Byzantine times. In recent years these problems have been the object of intensive research and several important works have been published as a result. To the books by Turyn, di Benedetto, Zuntz, and Tuilier listed in the bibliography we add the description of the tradition in W. S. Barrett's edition of the *Hippolytos* (Oxford 1964), which is important for the rest of Euripides as well. Further: A. Pertusi, "Selezione teatrale e scelta erudita nella tradizione di testo di Euripide," *Dioniso* 19 (1956), 111, 195; 20 (1957), 18, and "La scoperta di Euripide nel primo umanesimo," in *Italia medioevale e umanistica* 3 (1960), 101. I am grateful for K. Matthiessen's special kindness in permitting me a glance at the chapter on the history of the tradition in his edition of the *Hekabe*, as well as for his important remarks on the subject; see also his "Manuscript problems in Euripides' *Hecuba*," *Gr., Rom. and Byz. Stud.* 10 (1969), 293.

Because Euripides was chosen more often than the other tragedians for repeat performances from the early fourth century onward, the risk of contamination through actors' interpolations is correspondingly greater for his works.[2] Page has gone quite far in assuming such intrusions, but Barrett (op. cit., 46) also takes them into account. We mentioned in our chapter on Aischylos that the official state copy of Lykourgos probably did not put an immediate end to corruptions in the text; this seems even more probable for Euripides, since we must reckon with an especially wide distribution of his works in book form.

In our Aischylos chapter we also emphasized the special significance of Alexandrian philology, and of Aristophanes of Byzantium in particular, for our texts. Zuntz (35, 221) has recently stressed this for Euripides as well, based on the colometry of the lyric sections and their predominantly uniform transmission. Barrett (op. cit., 56) attempts to limit the importance of Aristophanes' work; this is correct only insofar as this learned edition cannot have supplanted all other versions, any more than the official text of Lykourgos did. Many variants preserved in papyri and manuscripts may derive from other sources, but the Alexandrian edition was undoubtedly the basis for the texts of the grammarians and the schools.

The transmission of the nineteen plays bearing Euripides' name (with the spurious *Rhesos*) consists of two blocks. As with the other two tragedians, here too we can distinguish a selection that comprises in this case not seven but ten tragedies: *Alk., Andr., Hek., Hipp., Med., Or., Rhes., Tro.,* and *Phoin.* To these is added the *Bakchai*, the only play that includes no scholia, though this is probably due simply to the quirks of the tradition. The position of the *Bakchai* outside the alphabetical arrangement, as well as its influence on the *Christus Patiens*, places it among the annotated dramas of the selection.

We can no longer assume with Wilamowitz that this selection was made by one and the same man in the second century A.D., who combined seven plays each of Aischylos and Sophokles with ten by Euripides for a school edition. Wilamowitz was convinced of this by the consideration that the last writer who knew of plays outside the selection was the elder Philostratos, but more recent papyrus discoveries have led to a new interpretation. On the one hand, fragments from the *Melanippe Desmotis, Skiron,* and *Phaethon* stem from as late as the fifth and sixth centuries A.D.; on the other hand, the predominance of the plays in the selection can be noted from the Hellenistic age onward. Thus everything indicates that the preference for individual plays (which were read and annotated more often) created or at least influenced the selection we possess. For we do not know whether the ancients possessed a separate edition of these ten dramas. Zuntz (254) stresses our uncertainty, and in fact we can demonstrate no more than a certain measure of probability. Indeed, the existence of such an edition is supported by the numbers of the plays by the three tragedians, and further for Euripides by the inclusion of the *Rhesos* for obvious thematic reasons.

The significance of the numerous repeat performances of Euripidean tragedies was correctly emphasized by Pertusi in the first of the studies cited above. He concluded that in the third/second centuries B.C. an edition was compiled of approximately thirty of the most popular plays; it was based on the Alexandrian text and acquired special importance in the MS tradition. However, after the convincing counterarguments of Zuntz (258), we cannot include this step in our history of the transmission. Also unconvincing is Tuilier's theory that the original selection from Euripides, like that of the two other tragedians, contained seven plays, to which *Rhes.*, *Tro.*, and *Ba.* were subsequently added to meet readers' demands.

The second block of our tradition comes from an ancient complete edition that was arranged alphabetically. Bruno Snell (*Herm.* 70 [1935], 119) proposed an illuminating hypothesis regarding the bibliographical basis for such a work: a papyrus edition of Euripides was constructed in such a way that each drama filled one roll; these rolls were placed in containers holding five rolls each. The texts of two such containers were converted into book form and reached Alexandria. One included *Hek.*, which also appeared in the selection, *Hel.*, *El.*, *Herakl.*, and *Hkld.*, the other *Kykl.*, *Ion*, *Hik.*, and the two *Iphigeneia* tragedies.[3]

The transmission of our texts in papyri and manuscripts must account for the following facts about the annotated plays of the selection (those in the alphabetical edition have their own history): the tradition exhibits such uniformity, especially evident in the colometry of the lyric sections, that the existence of a common archetype cannot be doubted. Its evaluation, however, must take into account that a large number of variant readings stand opposed to this uniformity of tradition, and that a significant portion of these variations and mistakes already appears in the ancient tradition as we know it from papyri. Their diffusion among the individual manuscript groups, however, deviates so sharply from the papyrus texts that it has been suggested, paradoxically, that the papyri were related eclectically to the codices. Gabriele Kliegl's dissertation "Studien zu den Papyrus-Fragmenten der ohne Scholien erhaltenen Tragödien des Euripides" (Munich 1966), leads to the assumption of a common tradition for this group.

In our chapter on the Aischylean tradition, we noted that today scholars have generally abandoned the thesis of Wilamowitz[4] that a single uncial codex with an abundance of marginal variants survived into the ninth century and became the source for all our manuscripts and that scholars selected their own readings from the numerous variations provided. To be sure, papyri offer texts with variations, but it is hard to imagine Wilamowitz's codex, monstrously overloaded with notations of this sort.

There are two ways to explain the existence of our texts. Both proceed from the probable assumption that several uncial manuscripts were preserved through the Dark Ages. The first theory claims that in the ninth or early tenth century some of these MSS—at least two—were transcribed into minuscules, which could explain the essentially bipartite medieval tradition. Such a solution is sought by Pertusi, who believes that the two branches of the tradition for the annotated plays diverge too widely to be traced back to the same medieval archetype, and also by di Benedetto (146) and recently Tuilier (180).[5] K. Matthiessen (see above) believes the problem should be left open.

There is another possibility. Since transcription was an extraordinarily painstaking business, it is conceivable that several uncial MSS were indeed available, but only one of them was transcribed. The scribe probably referred to one or several other MSS in order to introduce variant readings, either immediately or in later revisions. Thus the *codex unicus* suggested by Wilamowitz would again become a viable concept, although with considerable modification. This explanation is supported by Erbse;[6] Zuntz (272), after carefully weighing the facts, also leans in this direction, and W. S. Barrett (op. cit., 59) also seems to prefer this second possibility, though his discussion shows that a clear-cut decision is impossible.

Fixing a date for an archetype of the two discernible branches of the tradition involves hopeless problems. Tuilier suggests a date about 500.

Turyn (3–9) offers a synopsis of the MSS, to which must be added fourteen pages of a manuscript (Rylands Gaster Ms. 1689) from the safe of a London bank, where it was damaged in an aerial attack during World War II. Zuntz designates it as a copy of an edition of the triad (*Hek., Or., Phoin.*) by Triklinios in an earlier stage of his work.[7]

Of the two classes of the bipartite tradition, one contains only plays from the selection with scholia, the other offers the unannotated dramas from the alphabetical series as well. Its main witness is the Laurentianus 32, 2 (L), whose date Turyn (225) sets in the years 1300–1315.[8] Besides six plays of Sophokles, three of Aischylos, and Hesiod's *Erga*, it contains all of Euripides' plays with the exception of the *Troades* and the portion of the *Bakchai* after v. 755.

We also possess a manuscript (P) in two parts, the Palatinus gr. 287 and the Laurentianus Conventi Soppressi 172; it contains, along with the dramas of Sophokles and Aischylos's triad (*Prom., Seven, Pers.*), all eighteen plays by Euripides, augmented by the *Rhesos* and a fragment of the spurious *Danae*. It was important for the endlessly vacillating question of P's relation to L that Turyn (269), by dating P to ca. 1340, brought it closer in time to L. Another important advance, likewise the work of Turyn, came when he showed that the corrections in L not infrequently match the text of P, and that these corrections were made by the hand of Demetrios Triklinios. Zuntz then explained their relationship in a careful reexamination of both MSS. Although details here and there are subject to modification, his basic results cannot be questioned, despite Tuilier's efforts. Zuntz has clearly shown that the plays of the alphabetical edition in P were copied from L. On the basis of ink color he distinguishes three separate layers of corrections by Triklinios in L, and can establish that P was copied, probably in the same scriptorium in Thessalonike from which L originated, after the first but before the following two revisions. Zuntz establishes the great significance of Triklinios for the history of the text, and assumes that he united various branches in a "manuscrit de base." He obtained the plays of the alphabetical edition from a majuscule manuscript that Eustathios discovered and had transcribed ca. 1175. According to the schema proposed by Zuntz, Triklinios combined this MS with two further branches, one of which, stemming from an eleventh-century manuscript, included the plays of the selection (with the *Bakchai*). For these plays P does not depend directly on L, but on its prototype, through an intermediary stage. Only the *Rhesos* was copied directly from L to P. A third branch of the tradition that found its way into the "manuscrit de base" is assumed by Zuntz for the triad (*Hek., Or., Phoin.*), and derives from a MS that Triklinios in the margins provided with numerous readings of the Byzantines. A separate problem is posed by its very different representation in L and P. Zuntz attempts to solve this by assuming a different selection from the available variants of the prototype.

Of the other class of MSS, in which only the plays of the selection are transmitted, there are three manuscripts closely related in time: the Jerusalem palimpsest (Patriarchalbibl. 36), which offers more than 1600 verses from *Hek., Or., Phoin., Andr., Med., Hipp.* with scholia and variants;[9] the Marcianus 471 with *Hek., Or., Phoin., Andr., Hipp.* (up to 1234);[10] and the Parisinus 2713, in which *Tro.* and *Rhes.* are missing from the annotated plays. There is general agreement on the chronological proximity of these MSS, but suggested dates differ widely. Zuntz (35) favors an early date about the beginning of the eleventh century.[11] Turyn likewise proposes an early date for the palimpsest, but sets the other two codices in the twelfth century. Recently Tuilier has dated the entire group in the time between 1150 and 1200. He also puts a higher value on Par. 2713, which he considers the oldest of the three witnesses. To all these codices we add the Par. 2712, with all nine annotated plays, which Turyn convincingly dates after 1300.

Even this short synopsis suffices to make clear that our tradition for the unannotated plays stands on a much weaker basis than for the plays with scholia. This is dramatically demonstrated by *P. Oxy.* 19 (1948), 2223 from the second century A.D. It contains *Bakch.* 1070–1136, which come from a section for which we are dependent only on P. Variants and even plus-and-minus verses show the uncertainty involved here.

The shift in the evaluation of the medieval tradition that we described for Aischylos has been especially noticeable in the case of Euripides. Turyn (308) still believed it possible to display the results of endless toil in a richly detailed *stemma veterum*. But immediately Lloyd-Jones protested against such confidence.[12] Since then, as insight into the practices of the Byzantine scriptoria has increased, the concept of the open tradition has gained ground steadily. The vertical dimension of the stemmata is now seriously rivalled by the horizontal, which is determined by copious contamination of the manuscripts. Zuntz repeatedly offers insights into this type of transference of variant readings; Barrett offers a stemma (62) but vigorously emphasizes the important role played by MS contamination (54). Di Benedetto represents the most radical rejection of the diagram proposed by Turyn, but he exaggerates when he asserts that a separation of the two main classes of the tradition is merely hypothetical. Recently, Tuilier (287) offered an extremely complicated *stemma codicum*, but it is characteristic of the state of the problem that he draws in numerous cross-connections between the groups and MSS. Matthiessen correctly sums up the situation in a manuscript he has kindly lent me: the widespread contamination contradicts the confidence with which stemmata were drawn up, but this does not prevent us from establishing the dependent relationships; above all, it remains our task to delineate recognizable groups within the tradition.

The development just described has a far-reaching consequence for textual criticism: the belief that it is necessary to find the best branch of the tradition, the *codex optimus* if possible, and then to follow it through thick and thin, is now a thing of the past. Eclecticism, though much maligned, is the only methodically justified procedure.

Among the available editions, that of Wecklein (3 vols., Leipzig 1878–1902) still deserves special mention because of its careful and comprehensive apparatus. A prominent position is claimed by Gilbert Murray, 3 vols., Oxford 1902; II, 3d ed., 1913, but the individual annotated editions of Oxford, which are mostly based on Murray's text, show well how many questions remain open. Of the dual-language editions of the Budé series, prepared by L. Méridier, L. Parmentier, and H. Grégoire, with other collaborators, six volumes have appeared (Paris 1923–1961; the older texts are available in numerous reprintings; *Iph. Aul.* and *Rhesos* have not yet been published). The brief notes offer valuable assistance in interpretation. The four volumes of the dual-language Loeb Classical Library edition by A. S. Way, London 1912, were reprinted in 1958. In Spain, work has begun on a dual-language critical edition: A. Tovar, *Eur. Tragedias*, I (*Alk., Andr.*) Barcelona 1955; id., with R. P. Binda, II (*Bakch., Hek.*) 1960. The first two volumes (I: *Alk., Med., Hipp;* II: *Hkld., Hek., Andr.*) of a planned six-volume dual-language edition of the complete plays and fragments in Buschor's translation have appeared in Munich.

Editions with commentary are listed under the individual plays; however, we must mention here H. Weil's *Sept Trag. d'Eur.* (*Hipp., Med., Hek., Iph. A., Iph. T., El., Or.*) Paris 1868, 3d ed., 1905.

The scholia on the nine plays that (with the *Ba.*) formed the selection can be traced back through numerous intermediate stages to the commentary of Aristophanes of Byzantium. Several other names crop up in the scholia, the most important of which is Didymos. One of the fruits of his prodigious scholarship was the great commentary on Euripides, in which he compiled the research of earlier writers and formed the basis for the future tradition. Judging from attributions in the scholia on *Medeia* and *Orestes*, another especially influential commentary was that of a certain Dionysios, about whom we know next to nothing. The scholia were edited by Schwartz (Berlin 1887–1891) in the best edition of scholia that we possess for any tragedian. A final and easily distinguishable phase is represented by Byzantine commentators like Thomas Magister, Moschopoulos, and Demetrios Triklinios; for these we must still rely on Dindorf's complete edition of the scholia (Oxford 1863).

The fragments of Euripides' work are often so closely related in theme to the extant dramas that we will discuss the greater number of them in connection with the relevant plays. The constant increase in the number of papyri is a leading factor in the extraordinarily intensive labor devoted to these fragments and the problems of

reconstruction that they involve. To the important aids pertaining to all three tragedians and cited under Aischylos, we must add several excellent works specifically for
Euripides. Bruno Snell has added to the reprinting of Nauck's *Tragicorum Graecorum
fragmenta* (Hildesheim 1964) an appendix that assembles the additional fragments to
be gleaned from other authors. One fragment (477a) stems from the new Photios, who
seems to offer little of import for the tragedians. The extent to which the papyri have
advanced our knowledge becomes clear if we compare the *Suppl. Euripideum* by H.
von Arnim (Bonn 1913) with the collection of C. Austin published fifty-five years
later in the same series (Kleine Texte): *Nova Fragmenta Euripidea in papyris reperta*,
Berlin 1968. Further, B. E. Donovan, *Euripides Papyri*, i: *Texts from Oxyrhynchus*,
New Haven and Toronto 1969. H. Van Looy offers an index of all the identified and
newly discovered fragments with copious bibliography and an excellent historical
summary of the research: "Les fragments d'Euripide," *Ant. Class* 32 (1963), 162; addenda, 607. This was followed by his *Zes verloren Tragedies van Euripides*, Vlaamse
Acad., Klasse der Letteren 26 (1964), no. 51, with additions to the list; cf. Bruno Snell,
Gnom. 39 (1967), 326. Q. Cataudella has a thorough discussion of reconstruction
questions with an overconfidence that authors like Herodotos or Apollonios Rhodios
can be enlisted to aid in such attempts: "La ricostruzione delle tragedie Greche per-
dute," *Cultura e scuola* 17 (1966), 30. Webster placed special emphasis on the lost
plays in his book on Euripides. In an imposing volume, *Lustrum* 1967/12 (1968), H. J.
Mette has made available the material for these lost works, while F. Stoessl in his
supplement to the article on Euripides *RE* S 11, 658, offers a very handy and concise
synopsis, along with extensive bibliography.

Special mention should be made of E. G. Turner's treatment of *P. Oxy.* 2455
(vol. 27, London 1962), which is helpful for many specific questions. This papyrus
offers fragments from a collection of hypotheses to Euripides' plays, comparable to
the one known through *PSI* 1286. To this we add the conjecture of H. Hommel, "Euripides in Ostia," *Rivista Ital. di Epigrafia* 19 (1959), 109, that the verses of an inscription found in Ostia come from a Euripidean choral ode.

After a brief period of stagnation, translators have devoted their attention to
Euripides with renewed intensity. E. Buschor translated *Med.*, *Hipp.*, *Herakles*, Munich 1952; *Tro.*, *El.*, *Iph. T.*, 1957; *Or.*, *Iph. A.*, *Ba.*, 1960. Donner's translation was
revised by R. Kannicht and provided with an excellent introduction by Walter Jens,
Stuttgart 1958 (Kröners Taschenausg. 284f.). Stoessl has undertaken his own translations in order to complete the collection of dramas by H. von Arnim, *12 Tragödien
des Eur.* (2 vols., Vienna-Leipzig 1931): vol. i, Zurich 1958; vol. ii, 1968. Stoessl provided the individual plays with thorough introductions and also translated larger fragments from about the same period. A translation of all the surviving plays (except the
Rhesos, for which he prepared a dual-language edition; see on the play) was published
by D. Ebener in three volumes, Berlin 1966, also with good introductions. English
translations include those of Moses Hadas-J. H. McLean, i, New York 1936, and H. O.
Meredith, *Four Dramas of Euripides* (*Hek.*, *Her.*, *Andr.*, *Or.*) *Translated into English
Verse*, London 1937. We should also mention Gilbert Murray's translations of several
plays, which were quite influential in their time. Richmond Lattimore and David Grene,

the editors of the *Complete Greek Tragedies*, also contributed to the translations of all the plays in two vols., Chicago 1959.

The standard French translations were prepared by the various editors in the Budé series. In the venture *Il teatro Greco a cura dell'Istituto Nazionale del dramma antico* a series of Italian translations has appeared, most recently *Eracle* by S. Quasimodo and *Andromaca* by R. Cantarella. A survey of Czech translations of Euripides is given by K. Vysoky, *Listy filologické* 85 (1962), 76.

The later influence of Euripides in pagan and Christian antiquity is the subject of an excellent study (the best for any tragedian) by H. Funke in *Jahrb. f. Ant. und Christent.* 8/9 (1965/1966), 233. For Aristophanes' relationship to the tragedian see P. Pucci, "Aristofane ed Euripide," *Memorie della Classe di scienze morali e storiche dell'Ac. dei Lincei* 8, vol. 10, fasc. 5, 1961.

DRAMATIC WORKS

It is not simply a result of the greater quantity of extant material that we find in Euripides dissimilar elements juxtaposed more often than before. Webster (*Eur.*, 278) has called the poet's surviving plays "bewilderingly various" and Rivier (36) separates a group of masterpieces from the rest: *Alk.*, *Med.*, *Hipp.*, *Iph. A.*, and *Ba.* Others will choose differently but no one would wish to claim the same artistic quality for all the dramas. In the following pages attention will focus chiefly on those plays that best display Euripides' talents.

A series of reliable data offers a useful framework for the problem of chronology: 438 *Alk.*, 431 *Med.*, 428 *Hipp.*, 415 *Tro.*, 412 *Hel.*, 408 *Or.*; posthumous production is attested for *Iph. A.* and *Ba.* Allusions in comedy provide valuable assistance in dating, to which may be added linguistic and metrical observations. These last are especially significant in spoken verse, since statistics have established a fairly constant increase in the number of resolutions.[1] Much less helpful are references to contemporary historical events; scholars have occasionally gone too far in assuming such allusions.[2] As a whole, the chronology of the eighteen dramas can be established well enough that only in a few cases is there any appreciable room for doubt.[3] None of the extant plays is earlier than 438; only in the twenties does the transmission of plays become more frequent. Here, too, we are denied any insight into the early phase of the poet's career.

We know that Euripides made his debut in 455 with a tetralogy to which the *Peliades* belonged. Significantly, the figure of Medeia stands at the beginning of his career. Here her victims are the daughters of Pelias whom she induces to make the fatal attempt to rejuvenate their father. The remnants (Buchwald, 9; Webster, *Eur.*, 32) totally contradict Brommer's conjecture (*Arch. Anz.* 1941, 53) that this was a satyr play. Fragments from the end of a hypothesis have not furthered our knowledge.[4]

Of the poet's work between *Peliades* and *Alkestis* we know nothing for certain, but Buchwald (14) has demonstrated the probability that the *Likymnios* was parodied in the *Archilochoi* of Kratinos (fr. 1 Demianczuk) and should be dated ca. 450; perhaps, as Webster believes (36), it belonged to the same tetralogy as the *Peliades*. According to *Il.* 2. 661, Likymnios, a brother of Alkmene, was killed by Tlepolemos, son of Herakles. It is uncertain whether the play included the story of his son Areios (Schmid 3. 462; Webster, 36), whom Herakles brought under his protection to Troy, where he died.

The oldest of the extant plays, the *Alkestis* of 438, occupied the position within a tetralogy that is normally reserved for a satyr play.[5] Since the number of satyr plays known by title (Webster, *Eur.*, 5) is considerably less than the twenty-two tetralogies, we may assume that this is not the only case where Euripides avoided the satyr play. New finds of Aischylos and Sophokles leave no doubt that our poet's achievements in this genre were inferior to those of his predecessors.

Scholars have repeatedly made the mistake of forcing a comic interpretation on the *Alkestis* because of its final position in the tetralogy. Isolated burlesque features in the appearance of Thanatos or the drunken Herakles have been immeasurably exaggerated to support such a view. The *Alkestis* is a genuine tragedy, at least in the ancient sense of the word.

As for the history of the legend, Wilamowitz's theory that the story represents a human version of a divine myth has been generally abandoned; it is now thought that an ancient fairy tale about sacrificial death for the sake of love was combined with another that included a wrestling bout with Death.

Before Aischylos, Phrynichos had dealt with the material. From the meager fragments we may conclude that Death appeared with his sword to cut the hair offering, and that the wrestling-bout with him occurred in this version also. Otherwise we know so little about the play that we cannot even confidently allot it to the satyr plays.[6] Most probably we may ascribe to Euripides the detail that his heroine must sacrifice herself not on her wedding day, but only after a full life as wife and mother. How she was able to lead such a life, while constantly faced with the knowledge of the day on which she must die—that is one of those questions forbidden by the conventions of a dramatic work of art.

The prologue section begins with a speech of Apollo, who steps out of the palace of Admetos. This is the oldest example we have of the Euripidean prologue speech, in which we can see a resumption of the explanatory introduction invented by Thespis. Such monologue passages are often disguised by Euripides as a direct address; here it is a note of thanks for the house that became a place of gentle hospitality for the god who had been condemned to serve it after killing the Kyklopes. Right away (v. 10) we hear Admetos characterized as a ὅσιος ἀνήρ (pious man), and in the god's narrative it is not held against the king that he sought a substitute victim (after all, the god had created this possibility by deceiving the Moirai) and found only his wife willing.[7] Now the day of sacrifice has arrived; how the time limit was extended thus far, and how Alkestis knew when it would expire—these questions are left aside with the high-handedness of poetic license.

With coarse and blustering anapests Thanatos appears. The contrast between this gloomy fellow and the shining god repeats on a humbler level the scene from the *Eumenides* in which Apollo dismisses the daughters of the Night from his temple.

There the god threatens the monsters with his arrows; here too Thanatos is clearly afraid of the god's weapon. But in the following stichomythy he is calmed by Apollo, who tries persuasion—in vain. Apollo is enraged at his own impotence, but before departing he proclaims that a man shall come, sent by Eurystheus to fetch the Thrakian steeds; he will be granted hospitality by Admetos and will wrest Death's prize from him. Thus from the very outset the poet places the play's tragic situation under the aspect of a happy ending. He must rely on his skill to prevent this disclosure from blunting the tragic accents.

Certain of his mission, Death—here expressing what is apparently inevitable—enters the palace by the door through which Apollo departed.

The parodos of the chorus of Pheraian elders (77–135) frames two strophic pairs with anapests that accompany the entrance march and then the change in formation (we must imagine the servant making her appearance in the middle of the separating chorus).[8] The first pair of strophes continues the restless exchange of voices in the introductory anapests. The stillness within the house and the lack of signs of mourning cause uncertainty, and timorous hope fades quickly. In the second strophic pair the voices are united. Only Asklepios, Apollo's son, could help, but he was blasted by the thunderbolt of Zeus. The story of Apollo's penal service (in the prologue) is rounded off here; he slew the Kyklopes because they forged the thunderbolt for Zeus.

In the following first epeisodion (136–212) a servant comes out of the house and reports how Alkestis bade farewell to hearth and home—a deeply penetrating exposition of her character. Especially in the older plays, Euripides takes great care to prepare the appearance of central characters with earlier scenes: thus in *Med.*, *Hipp.*, and still in *Herakles*. We know of nothing comparable in Sophokles; a rough parallel might be found in the *Agamemnon* of Aischylos.

Announced by the chorus leader, the servant begins in a stichomythy and then delivers a lengthy report. This messenger speech is set very early in the play, which could not well have supported such an account about Herakles' struggle with Death.

We see Alkestis praying to Hestia for her children, we follow her to her altars, which she decorates, and we feel the sharp outbreak of pain when she throws herself on her marriage bed, after maintaining her composure for so long. The children cling to her garments, the servants weep—she speaks to each and offers her hand to all. The servant concludes the report by announcing that Alkestis, marked for Death, wishes once more to see the light and the sun.

In this scene, the woman's sentiments are differentiated from those of the men in a subtle and highly significant manner. The male chorus thinks only of the king. They lament for him in the stichomythy, using words that betoken their high esteem (144): οἵας οἷος ὢν ἁμαρτάνεις (What a man you are, who lose such a wife!) The maid's reply is cooler and detached: He does not yet know his loss before he has suffered it. This is repeated in reverse order and even more emphatically when the servant says (197) that Admetos would have been better off to die—"then he'd have it over with"—but now he must taste the fullness of his suffering. Here we see foreshadowed not the agon with Pheres, but rather the despair of Admetos as he returns home from the grave. Once again the chorus responds with a question about Admetos's condition.

In the following strophic pair of the first stasimon (213–237), a timorous request to the gods (first stanza) is followed by deep despair, thus setting the tone for the appearance of Alkestis and Admetos. The lament is continued in anapests (238–243) that again concern Admetos.

The chorus, which had combined to sing the stasimon, again separates into two semi-choruses, to make room for the couple's appearance.

The farewell and death of Alkestis are the subject of the second epeisodion (244–434). Here excited lyrics alternate with set speeches containing rational deliberation. The opening passage, two short strophic pairs with an epode, is composed in such a way that Admetos responds to the lyric verses of Alkestis with two trimeters each, but answers the epode with anapests.

Alkestis greets the light, recalls her maiden years in her homeland, but then, at the beginning of the second strophe, is seized with a vision of death, in which she thinks she feels the grip of the powers below. In his grief, Admetos cries προδῷς (250), a word that appears also at vv. 202 and 275. It might be translated as "betray," thus exposing the wretchedness of Admetos, but A. Rivier (op. cit., 288) has correctly reminded us of the meaning "deserere," and cited a decisive parallel to this situation in *Hipp.* 1456.

Now Alkestis begins her speech; we note the same technique that Euripides also uses in later plays (*Med., Hipp.*): after lyrics provide an outlet for emotion, a speech of calm deliberation follows. The Alkestis who speaks here is no longer the woman despairing in her marriage chamber or shaken by the vision of death; this Alkestis knows the greatness of her sacrifice, she can speak of it dispassionately, without disavowing her resolve. To think of idle narcissism in the face of such purely Greek epideixis is an unpardonable error. Alkestis also knows why she speaks of the greatness of her sacrifice: Admetos must requite it with the vow never to give their children a step-mother. Here a modern reader might miss words of tender love, of which the drama of this time was simply incapable, but he must not ignore what Alkestis says at 287: "I did not wish to live apart from you with orphaned children." Only the most arbitrary interpretation could make the line refer to the children alone. Further, it is important to point out that not once in the whole scene does the poet bring up the question how Admetos might have avoided the situation. An irrevocable, divinely ordained destiny bears down on the couple (247, 297; cf. 523).

The chorus leader vouches for Admetos's loyalty in two fine verses (326 f.) that separate the speeches. In general Euripides shows greater flexibility than Sophokles when a typical context demands such lines.

Who could deny the difficulties involved in the following speech of Admetos, with its lamentations and hyperbolic promises? The real question is whether the poet wanted to use it to make us perceive this character as contemptible and repugnant. When Admetos expresses the desire to have an image of his wife made and to lay it by his side in bed, does the poet consider this an unpardonable lack of taste? But we know of a *Protesilaos* by Euripides, in which the cult celebrated by Laodameia with the statue of her dead husband was a basic motif. Either the play preceded *Alkestis*, which we would like to believe, or else Euripides knew the motif from tradition.[9] However, when Admetos laments and wishes to free Alkestis from Hades like a second Orpheus, we should not forget that after her vow, the death of Alkestis has become inevitable destiny.

After two verses of the chorus leader that are again concerned with Admetos's suffering, Alkestis calls the children to witness the promise he gave her. Farewell and death follow in a stichomythy. Alkestis entrusts the children to her husband, who now must be their father and mother both; this act joins the couple once more before their final separation. Alkestis is not doubting the genuineness of Admetos's sorrow when she says, with a word of resignation (381), that time will soften everything, and the dead are nothing. But her last word is a farewell to her husband.

A pair of strophes follows, separated by two trimeters of Admetos, with the laments of his young son, who sounds movingly childlike in the strophe, more precocious in the antistrophe. The Hellenistic discovery of the child is yet to come.

After the chorus offers some consoling words, the scene is concluded with Admetos's directions for the funeral.

Of the two strophic pairs that form the following second stasimon (435–475), the first celebrates Alkestis and promises her songs at the Karneia of Sparta and in Athens. Because of the very nature of the *Alkestis* the common aetiological connection with existing institutions that usually appears at the end of Euripidean tragedies here occurs quite early in the play. With the admonition to Admetos to keep his promise, the second pair of strophes reflects the previous scene; the chorus's reproaches against the selfishness of the parents, who would not give up their waning lives for their son, anticipate a motif of the agon.

Herakles makes his entrance in the third epeisodion (476–567). Two stichomythies, one with the chorus leader and a longer one with Admetos, are framed by two shorter dialogues and separated by a short speech of Herakles. In the first stichomythy Herakles informs the chorus of his expedition for the steeds of the Thrakian Diomedes, and learns only now the dangers involved; in the second he is persuaded by Admetos to stay as a guest, despite the mourning in the palace. By skillful wordplay that both reveals and disguises the truth, Admetos deceives him about the identity of the "foreign woman" (cf. 646, 810) who lies dead in the house. In the final dialogue the chorus finds fault with this excessive hospitality and anticipates a reproach that we shall hear from Herakles himself in the finale: this sacrifice was made possible only by deceiving a friend.

Thus Admetos's conduct is seen to be ambivalent, but the third stasimon (two pairs of strophes; 568–605), dispels all doubt and blame with its high praise for the king. He is the host who extended guest-friendship to a god! Lyrics expand the image: we see Apollo, Orpheus-like, playing the lyre and surrounded by the beasts of the forest. The chorus ends on a note of irrational hope: Blessings will come to the pious man. Looking backward, the ode comments on Admetos's actions; at the same time it relates to the following scene by providing a cheerful contrast to the gloomy confrontation with Pheres.

The fourth epeisodion (606–961) exhibits typical agon structure. Two long speeches separated by two conciliatory verses of the chorus leader are followed by an excited stichomythy. This complex is framed by short dialogues. The bier with the corpse is brought on stage, and Admetos is calling upon the chorus to bid his wife a last farewell, when their leader announces the approach of Old Pheres, who is bringing offerings for the dead. Admetos rudely turns him away from the bier, bitterly accuses him of selfishness, since the old man refused to sacrifice himself, and finally renounces both his parents. Pheres requites bitterness with bitterness, and reproaches Admetos for the same reasons offered repeatedly by modern scholars: You killed your wife in your cowardly eagerness to live; you let her die and now you blame your parents for staying alive! In the stichomythy, both continue their sharp quarrel.

Does Pheres speak here the real truth about Admetos? We will take our stand on this question later, in the critical section; for now, suffice it to say that the worth or worthlessness of this accusation against Admetos is determined by the character of the man who makes it. In the final dialogue Admetos rejects his parents even more forcefully; then the funeral procession, after one last farewell from the chorus, leaves the scene. Choral anapests accompany the movement.

The stage is now empty, as in the *Eumenides* and the *Aias*, both times with a change of scene; this occurs again in Euripides' *Helena* and *Phaethon*, and in the spurious *Rhesos*. The fourth epeisodion (747–860) is constructed in a way familiar to us from the comedies of Aristophanes (*Wasps* 1292) and Menander (*Epitrepontes* 434). A servant reports the improper behavior of a person inside the house, who then himself appears on stage. The effect of the ensuing confrontation depends on mutual misunderstanding, a device exploited in many variations by the comedy of all periods. The servant complains about the noisy carousing of a stranger in the house of the dead queen, then Herakles comes in and confirms the slave's testimony with a protreptikos on enjoying the good life. In a stichomythy that is briefly congested at a crucial point (817), the two at first talk right past each other, then Herakles learns who the dead woman really was. The lightly applied touches of cheerful inebriation disappear in a flash after the truth is discovered. Herakles proclaims his resolve to wrest Alkestis from Death as he drinks the sacrificial blood at her grave, or else to bring her back from the underworld. He owes this to Admetos, who offered him such hospitality. The speech concludes with praise for this service, eclipsing initial words of reproach (816). Thus his attitude runs parallel to that of the chorus, renewing and confirming their commendation.

The third part of this lengthy epeisodion belongs entirely to Admetos, who comes back from the grave with the chorus. His suffering sets the tone for the kommos and is afterward expressed through clear but painful reflection. In the kommos, four anapestic passages of Admetos are followed by the individual elements of two strophic pairs, in which the chorus offers consolation, their voices divided in the first pair, united in the second. In the anapests of Admetos, the first and fourth sections describe the horror of the desolate house; in between we hear the rather stock lament (cf. *Med.* 1090) for the suffering a man must endure if he marries, and the third passage strikes an emphatic note with the question Admetos puts to the chorus: Why did you hold me back when I wished to leap into the grave?

Admetos's speech after the kommos is highly significant. He has not changed, nor is he burdened with regret, but he has come to a realization, which he expresses in v. 940: ἄρτι μανθάνω (only now do I understand). His situation, the very one occasioned by his wife's noble sacrifice, now confronts him with painful clarity: loveless isolation, no place to dwell in peace, and besides, the malicious gossip of his enemies, the κακοί, who will accuse him in the same way as did his father. The path by which he avoided his fated death has led him into misery (961).

The song of the chorus now flows more broadly in the fourth stasimon (962–1005). In the first strophic pair they sing of the relentlessness of ananke—before the concluding scene, in which we hear the "nevertheless" that points to salvation. In the second pair they turn to Admetos, bid him consider the necessity of his sorrowful destiny, and conclude with a smooth transition to praise for Alkestis and her sacrifice.

The final scene (1008–1163) is composed as a sort of agon between friends, and exhibits a corresponding form: two long speeches (here without intervening choral verses) are followed by a stichomythy that ends with a resolution into smaller verse groups. This stichomythy contains the issue of the situation developed in the two speeches.

Herakles begins immediately with a good-natured scolding (note the anadiplosis, 1017!), reproaching Admetos for deceiving him. The evaluation of this deception now undergoes a third change, for when Herakles, in his farewell speech, admonishes Admetos to continue offering pious hospitality to guest-friends, this sets the king's action, which before was branded a lie, now in a brighter light. Herakles' friendly revenge is a deception on his part that leads for Admetos to the confirmation of his fidelity. Herakles brings with him a veiled woman; he claims that he won her in a contest and demands that Admetos accept her in his house until he has survived his adventure in Thrace. Admetos refuses in a speech of some length. Euripides adds a subtle touch: it is this woman's very resemblance to Alkestis that makes the sight of her so unbearable. In the stichomythy Admetos again speaks of his pain and his resolve to remain faithful to his dead wife. Herakles understands and praises this but insists that his friend take the foreign woman into his house, so that, after much resistance, Admetos must finally grasp her hand. Here, at the decisive moment, the verse (1119) breaks into antilabai: Admetos holds Alkestis, returned to the light, and the words of salvation flow from the lips of her rescuer: Keep her, look at her, step from the darkness of pain into bliss! At first Admetos is incredulous, then he is all joy and thanks. Showing a fine sensibility, the poet has Alkestis remain silent—she must first be cleansed of her contact with the world of the dead. Herakles, however, cannot stay to share in the festive joy—here his character receives a light tragic touch—he must go on to his next struggle.

Choral anapests about the shifting plans of gods that counter all expectation (the same lines recur at the end of *Andr.*, *Hel.*, *Ba.*, and slightly modified in the *Med.*) conclude the play.

The structure of this, Euripides' oldest extant play, already shows the complete mastery of a poet who knew the stage. We can see this in the motif of Admetos's hospitality, which has a two-sided effect. It serves to characterize the grand seigneur, but it is also the essential prerequisite for the salvation of Alkestis. In a well-deliberated interlocking sequence, Euripides has divided the three scene blocks that contain the sacrifice of Alkestis and its effect on Admetos (136–434, 606–746, 861–961) by inserting two scenes with Herakles (476–567, 747–860), saving the union of all three figures in wonderful scenic harmony for the finale. A weakness in composition might have resulted from the fact that Alkestis drops out of the play as an active character after her all-too-early death. Euripides escaped this danger by playing out at great length the significance of her sacrifice. The prologue already predicts what will happen, but then we experience doubly the farewell of Alkestis: once with emotional intensity in the report of the maid, then illuminated rationally in the long scene with Admetos. The chorus does its part to maintain the central significance of her sacrificial death.

The most difficult problem of the drama is the character of Admetos; necessarily connected with this is the evaluation of Alkestis.[10] In his "Letters on the operetta *Alceste*," Wieland said that we cannot love this man and that his laments offend us. Goethe pilloried this as being non-Greek sentimentality in his farce "Gods, Heroes, and Wieland," but not a few poets and commentators have toiled to produce a spotless Admetos. Today two opposing fronts evaluate his character. Wieland's appraisal was energetically continued by van Lennep in his commentary and book on Euripides; he condemns Admetos on the basis of thoroughly modern categories. Von Fritz (310) grants that Admetos showed himself to be a decent man by keeping his promise of fidelity, but he sees him before Alkestis in a pitiful state in which he transgresses the bounds of good taste. However that may be, von Fritz has emphasized one thought that remains important for any interpretation of the play: the transformation from fairy tale to drama, in which the characters must come alive on stage, gives rise to a whole new set of problems, and much that was originally obvious now becomes doubtful.

The opposing front was headed by Wilamowitz, who stated in the introduction to his translation that the poet intended to make Admetos "into such an amiable man that he deserved the return of his wife." We would like to alter this view slightly, in that we cannot take offense at Admetos's happiness, but our interpretation runs much along this line. The play is so understood by A. M. Dale in her commentary, and recently by Steidle (132), with more subtle and profound argumentation. Here we can offer only the most important evidence. Three voices in the drama attest Admetos's noble character: those of Apollo (10, 42), the chorus (144, 569), and Herakles (857, 860, 1147). Also in his favor are his fidelity, which he not only promises but also preserves, and the depth of his awareness when faced with a deserted house. Of course it would be wrong to wish to explain away the difficulties presented by his farewell speech to Alkestis. But if his lamentations seem embarrassing—since all this is not really necessary—we must remember that a revocation of the sacrificial vow is utterly impossible. What happens now is destiny; significantly, Euripides has Alkestis say (297) that a god has simply ordered it this way; the poet may also have separated the promise from its fulfillment by a longer time period in order to show the couple in an irrevocably preordained situation. And then there is the scandal that has caused so much indignation: the sculpted likeness of his wife, which Admetos wants to place in his bed! The decisive statement about this was already made by Wilamowitz, with his reference to the Euripidean *Protesilaos*. We further note our analysis of the passage above. As for the accusations of Pheres, which in fact contain exactly those points which have led moderns to reject Admetos, we must focus our attention on the portrayal of the accuser in the play. It is not merely Admetos's conviction that Pheres refused to sacrifice his few remaining years out of loathsome selfishness; Alkestis says the same (290), and even the chorus condemns the aged parents (466). The Pheres who speaks the shameful line (766) "Once I am dead, evil gossip won't bother me" is not the man who should decide over our judgment of Admetos. This interpretation gains support when, after returning from the grave, Admetos foresees accusations of this sort in the mouths of ἐχθϱοί (enemies; 954) and κακοί (evil men).

It should already be clear from the previous paragraphs that we do not follow the interpretation of Alkestis as a sober and disillusioned wife who would surely never vow to sacrifice her life again if she had the choice. Strangely enough it is Wilamowitz who first took this view, which stands in marked opposition to his interpretation of Admetos and whose chief supporters are van Lennep and von Fritz, and also Kullmann (op. cit., 137), who judges Admetos rather as we do here, but believes that Alkestis has lost all her illusions about the meaning of her sacrifice. Such an interpretation seems to ignore the report of the maid, and we must also bear in mind that the *Alkestis* is not the only play in which highly emotional passages are followed by a rational discussion of the situation. But even in Alkestis's deliberative speech, we find line 287, which we have emphasized in our analysis. It can neither be taken as a reference to the children alone, thus bypassing Admetos (van Lennep), nor be dismissed as a report of her earlier decision to die (Kullmann). In this context it is also crucial that we not misunderstand the character displayed by the verses in which Alkestis, shortly before her death, hands the children over to Admetos as a pledge of their common bond. We can offer no better summing-up than this phrase from A. M. Dale's commentary: "and of course she loves Admetos."

In the interpretation proposed here we reject the view that the end of the play should be taken not as a liberating release from cares but rather as an ironic indication that such a denouement is in fact unsatisfactory (von Fritz, Kullmann). Recent editors have cast doubt also on the role of Apollo.[11] The rudiments (though nothing more) of a criticism of the god seem to be suggested by the fact that his good will leads only to new and greater suffering.

Thus we see the *Alkestis* on the first level as the story of a loving wife who sacrifices her life for her husband. But—and here we are basically following von Fritz—the fairy tale has assumed different features in the Euripidean drama. What was once an unproblematical solution is now seen to be the beginning of new sorrows. The king has escaped death, but at the cost of a life that is not worth living. He must come to realize this before the might of Herakles restores his wife to him. The experiences of both have proved difficult, but after sacrifice and insight their suffering has opened the way to a new life.[12]

The motif of voluntarily sacrificing one's life was a favorite of Euripides, especially if the sacrifice was for one's country (as in *Hkld., Erechtheus, Phoin., Iph. A.,* and probably *Phrixos*).[13] Here the categories of Aristotle's *Poetics* are no longer sufficient; the motif of voluntary sacrifice shows us how Euripidean tragedy seeks to arouse not only φόβος and ἔλεος (fear and pity) but also admiration. This is the start of a development that leads through Seneca to baroque drama and reaches its zenith in Corneille.[14]

The tetralogy that ended with the *Alkestis* began with the *Kretai*. According to schol. Soph. *Ai.* 1297, this play told the story of Minos's granddaughter Aerope, whom her father Katreus handed over to Nauplios to be drowned for unchastity. Nauplios, however, betrothed her to Pleisthenes. Webster (*Eur.,* 38), on the basis of the quite indefinite scholium on Aristoph. *Ach.* 433, assumes that Thyestes was one of the characters in this play. If so, then the Nauplios story must have been related in the prologue, and the courtship between Aerope and Thyestes could have been the main theme; it is doubtful whether we should also include the revenge of Atreus.[15]

The second play was *Alkmeon in Psophis*.[16] In his wanderings, Alkmeon, the killer of his mother, Eriphyle, comes to the mouth of the Acheloos, where he could find peace with Kallirhoe. In Psophis he was obliged to abandon Arsinoe, whom King Phegeus gave him to wife, and there too was left the golden necklace of Eriphyle. Kallirhoe desires to have it, and Alkmeon returns to Psophis to obtain the necklace by trickery. But the deception is revealed and costs him his life. However, Arsinoe (a character in the mold of Alkestis, in Schadewaldt's opinion) remains true to her former husband after his death, suffering greatly for her fidelity.

In the *Telephos*, the third play, the Mysian king, wounded by Achilleus, comes to Argos disguised as a beggar and, by abducting and threatening the young Orestes, forces the Greeks assembled there to provide a cure. The realism of presenting the king in rags was uncustomary: Aristophanes' mockery (*Ach., Thesm.*) shows that it caused great offense. The especially large number of fragments allows us to reconstruct this work with relative confidence.[17] E. W. Handley and John Rea made the important discovery that of the fragments previously ascribed to Sophokles' Ἀχαιῶν σύλλογος, *P. Berol.* 9908 (Berl. Klass. Texte 5/2, 64) certainly and *P. Ryl.* 978 most probably belong to the *Telephos* of Euripides.[18]

The *Medeia*, which has had an unparalleled impact on world literature, was awarded only third prize by the judges at its first performance in 431.[19] The story had its origins in ancient cult legends that told of a φόνος ἀκούσιος (unintentional murder) committed by Medeia when she attempted to make her children immortal in the temple of Hera Akraia. In the play, Medeia's promise to bury the children in that sanctuary and establish a festival for them refers to the graves of her children on display in Korinth and to the cult associated with them. As in many other instances, at the end of the play Euripides turns from his free adaptation of the myth, with its new interpretation of human problems, back to existing cult practices, as if the drama were an aition for those institutions. Based on our present knowledge we cannot determine whether Euripides was the first to make revenge the motive for Medeia's killing her sons. The confidence with which this view has been asserted in the past now seems unjustified, but we believe that Wilamowitz has made a fairly strong case for it.[20] If this is correct, then, following Page (op. cit., xxiv n. 5, after a suggestion from Beazley) and Buchwald (35), we could also assume that the revenge of Euripides' betrayed heroine was fashioned after the myth of Tereus and Prokne.

The hypothesis reports as the opinion of Dikaiarchos (fr. 63W) and Aristotle in the (almost certainly spurious) *Hypomnemata* that Euripides borrowed and adapted his *Medeia* from Neophron. In Diog. Laert. II. 134,[21] and in the *Suda* (s.v. Neophron) this has been inflated to the monstrous assertion that Euripides' work was in reality written by Neophron. Three fragments have survived (frr. 1–3N); the first accounts for the arrival of Aigeus by his seeking an explanation from Medeia of the oracle he received, while the second and longest corresponds to Medeia's monologue at 1021 and presents the Euripidean motifs in abbreviated form. The third fragment contains a prophecy, which diverges from Euripides' account, about Iason's death: he will hang himself. The most thorough treatment of the whole question is offered by D. L. Page in his edition of the play. In the course of a careful and mainly linguistic analysis he comes to the conclusion that a younger Neophron (assuming the elder to be in fact a nonimaginary person) composed an imitation of Euripides, which, perhaps because of the similarity of names, was later erroneously ascribed to a poet who lived before Euripides. In favor of the sequence supported by Page, one can note the obvious attempt to improve the motivation of the Aigeus scene.[22]

The prologue of the play is spoken by Medeia's nurse. Fear and concern underline her description of Iason's betrayal of Medeia and of her excessively violent reaction. In the second part of the prologue scene, the pedagogue comes on stage with the children. His dramatic function is to report the still unconfirmed rumor about the banishment of Medeia and her children. Like the first rumblings of an oncoming storm, the nurse had related in her prologue speech (36) that the mere sight of the children was hateful to Medeia; this motif recurs more emphatically at the end of this section (90): the pedagogue must keep the children away from their mother. In the third, completely anapestic part of the prologue, Medeia's painful cries are heard within the house as the nurse replies; for the third time mention is made of the danger which the mother now represents for her own sons. The nurse speaks soothing words to the children in order to send them into the house (89), but they remain, and so in the anapestic section (100), she must again urgently demand that they make haste, once more with a warning that the children should stay out of their mother's sight.[23] Here appears the key word (αὐθάδης, proud, defiant) for Medeia's nature, which is variously termed ἦθος, φύσις, and φρήν as Euripides probes for concepts in a way characteristic of his time. The second exclamation of pain that we hear from the house confirms the nurse's fears: Medeia curses her children. After new words of anxious concern, the nurse leaves the stage praising the life of moderation, but this represents only a brief pause before the following parodos of the chorus of Korinthian women (131–212). Their verses continue directly along the line of the prologue scene, both in the liberal use of anapests and in subject matter. Short, nonresponsive lyric passages of the chorus frame an arrangement composed so that a choral strophe follows anapests of the nurse and Medeia, after which come more anapests of the two women (here in the order B–A), followed by the antistrophe and finally an anapestic recitative of the nurse.

The grief of Medeia, who appeals to Themis and Artemis and now longs for revenge on Iason and his bride (163), is answered by explanatory comments from the nurse and miserable consolation from the chorus, which does, however, advance the plot by expressing the wish that Medeia come out of the house. The poet retards this section strangely: the nurse laments the fact that songs and lyre playing can bring festive joy but cannot comfort those in sorrow. The sharp chords struck in this opening scene fade out as the chorus intones the concluding verses, which name once again the oath-preserving Themis of Zeus.

The first epeisodion (214–409) begins with a speech of Medeia. As in *Alk.* and *Hipp.*, highly charged emotion is followed by calm and controlled discourse. Medeia considers at length how a foreigner should behave in the community and explains that she has come out to seek the sympathy of the women. Next she offers a rational account about the oppression of women, whose lot it is to be subject to men—a complaint that pertains more to the Athenian order of society than to the world of myth. But then Medeia separates her fate from that of women who have a country and a home. It becomes clear (260) that her will is indeed set upon revenge for Iason's crime, but that she has not yet decided on her method. This means that her hatred for the children, a main theme of the prologue, has not yet been connected with a definite plan for revenge. Should she find such a plan, she would like the support of the women. The chorus leader assures her of their assistance and announces the arrival of Kreon.

The function of this next scene with Kreon is to exert pressure on Medeia's will for revenge by severely limiting the time in which she can act. The portrayal of Kreon is a masterpiece of Euripidean characterization. The king attempts to disguise his inner weakness by assuming a bold front. His first words are a blunt and violent attack on Medeia. To her almost humble question why she must leave, he replies δέδοικά σε (I fear you; 282), which is the truth. Her long speech cannot dispel Kreon's distrust; beginning again he repeats even more forcefully his decree of banishment (321). Appropriately, an agitated stichomythy now begins, in which Kreon at first stands fast against Medeia's urgent pleas. But in verse 337, though still unyielding, he seems to weaken, and immediately Medeia seizes the opportunity to present a compromise request: Just this one day! And here Kreon gives in, sealing his doom. Another brilliant touch by Euripides: the king expends the rest of his energy in threats of violence, if Medeia should remain any longer. Then he reassures himself: Then stay this one day, for in it you cannot do harm.[24]

At the beginning of her speech (292) Medeia speaks at length of the position of the intellectually superior individual who is exposed to the hate and envy of society.

This passage deserves special attention, for although it is thoroughly integrated into the context, it represents as well an aspect of the struggle for the βίος θεωρητικός (theoretical life), which affected the life of Euripides himself.

In place of the customary intervening verses of the chorus leader, we find choral anapests (357–363), which, preparing for the Aigeus scene, pose the decisive question: Where can you find refuge?

Now follows one of Medeia's three great speeches which form the framework that determines the structure of the play.[25] The speech is not a pure monologue, for the chorus is addressed in the first section (365, 368, 377), but this contact soon dissolves and the rest becomes a soliloquy. Only at the end does the plural πεφύκαμεν allow vaguely for the possibility that the chorus is included in her statement. In this speech Medeia carefully considers how she might accomplish her revenge, but finds herself confronted with a serious obstacle. Kreon charged (287) Medeia with threatening the married couple and the bride's father with destruction; now their destruction is revealed as her firm resolution (375). The children are not yet included in her plan for revenge. Calmly and rationally she at first considers fire and the sword but then decides on poison as the method best suited to her. Now, however, her thoughts reach an impasse. Once the deed is done, where can she seek refuge? There still remains hope that an escape may be found (again, preparation for Aigeus); if so, then she can proceed with her deception. But if not—and here she abandons her cool deliberation and is swept away by emotion—she will kill her enemies with the sword, even if it means paying with her own life. With deep pathos she calls to Hekate, then summons up her own courage to dare all and maintain her pride as Helios's granddaughter. The effect is splendid: the calm flow of her careful consideration is stopped short when her plan seems hindered, at which point her passion boils up and assumes control.

The first stasimon (410–445) is sung in preparation for Iason's appearance. The world order is reversed: deceit and faithlessness are now attributes of men. The second strophic pair laments Medeia's fate and protests that oaths are no longer held sacred—a motif emphatically repeated in the agon. Indeed, in general the choral sections of the Medeia are quite closely connected with the dialogue scenes, thus refuting Aristotle's criticism (Poet. 18, 1456a 25).

The great agon between Iason and Medeia forms the second epeisodion (446–626). After a shorter speech of Iason follow two long speeches by the antagonists, separated by two verses of the chorus leader. They do not conclude with a stichomythy but rather by excited discourse that seems to strive toward such a form; here, however, the extreme harshness of the arguments allows only limited opportunity for compression into single verses.

Believing that the best form of defense is attack, Iason begins by reproaching Medeia, who brought exile on herself by her threats. Now he wishes to alleviate her distress, an offer that must strike to the depths of Medeia's pride: the traitor feigning concern! And so she too begins with a violent assault. After an emotional prooimion she lists her arguments.[26] First of all she recalls all that she did for Iason, although her murder of Apsyrtos is overlooked. This deed will be mentioned later (1334) as one

of Iason's reproaches. Bitterly she reminds the perjurer of his oath. Setting off on another tack, she takes up his promise to provide for her. This, for her, is nothing but
scorn, for where can she turn without a homeland? In his reply, Iason follows Medeia's sequence of thought. All of her services on his behalf he sweeps aside with an
argument that stems from archaic Greek thought, the double motivation of human
action. Medeia perceives her earlier deeds as her personal achievement, but Iason
sees them as the work of the gods, here of Kypris in particular. And what did this
barbarian woman gain upon entering Hellenic lands! Approximately at the same
point as Medeia (499–545), he too begins a new tack, attempting to show that his
new marriage will benefit his family. In three choral verses the women take Medeia's
side: betrayal remains betrayal, and none of Iason's arguments can undo his perjury.

The following dispute offers little that is thematically new. Medeia refutes Iason's fancy speeches by blaming him for not telling her a word of his planned infidelity. Iason repeats his offer of assistance, thus giving the epeisodion the form of ring-
composition. Proudly, Medeia refuses. The final words of both figures are characteristic: Iason calls the gods to witness that he has done what he could, but in the words
Medeia calls after him, the full force of her passionate jealousy breaks through: Go! I
know you can't wait to be with her! Make a marriage you'll soon regret!

The second stasimon (627–662) is again divided into two parts. In the first pair
of strophes we hear the chorus's reaction to the dispute: May Kypris spare me from
excessive love! The second pair then looks forward to the next scene: What a terrible
fate, to be without a homeland! No city, no friend will take you in!

The third epeisodion (663–823), with the Aigeus scene, first responds to the
chorus's song and removes the stumbling block from the path of Medeia's revenge.
This scene has been repeatedly criticized, from antiquity onward (schol. *Med.* 666).
Now it is a fact that the Attic king meets Medeia by pure chance; also, the Neophron
fragment shows that the need was felt for a more convincing motivation. But against
this must be set the great significance of the scene for the play as a whole, and further, the point stressed by Erbse (op. cit.) that the section is placed in the center of
the composition, surrounded by concentric scenes. Beyond this we must reckon with
the possibility that Aigeus was well known to the public through Euripides' *Aigeus.*[27]

This scene gives us the opportunity to make a formal observation about the
varied use of stichomythy. In the Kreon scene we find the technique employed on a
smaller scale; in the agon the form is avoided almost completely; now the scene with
Aigeus begins with a lengthy stichomythy. The dialogue partners exchange pertinent
information: Aigeus reports the strange oracle that he received to rid himself of childlessness, and which Pittheus in Troizen must explain to him; Medeia relates the
story of Iason's infidelity. Here it becomes clear (698) that she believes nothing of
Iason's arguments in the agon. The stichomythy is followed by Medeia's fervent plea
for protection, and Aigeus's agreement—on one condition: he himself cannot take
her from this land, but if she comes to Athens his house is open to her. Medeia
knows that she is pursued by the relatives of Pelias, and soon the Korinthians will
take up the chase. Therefore she binds Aigeus by a solemn oath.

The chorus accompanies Aigeus's departure with anapests (759–763), thus separating his scene from Medeia's following speech. This is addressed to the women of the chorus (765, 772, 797), who listen carefully (811), but it also contains elements of a monologue, especially near the end. She begins with unrestrained joy, elated that her path to revenge is now clear; then she informs the chorus of her secret plan (βουλεύματα; 772). She will feign reconciliation with Iason and request that the children be allowed to remain. She says she does this not so as to abandon them to the mercy of her enemies, but rather to destroy Kreusa with her gifts—a distant allusion to the motif, later to become so important, that the children are endangered by the Korinthians. Garments and jewelry smeared with poison will destroy the princess.[28] Then, after a clearly marked pause, she reveals the ultimate horror: the children too must die. Her justification for this is pure and simple: she wishes to annihilate Iason's entire house. The psychological problems involved are expressed epigrammatically in φιλτάτων παίδων φόνον (the slaughter of my dearest children); her hatred for the children is no longer dominant. Now she realizes that her first mistake was to abandon her father's house, but she will tread the path of revenge to the end. The speech concludes with a tenet of the ancient code of nobility, here in the mouth of a barbarian woman: to be severe with enemies and kind to friends.

The horrified chorus protests, but in vain. They forewarn her (818) of the pain she will feel as a mother who, in striking her children, strikes herself. Nothing can check Medeia; she sends for Iason.

Again, the third stasimon (824–865) points in two directions. The first pair of strophes, with their praise of Athens, reinforces the impression of the Aigeus scene. It is instructive to compare this ode with the praise of Kolonos in the *Oidipous* play of the aged Sophokles. Euripides, unlike his rival, puts great stress on intellectual values (827, 844), and behind the lovely description of a delicate walk through the bright-shining aether, we can recognize the teachings of a great physician of the time about the meaning of the environment. The second strophic pair reflects upon Medeia's terrible decision and at the same time points ahead to the events to come.

The plot is carried out in the fourth epeisodion (866–975). This scene is divided into two parts, again by an exact indication of the disposition (932). The feigned reconciliation is staged in the form of an agon: two speeches separated by choral verses. Then follows an abbreviated stichomythy. Medeia pretends that she has changed her mind, and again we find βουλεύματα (866) in the sense of a rationally considered plan. She calls the children from the house to greet their father. Here Euripides, the master of psychological insight, adds one of his finest touches to the portrayal of his heroine: Medeia, seeing her family reunited, illusion though it is, and seeing the children reach out to embrace their father, loses her composure and bursts into tears. The bitter hatred stressed in the prologue scene is broken; the children are no longer merely the means to revenge, they are Medeia's children and she, as their mother, now feels the pain that had been announced for the first time in her words (795) and that the chorus had predicted (861). The fate of the children now becomes the focal point for the entire scene, both in the painful intimations of their mother and in the meaningless utopia of a happy future described by their father. With a steady hand Euripides ties the threads that will come together in Medeia's great monologue. The second part of the scene advances the plot: Iason, with Kreusa's help, must obtain permission for the children to remain in Korinth. Medeia herself will support the request with precious gifts. Iason resists, here again in tones of generous concern, but is quickly overcome. The scene closes as the children are sent off, and in her last words—she hopes for good news—Medeia is once more solely the avenger, set in her purpose.

The fourth stasimon (976–1001) is woven tightly into the plot: no hope left to save the children (α), the bride is doomed as well (α'). Iason, most wretched, has destroyed them all (β'), but they must also lament the mother who kills her children (β'). Significantly, this last motif is set at the end of the ode in preparation for the following monologue.

The fifth epeisodion (1002–1250) comprises two parts, comprised by Medeia's great soliloquy and the messenger's report. The division is marked by a long passage of choral anapests, which basically serves the purpose of a stasimon.

The pedagogue has brought back the children, and joyfully announces that they may remain in the land. He attributes the painful reaction of their mother to the imminent separation. Impatiently Medeia sends him into the house.

Now she is alone with the children and confronted with the full weight of her decision. More than her other speeches, this passage is pure monologue, in which the forces within her rise up in opposition. Only once (1043), overwhelmed by the flood of emotion, does she appeal to the women of the chorus.

Medeia begins by addressing the children and speaks at first of the future as it might be if she relented. The children now have a house and a homeland, but she, an exile, must flee to strange lands. All her maternal hopes are shattered. Only in the last line of this passage (1038) does she come out with the terrible ambiguity: the children are going ἐς ἄλλο σχῆμα βίου (to another form of life), they are marked for death. But this very assertion—now become inexorable—causes an immediate reaction: the children's innocent smiles overwhelm their mother. As if the women could help her, she turns to the chorus. She cannot do the deed, her plan must be dropped (1044, 1048: βουλεύματα). She will take the children with her into exile, she will not inflict on her own heart twice the pain that Iason will feel. Her decision seems fixed, but can she bear it? To abandon revenge and be mocked by her foes? No, her hand will not falter! But once more her maternal instincts rise up against the rage of passion, against the adversary θυμός (seat of emotional impulses). She appeals to herself to spare the children. "There"—which can only mean Athens—they will live with her.[29] Then the fourth and last turning point, which now appears under a new aspect: It is too late. With a solemn prologue summoning up the chthonic spirits of malediction, Medeia swears that she will never abandon her children to the revenge of her enemies. Kreusa is already dying, trapped in the poisonous gifts (simultaneous events off-stage have a direct effect on Medeia's actions), the children are under the spell of Death, and with her own hand she must deliver the fatal blow. Now there is no turning back, only a last farewell fraught with all the suffering of a mother's heart. She sends the children into the house and concludes with a word of bitter insight into the struggle between the forces within her breast: the θυμός was stronger than the βουλεύματα; fiery passion emerges as the victor, the source of all evil. The thought sequence of this incomparable passage is by no means precise and unbroken. We will return to this in our critical section.

The chorus's long anapestic section (1081–1115) develops the topos that children cause pain and sorrow.

Quickly the messenger enters; he urges Medeia to flee and reports the demise of Kreusa and her father. But Medeia first wishes to hear the words she longs for, and so the messenger delivers one of those expansive reports in which the tragedian proves himself a master of epic narration. A special feature of these reports is their careful attention to realistic detail. Kreusa does not appear on stage, but how vividly we can imagine this vain, loveless creature! When the children arrive, she turns away insulted, but one glimpse of the dress and diadem, and all is forgotten. Iason has barely gone out the door with the children when she hastens to try on the precious gifts. She smiles at her reflection in the mirror, and turns her head to delight in the folds of her garment.[30] Then the poison eats into her flesh, and she dies miserably, along with her father, who throws himself over her.

After two unusually flat verses of the chorus leader, Medeia speaks her last and shortest monologue,[31] which moves from an appeal to the chorus quickly into self-apostrophe.[32] Here the motif that appeared at the end of the great soliloquy now becomes dominant: the children must die, but not by the hands of an enemy—so she must be the one to kill them. In the earlier speech it was the unholy power of the ϑυμός that determined her action; now, however, a situation of ἀνάγκη (necessity; 1240, 1243) has resulted. This alone fills Medeia's thoughts; she does not even mention revenge. While the speech opens in a declarative tone, soon it breaks into a series of imperatives, with which Medeia rouses herself to act. However, the speech also expresses all the pain she feels as the boys' mother, and echoes are heard from earlier passages, especially the great soliloquy. The decision is no longer subject to discussion. Though in the prologue she could look on her offspring only with hatred, now, as the reality of her vengeful deed presses closer, her motherly love asserts its right with increasing intensity.

Euripides has not only integrated the following choral ode (1251–1292) wholly into the plot, he has also allowed the action to proceed during the song itself. The first strophic pair is a single exclamation of horror: The earth and Helios, Medeia's ancestor, must intervene! We hear the children cry for help twice, in two pairs of trimeters inserted in the second strophe. More pitifully even than the chorus in the Agamemnon, the Korinthian women consider intervening, but they do not act. And in the second antistrophe, the allusion to Ino seems almost embarrassing. Yet it does serve the function of a pause as the emotion subsides before the next onslaught, with the arrival of Iason.

In the exodos scene Iason rushes to the palace. The poet adds one last ironic bond between him and Medeia. The same thought that ultimately determined her action now forces him to hasten: the children must not fall victim to the Korinthians' revenge. In a short stichomythy with the chorus leader he learns of their death. He is about to break down the gate, when Medeia appears on the roof of the skene in a chariot drawn by dragons, sent to her by Helios. The corpses of her children lie before her. Divorced from all human feeling she is now purely the demon of revenge, which she savors to the last. Scornfully she looks down on Iason; his long speech, filled with accusations, cannot move her hardened heart. The ananke motif is forgotten and when at the beginning of the following stichomythy Iason cries to her "But you too suffer," she speaks her most dreadful line: My pain is profit, so long as you cannot gloat in triumph! How different were her words in the soliloquy (1046)! The stichomythy ends with Iason's request for the children's bodies. Medeia offers a reply that would normally be proclaimed by a deus ex machina: she will establish a cult of expiation for the children, whom she will bury in the sanctuary of Hera Akraia. This is undoubtedly an attempt to link the play with existing custom. Once again Medeia pours out hatred and scorn in a final section of anapests, then she savors her last triumph. Iason begs for permission to hold the boys in his arms again, but in vain. He is left behind in despair; his concluding words, denouncing Medeia, are futile.

The chorus ends the drama with stock verses used in several of the plays, as we saw in the *Alkestis*; here they seem quite out of place.

The *Medeia* is bipartite in structure. The first part develops Medeia's situation and her unbounded desire for revenge, which is not yet directed at any specific target. A new and formidable obstacle, Kreon's decree of banishment, she deprives of its immediate effectiveness, but only with difficulty. The great agon presents the irreconcilable split between Iason and Medeia in further preparation for the act of revenge. The Aigeus scene, set at the center of the play, is pivotal. Now Medeia's path lies clear and she follows it, first in the plot and then in the murder of her children, with a constancy that is shaken only briefly by the forces within her. The concluding scene will be discussed below.

For a proper understanding of this drama much depends on the interpretation of the two main characters. We are especially indebted to von Fritz's insights concerning Iason.[33] He was able to challenge the popular conception that the poet intended to portray Iason as a hypocrite in the great agon scene. Iason's speech faithfully represents his own beliefs, his own view of the situation. He employs all the arguments he can think of, he delivers them with expertise, but he does not simply invent them. He is also serious when he claims that he did Medeia a favor by bringing her from a world of barbarism into the Hellenic order (536). Anouilh developed his *Médée* entirely from this basis. However, this line of argumentation cannot attempt to justify Iason's action. We cannot agree with von Fritz's assertion (350) that Iason adequately replies to Medeia's charge of breaking his oath when he explains his new marriage as a means of providing for his family. Iason does not take up the accusation of perjury because the point admits no argument—the oath, to which Medeia refers (160), which the nurse (169) and chorus (209) also mention, and which receives such strong emphasis in the agon (492), has clearly been broken. After all, Iason had sworn to remain faithful to his beloved, not to provide for her subsistence. Our own impression is well stated by the chorus leader (576): You have spoken skillfully, but justice is not on your side. Von Fritz has, however, correctly established that this agon reveals the irreparable discord between two people whose natures are essentially different, and that is the root of the conflict. Iason could not have chosen more fitting words if he had intended to wound Medeia to the heart.

As for the character of the barbarian princess, we must first clear up a mistaken notion that originated in antiquity and was recently revived in Zürcher's stimulating book on Euripides. The scholiast on v. 922 criticizes the character's lack of unity: Medeia weeps and laments, but still kills her children. This verdict betrays the influence of Aristotle, who demanded τὸ ὁμαλόν (consistency of character) and criticized the *Iphigeneia at Aulis* on this very point (*Poetics* 1454a 26). Zürcher has even spoken of a disintegration of character and an abrupt switch between θυμός and ἀνάγκη motifs.[34] But to assert that Medeia as avenger and Medeia as suffering mother have nothing in common but a name does not do justice to the poet, who was intimately acquainted with the furthest reaches of the human soul and knew that hatred and love, tenderness and fury, can exist simultaneously within it. The persistent influence of this Medeia throughout the millennia is largely due to the fact that her character is a unity of opposites.[35] To be sure, the phrase "psychological drama" has become something of a cliché in Euripidean studies, but it is incorrect to overlook the mastery of Euripides' psychological portraits, as Schlesinger (op. cit.) does, and substitute instead chance as the dominant factor in the sequence of action.

As we intimated in our analysis, the train of thought in the great soliloquy (1021) presents considerable difficulties. At the very start, Medeia's shift from her musings on the newly developed situation (the decree of banishment has been lifted for the children) to the grim reality of her murderous plan seem rather forced. But the real problem arises later: twice Medeia's maternal feelings attempt to subdue her passion and save the children (1040, 1056) and both times the thought occurs that she could take the boys with her into exile and live happily with them there. After the final, decisive turning point (the fourth in this speech), a new motif appears: the necessity of preventing the Korinthians from taking revenge on the children. Not a word about the possibility mentioned earlier, that they might accompany her into exile, nor of the reasons why this should no longer be possible. Solving this contradiction is our most difficult task in the interpretation of the passage.

The radical solution, the athetesis of lines 1056–1080 proposed by G. Müller following Bergk, has generally been rejected, and rightly so. Recently G. A. Seeck (op. cit.) offered a valuable survey of the various proposals, none of which is completely convincing, and himself undertook a perceptive analysis of the speech. He concludes with the athetesis of v. 1060–1063, thus doing away entirely with the motif that Medeia must kill the children herself to thwart the Korinthians' revenge.[36] The ταῦτα in v. 1064 would then refer to Medeia's plan in its entirety, which could not be reversed after she began its execution. There are two arguments against this solution. Seeck seems to us to place an undue restriction on v. 1059 when he interprets it only as the introduction to a general statement "the children must die," radically excluding the possibility of a connection with v. 1060, which refers to the danger from the Korinthians. The highly emotional form of v. 1059 results from Medeia's imagining her children in the hands of the Korinthians, a thought she cannot bear. Secondly,

however, the fear of revenge from the Korinthians has a very meaningful purpose
here, for in this way Euripides foreshadows the ananke motif at the end of the soliloquy, later to become the dominant theme of the last speech before the murder. Without this preparation the occurrence of the motif would seem quite abrupt. Steidle's
solution (158) appears most probable;[37] he believes that the plan to take the children
along turns out to be impossible because Medeia is so sorely pressed for time. Steidle
could also point to the version of Kreophylos (schol. 264), in which Medeia, after
murdering Kreon, cannot rescue the children because of their youth, and so brings
them to safety at the altar of Hera Akraia. Of course we are aware that Medeia never
explicitly mentions this consideration, unless we can read into v. 1064 a call for extreme haste, thus excluding the possibility of rescuing the children.[38]

Another serious difficulty remains: the contrast of θυμός and βουλεύματα in v.
1079. The specific question of a reference to Sokrates will be discussed later in connection with the *Hippolytos*. Almost without exception, scholars have seen the passage as a confrontation between the two opposing forces that carry out their devastat-
ing struggle within Medeia's soul. It is clear that θυμός represents irrational emotion,
but to what do the βουλεύματα refer? E. Christmann, following others, supported the
meaning of thought and deliberation in the practical sense, thus contrasting passion
and *ratio*.[39] We agree with him that although the word is used many times (769, 772,
1044, 1048) with reference to Medeia's plan for revenge, this does not justify our limiting its meaning here to this particular sense. Verse 1044 itself, with βουλεύματα τὰ
πρόσθεν (the earlier plans), shows that the word can also refer to deliberations of a
different sort, as v. 886 and Aisch. *Seven* 594 already establish beyond question. However, the limitation τῶν ἐμῶν βουλευμάτων (of my plans) contradicts a too general
interpretation of the word. H. Diller (op. cit.) attempts to resolve the difficulty by
construing κρείσσων not comparatively ("stronger"), but as "master over," thus eliminating the antithesis. Steidle (165) agrees; we are reluctant to recognize parallels
such as *Med.* 444 and *Ba.* 880 as conclusive in themselves, nor can we regard the
structure of the sentence as different from that of the homologous verse 965. Taking
up Diller's suggestion, but keeping the antithesis, we refer the βουλεύματα to the long
and shifting deliberations that precede the passage in question. In the course of these
reflections, the θυμός repeatedly asserts its power and emerges victorious at the end,
stronger than all rational thought. Thus we see in the antithesis a more concrete
reference to the scene, but we do not deny the possibility that the line also has a
general validity. From fragments 220, 572, 840 f. N it is obvious that the conflict between intellect and its counterforce was a persistent concern for Euripides.

A brief word about the play's conclusion. We still maintain our view expressed
some time ago that the finale is separate from the rest of the drama, that Medeia,
flying off on her magic chariot after she has greedily savored her triumph, abandons
the sphere of human misery and error, and fades totally into the realm of the daimonic. Aristotle (*Poet.* 1454a 37) criticized the conclusion as inorganic. The interpretation proposed here was opposed in a symposium on Euripides,[40] but has recently
received emphatic support from Schlesinger (op. cit.), and Erbse (op. cit.). In our analysis we emphasized the contrast between v. 1049 and v. 1362; such a conflict justifies

our speaking of the dragon chariot as the symbol of a solution that is only illusory, as Erbse has done. Whether Euripides deliberately intended us to perceive this discrepancy at the play's end is another question. We are skeptical here of the recent attempts to interpret many of the conclusions of Euripides' pieces ironically;[41] we prefer rather to take into account the tension between traditional myth and the Euripidean version.

In the tetralogy of 431 the *Medeia* was followed by the *Philoktetes*, which we discussed briefly in connection with Sophokles' play of the same title. The third play was the *Diktys*, named after the fisherman of Seriphos, who pulled the chest with Danae and Perseus out of the sea.[42] He then had to protect Danae from his brother, King Polydektes, until Perseus returned from his adventure with the Gorgons and turned the brutal king to stone. Based on Apollodoros (2. 4. 3) we may assume that at some point in the play, perhaps at the beginning, refuge was sought at an altar, a very common Euripidean motif. The concluding satyr play *Theristai* did not even survive into the Alexandrian age.

The *Herakleidai* was dated at 430 by Zuntz (*Political Plays*, 81); Pohlenz (2. 144) concurs. In fact there is much to be said for dating it between *Medeia* and *Hippolytos*. However, we will interrupt our chronological sequence in order to underscore those thematically related plays that represent a distinct phase of Euripides' creativity. Thus we now come to the discussion of the *Hippolytos* which, as a tragedy of passion, may be grouped close to the *Medeia*.[43]

Using as a basis the short song about the hunter Melanion in Aristophanes' *Lysistrata* (781), Radermacher has provided us with an excellent characterization of the personality type exemplified by Hippolytos.[44] The chaste youth who spurns the gifts of Aphrodite—usually an avid hunter—has become, in the figure of Hippolytos, the hero worshipped in Troizen with a cult in which brides make offerings of their hair before marriage. He had a cult in Athens as well, and in both places we find, curiously enough, a sanctuary of Aphrodite associated with his own. Characters like Hippolytos bore a natural affinity to the Potiphar's-wife motif, which is abundantly represented in Greek saga. Here the female role is given to Phaidra, a Kretan princess and the wife of Theseus.

Euripides had composed a version of the story about Phaidra's love for her stepson in his *Hippolytos Kalyptomenos* some years earlier.[45] All that we can really say about the date of this piece is that it was performed sometime between the *Alkestis* (438) and the *Hippolytos Stephanephoros* or *Stephanias* (428, given in the hypothesis), although it seems likely that the play stood closer in time to the *Medeia* than to the *Alkestis*. The prospects of reconstructing the first *Hippolytos* depend on the viability of the theory proposed by Valckenaer, that Seneca's *Phaedra* was essentially adapted from the *Kalyptomenos*.[46] While most scholars (including Snell) accept this confidently, W. S. Barrett, followed by Lloyd-Jones, is more cautious. The *Phaedra* of Sophokles furnishes ample cause for uncertainty, since we know very little about it; even the dating of the play between the two Euripidean dramas remains purely hypothetical, however plausible. But from all we know of Seneca's technique, Euripides really was his most probable model. In favor of Valckenaer's thesis, we know that

Seneca borrowed Phaidra's deathbed scene from the *Stephanephoros* and inserted it into his drama, which was based on another play. This increases the possibility that this source was indeed the *Kalyptomenos*. In any case some details about the earlier *Hippolytos* are tolerably clear. It was set in Athens; Theseus was probably absent on his journey to Hades, although this is uncertain. Probably there was nothing corresponding to Aphrodite's prologue in the second play; in the earlier version Phaidra or the nurse most likely spoke the prologue. An agon between Theseus and Hippolytos is suggested by fr. 439N. A deus ex machina must have prompted the glorification of Hippolytos in fr. 446N, in which the chorus, apparently in their concluding anapests, speaks of the honors received by Hippolytos because of his sophrosyne. But the most far-reaching alteration is noted in the hypothesis, which states that the extant *Hippolytos* is the later version, for in it the poet corrected the improprieties and faults of the earlier play. There Phaidra offered herself to her stepson, who covered his head for shame. This confronted the Athenians with more than they could tolerate to see on stage. The Phaidra of the *Stephanephoros*, who struggles with her passion to the point of self-annihilation, is quite different. And it was to this play that the judges awarded the first prize that Euripides won so few times.

The prologue of the extant work is spoken by an Aphrodite who resembles the goddess in the third book of the *Iliad*, in which she violently threatens Helen, forcing her into Paris's bed against her will. Here in Troizen there is a man who scorns her and honors Artemis alone. On this very day he will bear witness to her power with his own death. Her tool is Phaidra, whom she has caused to fall in love with Hippolytos during his stay in Athens to attend the mysteries. Here, in Troizen, where Theseus fled after slaying the Pallantides, her plan will be fulfilled. Phaidra is, to be sure, a woman of good reputation, but she must perish nonetheless. Her demise means little to the goddess, so long as she wreaks revenge. Aphrodite also knows (44) about the three fatal wishes granted to Theseus by Poseidon. The weapon that will cause Hippolytos's downfall is already poised to strike.

We have just heard from Aphrodite that Hippolytos stands in the shadow of death, and so the following exposition of Hippolytos in the fullness of his vitality is doubly effective. He enters with his hunting companions, who in a short lyric section follow his command and sing their greeting to Artemis, whose statue is in plain view on stage, as is Aphrodite's. Then Hippolytos prays to his goddess and offers her a garland from an untrodden meadow, where the bees hum and Aidos waters the soil. We can recognize a basic motif of nobility (familiar from Pindar[47]) when Hippolytos counts himself not among those whose knowledge is gained by instruction, but rather among those the essence of whose being is determined instead by their nature (φύσις). Now an elderly servant approaches with the modest request that he be allowed to offer some advice. In the following stichomythy he carefully leads up to his wish: Hippolytos should also greet the image of Aphrodite, she too a great goddess. Hippolytos refuses curtly. The spheres of his life are sharply and clearly characterized by devotion and total rejection (a goddess who works by night!). He leaves the stage with the semi-chorus, but the old servant prays that the goddess overlook the brash words of youth, for, after all, the gods should be wiser than men. This contrasts harshly with the speech of Aphrodite. The criticism of the gods in this passage is implied by the context; the messenger in the *Andromache* (1161) expresses it more directly.

The parodos of the chorus (121–169) is comprised of two strophic pairs, in which the dominance of glyconic rhythms corresponds to the hunter's prayer, and an epode. With much ornamental embellishment, the women of Troizen sing in the first strophic pair of the simple fact that they heard about the queen's sickness while doing the washing. Now they guess at the cause: the wrath of some destructive god, Pan, Hekabe, Korybantes, or Diktynna (β), or else the infidelity of Theseus (an ironic reversal of reality) or ill tidings from Phaidra's Kretan homeland (β')—in the epode they even suspect pregnancy.

The chorus introduces the expansive first epeisodion (170–524) with anapests; they announce the appearance of the nurse and arrange themselves in such a way that the large gate in the middle of the skene remains clear. These anapests are continued throughout the next section of the scene (176–266), which begins as Phaidra is brought on stage in a litter, accompanied by her nurse.[48] This passage serves to describe Phaidra's predicament with an almost clinical accuracy. Phaidra's entrance is beautifully motivated by her wish for fresh air and the light of the sun. But nowhere can she find comfort; she wants to go further, calls out for the crystal-clear spring, the field shaded by poplars, for a hunt in the forest and hills, for the race course. She seeks to commune with Hippolytos in the spheres of his existence. Then she collapses in shame and asks to be covered. The nurse, understanding nothing, replies to her ravings with helpless laments, but grants her wish and ends with the Euripidean topos (*Alk.* 882, *Med.* 1010): How a mortal endangers his peace and happiness when he loses his heart to another!

While the anapestic scene did nothing to advance the plot, the following section of trimeters now brings the revelation. It is composed of a lengthy, urgent speech by the nurse set between two stichomythies, and culminates in the old woman's exclamations of horror. In the first stichomythy between the nurse and chorus we learn only that Phaidra, for a reason she wishes to conceal, intends to starve herself to death—thus adding to the description of pathos in the anapestic section. Spurred on by the chorus, the nurse once again attempts to learn the secret—in vain. Only when the old woman remarks that Phaidra's death will compel her children to be subservient to Hippolytos does the queen react with a cry of pain, interrupting the verse abruptly. Still, the dialogue partners are divided by the misunderstanding of the nurse, who mistakes Phaidra's cry for an expression of loathing; but the silence has been broken and in a lively stichomythy the first hints are dropped: No, Theseus has not offended her—may she remain as blameless in his eyes (321). She wants to change her disgrace into honor (331). Such vague utterances do not help the nurse, so now as a last resort she turns to formal hikesia. Grasping Phaidra's knee and right hand, she refuses to let go until the queen has decided to say what her heart compels her to suppress. But Phaidra can only do so in roundabout ways, which the poet employs to recall the world from which she comes: Pasiphae, Ariadne, Krete. In another broken verse (352), she induces the nurse to utter the name of her beloved. The old woman's

reaction is one of despair and boundless horror. Earlier (236) she had asked which
divinity was destroying Phaidra, now she names Kypris, the terrible goddess who appeared before us in the prologue.

At this point a lyrical, predominantly dochmiac choral section (362–372),
which runs parallel to the lamentations of the nurse, marks a pause. The passage
finds its responsion much later in Phaidra's lament (669–679).[49]

Next follows a repetition of the phenomenon that we observed in the opening
scenes of the *Medeia*: Phaidra, regaining her composure, rises from her bed, joins the
women, and calmly delivers a long speech about her suffering and the way she intends to deal with it. Deepest emotion and rational deliberation are strictly divided
into separate sections. And just as Medeia begins with a broad and general line of
reasoning, so too Phaidra opens with an observation on the causes of human suffering.
Mortals lack neither knowledge nor wisdom, but rather the power to do what is recognized as right. They are hindered by the ἡδοναί (pleasures as temptations) of life,
such as long conversation and leisure and shame, of which there are two types: one
without reproach, the other a burden on ancestral houses. The difficulties involved in
this passage will be discussed in the critical section.

Because of such considerations she has begun to resist her passion. Euripides
allows Phaidra, like Medeia, to arrange her rational discourse carefully. Her first two
plans led to the third: concealment (we must add, in the hope that her love would
fade) and the will to suppress her desire were both unsuccessful; death alone remains.
She is firmly resolved to die, thus preserving the honor of her good name, and preventing herself from sinking into depravity, which, as Euripides remarks with aston-
ishingly keen sociological insight, begins in the houses of nobility and then sinks
into the broader masses of the populace.

In the intervening verses of the chorus leader, Phaidra draws the admiration
that she hopes to ensure for herself, but the following reply of the nurse has a completely different tone. The change in her attitude is presented, as always in Euripides,
abruptly and without intermediate stages, but the psychological motivation is convincingly supplied by Phaidra's speech. On first learning her mistress's secret, the
nurse was utterly horrified; now, however, confronted with Phaidra's calm and dispassionate resolve to die, she reacts differently, maternally, concerned only with saving the queen's life. She offers all sorts of commonplaces about the omnipotence of
Kypris, to whom even the gods are subject, and about the frequency of such cases—
she even brings herself to scold Phaidra for hubris in resisting her passion. She ends
by hinting that there are ways of dealing with love: charms and magic spells; women
know about such things.

In four verses (482–485) the chorus performs a sort of balancing act, calling the
nurse's advice helpful, and Phaidra's decision praiseworthy.

In the following dialogue, which is condensed into stichomythy near the end,
the nurse begins her assault: Noble words are useless; you need the man.[50] Phaidra
rejects this suggestion (498), but her resistance slackens noticeably (503). And when
the nurse speaks of love charms she has in the house (where she also wants to speak
with Hippolytos), Phaidra asks anxiously about their nature, but hope and desire are

now so powerful within her that she drops the matter and leaves everything to the nurse. She seeks once more to reassure herself by requesting that the nurse remain silent to Hippolytos—though this is exactly what she will not do. The ambiguity of the scene is masterfully executed. Love charms can either dissipate one's own passion or arouse it in the desired partner. When the nurse speaks of the things that are needed from Hippolytos (514),[51] the later effect seems more likely, and in fact it is mentioned specifically in v. 515. However, when Phaidra immediately afterward speaks of a salve or a potion, such methods seem rather intended to cure her own desire. Everything is deliberately left unclear.

The first stasimon (525–564) proclaims the dangerous power of Eros in the first strophic pair and cites the mythological examples of Iole and Semele in the second.

The second epeisodion (565–731) begins with an eavesdropping scene. Standing at the door Phaidra is horrified to hear within Hippolytos's wild imprecations against the adulteress. After a short stichomythy the chorus accompanies her outcries with dochmiac verses that first express worried curiosity, then horrified lament. At the end of this section (598) the chorus leader asks what Phaidra now intends to do, and receives the reply: to die, as quickly as possible. Her suicide plan is fixed once more, but how completely different are her reasons now!

Hippolytos rushes from the house. Phaidra hears his every word, but there is no indication that Hippolytos catches sight of her standing apart. In a spirited stichomythy the nurse tries in vain to appease the flaming indignation of the youth. But only after this dialogue does his anger truly break loose in a long declamation on the evil of women. The speech includes one of those utopian ideas for improving the world that occur frequently in Euripides; here the plan also serves to characterize the speaker: Women should not be responsible for reproducing humankind; instead, children should be bought in temples at whatever price the purchaser could afford. The poet adds a subtle touch: Hippolytos, in the first flush of anger, brashly sweeps aside his oath to keep silent, asserting that it was only his tongue that made the vow (612). This verse was able to be neatly lifted from the context and used as a weapon against Euripides.[52] But in actuality Hippolytos acknowledges that he is bound by the oath (657), and he sacrifices his life to honor it. His first disavowal is not only plausible, but also dramatically necessary, for it gives rise to Phaidra's uncertainty, which drives her to take dramatic action. A similar effect is intended by Hippolytos's promise to return with his father to observe how the women will behave when they face Theseus.

Verses 654 f. present another fine detail of characterization: How could I be evil when I feel soiled at the mere mention of such things! To be sure, he does not wish to be defiled, but there is also a trace of narcissism in these verses, as he exults in the image of his own perfection.

Phaidra's distress is released first in lyric verses (669–679, in responsion with 362–372), then in bitter reproaches for the nurse, whom she dismisses. One can perceive a tragedy within the tragedy in the fate of this old woman, guided by her primitive impulses, who for the sake of her beloved mistress overcomes her initial horror, only to bring on destruction where she hoped to give aid.

A carefully planned sequence is discernible in Phaidra's lines. Her lyrical passage is filled with despair; her suffering transcends the bounds of her existence (678). Verse 687 expresses this more clearly: the silence is broken, gone is the glory of an honorable death. But after the nurse departs, she decides on a new plan. Quickly she secures the chorus's promise to keep silent. She can assure her children of life with honor and make the best of what has happened. One thought dominates here: to avoid shame (715). In her final words, however, another motif is introduced, although we need not follow Zürcher (86) in suggesting a thematic split. Both factors are involved in Phaidra's intrigue: the concern for her name and honor, but also her undiminished passion, now turned to hatred. Hippolytos, proud and cocksure, shall not triumph over her; his wretched death will bind him to her in a final communion (κοινῇ μετασχών).

In the second stasimon (732–775) the chorus takes for granted that Phaidra must die (second antistrophe). In the first strophic pair they wish to take flight from the land, compensating for their embarrassing and total passivity. The second strophe recalls Phaidra's marriage journey from Krete, thus providing the transition to the present catastrophe.

The third epeisodion (776–1101) parallels the first, not merely in its great length, but also in that in their opening sections spoken verse is largely replaced by other meters, anapests and dochmiacs respectively.

From within we hear the nurse's cry for help; Phaidra has hanged herself. One semi-chorus hesitates, the other rejects any thought of intervention, since servants must already be present inside. Now Theseus enters; struck by his mournful reception he suspects that Pittheus has died and learns from the chorus of his wife's suicide. He has the doors forced open;[53] returning home as a θεωρός (envoy sent to observe a festival; 792) he must now look upon this θέα (spectacle, play).

The chorus laments in dochmiacs; Theseus joins in with a pair of strophes in which the same meter is interrupted by three pairs of trimeters.

Theseus now catches sight of the letter under his dead wife's arm, and in an extraordinarily agitated scene shot through with dochmiacs of Theseus and the chorus, Hippolytos is condemned to death by his father.[54] Earlier (849) Theseus had hailed Phaidra as the best of all women; now he is ready to pledge eternal fidelity (860). The ironic accent is here almost obtrusive. Horrified, Theseus reads the terrible accusation against Hippolytos, and hurls immediately one of the three wishes granted him by Poseidon as a curse against his son. The chorus leader tries to restrain him; in so doing she almost transgresses her oath of secrecy (892). Theseus, however, adds a decree of banishment. More later on the problems involved with the three wishes and the double verdict.

The chorus leader announces Hippolytos; she says that he comes ἐς καιρόν (at the right moment), perhaps intimating a hope that Hippolytos might defend himself successfully. The agon dashes any such expectation. In form it comprises two long speeches with spirited dialogue, which only in the second half becomes an occasionally interrupted distichomythy. Two shorter speeches of Hippolytos at the beginning and end frame the whole. He begins at the heart of the matter. Not a word of mourning for Phaidra, only the worried question about the reasons for her suicide. He presses Theseus further, who replies with general complaints about the corruption and hypocrisy of the world. Hippolytos is just beginning to suspect that he has been slandered when Theseus opens his long speech of accusation. In the prooimion he continues his criticism of the world's condition, but then shifts abruptly: There, look at this one! Filled with hatred, he evokes a picture of the hypocrite who boasts of divine friendship and the puritanism of Orphic sects, but in reality chooses the vilest paths. The dead woman is proof enough, against which sophistic tricks can avail nothing. Banishment—only this is mentioned by Theseus here—shall punish the blasphemer. The chorus must be silent; its verses express helpless despair.

Hippolytos, after a rhetorical prooimion in which he disparages his talents as an orator, takes up in careful order the first count of his father's accusation. His purity is sincere, his life spotless, of the pleasures of love he knows nothing. Then he attempts to invalidate the charge by a reductio ad absurdum: Neither Phaidra's beauty nor the thought of seizing power with her could be plausible motives for such a deed. Thus far we have heard a neat courtroom oration, but Hippolytos also wins our sympathy when, in despair, he vaguely hints at the truth without breaking his oath. In its two verses the chorus underscores significantly the meaning of the oath that Hippolytos tenders to clear himself.

As usual, the section of the agon following the speeches introduces no new arguments; instead, motifs used earlier are presented with heightened intensity. Theseus's decree of exile is escalated to the curse that Hippolytos wander wretchedly in strange lands; the youth's despair is deepened at being bound to his oath, although the thought that no one would believe him anyway (the chorus is ignored as a possible witness) does limit the ethical value of his steadfastness. Verse 1078 contains Hippolytos's curious wish that he might stand opposite himself to bewail his miseries. Of course this expresses his extreme isolation, but there is also a touch of that narcissism that we noted in connection with his self-indulgent boast of purity (654). When Theseus threatens to use force, Hippolytos gives up. With great composure he bids farewell to Athens and Troizen, calls to his friends, and departs.

In the first strophe of the following stasimon, the chorus delves deeply into the problems of a theodicy. The thought of the gods' rule comforts the soul. This is almost like an echo of the Aischylean hymn to Zeus (Ag. 165). But then reality intrudes harshly on all hopes, when one considers the fates of men. The antistrophe prays for a peaceful life of moderation. The second pair of strophes laments Hippolytos. The epode intensifies their sorrow to a painful outburst of emotion; the phrase μανίω θεοῖσιν (I am angry with the gods) contrasts sharply with the beginning of the ode.

The fourth epeisodion (1151–1267) presents the messenger's report about the catastrophe of Hippolytos, another epic masterpiece filled with realistic detail. There is an effective contrast between the melancholy but controlled tone of Hippolytos's departure and the thunderous onset of the disaster. Likewise impressive is the messenger's agonizing description of the uncanny certainty with which the beast sent by Poseidon drives the youth to his death.

This report is also framed by dialogues between Theseus and the messenger. Before the speech Theseus's words are filled with hatred, but afterward the flames of his passion are clearly diminished (1257)—another example of Euripides' fine psychological insight.

The fourth, very short, stasimon (1268–1282) sings of Kypris's power. The connection with the previous scene is not immediately apparent, but the praise for the goddess here contrasts effectively with the entrance of her adversary.

The exodos (1283–1466) begins with the appearance of Artemis (probably on the roof of the skene); in her entrance anapests she rebukes Theseus harshly.[55] Nor does she spare him in her following speech, in which she relates the true course of events; Theseus cries out in his terrible awareness. But her words soften near the end. Theseus acted with undue haste, but Kypris is really at fault. Artemis too acknowledges Phaidra's noble character (1301). We find it hard to believe that the poet did not consciously intend the dissonance at the end of the goddess's speech, when he lets her speak of divine justice that destroys only the wicked. Such a belief is sternly refuted by the dying Hippolytos and the later promise of Artemis to avenge herself on one of Aphrodite's favorites.

In an anapestic scene the chorus announces the arrival of the fatally wounded Hippolytos. Wracked by pain he bewails his fate, conscious of his moral worth even in the throes of death—he lays particular emphasis on his virtues in v. 1365. A renewed seizure of pain is expressed in the metrical shift to lyric anapests and iambics.

Now Artemis speaks to the dying youth, who hears her voice one final time. Her valediction is appropriate for a goddess who leads a life of ease, herself protected from death, as she parts from a beloved mortal. There is tenderness in her farewell, but also the cool and strict demeanor that cannot quite bridge the gap that divides two eternally separate worlds. Her final words, which after a stichomythy encompass a more lengthy speech, also have an institutional significance. The goddess proclaims that Hippolytos shall be honored as a hero, promising that the maidens of Troizen will cut their hair before marriage as a sacrifice to him, and further that choruses of virgins will commemorate his fate in song. Then, however, she commands that Theseus and Hippolytos be reconciled. As if to confirm Aphrodite's words in the prologue, Artemis calls human error the doing of the gods (1433). Hippolytos's farewell painfully stresses once more the gap between god and man: How easily you forsake our long companionship!

We might feel somewhat put off that the following scene of reconciliation results from Artemis's command, as Hippolytos himself admits (1442). But the chords he strikes in the stichomythy are so direct that we perceive only the human side of the action. This is another example of double motivation. The laments of Theseus and of the chorus conclude the play.

The events of this drama cohere so tightly that one almost hesitates to speak of a bipartite structure. Yet a certain parallelism becomes clear in the construction of the plot, which is interrupted only by brief choral odes. Two large scene complexes, the first and third epeisodia, prepare the way for the catastrophes of Phaidra and Hippolytos respectively. These two sections also correspond to each other in that the first begins with an agitated anapestic scene while the second presents passionate lamentation in lyric meters soon after the opening dialogue. In both, the silence of a character plays a decisive role; it is broken in the first instance, maintained in the second.

The considerably shorter second and fourth epeisodia also correspond to each other. In both, a death has become inevitable (Phaidra's in the second, that of Hippolytos in the fourth) while its accomplishment extends into the next scene. There is also clear responsion between the scenes that frame the drama, in the appearance of the goddesses and the related transposition of motivation to the level of a quarrel among Olympians.

It is not easy to answer why Euripides transferred the setting of the second *Hippolytos* to Troizen. The resulting difficulties receive thorough treatment in W. S. Barrett's commentary (34). Theseus rules in Troizen although the aged Pittheus still lives. In order for Phaidra to be able to dedicate the temple of Aphrodite ἐπὶ Ἱππολίτῳ while still in Athens, Hippolytos had to be present in Athens once for a pilgrimage to the mysteries. Perhaps the poet wished to connect the events more closely to the region that observed the cult of Hippolytos.

The change from the underworld journey of Theseus in the first play to the festival embassy in the second may be easily explained: in our play Phaidra must reckon with her husband's return—otherwise her letter would be meaningless.[56]

While we can assume that a divinity appeared at the conclusion of the *Kalyptomenos*, but not at the beginning, Euripides framed the *Stephanephoros* with the figures of Aphrodite and Artemis. This poses the most profound problem of the play's interpretation.[57] It is undoubtedly correct to emphasize the meaning of both goddesses as symbols for the forces that determine this tragedy of double destiny.[58] Thus it would be wrong to see in their opposition the real content of the drama. Its conflict develops between two human beings whose characters and modes of living are so utterly different that they cause their mutual ruin.[59]

And yet an interpretation that sees the goddesses as mere symbols does not do justice to the play. These are Olympian individualities who settle a conflict while formally placed on an upper stage, for whom the destruction of two mortals is a circumstance of secondary importance. To be sure, the poet is mainly concerned with the mortals, and not the divinities who determine their fates. It would be incorrect to claim that criticism of such divine intrusion represents the main content of the play. Conversely, however, we must not fail to recognize that Euripides shapes the attitude of these goddesses—which stems from the Homeric world—not in pious preservation of epic tradition, but from a detached critical standpoint especially evident in his treatment of Aphrodite. Defying any sort of concise formulation, the manifold levels of Euripides' divine characters are impressively displayed in the *Hippolytos*.

Phaidra's speech of rational deliberation (373) poses a number of difficult questions. When she speaks of the dangerous joys that cause men to fall against their better judgment, she lists only examples from women's lives, such as useless gossip or pleasant leisure. Αἰδώς will be taken up later. Now R. P. Winnington-Ingram (op. cit.) builds his thesis on the interesting idea that Phaidra is here depicting her own environment and its degenerating influences. Her later acknowledgment that it is in fact the houses of noblemen that breed such corruption for women coincides well with this view. Thus there would be a rational connection between the section under discussion and the following description of her own case.[60] Phaidra's painful recollection of her Kretan descent (337, 343) then complements the indictment of her milieu. The influences of environment and heredity should not obscure the fact that Euripides portrays Phaidra as a woman of noble character who would like to fashion her life on the model virtues of σωφροσύνη and εὔκλεια (discipline and good reputation). But the poet also shows us—and here we follow Winnington-Ingram—the opposing forces arising from her surroundings and predisposition, to which Phaidra succumbs, innocent yet guilty. Hippolytos's character is entirely determined by the two virtues just mentioned. He himself speaks of his φύσις (disposition; 79); it was given him through his descent from the Amazon queen. His environment is true to his nature: hunting and racing, the cult of Artemis, and friendship with youths of like mind.

No one yet has convincingly explained the business with αἰδώς in the list of inhibitions that Phaidra cites as the enemies of goodness.[61] Parallels like the Ἔριδες (forms of Strife) in Hesiod, Erga 11, or the διπλοῖ ἔρωτες (double Eros) in Euripides' prologue to the Sthenoboia (D. L. Page, Lit. Pap., 128), are instructive for the pattern of thought, but not for our particular question. Here, the fragmentary form in which the thought occurs is partly explained by the familiarity of the idea (Hesiod, Erga 317; Eur. fr. 365N, fr. 56 Austin). The difficulty lies in fitting the lines into the context of our passage. In no way can αἰδώς (shame) be counted among the ἡδοναί (pleasures); it must stand next to them.[62] This is syntactically possible but harsh. We must begin with the fact that the word designates an inhibition, usually of moral value, but as false modesty it can also obstruct a good deed. It is interesting that Plutarch, De virt. mor. 448 f., claimed to recognize in these lines a reference to the poet's own character. But how exactly does all this apply to the situation here? Is it the evil αἰδώς that prevents Phaidra from speaking, or turns her into a murderer to hide her disgrace? There might be a connection with v. 335, in which Phaidra yields out of shame to the nurse's supplication, but this is rather thin. Barrett believes the evil αἰδώς refers to Phaidra's indecisiveness, which prevents her from subduing her passion yet allows the nurse to have her way, but this forces us to grant the word a very wide range of meaning. The problem remains unsolved.

In Phaidra's remarks about the failure of wisdom to transcend the influences beyond reason's control, Bruno Snell[63] recognized the contradiction of Sokrates' precept that knowledge guarantees virtue. No one can deny that these lines sound like an echo of Sokrates; and the relatively small size of Athens and the intensity of Athenian intellectual life both increase the probability that the poet is indeed echoing the philosopher. It is also significant that Plato apparently refers to this passage in Prot. 352D. However, it remains doubtful that there is an even earlier allusion to Sokrates at the end of Medeia's great monologue (1078; see above).

Hippolytos's character has been subjected to various interpretations, as shown by his defense at the hands of Rivier (67) and the radical disapproval of G. Devereux, op. cit.: "Athenian aristocrat aping Sparta." Few will agree with such a verdict; Euripides has given this character the marks of immaculate purity and uncompromising piety, such that he sacrifices everything for the sake of his oath. But Hippolytos also bears the faults of his virtue. The self-conscious proclamations of his own spotlessness (654, 1455) overreach the bounds of the epideixis (display) natural to the Greeks and lead to that odd narcissism (1078) that we emphasized in our analysis. His brusque rejection of Aphrodite is an expression of chastity but as the denial of a great vital force it must also be seen as hubris. We agree with Barrett (op. cit., on v. 952) that Theseus's words do not make Hippolytos a disciple of Orphism, but he does seem close to that sphere of influence. In this context it might be relevant that the journey to Attika mentioned in the prologue (24) was undertaken for his initiation into the mysteries.

Theseus metes out a double sentence to his son: death from Poseidon and exile; he mentions only the latter in the agon with Hippolytos. Barrett (op. cit., 334) has shown clearly that this scene presupposes only the banishment decree, not the miracle expected of Poseidon. Moreover, only the intertwining of both motifs makes possible the dramatic sequence of events: Hippolytos goes into exile and is overtaken on his way by the curse. If a rational justification of the double penalty is demanded, one might suggest that Theseus is unsure of the effectiveness of the wishes, since he has never tested them. All three wishes were untried, for Barrett has recently established beyond doubt that this is the first one Theseus uses. Verses 888 and 1316 (τὴν μίαν; the first) indicate this clearly. The scholiast (on 46, 887, 1348), Cicero, De off. 1. 32, and Seneca, Phaedra 949 all speak of the third and last wish. They may have known another version that has been lost to us. In any event we can rule out the thought that Theseus could have brought Hippolytos back to life with a further wish. That would be an intrusion upon the world order that even Asklepios could not get away with.

The conspicuous masculine participles (1105, 1107, 1121) next to the feminine (1111, 1118) in the third stasimon led Verrall to the assumption of a double chorus divided into male and female voices. This view was accepted by Murray in his edition and more recently by Chromik (52). But it is out of the question to suggest here the hunter chorus introduced in the prologue.[64] Even if the male chorus is to be identified with the companions addressed in v. 1098—which cannot be ruled out—they are then immediately obliged to leave the stage with Hippolytos. Barrett (op. cit., 366) has assembled a telling list of arguments against the double chorus theory. It still seems best to follow Wilamowitz's assumption in his edition that in this general statement the masculine forms are used for the feminine. In his careful examination of the evidence for such usage, Barrett has invalidated many examples, but by no means all of them. He himself tries to resolve the difficulty with the ingenious emendation ξύνεσιν δέ τις ἐλπίδι κεύθων λείπεται, but even he is not totally satisfied. It will also be difficult to delete λεύσσων in the second strophe, which (despite variations in the tradition) picks up this form from the first strophe. But in no case should we try to divide the ode's cohesive sequence of thought between the men and women of a double chorus.

The two Hippolytos plays are not the only ones in which Euripides treated the Potiphar's-wife motif. In his Stheneboia the wife of Proitos of Tiryns craved the love of the morally scrupulous Bellerophontes.[65] The story is an old one; in the *Iliad* (6. 160) it is related by Glaukos of Anteia. A scholium to Gregorios of Korinth (Nauck, *TGF*, p. 567) provides useful information about the content of the play. Further details come from the Hermogenes commentary of Ioannes Logothetes (H. Rabe, *Rhein. Mus.* 63 [1908], 146). Stheneboia tries to procure the love of Bellerophontes, but in vain, for he feels obliged to Proitos who took him in and cleansed him of blood guilt. She then slanders him, causing her husband to send Bellerophontes on the adventure with the chimaira. He returns victorious, persuades Stheneboia to flee with him on Pegasos and drops her into the sea. A fisherman reports her death; Bellerophontes appears and justifies his actions.

It is a difficult task to reconstruct the play, for we must accommodate all the events described above, and two very considerable periods of time (the chimaira adventure and the deceptive flight with the fall of Sthenoboia) must be bridged with choral odes. Zühlke attempted to solve the first problem by assuming a lacuna in the prologue after v. 27, in which Bellerophontes narrated his conquest of the chimaira; later he returned to wreak revenge on Sthenoboia. This solution, slightly modified by Korzeniewski, seems tempting, but Webster rightly objects that the general drift of the prologue indicates that Bellerophontes has not yet rejected the advances of Sthenoboia. And so we must put up with the unusual time relationships.

Bellerophontes was the main character in the tragedy of the same name that should be dated before the *Acharnians* (v. 426 with schol.).[66] Of all the lost plays, this is the one we should most like to possess. Bellerophontes, stricken by disaster and quarreling with the gods, tries to ride Pegasos up to their seat in heaven, but he falls and dies.

Unlike the *Presbeia* (*Il.* 9. 447) the *Phoinix*,[67] produced before 425 (*Acharnians*, v. 421), presents its title character as an innocent youth who succumbs to passion and the intrigue of a concubine. The content can be essentially restored from the tale of Hieronymos Rhodios (fr. 32W.) about Anagyrasios, for we read in the *Suda* (E 1137) that Euripides transferred this local Attic legend to his Phoinix. We know that the concubine slandered the youth, that he was blinded, and that his father learned the painful truth. An agon between Amyntor and Phoinix, corresponding to that between Theseus and Hippolytos, may be inferred from the fragments. The *Phoinix* demonstrates how often Euripides varied a productive theme within a short span of time.

In the *Frogs* (863) the *Peleus* is mentioned in one breath with *Aiolos* and *Meleagros*, that is, with plays of erotic content.[68] Thus it is probable that this play dealt with the wife of Akastos of Iolkos, Astyadameia, who tempted and endangered the right-thinking hero. Since the *Peleus* precedes the *Clouds* of 423 (schol. on 1154), we may again assume that Euripides treated erotic themes of this type in plays produced within a short space of time.

In this same period of Euripides' productivity belongs the *Aiolos*, which was produced before the *Clouds* (schol. on v. 1371).[69] Owing to the discovery of a considerable portion of the hypothesis (*P. Oxy.* 2457; Austin, 88) we are now better informed as to how the poet made a tragedy of incest out of the story in the *Odyssey* (10. 7), in which the wind god had his sons and daughters intermarry. Makareus, the youngest of Aiolos's sons, impregnates his sister Kanake. He then advises his father to marry his sons to his daughters. Aiolos agrees and decides the matches by lot, which does not, however, unite the lovers. Before the hypothesis breaks off there is a reference to a nurse, who probably rescued the child while Kanake killed herself. It will be recalled that Nero sang and acted the part of Kanake in her birth pangs.[70]

Another drama typical of this period was the *Kretans*, about the pathological love of Pasiphae, wife of Minos, for the bull sent by Poseidon.[71] On metrical evidence, Austin dates the play before 430; Cantarella, about 433. Ancient myth here became moral outrage, but Rivier, interpreting Pasiphae's defense speech (Austin, fr. 82), makes a good case for believing that she appeared not as criminal but as the victim of divine wrath. Remnants include the beginning of the parodos, which introduces a chorus of initiates devoted to Idaean Zeus, Zagreus, and the mountain mother. We may reasonably assume that they were summoned by Minos to expiate the portent of the twin birth. New papyri have also brought to light verses from a stichomythy in which Minos describes the hybrid monster, the Minotaur, to another character, perhaps the chorus leader. It is probable that Daidalos had a role to play and that Ikaros's fall was included, just as some god most likely arranged for Pasiphae to be spared and the Minotaur confined at the end.

We have few clues to the date of the *Chrysippos*.[72] Reconstruction is aided by the Pisander scholium on *Phoin*. 1760. Laios abducted the handsome son of his guest-friend Pelops. Chrysippos then took his own life out of shame. (Euripides condemned pederasty, as we know from his treatment of the motif in *Kyklops*, *Hik*. 899, and fr. 362. 24 from the *Erechtheus*.) Fragments 840 f. N recall Phaidra's speech in the *Hippolytos*. In the first, Laios apparently names the force of nature (φύσις) as the victorious opponent of wisdom (γνώμη), while his dialogue partner laments that man knows what is good but does not act accordingly—an evil foreordained by the gods.

Unlike Sophokles, Euripides made the love of Haimon and Antigone a main theme of his *Antigone*.[73] Fr. 165N sounds like a reply to Soph. *Ant*. 563. That would give us a terminus post and a time period supported by the number of resolutions in the trimeter. Reconstruction attempts must take into account the material similarity between the plays, well attested by the hypothesis to Soph. *Ant*. and the scholium on 1350. In Euripides, Haimon took part in the burial of Polyneikes and came into conflict with his father. But a deus ex machina, probably Dionysos (cf. fr. 177N), effected a happy resolution: Haimon married Antigone, who bore him a son, Maion.

We add here two dramas whose events were determined by Eros. Whereas Sophokles dealt with the fetching of Neoptolemos from Skyros in, his *Skyrioi*, Euripides chose as his subject the seduction of the princess Deidameia by Achilleus, whom Thetis had brought to Lykomedes in women's clothing.[74] We know this, and that Diomedes was dispatched (with Odysseus we may surmise), from a fragment of the hypothesis in *PSI* 12. 1286. The complication probably arose from Deidameia's confinement, the revelation of Achilleus's true nature, and the conflict between love and heroic mission.

The *Meleagros* is assigned to the later career of the poet, on the basis of its usage of trochaic tetrameter (fr. 536N).[75] The fragments reveal an expansive plot, which led from the departure on the hunt for the Kalydonian boar to the quarrel over its hide, which Meleagros promised to Atalanta. Then followed the slaying of Thestios's sons, who claimed the hide, and finally the death of Meleagros caused by Althaia's magic firebrand; she was exacting revenge for her brothers. It is uncertain whether fr. 533N comes from the nurse's report of Althaia's suicide.

Among the extant works, we possess a group of plays that belong some time before the tyche dramas of Euripides' late career. They are dated in the twenties and some of them, like *Hkld.* and *Suppl.*, betray the influence of contemporary politics in their especially patriotic attitude or, like the *Andr.*, in biting attacks against Sparta. The chronology of these plays is not entirely clear. We will begin with the *Hekabe* because of its thematic similarity to the θυμός tragedies discussed earlier.[76]

The epic cycle supplies the basis for the first of the play's two main themes, the sacrifice of Polyxena at the grave of Achilleus, who appeared to the Greeks before their departure and demanded a sacrificial victim. According to the excerpts of Proklos, in the *Iliupersis* Demophon and Akamas slew Polyxena on the grave of Achilleus, and the *Nostoi* relates that the hero's ghost appeared to the group around Agamemnon when they were ready to embark and warned them of the coming disaster. But we have no way of knowing when the version developed that the Greeks sacrificed Polyxena at the grave of Achilleus to fulfill the hero's demand. It is said (*PMG* 557) that Simonides composed the most thrilling account of this apparition, but this says nothing of Polyxena. We know little about Sophokles' *Polyxena*,[77] but it seems quite probable that Euripides' report of the quarrel that arose in the Greek camp about sacrificing the girl (*Hek.* 116) echoes a scene in Sophokles' play in which Agamemnon pleaded for her life. This receives some support from Seneca's *Troades*, in which Agamemnon opposes the killing of Polyxena. In Euripides it is the sons of Theseus who demand the sacrifice; this reflects the situation in the *Iliupersis*, in which they slew the girl.

For the treachery of Polymestor, who kills his ward Polydoros to usurp the treasure and then is horribly punished by Hekabe, we have no evidence whatever for any version before Euripides.[78]

The dating of the *Hekabe* has been unnecessarily complicated by the ill-founded conjecture (417 B.C) of Schmid (3. 464). Two passages of Aristophanes' *Clouds* (160, 171) contain allusions to verses of *Hekabe*. It is inadvisable to attribute both lines of the comedy to the play's revision, since they come from sections which, according to the *Clouds'* seventh hypothesis, were not subjected to the diaskeue.[79] There is no reason to reject the date before 423 supported by Wilamowitz (*Herakl.*, 1. 144. 51).

The shade of Polydoros speaks the prologue and offers much relevant information. He relates how Priamos sent him with valuable treasures to his guest-friend Polymestor in the Thrakian Chersonese, and how Polymestor slew him to get the gold. Now the Greeks, returning from Troy, have landed in the Chersonese and brought with them Polydoros's mother, Hekabe, as captive. His corpse is tossing in the surf, where a slave woman will find it. At the end he announces the entrance of Hekabe, who has been frightened by his apparition.

The significance of this prologue as a connecting link between the two plot lines is obvious, the more so as the ghost also related the appearance of Achilleus over his grave mound and his demand that Polyxena be sacrificed to him. Already we note a difficulty in the setting. According to v. 35, the assembled Achaians are idling in camp on the Thrakian Chersonese, while the grave of Achilleus is located in the Troad, on Cape Sigeion. One might object that the two places were not so far apart that swift communication between them would be unthinkable, but later we find the entire Greek army (521) attending the sacrifice at the grave. We must simply accept the fact that the poet switches around with the settings, both of which are necessary for him, to suit his needs.[80]

Now follows a lengthy anapestic section (59–215) in which Hekabe's lines before the entrance of the chorus are quite closely connected in theme with the parodos, while the subsequent scene between Polyxena and her mother anticipates the action of the first epeisodion.

Hekabe drags herself on stage, propped up by servants. Horrible dreams have upset her; she fears for her son in Thrace and she is alarmed by the news that Achilleus appeared at his grave and demanded the sacrifice of a Trojan woman. Thus the two stations on Hekabe's path of suffering are foreshadowed by intimations which are as yet unclear.[81]

The chorus enters, individually or in separate groups; the parodos is not a song by the captive women, but an anapestic recitative of the chorus leader, in which she tells of Achilleus's demand, the dispute between Agamemnon and Theseus's sons, and the decision carried by Odysseus against Agamemnon's opposition. Now Odysseus will come to fetch the girl. The following section (154–215) is composed in lyric anapests with an abundance of spondees. Strophic arrangement seems discernible in that Hekabe's lament, which she concludes with a call for her daughter, is answered by an antistrophe of Polyxena.[82] In between comes a section of spirited exchanges in which Hekabe informs Polyxena about the threatening disaster. The girl's magnanimity is brought out beautifully in her lament, which is not for her own lot, but solely for the suffering of her mother.

The first epeisodion (216–443) exhibits a special structure (more or less repeated in the finale) through the interaction of three people who differ not only in character but in their attitude toward the present situation. Odysseus enters, and the poet first presents us with a section composed like an agon (229!). An introductory dialogue (which turns into a short stichomythy) is followed by long speeches with attack and entreaty on one side, defense on the other. Hekabe prepares for her speech in the stichomythy, recounting all the details about Odysseus's mission as a spy in Troy, how he was recognized by Helen, and only saved by the mercy of Hekabe. Odysseus confirms everything and proffers his thanks. At this point Hekabe begins her speech, which twice mentions Odysseus's debt of gratitude, with an intervening attack on the senselessness of human sacrifice. She concludes with a fervent appeal to Odysseus to use his influence and prevent the sacrifice. Three dividing verses of the chorus leader support her request.

Odysseus replies as the executive official of the army, a timeless role. He curtly dismisses his personal obligation with a mean trick of sophistry: he is prepared to save Hekabe, but she is not the one whose life is in danger. The crux of his argument is the obligation of gratitude as he sees it: Achilleus, who gave up his life in battle, must have the victim he demands. It is necessary to honor the dead in this way if one expects sacrifice from the living. Finally, he resorts to insult: Barbarians may do as they please, but Greek custom honors the dead! The irony is heavy as Euripides lets this ungrateful Odysseus speak at great length about the need for gratitude.

Hekabe sees that her words have been useless; now she urges Polyxena herself to assail the relentless commander. However, the girl speaks not as a suppliant, but more like a mediator settling a dispute. Pointedly she tells Odysseus, who once in entreaty seized Hekabe's garments with a grip tight as death (246), that he need not conceal his right hand, nor turn away his countenance—he need not fear any gesture of hikesia from her. She will go with him without opposition. Death is better than the slave's lot that threatens her after the collapse of their proud grandeur.

The chorus leader and Hekabe praise the girl's noble attitude, but the mother does not give up the fight. She herself should be killed for Achilleus instead of Polyxena. The curt denial of Odysseus sums up all that he has to say in the form of address ὦ γεραιά (Old woman! 389). Then Hekabe wishes at least to die with her daughter. In a brief, sharp stichomythy she pits her stubborn will against the refusal of Odysseus. Violence threatens when Polyxena intercedes anew: Resistance is senseless; it is time to say farewell. In the following stichomythy with her mother, Polyxena, marked for death, breaks down in lamentation; after her heroic stand she allows her heart to speak. Again the poet links the two sections of the play: Polyxena consoles her mother with the thought that Polydoros still lives among the Thrakians, while Hekabe, in dark premonition, doubts this as well. Hekabe's final words to Polyxena as she departs with Odysseus express again her utter despair but also hurl a curse at Helen, who bears the guilt for the whole disaster. She should be led off to death like Polyxena. Lightning-swift, the desire for revenge that will later determine Hekabe's actions penetrates all her suffering.[83]

In the first stasimon (444–483) the frightened captives ask where their path into slavery will lead them. The whole second strophe is devoted to Athens, where the slave's lot seems not to be so terrible: they would weave chariot processions and Titans' battles into the borders of Athena's robe.

In the second epeisodion (484–628) the herald Talthybios enters with news for Hekabe, who lay covered on the ground during the ode (486). The aged messenger is clearly moved by the sight of the woman, old like himself, overwhelmed by grief. Shaken with emotion and drawing on his painful and plentiful experiences in life, he speaks words that resound far and wide through Euripidean tragedy: Should we believe in the order of Zeus, or does chance (τύχη) alone govern all human events?

Hekabe clings to her last hope: Have you come to fetch me for the sacrifice? Talthybios destroys her delusion. He has come to summon Hekabe to the burial of her daughter. He reports the heroic death of the princess, who gave herself to the sword free from restraining hands, and by her honor was victorious over the conquerors of her homeland. In the dividing verses that follow, the chorus leader sees only suffering; in Hekabe's speech this pain is combined with pride in her child's death. Here (591) follows one of the strangest reflections in Euripidean tragedy: Is it not remarkable that care and nurture make all the difference for soil, whether good or bad, but that an ill-natured man is always bad and a good man always good? Whence comes this? Is it hereditary or is it a result of upbringing? Certainly good upbringing can teach nobility. He who has learned this knows how to measure Evil by the standard of Good.

After this thought, which is drawn out over eleven lines, Hekabe recovers her composure: Whither have my thoughts wandered? (603). This desperate pondering and unsure groping reflect the debate introduced by the Sophists that remains controversial even today: nature or nurture? The old conviction of the noble order, supported so mightily by Pindar, that inborn nature determines everything, is starting to topple.[84]

Then Hekabe prepares to bury Polyxena. She wants to beg for jewelry from the captive women who live in her tent. In deep resignation she leaves the stage. Previously she had sent an elderly servant woman (age and frailty dominate the scene) to the shore to fetch water for the final lustrations. There she will find the dead Polydoros.

In the short second stasimon (629–657; one pair of strophes with epode) the chorus sings of Paris's journey to fetch Helen, the cause of all their misery. A noteworthy thought is voiced in the epode: weeping wives and mothers sit on the banks of the Eurotas as well. Here we find anticipated a theme of the *Troiades*, that war blasts both the conquered and the conqueror.

As the third epeisodion (658–904) opens, the servant returns, having found the corpse of Polydoros on the shore. A short dialogue with the chorus leader follows, then Hekabe emerges from her tent. The shrouded body allows the poet the opportunity to intensify to the utmost the pain of Hekabe's recognition: she guesses first that it is Polyxena, then she imagines Kassandra; only after the cloth has been lifted does she recognize the collapse of her final hope.

A kommos follows with spoken verses of the chorus leader and servant; in Hekabe's section dochmiacs predominate, though single trimeters are interspersed. She sets the tone for her lament when she sings of the βάχχειος νόμος (bakchic mode). We must perceive the turbulent force of her grief in the intensity of this song if we are to understand Hekabe the mainad at the end of the play.

Agamemnon enters—another significant link between the two halves—to bring Hekabe to Polyxena's burial. He is surprised to see the corpse but receives at first no explanation. To understand the following scene we must remember that here two people face each other who were until recently archenemies. Hekabe realizes the difficulty of her situation: she must make Agamemnon her ally. For this purpose Euripides makes use of the "aside" to an extent unprecedented in a tragic play, though it is quite common in comedy. She deliberates at some length: should she plead with him? Agamemnon, puzzled, addresses her as she stands apart, speaking to herself. Finally she makes her decision and falls as a suppliant at the king's feet. The poet, not wishing to burden her lengthy plea (787–845) with a narrative of events, has already provided this information in a skillfully constructed stichomythy (761–786). In her speech Hekabe appeals first to the king's sense of justice. She names nomos as the highest authority over the gods, calling it the cause for our belief in divinity and for our distinction between just and unjust—again reflecting the intellectual disputes of Euripides' time.

The central passage of her speech is an outburst of despair. Agamemnon has turned away, all attempts at persuasion seem fruitless. Hekabe summons her courage and tries a new tack. Agamemnon has Kassandra as his concubine and shares his nights with her. Kypris must help her. Her speech ends in a series of desperate entreaties. In four verses the chorus leader speaks of the mutability of things: enemies shall become friends.

Agamemnon is beautifully characterized as the man of high rank who does not wish to be harsh yet is beset by misgivings.[85] His words make it clear that of all Hekabe's appeals, only the reference to Kassandra has influenced him. But what will the army say to this? Polymestor was considered his friend. Will he be accused of bias for Kassandra's sake? But Hekabe calms his fears. Agamemnon need not be an accomplice in her revenge; it is enough if he permits it. She merely hints at the form of punishment she has in mind for the Thrakian king. In sufficient numbers, women can accomplish much. She sends her servant to Polymestor, who is to come with his children. Agamemnon must postpone the burial of Polyxena, that she might share the pyre with Polydoros. Agamemnon is relieved that nothing more is required of him; now he can close the scene with fulsome words about the just requital for good and evil.

The third stasimon (905–952) comprises two strophic pairs with an epode. This is our first encounter with the narrative choral ode, here still in the developing stages (Kranz has spoken of dithyrambic stasima). Relevance to the play as a whole is not lacking, but even so the poem seems to exist on its own, apart from the plot. The subject of these strophes is a sort of *Iliupersis*: they conclude with a curse on Paris and Helen.

Polymestor enters, feigns sympathy, and covers up with the lie that he was just on his way to see Hekabe when the servant arrived. Hekabe avoids looking at Polymestor's face, claiming her terrible sorrow as an excuse (968–975)—a fine touch of subtle psychological portraiture. In reality she fears that she might not be able to conceal her hatred. Now she orders him to dismiss his servants, since she has a secret to impart to him. With her question about Polydoros, to which the king offers a reassuring reply, she once more highlights his total depravity, before offering his greed the bait with which she plans to trap him. In this stichomythy the poet employs two motifs: first, the secret of the location of the gold that lies buried in Ilion. For this reason Polymestor was summoned with his children, that they too might learn the hiding place. Then, however, Hekabe speaks of gold that she has brought with her and concealed in her tent; thus she lures him to the women. The scene is filled with the irony of double deception: Polymestor dissembles friendly loyalty; Hekabe, absolute faith in his words (990, 1000, 1004).

After a short iambic-dochmiac passage in which the women of the chorus announce the punishment to come, we hear Polymestor's screams of pain, which are answered by verses of the chorus leader (or of individual choristers). Hekabe emerges from the tent and proclaims the consummation of her revenge. Here we run into the ever-recurrent problem of the ekkyklema. When Hekabe promises that the chorus will also see the murdered children (1051), one might think of the rolling platform; στείχοντα (1050) and χωρεῖ (1053), spoken by Polymestor, indicate rather the opening of the central door. Polymestor staggers from the tent, partly crawling on all fours; his monody in dochmiac rhythms must be imagined accompanied by a mime of groping and searching for the children, with the complete helplessness of a blind man. Two verses of the chorus leader, weighing the punishment against the crime, mark a pause, after which Polymestor in total despair calls for his Thrakians, the Achaians, and the Atreidai.

Agamemnon has heard his screams, and after a short choral dialogue an agon develops, which adds to the two opponents a third speaker who decides the outcome, as Polyxena did after the agon between Odysseus and Hekabe. There is a further parallel in that the χάρις motif (of obligation through kindness) plays a role in this scene also. After relating what happened in the tent Polymestor twice asserts that he slew Polydoros to help the Greeks. A section of the agon has here taken over the function of a messenger report.

After the four dividing verses of the chorus leader, who protests against Polymestor's insults to women, Hekabe begins her speech with one of those utopian wishes that the poet, deeply distressed by the world's condition, so likes to set in the mouths of his characters: Good men should also be good speakers; no evil man should be able to blind others with his words. Then she accurately destroys Polymestor's arguments: Why did he not slay Polydoros to please the Greeks when Troy was still strong? Why did he keep the treasures for himself? She concludes with the urgent demand for justice. Prooemium, argumentatio, and peroratio are quite clearly marked off in this speech.

Agamemnon is convinced; he condemns the defiler of hospitality.

At the end of many Euripidean tragedies we get a glimpse into the future of those involved—generally given by the deus ex machina—and an aetiological connection with some cult or locale. Here Euripides has given both a peculiar form. A distich of Polymestor introduces a stichomythy, first between him and Hekabe, then between him and Agamemnon. Dionysos, the god of his land, has told him that Hekabe will be transformed into a bitch and will give the promontory of Kynossema its name. Hekabe is unperturbed by this, so long as Polymestor has atoned. Verse 1274 is very close to v. 1362 of the *Medeia*. Then she hears more: Kassandra will fall victim to Klytaimestra. Here the dialogue turns to Agamemnon. He too will die by the hand of his wife. In great agitation (antilabai) the king forces him to be silent, then commands that he be abandoned on a deserted isle. Now it is time to bury both victims, then the journey home will begin. His prayer for a happy return is darkly overshadowed. Again we learn that in this war conquered and conqueror both are marked by destiny.

In the final anapests the chorus prepares to tread the path into slavery.

The bipartite composition of this play is as undeniable as the art with which Euripides has fashioned a whole from the two halves. The dramatic sequence of the first section is exactly the opposite of the second.

The tragedy of Polyxena is gradually communicated to Hekabe in the reports of Achilleus' demands; then Odysseus comes to fetch the girl, but there still remains hope that the horror may be averted. A lengthy struggle ensues, until Polyxena, with great composure, decides the issue. Talthybios reports the completion of her fate. Conversely the Polydoros section begins with the revelation of the catastrophe as a fait accompli. The rest of the action is devoted to the preparation and execution of revenge. Parallels may be discerned between the two halves: each presents a long scene of pleading and persuasion which is fruitless in the first part, successful in the second. First we see Odysseus, the executive official, then Agamemnon, the man dominated by personal motives. The characters are contrasted beautifully. We recall also the repeated use of the χάρις motif.

The poet has done so much to connect the two halves it is difficult to understand those scholars who believe that Euripides tacked the Polymestor story onto his original conception of a tragedy of Polyxena.[86] The apparition of Polydoros has a binding function similar to that of the *Telemacheia* before the two parts of the *Odyssey*. We emphasized the individual links in the course of our analysis; it is also relevant that Hekabe first guesses that the shrouded corpse of her son is the body of Polyxena.

However, the poet could really achieve the unity of the drama only from within, and he owes his success to the fact that each event derives its meaning only in connection with the central figure of Hekabe. Steidle (44) has done much to show the essential unity of her character. One cannot speak of a radical change, but rather of a single continuous line of development. Euripides has set its beginning in the past when, in the scene with Odysseus, he shows us a Hekabe who had provided an enemy with an escape from a deadly situation. Already, at the play's start, terrible blows have smitten her. But she still has children. Then hope after hope crumbles to nothingness, until excess of suffering is vented in an excess of bestial revenge. Goodness, even tenderness, and insatiable vindictiveness dwell within one and the same soul; those who see a split in her character are as unjust to the poet as the detractors of his Medeia.

It is difficult to say whether Euripides really wished to show us the moral "degeneration" (G. Kirkwood, op. cit., 67), the collapse of arete (Conacher, 163), in his heroine. Without doubt, the killing of the children deprives Hekabe of all traces of humanity and her transformation into a dog is a sort of ultimate verdict, beyond its aetiological function. Yet, for all that, we must understand her as the victim who is dragged down by continuous suffering into a perversion of everything human, a process that culminates in her transformation into an animal. The poet has done much to help us understand this path.

We would overtax the play if we were to seek in it a specific statement about human sacrifice.[87] Hekabe's criticism (261) appears quite peripheral in the agon with Odysseus. She herself would not object if Helen were the victim.

The poetry of the *Hekabe* shows us the forceful advance of the actor's song, for which the entrance monody of Alkestis and the lament of Theseus over Phaidra's corpse provide earlier examples. In the *Hekabe* the entire opening section after the prologue is composed in lyric. Lamentation in song follows the report of Polydoros's death (684) and the blinded Polymestor vents his pain and rage at some length in the same form (1056).

We cannot date the *Andromache* to an exact year,[88] but sometime in the middle of the twenties seems very probable, which would place it close in time to the *Hekabe*.[89] The scholiast on v. 445 offers much valuable data. He infers (φαίνεται; "it seems") that the play was written at the beginning of the Peloponnesian War; it was not produced in Athens, since evidently the title could not be found in the didas-kaliai.[90] It is difficult to evaluate the statement (probably referring to a remark in the *Pinakes*) that Kallimachos knew of a rival claim to authorship for a certain Demo-krates. Schmid (3. 397. 4) believes he was the χοροδιδάσκαλος (chorus master) who had charge of rehearsals. Goossens (386) thinks the name is a pseudonym, while D. L. Page (op. cit., 221), following T. Bergk, suggests that the Argive lyric poet Timokrates was really meant. This poet would have written Andromache's quasi-Doric elegiac lament (103), a form unique among the extant tragedies.

Euripides composed this spirited interplay among three representatives of dif-ferent regions (Troy, Phthia, Sparta) using diverse elements from the tradition. That Andromache was allotted to Neoptolemos as war booty could be found in the *Iliuper-sis*. The Molossian kings derived their ancestry from Achilleus, through the child Andromache bore to her new master. Pindar (*Nem.* 7. 38) mentions that the Molos-sians were ruled by the descendants of Neoptolemos. For the second part of the play the remarks of Eustathios (*Od.* 1479. 10) about Sophokles' *Hermione* are quite signifi-cant. In that drama the grandfather, Tyndareos, gave Hermione to Orestes while Men-elaos was absent. A conflict arose, since Menelaos had promised her to Neoptolemos at Troy and now took her away from Orestes.[91] But Orestes got her back when Neop-tolemos was killed at Delphi. According to Sophokles he had gone there to demand that Apollo provide requital for the death of his father. Pindar offered another story in the *Paean for the Delphians* (fr. 52 f. Sn.): the god slew Neoptolemos as punishment for the cruel murder of Priamos. But Pindar's poem offended the Aiginetans, who de-sired a more glorious end for the descendant of their Aiakos, and therefore in *Ne-meian* 7.42 the poet arranged things so that Neoptolemos came to Delphi and was slain in a quarrel over sacrificial meat. After this, however, the Delphians held his memory in high honor.

The hypothesis of our play, which preserves for us the verdict of the Alexandri-ans and judges the work rather harshly, rightly emphasizes the fine composition of the prologue. Andromache speaks of her fate, which has placed her at the mercy of Neoptolemos after the fall of Troy. Euripides compresses the tragedy of her lot in the single particle γέ (25; cf. 36, 38). She has borne a child, Molossos, to the son of Achil-leus—she could not deny herself to him, he was her master! She lives with him in the Thetideion, where the sea goddess once dwelt with Peleus. Thetis is here fore-shadowed as dea ex machina. Neoptolemos has left the control of the land in the hands of the aged Peleus. This is necessary for the plot, since the old man must appear in a position of power. For Neoptolemos has gone to Delphi to beg forgiveness from Apollo for the audacity with which he once demanded that the god atone for the death of Achilleus. Hermione, the lawful wife of Neoptolemos, sees that her chance has come to rid herself of the concubine and her child as well. To assist her, she has summoned her father, Menelaos, from Sparta. But Andromache has hidden the boy and fled to a sanctuary of Thetis near the house, another example of one of Euripides' favorite motifs, the flight to an altar.[92] Rarely does a Euripidean prologue have such an abundance of intricate background information to relate. The praise of the Alexandrians was well deserved.

A maidservant, who has remained loyal to Andromache even after the sack of Troy, enters and bears the ill tidings that Menelaos has left the house to fetch the boy from his hiding place. In a short, agitated stichomythy Andromache persuades the maid to call Peleus for assistance. It is her last hope, since other messages have failed.

Andromache is alone once more. After a short prelude in trimeters she begins her elegiac lament (103–116), the only example of such a composition among all the rich and varied forms of Attic tragedy. Her entire tale of woe from the ill-fated marriage of Paris to her supplication at Thetis's altar is contained in these distichs.

The parodos (117–146) presents the chorus of women from Phthia. In both strophic pairs (especially the first) the hexameters echo the elegiac meter. The women take pity on the foreigner and wish to help (α) but can do no better than advise her to leave her asylum, since Andromache's situation is hopeless (α' and β); they themselves are afraid they might offend Hermione (β'); φόβῳ δ' ἡσυχίαν ἄγομεν (out of fear we keep silence), the typical expression of a timid chorus.

In our text, Hermione's entrance is set directly at the beginning of the first epeisodion (147–273), so that Musgrave assumed the loss of transitional choral verses. This seems advisable, not merely because such verses are regularly employed, but the words ὑμᾶς . . . ἀνταμείβομαι λόγοις (I reply to you; 154) demand it, since Hermione here clearly answers the chorus.

The following agon, in which the two women confront each other, is very tightly constructed. In place of the usual preliminary dialogue we find only a few verses addressed to the chorus at the beginning of Hermione's long speech. But these brief lines are a masterpiece of characterization for this vain and foolish female, puffed with pride over her finery brought from Sparta. She makes a wild attack on Andromache, accusing her of a plot to drive her from the house, of making her hateful to her husband and barren besides by means of a magic charm. With a meager display of logic she threatens her with certain death, the Nereid's asylum notwithstanding, but adds immediately that only the utmost humility and self-abasement could save her. She who sleeps with the son of the man who slew her husband is a true barbarian!

After the usual two dividing verses of the chorus (here on women's jealousy) Andromache replies. Following a prooimion about the disadvantages of her position as a slave, she refutes Hermione's charges with a reductio ad absurdum: what could she, captive and aging, hope for in this house? No black magic spoiled the Spartan woman's relations with her husband; rather, it was her proud manner, devoid of feminine modesty. Andromache certainly demands a bit much of her opponent when she invokes the Thrakian institution of polygamy and sets herself up as a good example, since she even suckled the bastard children of Hektor. Here she really is the Trojan barbarian, though we must not forget that in an agon any weapon is justified. Of course she is the victim and no shadow of adultery falls on her (25, 36, 38, 390), but Neoptolemos has created a situation in his house that would have provoked to conflict even a creature of higher integrity than this Hermione.

After two verses of the chorus leader, a meaningless admonition to reconciliation, Hermione, with two verses of her own, opens the stichomythy that we expect after the speeches of the agon. As usual, the quarrel intensifies, but no new arguments are introduced. Death threats clash with the invocation of a suppliant's rights. Not until her short concluding speech does Hermione hint that she possesses a lure that will induce Andromache to leave the altar, an adumbration of the next epeisodion. Andromache closes the act with a general statement about the wickedness of women; strangely enough she includes herself in this remark with the use of the plural (273; cf. 353).

The first stasimon (274–308) begins with dactyls, echoing the elegy and parodos. In two pairs of strophes the chorus sings of the disaster brought on Troy by the judgment of Paris. If only his mother had killed him, as Kassandra commanded!

The second epeisodion (309–463) presents the miserable aristeia of Menelaos, this too in the form of an agon, but atypical in that a shorter speech of Menelaos comes between two longer speeches of Andromache. Verses of Menelaos take the place of an introductory dialogue. He has found Andromache's child, boasts with foolish pride that he has outwitted the woman, and gives her the choice either of dying herself or witnessing the death of her boy. Andromache begins her first speech with an observation on the false reputation that settles on the unworthy. Then she turns to Menelaos, who would disgrace himself by committing murder and make Neoptolemos his enemy. Neoptolemos will drive Hermione from the house, no one will ever want to take her as a wife. She herself is confident of her innocence. But Menelaos has already demolished Troy, all for the sake of a woman. The myth becomes, in anticipation of a later development, material for the dispute.

In his reply Menelaos brushes aside Andromache's arguments as σμικρά (paltry). He is helping Hermione in a matter of the utmost importance to a woman. He has complete control over Neoptolemos's slaves, for all property is common among friends. He concludes with the alternative: You or the boy!

The tone of Andromache's second long speech is markedly different from the first. Where before she employed reasoned argument, here she pleads for her life and, recognizing that her entreaties are useless, pours out her grief in a lengthy lament for her past and present fate. Then she abandons her asylum and delivers herself unto death to save her child. At the end of her speech she reverses significantly the sentiment of many Euripidean characters that children bring pain and worry. To be sure, the childless suffer less, but this well-being is in reality misfortune.

The chorus leader is here more expansive than usual (four lines), but Menelaos ignores her advice completely. Now he reveals the ultimate in depravity and meanness: his servants must seize Andromache; Hermione will decide as she sees fit whether the boy will live or die. In a short stichomythy Andromache's indignation clashes with the cold cynicism of Menelaos. Andromache's emotion has increased steadily in her two long speeches; now it breaks through completely in her short third speech, concluding the epeisodion. She heaps passionate abuse on Sparta, but then composes herself and, proudly contemptuous of her enemies, declares her readiness to die.

The second stasimon (464–493) first expresses bits of general wisdom: No good ever comes of bigamy (α), nor from dual control of the state (α'), nor from having two helmsmen on a ship (β). Here, as often, the second antistrophe switches to the particular case: the Lakonian woman plans to murder wickedly the unfortunate captive from Ilion. The requital is yet to come, a clear adumbration of Hermione's despair.

The third epeisodion (501–765), whose central position and importance is obvious from its length alone, connects quite effectively the extreme and apparently inevitable predicament of Andromache with the peripeteia.

Andromache is led out of the house, bound and with her child. In an epirrhematic arrangement two strophes containing the lament of Andromache and the boy in soft glyconics are followed by anapests of Menelaos. The verses of Molossos are not yet couched in the language of a child, but are rather more convincing than the antistrophe of Eumelos's lament in the *Alkestis* (406). The anapests of Menelaos after the antistrophe are particularly harsh and echo the image in the *Iliad* (16. 34) of the cruel inflexibility of the cliffs and sea. There seems to be no escape, when suddenly Peleus arrives, announced by the chorus leader, with a servant guiding his steps (551). The nucleus of this scene is an extensive agon between him and Menelaos, who adds rejoinder and counterplea after the old man's two expansive speeches. To this lengthy accusation corresponds the extended composition of the preliminary dialogue between Peleus and Andromache. A similar dialogue concludes the long epeisodion in ring-composition. Peleus learns from the captive of the fate threatening her and immediately commands that she be released from her bonds. This leads to a stichomythy, quickly compressed from double to single verses, in which Menelaos makes some weak excuses in an effort to countermand the order. Then Peleus moves into his long invective, attacking Menelaos, the ladies' man and coward, the instigator of immeasurable calamity; beyond this the indecency of girls' training in Sparta is also criticized.

The chorus leader separates the long speeches here with three insignificant verses about starting a great feud for a small reason, then Menelaos replies in a speech of approximately equal length.[93] He repeats his now familiar arguments: the concubine is from an enemy city, and should not bear children in Greece; he is concerned for his daughter, who desperately needs his help to prevent the destruction of her marriage. He covers up his subjection to Helen, as Helen herself excuses her guilt in the agon of the *Troiades*: divine will determined her actions. He closes with a sharp blow to Peleus, again using myth as material for argument: he was right not to kill Helen, and it would also have been better had Peleus not murdered his stepbrother Phokos.

The two dividing verses of the chorus leader contain a useless "Desist!" In his response Peleus proceeds from the general to the particular and then takes action. He begins with a democratic attack against the unfair custom that the individual general reaps the benefits of the courage and toil of the many after a victory. The thought is spun out to such length that it acquires significance independent of the context. Only afterward does Peleus apply it to the Atreidai, but then he becomes vehement, expels Menelaos and his barren daughter from the house, and threatens them with the terrible anger of Neoptolemos (thus preparing for the change in Hermione's attitude). Now at last he loosens Andromache's bonds and raises her to her feet. During the long speeches mother and child have been huddled together to evoke our sympathy.

The chorus leader's following two verses about the rude manners of old men seem rather odd. They are perhaps to be construed as a warning to Menelaos. His retreat is simply pitiful. He still reviles Peleus at the beginning and end of his speech, but then he suddenly remembers that he must deal with a recalcitrant city back home and so has no time to waste. In this light it is difficult to take seriously his threat to return and set matters straight with Neoptolemos. He leaves, while the poet arranges the remaining characters in a group like the one in the *Herakles*, in which the hero enters the palace with the rescued children. Andromache and Molossos now lead the aged Peleus, who in a final dialogue promises the mother safety after all her sorrows. He speaks of his own might in bold tones that border on the mildly comic. This is not without parallel in Euripides (*Hkld., Ba.*) but here it is unintentional.

The third stasimon (766–801) comprises one pair of strophes with epode. After praise for the safeguards provided by noble lineage (α) there follows the condemnation of unjust violence such as Menelaos intended (α′), and in the epode the chorus praises the previous deeds of Peleus.

The fourth epeisodion (802–1008) marks the beginning of the second part of the play, opened by a speech addressed to the chorus by Hermione's nurse as a sort of prologue. She reports the complete collapse of her mistress, which should not be taken as an admission of moral guilt, but simply as a result of the fear she now feels, left all alone, for the consequences of her attack. Only with difficulty do her handmaidens restrain her from suicide; she tears herself loose from their grip and rushes on stage. In a kommos (825–865) interrupted by trimeters of the nurse, Hermione sings passionately of her fear and her wish to die. The transition from self-confidence, as long as Menelaos stood behind her, to unbridled despair is harsh and abrupt but thoroughly plausible, given the woman's character as the poet reveals it. When Hermione asks (859) to which divine image she should flee, we perceive the reversal of the situation and the correspondence between her new predicament and the one she brought on Andromache. The nurse tries to calm her, without success, but then the chorus leader announces the arrival of Orestes, who represents the peripeteia of the second part, corresponding to Peleus's role in the first section.

Here Euripides has inserted a minor but effective retardation in the plot. Orestes speaks first to the chorus leader, revealing his identity and mentioning that he would like to visit his relative, Hermione of Sparta, while on his way to Dodona. At her nurse's suggestion Hermione has entered the house, or is just about to. Since a restless coming and going hardly suited the poet's purpose, we might best imagine that she remained standing at the door, overheard the conversation with Orestes, and now falls at his feet hoping for deliverance. In the driving tempo of a stichomythy she tells Orestes what has happened: Peleus took sides with the baser cause (914) — not a trace of insight or repentance on her part. No case can be made for her moral salvation (despite Schmid, 4. 403). When Orestes reproaches Neoptolemos for keeping two women in the house (909) he naturally shows some bias, but as the chorus passed the same judgment (465) we must not overlook the fact that Neoptolemos is also partly responsible for all the confusion.

Hermione begins a longer speech (920), which in many respects recalls the rationalization of Phaidra (373). Otherwise than in many similar Euripidean speeches, here the train of thought runs from the particular case to the general. First she makes a passionate appeal for help, then blames her folly on the insinuations of evil women. This leads to an observation on the disastrous effects of evil association with women, and when Hermione finally commands that houses should be shut tight with bolts and bars, it seems her words (φυλάσσετε; Watch! 950) are addressed surely not to the chorus but to the theater audience.[94] Euripides appears to have more than a slight personal investment in these reflections, but he does permit the chorus leader to protest mildly (in three verses) against such a harsh disparagement of her own sex.

Now Orestes discloses that his arrival was not fortuitous; spies informed him of the dissension in Neoptolemos's house, and he is exploiting it to assert his earlier claim to Hermione. For Menelaos had promised her to him but then gave his word to Achilleus's son while at Troy.[95] Neoptolemos made good his claim and scorned and abused Orestes, who now wants to rescue Hermione from her distress and bring her back to Menelaos. When Hermione expresses concern that Neoptolemos or Peleus might prevent her escape, Orestes goes a step further in his disclosure: Neoptolemos will not return from Delphi. Orestes has set a deadly trap for his enemy; he can rely on his accomplices to carry it out (999). In a typical contamination of motifs Orestes says that Neoptolemos will fall at the hands of the god whom he once insulted and through his well-prepared scheme.

It is significant that after Orestes' appearance the chorus sings in the fourth stasimon (1009–1046) of the calamity that the war against Troy brought. We must accept the fact that in the first strophic pair the women of Phthia sing a lament for the fallen city of their enemies. The second strophic pair relates the murders of Agamemnon and Klytaimestra and mentions a far-reaching disturbance that left Greece desolate and then passed over to Phrygia; here we catch a preview of the *Troiades*, which depicts the conqueror and conquered in the catastrophe of war. And when in the second strophe, after the mention of Orestes' matricide, the chorus breaks off with an appeal to the god and the question πῶς πείθομαι (How am I to believe it?), the essence of the poet's *Elektra* is here already expressed.

As the finale (1047–1288) begins, Peleus enters in a state of great agitation; he has heard rumors of Hermione's escape, confirmed in a short stichomythy with the chorus in which he also learns of the danger to Neoptolemos in Delphi. Quickly he tries to send off a warning when suddenly a messenger arrives and reports the death of Neoptolemos in a spirited conversation with both Peleus and the chorus leader. The old man almost collapses, then raises himself wearily to hear the messenger's story. All has transpired as Orestes predicted. His plot and the god's will have stricken Peleus's only grandson. Orestes' slander had the desired effect. No one believed that Neoptolemos came with the pious intention of effecting a reconciliation with Apollo. Euripides masterfully depicts the attack of a cowardly mob on Achilleus's son, who snatches weapons from a temple pillar, holds his own against the throng, and even puts them to flight. But the god proves decisive; a voice from the sanctuary summons the mob to a new attack, and this time Neoptolemos succumbs. The messenger ends by reproaching Apollo: he teaches others justice and yet bears a grudge like a man of bad character. We recall the words of the servant in the *Hippolytos* (120).

Anapests of the chorus leader announce the bearers of Neoptolemos's body. The lamentation resounds in a kommos (1173–1225). Dactyls dominate the first strophic pair (interrupted by two trimeters of the chorus leader), a clear echo of the opening section. This passage is given to Peleus, who bewails his grandson and the marriage to Hermione but also laments the hubristic demand that the god be called to account for Achilleus's death. In the second pair of strophes (primarily trimeters) Peleus's laments combine with those of the chorus. The appeal to Thetis prepares us for the Nereid's arrival. Choral anapests announce the goddess's entrance. Since they speak of her path through the radiant aether, it seems certain that a machine was employed to fly her in. Thetis restores order quickly but carefully and offers consolation. Here again Euripides could not resist concluding his play with the foundation of a cult, for the grave of Neoptolemos was displayed at Delphi and received honors annually (Paus. 10. 24. 6). Andromache shall journey to the land of the Molossians and there marry Helenos. Her son, however, will become the ancestor of the local kings. To Peleus she promises immortality; he will dwell in the palace of Nereus and be able to visit, dry-shod (the detail seems pedantic), Achilleus on the isle of Leuke. Thetis delivers an extremely specific set of instructions, bidding Peleus to bury his grandson and then wait for her on Cape Sepias. The poetic atmosphere thins somewhat in Peleus's final words, too. He promises to arrange for the obsequies according to her orders and to wait where he once won Thetis in hand-to-hand struggle for her love. His final statement, that a marriage from a noble house is preferable to an ignoble match, even if it offers a rich dowry, falls completely flat, however relevant it might be to the plot. The chorus departs chanting anapests familiar to us from the conclusion of the *Alkestis*.

The division of the play into two parts of unequal length is clearly marked by the departure of all the previous participants at the end of the first, larger section (795) and by the prologue-like entrance of the nurse after the third stasimon. The parallelism of the two parts has often been emphasized, and with good reason. In both, a situation of extreme despair is followed by the appearance of a new character who effects the rescue. Both sections are concerned with the fate of a woman, and the utterly different personalities of Andromache and Hermione yield an effective contrast within the formal parallelism.

But all this does not yet answer the question of the play's unity. The various

attempts to solve this problem are neatly summarized by H. Erbse (op. cit., 276).
Some seek the focus of the plot in the figure of Neoptolemos, others in Hermione.
Erbse suggests Andromache. He cites a number of convincing connections between
the two sections of the plot dealing with Andromache and Hermione respectively but
claims support for his thesis by assuming (like Kamerbeek, op. cit., 47) that Andromache, who must have come with Peleus, is present in the final scene. But can
γυναῖκα δ᾽ αἰχμάλωτον, ᾿Ανδρομάχην λέγω (the captive woman, Andromache I mean;
1243) really imply her presence on stage? We have always doubted that possibility
and find now that Steidle (118, with bibl.) is equally skeptical. We also agree with
him that παῖδα τόνδε (this boy; 1246) does not necessarily prove the presence of Molossos.[96] And even if mother and child were on stage we would have to construe Andromache's silence as an even clearer sign that her role in the play is finished, instead
of assigning it a deeper significance. Rather it seems advisable, with Conacher (173)
and Steidle (129), who were anticipated by Hartung, to consider as the unifying
theme of the play the fate of a house into which a bad marriage has brought disorder.

Although a certain dramatic unity can be established in this manner, the previous paragraph clearly shows that we must search in order to find it, and the solutions proposed differ widely at that. It has never yet occurred to anyone to search for
the unity of the *Oidipous* or the *Medeia*, and so we would do well to admit that the
Andromache is constructed differently, more loosely than the aforementioned plays.

In this play Euripides has composed a spirited and fast-paced interplay among
sharply drawn characters from three different camps: Trojan, Spartan, and Thessalian.
The scenes that revolve around Andromache's fate are filled with strong emotion. For
all this only an overly zealous apologist could deny that the *Andromache* is not one
of those plays in which we are called to reflect upon the great problems of human
existence. To some extent the evaluation in the ancient hypothesis is just: τὸ δὲ
δρᾶμα τῶν δευτέρων (the drama is second-rate). Yet in no way should one charge the
poet with carelessness in the disposition of time within the plot, as Schmid (3. 404)
and Pohlenz (2. 121) do. They suppose Orestes to have prepared the murder of Neoptolemos in Delphi by means of helpers, to have followed his enemy all the way from
Phthia (thus with Hermione!), and then to have carried out the deed himself before
the god's temple. The last stasimon would have to bridge the significant span of time.
But actually everything fits together perfectly.[97] When Orestes comes to Hermione,
he has already set the trap at Delphi and need only rely on his helpers (999). He himself does not return to Delphi, but instead brings Hermione to Menelaos (984). His
accomplices and the god carry out the work at Delphi without him. Even Wilamowitz was moved by verses 1115 f. to assume that Orestes was present at the murder.[98]
But the line should be printed without punctuation and it means "of all these things
Klytaimestra's son was the one and only schemer." Lines 1075 and 1242 refer to Orestes purely in the sense of instigator. The word χερός in v. 1242 does not contradict
this since it appears in a similar context at v. 997, where Orestes speaks of his preparations for the attack. How carefully Euripides has here arranged time relationships
may be seen in the curious circumstance that Neoptolemos spends three full days
viewing Delphi before he attempts his reconciliation with the god. Thus Orestes has

time for his intrigue and for the journey to Phthia, while others fulfill his design.

To what extent are the invectives of Andromache and Peleus against Spartan manners connected with the atmosphere of war at the time Euripides wrote the play? The question involves the larger problem of deducing the poet's personal opinions from his work. Following those who negate too strongly the possibility of doing this (an almost obligatory reaction to earlier exaggerations), Webster (28)[99] and H. Erbse (op. cit., 286) have recently denied possible allusions to the war. Steidle (128) is more cautious, judging that the passages in question are "difficult to understand entirely without any contemporary historical points of reference." And in fact one must agree with those authors, from the scholiast (on v. 445) to Conacher (170), who believe that the attacks on Sparta cannot simply be separated from the atmosphere of a time when Athens was fighting with this state for its very existence. That they also fit well into the context of the plot is perfectly reconcilable with this view. However, H. Erbse is quite right to protest against all attempts to connect specific passages with specific historical events, as Conacher was also correct to reject Kitto's interpretation that the entire play constituted an attack on Sparta's *Machtpolitik*.

Despite the differences in their execution, the *Herakleidai*[100] and the *Hiketides* (*Suppliants*) bear a certain thematic similarity: both praise Athenian resistance against injustice and the readiness of the Athenians to help the oppressed.

Tradition offered the poet essential motifs for the *Herakleidai*. Aischylos had written a drama with the same title and same basic theme.[101] Fr. 361N, 111M leaves no doubt that Iolaos was rejuvenated in the earlier Aischylean version. Pindar told of his victory over Eurystheus (*Pyth*. 9. 81). We cannot be so sure about the role of Makaria. Zuntz (*Pol. Plays*, 111) has adduced telling arguments against the old theory of Wilamowitz (*Kl. Schr.*, I, 62) that the girl's anonymity in the play suggested her invention by Euripides.

Of decisive importance for dating the play is Eurystheus's prophecy that his grave in Pallene will be a strong protection against invading enemies. According to Ephoros (in Diod. 12. 45. 1) the Spartans spared the Tetrapolis during their second invasion of Attika (430) because the Herakleidai were once granted refuge there. On the other hand Thukydides (3. 26. 3) speaks of a complete devastation of Attika in 427. Thus Wilamowitz (*Anal. Eurip*. 1875, 152) set the play's date after 430 and before the summer of 427.[102] Zuntz (*Pol. Plays*, 83) showed that doubts remain about the stringency of his conclusion and the certainty of his premises; he lays the emphasis on v. 1042, in which Eurystheus promises to arrange a disastrous return for invading enemies. It is difficult to imagine this being said after the Spartan devastation of Attika in the summer of 430, so Zuntz's date in the spring of that year seems quite plausible. On the basis of metrics T. B. L. Webster set the play close to the *Med*. and *Hipp*.[103]

In the prologue section of the drama Iolaos's introductory speech is immediately followed by vivid action with the entrance of the Argive herald. Iolaos begins with a general observation that sets the basic tone for the play: The just man, who is always concerned for his neighbor's well-being, is contrasted to the selfish man, who is a burden and a detriment to the community.[104] He bases this remark on his own experience, thus beginning the exposition: once comrade-in-arms to Herakles, he is now the guardian of that hero's children. Eurystheus pursues them from one place of refuge to the next, demanding that they be surrendered to him for execution. Now only Athens remains open to them, and so they have come to Marathon and its precincts. The phrase (32) is intentionally chosen in such a way that we do not imagine the site itself; later (80) the Tetrapolis is mentioned, to which Marathon belongs. Immediately afterward Iolaos says that the two sons of Theseus inhabit this region and that the refugees have come to the borders of Athens for that very reason. Here we encounter an ambiguity (we decline to speak of a contradiction) that runs through the play: the scene is set in the Tetrapolis, as demanded by the tradition, but the protection of the refugees is understood as being the accomplishment of Athens.[105]

Iolaos has ensconced himself with the boys at the altar before the temple; inside Alkmene watches over the girls. Only Hyllos has departed with his grown brothers to search for a new refuge, in case they should be driven from this land. Even as the old man ends his speech the threat takes shape: a herald enters (his name, Kopreus, is not mentioned in the play), wants to lead off Iolaos and the suppliant children, and knocks the old man to the ground at the end of their spirited dialogue. Iolaos calls for help, and in light of the remarks in the previous paragraph it is characteristic that he appeals to those "who have long dwelt in Athens." And just as characteristically the entering chorus immediately afterwards (80) introduce themselves as settlers in the Tetrapolis.

The two strophes of the parodos begin after two trimeters (75–110; the end of the antistrophe has been lost and in the strophe a verse is missing after line 76); they are composed as a dialogue throughout, the chorus alone making use of both spoken and lyric verse. In this singular passage the emphasis is entirely on movement. In the exchanges of the strophe Iolaos gives his name and explains his situation. In a sort of enjambment of the thought connection, he presents his request for protection at the beginning of the antistrophe, at which point the herald immediately intercedes with the Argive claim to the refugees. Now he joins in a dialogue with the chorus; before the lacuna we still catch his main argument against the first inclination of the citizens to help: It is well to heed good advice and keep your hands out of these matters! When the first epeisodion (111–352) begins after the gap in our text, we find the chorus leader involved with the herald in a dialogue that prepares us for the entrance of Demophon, son of Theseus. He is accompanied throughout by his brother Akamas. The poet has not separated the pair, united since the *Iliupersis*, but allows only one a speaking role.

After a brief explanatory introduction, an agon develops in the form familiar to us from the *Hekabe*: Demophon will arbitrate the dispute. The herald begins boastfully: I am an Argive (134; repeated immediately, 139). He first develops a rather specious point of law: criminals condemned by Argive law must be extradited to that state. But he quickly abandons this slippery ground and expounds at some length the motif of sheer profit. To win the powerful Eurystheus as an ally by granting him this favor is surely better than beginning an unjustifiable war with Argos. He mentions how many other cities have already rejected the refugees, thus setting the Athenian position in an even brighter light.[106] It is difficult not to see some contemporary reference behind his assertion that Athens has often chosen the weaker instead of the stronger for her allies.[107] *Audiatur et altera pars*, says the chorus leader in his two dividing verses and then Iolaos begins. He easily demolishes the false legal basis of the herald: We were banished from Argos, but not from all Greece! Then, with an appeal to Athens' pride, he forcefully counters the herald's κέρδος argument with the motif of χάρις, setting obligation over profit.[108] He invokes the lineage of the Pelopidai to establish the commitment of family ties, recalls his part in the Amazon expedition of Theseus and that hero's liberation from the underworld by Herakles. Once again a myth extraneous to the plot is used for the purpose of argument. At the end emotion overwhelms the speaker. He is nearly reduced to stuttering out his plea.[109]

The chorus leader takes Iolaos's part (232–236) and Demophon decides for the refugees. Zeus, bonds of kinship, and the disgrace of servitude, should he yield, are the determining factors. In the stichomythy with the herald that follows his speech the ruler stands by his decision. When Kopreus tries to use force, Demophon threatens to do the same and must be restrained by the chorus from striking the herald. This suggests an earlier version according to which the Athenians killed the herald in indignation.[110] As he retreats, Kopreus threatens war but is rudely dispatched by Demophon.

Worried anapests of the chorus leader mark a pause, then the excited flow of action resumes in speeches by the participating characters. Iolaos offers profuse thanks and admonishes the sons of Herakles to be grateful to their rescuers (a reminder of Spartan ingratitude). They must never raise their spears against Athens![111] Four verses of the chorus leader echo the praise lavished by Iolaos. Demophon thanks him for his kind words and explicitly accepts the obligation of χάρις imposed by Iolaos upon the Herakleidai. Then he makes his dispositions: citizens must be levied, scouts dispatched, victims sacrificed. He emphatically orders the old man to go with the children into the house (what house? He must mean the temple, in which Alkmene has hidden the girls). But Iolaos wishes to remain at the altar of Zeus until the victory of the just cause. He projects the conflict into the sphere of the Olympians: Attic Athena will not endure a defeat by Argive Hera.

The short first stasimon, one strophic pair with epode, covers a considerable span of time until the return of Demophon. It strikes a tone of bold confidence in the justice with which the city that loves peace will now meet the attack. The πόλις εὖ χαρίτων ἔχουσα (city well furnished with charis; 362) is Athens, on which all light is focused.

The second epeisodion (381–607) brings Demophon (with Akamas) back on stage. Iolaos asks why his countenance looks so troubled—one instance in which the rigidity of the mask is ignored. Now Demophon reveals that all is in readiness for battle, but the seers have proclaimed a terrible condition for victory: a maiden of noble blood must be sacrificed. Here, as in other plays, human sacrifice is not an ethical or religious problem but simply a requisite of the myth. The only aspects relevant for Euripides are the human troubles and attitudes that come about as a result. Thus Demophon confesses here that this demand is impossible for him to fulfill. He could never expect his citizens to offer such a sacrifice. The chorus leader also despairs (425 f.): Will the gods thus prevent us from aiding the foreigners?

Now it becomes clear that the rescuers' spirit of sacrifice makes the same demands on those who are to be saved. But how shall this happen? Iolaos's frightened speech expresses his utter despair but also his noble sensibilities. He reproaches deceitful *elpis*, but not Demophon, who shall remain certain of their gratitude for his goodwill. But then hope springs up anew. He offers to sacrifice himself as the victim of Eurystheus's hatred. The chorus leader reacts against this out of fear that the city might be blamed for surrendering the foreigners; Demophon refutes the plan quite rationally. Eurystheus does not care about the aged Iolaos but about the children, who might later seek revenge. There appears to be no way out; he can only admit his fear and helplessness. Then Makaria (not named in the play) steps onto the scene. Her concern has overcome her maidenly modesty and forced her to leave the temple. The moment she learns of the new situation from Iolaos her decision to sacrifice herself stands fixed. In her speech she justifies it with the same rationalism that moves Antigone to make her much-maligned calculations and that has been criticized so often in Alkestis. Athens will not surpass her in honor. And what would be her fate should she live? To wander and be despised. The chorus leader is filled with admiration, as is Iolaos, but he thinks it would be fairer to cast lots among the maidens. Here Makaria reaches her full pride as a true daughter of Herakles: not by the chance of the lot, no; of her own will she offers herself to be sacrificed. Iolaos has no more objections but he cannot grant her request to be allowed to die in his arms—it would be too much for him. Now she begs to end her life in the hands of women, which Demophon grants her. Makaria speaks her last farewell in the calm consciousness of the worth and greatness of her sacrifice, which again likens her to Alkestis. The earnestness with which she consigns the rearing of the children to Iolaos, too, parallels the farewell scene of the earlier play. Then her words express composed resignation. Her sacrificial death is the wealth she takes with her, if anything exists below; but it is better to think that nothing of the sort is really true. Where can one turn if death is not peace and cure for all ills? Demophon leaves with Makaria; after a farewell of praise Iolaos asks to be led to the altar and there covered over.[112]

The brief second stasimon (608–629) reflects on the events of the previous act. The strophe proclaims the ancient bitter wisdom: all human destiny is subject to uncertainty and ruled by the will of the gods. But the antistrophe attempts to encourage Iolaos: through all the adversities of fate strides true nobility, as exemplified by Makaria, untouched: ἁ δ' ἀρετὰ βαίνει διὰ μόχθων (Human excellence strides through distress).

In the third epeisodion Euripides, as he often does, imparts important information and decisions in a stichomythy. A servant of Hyllos comes bearing good news: the boy has assembled an army and combined it with the Athenians'. But his message is not delivered immediately. At first the servant falters as he catches sight of Iolaos lying on the ground (633). The frailty of the old man is heavily emphasized at the beginning of the stichomythy to set in relief his later decision to fight. But as soon as he hears of Hyllos he stands up straight and calls out loudly for Alkmene. She misunderstands his shout as a call for help and mistakes the servant for an attacker. In the threatening words with which she opposes her supposed enemy, Euripides foreshadows the Alkmene of the final scene.

The stichomythy commences now as Iolaos explains to her who the man is. After her jubilant greeting the form begins again as a three-part exchange but then continues between Iolaos and the servant. The latter reports about the disposition and readiness of the army; then a short dialogue (677–681) introduces a surprising new motif. The servant wishes to join in the battle and Iolaos announces that he will do the same. He sets his firm will against the servant's objections; he can take his weapons from the votive offerings in the temple.[113] The chorus offers a warning in anapests, then Alkmene intervenes and bids him be mindful of their helplessness, should he leave them behind alone. He refers them to Zeus for protection and thus provokes from her a bitter word about the god (719) that reminds us of his role in her life.

Iolaos has gone into the temple with the servant; now they return with armor and weaponry. The servant wants to carry the heavy weapons until they reach the battlefield; Iolaos, propped up by his spear and the servant's arm, urges haste. The servant replies that it is really the old man who slows them down. The scene contains elements of the grotesque, of which we will have more to say later. It closes with Iolaos calling for the strength of his youth: then he would certainly take care of Eurystheus. His request is later fulfilled by a miracle.

The third stasimon must bridge the elapsed time of the battle with its two strophic pairs (748–783). The ode begins with an appeal to earth, sun, and moon. The forces of the cosmos should raise their voices to the immortals and announce to them the imminent battle (α).[114] Terrible is Mykenai's wrath, but it is shameful to yield up suppliants. Zeus will help (α'). Then the chorus prays to Athena, strangely invoking her as mother, mistress, and protectress of the land (β); she will be honored always with sacrifices and always with song and round-dance at the month's waning.[115]

The fourth epeisodion (784–891) presents the messenger's report of the battle. In his remarks on the dramatis personae of the manuscripts, Murray identifies the ἄγγελος (messenger) listed there with the servant of Hyllos who accompanies Iolaos into battle and brings in the captured Eurystheus in the final act. Such a triple role seems curious enough in itself, and in fact must be rejected, because at the beginning of the scene Alkmene promises the messenger his freedom, and he is careful to remind her of this when he finishes. Therefore, he must be a slave to Alkmene, not the servant of Hyllos. And the misunderstanding of v. 646 is only possible if Alkmene does not know him at all.[116]

After a brief choral dialogue the messenger first reports Hyllos's vain attempt to settle the conflict by a duel with Eurystheus, and then he describes the course of the battle. He uses typical motifs and phrases (838!); the extraordinary vividness of many Euripidean messenger reports is not to be found here. But also it is clearly the poet's intention to spare the Argives in this account of the battle; the messenger himself praises their valor. The high point of the narrative is Iolaos's prayer to Hebe and

Zeus to be rejuvenated for one day, and the miraculous fulfillment of his wish as two stars descend onto the yoke of his chariot. The subsequent events are intimated rather than described: the youthful Iolaos catches up to Eurystheus's chariot by the Skironian cliffs and binds his opponent. Alkmene thanks Zeus, but not without a quiet reminder that his help was long in coming. To the children she announces salvation. Then she asks why Iolaos thought to take Eurystheus alive. Her own thoughts are quite clear: she calls it foolish to renounce revenge. She learns that Iolaos spared Eurystheus only to grant her the triumph over their enemy.

The two strophic pairs of the fourth stasimon (892–927) celebrate the victory in a moderate, reserved manner. The first strophe sings of festive joy, which the antistrophe connects immediately with justice and religious awe. Then comes praise for the deified Herakles (β) and the related thought that Athena was once the guardian of Herakles and now her city has rescued his descendants (β').

In the concluding scene (928–1055) the servant who left with Iolaos returns with the captive Eurystheus. The poet himself emphasizes that the mention of the king's name corresponds more to dramatic convention than reality, since Alkmene knew her enemy well enough before this. Both Hyllos and Iolaos are off setting up a trophy for the victory, which explains their absence.

With bitter hatred Alkmene confronts her enemy with all that he has done to her son and his children. She vents her unbridled vindictiveness: one death is insufficient punishment. In the ensuing stichomythy (961–974) she is opposed by an interlocutor, who tries to restrain her from killing Eurystheus with an appeal to the Athenian custom of sparing prisoners. It is difficult to determine who this second speaker actually was.[117] Zuntz is certainly right to reject Murray's conjecture that the first three verses of the stichomythy should be given to three different speakers. Alkmene has only one partner. Zuntz follows Tyrwhitt and believes it was the servant who brought in Eurystheus. However, if one assumes that the chorus leader refers not to a specific command but to the general Athenian nomos, and if one connects his remarks (965 f.) to the previously mentioned προστάται (rulers of the land), then his subsequent mild attitude appears curious to be sure but is no decisive obstacle against choosing him as the most obvious character to object to Alkmene's harshness, as Conacher and Schwinge have recently done. That Alkmene, when she begins her comprehensive reply, speaks of her obligation to the city supports this identification. She does this almost in the form of a praeteritio; in reality she wants only revenge and fears no reproach. The chorus leader concedes that her bitterness is justified and no longer opposes her wish to kill Eurystheus. Now the king himself speaks. Thus far we have witnessed the persecution of innocent refugees by a cruel despot, but now new motivations are introduced on two levels. To complicate matters in a typically Euripidean manner, the poet introduces the gods into the play. When Eurystheus explains that his actions were dependent on Hera's will, are we to see this as a shabby excuse or as a serious claim which exonerates him? Hardly the latter, for even were we to assume that the poet intended this added myth to be taken seriously, mortals still remain responsible for all that they do in accordance with divine will, even in Homer. Eurystheus the mortal, however, reveals himself as a timid man driven by fear, afraid that the children of Herakles might grow up to take revenge on him.

Now the chorus leader once more advises that the prisoner be spared; Alkmene, however, suggests instead a shameful deal. She will have Eurystheus killed but will surrender his corpse to the Athenians for burial. Eurystheus finally yields to his fate. In his last speech he assumes the formal position of a deus ex machina. As Apollo once prophesied, his grave will ensure the protection of the city that wished to spare him against an attack of the Herakleidai, should they ever (as they did indeed) forget their debt of gratitude. Filled with scorn, Alkmene exults: Why hesitate to kill this man, whose death will bring such profit? Her final words pose another difficult problem. Eurystheus's corpse is to be thrown to the dogs. Is this the last gasp of her vindictiveness, as Zuntz assumes (*Pol. Plays*, 37. 8)? A cynical disregard for the agreement just made? Without any response from the chorus, who express satisfaction in the concluding anapests that Athens remains free of pollution? Are we supposed to recognize a ferocity bordering on madness, since Alkmene in one breath speaks of the corpse's usefulness and then wants to throw it to the dogs? Nothing can be solved by conjectures, as Zuntz shows. But it is hardly possible to accept the text as it has been transmitted. Whoever is inclined to reconsider Wilamowitz's old theory of a later revision will seek the solution along that line.

In establishing Eurystheus's grave as a protection against the perfidy of the Herakleidai (Spartans), Euripides intended his audience to see a reference to the current political situation. But the way in which he accomplishes this purpose is significant for his view of the events of this world. Justice, goodwill, and moral discretion are lofty values. They are represented in the play by Iolaos, Makaria, and Demophon, while Eurystheus threatens to destroy them. At the conclusion, however, the evil king finds his counterpart in Alkmene, who, in her excessive vindictiveness, tramples upon the order of justice just as he had done in his fear of becoming a target for avengers. This final act casts a shadow over the entire play. The opponents of the forces that could guarantee order and meaning in human existence have the last word.

Structurally, the plot follows a single ascending line up to the victory and liberation. The demand for a sacrificial victim marks a retardation that is soon surmounted by Makaria's intervention. But once the pinnacle is reached, it is broken off by the conclusion. Of course one can take into consideration the question of the treatment of prisoners of war—a topic of some relevance at the time—but Zuntz has shown that this in no way exhausts the function and meaning of the conclusion, as our analysis also tried to make clear.

There is one problem connected with the *Herakleidai* that in our opinion has not yet been satisfactorily solved. In his "Exkurse zu Euripides' *Herakliden*" (*Herm.* 17 [1882], 337), Wilamowitz, following Kirchhoff, supported the thesis that the play is preserved in a mutilated and revised form: most importantly, that a section after v. 646 is missing; it would contain the report of Makaria's sacrifice and a lament for her death. Further, he thought he discerned passages that had been retouched by the reviser (353–380, 672 f., 819–822, perhaps 642–658). This interpretation has been contradicted by so many scholars, including Zuntz, that today it seems passé.[118] But it would be wrong to ignore the arguments that suggest the loss of a report about Makaria's sacrifice. The absence of such a report is curious in itself. The self-sacrifice of Menoikeus in the *Phoinissai* is a different case altogether. Further, the hypothesis contains this sentence about Makaria: ταύτην μὲν οὖν εὐγενῶς ἀποθανοῦσαν ἐτίμησαν (they honored this girl who died nobly). It is indeed quite difficult to refer this to the praise of her decision rather than to her death. Makaria's request to die in the hands of women (566) makes more sense as preparation for a situation to be depicted later than as a momentary wish without any apparent consequences. Then there are lines 821 f. about the sacrifice offered by the priests before the battle: ἔσφαζον, οὐκ ἔμελλον, ἀλλ' ἀφίεσαν / λαιμῶν βροτείων εὐθὺς οὔριον φόνον (they sacrificed, did not hesitate, but immediately spilt from human throats the blood that brings good fortune). Here Zuntz (*Pol. Plays*, 153) was quite right to assert that the lines are intolerable as a report about the sacrificing of Makaria—intolerable, we might add, if Euripides is supposed to have written them for that purpose.[119] Against the attempt of J. Barnes and E. B. England to understand βροτείων proleptically and to derive from βρότος the word "blood," Page (35) has correctly emphasized the lack of any comparable instances. In particular it is contradicted by *Iph. A.* 1083 f., a parallel that incidentally forbids conjectures for our passage. Thus the reference to human sacrifice seems as unavoidable as the assertion that Euripides would never have disposed of Makaria's death in such a manner. But then we are left once again with Wilamowitz, who ascribed the questionable lines to a reviser who deleted the report of the girl's slaying and replaced it with the extremely clumsy reference in the messenger-report. In addition there are the lines in Stobaios quoted from the *Herakleidai* but which are missing from our version (fr. 852 f. N, perhaps also fr. 854). Our tradition is certainly not beyond questioning, but Pohlenz (2. 145) was hard pressed to set it at nought. Finally, the play with its 1055 lines is conspicuously shorter than the other Euripidean tragedies. We would like to add one more consideration, without exaggerating its significance. After Makaria departs, Iolaos commands the children (603) λάβεσθε κεἰς ἕδραν μ' ἐρείσατε (Take me and put me on the seat!). Thus he is brought to a sitting position, evidently leaning on the altar, as the women in the *Bakchai* (684) sit leaning against the pine trees. But then when Hyllos's servant enters, he asks (633) τί χρῆμα κεῖσαι; (Why do you lie there?). When and why has Iolaos sunk to the ground? How can the servant speak of the old man's κατηφὲς ὄμμα (downcast eyes) when Iolaos has had himself covered over (604)? If one assumes the loss of a report about Makaria's death the change in Iolaos's position is perfectly understandable. His readiness to give in to pain and his weakness are apparent from other passages in the play.

None of the arguments summarized here is convincing—that troublesome line 822 is the most serious—and it is always worth noting that the addition of uncertain quantities can never yield a certain result. We must rely on relative probability, and this seems to indicate some sort of revision.

It is not easy to decide how we are supposed to interpret the scene with Iolaos and his armor. Did the poet wish to extend the grotesque elements to the limits of the ridiculous, or to surpass those limits? We can only say that Euripides would have placed in a very bad light the earnest prayer of Iolaos at the end of the scene as well as his miraculous rejuvenation if a mime with an intentionally ridiculous effect had preceded those events. It is another question entirely whether the poet went a step too far—and not only for our modern sensibilities—and thus challenged us to interpret the scene comically.[120]

Suppliants also initiate the action in the *Hiketides* (*Suppliants*).[121] The retrieval of the corpses of the Argive attackers who fell before the gates of Thebes was already treated by Aischylos in the *Eleusinioi*.[122] Plutarch has preserved for us (*Theseus* 29) the important detail that in Aischylos, Theseus won back the bodies not by battle but by persuasion. This is the version adopted by Isokrates in his *Panathenaikos* (168). It is uncertain whether we should connect with this Plutarch's statement that Theseus, at the request of Adrastos, buried the leaders' bodies at Eleusis, where Euripides sets his drama. It begins, like the *Herakleidai*, with a pre-arranged scene of hikesia, but with one difference: here the chorus itself is assembled on the altar in supplication, thus eliminating an actual parodos. The scenery represents the anaktoron of the Eleusinian goddesses; at its entrance lies Adrastos among the sons of the fallen heroes, who form a secondary chorus. In this and similar cases, as in the *Herakles*, it is not easy for us to imagine that the corresponding groups arranged themselves before the eyes of the spectators. And yet such must have been the case, for neither did the theater of Euripides employ a curtain, nor could the ekkyklema be used for such large groups of people.

The composition of the chorus cannot be analyzed rationally. Since maidservants sing from v. 71 on and in vv. 598 ff. Aithra cannot, following the MSS allotments, be the partner of the mothers (she left the stage at v. 364), but instead the maidservants should probably be given these lines; it is tempting to see in these servants one of the semi-choruses.[123] But if the mothers compose the other, then the number seven, which is stressed repeatedly for the women and the graves, poses further problems.[124] Iokaste cannot be numbered among the mothers present, any more than the mother of Amphiaraos, who was swallowed up by the earth. Tydeus's mother was not an Argive, and few would suspect that the huntress Atalanta, mother of Parthenpaoios, was present either. The mothers appear as a collective that defies individual identification and is determined by the number associated with the seven gates of Thebes (cf. 131, 588, 1221). We really do not know how to arrive at the requisite number of fifteen chorus members. An eighth servant is unlikely; perhaps there was a chorus leader separate from both groups.

The prologue speech here fits especially well into the plot. At the altar of the local gods Aithra prays for prosperity for herself, Theseus, and Attika. Her prayer is prompted by the sufferings of the foreign women she sees before her. Huddled around the altar are the mothers of the leaders who stormed Thebes and died before its seven gates. They all must suffer the fate that Kreon intended for Polyneikes in the *Antigone*. Thebes refuses to surrender the bodies, thus preventing their burial. Already (19) we hear that this act violates a principle established by the gods, as Theseus also will later (563) speak of an ancient nomos of the gods. Aithra has sent a herald to summon Theseus, who must decide.

It matters little whether we designate the following choral passage as the parodos (since it fulfills this introductory function) or as the first stasimon. Urgent pleas and expressions of grief fill the first strophic pair; in the second the chorus appeals to Aithra as a sympathetic mother who must persuade her son to intercede on their behalf. The third strophe is given to the passionate lamentations of the maidservants, and once again we must confess our uncertainty as to the arrangement of the choral parts. Were the previous sections sung by the entire chorus, or only half, or even (in the first strophic pair) by individual voices? The final antistrophe escalates the desperate lament to a wish for death. At the beginning of the first epeisodion (87–364) Theseus arrives, looks at the suppliants in astonishment, and learns of their request from Aithra in a brief expository stichomythy. A few verses provide the transition to a long stichomythy with Adrastos, who fills in the background of the Theban disaster. Here two passages appear to involve a serious contradiction, which can, however, be resolved by a closer scrutiny of the text. Adrastos tells of Apollo's oracle that directed him to give his daughters to a boar and a lion. He thought to fulfill the oracle by marrying them to Tydeus and Polyneikes. Theseus is extremely displeased and later reproaches Adrastos sharply for this decision (219). The same Theseus condemns Adrastos just as harshly for not heeding the prophecy of Amphiaraos, who discouraged the expedition (159): οὕτω τὸ θεῖον ῥαδίως ἀπεστράφης (So calmly you rejected divine words?). Does Theseus here, as has often been supposed, presume to slight the Delphic god? But the word ἐξελίσσεις (unfold, explain; 141) solves the problem. Adrastos's choice in marrying off his daughters was merely one interpretation of the oracle—but it is not certain, in fact it is highly improbable, that it was the correct one. Significantly, we do not find here the detail usually connected with the story, namely that the escutcheons or the pelts worn by Tydeus and Polyneikes led to their identification as boar and lion; Adrastos merely compares their struggle over nightly lodgings to the fighting of two wild beasts, evidently a hasty conclusion Theseus can blame as the cause of their destruction.[125]

The dialogue leads into a long speech by Adrastos (a lacuna after 179) in which he assumes the role of advocate for the mothers' cause and presents their plea for help. He explains that they must turn to Athens, for Sparta is crafty and brutal—a pointed reference, since Zuntz's date of 424 puts us in the very midst of the Archidamian war.[126]

Unlike in other plays, the chorus is here directly involved in the action, so the two dividing lines of the chorus leader simply repeat Adrastos's request. At first Theseus replies in quite general terms, expounding a view of the world in which Adrastos's actions are necessarily seen to be nonsensical. The passage is relevant enough to the context, but we should recognize that it also stands independently of the play as an echo of contemporary philosophical debates. Of course we must also warn against rashly equating these verses with the opinions of the poet. Euripides hardly ever (Herakles 673 may be excluded) confesses his personal beliefs, but he felt deeply involved in the pressing problems of his era, and allusions to these are to be found everywhere in his work.[127]

Theseus develops his image of the best of all worlds, in which the gods favored man with reason and language, assured him of nourishment, and gave him the advantages of civilization. He also includes prophecy through the observation of sacrificial victims and the flight of birds, which is probably meant as a barb against Adrastos, who disdained the words of Amphiaraos. It is worthwhile to compare these lines with the first stasimon of the *Antigone*. There Sophokles depicts man's tempestuous drive for progress in all directions, which must be limited by εὐσέβεια and δίκη (piety and justice). In Euripides, speculation about the evolution of human culture leads to the more static picture of a well-ordered world, maintained by the healthy influence of self-control (σωφροσύνη), that does not seek to be more clever than the gods who established the world order. But against this very order (here construed in a thoroughly religious sense) Adrastos transgressed when he foolishly married off his daughters and then amidst the resulting confusion disregarded the voice of a prophet (230). At its conclusion the speech again echoes contemporary social debates. Who preserves the order that Adrastos disturbed? Not the haughty rich nor the rebellious proletariat but the middle class maintains security. Somewhat abruptly (246) Theseus says no to Adrastos.

The chorus leader blames the disaster on the hot-headedness of the youths, which merits indulgence, but Adrastos proudly declares that he has not come to Theseus to find a judge but a helper;[128] then he bids the mothers leave, but they refuse to admit defeat. In trimeters, whose beginning is lost, the chorus leader entreats Theseus (263–270); then follow passionate pleas in dactylic meter, which, following Hermann's example, should probably be distributed among individual choristers. They produce the desired effect on Theseus indirectly, through Aithra; the son is deeply moved when he sees his mother in tears. In a terse stichomythy enlivened by antilabai Aithra begs permission to speak at length. After a brief prooimion in which she claims the right, though a woman, to offer good advice, she carefully leads Theseus out of his error. He saw only the folly of the Seven when they attacked Thebes, but apart from this stands the serious injustice done to the corpses. She places nomos emphatically in the foreground. Principles that are upheld in all Greece, principles on which depend the very existence of the civil community, are at stake here. Once again myth must serve the argumentation. Did not Theseus undertake a less significant struggle with a wild boar (of Krommyon)? How can he refuse his help now? In an urgent peroratio Aithra calls on him to champion justice and morality for the honor of Athens.

The chorus leader offers thanks in her two dividing lines, but Theseus first asserts once more his own side, repeating his charges against Adrastos. Then, however, he submits to his mother's pleas. It is his duty to punish injustice and here also to preserve the rights of the dead. He desires now that the city pass a resolution; δόξει δ' ἐμοῦ θέλοντος (it shall approve it in accordance with my wish; 350). Then he will assemble an armed company to add weight to his envoy to Thebes, and, if necessary, do justice with force. With words of fervent piety he accompanies his mother back to Athens.

In two quite short strophic pairs (365–380) the first stasimon (if we consider the first ode as a substitute for a parodos) sings of thanks, hope, and praise for Athens. Despite its brevity the ode must cover the lapse of time until Theseus returns.

In the second epeisodion (381–597) Theseus comes on stage with a herald whom he instructs to make an amicable settlement with the Thebans for the burial of the dead. If they refuse, violence will ensue; the troops stand in readiness by the sacred spring of Kallichoros in Eleusis. Theseus's entrance with an unintroduced command directed to a person who enters with him recalls the topos in comedy in which two characters come on stage engaged in conversation. The liveliness of the scene is increased when the Theban herald enters opposite the pair, thus making the dispatch of the Athenian messenger superfluous. The lengthy remainder of the epeisodion is devoted to a two-stage agon in which the first section presents arguments of a general nature, the second narrows the dispute to the particular case.

The introductory dialogue is short, since the Theban herald immediately gives the cue for the first round when he asks for the τύραννος (monarch). Theseus sets him straight: here there is no individual who rules, the people themselves exercise power in an annual succession of authority. More resolutely even than Aischylos in his *Suppliants*, Euripides has here brought the mythical kingdom into a utopian synthesis with the democracy of his own day. This allowed him to compose a constitutional debate in which each speaker clearly outlines the abuses inherent in the opposing system. We need only recall the third book of Herodotos to understand the intensity with which such questions were discussed in the fifth century.

At the end of his lengthy disquisition Theseus rudely and impatiently orders the herald not to chatter but to say why he has come—we might see a touch of the comic here, but it is surely unintentional.

After two insignificant verses by the chorus leader (such lines, which normally divide two speeches, are lacking in the first agon), the herald presents his case. To his refusal to surrender the corpses he adds the demand for the banishment of Adrastos, making the already tense situation unbearable for Athens. The herald's warning about a violent counterattack, about starting a frivolous war, his praise of peace—all this sounds insincere and untrue after his opening words. He concludes by reproaching Theseus for drawing his sword on behalf of blasphemers marked by the wrath of Zeus.

We now hear two somewhat formal verses of reproof from the chorus leader after which Adrastos, whom the poet does not wish to leave entirely speechless, lets fly a scornful epithet. But Theseus interrupts him in mid-line and presents his case himself. He declares briefly that he need not take orders from Kreon; then he takes up the leitmotif of his remarks: Panhellenic nomos (cf. 671) obliges him to defend the just claims of the dead (525). Whence man came into the light, there must his parts return: the πνεῦμα (breath) to the aether, the body to the earth.[129] Then Theseus places the principle common to all Greeks in the center of his speech, his rational justification here being that any violation of this law would have to break the courage of those in battle. However, when he finally offers the alternatives, surrender of the bodies or war, he speaks of the νόμος παλαιὸς δαιμόνων (the ancient law of the gods) that

Athens will never abandon. His abrupt conclusion is preceded by a general remark in favor of conciliation, which sounds somewhat peculiar in the context: life is a struggle with ever-changing success, but only the δαίμων wins: the unhappy man honors him to attain happiness, the happy man, to keep it.

Two encouraging verses by the chorus leader are followed by the typical stichomythy, which only hardens the resolve of both parties to fight. The herald withdraws, followed by Theseus after he has commanded his men to maintain the utmost readiness but carefully separated his cause from that of Adrastos. He will oppose the foe with the gods, who honor justice. Man's ἀρετή (excellence) is nothing if it is not joined to the gods' will.

Now follows the second stasimon (508–633), whose two strophic pairs are to be distributed among various voices, including probably those of the maidservants, but by no means that of Aithra, as the manuscripts claim. Fear for the outcome of the battle, a struggle between doubt and faith in the gods, and finally, a plea to Zeus form the content of the ode.

The song of the chorus covers the expedition and battle; the third epeisodion (634–777) is given to the messenger. He did not participate in the fighting; he is a vassal of Kapaneus, captured during the futile assault of the Seven. The reason for this appears in v. 651: from a tower in Thebes the man could see the events below in overview. In the introductory dialogue he reports the victory, which he then describes at length.[130] Euripides took great pains—more so than in the *Herakleidai*—to describe accurately the dispositions for the battle, the troop movements, and the fighting itself. Nonetheless, the speech does not attain nearly the mastery of other messenger reports; comparing it with the battle narrative in the *Persians*, we can note here the standardization of certain features that were later to recur among the historians. There is an effective contrast between the cry of the Athenian herald and the gloomy silence of Kreon, and a nice display of Attic sophrosyne by Theseus, who declines to invade the city after the battle is won.

The chorus leader rejoices, but Adrastos bows before the will of Zeus, who denied success to the unjust campaign of the Seven (here we learn that Eteokles offered a settlement on reasonable terms), but punished the arrogance of the Thebans. The doubts raised in the previous stasimon (612) are dispelled in these words of Adrastos.

At the end of his speech Adrastos, asking for details, initiates an expository stichomythy, in which we learn from the herald that the corpses of the Seven, piously tended by Theseus, have been brought along; the other bodies were buried on Kithairon.[131]

Adrastos concludes the scene with words of lament that set the tone for the following section.

The third stasimon (778–837) consists of two parts. The first strophic pair sings of joyous victory and mothers' grief, followed by the familiar topos of the advantages of childlessness and the unmarried state. Then anapests, announcing the funeral procession, mark a division. Apparently the lines accompany a shift in the position of the chorus. The following strophic pair (with epode) is pure lamentation, a kommos sung by Adrastos and the mothers.

The fourth epeisodion (838–954) begins with difficult verses. Theseus says to some unidentified person that he wished to ask him a question in the midst of his lament for the army but refrained; now he sees Adrastos and turns to him. It was a desperate solution Murray suggested when he had Theseus enter conversing with some Argive leader (who remained mute) and then speak to Adrastos. Line 381 offers an approximate parallel, but there the situation is clearer and simpler. Rather one might imagine that Theseus enters during the kommos, but does not wish to interrupt and only then catches sight of Adrastos. However, it is not easy to assume that Theseus wanted to ask the chorus about the merits of the fallen warriors, and στρατῷ in v. 838 remains odd in any case. The text of this section is certainly corrupt.

Theseus now asks Adrastos about the outstanding valor of the fallen leaders: whence did it arise? This information will be a lesson for young citizens, yet it would be ridiculous to ask about the opponents of each individual captain. The reason he gives for this, namely, that in the heat of battle clear observation is totally impossible, does not really support the theory that Euripides was here polemizing against the *Seven* of Aischylos. But since such criticism is quite unmistakable in *Phoin.* 751, there may well be a passing allusion to Aischylos's detailed description of the seven pairs of warriors in this section as well. But it is more important that Theseus in this curious passage, in which hubristic chieftains of the Argive expedition suddenly appear as idealized and laudable heroes, avoids their martial aspect in praising their merits. And so the following funeral speech of Adrastos incorporates the fallen chiefs into his picture of civic virtues, corresponding to the order of a rational world that Theseus described earlier. Kapaneus, despite his riches, modest and the enemy of all luxury; Eteoklos poor but proud and the enemy of the wicked; Hippomedon raised in strict self-discipline; Parthenopaios, the foreigner who fitted so well into the Argive community; Tydeus, whose mastery in arms, however, does shine forth in the description. In discussions of this speech reference is often made to Attic funeral rites, but Zuntz has quite rightly emphasized its unique orientation toward the individual personality. The dissonance between this version and the earlier image of the Seven cannot be lightly dismissed. It was undoubtedly the poet's intention to portray them as heroes worthy of the laments lavished upon them.

The conclusion of this speech is as curious as the rest. Adrastos remarks on the possibility of teaching virtue, ending in the command: οὕτω παῖδας εὖ παιδεύετε (So educate your children well!). But to whom does he address this admonition if not to the Athenians assembled in the theater? The problem of heredity or education, subjected to intense discussion by the Sophists, greatly stimulated the intellectuals of the time. Earlier, the *Hekabe* reflected these debates in a passage (592) that appears strange in the context; here the language has become much more definite, expressing an unlimited optimism in the power of education.

It is understandable that after this speech the poet was anxious again to strike the keynote of maternal lament in a short lyric strophe. Then Theseus adds to Adrastos' praise, which had been limited to the five leaders whose bodies were present onstage. He interprets (differently from the herald, v. 500) the disappearance of Amphiaraos as evidence of the god's approval and can praise Polyneikes from his personal knowledge of him. Then a stichomythy with Adrastos develops, containing important stage directions. Kapaneus, struck down by the thunderbolt of Zeus, must be buried separately from the others, near the temple in the background. This is well motivated on religious grounds, but also sets the scenic dispositions for the Euadne act. Theseus opposes Adrastos when he invites the mothers to approach the bodies of their sons (to accompany them to the pyre). The sight of the mutilated corpses would be unendurable for the women. We understand that the chorus has to remain in the orchestra, but must assume, to avoid contradiction, that the mothers' wish to embrace the bodies (815 ff.) is not fulfilled in the play.

Adrastos, who has become quite didactic in the second part of the drama, now concludes the scene with a remark on the folly of war.

In its single triad, the fourth stasimon (955–979) contains the lament of the now childless mothers. Then anapests provide the transition to the fifth epeisodion (980–1113). The chorus leader sees the grave of Kapaneus, already arranged, and the graves of the others apart from the sanctuary; she also sees Euadne, wife of Kapaneus, on top of a cliff near the pyre of her husband.

Here more than ever we must confess how inadequately we know the Attic stage. Desperate solutions have been suggested.[132] It seems best to assume some sort of structure on the stage roof (cf. 987 f.) that was disguised as a cliff and could be mounted and left from behind. Smoke rising behind the skene could have symbolized the pyre of Kapaneus.

The entire epeisodion—the aria of Euadne (a strophic pair interrupted by three choral trimeters), who sings of the happiness of her distant marriage and her readiness to die; the appearance of her father Iphis, who comes to his dead son Eteoklos and in search of his daughter; the stichomythy, in which Iphis tries in vain to restrain Euadne from leaping onto the pyre; and finally his speech of lament—forms an act complete in itself, which heightens the collective grief of the mothers through its highly pathetic portrayal of an individual destiny.

Anapests (1114–1122), to be allotted to the semi-chorus of mothers (note the address to the servants), introduce the second kommos of the play (1123–1164). The lament, comprising three strophic pairs, is sung in spirited exchanges between the mothers and a secondary chorus of boys who have come bearing the funeral urns of their fathers.[133] Here appears the revenge motif provided by the myth of the *Epigonoi*. If we follow Murray's arrangement of this problematical section, this motif is given to the boys (1146), with the mothers opposing the idea (1147).

Theseus enters (with Adrastos?) during the kommos or at the end, in any case after the boys. He reminds the mothers and Adrastos of Athens' favor and requests the thanks of Argos, which Adrastos then promises him. They have already bidden each other farewell when Athena appears (more likely from the machine than on the roof). She orders Theseus not to be satisfied with a promise but to bind Argos with a solemn oath never to attack Athens and to defend against the invasion of others (presumably Sparta). Theseus keeps at home a tripod that Herakles once entrusted to him to be dedicated at Delphi.[134] On its hollow he must inscribe the text of the oath and then consign the trophy to the Pythian god. The aetiological nature of these concluding speeches makes it quite certain that this refers to some monument visible at Delphi. Then Athena turns to the boys and promises them—continuing the motif from the kommos—victory over Thebes in time to come. Words of pious submission from Theseus and anapests, in which the chorus declares its readiness to take the oath, conclude the play.

Although one can hardly claim for the *Suppliants* the compactness of composition that distinguishes Euripides' masterpieces, nonetheless the poet has produced a neatly arranged whole. Despite a certain independence of some sections, the continuity is never broken. The play was maligned even in antiquity, as shown by the foolish remark of the scholiast on Soph. *Oid. Kol.* 220 that Euripides inserted the expository dialogue between Theseus and Adrastos to make the drama longer.

The first two thirds of the play present a formal hikesia and its fulfillment. The issue is set against a background of great significance in terms both of ethics (Theseus against Adrastos) and of politics (Theseus and the Theban herald). When the corpses are brought in the supplication is over; then follow the funeral rites, which comprise an Adrastos act and an Euadne act, clearly marked by the two kommoi. The self-contained nature of these acts reinforces our judgment that the poet was concerned more with the effect of the individual parts than with their seamless interconnection.

In the meager remnants of a hypothesis our play is termed an ἐγκώμιον Ἀθηνῶν (encomium of Athens). In his excellent discussion of the drama (*Pol. Plays*), Zuntz has correctly judged the value of this designation. All attempts to derive from it justification for detailed historical research and to come up with specific dates have gone astray.[135] We have already remarked (note 126 above) that neither the events after the battle of Delion nor specific treaty agreements with Argos can provide us with definite points of reference. On the other hand, the play is indeed an encomium of Athens, and its basic attitudes are determined by the situation of the Archidamian war. The relationship to Argos, which was always a matter of the utmost importance, plays a significant role in the overall conception of the drama and especially in the finale. Further, it is understandable that even after Perikles' death his political principles were still the subject of heated debate. When Theseus binds Argos by offering aid, he is operating on the principle espoused by Perikles in Thukydides (2. 40. 4). And when the king of Athens wishes to consult his people about the oncoming war (349), but nonetheless is certain that their decision will coincide with his will, we recognize the position of the leader in a democratic community. This does not mean that we should simply equate Theseus with Perikles; Goossens (433) has gone too far on this point.

More forcefully than in other plays, the problems of an era filled with controversy demand our attention in the *Suppliants*. Questions of constitution, of social structure (with an emphatically positive evaluation of the middle class), and of education were brought out in our analysis.

We come now to a separate problem. The *Suppliants* with its portrayal of a successful bellum iustum, with the character of a Theseus borne by a faith in god that appears wholly justified, stands as a *pièce bleue* in the work of a poet whose judgments on the possibilities of human action and existence are generally much more skeptical. This has led to extremely arbitrary interpretation of the play, the most glaring example being Norwood's thesis that the drama is a patchwork, assembled by some dismal fellow in the second century A.D. by contaminating one play by Euripides with another. The verdict remains isolated, but others, in the manner of Verrall, like Blaiklock (65), Greenwood (92), and Fitton (op. cit.) have tried to read Euripides' own opinion between the lines; they base their views of the play's meaning on a condemnation of Theseus and his battle.[136] Conacher stops far short of this, but also likes to perceive ironic overtones. He stresses the fact (98) that Theseus, though he speaks of the νόμος παλαιὸς δαιμόνων (the ancient ordinance of the gods) at v. 563, otherwise in the debate with the herald refers more rationally only to a Panhellenic law common to all peoples (526, 538). But a contradiction within these three passages, which all occur in the same speech of Theseus, does not exist at all. The Panhellenic law takes into account a right of the dead guaranteed by the gods. We are to take Theseus seriously when he harmonizes his world view based on reason with the belief in the dependence of all human action on the gods. The result, however, is not perfectly consistent—to this extent we agree with Conacher. The same speech also contains the odd—one is tempted to say, truly Euripidean—statement that the δαίμων (daimon; here almost in the sense of "divinity") always profits in the fluctuations of human destiny.

More important is the question whether the sons' future revenge expedition against Thebes casts a shadow over the conclusion of the just war and the oft-intoned praise for peace, whether the play concludes with an ironic reversal, as is evident at the end of the *Herakleidai*. The resistance of the mothers (1147) seems to point in this direction, but we do not believe that the motif carries such weight that one can draw conclusions from it for the interpretation of the play. The story of the expedition of the Epigonoi was simply a part of the legend given in the epic tradition.

But the strangest section of the play is still the funeral speech of Adrastos. We have attempted to interpret it as an inversion of the earlier image of the Seven, but we are aware of the difficulties involved. Nonetheless we cannot agree with an ironic-satirical interpretation that would destroy the play's unity, as suggested by scholars from Wecklein to Conacher.[137]

Close to the *Suppliants* in theme, time, and spirit is the *Erechtheus*, a mythical play of Attic history and, in its way, also an ἐγκώμιον Ἀθηνῶν (encomium of Athens).[138] It stems from the period in Euripides' career when the poet took an especial interest in the fate of his city. Calder (op. cit.) has proven that the year 422 (considered by Goossens and recommended also by Webster) remains the most probable date. Calder also deserves the credit for eliminating the old and long overestimated hypothesis of Wilamowitz that the *Erechtheus* was produced in the same trilogy with the *Suppliants*.[139] The numerous fragments, some of considerable length, that have now been augmented by the Parisian *P. Sorb.* 2328 (fr. 65 Austin) permit us to recon-

struct with confidence many sections of the play. According to fr. 349N, 39 Austin,
Poseidon probably spoke the prologue. The Thrakian Eumolpos threatened Athens,
whose king Erechtheus sought counsel from the oracles at Delphi and Dodona (fr.
367N, 58 Austin). He was told the city could only be saved if he sacrificed his eldest
daughter. From his conversation with his wife, Praxithea, we still possess her speech
(fr. 360N, 50 Austin), in which she consents to the sacrifice out of patriotism, and
justifies the act with rational arguments. If fr. 2R from the *Erechtheus* of Ennius with
the lament about pitilessness refers to the king's daughter and derives from Euripides,
if further, fr. 361N, 52 Austin and Ennius fr. 1R express the girl's proud willingness to
die, then we could conclude that there was a change from her fear of death to the
acceptance of the sacrifice, similar to that in *Iphigeneia at Aulis*. Also preserved is a
longer speech of Erechtheus (fr. 362N, 53 Austin), who before he departs for battle
instructs an adopted son (Ion? Xouthos?) in the proper way to live. The closeness of
this play to the *Suppliants* is evident in a further detail. In fr. 352N, 42 Austin,
Erechtheus says that men may join battle only with the gods on their side, never
against their will. The agreement with *Suppl.* 594 ff. is perfect. Here too the praise of
peace plays its role, as the fragment of a choral ode shows (fr. 369N, 60 Austin). The
chorus was made up of the city elders; from fr. 351N, 41 Austin, we can assume a
secondary chorus of women, this again showing a certain parallel to the *Suppliants*.
Thanks to the Paris papyrus we are well informed about the conclusion. We can discern the end of the final stasimon with the transition to the messenger's entry, as
well as sections of a stichomythy between him and Praxithea with the announcement of Erechtheus's victory and death. The ensuing report is lost, the text resumes
again with the end of a threnos that concludes in terror of the earthquake sent by
Poseidon, the father of the vanquished and slain Eumolpos. The following speech of
Athena is for the most part preserved. She calms Poseidon and orders that cult honors
be granted the victims of the conflict. Line 69 confirms for our play the detail reported in Apollodoros (3. 15) and Hyginus (46): the sisters of the martyred girl killed
each other because of an oath (Hyginus). Athena has settled their πνεῦμα (breath) in
the aether and withdrawn them from Hades. This recalls a current belief of the age
but here signifies the deification of those worshiped in time to come as the Hyakin-
thides. With the σηκὸς ἐμ μέσῃ πόλει (holy place in the middle of the city) for the king
who receives the epithet Poseidon, Athena is of course alluding to the Erechtheion.
This need not refer to a specific phase in the history of this structure; Calder's hypothesis (op. cit., 156) that in 422, when the play was produced, the general assembly
concluded the construction of the new Erechtheion, lacks a firm foundation, as he
himself conscientiously points out.

In his *Theseus*, produced before 422 (schol. Ar. *Vesp.* 313), Euripides dramatized the adventure with the Minotaur. The Athenian national hero was probably
represented in his role as the savior of the city's children. Ariadne's love must have
been an important theme. All else remains uncertain.[140] A precious fragment (382N)
with a shepherd's description of the name Theseus is important for the advance of
the Ionian alphabet before it was officially introduced by Eukleides.

We have no real clue to the dating of the *Herakles* other than the resolutions in the trimeter, and not the least reason for our uncertainty is that the play's content makes it unique in the Euripides canon.[141] Some time close to the *Troades* of 415 is a probable estimate.

Euripides gave the play its intellectual form by making an ingenious transposition in the biography of the hero. According to the ancient legend (Apollodoros 2. 72 ff., 127), Herakles slew his wife and children in a fit of madness. As atonement he had to perform his labors as the slave of Eurystheus. Euripides reverses the order. In his version, Herakles, as he returns from Hades, has completed his struggles, and only then does he succumb to madness and kill his family. The meaning of this reversal is also the meaning of the play. The poet provides a purely human motivation for the Twelve Labors. Amphitryon had to flee from Argos, since he had killed Elektryon, father of Alkmene, in an unlucky accident. In order to alleviate his father's fate as well as to gain permission for himself to live in his homeland again, Herakles entered the service of Eurystheus. That another motive, the wrath of Hera, claims its place directly beside this one, is characteristic of the way Euripides juxtaposes human action and suffering with traditional myth.

This play too begins with a scene of refuge at an altar. While Herakles was off on his underworld adventure, the usurper Lykos killed Kreon and seized power in Thebes. Now he plans to kill Megara and the children of Herakles to protect himself from future revenge. The threatened family has fled with Amphitryon to the altar of Zeus, which Herakles erected after his victory over the Minyans. This detail is quite important. Zeus is called "savior" (48); with him the persecuted seek refuge. His protection seems to be confirmed in the timely return of Herakles, but where is the succor of Zeus, who is called the hero's father, when Herakles is plunged into fearful suffering?

The play begins with an expository prologue speech by Amphitryon, which, without the artifice of a preliminary apostrophe, begins at once with events from the distant past. He unfolds at length the lineage of Kreon's daughter Megara, describes in detail the destinies that once brought him and Herakles to Thebes, where Lykos has now seized despotic power and rages against his enemies. When the old man finishes, Megara speaks of past happiness and present sorrows. From her opening speech we know already that the children are the center of her concern. Her question whether Amphitryon knows of a way to escape itself betrays the hopelessness of the situation. The following brief discussion serves to characterize the two speakers: Amphitryon considers only the possibility of postponing their death, while Megara sees no salvation in delay.[142] So too the short speech with which Amphitryon concludes the prologue scene offers only vague hopes for rescue.

The parodos (107–137) brings on stage the chorus of Theban elders. The strophe, stressing repeatedly the frailty of old age, immediately dashes our hopes that these men, however sympathetic, could offer even the slightest assistance. The antistrophe completes the image of their laborious gait; the epode again directs our attention to the children, whose radiant youth must fall victim to death.

The first epeisodion (138–347) is a Lykos act, in which the usurper presents himself in all his base brutality. It is interesting to note that the interplay among the three sharply differentiated characters is developed entirely in long speeches. Neither Amphitryon nor Megara establishes a point of contact with Lykos based on good or evil, as the stichomythy would demand.

Lykos immediately launches a rude attack against the refugees. How long and with what hope do they wish to delay their death? Then he reviles Amphitryon, who boasts of Zeus's partnership in his marriage (this theme recurs several times in the play, though the terms are never clearly defined), and Megara, who prides herself on her husband's deeds. As for Herakles, he is a cowardly archer who never held a shield. Finally Lykos reveals his motive: he has slain Kreon, Megara's father, and will not permit any who might avenge him to reach manhood.

Amphitryon answers in a long speech (170–235); its disposition is clearly marked (174). Let Zeus himself assert his share in Herakles' birth. Again the theme of double paternity is left quite unclear. On the human level Euripides needs Amphitryon as the father to extract a touch of pathos from his relationship to Herakles; Zeus as begetter, however, involves the problems of the mythical world of the gods.

Then Amphitryon offers his description of Herakles' deeds and delivers a detailed defense of archers as opposed to lancers. Here we catch an echo of the debates conducted in Athens and elsewhere by the proponents of both types of weapon.[143] Then Amphitryon returns to the situation at hand. That the children should die for the sake of Lykos's cowardice! Instead, he should let them pass freely from his land (Amphitryon does not give up hope). He concludes with a lengthy indictment of Thebes and Greece for their ingratitude.

The dividing verses of the chorus, which acknowledge the rhetorical skill of Amphitryon, are unbearably feeble, but Lykos puts an abrupt end to the protest, sends out woodsmen for the purpose of asphyxiating the refugees in a fire set by the altar, and intimidates the chorus with threats. In doing so, however, he gives them the cue to break their silence. It is uncertain whether the following speech (252–274) should be given to the chorus leader alone or distributed among the individual choristers.[144] In any case the speech contains different nuances of rising opposition and a resigned awareness of their own weakness. This would fit well with the distribution to different voices.

Now Megara intervenes. Her great composure and insight into the necessities of her situation place her above the quarrel. Pitiable death by fire, senseless hope, or miserable begging—she rejects all equally. All that remains is to overcome destiny by taking it upon oneself. Now Amphitryon takes her side. He was concerned only for the children, who are repeatedly set in the foreground that we may fully perceive the horror of their end. Amphitryon has one last request: to die before they do, so as not to hear their screams of death. But Megara asks permission to put the children in their funeral clothes inside the house. The tyrant graciously grants her request.

Amphitryon remains alone on stage. Passionately he denounces Zeus, co-father of Herakles, adulterer who abandons his own kin as no mortal would ever do. Herakles' arrival will refute this charge, but only to redouble its power in the second part of the play.

The first stasimon (three strophic pairs; 348–441) is a splendid praise of Herakles; in this superbly constructed drama it foreshadows his arrival but at the same time contrasts sharply with his dreadful ruin. If we separate the journey to Nereus included in the Hesperides adventure and the Atlas episode, we arrive at a dodekathlon that differs slightly from other versions, such as the metopes at Olympia. The canon is not fixed.

Each strophe and antistrophe has a glyconic refrain, which attests the influence of hieratic poetry.[145] From the refrain of the first strophe on, the ode is so composed that each strophic element and refrain celebrate one labor of Herakles. In the second antistrophe and refrain this arrangement is somewhat modified, in that both parts deal with the Hesperides adventure. Then follow in quick succession: the Amazons (third strophe) and Hydra and Geryoneus (refrain). Significantly, the final antistrophe concludes the ode with the Hades adventure, thus providing a logical transition to the lament for the destitution of the children and the weakness of the old men.

The second epeisodion (442–636) presents the first of the two peripeties, the ἄνω ὁδός (ascent). A dark pall still clouds the opening section. Announced by choral anapests, Amphitryon, Megara, and the children emerge from the house in mourning. Now, in the absence of the despised Lykos, Megara speaks quite differently. She laments the fate of her children whom she bore for a future of happiness and fame. With tones of the utmost tenderness, recalling Medeia's great monologue, she clasps the children in a final embrace and subsumes their laments in her suffering. In her appeal to Herakles in Hades, in the ἄρηξον, ἐλθέ (help! come! 494), we see that within her there still glows a spark of hope that she proudly concealed from Lykos. Her cry also prepares us for Herakles' arrival. Amphitryon begs for Zeus to send help at the eleventh hour. Then with a melancholy remark about the frailty of human destiny he bids farewell to the aged members of the chorus.

Megara's shouts announce the turning point. Out of incredulous doubt that Amphitryon at first shares breaks joyful certainty: Herakles is coming! And immediately her concern focuses again on the children: they must cling to their father's robes and never let him go.

Herakles' words as he enters (523–530) correspond exactly in function to numerous entrance monologues from New Comedy: greeting of the house, bewildered description of the group at the altar, decision to address his wife. Amphitryon manages only a brief outcry (531), before Megara, excusing herself politely for interrupting the old man, takes over the conversation. In a long stichomythy of lively questions and answers, Herakles learns all that has happened. In a wild speech (562–582) he vows to take boundless revenge. So passionate are his words that they have been taken as the departure point for an interpretation that claims to find Herakles' madness present in him even before the arrival of Lyssa. But the chorus leader expresses his full approval, which seriously undermines this view. When Amphitryon warns against haste (587), he is not trying to stifle his son's wrath but to indicate the dangers lurking in the city. But Herakles has already taken precautions; he arrived unseen. Therefore, he can follow his father's advice and await the arrival of Lykos inside the house. In a brief stichomythy Herakles, now pressed by other concerns, informs

Amphitryon about his adventure in Hades. Kerberos he left in Hermion. Eurystheus still knows nothing of his return. This hurried conversation is important, because in it we learn that Herakles rescued Theseus. The poet passes over the hubris of Theseus's journey to the underworld, for later we must see his character in untarnished splendor.

The act closes with one of the most touching scenes Euripides ever composed. Again he focuses on the children. Herakles wishes to enter the house with them, but this proves to be difficult, for the boys will not let go of him. And so he must grasp them with his hands and pull them along behind him like a ship dragging barges. We must keep this image in mind.

Herakles' enormous strength reminds the chorus painfully of their own weakness. And so in the first strophe of the second stasimon (637–700) they sing of the hardships of old age, which they wish would disappear into the waves or the upper air—an imitation of the cult form of ἀποπομπή (sending away).[146] In the antistrophe we encounter another of those Euripidean utopias that are a bizarre result of the poet's criticism of the world's condition: good men should have a double life, renewed youth after death.[147] When Euripides wrote the *Herakles* he was close to, or already, seventy years old. Thus the vow of the chorus (β) never to leave the service of the Graces and Muses comes from the poet's heart as well. The connection with Herakles is maintained, but in fine ring-composition this vow to the Muses is repeated at the end of the stichomythy. As the paean is sung in Delphi to Apollo, Savior and Healer—thus the second antistrophe—the chorus will sing paeans to their liberator, who by his deeds surpassed even the nobility of his lineage from Zeus.

The third epeisodion (701–762), uniting brevity with the utmost suspense, first presents a scene in which short sections of dialogue frame a stichomythy. Lykos comes to carry out his wicked deed, and Amphitryon lures him into the house with the pretext that Megara has fled to the hearth inside.[148] A kommos follows, accompanying the death of Lykos. Excited dochmiacs are interrupted by the chorus leader's trimeters; in the midst of it all we hear the screams of the tyrant. In this section a theme is brought up which the third stasimon (763–814) will continue. The justice of the gods is vindicated; they punish wickedness and protect the good.[149] The two strophic pairs are constructed in such a way that each strophe calls out for rejoicing while the antistrophes proclaim the just rule of the gods. The second antistrophe praises Zeus in particular, who, by leading the hero from the world of the dead to a radiant victory, has shown himself to be a true partner in the begetting of Herakles. If the play ended here, we would have a drama that leads from misery and doubt to a grand and glorious theodicy. But it would not be Euripides.

The second part of the play contains no stasimon arranged in formal strophes. Horror and lament demand other forms, and the course of the plot will not stand for any lengthy interruptions. The demarcation of episodes is wholly arbitrary. With these reservations in mind we will mark off verses 815–873 as the fourth epeisodion. As it opens, startled verses of the chorus members (three voices can be distinguished) describe a fearful apparition. A flying chariot has descended onto the roof of the house; in it are Iris and Lyssa, the latter the gorgonlike demon of madness. Again we

must regret our scant knowledge of the ancient stage. The use of the machine is beyond doubt, as Lyssa's command that Iris rise up and return to Olympos indicates
clearly enough. Dummy horses are out of the question, but a winged chariot is easily
conceivable after the *Prometheus* of Aischylos. The difficulty begins when we hear
(880) that Lyssa drives her team with a goad; Iris, therefore, must have flown away
without it, and the daimon rides it into the house. We have no idea how the stage
roof was adapted to permit this operation.[150]

Iris introduces herself and Lyssa and reassures the old men. Her arrival concerns one man only. With extreme cynicism she exposes the rule of the Olympian
deities, creating the sharpest possible contrast to the piety of the previous choral ode.
As long as Herakles was performing his labors, Zeus protected him. Now the hero is
finished, and Hera can plunge him into misery. Iris zealously asserts that her will is
one with that of her mistress (832). She goads Lyssa on to utter frenzy, so that Herakles may know their wrath and Hera's and suffer punishment. Punishment for what?
She has just spoken of his great deeds.

Euripides could not have shown the depravity of this action more forcefully
than with the objection of Lyssa, who warns Hera: This man has pacified land and
sea; alone he upheld the honor of the gods that blasphemers threatened. The dialogue
becomes heated; trochaic tetrameters are introduced, the earliest to be found in
Euripides.[151] After a brief exchange Lyssa calls Helios to witness that she acts against
her own wishes, but then she becomes merely the tool of Hera, kindles the firebrand
of madness, and penetrates into the house.

In place of a stasimon there follows a choral section (874–908; probably distributed among various voices), filled with fear and lament; it is interrupted by the
desperate cries of Amphitryon from within. A storm breaks loose and causes the roof
to collapse. Thus the terrible events inside the house are projected without. The messenger's report does not even mention the storm or the collapse, but according to his
speech Herakles is bound to a pillar that probably toppled when the house shook.
The motif is left unclear; the poet uses it where he needs it.

The following messenger scene (909–1015) may be considered as the fifth epeisodion. In place of the usual introductory dialogue in trimeters we find here a short
lyrical scene between messenger and chorus. But here again the decisive message is
delivered before the detailed report: the children are dead. The following narrative is
one of the most perfect of its kind. In broad description the poet brings the disaster
gradually nearer; his portrayal of Herakles' mental derangement, drawn with truly
clinical accuracy, has won deserved praise. With uncanny steadiness the action intensifies to a furioso of horror. The bow and club of their own father kill two of the
children; in vain Megara flees with the third as one shot strikes down both. Herakles
is about to commit the final outrage, the murder of his father, when Athena hurls a
rock against his chest and knocks him into a deep sleep. He strikes against a broken
pillar to which he is then bound.[152]

A brief astrophic ode (1016–1038) sets the monstrous event next to the mythical examples of the Danaids and Prokne. The door opens, and Herakles is seen bound
to the pillar; beside him lie the corpses.[153] Three transitional verses of the chorus

leader announce the arrival of Amphitryon. The kommos that now begins (1042–1087) develops into a formal mime: Amphitryon, deathly afraid that his son will wake up, first demands that the chorus be perfectly quiet, then almost flees in panic.

The concluding section (1089–1428) begins with a speech of Herakles, now fully awake. The madness has left him, and he remembers nothing; he cannot understand his present situation. Abandoning recent events his thoughts dwell on Hades, whence he has come. Has he returned there? In a long stichomythy with his father he is confronted with the knowledge of his deed. He is again in his right mind, and Amphitryon can loose his bonds.[154]

Herakles' situation is equivalent to that of Aias when he recovers his senses. And his first action is also the same: his own road to death is all he sees before him. Now Theseus enters. His arrival is well motivated: he has heard of Lykos's coup and now wishes to help his friend, who liberated him from Hades. The poet has him misconstrue the events. Do these corpses mean that he has come too late? He is enlightened by Amphitryon; Herakles covers his head in shame before his friend. Earlier Amphitryon led his son to the knowledge of his deed in a long expository stichomythy; here the poet varies the form but not the function: Theseus speaks in iambics, Amphitryon reports in lyric verse.[155]

Now Theseus knows the identity of the shrouded figure, and he turns to him in his speech. A mighty struggle begins, in which Euripides contrasts the two greatest heroes of a heroic world which is no longer that of the epic. Neither the Homeric Achilleus nor Odysseus could have participated in this conversation. The classicism of the fifth century has now ripened to bursting, and new ideas and new attitudes have sprung forth.

Theseus speaks to Herakles of his gratitude and readiness to requite him for his rescue. Then he pulls the cloak from his friend's head, and Herakles speaks. A stichomythy develops between the two, in which Theseus rejects the thought that a mortal could stain the realm of the gods. It is instructive to compare these words with Kreon's statement to the same effect in the *Antigone* (1043). But while Kreon thus seeks to conceal his flagrant blasphemy, Theseus speaks from an enlightened piety that can distinguish between the divine and human spheres. He cannot endure Herakles' angry protests against the gods (1244). However, as soon as he hears of his friend's resolve to die, he reproaches him for speaking like a common man (ἐπιτυχόντος ἀνθρώπου, 1248). Again we must recall the Aias of Sophokles to evaluate correctly the change in concepts.

Herakles still resists. In a lengthy speech he evokes the image of a life not worth living. What city would take him in? Even land and sea would refuse him. Twice he denounces the gods and foreshadows his disavowal of their existence in a later speech. Zeus—ὅστις ὁ Ζεύς (whoever Zeus is)—begot him as an enemy of Hera. We must compare this with the hymn to Zeus in the *Agamemnon* (Ζεύς, ὅστις ποτ' ἐστίν, Zeus, whoever he may be; 160) to measure the gap between two worlds.

Here, as in the whole play, both Zeus and Amphitryon are indiscriminately called Herakles' father (1258, 1263, 1265).

However, at the end of his speech Herakles asks who would now ever pray to a goddess like Hera, who destroyed the benefactor of Greece for the sake of her marriage bed.

Dividing verses of the chorus (1311 f.) acknowledge that Herakles is the victim of Hera.[156] Theseus, however, launches a second, redoubled attack on his friend's decision to die. He takes his first argument from myth, which recounts many evil deeds of the gods, though these faults never destroyed their Olympian essence. But then he tells Herakles what he can promise him: acceptance in Athens, purification, and high honors in his lifetime and after death. This refers to the numerous temples of Herakles in Attika; thus Theseus here introduces the aetiological element of Euripidean finales.

Herakles entirely dismisses the consolation Theseus offered from myth. Earlier (1315) Theseus made the reservation "if the stories of the singers are not lies"—but of this Herakles is certain. In the spirit of Xenophanes he asserts that the tales of adultery and violence of the gods are the deceptions of the poets; true divinity is wanting in nothing.[157] Such a view also negates the myths of Zeus's love for Semele and Hera's jealousy. We will return to this point.

However, Theseus's remark that suicide is the resort of a lesser man has some effect. Now Herakles says to himself that this would be cowardly evasion unworthy of the hero, and he speaks the splendidly bitter line ἐγκαρτερήσω βίοτον (I will persevere in life; 1351).[158] Not Aias, who falls on his sword, but Herakles, who will bear his misfortune, is the new model for heroic conduct. Now he gives instructions for the burial of his victims. The children are to be laid on Megara's breast; thus will he reestablish in death the communion he took from them while they lived. He is again the father who tenderly embraced his rescued children but a short while ago; now he bids them a heartfelt farewell. Only after some hesitation does he again take up the weapons with which he committed his fearful deed, but then he asks Theseus—a step toward reentering life—to help him bring Kerberos to Argos. Unabashedly, as if the beginning of his speech did not exist, at the end he names Hera as the cause of all his misery (1394).

Now Theseus intervenes; he bids his friend come with him and offers him his hand in support. The stichomythy becomes an emotional three-way exchange when Amphitryon joins in, and finally dissolves into brief words of painful farewell in the antilabai at the end. Then Herakles is ready to follow Theseus, whose friendship is the only possession he has left.

Here the poet employs a word responsion that is hardly equalled in importance in all of ancient tragedy. In the rescue scene Herakles has trouble with the children, who cling to his robes; they refuse to leave him and so he drags them along like ἐφολκίδας, as a ship pulls barges behind it (631). Now, however, overwhelmed by suffering he must cling to Theseus for support, must be led—actually dragged—by him, and in one of the final verses (1424) recurs the word ἐφολκίδες, now spoken about the hero who brought to his kin the light of salvation and then the blackness of death.

With two dimeters of anapestic lament the chorus leaves the stage.

Few dramas divide so sharply into two parts with the second action entirely the reverse of the first. Yet, such is the *Herakles*, which begins the second section with a prologue scene between Iris and Lyssa. But in no comparable play are the parts by antithesis so tightly bound to a whole as in our play. It is the antithesis between the radiance of the rescuing hero and his abysmal plunge into the blackness of suffering, the antithesis between the confirmation of trust in gods who protect the good and the cruel negation of that belief. Though Carrière (op. cit.) proposed that Euripides later tacked on the portion after v. 815 to the Herakles-Lykos section, both form and content of the play refute his hypothesis. Kamerbeek (op. cit.) rightly emphasized the unity of the drama, yet we would prefer to modify slightly his assumption of a tripartite structure, in that we consider the antithesis of the two main sections joined at 815 to be the real principle of construction.

In his edition Wilamowitz offered an interpretation of the play that has enjoyed widespread influence.[159] In his view the forces that break out in madness are already present in Herakles from the start; his crime stems from the same roots as his heroic greatness, so that he exemplifies the inadequacy of the Doric masculine ideal. This interpretation has been justly opposed, and Wilamowitz himself (*DLZ* 1926, 853) later abandoned it as out of date.[160] In reality nothing of the derangement brought on by madness is present in the hero's nature. It comes entirely from without; from what source is another question, to be discussed presently. In any case the source is rooted in powers before which man in the insecurity of his existence is utterly helpless, powers whose effect cannot be understood rationally and is not bound to any ethical norms. They cannot be analyzed from the Aischylean standpoint of δράσαντι παθεῖν (the doer must suffer), nor can they be venerated with Sophoklean piety as forces withdrawn from human understanding but sprung from the lofty world of the divine. The irrational element intrudes on human life, either as a destructive or (as in the later plays) a playful force, hurling its victims into confusion.

The role of the gods in Euripides is problematical enough; in the *Herakles* the question leaves us completely at a loss. Do not vv. 1340–1346 simply pull the very foundation out from under the play? How are we to tolerate this passage in a drama where gods appear on stage, and Hera's resentment is repeatedly stressed as the cause of the entire disaster? Attempts to harmonize the discrepancies, by which modern scholars have occasionally (see my remarks on the *Ion*) tried to present Euripides as a believer in the traditional religion, are entirely misguided. The patent dissonances cannot be explained away. Our task is to grasp the facts of the case: the play contains two dramas based on very different assumptions. First, we have the story of a man who rescues his family from extreme danger but then goes mad and tragically destroys them—a completely self-contained human destiny. The other story is purely mythical, of the hatred of a jealous goddess who drives a great hero to extreme misery. The fact that the motifs can be separated in this manner, as would be impossible with any other ancient tragedian, gives us an insight into the unique position of our poet regarding the mythical tradition. It is his only source for dramatic material, but it cannot offer him the spiritual and moral postulates for his world view. These he creates for himself in a constant struggle with the problems of a troubled era, in the midst of great social and political upheaval. If we speak—with slight exaggeration—of two dramas in one, we are aware that these two conceptions exist in a state of constant interference, that there are gaps, tears, and friction. But in the protest lodged by Herakles against the traditional picture of divine nature, the long-smouldering contradiction suddenly bursts into the open; the poet shakes the only foundation on which he can build his structure. For a moment the colorful curtain of myth is torn away, and we see with the poet a purer world of the gods, in which such an occurrence would be unthinkable. But only for a moment, for immediately Hera returns in her established mythical role.

A brief word is necessary about the character of Theseus. The parallel to the *Suppliants* is unmistakable. In both plays the Attic hero appears as the representative of enlightened knowledge about the conditions of human existence, filled with a piety that maintains proper distance and is ready to offer a helping hand to the unfortunate. In the *Herakles* Theseus represents the ideal of friendship that can be a refuge for Euripidean characters amidst the threats and hardships of life. For all that, we must not overlook the differences that separate this Theseus from the same figure in a comparable role in the *Oidipous at Kolonos*. In both plays he displays understanding and readiness to help; in the *Herakles* these qualities are strengthened even more by the motif of gratitude, but in Sophokles we perceive the unmatched tones of warm humanity, of gracious sympathy, that are lacking in Euripides' Theseus, who speaks rather from his knowledge of righteousness.

Only for the year 415 do we have uncontestable evidence for a thematically unified Euripidean trilogy. The extant *Troades* was the third play. The assumption of other thematic trilogies remains conjectural. The most likely candidates for such a form—according to the hypothesis, which is admittedly mutilated—are the *Dinomaos, Chrysippos,* and *Phoinissai*.[161] Wilamowitz's suggestion that *Aigeus, Theseus,* and the first *Hippolytos* belong together remains uncertain;[162] there is a possibility that *Temenos, Temenidai,* and *Archelaos* formed a trilogy. For other poets we know of a *Pandionis* by Philokles and an *Oidipodeia* by Meletos. The fact that all the confirmed trilogies belong to the years after 420 led Webster to an interesting conjecture.[163] He proceeds from the assumption (which I too consider probable) that Aischylos was the originator of the thematic trilogy. He believes that about 449 a change in production took place, such that on a given day one play was presented by each of the competing poets. Not long before 415, however, all three groups of actors (including the victorious protagonist of the previous year) were placed at the disposal of each poet, so that an occasional return to the trilogy was promoted under the aspect of the actors' agon, since during the production of a trilogy on one festival day all the competing actors had a chance to perform.

The first play of Euripides' trilogy was the *Alexandros*; the Strasbourg papyri are of some help in reconstructing it.[164] The basic elements of the plot are known. Paris, who was exposed on Mount Ida and raised by shepherds, takes part in a contest at Troy without being recognized; he is victorious. There is an attempt to murder him, instigated by Deiphobos and Hekabe, from which Hektor refrains. Paris flees to an altar, is recognized by his mother, and is welcomed to Troy—to the city's ruin. Kassandra played an important role with her prediction of the coming catastrophe.

Whether this came at the beginning or the end of the play is unknown. According to the view of Snell and Webster, the words of the prophetess formed a prelude to the entire trilogy; D. Lanza and G. Hanson suggest that her speech was the conclusion. For the chorus, the women of Troy seem more likely than the men, since we know of a secondary male chorus from the scholiast on Eur. *Hipp.* 58: shepherds came with Paris.[165] Much must remain uncertain, since Ennius is not always a reliable source. It is tempting to assume with Hanson that there was a confrontation between Paris and Hekabe before the anagnorisis. This would be a further parallel to the *Ion*, which, like the *Kresphontes*, contains an attempted murder of a son by his mother that is prevented at the last moment.

The second play, the *Palamedes*, dealt with a theme previously treated by both Aischylos and Sophokles.[166] The setting was the Greek camp before Troy. Odysseus, jealous of the resourceful Palamedes, contrived his ruin by falsely accusing him of betraying the Greek cause. His brother Oiax reported the events back home using written symbols (which Palamedes invented) on an oar. It is possible that Nauplios, Palamedes' father, who wreaked revenge on the returning Greeks by means of deceptive fire signals on Cape Kaphereus, made an appearance in this play.

As meager as our knowledge is of these lost plays, we can still say that the connection between the individual dramas of this trilogy was far looser than, say, in the *Oresteia*. The *Troiades* (*Trojan Women*) did not conclude a unified composition in the same way as the *Eumenides*.[167] For this reason its independent value is correspondingly greater.

The prologue scene opens with a speech of Poseidon, who here, unlike in the *Iliad*, is not the enemy of Troy. Euripides excludes the motif that Laomedon tricked the god out of his due for building the walls; his disposition toward the city remains kindly. Now, however, he surveys its smoldering ruins; the destructive will of Hera and Athena has proved too strong. The Skamandros echoes with the laments of captured Trojan women, who are just now being allotted to the victors. We hear that Helen is among them, in anticipation of her later appearance. Then the god points to the motionless Hekabe, as though she were a painting; she lies prostrate in grief before the captives' tent. She has lost Priamos and her children; of the sacrifice of Polyxena at the grave of Achilleus she is as yet unaware. Kassandra has been allotted to Agamemnon. Of the three great acts that determine the structure of the drama (Kassandra, Andromache, Helen) the first and last are foreshadowed here.

Just as the god bids a melancholy farewell, Athena approaches, and in a long conversation (distichomythy, stichomythy, concluding speeches) she asks Poseidon, who is astonished at her change of heart, to help her punish the Greeks.[168] Lokrian Aias's impious crime against Kassandra has seriously offended divine law: now the bolts of Zeus and Poseidon's help must destroy the returning Greek fleet. Poseidon gladly offers his assistance. The geographical hyperbole in his description of the shipwrecks that will fill the entire Aegean with corpses foreshadows the baroque features of Senecan tragedy.

The entire next section—Hekabe's monody, the parodos of the chorus, the con-

frontation with Talthybios, and the appearance of Kassandra in a bakchic frenzy—
strikes a single note of lament, constantly repeated and steadily intensified.

Still within the prologue are Hekabe's anapests (98–152) that move from recitative to lyric. In the first passage Hekabe rallies her strength to lift her head up from
the ground; her body remains prostrate and after v. 138, only half erect.[169] Lament for
her lost homeland is followed by the expression of physical pain that the old woman
suffers lying on the hard ground. Then, in a near visionary outburst, she summons up
(as the anapests become lyrical) the image of the Greek ships that caused Troy's ruin
for the sake of a shameful woman. A powerful period (122–137) unfolds, betraying the
influence of the new dithyramb. The obscure phrase (128) for the twisted ropes is
well suited to this style. Then the anapests return to Hekabe's personal lament and
conclude with a call to the captive women.

The parodos (153–229) brings on stage first one semi-chorus, then the other.
One could imagine that the paraskeniai were arranged to represent the tents of the
captives and that the procession of women passed through the two side entrances.

The two strophic pairs of the parodos (lyric anapests) present first an animated
exchange of verses between Hekabe and the chorus, while the second pair belongs
exclusively to the latter. In both we should assume that the lines were distributed
among the individual choristers.

In the first strophe Hekabe's warning not to let Kassandra come outside prepares us for the girl's appearance. The antistrophe accompanies the procession of the
second semi-chorus, and introduces a series of excited questions (interspersed with
lament) about the imminent lottery. Athens appears as their wish and hope, Sparta as
the despised counterpart. This is justified in the play by the characters of Helen and
Menelaos, but the barb will not have displeased the Athenian audience. If not Athens, then the chorus hopes for Thessaly, Sicily, or southern Italy—regions, that is,
where Athenian interests were invested at the time.

Recitative anapests of the chorus leader, announcing Talthybios and ending in
the fear of being enslaved in a Dorian land (Talthybios comes from Agamemnon),
open the first epeisodion (230–510), a Kassandra act with a prelude supplied by the
herald. This introductory passage displays elements of a kommos, as Hekabe's verses
(mostly dochmiacs) respond to trimeters of Talthybios.

At first Talthybios's message expands on Poseidon's prologue speech. Kassandra is allotted to Agamemnon, not as a slave, but as his concubine. Polyxena attends
the grave of Achilleus. Euripides presented her story as a main theme of the *Hekabe*;
here, with fine artistic tact, he does not pass over her fate but weaves it as a thin
thread into his elaborate web.[170] Hekabe does not yet understand the import of the
herald's words; only later do the character and her lot emerge in full clarity. Then
Talthybios offers new information: Andromache must follow the son of the man who
slew her husband; Hekabe has fallen to Odysseus. She replies with a savage outburst
of hatred. Unlike in the *Hekabe,* here neither Odysseus nor Agamemnon appears on
stage; they function behind the scenes as the representatives of insensitive power.

Instead of answering the chorus leader's question about the fate of the other
women, Talthybios demands that Kassandra be brought forward. Torchlight from

within the tent makes him uneasy. Are the women trying to burn themselves to death? But then Kassandra dashes onto the scene, torch in hand.

The prophetess, whose vision penetrates time and space, recalls the magnificent figure in the *Agamemnon*, if only because she alternates between ecstatic raving and rational argument. But while Aischylos's character focused a harsh light on the past of the House of Atreus, the vision of this Kassandra extends only into the future, triumphantly disclosing the catastrophe of the victors: Agamemnon slain, his avenger a matricide, Odysseus condemned to wander for ten long years. As in Aischylos, the motif that Kassandra's prophecies were never believed remains far in the background; it may be present, if at all, in the doubting words of the chorus leader (406 f.). Our Kassandra again differs from the Aischylean character in that she bears no guilt for refusing the love she promised to Apollo.[171] He has allowed her the sanctity of a priestess (41, 252), and even when she puts aside the fillets of the god she calls him φίλτατος (dearest of the gods; 451).[172] Although Euripides' language lacks the unparalleled power of Aischylos's, in the skillful blending of madness, irony, reflection, and triumph he comes near to equalling his predecessor. But he adds a purely Euripidean touch when Kassandra herself speaks of the coexistence of heterogeneous elements in her discourse (366 f.).

The main section of the Kassandra act is composed in symmetrical form. To the ecstatic monody (308–341; dochmiacs with glyconics and iambics), a horrible mock hymenaios, correspond at the end excited trochaics (444–461), in which the prophetess speaks of her own destined death, removes the fillets of Apollo, and leaves as one of the three Erinyes to destroy the house of the victors. In between come two speeches of Kassandra. The first begins with a highly emotional proclamation of the disaster that she will bring down on the Atreidai; but then, with a rather dry description of her theme (365), she sets out to prove in near-pedantic fashion that the Trojans, who fought for their homeland, were better off than the Greeks, who suffered and died in a strange land. Near the end she develops the idea of fame that will recur again later (1242): Hektor was able to prove his worth! Not without a touch of sophistry (how different in 498, 597!), even Paris is glorified here as the spouse of Zeus's daughter. War should be avoided, but if it is inevitable, an honorable downfall is yet a crown of fame. In ring-composition, a renewed declaration of revenge, in which Kassandra herself will be instrumental, concludes the long speech. The second is shorter; it continues in tetrameters. Now she turns to Odysseus, doomed to wander miserably,[173] and to Hekabe, who was destined by Apollo's word not to be the slave of Odysseus, but to die in her homeland. Here Kassandra echoes the prophecy at the conclusion of the *Hekabe*.

Between Kassandra's two speeches stands one by Talthybios, in which he asserts his role as Agamemnon's servant, unmoved by the seer's prophecies. As for his captain's love for the crazed girl, he can only shake his head. Euripides has not imbued this character with the same human warmth and wisdom of old age possessed by the Talthybios in the *Hekabe*. And yet he is not merely a cruel myrmidon of the mighty; with a certain shyness he conceals Polyxena's death (262 ff.) and repeatedly expresses sympathy with the victims of brute force (709, 1130, 1269, 1284); he can barely discharge his duty when he must demand the death of Astyanax, for his inner emotion breaks through (786), and he can even wash the tiny corpse while crossing the Skamandros (1151) and help with burial of this most innocent of victims.

The herald having left with Kassandra, the chorus leader cries out to the women, for their mistress has collapsed to the ground. Hekabe refuses support and must be imagined prostrate on the stage during the following speech. When servants lift her up (505) she desires only to be led to her resting place on the rocky ground, where she remains during the following choral ode and the Andromache act.[174] With a long speech of lamentation she concludes the act. Her appeal to the gods (469) is rendered meaningless by her knowledge of their past failures to offer help, ὅμως δ' ἔχει τι σχῆμα . . . (yet one calls on the gods nonetheless . . .). Previous happiness only makes present suffering worse. Her frightened question about Polyxena reminds us that Hekabe still knows nothing of her fate; she cherishes yet a glimmer of hope that will soon be extinguished.

The first stasimon (511–567) contains a triad that recounts the fall of Troy in choral lyric style. Individual images leave a strong impression: the crowd thronging at the gate to receive the fatal horse, the festive joy, the sudden outbreak of terror.

The second epeisodion (568–798) presents a clearly delineated Andromache act. In anapests the chorus leader directs Hekabe's view to the cart loaded with Hektor's armor and other booty; Andromache sits on it, the child Astyanax at her breast. Andromache's section, like those of Hekabe and Kassandra, also begins with lyric verses of great agitation. The kommos between her and Hekabe (577–607; three short strophic pairs) consists mostly of painful outcries in short cola; only near the end do we find structured sentences. Andromache sings of the hostile temper of the gods that destroyed Troy, this in preparation for the later reproaches of Hekabe and the chorus. In the following distichomythy between the two women, Hekabe calls the gods the cause of Troy's downfall (612) but immediately adds ananke as well (616).

Set at the approximate center of the play, this dialogue connects various threads in the plot. Hekabe's description of Kassandra's lot reflects back to the previous act, while Andromache now reveals the truth about Polyxena to her mother. However, she does not enlarge on this motif but quickly passes over it with the thought that the dead girl's fate is better than her own. Hekabe objects that hope is always a refuge for the living, thus foreshadowing her stronger assertion of an ultimate (tragic) faith in a later speech (702).

In an extended lament Andromache now speaks of what lies in store for her. She had lived as a model wife, keeping house and avoiding the gossip of other women. This picture of bourgeois propriety seems strange in the midst of the collapse of a great kingdom, but we need only recall Phaidra's speech in the *Hippolytos* (383) to realize that the question of woman's position and duties was a lively issue in Athens at this time.[175] But Andromache's reputation was her downfall, since for this reason Achilleus's son desired her as his wife. How could she live with the son of a man who had killed her husband? (This problem was confronted in the *Andromache*.) Her praise of the slain Hektor assures us that she will never forget him. She concludes in ring-composition: Polyxena is better off than she.

After the dividing verses of the chorus leader, who reflects on her own fate after hearing Andromache's lament, Hekabe replies. She describes her pain with an elaborate nautical simile, but then advises Andromache to be a good wife to her new master, for hope still remains. The unfortunate queen hopes for Astyanax; he will grow up, Andromache will have other children, Troy can one day rise again.

Immediately the blow falls that smashes this final hope. Talthybios comes, deeply distressed, to report the horrible news that the Greeks, at Odysseus's insistence, will cast Astyanax from the city walls. The message is related in a stichomythy, after which he counsels the women to abandon all thought of resistance; in resisting they would only forfeit the final favor of burying the child.

The following speech of Andromache numbers among the most beautiful that Euripides ever wrote. Comparison with the first great speech of Kassandra or the previous speech of Andromache shows the multiplicity of resources the poet had at his command. Here we find no rational argumentation, no rhetorical exertion; all is genuine, direct emotion. In the moving farewell of mother to son we hear tones reminiscent of Medeia and Megara. Then she breaks out in passionate bitterness against the Greeks, against Helen above all (preparation for the next act). In a paroxysm of pain she leaves the stage. The concluding trimeters of the chorus leader (781 f.) again name Helen as the cause of all their suffering. In a brief anapestic scene Talthybios, himself oppressed by his task, hastens to lead the child away. Hekabe's farewell expresses her utter despair.

Of the two strophic pairs of the second stasimon (799–859), the first continues the tale of the fall of Troy begun in the earlier ode and sings of the expedition that Telamon undertook with Herakles, of the destruction of the city, and of Laomedon's death. The second pair, however, reproaches the gods. Zeus took Ganymede up to Olympos, but this brought Troy no advantage. Even Eos, who had taken Tithonos as her husband, stood by and watched as the city fell to ruin.

The third epeisodion (860–1059) is a Helen act. Menelaos comes to fetch his unfaithful wife.[176] He defends himself against a charge with which he is quite familiar: he did not advance against Troy for the sake of a woman, but to punish the violator of his hospitality. The Greeks have handed Helen over to him, but he first wishes to take her back to Hellas and then kill her. This postponement already sounds suspicious, and none of the spectators, who all knew the fourth book of the *Odyssey*, could believe even for a moment that Menelaos would keep his word. But Hekabe does believe it; the thought of just punishment for Helen raises her once more from the depths of despair and she expresses her hope in the strangest prayer ever intoned in Greek tragedy.[177] It is addressed to Zeus, who upholds the earth on which he keeps his throne. But this is not the Zeus of myth, it is a force past comprehension. Ὅστις ποτ' εἶ σύ (whoever you may be), a clear echo of the *Agamemnon* (v. 160), does not signify here the vast abundance of the ineffable, but instead gnawing uncertainty. Is this god the necessity of nature, is he the nous of mortals? The influence of contemporary natural philosophy, of Anaxagoras and others, has long been recognized in this passage. Hekabe prays to this power which for her ensures the just direction of men in its silent movement. Again her hope is renewed, no longer for Troy, but for the execution of justice, the punishment of Helen. But her belief is deeply ironic, for we know that this hope is also illusory and that Helen will triumph.

It is difficult to say why the poet has Hekabe offer a prayer that does not perhaps reflect his own conviction but certainly his striving for an enlightened conception of god. It may help to consider that Euripides could hardly have Hekabe pray to the Zeus of myth—she has long since given up hope in gods of that sort.

In a three-way dialogue Helen defends herself against being treated like a criminal, and again it is ironic that Hekabe is the one who persuades Menelaos to let Helen speak. She anticipates a victory that she then achieves—though hollow, in word only—but in so doing she exposes Menelaos to Helen's seductive charms, of which he was justly afraid (891).

Helen first denounces Hekabe, who gave birth to Paris, and then the old man who let him live;[178] then she bases her defense entirely on arguments supplied by myth. With a conjurer's sleight she turns the judgment of Paris to her glory: if another goddess had won, it would have meant the domination of Asia over Greece. But when Paris came to Sparta, where Menelaos left her alone with his guest, he came with a powerful goddess. Who could withstand Aphrodite? After the death of Paris all her attempts to escape and return to the Greeks were thwarted.

The chorus leader is here given three verses in which she entreats Menelaos not to be misled by this speech. Hekabe then proceeds to destroy the mythical tissue of excuses. Not that she denies the goddesses; on the contrary, she takes their side and explains that the tales told about them are self-contradictory nonsense. What Helen called Kypris was really her own nous that was deluded by the beauty of Paris and by Trojan luxury. After a pause (εἶεν, 998, approximately in the same position as in Helen's speech, 994) she refutes Helen's lies about her abduction by force and attempted escapes from Troy. Quite the opposite: Hekabe urged her to flee, without success. In a final appeal she exhorts Menelaos to kill his faithless wife.

It is not easy to interpret this agon.[179] Does Hekabe simply unmask Helen, or is her defense also justified to some extent? We can immediately settle the dispute about Helen's alleged escape attempts: Hekabe here refutes beyond doubt her opponent's purposeful lies. In the rest of the section, however, two stories are set against each other that exist on entirely different levels. We recall our remarks on the *Herakles*. The story of a woman who fell victim to quarrelling goddesses is opposed by the other story about an amorous woman who was smitten by a handsome prince. Myth versus psychology. The clash of the two spheres results necessarily in criticism of the myth, here as in the *Herakles*. Helen, who appears as the guilty one in the play, can defend herself as she does; the myth is there after all.[180] But for Euripides the myth is flawed, and these flaws are exposed by Hekabe, and justifiably. Rhetorically, she wins a victory, but the final dialogue (again among three characters) leaves no doubt that reality will turn out otherwise. Hekabe knows why she demands that Menelaos and Helen return in separate ships.

Again in the third stasimon (1060–1117) the two strophic pairs are divided in content. The first contains an accusation leveled directly against Zeus.[181] He has abandoned Troy, and the chorus wonders if the god on his heavenly throne cares at all about the city's misery. In the antistrophe the women's grief finds release through the curse on Menelaos, whose ship they pray will be shattered by Zeus's thunderbolts.

The entire exodos (1118–1332) is an extended threnos, in which the lament for Astyanax is overwhelmed by the mourning for Troy as it collapses in smoke and flames. Talthybios comes with the corpse of Astyanax and reports the hasty departure of Neoptolemos. Andromache, whose farewell moved the herald to tears, requested of her new husband the shield of Hektor in which Hekabe is to bury the child. While crossing the Skamandros, Talthybios washed the boy's corpse; now he leaves to dig a grave.

Hekabe delivers the funeral speech for Astyanax and first denounces the senseless fear on the Greeks' part that led them to the brutal murder of an innocent child. Then she finds words of moving fervor for all the hope lost with Astyanax, for his childlike tenderness, for the love he gave and received. Again we perceive that delicacy of feeling that Euripides could evoke so masterfully when dealing with child relationships.[182] But the shield on which Astyanax now lies and that still bears the trace of Hektor's arm on its inner strap and of his sweat on its rim, awakens in Hekabe the memory of her dead son. Her long speech of lamentation (1156–1206) continues into the following kommos (1207–1250). The women of the chorus follow her bidding and adorn the corpse with whatever they have managed to save from the disaster. Their cries of woe respond to the verses with which Hekabe accompanies the obsequies. In her final words a new note is struck: the gods abandoned Troy. But if they had not caused its destruction, the fall of the city could never be celebrated in song by later generations. This thought, which recalls Kassandra's more rational argumentation (394 ff.), bears no heavy emphasis, but it corresponds fully to the Greek conception of what can last of human destiny.

Choral anapests mark the transition from the lament for the child to new terror. Over in Ilion men are seen lighting more fires with torches. By way of rational explanation for this, one might say that the Greeks wished to destroy everything that was left to be destroyed before they departed. But the play as a work of art demanded a final climax, which the burning provides. Talthybios comes, calls to his men to make haste, and orders the women to prepare to leave their homeland when the trumpet sounds.

The play ends in a paroxysm of suffering. After a short speech of lament, Hekabe tries to leap into the flames, but Talthybios has her restrained and kept safe for Odysseus. A kommos in lyric iambics with a rapid exchange of voices between the chorus and Hekabe forms the conclusion. The women hurl themselves to the ground, beat the earth with their fists, cry out their distress to the dead below. Then comes the sound of the fortress crashing down: the forces of destruction rage as in earthquakes and floods. From this inferno the women march away, Hekabe trudging slowly into slavery.

With this trilogy, and its satyr play *Sisyphos*,[183] Euripides took second place to Xenokles, who produced *Oidipous*, *Lykaon*, *Bakchai*, and *Athamas*. Ailian (*Var. Hist.* 2. 8) could explain this only from the stupidity or corruptibility of the judges. Or was it difficult for the Athenians to endure such an abundance of suffering? In Plutarch

(*Pelop.* 29) we read the story of Alexander of Pherai, who left the theater during a performance of the *Troiades*. He was ashamed to let the audience see him, who had murdered so many without pity, weep for Hekabe and Andromache.

Only a pedant could dispute the unity of this magnificent work or quibble about its structure. This is not to say that the paratactic construction of the drama does not differ from that of other plays, in which a consistent plot is developed point by point from exposition to conclusion. The scenes are set side by side—not without important relationships between them, but it is true that they *are* set side by side rather than fused together. The play's unity lies in the constant reference to Troy and in the character of Hekabe. Its construction is crystal clear. After the independent scene with the gods, the drama begins with expansive lamentation, and it ends in the same way. In between are set three clearly delineated acts that present the fates of three women. The main accent lies on the central section, for Andromache's lot is the hardest. The poet also lays special emphasis on the Andromache act by including within it the change from the last chance for Troy's future to the utter extinction of any such hope.

In this play as in others, scholars have greatly exaggerated the extent of contemporary references.[184] Conacher suggests (136) that sorrow and indignation resulting from the Athenian atrocity at Melos could have been determining factors in the play's conception; such a possibility cannot be simply refuted, still less proved. However, following the modern trend of avoiding historical interpretations, some have gone so far as to reject a view of the play which had previously been accepted as fact.[185] Thus, we are no longer to see in the play an indictment of war or to connect it with the situation in Athens at a time when the planned invasion of Sicily was everyone's concern. Here it appears that a principle that was certainly justified as a reaction against earlier exaggerations has been taken too far. To be sure, the poet reflects the misery of war primarily in the fate of the women, but are they not the most suitable medium for what he had to say? However, the glorious mention of the Greek west (220) indicates nothing more than the interest that these areas aroused at that time. In all these questions one is falling nowadays too easily into a rigid either-or position. Steidle (55) correctly states "that Euripides wished to represent human suffering, as it were, in an extreme case, in its entire weight and paradoxical incomprehensibility." But this does not exclude the possibility that the poet presented in this excess of suffering the terrible absurdity of war, or that such a presentation in the Athens of 415 would necessarily be interpreted as a warning.

Together with the Euadne scene in the *Suppliants*, the *Troiades* presents our most difficult problem of staging. We offer two opposing views. Wilamowitz commented on the action at the end of the play: "quin re vera scaenam vel potius proscaenii tabulamentum flammis adesum theatrales operae proiecerint, non licet dubitare."[186] On the other hand, Hourmouziades (122) prefers to leave almost everything to the imagination. The tents provided for the captive women were visible. "The destruction of Troy . . . forms an elaborate background, vividly described though invisible, in the *Troiades*." He believes the fires were represented by a group of torch bearers who marched across the stage from one parodos to the other. This is an acceptable solution for the section in which Talthybios gives his orders (1260). It is not so easy to accept that in the imagination of the spectators the women's tents were simply transformed at the end into the ruins of Troy. This specific difficulty is closely bound to the general problem of how much the poet could impute to his audience's imagination and how much was actually seen.[187] For the *Troiades* the solution probably lies between the two aforementioned extremes. Smoke rising behind the skene could have suggested the fire. Probably more smoke came from the skene itself, since Hekabe's attempt to hurl herself into the flames can hardly have been presented without some tangible scenic aid. As for the extent to which the skene wall represented the walls or fortifications of Troy, while the paraskenai were used for the captives' tents, any suggestion must remain purely hypothetical.

With the exception of the *Bakchai*, no other Euripidean drama poses so many difficult problems as the *Elektra*.[188] The uncertainty begins with the dating. August Boeckh was the first to see a reference to the Sicilian expedition in the verses 1347–1356 of the Dioskouroi, and accordingly dated the play to 413. H. Weil (*Sept. Trag.*, 569) then referred the passage specifically to the relief expedition launched by Demosthenes in the spring of 413 (Thuk. 7. 17) and so he arrived at the Dionysia of 413. This date was long accepted as certain until it was opposed by G. Zuntz who won such a following that the play is now most often dated between the *Suppliants* and the *Troiades*.[189]

Zuntz was able to eliminate the previously assumed reference of verses 1280 ff. to the *Helen* produced in 412. This justification of the heroine was not invented by Euripides (cf. Kannicht, *Helena*, Heidelberg 1969, 1. 31). As for the Sicilian argument, here we must examine the passages in question very closely. It cannot be said that the Dioskouroi have left their duty of rescuing ships (1241) and then return to it later (1347). In the first passage they perform their special task, to which they are summoned in the splendid hymn of Alkaios: they save a ship in deep distress at sea. No such action is even hinted at in the second passage. There σῴσοντε refers to the safe protection of a fleet, a function that differs completely from the first instance.[190] And the specific mention of the Sicilian sea cannot be so easily taken as a general remark without particular significance.

The protest against the exaggerated search for contemporary historical references, which was a reaction against the offences of earlier scholars, cannot justify a general prohibition that would decide our question.[191] Zuntz must be credited with releasing *Elektra* from too close a connection with *anagnorisis-mechanema* plays like *Hel.* and *Iph. T.* This difference, however, tells us nothing about the chronological relationships. We need only refer to *Iph. A.*, *Ba.*, and *Alkmeon in Korinth* to show how variegated elements can coexist within a limited period of creativity.

The weightiest arguments that Zuntz brings to bear are based on metrical analysis. All the plays from the *Herakles* and the *Troiades* on contain trochaics, but the *Elektra* does not. Vögler (op. cit., 61. 26) was able to show that the density of the trochaics changes quite irregularly. The observation of resolutions in the trimeters, for which Zuntz can refer to excellent preliminary studies, is of greater weight.[192] The percentage of resolution increases between the *Alkestis* (6.2%) and *Bakchai* (37.6%)

with a regularity that can almost always be verified.[193] Yet the "almost" is a necessary qualification. From the *Medeia* (431 with 6.6%) to the *Hkld.* (5.7%) to the *Hipp.* (428 with 4.3%) we note a considerable drop, followed by a jump to 11.3% in the *Andromache*. Later we find another decrease from the *Helena* (412 with 27.5%) to the *Phoin.* (25.8%). But are these statistics sufficient to prove the viability of dating the *Elektra* (16.9%) between the *Troiades* (415 with 21.2%) and the *Helena* (412 with 27.5%)? Despite A. Vögler's earnest efforts (op. cit.) serious doubts remain.

We are left with a dilemma. To give preference to the metrical argument necessitates the elimination of a reference to the Sicilian expedition that seems undeniable; to reverse the emphasis would entail our ignoring the metrical evidence. It is understandable that W. Theiler recently resorted to the "theory of the drawer": "The *Elektra*, composed in 419/418, remained in the drawer until its production in 413."[194] At that time the allusion to Sicily was inserted in the play. This expedient, which cannot be supported by anything we know about the production of the ancient dramatists, is as unsatisfactory here as in the similar attempt to keep the *Suppliants* among the early works of Aischylos.[195]

We have considered it more correct to outline the problem in all its perplexity than to dictate a solution. Yet, after all, it seems more difficult to evade the metrical evidence than to deny the historical allusion. But that is not to say we can do this with a good conscience.

The prologue section is exceptionally rich in exposition. It begins with the speech of a peasant farmer, the husband of Elektra. His address to the land is followed immediately by rather dry but very informative narration recounting Agamemnon's expedition to Troy, and his murder in Argos after which Aigisthos seized power. The latter wished to kill Agamemnon's children as well, but the king's aged tutor sent Orestes safely to Strophios in Phokaia, while Elektra, now of marriageable age, was protected from Aigisthos by her mother. Despite all reservations—Klytaimestra is called ὠμόφρων (savage-minded), and is said to have feared φθόνος (ill will) if she killed her children—her actions still appear less reprehensible than the plan of Aigisthos. Her alternative was to marry Elektra to a peasant far from Mykenai who was of noble lineage but now completely impoverished. He has not touched the bed of the princess. This is relevant to the plot, since at the end of the play the Dioskouroi give Elektra to Pylades in marriage. But the motif also has its own significance, since the nobility of the poor man justifies new standards of moral values divorced from social rank.[196] When Orestes later (384), in a remark seemingly directed to the general public, recommends ὁμιλία and ἤθη (behavior in the community and character) as criteria for judging men, Euripides anticipates the social commentary of Menander.[197]

Elektra enters speaking a monologue which, with its address to Night, might itself have opened the play. On her head she carries a vessel for fetching water. Not that she need perform such menial tasks, but she does it to publicize the disgrace Aigisthos inflicts upon her. With this one touch the poet beautifully characterizes the excess of her deep and hostile bitterness. In her first words we hear nothing of her father's murder, but only what Klytaimestra and Klytaimestra's lover have done to her. The peasant enters the conversation and tries to dissuade her from her task.

Elektra praises his disposition but feels obliged to help him in his poverty; thus the act of fetching water, first seen as a gesture of defiance, now appears in a different light. Both leave the stage as Orestes now enters with Pylades, who remains mute throughout the entire play. Orestes addresses his friend, but the speech is basically an entrance monologue for the purposes of orienting the audience. We learn that he has visited his father's grave at night and offered sacrifice there. Now he wants to remain here by the land's borders, find his sister, and accomplish the revenge commanded by the god. Meanwhile day has broken; he sees a woman approaching with a water jug and suggests that they listen in on her conversation. A curious notion, for how could Orestes guess that this solitary figure would talk or sing? The eavesdropping scene is fast becoming a standard device.

Elektra returns from the well and sings a monody in two strophic pairs, each of which contains a mesode (without responsion). The song begins with a rather awkward self-description intended by the poet to be overheard by Orestes. The rest of the poem is entirely devoted to a lament for her murdered father that establishes a bond with her brother's task even before they meet. The imperatives within the monody are difficult. With a single exception they are addressed to herself; however, θές in v. 140 must be directed to a maidservant who did not enter with Elektra but appeared only briefly for the purpose of removing the vessel.

The parodos (167–212), in one strophic pair divided equally between chorus and Elektra, picks up to a great extent the meters of the monody (glyconics and choriambic dimeters). The neighboring women have come to invite Elektra to a festival at the temple of Hera; Elektra declines amidst complaints about her menial lot (207, cf. 1004). Again it is characteristic that, although she could receive fine clothes and jewelry from the women, she refuses everything, deeply embittered. In this way, too, she contrasts her despair of divine help to the pious assertions of the chorus (193).

At the beginning of the first epeisodion (213–431) the chorus leader first reacts to Elektra's lament in two trimeters. She mentions the guilt of Helen, of which the Dioskouroi will absolve her at the end of the play.

Orestes and Pylades emerge from their hiding place. Elektra fearfully tries to flee, but Orestes holds her back and introduces a stichomythy that runs over seventy verses. Elektra's fear and resistance disappear immediately when Orestes promises news of her brother. Now the stichomythy, as so often, is used to supply information. Elektra hears that her brother lives and inquires after her, while Orestes learns his sister's circumstances and her uncompromising will to assist him in their revenge, which is to culminate in the long-desired murder of Klytaimestra (281, 283).

The situation is peculiar. Orestes knows with whom he is speaking, but Elektra does not. That she does not recognize her brother is convincingly explained by their early separation (283 f.). That Orestes does not reveal his identity might perhaps be explained by the presence of the chorus (which is, however, so often either ignored or sworn to silence). But Elektra's reassurance in 273 takes care of that. It cannot be disputed that the poet has overextended this situation of one-sided recognition.[198] At the beginning of the stichomythy he can use it to turn a couple of nice phrases (222, 224), but its further exploitation in 282 is obtrusive.

After the rapid exchange of questions and answers Orestes demands to hear more. The long description by Elektra that follows adds little to the overall situation but enhances the portrayal of her sorrows and the rulers' hubris with effective strokes of violent emotion.

Returning from the field, the peasant enters with a parodos. In a brief dialogue he learns what Elektra knows about the strangers and hospitably invites them to enter his house. After he leaves, Orestes reflects at length on the uncertainty of criteria like lineage, wealth, and martial valor, by which men are judged. All is doubtful, as proved by this gallant man clothed in poverty. Here occurs the admonition, mentioned earlier, to judge according to ὁμιλία and ἤθη. It is men like this who uphold state and family. Once again Orestes plays on his concealed identity; then he enters the house. The peasant must appear on stage again to hear Elektra rebuke him for thoughtlessly inviting strangers into his destitute house. Now she sends him to Agamemnon's aged caretaker, the same one who rescued Orestes as a child. He lives as a shepherd in another region and must bring some meat to accommodate the guests. When he hears of Orestes he will come gladly. The peasant sets off, reflecting that money can come in handy sometimes. He then disappears from the play, but the Dioskouroi do not forget him when they make their final settlement (1286).

The first stasimon (432–486; two strophic pairs with an epode) begins with an apostrophe to the ships that once bore Achilleus to Troy with Agamemnon (α). Then the ode flashes back to the expedition of the Nereids, who brought the magnificent weapons to Achilleus (α'). Shield, helmet, armor (β, β'), and sword grip (γ) are described. The conclusion offers a somewhat tortured connection with the plot: The leader of such warriors was slain by Klytaimestra! For this she will pay with her life.

The second epeisodion (487–698) opens with the entrance of the old man summoned by Elektra. An exile from the city (412), he has wearily toiled along the path to her cottage.[199] After greeting Elektra, he offers his meager gifts for the sustenance of the strangers. The motif of joyful expectation of their news about Orestes (415) is postponed until v. 547, for other events take precedence. The old man has passed by Agamemnon's grave to pay his respects and found there a sacrificial black sheep (the color of offerings for the dead) and a lock of blond hair. Could Orestes have returned secretly? He suggests ways of making sure: Elektra should compare the lock with her own hair or place her foot in the tracks near the grave or recognize her brother by a garment that he wears. All these methods played a role in the anagnorisis of the *Choephoroi*. Elektra dismisses them as nonsense, using critical logic to prove her point. The controversial evaluation of this section will concern us later.

Orestes and Pylades emerge from the house, the old man observes them with increasing curiosity, and Orestes, who has learned from Elektra that this was the man who once rescued him, asks his sister in amazement what the old man is about. The old man too then enters the conversation, which soon develops into a stichomythy with Elektra, to whom he discloses the identity of the stranger. He recognized him by a scar over his eye, and this token convinces even the critical Elektra. Now we might expect to find, as in plays like the *Iphigeneia in Tauris* or the *Helena*, a highly emotional duet between the reunited siblings, but the poet instead inserts only a few verses, quickened by antilabai, to express their joy and even these lines culminate in the thought of revenge (581).[200] It remains for the short dochmiac section of the chorus (585–595) to strike a jubilant note. The paucity of expression results from the poet's intention to place the main emphasis on the deed of revenge. He could hardly endow brother and sister, whom we shall see after they murder their mother, with tones of tender intimacy in the anagnorisis scene.

Abruptly Orestes comes to the point (596). There follows a predominantly symmetrical structure in which shorter dialogues, first between Orestes and the old man, then between Elektra and Orestes, frame an overly long stichomythy (612–684). The development within the stichomythy determines the change of partners in the two bordering dialogues. In a series of exchanges with Orestes the old man suggests that the youth kill Aigisthos outside the city as he offers sacrifice to the nymphs, for which preparations are now being made. When the talk turns to Klytaimestra, Elektra assumes the role of dialogue partner with the old man, by way of a brief three-way conversation (647–650). The matricide will be her job. She reveals her plan to lure Klytaimestra to the country under the pretext that she, Elektra, has given birth and requires ritual purification. The stichomythy concludes with twelve verses arranged in four triads.[201] They form a sort of abbreviated version of the kommos in the *Choephoroi* of Aischylos. A prayer to Zeus and Hera (the Argive goddess) is followed by an appeal to their father below, who must assist in the accomplishment of revenge.

In the final dialogue Elektra takes the lead. Orestes must kill Aigisthos, but in case the assassination is aborted she will keep a sword nearby to take her own life. Orestes only has to speak a word in agreement (693).

The second stasimon (699–746) is a two-strophic song narrating how Thyestes cheated his brother Atreus out of the golden lamb and how Zeus, enraged by this, reversed the course of the sun. To be sure, the ode about ancient guilt in the House of the Atreidai is not without relevance to the play, but on the other hand it stands by itself and does not serve, as in comparable treatments of the theme by Aischylos, to integrate new events into an older context of guilt and expiation.

Choral odes with two strophic pairs often present a special twist in the last antistrophe. Here the chorus cancels out its own song by confessing doubts about the truth of the story. How can the guilt of mere mortals have caused the sun to alter its path! But of course myths intimidate men and therefore promote the worship of the gods. The passage stands next to Herakles' words on the fabrications of poets as an impressive example of criticism of the gods.

The subdivision of the following sections into epeisodia is necessarily somewhat artificial, since fixed choral passages are largely absent. If we assume that the brief anapestic choral section beginning at v. 988 takes the place of a stasimon, then vv. 747–987 can be considered the third epeisodion, with Aigisthos as the focal point.

A highly dramatic prelude prepares us for the entrance of the messenger. The chorus and Elektra have heard a scream from afar, and Elektra fears the worst; she is ready to kill herself when the messenger arrives announcing victory. Here Euripides employs a favorite technique for increasing suspense, and with excellent results. An expansive, highly detailed description of Aigisthos's invitation to the strangers and the preparations for the sacrifice unfolds, then the action follows in a flash. Aigisthos falls, and the servants recognize their true master.

The messenger-speech joins onto a jubilant epirrhematic composition (859–889) in which the two choral strophes are answered by trimeters of Elektra. Orestes, announced by the messenger at the end of his report, enters with Pylades and receives the garland of victory from Elektra's hand.[202] Orestes thanks the gods and yields the corpse to Elektra to dispose of as she sees fit. In a short stichomythy she suggests hesitantly that she deliver a diatribe against the dead man. Orestes agrees, saying that their hostility knows no reconciliation. To appreciate the crass excesses of this scene the Greek spectator had to recall the noble words of Odysseus (Od. 22. 412), who forbade Eurykleia to rejoice over the slain suitors.

The long diatribe of Elektra (907–956) numbers among the most unpleasant passages Euripides ever composed. On the whole it sounds like a rather unsuccessful exercise for a class in rhetoric. The crimes of Aigisthos are barely touched upon (914); in the remainder we hear declamations on the constant faithlessness to be expected from an adulteress, on the superiority of φύσις (inborn nature) over money, on the trifling worth of a handsome man—at which point Elektra even acts the blushing virgin. Only her remarks on the miserable role of Aigisthos in his marriage have any real relevance to the dead man. The speech is difficult to understand. Hatred and contempt swell in the heart of Sophokles' Elektra too, but how different is the level on which she speaks! Of course it should be noted that Euripides bypassed many arguments here to use them more effectively in the agon with Klytaimestra.

The chorus sums up this flat speech with an equally flat allusion to Dike; then Orestes orders that the corpse be brought inside. Meanwhile, Elektra catches sight of her mother approaching the cottage and informs Orestes of her arrival.[203] An interjection betrays his uneasiness, and he asks the question that he addresses to Pylades just before committing the murder in the Choephoroi (899): Can I kill my own mother? There the reminder of Apollo's order sufficed, but here Elektra is hard put to strengthen Orestes' earlier resolve (614 if one follows Wilamowitz in deleting 600). He is beset with grave doubts. The god proclaimed folly, indeed, an evil spirit may have given the terrible order instead of Phoibos. Elektra replies, "Then who is wise, if not Apollo?"—foreshadowing the criticism of the Dioskouroi on this very point (1246, 1302). Finally, Orestes is convinced. His fears, wholly alien to Elektra, are not allayed, but he enters the house to kill their mother.

The submissive and flattering anapests (988–996) with which the chorus greets Klytaimestra serve two ends. When the women praise her as the sister of the Dioskouroi, this prepares us for their entrance ex machina; when they sing of her τύχαι (fate) and καιρός (critical moment) we are reminded that death awaits her.

Any poet who released the character of Elektra from her modest role in Aischylos had to stage a great confrontation between her and her mother. The differences in the composition of this scene by Sophokles and by Euripides provide an insight into the independence of the two dramas. The thematic sequence is largely the same in both. Klytaimestra begins on the defensive. Her most important argument is the sacrifice of Iphigeneia; Euripides adds Agamemnon's love for Kassandra. In both plays

Elektra destroys her mother's attempts to vindicate herself and emerges the moral victor. But what distinguishes the two speeches, so similar in content, is the portrayal of Klytaimestra. In Sophokles, the victim is a demonic woman who stands by her deeds to the end, while in Euripides, she is a sinner who regrets her past actions (1105) and is led to execution.

The Klytaimestra act (998–1146), which, with the reservations cited above, can be designated as the fourth epeisodion, is rich in subtle characterization. The aging queen steps down with difficulty from her chariot. Captive Trojan maidservants assist her, in recompense for Iphigeneia. What recompense! But Elektra immediately joins the slaves, claims herself to be no different, because of her mother's sin. So too in the brief interlude between the long speeches she requests with feigned humility permission to speak freely. But Klytaimestra has only a word of resignation for her daughter's sharp denunciation of her love affair (1102): You always loved your father best. In the verbal exchanges after the agon, which contain only short stichomythies, she imagines that Elektra might be reconciled with Aigisthos (1119). With drastic irony her daughter replies that Aigisthos dwells in her house (as a corpse), which Klytaimestra can only misconstrue as a renewed declaration of hostility. But when she enters the house in which she is to die, Elektra warns her with scornful solicitude to be careful of her fine garments in the grimy cottage. Her final words to Klytaimestra, that she will offer due sacrifice to the gods, is horribly ambiguous. She remains yet a moment on stage and speaks triumphantly of the imminent murder. The situation is reminiscent of Klytaimestra's in the *Agamemnon* before she follows her husband into the palace.

A small detail can further illuminate our earlier remarks. In Sophokles, an enraged Klytaimestra addresses her daughter as θρέμμ' ἀναιδές (shameless creature; 622); not once do we hear the word Euripides uses three times (1057, 1106, 1123): τέκνον (child). His Klytaimestra cannot be absolved of her crimes, but she is weary of them and they weigh heavily upon her (1105). She needs no dream to shake her confidence. This motif, used so effectively by the two earlier dramatists, is absent in Euripides.

A short pair of strophes by the chorus (1147–1164), recalling Klytaimestra's crime, prevents us from judging her too leniently.

Now we hear her pleading and death screams from within the cottage. The chorus leader's remark (1168 ff.) foreshadows a change of heart, but she remains indecisive as yet. Klytaimestra's death at the hands of her children is woeful, but horror is being requited with horror. However, the trimeters (1172–1176) announcing the entrance of Orestes and Elektra speak only of the misfortune of the Tantalids.[204]

The following kommos between the chorus and Orestes and Elektra (three strophic pairs; 1177–1232) shows the avengers in a completely different attitude. Nothing remains of their indignation and their vengeful will; they are frightened and broken as they confront the reality of their deed. The poet shows us no transition between the two postures, no gradual ascension of a new awareness. This is that intermittent treatment of psychological phenomena that will be discussed more fully when we come to *Iphigeneia at Aulis*.[205] In the first pair of strophes Orestes' despair is answered by Elektra's admission that she bears the guilt for the matricide, and the chorus, now condemning her action, confirms that she drove her brother to the awful deed (1204).[206] This is correct with respect to the scene of Klytaimestra's approach; but it is one-sided if we recall that Orestes returned to Argos with his will set upon revenge. In any case, however, it shows what the poet wished to emphasize.

In the following two strophic pairs the tormented siblings recall their deed once more; we hear how Orestes covered his eyes at the fatal blow, how Elektra grasped hold of the sword as well. Then they cover over their mother and her wounds.[207]

Announced by choral anapests, the Dioskouroi appear on the roof of the skene. From v. 1240 we learn that Kastor is the one who speaks. His mute companion, Polydeukes, is the divine counterpart of Pylades beside Orestes. Kastor judges the events with epigrammatic brevity: Klytaimestra paid in accordance with justice. As for Phoibos—but he is the lord of the Dioskouroi. This aposiopesis does not, however, silence the blunt criticism: himself wise, the god commanded folly. That the events are then (1248) connected with Zeus and Moira should not lead us to further theological speculation; it is simply a paraphrase of "what's done is done." The same holds for vv. 1301 f., which unites Moira, ananke, and the unwise words of Apollo. Even the reference to the ancestral curse (1306) remains wholly peripheral. Human destiny alone is involved, and no metaphysical aetiology can make it bearable.

The Dioskouroi carefully restore order from the wreckage. Orestes is to give his sister to Pylades in marriage, but he himself must leave Argos, hunted by the terrible Furies. In Athens he will find refuge at the image of Pallas and be acquitted before the court of the Areopagos, the votes being equal. Aigisthos will be buried by the Argives, Klytaimestra by Menelaos, who has just arrived in Nauplia on his return from Egypt (Od. 3. 311). Menelaos has brought along the innocent Helen, who was staying with Proteus in Egypt while the Greeks fought over a phantom. Pylades must settle the worthy peasant in Phokaia, and reward him suitably. When he is called Orestes' brother-in-law in name only, we are reminded that Pylades will marry a still virginal Elektra.

The anapestic conclusion begins with verses whose allotment is difficult; it seems best to follow Murray and Denniston in their editions.[208] The chorus and Elektra request permission to ask questions and are informed that the forces of destiny prevented the Dioskouroi from interceding on behalf of their sister, Klytaimestra, and that Elektra, while not constrained by Apollo's commandment, was forced by the ancestral curse to share in Orestes' fate. Here the poet answers the questions the spectators might raise.

The body of the anapestic section shows that the Dioskouroi can put much in order but cannot prevent the worst suffering. Orestes and Elektra, reunited but a short while ago, must part forever, marked by the murder. Even the gods take pity on their sorrows (1327). But then the Dioskouroi send Orestes on his way, while they hasten to the sea of Sicily. With a word of subdued resignation the chorus bids them farewell.

Earlier in our discussion of the dating question we remarked that Zuntz cor-

rectly separates the structure of this play from that of the *Iph. T.* and the *Helena*.[209]
To be sure, anagnorisis and mechanema play a role in the *Elektra* too, but there is a
significant difference: in the two other plays, a completely unexpected recognition
places the separated characters in a critical situation, from which they finally escape,
while in the *Elektra*, the brother seeks out his sister from the very start. The relationship of the individual parts of the play to the matricide is the real structural problem
in the *Elektra*. Of course the murder of Aigisthos is a prerequisite for this, but its
accomplishment occupies so much space that it becomes something of an end in itself. However, one cannot deny that the contrast between the two murders, which
becomes quite evident in the situation after their execution, does much to isolate the
matricide as the deed that is truly outrageous and intolerable. Thus we can understand the composition as a whole as one that aims toward this act, although the plot
line is frequently diverted by the independent nature of certain sections, without,
however, quite losing sight of the final goal. Thus it is in the lengthy exposition of
Elektra's misery and her unbending defiance, in the two-staged anagnorisis with the
undue protraction of the first stage, in which only Orestes recognizes his sister, and
thus it is in the expansive Aigisthos section. Episodic characters like the peasant and
the old man are dropped from the play after they have performed their limited functions.

The play justly takes its name from Elektra. She plans the intrigue against her
mother, as in the *Iph. T.* and *Hel.*, where the mechanema is devised by women; she is
the driving force at the decisive moments. The chorus expresses this clearly in the
conclusion. But this must not lead us to conclude that Orestes is misled by her or is
merely a subsidiary character. He comes home set on revenge, he overcomes his misgivings, and he delivers the fatal blow. Thus the play is a tragedy of both brother and
sister, culminating in their sorrow as they part forever.

Aischylos saw Orestes' deed in the context of the succession of guilt and expiation over generations and placed it within the development of a new and just order
embracing both polis and kosmos. Sophokles shifted the problematic matricide far
into the background, in order to show the distress and perseverance of a great soul;
Euripides depicts the destiny of two people who are driven to action by a horrible
chain of events, but also by hatred and bitterness: however, the deed is more than
they can bear, and it breaks them. Apollo's command is no longer the decisive factor,
and in this context it is highly significant that Elektra, the most avid proponent of
matricide, is not constrained by the oracle at all. The ancestral curse mentioned by
the Dioskouroi (1305) remains a completely marginal motif borrowed from tradition.
Next to such a traditional mythical motif, which, as in the *Herakles*, can no longer
withstand the new criticism, stands a purely natural and human theme that, for
Elektra at least, leads from misery, despair, and passion to a deed that should never
have been committed and that destroys its perpetrator.

One of the perennial problems of scholarship in our field is the question of the
chronological relationship between the Sophoklean and Euripidean *Elektra*. A sam-
pling of the numerous opinions: F. Kraus, *Utrum Soph. an Eur. El. aetate sit prior*,
Progr. Passau 1890; V. d'Agostini, "Sul rapporto cronologico fra l'El. sof. e l'El. eur.,"

Riv. Stud. Class. 3 (1955), 1; W. Theiler, "Die ewigen Elektren," *Wien. Stud.* 79 (1966), 102; and A. Vögler, op. cit., with further references.[210] Both sides of the question have always been well represented. We remain skeptical, since the independence of both plays will not admit of a clear decision. That two outstanding scholars have reversed their positions regarding priority is most revealing: Wilamowitz changed from Euripides to Sophokles, *Herm.* 18 (1883), 214, and 34 (1899), 57, 2; Diller went the opposite way, *Ant. u. Abendl.* 6 (1957), 166 = *Soph.*, Wege der Forschung 95, 1967, 206, and *Serta Philol. Aenipontana* 1962, 96, with *Soph.*, Wege der Forschung 95, 1967, 4.

Another long-disputed problem seems now to be cleared up. The way in which Elektra picks apart all the elements of the Aischylean anagnorisis certainly makes a strange impression. Therefore, there have been frequent attempts to delete the lines; sometimes the criticized verses in Aischylos were cut as well.[211] Recently, however, the authenticity of the Euripidean passage has been justly defended, which of course presupposes the section in Aischylos.[212] Euripides again criticizes Aischylos unmistakably when, in the *Phoinissai* (751) he has Eteokles say that it would be an idle waste of time to recount the names of the warriors at the seven gates, when the enemy already stands before the walls. These considerations do not exclude Matthiessen's more profound interpretation (op. cit., 122) of the passage as showing how difficult man's advance from apparent knowledge to truth is.

In theme and execution two Euripidean dramas are so similar that it seems probable they were written about the same time, a conclusion also supported by other evidence, such as metrics: the *Iphigeneia in Tauris* and the *Helena.*[213] The latter play can be dated securely to 412. Setting the *Iph. T.* before or after this date has proved to be a much discussed problem, but today *Iphigeneia* is generally accepted as the earlier of the two, probably rightly.[214] Thus 414 or 413 seem the likeliest years for production.

For the *Iphigeneia in Tauris*, we find basic elements of the plot given in the *Kypria*, in which Artemis snatches away Agamemnon's sacrificial daughter to the land of the Taurians.[215] The epic tells us that there she became immortal, which indicates that her nature was originally divine, as indeed an Artemis Iphigeneia was worshipped in Hermione (Paus. 2. 35. 1). The Taurians knew of a goddess whom they called the Virgin, and to whom they offered human sacrifice (Herodotos 4. 103). This goddess was recognized by colonists as Iphigeneia (according to Herodotos) or else Artemis, but, as we just saw, this amounts to more or less the same thing. The rationalizing tendency operative in Greek myth then made Iphigeneia into a priestess of Artemis, who in Euripides, characteristically, sometimes comes to oppose her goddess. The cult also included the temples to Artemis in Halai and Brauron, and the sacrificial customs there.

We have no convincing evidence that the expiation of Orestes was ever connected with Iphigeneia's fate before Euripides. It has been suggested that in Sophokles' *Chryses*, parodied in the *Birds* of Aristophanes (414), it is presumed that Orestes made away with his sister and the statue of Artemis, but Hyginus, *Fab.* 120 f., is a totally unreliable source for reconstructing this play. It could just as well have been about the wanderings of Chryses, son of Agamemnon and Chryseis, in search of Iphigeneia and the foundation of the city Chrysopolis.[216]

The section of the drama before the parodos exhibits a compositional technique first encountered in the *Hipp.*, wherein the two "parties" involved in the play are introduced one after the other. In both plays a prologue speech is followed by a dialogue scene. In our drama Iphigeneia begins immediately with a narrative that proceeds from Pelops and leads to her own fate. Now she is the priestess of Artemis in the land of the Taurians and consecrates human sacrifices to the goddess, although—freed from this by the poet—she need not slaughter the victims with her own hand.[217]

Not until v. 42 do we learn that Iphigeneia has left the temple for a breath of air, hoping to find relief in her deep distress—a motif much used later in erotic literature. She dreamed of the collapse of her ancestral home; only one pillar remained standing. This column had blond hair and spoke with a human voice. Euripides displays an intimate acquaintance with the world of dreams in the subtle confusion of images here: Iphigeneia performs her Taurian rite and sprinkles the supposed victim as she weeps. She can interpret the dream only to mean the death of Orestes, for her sprinkling means death. Now she wishes to pour libations to her supposedly distant dead brother (thus doubly missing the truth). But for some reason her maidservants have not yet arrived. She returns to her quarters in the temple.

Cautiously looking about, Orestes and Pylades come onto the empty stage. A brief stichomythy is followed by a longer dialogue. They see the altar reddened with blood, the armor of the victims dedicated in the temple, and realize they have reached their goal. Euripides skillfully manages the improbability that Orestes, after his long journey, begins to speak of the reasons why he came; in an appeal to Apollo he recalls how the god promised him release from his troubles if he could bring the image of Artemis to Attika.[218] But he begins to lose heart; Pylades encourages him and develops a plan to force a way into the sanctuary between the triglyphs (where the fully developed temple would have metopes) when night falls. Until then they will remain hidden.

The parodos of the chorus of captive Greek women (123–235) is composed in lyric anapests; Iphigeneia joins in, giving the passage a kommatic structure, as is frequent in Euripides.[219] The chorus introduces itself in very ornate verses and asks the reason for Iphigeneia's summons. She then laments the death of her brother; the poet avoids repeating the dream narrative but instead describes the libation at some length. Thus the prologue speech of the mistaken sister and her verses in the parodos frame Orestes' appearance most effectively. The chorus joins in the lament. They sing of guilt and suffering in the House of the Atreidai, but this expansion of the mythical background is in no way intended as a revelation of deeper meaning. Iphigeneia concludes the parodos with a monody in which she bemoans the misfortunes of her life and ends in mourning for Orestes.

In the first epeisodion (236–391) the action begins: the strangers are discovered and captured. A herdsman comes on stage. As always, the brief introductory dialogue, partly in stichomythy, presents the facts. We also hear that one of the youths is named Pylades; the other's name is unknown. A messenger-report follows, the first of two at the edges of the play, a jewel of Euripidean storytelling. In a rock crevice someone has discovered the two strangers. As elsewhere (*Andr., Ba.*) Euripides brilliantly brings to life individuals from the crowd. A pious man thinks they are gods and offers a prayer, but an insolent and more adventurous type ridicules him and suggests capturing the strangers. Then the madness seizes Orestes, and he attacks the herd with his sword. The herdsmen band together for an attack, but they are hard-pressed to overcome the two men, both armed with swords, by throwing rocks. Finally the youths yield and now the king is sending them off to be sacrificed.[220]

In a speech that is essentially a monologue despite the address to the chorus (351; in Medeia's speeches the case is similar), Iphigeneia begins with an appeal to her own heart, then speaks of a change within her: after the dream of her brother's death, she feels no more pity for captured Greeks. Here in the byplay with people who each have mistaken thoughts about the other, the irony is carried to extremes. Iphigeneia laments that Helen and Menelaos were never driven to the Taurian shore to pay for what Aulis did to her. It becomes evident that the trauma has remained with her since that day of sacrifice. Once again her lament returns to Orestes; then she jumps abruptly (many have postulated a lacuna) to rational discourse about her goddess. Whoever has blood on his hands or has touched a childbed or a corpse is barred from her altar, but Artemis herself permits men to be slaughtered on it! All lies, like the story of the meal of Tantalos; the Taurians, who themselves offer human sacrifice, impute the custom to their gods. No god can be bad. Once again Euripides has one of his characters oppose the tradition.

The first stasimon (392–455; two strophic pairs) exhibits the typical form, in that a train of thought is carried through the first three elements, while the final antistrophe brings new material.

From what land do the strangers come? (α). Has love of gain driven them to the sea? (α'). How did they endure the long journey? (β). Now, however, the chorus picks up Iphigeneia's wish: If only Helen would come here, a welcome sacrifice! Even better would be for a Greek ship to come and free the women from slavery. To see their homeland even in a dream would be happiness (β'). The motif of longing introduced here will dominate the second stasimon.

The second epeisodion (456–1088), the great centerpiece of the drama, is subdivided by a kommos and enhanced with other lyric passages.[221] It begins with anapests in which the chorus leader announces the arrival of the bound captives. May the goddess accept the sacrifice, if it so please her—such is not the way of the Greeks. A protest that is mild in form but whose sense is clear.

In the section of this epeisodion before the kommos Euripides plays out very effectively the suspenseful situation in which brother and sister stand face to face, each convinced the other is dead. As soon as Iphigeneia sees the youths, her earlier resolution to feel no pity disappears. She has their bonds removed and laments their fate. Orestes, however, brusquely rejects her sympathy. In the introduction to the long stichomythy (492–569) that now develops between the siblings, Euripides had to make allowance for a certain difficulty.[222] Iphigeneia knows only Pylades' name and wishes to begin conversation with him. Instead Orestes answers, concealing his own name with rather artificial excuses. The first spark is struck when he names Argos as his homeland. Now the questioning begins in earnest. Iphigeneia asks about Troy, about the return of the despised Helen and, characteristically, about Kalchas, whose prophecy led her to the sacrificial altar in Aulis. She also inquires about Odysseus and Achilleus. We await the bewildered question of Orestes which comes at v. 540: Who are you, who know so much of Hellas? But a noncommittal answer postpones once more the imminent recognition. Iphigeneia's questions bring it ever closer, and still do not suffice: she hears of Agamemnon, of his demise at Klytaimestra's hands. Orestes does not want to go on (554), but he must say it: Klytaimestra was slain by her son. Iphigeneia even hears that her family believes her dead. Still the veil is not lifted, not even with her last question about Agamemnon's son; but she does learn that her brother lives and thus that her dream deceived her. Orestes picks up on this at the beginning of his following speech: the gods are deceivers. Woe to him who, misled by oracles, is broken by misfortune!

Here (576) the chorus leader wants to join the conversation, eager for information about her own family, but this request is completely ignored. Iphigeneia has meanwhile come to a decision. The man from Argos, as Orestes is known to her, must bring to her homeland a letter written long ago, and thus save his life. Friendship and a sense of right and fairness—the voyage was undertaken for his sake after all—induce Orestes to demand that Pylades return in his place. In a short stichomythy Orestes asks about the manner of his impending death and about his grave. Once again, here almost obtrusively, the poet seeks to exploit the situation: If only my sister's hand would care for my corpse! And Iphigeneia promises to fulfill his sister's duty. Then she goes into the temple to fetch the letter.

A centerpiece within the drama's centerpiece is formed by a short lament-kommos between the chorus and the friends (643–657) and a longer dialogue between the latter pair (658–724). Orestes' amazed comment about the maiden's knowledge echoes the previous scene; then follows a friendly agon, in which Pylades refuses to abandon Orestes.[223] He clearly explains his double motive: friendship and the fear of men's reproach. Orestes turns down his sacrifice and breaks out in complaints against the god who deceived him. Pylades, ever the cooler head, contradicts: It's always darkest before the dawn. Thus he anticipates the finale that will justify the god, without of course undoing the sufferings of mortals along the way.

Iphigeneia comes back with the letter, leading to the artful anagnorisis on which Aristotle bestowed such high praise (Poet. 16, 1455a 18). In a stichomythy she promises Orestes that Pylades will go free and binds Pylades with a solemn oath to deliver the letter to her family. It is a nice touch that the youth characterized as the more prudent brings about the turning point by this very quality; for what would happen, he asks, if he lost the letter in a shipwreck? Iphigeneia will teach him its contents by heart. How she does this, undisturbed by the friends' exclamations, how Pylades now fulfills his mission by simply handing the letter to Orestes, how Iphigeneia (here a Greek woman like Penelope) first demands exact details from the past before she can believe the miraculous—all this displays Euripides' total mastery of stagecraft.

Once assured, the recognition is followed by an amoibaion between the siblings (827–899), rich in sound and phrasing, in which trimeters are given to Orestes and heavily dochmiac verses to Iphigeneia. Joy prevails at first (another fine touch: in her excess of happiness, Iphigeneia turns to the women of the chorus), but Orestes recalls the painful lives both have led (850), and immediately the vision of Aulis returns to haunt Iphigeneia. Now Orestes shudders: how close his sister came to killing him! And what will happen now? How can they escape from their predicament? Iphigeneia concludes the amoibaion utterly perplexed.

One of the functions of this lyric section is to provide a smooth transition between the anagnorisis and mechanema, for in the following section the three make plans to escape safely. Not right away, however: the calmer Pylades' admonition to think about the future is at first ignored by Iphigeneia. In a stichomythy, she asks about Elektra and the reason for Orestes' wanderings. He now recounts how he was accepted in Athens, though still treated as a sinner. The aition for the custom of drinking at separate tables and not from one common mixing bowl at the Choes feast is skillfully woven in. Then Orestes tells about the trial before the Areopagos, at which he was defended by Apollo and acquitted. Euripides was probably the first to add the detail that not all the Erinyes accepted the verdict and that some continued to persecute Orestes, so that he again sought instruction from Apollo, who sent him to Tauris to bring back the statue.[224] With a forceful shift at the end of his long speech, he begs his sister to save him and the family. Iphigeneia is willing to let the friends escape with the statue and to sacrifice her life. Orestes refuses: he will not add his sister's murder to his mother's, nor is this the will of Artemis, who once saved Iphigeneia. The dialogue is compressed into a stichomythy between the siblings. Iphigeneia rejects two suggestions of Orestes. She will not assist in a plot to kill the king. Her unelaborated οὐκ ἂν δυναίμην (I could not do it; 1023) seems subtly to anticipate Goethe's Iphigeneia. It would be impossible to steal the statue at night, because of the guards' watchfulness. Orestes is on the brink of despair when feminine cunning finds a way out. Iphigeneia will pretend that it is necessary for her to purify the statue and the youths at the seashore, and from there they can reach Orestes' ship.

Orestes still insists that they bind the chorus to secrecy. This is done at greater length than in similar cases. The deciding factor is Iphigeneia's promise to bring the women home later.

We understand that it is not easy for the women to conceal the escape of the fortunate ones back to Greece when they themselves long for this so intensely. The second stasimon (1089–1152)—sung after the friends have hidden inside the house and after Iphigeneia has concluded the lengthy epeisodion with a prayer to Artemis—attests to their longing. The motif introduced at the end of the first stasimon dominates this fine example of Euripidean lyric. They long for Delos (α); how painful the memory of the day that stole their freedom (α'); you, mistress, travel home amidst the sounds of Apollo's lyre and the flutes of Pan (β); if only I had the wings to hasten to my family's home and there to dance the round dance! (β′).

At the beginning of the third epeisodion (1153–1233) Thoas enters to attend to the sacrifice. Once again, in the change from the brusque question about Iphigeneia (Where's the Greek woman who keeps the temple?) to his respectful address to Orestes (Ἀγαμέμνονος παῖ; 1158) one may observe the subtle nuances of which tragic diction is capable, even in formulaic utterances. The outwitting of the king follows in a long stichomythy, whose tempo is accelerated at the end by the antilabai in the trochaic tetrameters. This Thoas is a gullible barbarian who rushes blindly and eagerly into the trap set for him. The audience would relish the artful deception with which the Greek woman weaves a web of truth and fiction for the king, such that he finally praises her loyal precautions (1180, 1202). The poet has Iphigeneia play her game with the unsuspecting king longer than necessary, leading the king himself to assert that the Greeks cannot be trusted, and eventually even bringing him to cover his head at the departure of the escape party. The context heightens the effect of the king's exclamation, when he hears of Orestes' matricide (1174): Apollo, no barbarian could have done it![225] When he calls on the god who commanded the murder, we hear a repetition of the earlier rejection of Apollo's oracles by the Dioskouroi at the end of the *Elektra*.

Iphigeneia concludes the trochees with an ambiguous prayer to Artemis, who will inhabit a pure house of happy men. Thoas goes into the temple, whereupon the chorus sings the third stasimon (1234–1283), whose pair of strophes contains a hymn to Apollo: it tells how he was born on Delos; how, when still a child in his mother's arms, he shot dead the python (a vase-painting depicts this scene[226]); and how later, when his oracle was again endangered, he begged for and received Zeus's protection. The bold child and laughing god—these are features that foreshadow the Hellenistic style of mythologizing as we know it from Kallimachos's *Hymn to Artemis*. The ode's connection to the plot is loose but significant. Apollo is the brother of Artemis, whose image he has ordered brought to Greece, and the end of the play will confirm that his prophecy was correct. If one tries to reconcile this with the accusation heard earlier, one fails to recognize the dissonances in Euripides' work that result from his attitude toward the tradition and his thematic dependence upon it.

The messenger-report of the exodos (1284–1496) is preceded by two introductory dialogues. In the first, between the messenger and chorus leader, the latter vainly attempts to cause delay by leading the messenger astray. Right away the women of the chorus are under suspicion of being accomplices. Thoas comes out of the temple, drastically exposing the lie of the chorus, and learns first the gist: Iphigeneia and the youths are escaping with the statue. The surprising twist of their probable failure is saved for the following report. As in the first messenger-speech we are again by the seashore; Thoas's people become suspicious, discover the ship ready to embark, and are bested in their attempt to halt the refugees. The particularly vivid account of the battle emphasizes the superiority of the Greeks. But then, as the ship leaves the harbor, a powerful wind rises and drives it back to land. Oars are no help; the Taurians wade into the water and prepare to catch the fugitives. The messenger does not await the outcome—a skillful way of avoiding another battle description and adding a touch of suspense. The chorus cries out in pain. Thoas, however, mobilizes all citizens to ensure the strangers' capture. They shall die a miserable death, and the women of the chorus shall also receive punishment. But then Athena appears.

Rarely elsewhere can we see so clearly how careful Euripides was to connect in the finale his often loose adaptation of the myth with the facts of its cult, thus legitimizing the new version for the audience. The escape is about to succeed; the ship need only pass out of the harbor, when suddenly the wind drives it back because Athena must appear, proclaim the future, and found institutions in Attika. Orestes must erect a temple at Halai, and keep in it the statue of Artemis, who will be worshipped there as Tauropolos. The custom of scratching a man's neck at her festival (a survival of ancient human sacrifices) will recall the time when Orestes, the victim, escaped. Thus the goddess herself is freed of the stain of human sacrifice by more refined Greek manners. Iphigeneia, however, will become priestess of Artemis in Brauron and after her death will receive as offerings the garments of women who died in childbirth—further proof of her identification with Artemis. Orestes will lead the women of the chorus out of the country;[227] a few verses, probably referring to his further destiny, have been lost. The text resumes with an allusion to the goddess's help before the Areopagos and the declaration that an equal vote means acquittal for all time. The end of the goddess's speech is curiously abrupt: Orestes must take his sister away, Thoas should put aside his anger. The brief word to the king hearkens back to the beginning, where the goddess explains the situation to him and leaves no doubt that Orestes is saved, since Poseidon has already ensured smooth sailing.

Thoas gives in completely. His assurance that he is not angry with the fugitives does not, however, signify noble renunciation, but only pious obedience. Choral anapests with a benedictory wish for the homeward bound travellers and a thankful prayer to Athena conclude the play. The appeal to the goddess of victory for success in the dramatic competition, repeated in much the same way in the *Or.* and *Phoin.*, stands outside the framework of the drama.

The *Iphigeneia in Tauris* displays a clear and easily recognizable structure.[228] Anagnorisis and mechanema follow each other without being separated by a clear caesura. Rather, the *amoibaion* after the recognition provides a smooth transition. The play is constructed in the form of a triptych. The significance of the lengthy central section, the second epeisodion divided by the kommos, has already been emphasized. It is framed by the first and second stasima, in which the note of longing struck in the first ode is continued in the second. The two side panels, approximately balanced in length, consist of the introductory section, which leads up close to the recognition of the siblings and is subdivided by the lyrics of the parodos, and of the finale, with the execution of the deception; these parts are punctuated by the third stasimon. This lucid composition nonetheless conceals a certain inequality in the treatment of the two main themes of anagnorisis and mechanema. The recognition does not occur until well after the middle of the play; again and again it is artfully postponed to exploit the situation for the greatest effect. And even when it comes, the recognition is not swift but gradual; both siblings are incredulous and amazed, and their doubts must be elaborately refuted: first Orestes', then Iphigeneia's. However, after the detailed and suspenseful planning scene, the escape is carried out with great speed. The naïve compliance of the king eliminates further obstacles. From this standpoint it is also significant that the sudden gale blows the fugitives back to land, thus creating yet another critical situation.

The scholia on Aristophanes, *Thesm.* 1012, 1060, and *Ran.* 53, confirm that Euripides produced the *Helena* and the *Andromeda* at the Dionysia of 412.[229] What a stir was caused when the adulteress who appeared so evil in the *Troiades* (performed just three years earlier) now became the paragon of chaste conjugal love we know from the remark of Mnesilochos (*Thesm.* 850): he wanted to imitate καινὴν Ἑλένην (the new Helen).

The material basis for this play was given by the *Palinodia* of Stesichoros, who is traditionally supposed to have won Helen's forgiveness and the restoration of his eyesight by composing a poem about a phantom, for whose sake the Trojan War was fought, while the real Helen remained pure and faithful with Proteus in Egypt. A papyrus with remains of a hypomnema to the melic poets (*P. Oxy.* 2506, *PMG* 193) surprised us by quoting two palinodiai, but it seems quite possible that the opening verses given there belong to parts of the same poem.[230] Especially valuable is the detail that Helen stayed in Egypt with Proteus, which shows that Euripides followed Stesichoros in choice of setting as well.[231] Relocating Helen in Egypt was easy enough for the choral lyricist after *Od.* 4. 125, 228, and the Egyptian adventures of Menelaos.

Tzetzes' remark (*Lyk.* 822; I 71 Scheer) that Hesiod was the first to introduce the phantom story (fr. 266 Rz.) is today considered incorrect, and rightly so.[232] We note in passing the rationalization of Helen's stay in Egypt found in Herodotos (2. 112); it is of no importance for the drama.[233]

Euripides brought dramatic movement into the legend by inventing the characters of Theoklymenos, Proteus's violent son who desires Helen, and Theonoe, his noble sister gifted with prophecy.[234] Thus he created a framework for the plot that corresponds to that of the *Iphigeneia in Tauris* in many respects. But we must not overlook the fact that the *Helena* is determined by the interplay of appearance and reality to a much greater extent.

As in the *Iphigeneia T.* the title figure delivers the introductory prologue speech; she appears as a refugee before an altar, for to escape the advances of Theoklymenos, Helen has fled to Proteus's grave. The setting is described and Proteus's two children, Theoklymenos and Theonoe, who are so important to the plot, are introduced. When Helen mentions that the girl's name as a child was Eido, we conclude that this character was derived from the Eidothea of the *Odyssey* just as the good Proteus was from the mythical Old Man of the Sea.

Then Helen recounts her lineage from Zeus and Leda—if the story is reliable (21). Repeatedly Euripides reminds us that the myths have become unstable and are on the way to becoming mythology. The goddesses' quarrel over the prize for the most beautiful determined Helen's fate. She was supposed to fall to Paris, but the bitter Hera deceived him with a phantom οὐρανοῦ ξυνθεῖσ' ἄπο (fashioning it from heaven's air; 34). Here it is highly questionable whether we should identify this with the aether, which has such important meanings for Euripides.[235] The aether appears right afterward in another context (v. 44), and later the phantom is consistently (705, 707, 750, 1219) referred to as a cloud, such as that used by Zeus to deceive Ixion. The Helen phantom became the πρόφασις (occasion) of the Trojan War, whose αἰτία (cause) was simply that Zeus desired to unburden the earth. The real Helen, however, was transported to Egypt by Hermes, who entrusted her to Proteus. But now her name, though not her body, is covered with shame and hated by the Greeks. All that keeps her alive is Hermes' prophecy that she will be reunited with Menelaos and see her homeland again. But the courtship of Theoklymenos now adds to her troubles.

As in *Iph. T.* the other side is introduced in the prologue right after the opening monologue. But here Helen cannot leave the stage, and the character who now enters is not the main character of the counterplot, but Teukros in an episodic role. His scene performs various functions: his first words give expression to the Greeks' hatred of Helen, while the development of the dialogue sharply accents the grotesque aspects of the situation caused by the phantom Helen. Teukros must content himself with believing in a deceptive similarity. The section has the common form of two shorter dialogues framing an extensive stichomythy. In it Helen asks a great many questions about Troy, the Greek heroes, and her homeland (Leda's suicide, the uncertain fate of the Dioskouroi). Most important for her and the play, Teukros says that Menelaos is missing, and he then heightens this with the report that in Greece her husband is considered dead. Thus, his information serves the same purpose as does Iphigeneia's dream, by which she was falsely convinced of the death of Orestes. Another function of the passage is to prepare us for the decisive role of Theonoe. Teukros hoped to consult her prophetic powers for help in sailing home, but now, warned by Helen that Theoklymenos hates all Greeks, he abandons his plan and leaves.

The parodos (167–252), comprising two strophic pairs and an epode, is kommatic in character, as in the *Iph. T.* After a short dactylic prooimion Helen appeals to the sirens and to Persephone to resound her lament (α). When her strophe ends, the chorus of captive Greek women appears (again we recall the *Iph. T.*), having come from the washing place (like the chorus of the *Hippolytos*) to find her on hearing her mournful cries (α'). In the second strophe Helen recounts all her anguish, having lost her good name as well as her mother, brothers, and husband (β); in the antistrophe the chorus faithfully echoes her words (β'), but there is a significant progression from v. 204, in which Menelaos is mentioned as missing, to v. 226, where he is considered dead. Helen later again says quite explicitly (279, 308) that her husband is dead, contradicting Teukros's testimony. Like Iphigeneia's dream, here a rumor is magnified into certainty, in order to lower hopes as far as possible before the anagnorisis. The epode of this predominantly trochaic system is a monody by Helen, which repeats the phantom motif in the form of a lament.

The following sections cannot be accurately divided into epeisodia and stasima; the first real stasimon does not come until v. 1107. Up to that point Euripides has chosen a freer style of composition, in which dramatic action alternates with rich, lyrical passages. The parodos, together with the great amoibaion (330–385), frames a spoken section primarily devoted to Helen, so that the play up to the departure of the chorus forms a triad.

In a long speech in which Helen bewails the disgrace to her name and the loss of her mother, brothers, and husband, the poet depicts once more—for the third time—the grotesque situation created by the phantom.[236] The lament concludes with Helen's resolution to die. After a brief stichomythy, at the beginning of which Helen turns the unsure testimony of Teukros into a definite report, the chorus leader advises her to consult the prophetess Theonoe in the palace to make certain of Menelaos's fate. Without pause the dialogue is transformed into a lyric amoibaion, in which Helen again bemoans her lot and proclaims her willingness to die if Menelaos no longer lives. She enters the palace with the chorus, one of the rare cases when the stage is left empty during the course of a play. Now the lengthy prelude comes to an end; in it the dramatic essentials were not merely introduced but forcibly stamped upon the spectator's mind.

For a second time the counterplot takes over: after Teukros, Menelaos himself appears, another hero in rags. Since the *Telephos* the public must have learned to put up with such things more easily. A sort of Menelaos act (386–514) again displays the form of a triptych: two long speeches surround a dialogue conducted as stichomythy. Menelaos's first words begin like a proper prologue speech with genealogy and self-presentation. The slightly bombastic tone is probably meant to accentuate the contrast to the beggarly garb of the shipwrecked sailor. His ship is shattered, his comrades are guarding the supposed Helen, and he wanders around now to find provisions.

An old portress rudely dismisses the tattered Greek from the palace, but at least she informs him in the stichomythy and adjoining short speech that he is in Egypt and that Helen, the daughter of Zeus and Tyndareos from Sparta, lives in the palace, having arrived shortly before the expedition against Troy. Menelaos is thrown into utter confusion and considers the possibility of multiple duplicate names, showing himself to be firmly trapped in the world of appearances, the example of a man who goes astray just where he is confident about his reason. In the second part of the speech Menelaos decides to wait for the master of the house, but he hides himself cautiously (probably in a parodos).

The chorus reenters with Helen, singing a brief song (515–527) that proclaims Theonoe's response: Menelaos lives and is still wandering. These lines might be taken as the rudiment of a stasimon.

Now follows the great central scene-complex (528–1164), heightened only once by lyric; it corresponds to the large middle block between the first and second stasima in the *Iph. T.* In keeping with the play's tangled plot lines, the sequence of action in the *Helena* is considerably more eventful.

For the five parts of this section, R. Kannicht (op. cit., 2. 150) has well described the rhythm in the alternation of two- and three-figure scenes, of which the latter are approximately double the length of the former.

In the first scene (528–596) Helen approaches the grave for protection after

Theonoe has assured her that Menelaos is still alive. Euripides carefully leaves open the further course of events by having Helen forget to ask the omniscient prophetess whether Menelaos will yet be saved. This is nicely motivated by her joy at hearing the good news. Timidly, Helen asks when her longed-for husband will ever return, when suddenly she catches sight of Menelaos, thinks she is being pursued, and reaches the place of refuge in great agitation. A stichomythy in which questions and answers are hurriedly exchanged brings recognition on one side only—under the circumstances at this point, all that was possible. The different situation of the two characters is brilliantly exploited for the retardation. Through Theonoe, Helen was prepared: she can understand that Menelaos stands before her as a shipwrecked sailor; she recognizes him and falls into his arms. But Menelaos's speculations about identical names have thrown him off the track; he believes that his Helen (in v. 571 we hear that one was enough for him) is guarded by his comrades and so he repulses the stranger. As he turns to go and it appears that all will be ruined by his delusion, one of his men enters to report that the illusory Helen, after an explanatory statement, vanished into thin air. This next section runs from 597 to 760 and is again tripartite.

The servant arrives in haste and relates the miraculous disappearance of the false Helen.[237] By an amusing twist, he only now becomes really confused, and mistakes the real Helen for the missing phantom. Everything seems upside down. But now Menelaos realizes the truth, and after a brief word of confirmation, in a long amoibaion (625–697) the couple mingle their joy at being reunited with the pain from all their sorrows, which no one can undo.[238] Unlike in the *Iph. T.* the smooth transition here from anagnorisis to mechanema is postponed until a later section. Rather, the amoibaion serves to inform Menelaos about what really happened. The third part of this section corresponds to the first as a dialogue between Menalaos and the aged servant. The latter's role is elevated above that of an episodic character. He, too, learns the truth and may greet his mistress with affection. Menelaos sends him to his companions, who are to await further events by the shore. As he departs the old man vents his displeasure with prophets like Kalchas or Helenos who knew nothing of the truth. The best prophets man can rely on are γνώμη and εὐβουλία (reason and good counsel). In particular, the second word was a programmatic term at the time of the Sophists.[239]

The midsection (761–856) of this five-part composition provides the transition from anagnorisis to mechanema, but also the exaltation of the two lovers, marked by their great pathos. This section is again divided into three, as two dialogues approximately equal in length frame a highly emotional stichomythy. In the first, Helen wishes to hear of Menelaos's wanderings. Since a more lengthy account would entail an unwelcome delay in the action, the poet allows Menelaos to name a few important stations of his woeful journey in the form of praeteritio. The transition from the troubles of the past to the dangers of the future is skillfully accomplished. Menelaos is reflective: Ten years of war at Troy and then seven years of peril on the sea! Helen: A long time to suffer, and now the sword threatens you here! At this point the stichomythy begins. Menelaos learns of Helen's flight from the untoward advances of

Theoklymenos and hears also that this man would kill him. Here, as in the *Iph. T.*,
they start to search for a means of escape, at first without success. Menelaos refuses
to flee alone; Helen says it is impossible to kill the king of the land. Although the
woman does not yet hit upon the saving deception, she shows the way that could
lead to it. The figure of Theonoe makes for a much richer plot than in the *Iph. T.* The
prophetess can save them if she remains silent: otherwise Menelaos is lost. They
swear a solemn oath to die together if their plans fail. In a heroic gesture worthy of
the heroes at Troy, Menelaos determines to win the desperate battle; Helen vows to
end her life with him.

There is a small, very subtle detail in this scene of pathos: Menelaos still finds
it difficult to associate with Helen the concept of uncompromising fidelity. Twice
(794, 834) he raises doubts, until finally assured by Helen's sworn willingness to die.

The following scene is composed quite symmetrically. Two long speeches of
Theonoe frame speeches of Helen and of Menelaos, which, if with Hermann (and
now also with Kannicht) we delete v. 905, are exactly equal in length. In design these
resemble the speeches of an agon (cf. Ludwig, 43).

The entrance of Theonoe, which introduces the great judgment scene (857–
1031), is accentuated by ritual solemnity. A maidservant purifies the air with sulphur
fumes, in order that the prophetess might breathe the immaculate πνεῦμα (breath) of
heaven; another cleanses the path with the flame of a torch. Theonoe can point out
the correctness of her prophecy: Menelaos is here. But what danger threatens him!
On this very day Zeus presides over an assembly of the gods, which will decide his
fate. Hera wants Menelaos to return to inform all the world that Paris abducted a
phantom, but Kypris has every reason to prevent this. Theonoe finds herself faced
with the decision either to surrender Menelaos to her brother as Aphrodite wishes, or
to save the pair in compliance with Hera. The end of her speech is difficult, but in
any case the surrender of Menelaos remains a distinct possibility.[240]

Helen and Menelaos try to win Theonoe's protection with their speeches,
which are divided by three verses of the chorus leader in the role of a chairman.

Helen, throwing herself at Theonoe's feet, bases her plea entirely on the claims
of justice, which must entail an obligation for the pious prophetess. By divine decree
Hermes handed her over to Proteus for safekeeping. Not to give her back would be a
sin against the gods and the dead man. Menelaos's speech revolves around the same
argument. With great effect he appeals to the girl's father in the grave and demands
the return of his wife, received by the old man in good faith. However, the tone of
this speech contrasts most sharply with that of Helen. We hear no desperate pleading
but a confident insistence upon the justice of his claim. The conclusion receives special emphasis with the alternatives that Menelaos either fight a life-and-death battle
with the king or else kill himself on the grave with Helen.

The dividing verses are characteristic of the attitude of choruses: May
Theonoe so decide that all may be pleased. But the prophetess has decided already, as
is consonant with her φύσις (nature) and the sanctuary of Dike that she keeps within
her. She will side with Hera, for it would be blasphemy not to return what was given
in confidence. But punishment threatens the sinner, be he dead or alive. This is ex-

plained especially with regard to the deceased: their νοῦς (brain) lives no longer (it has no body in which to operate), but man does possess an immortal consciousness (γνώμη, mind, intellect) that enters the aether (and in which his deeds endure). So she cannot assist even her brother in a misdeed. Then she breaks off: But now you must contrive the escape yourselves; pray to Kypris that she allow your return voyage, and to Hera, that you remain in her favor.

The fifth section (1032–1106) of this scene-complex takes the form of a distichomythy between husband and wife, with a concluding speech by Helen. Again they try to make plans. Helen had demanded that Menelaos find a way out, but he fails. Neither is it possible to escape by land nor would Theonoe permit him to kill her brother. As in the *Iph. T.*, here too it is the woman who finds the solution. Menelaos will report as messenger the news of his own death; then Helen will request a ship to perform an empty burial at sea, and on it they will escape. Then, as Theonoe advised, she prays to Hera and Aphrodite. Her prayer to the love goddess is that of a heroine, more a command than an entreaty.

Only now does the chorus sing the two strophic pairs of the first stasimon (1107–1164). The first pair has a tangible connection with the plot. The chorus wishes for the voice of a nightingale, to bewail all the suffering brought on Trojans and Greeks by Paris and the phantom. In the second strophe the chorus confesses ultimate uncertainty about the nature and influence of the gods. Their will is incalculable. For proof, look at Helen—who is after all, the child of Zeus.[241] The second antistrophe is a vigorous protest crying out in the maze of history against the madness of war. Here speaks the poet of the *Troiades*. No Athenian could hear these lines in 412 without thinking of the disaster of his own city.

Now follows a short Theoklymenos act (1165–1300), at the beginning of which the king enters in a state of great agitation. He is returning from the hunt, piously greets the tomb of his father (his appreciation for the honors of the dead will also determine his actions later), and becomes sorely distressed when he does not find Helen. He has already heard of a Greek who is roaming about, undoubtedly plotting her abduction. Then Helen emerges from the palace with shorn head, dressed in mourning. A lengthy stichomythy begins, first between Theoklymenos and Helen. The false report of Menelaos's death is given broad play; Helen feigns reconciliation and willingness to marry Theoklymenos, but before this the proper sacrifice must be offered for her drowned husband. Lines 1205 and 1225 (textually difficult) add a dash of irony. The king's slight doubts are eliminated by Helen, who boldly plays on the omniscience of Theonoe. When they come to the actual procedures, she turns the king over to Menelaos, whom she already pointed out at v. 1203 crouching by the grave (which must have been a rather large structure). He receives everything necessary for the plan: ship, sacrificial gifts, even armor, and skillfully parries the suggestion that he perform the ritual alone. Finally each of the three characters makes a remark about the situation from his own point of view, then all enter the palace.

The second stasimon of the chorus (1301–1368) is one of the strangest odes in all Greek tragedy. Its two strophic pairs tell the story of Kybele-Demeter's search for her abducted daughter, of the earth's desolation because of her anger, and the final reconciliation. Since bakchic motifs are also present (1358) the ode is an early example of syncretistic ideas.[242] The textually difficult second antistrophe tries to supply a connection with the plot by mentioning Helen's transgressions against the Great Mother. This motif is completely peripheral to the content of the drama; a real connection is not to be found. But the ode is particularly important because it attests to the interest in orgiastic cults that Euripides developed in his later years.

This ode is followed by a short epeisodion (1369–1450), in which the suspenseful situation before the success of the ruse is once more exploited for a special effect. First, Helen enters alone and describes, without an introductory dialogue with the chorus leader (and quite in the style of New Comedy), how inside the house Theonoe affirmed that Menelaos was dead, while the real Menelaos was even given armor by Theoklymenos. Helen's hasty plea that the chorus be silent, and her very vague promise (ignored in the epilogue) to come back for the women later are neatly excused by the poet with the arrival of the king. A thorough treatment of these motifs (cf. again the *Iph. T.*) would unnecessarily have overburdened these scenes, already so rich in themes.

Theoklymenos enters with the newly dressed and armed Menelaos and a retinue of men bearing the offerings for the dead. The comical effect of his blind zeal was enhanced by visual means. Helen then joins him in a dialogue that soon is compressed into stichomythy. Twice she must prevent the failure of her plan, for Theoklymenos repeats his earlier suggestion that Helen not go along, for she might hurl herself into the sea out of grief; then, however, he wants to accompany her himself. All obstacles are finally removed and the king commissions the stranger to lead the ship. Before departing he orders the palace to be gaily decorated for his coming marriage. Menelaos offers a prayer to Zeus, the prayer of an upright hero: Truly, we have suffered enough![243] Then he leaves with Helen for the beach.

The following stasimon (1451–1511), the third of the odes set comparatively close together in the second half of the drama, corresponds in tone and theme to the related ode of the *Iph. T.* (1089). In thought the chorus accompanies Helen back to her homeland, and they long to imitate the migrating birds. The reference to the Dioskouroi prepares us for their entrance at the end.

The exodos unfolds in three sections. A messenger comes in and proclaims to Theoklymenos in the introductory dialogue, as is customary, the gist of what has happened; then he delivers his detailed report. At first the broad narrative flows along calmly, but then follow in dramatically swift succession the battle between the Greeks and the Egyptians on the ship, the victory of Menelaos's men, and the successful escape.

Especially effective are the trochaics in the following scene, which begins with Theoklymenos's outburst of wrath. He can no longer reach the ship, but Theonoe will pay for concealing Menelaos's identity. In spirited antilabai the chorus leader steps in to oppose the king.[244] Her determined resistance, even to the point of sacrificing herself, seems incapable of saving Theonoe, when suddenly the Dioskouroi appear. They bid Theoklymenos bury his anger, for these events were fated, and Theonoe acted according to the wishes of her father and the gods. Then they turn to their sister, as Athena does in the *Iph. T.* when she speaks to Orestes from afar, and since the play could not end without an aetiology, Helen learns that after her death she will be granted a cult with her brothers, and that the island on which she first stopped to rest during her abduction will be named for her. Menelaos, for his part, will dwell in the Isles of the Blessed. Like Thoas, Theoklymenos too forgets his resentment quickly. His final word is in praise of the noble Helen. The concluding anapests about the many forms of divinity (familiar to us since the *Alkestis*) fit here especially well.

Despite the freer composition of the *Helena* in comparison with the earlier plays, we can still distinguish a well-defined arrangement as a sort of triptych. An extensive central section begins with the reappearance of the chorus (514) and ends with the first stasimon (1164). The side panels are comprised of the opening scenes with the exposition of the still-separated couple and the execution of the intrigue, which begins with the entrance of Theoklymenos. The course of both sections is determined by two lyric passages, the first by parodos and amoibaion, the finale by two stasima. In this analysis I have tried to show how strongly the individual sections within the larger divisions also exhibit a tripartite structure.

Thus we find a certain compositional parallel to the *Iph. T.*, but in the distribution of the two main themes the plays differ significantly. While in the *Iphigeneia* the recognition plot clearly predominates over the mechanema, this situation is reversed in the *Helena*. Here the transition (smooth in both cases) between the two actions occurs at vv. 777 f., considerably before the midpoint of the play. This results from the insertion of the Theonoe scene, so important for the dramatic complication.

The greater length of the *Helena* is an expression of the richer development of motifs; thus, at the start, the counterplot is presented through two characters, Teukros and Menelaos. From observations of this sort it seems probable that in the later play Euripides elaborated on a structural form developed in the *Iphigeneia*.

The assessment of the *Helena* has led to sharply conflicting opinions: we contrast Zuntz's attempt (op. cit., *Entretiens*) to discover philosophical profundity beneath the superficial effect of the plot, with Webster's judgment (*Eur.*, 201): "The *Helen* should not be taken too seriously." Now by adding elements of his own invention (Theoklymenos, Theonoe), Euripides was certainly out to transform the *Palinodia* of Stesichoros into an absorbing play full of surprising twists. What resulted was a foreshadowing of the Greek novel. A couple bound faithfully in love is separated and finally, after adventures, wandering, shipwreck, and threats by an infatuated third party, are happily reunited.

But does the play make any more profound statement? The question centers on the judgment scene with Theonoe. This we can neither dismiss as mere embellishment nor overburden with theological ideas. First of all it is undeniable that the poet used the prophetess strictly according to the dramatic necessities of his plot. As a seer, Theonoe knows past and future—this is stated explicitly (13, 923), yet she can only suggest to the threatened couple that they find a means of escape by themselves, and she sees her own fate exposed to unknown dangers. Actually the situation is much the same as in Aischylos's *Eumenides*, where an omniscient Apollo must take up a struggle whose outcome depends on a vote.

Zuntz deserves the main credit for correcting the mistaken opinion that Theonoe's position settles the gods' quarrel over the fate of Menelaos. What she in fact does is stated clearly in v. 1005: she votes with one of the opposing divinities; indeed, in her position she has no choice. However, the sanctuary of Dike that she bears within her (1002) obliges her to seek her decision along the path of righteousness, as the Dioskouroi confirm. And it is precisely here that her character transcends the limited importance of a dramatic tool. Her initial concern to partake only of the pure breath of heaven signifies her awareness that she is bound to a divine power from which she derives both her prophetic gift and her knowledge of justice. This godly domain might perhaps be identified with the aether, which plays such a large role in Euripides.[245] According to Theonoe (1013), this is also where the immortal consciousness of the νοῦς goes after its separation from the body. The remarkable passage (thoroughly discussed by Kannicht) is based on ideas current in the philosophy and theology of the time; Euripides plays with them quite freely, since he is not attempting to communicate a dogmatic system of belief. We would not go so far as to consider the Theonoe scene the spiritual center of the play, but we fully recognize that the poet portrays this figure as the possessor of pure divine knowledge.

Compared with the arguments with which mortals fight for and achieve justice, the jealous quarrel of the goddesses appears petty and despicable, and the poet intends this. The tension between his thought and traditional conceptions is perceptible in this play too, as in Helen's doubts about the story of her parentage (21), in the servant's criticism of prophecy (744), and especially in the final strophe of the first stasimon. Yet these motives never achieve central importance in the *Helena*. In A. M. Dale's excellent phrase (xv): "this is not an angry play."

In the search for historical allusions the *Helena* has not been spared.[246] The results are not convincing, though the invective against the war (1151) is surely inseparable from the mood of Athens in 412. We might also ask whether Euripides did not write this colorful and imaginative play, complete with a happy end, precisely as an escape from the afflictions of the time.

L. Radermacher raised the question whether the *Iph. T.* and the *Helena* were tragedies in the real sense, and Rivier (130, 178) claims to recognize in the time around 412 a more untragic period of Euripides' work.[247] Of course we must distinguish between the ancient and modern concepts of tragedy; but since our conception of the tragic is largely derived from plays like *Oidipous* and *Medeia*, the contrast presented by *Iph. T.* and *Hel.* is also highly significant for Attic tragedy. Here man is no longer at the mercy of a fate that can be cruel and unfathomable but yet so full of divine power that it ennobles him even as it annihilates. No longer is the interest directed at primeval human forces welling up from the depths of the soul. Tyche emerges as the new power.[248] Her games are dangerous, but of a lighter sort than the confrontations between man and god in Sophokles. Nor is the result tragic annihilation; the bark of human destinies now must pass through many reefs, but at the end it sails—literally and figuratively—happily out to the open sea. To be sure, the poet is not so much concerned with these games of Tyche as he is with the people who withstand its test and combat the tangles of fate with good counsel (εὐβουλία, catchword of the Sophists' era). And amidst all these threats, surprises, and solutions the human soul starts to soar, and we perceive new tones of longing, of sorrow, and of loving embrace. The form best adapted for the expression of this emotion is the actor's song.

Together with the *Helena* Euripides produced the *Andromeda*.[249] On Poseidon's orders the daughter of King Kepheus of Ethiopia and Kassiepeia is to be exposed to be devoured by a sea monster. The reason was probably the motif known from Apollodoros (*Bibl.* 2. 43 f.) and Hyginus (*Fab.* 64) that the queen considered her daughter more beautiful than the Nereids. Perseus came to the rescue and won the love of Andromeda. This does not give us much of a plot, and therefore with Webster (*Eur.*, 198) we consider the possibility that the second half of the drama contained an intrigue in the style of the *Iph. T.* and the *Hel.*, perhaps involving the unsuccessful attack of an earlier lover of Andromeda with the collaboration of Kepheus (Hyginus). The scholiast on *Thesm.* 1065 confirms the appeal to Night as the beginning of an anapestic prologue by Andromeda, who is fettered to a rock. This is important for our assessment of the prologue composition in the *Iphigeneia at Aulis*. The fragments also reveal that Euripides contrived a special effect by having an echo respond to the young woman's laments.

The new intimacy that we discussed in connection with the *Helena* is much in evidence in the *Ion*.[250] No agreement has yet been reached concerning its date. On the one side stand those who base their estimates on references to contemporary history.[251] But the mention of Rhion (1592), which Alkibiades tried to fortify in 419 (Thuk. 5. 52), does not necessarily mean that the play was produced immediately thereafter. Of greater weight is the question how long into the Peloponnesian War did the tendency in the denouement to base Athens' claim to Panhellenic hegemony on genealogical inventions remain acceptable. It would be too rigid to assume that this would no longer have been possible after setbacks like the battle of Mantineia (418). However, the revolt of the Ionian allies in 412 does fix a rather probable boundary. If we accept this, then we can reach agreement with the other group of scholars, who proceed from stylistic and metrical considerations.[252] Especially significant here are the resolutions in trimeter. A glance at the table in K. Matthiessen (Hypomn. 4, 170) shows the difficulty in dating the *Ion* (25.8%) before the *Troiades* (21.2%). While the consistent increase in the number of resolutions is certainly not a rule without exception, the orderly sequence—especially impressive in this time period—would be too violently interrupted. If we grant auxiliary importance to structural and stylistic arguments, then the estimate 414 or 413 proves to be the most probable date.

The figure of Ion and his significance for Athens were given to the poet in a tradition that we encounter in Herodotos (8. 44), where the Athenians, after numerous name changes, were called Ionians after their field commander Ion, son of Xouthos. The names of the ancient Athenian phylai supposedly stem from his four sons (5. 66), and in another passage (7. 94) Herodotos derives the name of the Ionians from Ion. Xouthos appears in Hesiod (fr. 7 Rz.) with Doros and Aiolos as the sons of Hellen.

According to Pausanias (7. 1. 2) his brothers drove him from Thessaly after Hellen died; he fled to Athens and received the daughter of Erechtheus as his wife; she bore him Achaios and Ion.

It remains uncertain whether Apollo's role as Ion's father is the invention of Euripides or simply traditional, although much speaks for the latter.[253] We note another variation, significant in the context of Athenian power propaganda, which also cannot be traced back before Euripides: in the drama Doros and Achaios appear as the sons of Xouthos by Kreusa, while in Hesiod Doros and Aiolos are his brothers.

The prologue speech is given to Hermes, since only a god can know about the tangled circumstances surrounding Ion. He introduces himself with his genealogy, and then relates how on the northern slope of the Akropolis Apollo enjoyed the love of Kreusa, daughter of Erechtheus, how the young woman exposed the infant in the place where the god lay with her and gave it an amulet of golden serpents, according to the custom handed down from Erichthonios. The god cared for the boy and ordered Hermes to bring him to Delphi. There he grew up, appointed temple steward by the community. Later Kreusa married Xouthos, but their marriage remained childless. Now the couple will come to Delphi to seek advice from the oracle. Apollo plans to give Ion to Xouthos as his putative son, and then bring about his recognition by the mother in Athens. Hermes sees Ion coming and hides himself in a bay-covered hollow to watch the outcome of events.[254] This has no further significance, but it serves as a belated motivation for his appearance in the role of an inquisitive servant.

From the prologue we can clearly see how intent Apollo is to direct events by his influence on human beings. He has arranged it so that Kreusa can bear her child unnoticed. He has manipulated the Delphic priestess, who was not particularly pleased with the foundling's appearance at the temple's steps, and now he leads Kreusa and Xouthos, who undoubtedly had to remain childless for this very purpose, to his sanctuary, so that he can play his trick with the fictitious paternity of Xouthos. To this extent his effectiveness extends into the realm of Tyche. We shall see later on whether the god really can rule over this power as he pleases. Hermes also wants to see this, especially since his older brother believed he could keep his intentions secret.[255]

Already the poet boldly strikes the note of Athenian glory (8, 29; later 262) that resounds so forcefully in Athena's final speech.

Unlike the Iph. T. and Hel., here the prologue section before the parodos shows us only one side of the action to come. Ion steps out of the temple and sings a monody, which is basically a mime, as is especially obvious in the concluding lines. The section (82–183) is clearly divided into three parts. Two anapestic passages, the first in recitative, the second in melic anapests, surround a pair of strophes in Aeolic meters. The opening anapests evoke the image of a Delphic morning, whose clear purity finds its counterpart in the youth who joyfully serves his god. Here Euripides displays the same talent for describing nature as in the magnificent morning song of the Phaethon. Ion then turns to his task of sweeping the temple steps. In the strophic pair he lingers over the happiness of his pious service, and he unknowingly hits upon the truth when he names Apollo his begetter and father (136) because the god allowed him to grow up in his temple. The lyric anapests are then full of mimetic movement; they accompany the zeal with which Ion frightens birds of all kinds from the sanctuary.

The parodos of the chorus (184–236) is also a brief mime: the women admire the temple's decorations. As in the *Iph. T.* and *Hel.* the parodos exhibits the title figure as the dialogue partner of the chorus, but here the rhythm is different. The chorus of Athenian women who accompany Kreusa marvel at the temple sculptures and identify the figures. It is highly unlikely that these were actually represented on stage.

The first strophic pair is divided symmetrically between semi-choruses; the second strophe increases the tempo with the exchange of question and answer among individual choristers. In the antistrophe Ion, in a singular manner with recitative anapests, joins in a lively conversation with the women, answers questions, and gives instructions for a sacrifice before entering the temple. Still in the ode, and not in the usual anapests, the chorus announces Kreusa's arrival.

The first epeisodion (237–451) contains one of the most beautiful scenes in all of Euripides' dramas, the confrontation between mother and son, still unknown to each other; they are led along the path to anagnorisis, by the growing sympathy each feels for the other, as far as possible before this line is abruptly broken off. On seeing the temple Kreusa bursts into tears and replies to Ion's sympathetic question in obscure phrases about the capriciousness of the gods' dealings with mortals. A further question from Ion leads to a long stichomythy after two sets of distichs; the conversation takes numerous turns, almost completely without makeshift verses (256–368). Ion's questions concern Athens, Erichthonios, the Earth-born, and the children whom Erechtheus had to sacrifice.[256] Kreusa answers calmly and objectively, until Ion asks (283) about the Makrai cliffs on the slope of the Akropolis and speaks of Apollo's preference for that spot. Thereupon Kreusa groans in painful recollection, but the conversation quickly shifts over to her husband Xouthos and his lineage. Again the dialogue touches on Kreusa's personal fate when they speak of the oracle that might cure the childlessness of the woman who in truth is not childless at all (306). She evades the issue with a question to Ion about his own fate; her words (308) express deep sympathy for the youth. The tale of the motherless Ion cuts straight to her own heart (320). She, who kept silence for so many years, is now overwhelmed by the desire to speak of her fate, but again she chooses to conceal the truth by pretending that it was another woman, a friend of hers, whom Phoibos violated. At this point the lines of their fates seem about to touch. Kreusa: The exposed child would be your own age (354). Ion: How similar is our lot (359).

Kreusa has hastened ahead of her husband to receive a secret response from the god, but Ion, who at first refused to attribute to his god the actions alleged by the woman, now dispels her hope for an oracle. In a speech that develops out of the stichomythy he warns against questions that require from a god an admission of guilt.

We expect no more from the chorus leader than the three insignificant verses that follow about the mutability of man's fate. Kreusa, however, denounces the god who did not save his child and refuses to speak to the mother. Then she asks that Ion

keep her story secret, since she sees Xouthos approaching. His opening words characterize him as a man pious toward god and wife. He greets both and asks if his late
arrival worried Kreusa. He has just received the response from Trophonios that the
two of them will not return home childless. The poet adds a subtle touch: Kreusa
immediately prays to the mother of the god who caused her pain and sorrow. Xouthos
now wants to learn more from the oracle and questions Ion about the official interpreters. This is the first contact—still wholly formal—between these two men. Then
Xouthos enters the temple; here Euripides, ever concerned with the πιθανόν (plausible), explains away Xouthos's failure to perform the required sacrifice (mentioned
earlier by Ion, 228) with a reference to a general victim offered that day for strangers.
However, before leaving the scene Kreusa demands that the god make amends for his
previous misdeeds and then says—a statement of profound significance for the appreciation of human suffering—that he can never really do so entirely (427). The speech
of Ion, who remains on stage, is artfully composed. What does this strange woman
mean with her laments? But why should I care? I have my sacred duties to perform.
However, her story continues to disturb him, and he delivers a precocious sermon to
his god on what divine beings ought not to do if they demand morality from mortals.

The first stasimon (452–509) appeals to Athena and Artemis for beneficial
prophecies for the house of Erechtheus (α) and praises the flourishing of races in children (α'). The epode sings of the Makrai cliffs where Pan and the Sisters of Dew dwell
and where the sorrowful fate was played out that Kreusa related as the lot of a
stranger.

At the beginning of the second epeisodion (510–675) Ion, who has in the meanwhile filled the sacred water stoups, asks if Xouthos has already come out of the temple. The scene, which introduces lively movement, is composed in trochaics, changes
into stichomythy as soon as Xouthos arrives, and then quickly breaks into antilabai.

Impetuously Xouthos greets the youth as his son, as the god's oracle proclaimed him to be. Ion draws back, doubts for some time; but in a formal hearing
with Xouthos he is finally convinced that the man might have begotten him as a
result of an amorous adventure in Delphi many years back.[257] Another fine touch:
Ion's questions turn immediately to his mother, about whom Xouthos knows nothing; with verses of longing for the unknown woman, Ion concludes the scene.

The god's trick has succeeded, but the initial result is to separate mother and
son even further. The false happiness of Xouthos contrasts with Kreusa's genuine suffering, to which the chorus refers without knowing the truth, in the dividing lines
566–568. A deceptive anagnorisis has taken the place of the expected one, and under
the illusion of a solution endorsed by Apollo, everything has in fact become utterly
confused.

The second part of the act (in trimeters) presents an argument between Xouthos and Ion that takes the form of an agon. Xouthos also thinks of Ion's mother and
hopes to find her, but this is overshadowed by his hope for future happiness. Ion cannot share this hope and expresses his misgivings in a long speech. The Athenians will
look askance at the foreign bastard; his stepmother will hate him. Again we note a
very fine stroke of characterization: he not only fears the woman (he knows her al-

ready) but also pities her. He ends with a declamation against tyranny, to which he contrasts his peaceful happiness in the service of the god.[258] Here already we can see the nucleus of the debate about contrasting ways of life held by Amphion and Zethos in the *Antiope*.

The chorus leader agrees with Ion, but Xouthos will hear nothing of such renunciation. He is, however, concerned with sparing Kreusa's feelings. When the birth is belatedly celebrated in Delphi and when Ion is brought to Athens, the boy is not to appear as Xouthos's son but as his guest. Only later will Xouthos induce Kreusa to accept Ion as his son and heir to the throne. Here the poet illumines the grotesque side of the situation: Xouthos and Apollo both wish to wait for a favorable opportunity in Athens, though with quite different purposes in mind.

In this scene Xouthos gives his supposed son the name Ion (as Apollo's slave he had none) because he met him as he came out of the temple. The tragedians, Aischylos and Euripides in particular, delight in such etymologies.[259]

Once again Ion expresses the desire to find his mother, here with a special twist that will later prove true: may she be an Athenian, so that as a fully enfranchised citizen he may be granted the right of free speech.

The second stasimon (676–724), which is rich in dochmiac rhythms and, like the first, contains only one triad, shows us the chorus actively participating in the action of the plot, thus proving that Aristotle's judgment of Euripidean choruses (*Poet.* 18, 1456a 27) is by no means valid in every case. The chorus raises serious doubts about the oracle, laments the lot of Kreusa, and in anticipation of the intrigue to come, hopes for the intruder's death.

The third epeisodion (725–1047), composed as the broad centerpiece of the play, centers on Kreusa and presents her desperate decision to take revenge.

Kreusa enters conversing with an old man, the former tutor of Erechtheus, who now in his loyalty is like a father to her. Here again we note a feature of mime: the old man can hardly manage the steep ascent to the temple.

Then follows a spirited three-way dialogue between Kreusa, the old man, and the chorus leader which, in its progression through the lyric (heavily dochmiac) verses of Kreusa, assumes the character of a kommos.[260]

Xouthos has ordered the chorus to remain silent on pain of death (666). This is something different from the secrecy requested by oppressed characters in other plays. Here only brief deliberation is necessary (758, 760) before the women of the chorus, who have already revealed half the truth, break their silence completely. In a very real sense the chorus here becomes an active character. Indeed, they even interpret the oracle in a way that goes beyond the actual message and strikes straight to Kreusa's heart: Never will you hold children of your own in your arms!

The old man asks about the name and mother of Xouthos's supposed son; then he turns in two speeches to Kreusa, who, stricken with pain, remains mute for some time. To Xouthos he imputes a trick planned long in advance (and chronologically quite improbable) to smuggle a bastard into his house. Ion and Kreusa, archenemies, are supposed to live under one roof. One or the other must yield. Kreusa must kill her husband and stepson; he himself is ready to do away with the youth in the tent where he is celebrating with Xouthos.

The continuation of the intrigue is delayed by Kreusa's monody (859–922), a passionate outburst that forms the centerpiece of this midsection. In these lyric anapests, sparingly interspersed with dochmiacs, pain and indignation stream forth with unparalleled intensity. Here a tortured woman breaks the seal that has barred her lips for years: now she reveals all that Apollo did to her. She hurls wild accusations at the god who took her love and then abandoned her, helpless, to misery.

This monody is a masterpiece of Euripidean emotional expression, but it also has an important function within the whole. After this outburst Kreusa is changed; now she is desperate enough to do anything.

Her dialogue with the old man quickly shifts into a long stichomythy (934–1028), which as in *Iph. T.* and *Hel.* contains the arrangement of the planned assault.[261] First, however, Kreusa explains to the old man in detail what he heard only piecemeal in the monody. A realistic detail is added: at the time the old man suspected something was wrong (942, 944). The stichomythy offers a suitable form for her faltering report, but the narrative provides the basis for the planning, which the old man initiates in v. 970. As in *Iph.* and *Hel.*, here too the first suggestions of the male partner (burning of Apollo's temple, murder of Xouthos) are rejected as unfeasible or contrary to Aidos; only the thought of killing the bastard kindles Kreusa's interest. But open violence, such as the old man advises, is impossible, and so he ends up at a loss, a pause that also occurs in the counseling scenes of the related plays. But now the woman knows what to do. In a bracelet on her wrist she carries two drops of the Gorgon's blood—one heals, the other kills—a gift from Erichthonios. With the poison the old man must kill Ion in Athens. But he corrects his mistress's plan: everyone would suspect her of the murder there; it must be done in Delphi. A brief dialogue with a mutual call for action concludes the epeisodion.

The third stasimon (1048–1105) contains two pairs of strophes. The first summons up the goddess of the crossroads to aid in the plot, for failure would mean death for the mistress. The second strophe sings of the disgrace that the foreigner would bring to Athens' festivals; the antistrophe, as often, becomes more general and reproaches men who, themselves so faithless, compose poems about the infidelity of women (cf. *Medeia* 410).

The fourth epeisodion (1106–1228) presents the messenger act. As always the character first reports the essentials in a brief introductory dialogue with the chorus leader: the plot has failed; Kreusa is condemned to die by stoning.[262] In the subsequent narration Euripides' method of presenting first a slow and detailed introduction, then quickening the pace as the decisive events follow in short order, here becomes highly stylized. The festival tent in all its dimensions, the tapestries with their embroidery, the guests, are all described in minute detail, as is the account of the murderous attempt itself. An improper word uttered aloud required the guests to fill their cups anew. The plot was revealed when a dove that drank from the spilled wine perished miserably. The seizing of the old man, his confession that implicated

Kreusa, and her condemnation—all this is told in that accelerando that characterizes the conclusions of most Euripidean messenger-reports.

The messenger departs without the usual final dialogue, and in place of the expected stasimon the chorus, filled with anxiety about Kreusa's fate and their own as well, sings a brief astrophic ode (1229–1243), followed by anapests (1244–1249). The choral odes in the *Ion* are shorter than in other plays; in this way the poet saved space for the lyrical passages by Ion and Kreusa.

The exodos (1250–1622) is bipartite. At first it moves incessantly further downward, toward the catastrophe. Now only the refuge at Apollo's altar prevents Ion from murdering his mother, as she nearly murdered him. The upward path begins with the appearance of the prophetess and ends in the order arranged by Athena. The form of this final section is determined by three long stichomythies, followed by the joyful solution, which is played out at great length in speech and lyric.

In a short trochaic section broken up by antilabai (1250–1260) Kreusa rushes on stage and is hastily advised by the chorus leader that only asylum at the altar can protect her. Two speeches of Ion, the first with a savage denunciation of his enemy, the second with a complaint about the improper laws guarding suppliants' rights, frame the stichomythy in which Kreusa turns to accuse the one who would intrude in her home.[263] The situation has come to a standstill. But now the Pythia emerges from the temple. In a stichomythy with the enraged Ion—the second of three in quick succession—she checks his revenge and hands over the chest with the articles that were exposed with him so long ago, the prototype for the countless *crepundia* of New Comedy. She expressly states that it is the god's will that he receive these things, which are to help him find his mother, on the very day of his departure from Delphi. After commanding Ion to begin the search for his mother, she leaves the stage.

In verse 1356, which is certainly to be given to Ion despite the MS tradition, he has already proclaimed his longing for his mother; he is ready to wander through Europe and Asia to look for her. Now, deeply moved, he holds in his hands the basket in which she once abandoned him. Filled with tenderness, he laments not merely his own lot, but also that of his unknown mother. As in the *Helena*, with the dangerous suggestions of Theoklymenos, here too the path to a successful resolution is seriously jeopardized: Ion plans to dedicate the chest unopened to the god—for he might discover that he is the son of a slave woman. But then he reflects: has not the god himself given him the means for finding his mother?

He starts to open the chest; Kreusa looks on closely, becomes excited, and leaves her refuge at the altar. In a masterfully executed stichomythy (with amplifications at the beginning and end) the poet juxtaposes Kreusa, who already knows the truth and is transported with the joy of recognition, to Ion, who at first is hostile, then seems unsure, until he is finally convinced by a careful examination of the chest's contents. A magnificent progression runs through the three stichomythies that sustain this section: savage animosity—admonition and the transferral of the decisive objects by the Pythia—carefully checked proofs leading to recognition, and an outburst of joy: ὦ φιλτάτη μοι μῆτερ (Oh dearest mother mine! 1437).

Now they fall into each other's arms, who were mortal enemies just moments before. As in the *El.*, and later in the *Iph. T.* and *Hel.*, the recognition is followed by an amoibaion with lyric verses of the female partner and iambics of the male (1439–1509).[264] Kreusa pours forth her jubilation, but Ion's remark that his father should also share their joy leads to the final, necessary clarification. Haltingly Kreusa tells of Apollo's love and experiences once more the painful moment when she had to abandon the child; the sympathy which Ion earlier felt for his unknown mother he now extends to Kreusa, sent to him after so many years (1497).

Two conventional verses from the chorus leader provide the transition back to dialogue. The play might have ended here. Mother and son could have decided what to tell Xouthos. But the poet needs Athena, who has much good news to proclaim to her city, and so in this dialogue he raises doubts in Ion's mind, after first praising Tyche. Is Kreusa trying to cover up an affair with a mortal? And how strange is the god's behavior! But then Ion is standing right by his temple, so he will ask him point-blank. He is just about to enter when the goddess appears on the skene roof (1549).[265]

Her reason for coming is worthy of note. She fulfills the request of Apollo, who avoids showing himself to Ion and Kreusa, for fear of being reproached for past events. His clever sister is his trusty advocate. She confirms Ion's divine paternity and skill-fully presents the deception as a gift to Xouthos so as to allow the descendant of Erechtheus to rule over Athens. Of course the god had a different plan in mind: Mother and son were to be reunited only in Athens. But Kreusa's plot forced him hastily to intervene; from v. 1565 we are to conclude that Apollo was carefully directing events when the disturbing word was spoken at the feast, when the dove was poisoned, and later when the Pythia appeared.

Instead of establishing a cult, as dei ex machina so often do, Athena here provides a look into the glorious future of Athens. Ion will be ruler; the four Attic phylai shall be named after his sons (Herod. 5. 66); the islands and coasts of the Aegean will be colonized by the Athenians; and their population will be called Ionians, after their ancestral lord. To Xouthos, however, Kreusa will bear Doros and Achaios, so that these tribes too will have originated in Athens. To show how perfectly Apollo ordered everything the goddess looks back once more on what has happened, and admonishes all to let Xouthos believe that Ion is his own son.

In trochaics the son and mother respond to Athena's words. Ion politely tones down his earlier doubts of Apollo's paternity, and Kreusa declares herself reconciled and compensated for her suffering. But can we forget that she previously (427) denied the possibility of a complete compensation?

Both begin the journey to Athens, and the goddess promises to accompany them with her favor. In four trochaic tetrameters instead of the more usual anapests, the chorus praises the god and sees correct faith in god confirmed. For in the end the good man gets his reward; the wicked, the fate he deserves.

Unlike the *Helena*, the *Ion* exhibits a regular sequence (tending toward a five-act composition) of spoken scenes, often with passages of song, and choral odes (mostly short). A lengthy and thematically weighty central section occurs here again as the third epeisodion. The clearly arranged structure is given dramatic life through the constant change in situations, which contrast ironically with each other. Two confrontation scenes, Kreusa-Ion and Xouthos-Ion are brilliantly opposed: in the first, we find suppressed tones of warmth, a contact between the partners, and a fleeting glimpse of the truth; in the second, brash insistence on the one side, cool resistance on the other, and complete entanglement in illusion. Kreusa's attempted murder is the grotesque reversal of the first dialogue between two characters who meet in love and sympathy; this in turn is reversed in the scene where Ion demands Kreusa's life.

Three stages of development can be discerned: a first part, in which mother and son meet each other (and come so close that the god would only need to proclaim one word to Kreusa to clear up everything); this part finds its fulfilling continuation in the finale. In between lies confusion upon confusion, all caused by the god who initiated a false anagnorisis. This is set right by the real recognition, although Xouthos must be content with the appearance of truth.

The glorification of Athens and propagandistic support for her Panhellenic claims are obvious enough in Athena's speech. Athenian power need not have been at its height when these words were spoken; they are perfectly imaginable at the very time when those achievements were most endangered. The goddess speaks them with emphasis, yet it would be incorrect with Schmid (3. 556) to make the *Ion* the last "political" play that Euripides wrote in his homeland. The supporters of a historical interpretation, like Grégoire in his edition and Delebecque, also exaggerate the importance of this section, which belongs to the drama but does not define its purpose.

The role of the god in the play is a much discussed problem. Of course the ludicrous rationalism of A. W. Verrall is now only of historical interest.[266] In his view Ion actually was the natural son of Xouthos, Kreusa had exposed an illegitimate child, and all ran according to the will of a deceitful priesthood! But Murray (118) and Norwood (238) have a defensible point when they see in the play an attack on the world of the gods and on Apollo above all. Wilamowitz made a similar judgment in the introduction to his edition. Their view is rejected by those who seek the answer along the lines of more recent attempts to reduce if not eliminate the poet's opposition to popular religion whenever possible.[267] The attempt to interpret the Apollo of the *Ion* as a model of divine care and sublime rule, as Athena proclaimed (Apollo has done all things well; 1595), based on Kreusa's expression of gratitude and the heavy dose of poetic justice in the concluding statement, fails for the following reasons: the suffering that Kreusa had to endure to serve the god's pleasure cannot be erased. She speaks of it often enough and also says that complete compensation is impossible (427). The god confirms this strikingly when he dispatches Athena to escape reproach for "earlier things." One need only compare the Apollo of the Diomedeia in the *Iliad* or the statue from the west pediment at Olympia to realize what has become of the Olympian figure in Euripides! Further, the god himself is exposed to the games of Tyche, which is something different from the ironclad fate to which even the gods of the old faith were subject. The chorus that refused to keep silence has thwarted Apollo's plan to reunite the pair in Athens; instead, mother and son were on the point of killing each other. In any event, Apollo provided assistance at the last moment, but he had to learn the truth of Odysseus's statement in the *Kyklops* (607): τὰ δαιμόνων δὲ τῆς τύχης ἐλάσσονα (the gods' power is weaker than chance).[268]

The god who ravished a beautiful princess on the slope of the Akropolis certainly belongs to an ancient legend that should not be judged too severely, but we are in no way guilty of a rigor foreign to antiquity if we find the manner in which Apollo palms off his own child on Xouthos highly dubious and irreconcilable with the phrase, "If gods err, they are not gods" (fr. 292N).[269]

I must say immediately that even so, I think it wrong to believe that Euripides composed the *Ion* for the purpose of picking apart traditional religion. Certainly he had begun to feel doubts about it: when he operates the mythological machinery, he also includes criticism of it, which pierces again and again the surface of the tradition.[270] In no way, however, does it represent personal concerns for the sake of which the poet wrote his dramas.

Neither the political elements nor the criticism of the tradition provides the key for understanding the play. As in Euripides' other works the focus is on man, and, as in many of the later works, on man in the whirlpool of a fate that offers him extreme danger and liberating salvation, causing his soul to resound in lament and jubilation. In few other characters can we perceive these rich tones more strongly than in Kreusa. Of course the question of whether everything is joined in a perfect unity, whether the woman who suffered in silence is readily reconcilable with the mad avenger—this is a question that must at least be asked. The poet has certainly done much to make the transition more tolerable for us. He gave Kreusa the old man as the driving force, and in the great monody portrayed the agonizing pain of a woman who must renounce her child forever, while the god who seduced her presents her husband with a child. Rivier (123) has especially brought out this side of Kreusa's character. Nonetheless the comparison occasionally made with Medeia rather underlines the difference between the two women. The magnificent unity of that character—precisely in her dissonances—this Euripides did not achieve in his characterization of Kreusa. Instead she confirms the remark of Jakob Burckhardt that it was Euripides' manner "to exploit to the fullest the feeling of an individual character in a particular scene."[271]

The three previous plays show how Euripides was repeatedly able to contrive new effects from certain motifs. The same probably holds true for a whole series of lost plays and their basic themes. How much human ἄγνοια (ignorance) is exposed to the games of Tyche is never more glaringly evident than when close relatives are near to destroying the life of the one they love best.

The *Aigeus* was already mentioned in connection with the *Medeia* (at n. 27, above). For its subject matter we can rely with some confidence on Apollodoros (1. 4–6). Theseus comes to Athens, unrecognized by his father, and finds there Medeia, his hostile stepmother. She apparently is responsible for sending him off against the Bull of Marathon, and prepares his death by poison after his successful return. Theseus's sword (Aigeus once left it for his son in Troizen) leads to the recognition between son and father, and to Medeia's exile.

In the *Alexandros*, discussed above as a play from the Trojan trilogy, chance and man's ignorance again endanger close relatives. This motif is well attested for the *Kresphontes* as well.[272] The date of performance for Aristophanes' *Georgoi* in which (fr. 109K) the beginning of fr. 453N is parodied, gives us a terminus ante around 424. Thus it appears that Euripides chose motifs of this sort even in his earlier works. The fragments confirm that the essential story is preserved in Hyginus, *Fab.* 137. Polyphontes, king of Messenia, killed his brother Telephontes and seized his power and his wife, Merope. She has her son Kresphontes brought to a friend in Aitolia while he is still a small boy. Polyphontes has set a price on his head (as Aigisthos does with Orestes, Eur. *El.* 33). On reaching manhood Kresphontes returns to take revenge, but in order to get near Polyphontes pretends to be his own murderer. Believing that he speaks the truth, Merope tries to kill the stranger, whom she does not recognize, but this is prevented at the last moment. In Hyginus this occurs when an old man, who knew Kresphontes, intervenes. How far this corresponds to Euripides' version must remain conjectural, for the new *P. Oxy.* 2458 poses a number of unsolved questions. Merope feigns reconciliation with Polyphontes, and her son kills him at a sacrifice (as Orestes does Aigisthos). The drama was, as the quotations in Nauck show, extraordinarily impressive.

Parallels to the *Ion* can be seen in the *Antiope*,[273] and it seems that no long interval separated the two plays, since the latter was produced a few years before the *Frogs* (405), according to schol. Aristoph. *Ran.* 53. Hyginus states explicitly that *Fab.* 8 is a reproduction of Euripides' play. Basically the facts agree with Apollodoros 3. 5. 5. Numerous fragments, including a Flinders Petrie papyrus (1, 1891, 1), permit a tolerably certain reconstruction.

Antiope bears Zeus the Theban Dioskouroi Amphion and Zethos and exposes them at Eleutherai on the Attic-Boiotian border, where a shepherd finds and raises them. She then flees to Epopeus of Sikyon but is captured by her uncle Lykos, who enslaves her to his cruel wife, Dirke. This is the background, related by the speaker of the prologue (the shepherd? Dionysos?). Antiope was able to free herself miraculously and escape to her sons, who have since grown up. Zethos takes her for an impostor and refuses to receive her. Dirke, who pursues Antiope with an auxiliary chorus of mainads (men of Attika formed the main chorus), threatens her with death. In the nick of time the shepherd brings about the recognition of the mother by her sons. They kill Dirke, whom they tie to a wild bull, and lure Lykos into their cottage. He too is about to die when Hermes steps in ex machina, rescues Lykos, but then establishes Amphion as ruler.

The play's main attraction was the agon between the two brothers, in which Amphion defended the βίος θεωρητικός (life of contemplation), Zethos the βίος πρακτικός (life of action). The widespread influence of this debate on Western literature and thought extends as far as the discussion between the two brothers Prometheus and Epimetheus in Goethe's *Pandora*.

Murder within families is not always prevented; it can also be committed in ignorance and thus become the horrible punishment for a deceitful attack. The *Ino*, produced before 425 according to Aristoph. *Ach.* v. 434, shows that Euripides based even relatively early plays on extremely complex situations.[274] The *Ino Euripidis* of

Hyginus (*Fab.* 4) tells us the contents. Athamas, king of Thessaly, has two sons by Ino. When she leaves him he gives her up for lost and takes Themisto to wife, with whom he also has two children. Later he learns that Ino lives as a bakchant on Mount Parnassos, and he has her brought to him. He conceals her identity and gives her as a servant to Themisto. But the queen wishes to eliminate the two stepchildren and so tells Ino at night to put black covers on these boys' beds and white covers on those of her own. Ino does the reverse and Themisto kills her own children; when she learns the truth, she dies by her own hand. The conclusion of the play remains obscure. That Athamos in madness killed his elder son, Learchos, while hunting still belongs in the plot, if we can trust Hyginus. But that Ino fell into the sea with Melikertes and became a goddess was perhaps predicted by a deus ex machina, most likely Dionysos.

We cannot place too much confidence in the testimony of Hyginus, especially where he quotes no sources. So it remains uncertain whether *Fab.* 86 reproduces the contents of the *Pleisthenes*,[275] which should be dated before 414, based on the parallel between fr. 628N and Aristoph. *Av.* 1232. That Atreus here kills Pleisthenes as the supposed son of Thyestes, when in reality he is Atreus's own son, would certainly fit well in this group of motifs.

The story of the seduced young woman who exposes her child and later finds it again through a special providence, as we saw in the *Ion*, recurs in a number of Euripides' plays. In tragedy the seducers are gods; in New Comedy, which would be inconceivable without this motif, their place is taken by enterprising young men.

Of the two *Melanippe* dramas, the *Melanippe Sophe* is easier to reconstruct.[276] The scholium on *Lysistrata*, v. 1125, confirms 411 as the year of production. The prologue, spoken by Melanippe, is preserved for us by the commentary of Joannes Logothetes on Hermogenes (H. Rabe, *Rhein Mus.* 63 [1908], 144). This and *P. Oxy.* 2455 assist us greatly for much of the play. The extant section of the prologue offers a lengthy genealogical introduction; the background to the story must have been provided in the lost part. During the one-year exile of her father Aiolos, Melanippe lay with Poseidon and gave birth to twins, whom she concealed in a cowshed on the god's instructions. The dramatic action probably began when herdsmen found the boys being suckled by a cow and brought them to Aiolos as a preternatural marvel. His father, Hellenos, persuaded him, apparently against some opposition, to burn the twins, and Melanippe was ordered to dress the children for death. In a speech whose outlines are still dimly perceptible, she protested for the children's sake, without revealing the truth. Being σοφή (clever), she tried to prove that the belief in a monstrous birth was nonsense and that killing the children would be murder. The rest of the play is unclear; in any event it must have presented the revelation of Melanippe's motherhood and, perhaps through Hellenos, a further threat to their lives. Only thus does it make sense that Melanippe's mother, Hippo, appeared at the end and assured the twins Aiolos and Boiotos their place in the royal house.

We are considerably less certain in reconstructing the *Melanippe Desmotis*.[277] Hyginus, *Fab.* 186, and Diodoros, 4. 67, are unreliable sources. The setting seems to have been southern Italy, in fact Metapontum, where Melanippe, impregnated by Poseidon, was brought to King Metapontos, and where she was treated like a captive.

The twins she bore were exposed. The king's wife was given the children, without knowing their real identity, by a shepherd, and she raised them as her own. The plot was set in motion when the queen decided to eliminate the two foundlings, who had since grown up. Her motive cannot be accurately determined. But despite doubts raised by Van Looy, the version given by Hyginus still seems the most probable. As his story goes, the queen later bore children herself, so that she wished to rid herself of the twins. In any event, in the large fragment from the messenger-speech, a participant in the plot, which was to be carried out by the queen's two brothers while on a hunt, reports to her how the twins slew their opponents and put the servants to flight. How Melanippe was freed, how mother and sons were reunited, and how a god, probably Poseidon, granted the twins royal privilege and perhaps even brought about Melanippe's union with Metapontos, the queen committing suicide—the details of all this are lost to us.

Here we must remark that one of the two *Tyro* dramas of Sophokles dealt with related themes. Tyro, impregnated by Poseidon, secretly gives birth to twins, Pelias and Neleus, and exposes them. When they grow up they recognize their mother and punish their stepmother Sidero, who had tormented Tyro. Based on the scholium to Aristoph. *Av.* 275 the play can be dated to 416 at the latest (since Sophokles did not produce a play in 415), but we cannot ascertain its chronological relationship to the *Melanippe Desmotis*. The other thematically related plays *Antiope* and *Hypsipyle* (see below) come later.

In the *Alope* the poet dramatized the fate of the daughter of Kerkyon by Eleusis, who bore to Poseidon a son, Hippothoon.[278] One shepherd finds the child and gives it to another one, but wants to keep its costly garments. The result is a trial before Kerkyon, who discloses the truth. Menander ingeniously transposed this scene into his *Epitrepontes*. The resolution was probably effected by Theseus, who slew Kerkyon.

The *Auge* belongs in the later phase of Euripides' career.[279] Important for the reconstruction is Moses Chorenensis, *Progymn.* 3. 3. There we learn that Herakles violated Auge, priestess of Athena and daughter of Aleos, at a festival one night in Arkadia. Auge gives birth in the temple, and Aleos has the child exposed, threatening his daughter with death. Herakles, who returns to the land, recognizes Auge by a ring he left with her, saves her from death, and rescues the child. But now Moses Chorenensis continues the story unexpectedly: Teuthras, king of Mysia, marries Auge and adopts Telephos. This agrees with Strabo (13. 615), who refers to Euripides. If all this belongs in our play, we must assume that Herakles initially saved Auge from death, but that Aleos insisted that mother and child be put in a chest and cast out to sea. A deus ex machina (Athena?) could have sanctioned this by prophesying a glorious future for the child, so that Herakles finally consented. This remains conjectural.

From this play we know of two fragments that attest the breakthrough of a new mode of thought challenging tradition. In fr. 266N, Auge accuses Athena of delighting in the sight of bloody spoils and fallen heroes, but of shunning a birth (in her temple). Based on Menander's *Epitrepontes* (689), fr. 920 has found its place in the

Auge. It is a programmatic statement of the sophistic theory about natural law: ἡ φύσις ἐβούλετ', ᾗ νόμων οὐδὲν μέλει (Nature willed it so, caring nothing about laws).[280]

For the *Danae* we learn from Joannes Malalas (*Chronogr.* 2, p. 34, 17th ed. Bonn) no more than we could guess from the title:[281] Zeus impregnates the daughter of Akrisios in the form of golden rain; her father places her and the child in a chest and puts them out to sea, as Aleos did to Auge, if our attempt to reconstruct that play is correct. As with the *Danae* of Sophokles, we have no reliable evidence for dating the piece.

The motif that twins who were abandoned after their birth find their mother many years later and rescue her from dire peril, was used by Euripides in the *Antiope* and *Melanippe Desmotis*. The abundance of variations he had at his command becomes especially evident when we consider the *Hypsipyle*, which according to the schol. Aristoph. *Ran.* 53 was produced around the time of *Antiope* and *Phoinissai* and preceded the *Frogs* by a few years.[282] *P. Oxy.* 852 offers considerable portions of the play, to which are added fragments of the hypothesis in *P. Oxy.* 2455, fr. 14. In the prologue Hypsipyle filled in the background of the story. She is the daughter of King Thoas of Lemnos, where Iason landed on his expedition with the Argonauts. To him she bore the twins Thoas and Euneos, whom Iason took with him on the Argo. Later she fled, to avoid having to kill her father during the atrocities of the Lemnian women. Now in the service of Lykourgos and Eurydike of Nemea, she takes care of their child, the young Opheltes. Her two sons come on stage before the parodos begins (~ *Iph. T.*); Thoas, their grandfather, has given them the golden vine, gift of his father, Dionysos, and sent them off to search for their mother. Hypsipyle comes out of the house when they knock, and, as in the thematically related plays, mother and sons confront each other without recognition. When Hypsipyle praises the mother of such children, we recall the exact parallel in the *Ion* (308). The parodos of the chorus of Nemean women is composed in the form of an antiphony with Hypsipyle (~ *El.*, *Hel.*, and Soph. *El.*); the chorus bids her to forget her sorrow and come to the pasture near Nemea, where the Seven have marshaled their armies against Thebes. In the following scene Amphiaraos enters and asks Hypsipyle where he can find pure water for a sacrifice. We can discern a stichomyth, in which he tells of the expedition against Thebes and the betrayal of his wife, Eriphyle, which forced him to take part. Webster groups *Hypsipyle* together with the *Antiope* and *Phoinissai* to form a trilogy. This would explain the broadly developed role of Amphiaraos.

For a large portion of the play we possess only meager fragments, but the basic course of the plot can be determined. Hypsipyle accompanies Amphiaraos to the spring, which is guarded by a snake. The serpent kills Opheltes when his guardian leaves him alone while helping to fetch the water. Hypsipyle rushes on stage in despair; a lengthy section of the text takes up where she defends herself against Eurydike, who has accused her of killing the child. She is about to be executed when Amphiaraos arrives, relates the true course of events, and defends her. The child is to be buried and the Nemean games founded in his honor. In the contests that now begin, Thoas and Euneos are victorious, much to the displeasure of Eurydike. The questions remain open when and how the anagnorisis took place between the mother and her sons. Here Amphiaraos may have played a decisive role, perhaps in connection with the contests, and he probably also persuaded the queen to allow Hypsipyle to depart with her sons. His farewell speech and the amoibaion of the reunited family have been preserved. Once again the male partner (Euneos) is given trimeters, while Hypsipyle sings.[283] The concluding lines, which are not extant, were spoken by Dionysos.

P. Oxy. 2455 with the alphabetically arranged hypotheseis to Euripides has proved beyond all doubt that there were two Phrixos dramas (frr. 14 and 16; Austin, p. 101).[284] We also know now that fr. 821N represents the beginning of the first Phrixos; fr. 819N, the beginning of the second. It has furthered our knowledge considerably to learn from the new hypothesis that Apollodoros 1. 9. 1 and Hyginus, Fab. 2. 3–5, 3. 1, are generally reliable reproductions of the latter play. The setting was Orchomenos, where Athamas had two children, Phrixos and Helle, by his wife Nephele. When she abandoned him he married Ino. How Euripides handled the time relationship between Athamas and the two women cannot be ascertained. In any case Ino, as the evil stepmother, tried to get rid of Phrixos. She persuaded the women to roast the seed corn. When famine broke out and Athamas sent a messenger to Delphi, Ino bribed the latter to report that the oracle demanded the sacrifice of Phrixos. W. Schadewaldt, op. cit., has incorporated a Florentine papyrus (D. L. Page, op. cit.) into the play and concluded that Phrixos, apparently against the opposition of his father, voluntarily agreed to be sacrificed. But then pity overcame the false messenger and he revealed the truth. Athamas handed over the guilty woman to Phrixos and Helle for punishment, but a messenger reported that Dionysos saved Ino by striking the siblings with madness. Probably Dionysos ex machina then related their rescue by their mother, Nephele, and promised that Phrixos would be welcomed in Kolchis after his miraculous journey on the ram. Recently, two fragments have been added: P. Oxy. 2685 (edited by J. Rea in vol. 34), which belongs in the scene with the preparation for the sacrifice, and five verses on the relationship between the gods and Tyche. They are confirmed for the drama by a Florentine papyrus with an anthology of sententiae.[285]

Still unsolved is the question of the contents of the first Phrixos. Here Athamas was king in Thessaly, but this does not prove that the plots of the two dramas were completely different. One need only recall the two Hippolytos dramas. If we follow Van Looy (182) in accepting as certain Turner's restorations in the hypothesis ἐμη]χανᾱτο (contrived) and συνκαλέ[σασα (after she summoned together), it seems most likely that Euripides treated this material twice, as he did the fate of Hippolytos. The other possibility, considered by Webster (Eur., 131), that the two plays were separated by an interval of time similar to that between the two Melanippe dramas, and that the first Phrixos was set in Kolchis, would only be viable if the two verbs quoted above belonged to the prologue speaker's account of the background information.

For the dating of the Phoinissai our most reliable source remains the scholion on Aristoph. Ran. 53, where it is named with Hypsipyle and Antiope as an example of Euripides' works after the Andromeda of 412.[286] Since Euripides left Athens shortly after 408, we are left with 411–408 as the boundaries, within which 409 seems rather probable.[287] The severely damaged hypothesis of Aristophanes of Byzantium names *Oinomaos* and *Chrysippos* in an uncertain context. To correct an earlier statement, I would no longer agree with L. Deubner (*Sitzb. Berlin* 1942/4, 12), who believed the three plays were connected in a trilogy. With greater probability, Schwartz, in his edition of the scholia, suggested thematic relationships. On the *Chrysippos* see below; so little is preserved of the *Oinomaos* that we cannot say whether it dealt with the same material as Sophokles' like-named drama, the love of Hippodameia and the death of Oinomaos in the race with Pelops.[288]

That the *Phoinissai* formed a trilogy together with *Antiope* and *Hypsipyle* is a hypothesis proposed by Webster (205) and supported both by the Aristophanes scholium just mentioned and thematic considerations.

The portion of the play before the parodos is devoted to the exposition of the women who stand between the hostile brothers. Iokaste delivers the prologue speech. Unlike in the *Helena*, here the details of locale and genealogical relationships are preceded by a highly elaborate appeal to Helios. Then comes the background: how Laios transgressed Apollo's order not to beget children, how Oidipous was exposed, rescued, and raised by Polybos; here the king's wife passes off the foundling as her own son. The fatal meeting between father and son at the Phokian crossroads is motivated in a very significant way: both wish to consult Delphi, Oidipous about his parentage, Laios about his exposed child. Iokaste remains alive after Oidipous's discovery and blinding, unlike in Sophokles' version. His sons hold him captive to conceal the disgrace, but for this they reap his curse: they shall divide their inheritance with the sword. To escape that fate they agree to alternate as rulers annually. But hardly has Eteokles come to power, when he exiles his brother and refuses to yield his authority. In Argos Polyneikes marries the daughter of Adrastos and collects an army with the help of his father-in-law; as its captain he now stands before the gates of Thebes. Iokaste has him summoned by a messenger, hoping to reconcile the brothers at the last moment. She concludes with one of those prayers that mix reproach with petition, as often in Euripides: Zeus, if he is wise, cannot always smite the same man with disaster.

After her exit the pedagogue of Antigone appears on the roof of the skene, which in this play is not needed for any god. He carefully looks about to make sure no one is near the palace; then he bids the girl ascend the stairs.[289] The following teichoskopia is composed as an amoibaion that recalls the passages after the anagnorisis in the previous plays insofar as the male partner speaks in trimeters, but here Antigone does so as well, alternating with lyric verses (predominantly dochmiacs).[290] The pedagogue identifies for the girl the enemy captains who were portrayed in the great centerpiece of Aischylos's *Seven*. In Euripides, however, the sequence is entirely different, and Eteoklos is left out, since his name sounded too much like Eteokles. Antigone is nicely characterized in her fluctuation between fear and sisterly longing. She has just cursed Parthenopaios for attacking her city when, at the sight of Polyneikes, she desires only to embrace her long-lost brother. The maiden's appeal to Artemis, the virgin goddess, and the admonition of the pedagogue to return to the house now that the chorus is approaching, conclude the prologue section.

The censorious first hypothesis condemns the teichoskopia as a superfluous intrusion in the drama. We judge otherwise and see in the scene the broadly developed image of the danger threatening Thebes. Moreover, the character of Antigone supplies the connection between the fate of the city and that of the Labdakidai.

The choice of chorus, which now enters with two strophic pairs (202–260; the first with epode), is original, and a happy one. In this plot, which is full to overflowing, there was no place for a chorus to act with the intensity of the Theban women in the *Seven*. On the other hand, for the odes there had to be some connection with Thebes. These conditions are fulfilled by the chorus of Phoinikian girls from Tyre, who are stopping in Thebes on their way to Delphi as a living votive offering to the god, for Kadmos, the founder of Thebes, had once come from Tyre on his search for Europa.

The chorus introduces itself and sings of its dedication to Loxias (first pair), full of longing for the holy place (epode).[291] The second strophic pair expresses the maidens' concern for their related city, their fear of the imminent battle. At the end the chorus explicitly acknowledges the right of Polyneikes to demand his share of rulership.

At the beginning of the first epeisodion (261–637), Polyneikes comes on stage with an entrance monologue that again anticipates the technique of New Comedy. The unnatural side of his situation is harshly emphasized. His home city has become a hostile land, in which he moves only with the utmost caution, now trusting in his sword, now in the altars as places of refuge. A brief dialogue with the chorus leader presents the mutual introductions, then the chorus, changing to lyric meters after two trimeters, calls Iokaste from the palace, while they greet the newcomer in oriental fashion, with proskynesis.

Iokaste enters—she lays great stress on the weariness of her aged steps—and begins with a long, largely dochmiac aria (301–354). Her maternal joy flows forth unrestrained. Then she bewails the fate of Oidipous and Polyneikes' marriage in a foreign land, far from his mother. For her, too, as well as for the pedagogue (154) the justice of Polyneikes' cause is beyond doubt (319). Her final verses express the well-known multiplicity of motivations: Do iron, the quarrel and the father bear the guilt, or did divine will upset the House of Oidipous?

A passage follows (357–442) with the familiar tripartite structure, in which two speeches of Polyneikes frame a stichomythy between him and Iokaste. He describes his feelings of bitterness; he had to enter the city like enemy territory—his own homeland, the sight of which moved him so deeply. Iokaste answers his inquiry about his father and sisters with a short lament, for she herself is full of questions, which are asked and answered in the following stichomythy. She inquires about the suffering and misery of banishment, and no Athenian present could have suppressed the thought of the many political exiles in the Greek world at that time, whether the poet himself had this in mind or not. Question and answer then center on the dramatic arrival of Polyneikes together with Tydeus in Argos and on the marriage he celebrated there.

In his second speech he reports on the expedition, of whose questionable nature as an attack on his home city he is fully aware. He hopes that his mother can reconcile the differences, but at the end (438 ff.) offers his motives for fighting, which many scholars have deleted.[292] They are, however, thoroughly relevant and spring from the pressing want that the exile suffers. The lines add an essential element to the generally emotional lament for his homeland. In no way, though, should these verses lead us to distort our image of Polyneikes into that of a man driven by unscrupulous greed. Neither does Aischylos intend to cast a shadow over his Orestes with *Choe*. 301.

Three verses of the chorus leader announce the arrival of Eteokles, who comes from drawing up his armed forces, wanting to hear the verdict for which his mother brought "that man" into the city. With an admonition directed sternly to Eteokles, more mildly to Polyneikes, Iokaste introduces the agon, which is conducted before an umpire, as in the *Hekabe* and *Troiades*. She bids Polyneikes speak first, and he justifies his legitimate claim and is ready for reconciliation—but also for war. In the *Seven* of Aischylos the question of justice remains in the background; Polyneikes there appears as the brutal attacker justly rebuked by Amphiaraos, and Eteokles as the dutiful defender of Thebes; but Euripides has reversed the distribution of light and shadow. Though he cannot free Polyneikes from the taint of an attack against his homeland, the poet does grant him the legitimate claim, and has characterized him as the better of the two brothers by virtue of his readiness to be reconciled and his love for his city and his mother. Only thus could Euripides achieve the ethical basis for the great agon scene, which would have been unthinkable with the Polyneikes of the *Seven*.

Eteokles begins his speech as if he were a pupil of the Sophists instructed that man is the measure of all things. If the same thing appeared to everyone as good and wise, there would be no strife. As things are, nothing is equal except in name, but what lies behind the names is a different matter (ὄνομα-ἔργον antithesis). Then follows a passionate defense of his lust for power, which he calls Tyrannis, to name the highest of all divinities. We might be listening to Kallikles or Thrasymachos. But Euripides does not make Eteokles totally one-sided; he too has a correct idea to his credit: his brother should have begun negotiations before resorting to force; πᾶν γὰρ ἐξαιρεῖ λόγος (for words can accomplish all; 516)—here we recall the ode in the *Helena* (1151). Finally, however, he returns to his initial assertions.

Iokaste replies to the brothers in a speech of admonition, which approximately corresponds in length to the other two speeches combined.[293] She turns first to Eteokles and calls by the correct name the power that drives him. It is Φιλοτιμία (Ambition), the worst goddess of all, to whom she contrasts Ἰσότης (Equality), the force of order among men and in the cosmos. The recollection of *Suppl.* 407, but also of Sokrates in the *Gorgias* (507e), is unavoidable. And when she reproaches him for foolish greed, we are reminded of the concept of πλεονεξία (avarice), which later plays such a great role in moral philosophy. Finally, she warns Eteokles that he must choose between tyranny and the welfare of the state, for his defeat would mean its destruction. Framing this section, the word φιλότιμος (ambitious) appears in the final line (567). In a briefer speech she talks to Polyneikes and reverts to the last argument used against

Eteokles: To destroy your homeland, what a victory! And if you are beaten, how you will return to Argos!

But Iokaste's speech falls on deaf ears, as do the three verses of the chorus leader with her appeal to the gods. Lively tetrameters now begin, whose tempo soon escalates to a stichomythy between the brothers, which after a few verses breaks into continuous antilabai. After v. 618 Iokaste joins the dialogue as a third partner. But the lines of battle have already been drawn; only accusations are hurled back and forth. Once again the poet contrasts the character of the two brothers, as Polyneikes expresses the wish to see his father and sisters, while Eteokles bluntly refuses the request. The reciprocal murder of the brothers is foreshadowed when Polyneikes says (594) that whoever strikes him with the sword will suffer the same fate and when Eteokles (620) asks where his brother will be stationed, so he may oppose him face to face.

The short concluding speeches correspond to those that precede the stichomythy, with the distribution reversed. Now Polyneikes has the longer section, in which he once more combines lament and hatred. Eteokles departs with two verses that refer to the belligerence inherent in his brother's very name.[294]

The first stasimon (638–689) initiates a series of beautiful choral odes that connect Thebes' past with the events of the drama. One pair of strophes with epode, exhibits in its rich imagery, diction, and syntax the new "dithyrambic" style that became fashionable in the late fifth century and provoked the scorn of Aristophanes.[295] The chorus sings of the founding of Thebes by Kadmos and the birth of Dionysos (α), of Kadmos's battle with the serpent and the sowing of its teeth (α'). The epode calls on their ancestor Epaphos and on Persephone and Demeter to protect the city.

While the first epeisodion served to eliminate any chance for a possible reconciliation, the second (690–783) has more of a preparatory character. A confrontation scene with a very realistic introduction (the one sends for the other, while the other has been searching for him for some time) brings together Eteokles and Kreon. Again we note the schema of a stichomythy framed by a dialogue and a speech.

In the introductory dialogue an important change takes place. In Kreon's words, Polyneikes and the collapse of negotiations appear in a different light. The attacker thinks himself greater than Thebes and puts all his trust in Adrastos and the army. In the rest of the play, we should think not so much of the legitimate claims of the one, as of the unrestrained desires of both for war and possessions.

In the stichomythy, various aggressive suggestions of the younger man (battle in the open field, nocturnal raids, attack at mealtime) are rejected by Kreon until, when Eteokles impatiently asks what he is supposed to do (surrender, perhaps?), Kreon finally comes out with the suggestion to man the seven gates.

In the concluding speech Eteokles declines to list the names of the individual defenders. This is certainly well motivated by the urgency of the situation, but it cannot be separated from the great central section of the *Seven*, which Euripides is clearly criticizing.[296]

Then Eteokles makes the final arrangements. Kreon, as χύριος, is to take care of Antigone's wedding (looking ahead to the concluding section), and is to send his son Menoikeus to Teiresias for consultation, which Eteokles, having offended the prophet, cannot do. This prepares us for the following Menoikeus act. Should the city be victorious, Polyneikes must not be buried in Theban ground (a motif in the finale). This edict must of course be deleted by those scholars who remove any reference to Polyneikes' burial from the final act. More will be said on this later, but here two remarks are necessary: in no way is Eteokles' edict senseless, since even if the battle is won, he can reckon with his own death. Further, it is to be noted that the prohibition pertains only to Theban ground, and—unlike Kreon's command in the *Antigone*—does not exclude burial in some other place.

The second stasimon (784–833) continues the theme and style of the first, but reverses the accents within its single triad. Strophe and antistrophe, lamenting the misery of war and Oidipous's fate, which led to his sons' quarrel, are directly related to the plot, while the epode reaches far back into Thebes' mythical past with the Spartoi, Harmonia, and Amphion.

The third epeisodion (834–1018) is a Menoikeus act. In this midsection of the drama the fates of the Labdakidai and the Spartoi (through Menoikeus) are interwoven with the destiny of Thebes.

Teiresias steps on stage, accompanied by his daughter and Menoikeus. In a dialogue with Kreon he relates that he comes from Athens, where he gave good counsel for the fight against Eumolpos and was given a golden wreath. The Athenians, who were familiar with the poet's *Erechtheus*, knew that Teiresias's advice referred to the sacrifice of the king's daughter, and must have expected similar instructions for Thebes. But the prophet's comparatively long speech (865–895) first presents a retardation. We learn that Teiresias incurred the animosity of the sons of Oidipous because he rebuked them for their treatment of their father. The old man's curse will bring them death by their own hands—the prophet knows their end. The first measure necessary to save Thebes would be that no member of Oidipous's stock—neither ruler nor citizen—remain in the city. This prepares for Kreon's banishment of Oidipous later. Yet there is also another way, but the prophet wishes to conceal it and depart. Thus we have a situation which is similar to the Teiresias scene in the *Oidipous Tyrannos*. Here, however, Kreon extracts the truth not by vehemence but by persuasion, in the stichomythy that follows. Now Teiresias reveals that Menoikeus must be sacrificed for the salvation of the city. Horrified, Kreon resists (920: This is no longer the same man) and begs the prophet on his knees to keep secret his terrible demand, which Teiresias sternly declines to do. Here there is a contradiction. The same Teiresias who was about to leave, in order to spare Kreon's anguish, now refuses emphatically to withhold his counsel from the city. Bruno Snell (op. cit.) has noted that the scholia offer the following version as a variant to 915: τί δή με δράσεις; παῖδα μου κατακτενεῖς (What will you do to me? Will you murder my child?); this would smoothly join 928, and Snell believes we are faced with the alternative that either the transmitted verses 915–927 are an interpolation, which suppressed the genuine verse 915a, or conversely, that the line was meant to bridge the gap left when the longer section was eliminated. After careful deliberation, he comes to the conclusion that the longer version is the genuine text. We believe this is correct. Even assuming that the lines were interpolated, we are still not rid of the contradiction. For there is also verse 973, in which Kreon says that the prophet will pass on his knowledge to the authorities.

Teiresias explains the meaning of the sacrifice. Ares is angry with the city because Kadmos slew the dragon. Now one of the Spartoi, who sprang from its teeth, must die.[297]

The prophet has left. Kreon remains determined to save his son and orders him to flee immediately. In a short stichomythy he points him the way, far off to Dodona. Menoikeus pretends to obey, but when his father leaves, he proclaims in a monologue (despite the address to the chorus) his resolve to kill himself, to fall from the ramparts of the city into the ancient lair of the dragon. The poet gives the unselfish boy, the only truly bright figure in the drama, a speech of great pathos.

The third stasimon (1019–1066) conjures up the horror brought over Thebes by the Sphinx, when she snatched away youths in her talons (α). Now—so we infer—another one must lose his life. In the antistrophe the chorus sings of Oidipous's solution of her riddle, and of the disasters that followed up to the battle between the sons. Against this background the image of the heroic youth shines all the more brilliantly.

In this play events off-stage decide two fates: that of the city and that of the hostile brothers. Unlike Aischylos, who combines both in a short messenger scene, Euripides has composed the fight for the city and the confrontation of the brothers in two separate messenger acts with detailed reports, of which each is bipartite, the longer section followed by a shorter.

In the fourth epeisodion (1067–1282) the messenger rushes on stage and summons Iokaste from the house. With a mother's concern she asks first about Eteokles, then Polyneikes, and learns that both still live. The messenger also reports the Theban victory in this initial dialogue and then begins his narrative. We might note that this anticipation of the essential points, before the long expansive report, repeats on a smaller scale the function of the prologue speech before the development of the plot in many plays.

Reaching back the messenger begins with the self-sacrifice of Menoikeus and Eteokles' manning of the gates. We must simply accept the fact that the opposing army, which in the scene of the teichoskopia was already marshaled on the banks of the Ismenos and Dirke (101), now marches on from Mount Teumesos (1100).

A section follows (1104–1140) in which the seven attackers (the same as in Aischylos with Adrastos in place of Eteoklos) are assigned to the seven gates. The precise description of the blazonry is a conscious variation of the corresponding section in Aischylos's drama. These lines overextend an already lengthy messenger-speech; moreover, they represent an unwanted repetition of the teichoskopia. Most probably they can be deleted as an interpolation. In the view of W. H. Friedrich they serve as a substitute passage if no appropriate singer could be found for the amoibaion of the teichoskopia.[298] This is possible, if one accepts his atheteses in the final act.

In the report follow the individual ventures of Parthenopaios, Tydeus, and Kapaneus. After their defeat Adrastos sounds the retreat, the Thebans pursue, and the first section of the report ends with a confused battle situation, but one favorable to the beleaguered city.

This section contains many brilliant narrative details, like the onrush of Kapaneus, but we must reiterate our observations for the *Herakleidai* and *Suppliants*: the great vividness of Euripidean narration is diminished when he describes military operations. They are not the forte of a poet who despised war.

Now Iokaste yearns to know her sons' further plans. She senses that the messenger is holding something back and in a short stichomythy forces him to speak. In the second section of his report he relates how Eteokles suggested a duel with his brother to decide the issue, how Polyneikes instantly agreed, and how both donned their armor. Then prophets, to whom the sacrificial fires flash the signs for victory and defeat (both are the lot of the brothers), supply the delay the poet needs until the second messenger act can begin. Greatly agitated, Iokaste follows the messenger's advice to prevent the worst at the last moment, and calls Antigone from the house. In a brief stichomythy that breaks into antilabai, she directs the young woman to hasten with her to the battlefield; she is resolved to stop the fight or die with her sons.

The short fourth stasimon (1283–1306) now no longer interrupts the plot with a flashback to Theban history; instead the single strophic pair reflects the previous action in sympathy for the mother and in lament for the hapless brothers.

Afterward begins the section we designate as the exodos, but the choral anapests 1480–1484 clearly mark off a second messenger act; only after this does the real conclusion begin.

Before all this Euripides inserts a short scene bringing Kreon on stage.[299] He is completely overwhelmed by his suffering for Menoikeus and seeks his sister to care for the corpse. But the messenger enters immediately and in the introductory dialogue with Kreon announces the death of the brothers and of Iokaste. Again his report, here interrupted by two verses of lamentation from the chorus leader (1425 f.), is bipartite, so that the brothers' duel and the death of Iokaste form separate narratives.

The description of the fight is sharply accented by the terrible prayers of the brothers. Each demands the other's blood, each appears here equally base and guilty. Again we remark that battle descriptions are not Euripides' forte, despite his efforts to develop suspense and surprise. To be sure, the first phase of the duel, up to Eteokles' slip, exhibits the poet's mastery of realistic detail, but then he demands more of us than we are able to believe. Eteokles, his calf pierced by the spear, fights on, thrusts his lance into his brother's breast, and when the spearhead is broken off, smashes his opponent's shaft with a stone. Then both reach for their swords. Polyneikes, who fights despite the deep wound in his chest, is done in by a trick of his brother's, but, in the very throes of death, delivers the coup de grâce by a blow to Eteokles' liver.

The second part of the report presents Iokaste's end. She arrives just in time to accept the final loving gesture of the dying Eteokles and hear the last words of Polyneikes. In the tenderness with which Polyneikes remembers his mother, sister, and even his dead brother, the poet once again distinguishes his character from that of Eteokles. His request for burial in the earth of his homeland is important for the final section. Iokaste seizes one of their swords, buries it in her neck and sinks down next to her two sons, embracing them in death.

After the death of the brothers a quarrel arises, each side claiming victory. Another battle is joined, in which the Thebans, after heavy losses, finally put the Argive forces to rout.

After the choral anapests, which really take the place of a stasimon, the conclusion begins, at first in the form of a great threnos. Questions of composition and authorship arise from the introduction of new elements in the plot, or of motifs that had merely been intimated earlier.

The corpses of Iokaste and the brothers are brought on stage. Antigone accompanies them and sings a long monody of lament (1480–1538), at the end of which she calls Oidipous from the house. An amoibaion follows between father and daughter, in which the blind old man learns what has happened, amid much lamentation. His curse—Antigone says it plainly—has brought destruction on his family.

The dividing verses of the chorus leader (1582 f.) here mark a welcome pause.

After a long silence Kreon speaks. Enough lamentation! Eteokles has invested him with supreme authority and the supervision of Antigone's wedding with Haimon, but Oidipous must now depart from the land. Kreon is stretching it a bit when he refers to a specific instruction of Teiresias in support of the banishment (1590), but the prophet's words (886) could probably admit such an inference.

Oidipous replies with a lengthy speech of lament (1595–1638) in which he looks back on his miserable life.[300] Damned from the womb, he has suffered blow upon blow. Thus he believes that the gods persecute him, for even the curse on his sons was the work of daimonic influence. Nowhere do Sophokles and Euripides contrast more sharply than here. The Oidipous of the elder tragedian sets himself against the monstrous will of the gods with a greatness that is not diminished by misery; indeed only then does it prove its real worth. The Oidipous of this play is one shattered by hostile powers, a broken man. Only when, despite his helplessness, he refuses to deny his noble nature and beg Kreon on his knees, does he retain something of the force of his prototype.

Kreon harshly repeats his banishment decree and now forbids anyone to bury Polyneikes on Theban ground under penalty of death.[301] Antigone, however, must remain inside the house until her wedding with Haimon.

And so at the play's end, more and more fuel is added to the fire. We find ourselves in a maze of tensions, which are first released in a stichomythy between Kreon and Antigone (1646–1682).[302] Previously Antigone bemoaned her father in a short speech and asked why Kreon expelled Oidipous and forbade the burial of Polyneikes in his homeland. Kreon mentions the instructions of Eteokles and Polyneikes' crime against the city. Here we note a discrepancy. "Would it not be just to throw him to the dogs?" says Kreon (1650). But Eteokles (776) and Kreon himself just a few lines earlier (1630) had spoken only of forbidding the burial at Thebes. There Kreon says explicitly that the corpse should be hurled beyond the city border. Whoever found it was obliged to give it burial, according to Greek custom. One might ascribe the amplification in our passage, which recalls the Kreon of the *Antigone*, to the heat of the moment, but it remains curious.

Kreon breaks off the discussion (1656): The dead man stays unburied. Then Antigone: I will bury him, even though the city forbids it. The debate has reached an impasse, but one twist is left. Kreon wants Antigone brought into the house, but she will not leave Polyneikes. Kreon attempts to persuade her: This is god's decision, girl, not yours. Antigone answers curtly, and curtly Kreon repeats his decree. Now Antigone invokes the memory of Iokaste, and when Kreon remains unmoved, she begs further for permission to wash the corpse, to bind its wounds. All is denied her, and when she tries to kiss the body, Kreon gives her a new cue: These lamentations do not befit your wedding. Here Antigone leaps to a final, most vehement exchange: Do you think I would be your son's wife, as long as I live? Rather, on the wedding night she would become a Danaid. She wishes to leave the country with her father. Finally Kreon gives in: You are noble, but foolish, and you shall not murder my son. Go! With that he walks off stage.

Without a pause, this stichomythy runs into another between father and daughter (1683–1706). Oidipous is prepared to wander alone in misery, but Antigone does not sway from her resolve to accompany him. Now she leads him to the bodies for a last loving embrace. At the end Oidipous reveals that he knows the goal of his journey. An oracle will be fulfilled, which will lead him near Athens, to Kolonos, sacred to the god of horses.[303]

An amoibaion follows (1710–1757), which in its first and longer section accompanies the departure of the pair with laments. But then (1743) Antigone returns to her decision to bury Polyneikes, even if it costs her life. Oidipous's suggestions, all of which Antigone rejects, are quite difficult: Go to your friends, pray at the altars, go to the mainads of Bromios!

Six tetrameters of Oidipous conclude the scene. They begin with a quote from the *Oidipous Tyrannos* (1524), speak of the sorrows of the man who once solved the Sphinx's riddle, and end with the resignation of man faced with necessity ordained by the gods. Choral anapests requesting the victory prize conclude the play in the same way as in the *Iph. T.* and *Or.*

The structure of this drama was already much criticized in antiquity. The first hypothesis condemns the teichoskopia, the attempt at reconciliation, and the banishment of Oidipous as superfluous "padding." More recent scholars have carried on the hostile tradition, although few are as harsh as Howald, who (171) speaks of total disintegration or total compilation. A good overview of the history of scholarly opinion is offered by W. Riemschneider (op. cit.), who himself attempted to find the unity of the play in its concentration on the fate and salvation of the city. His solution is one-sided and the interpretation leading up to it is occasionally forced. But he deserves credit for liberating our judgment of the play from a purely external point of view. I too must confess that I have formed a different picture of the structure of the *Phoinissai*. Only I do not believe that the city alone provides the context for the whole, but rather the interweaving of its fate with that of the Labdakidai. What Aischylos formally separated into two movements that are brought into harmony only at the finale is shown here as an indissoluble unity from Iokaste's prologue speech and the teichoskopia onward.

In this view the Menoikeus act, placed near the center of the play, is also central to its structure, dividing the rising and falling actions of the drama; the exposition of the situation, the attempt at reconciliation, and the tactical preparations determine the rising action, with the two great messenger acts and the lament as the denouement. The appearance of new motifs in the conclusion is a separate problem.

In addition, Ludwig (130) has well pointed out that the play is clearly divisible into five parts. His schema delineates 638–1066 as the great centerpiece, in which the cycle of the first three stasima frames the second and third epeisodia with the preparation for the decisive action. Moving from the middle outward we find that the first epeisodion corresponds to the two messenger acts, being concerned with the fate of the brothers and involving Iokaste; similarly, the opening section (prologue and parodos) and the conclusion are associated by assigning Antigone a special role.

The main problem of this play, which involves a number of individual questions of interpretation, is this: To what extent is this drama, which was widely read in antiquity and was included in the Byzantine triad together with *Hekabe* and *Orestes*, contaminated by interpolations? In my analysis I repeatedly referred to questions of this sort. The entire complex of problems again became the subject of heated controversy with the publication of Fraenkel's studies (op. cit.). Regardless of to what extent one agrees with his deletions, his article deserves credit for shaking conservative textual criticism (itself a product of the reaction against frivolous athetizing and wild conjectures) from its complacency and for showing the need for a thorough review of the problems. H. Diller and H. Erbse have responded to this challenge in their works cited above.

In questions of this sort one often forgets that by their very nature they cannot be solved along the lines of a mathematical problem—unless, that is, we could exactly determine how many linguistic anomalies, how many contradictions, and how much disregard for dramatic coherence can be expected of a poet. Since no one is capable of drawing such sharp distinctions, there is a whole series of cases in which the recognition of our abiding uncertainty serves the purposes of scholarship much better than doctrinaire decisions. The gradations from total certainty, which may still be achieved in many instances, through the various stages of probability to the realm of pure conjecture, should be present in the mind of every scholar devoted to philology.

Earlier in this analysis I remarked that many of Fraenkel's deletions have met with justified refutation. It is impossible to discuss each individual case here, but the problems of the concluding section do seem to demand a more thorough consideration.

In the discussion care was taken to emphasize the opposition of concurrent motifs present in the final act, which has driven some scholars to perform major surgery. The most radical view is represented by Page (22), who disputes the authenticity of the entire section from 1582 to the end. Friedrich (op. cit.), in deleting lines 1627–1634 and 1639–1672, has removed from the exodos all references to the burial ordinance, and also athetizes Eteokles' instructions on the same matter (774–777). H. Erbse defends them with good reasons. Friedrich, later followed by Fraenkel, tries to prove that Polyneikes' request for burial (1447) is a mere addition for the sake of characterization and of little relevance to the plot. He is rightly contradicted by H. Diller (op. cit., 649).

Schmid (3. 862) already attempted to refute the atheteses listed above; W. Riemenschneider was not yet able to discuss them, but interprets the exodos as genuine. Both propose only one deletion in the final amoibaion; this will be discussed below.[304]

Going further than Friedrich, E. Fraenkel (op. cit., 104 ff.) extends his athetesis beyond 1627–1634 to include the dialogue between Antigone and Kreon (1637–1682). In so doing he assumes that genuine lines have been lost in later revisions.

No one would maintain that the flow of the final section is entirely smooth. The worst offense is the thematic opposition between Antigone's desire to depart into exile with Oidipous and her resolve to bury Polyneikes in defiance of the decree. The scholium on v. 1692 (although identified as Byzantine by Schwartz) already raised the question when Antigone planned to do this. But Diller (op. cit., 648) has correctly pointed out that, if we eliminate the burial prohibition, the vehemence with which Antigone rejects her marriage with Haimon is incomprehensible. Even if, following Friedrich, lines 1676–1678 (in any case also 1675 and 1681 f.) are removed, verse 1673 still remains with its full force.

Thus the various attempts to save the burial motif for the exodos deserve serious consideration. Quite some time ago I. A. Hartung suggested that Oidipous could have died in Athens, after which Antigone could have returned to Thebes; or she might have hidden her father outside Theban territory and come back to bury her brother secretly.[305] H. Erbse (op. cit., 32), who is extreme in his defense of the transmitted text and retains the passage 1737–1757 in its entirety, has selected the first of these possibilities. Thus Oidipous's advice that Antigone should go to her friends, the altars, and the mainads (1747) would refer to the time of her return after her father's death. But this interpretation requires us to fill in so much that we would have to accuse Euripides of creating an obscurity that was bound to cause confusion.

Snell (op. cit., *Ges. Schr.* 181. 2) concurs with the atheteses of those sections in the conclusion that refer to the burial prohibition, and deletes 774–778 as well. But he asserts the importance of verses 1447–1450 and so must speak of the inconsistent handling of this motif as a weakness in the play. We believe that this very consideration, which Snell puts forward so soberly, represents an objection to the proposed deletions.

If there is any solution which avoids such a hypothesis, then it must be sought through a precise interpretation of lines 1643–1672, as was attempted above. After Kreon again asserts that no one will bury Polyneikes (1664), Antigone no longer replies by affirming her decision to inter her brother even at the price of her own life; instead, she begins to plead and then retreats step by step: the final lustrations, the binding of the wounds, the kiss. She has failed in her resolve.[306] But Kreon's mention of her marriage provokes her to further resistance, and here the king must yield and let her depart.

If one accepts this explanation—it seems the most probable—then verse 1745 with the renewed assertion of Antigone's intention to bury her brother is insupportable. Thus we come back to Wilamowitz (*Sitzb. Berlin* 1903, 587), who defended the conclusion but deleted the section from v. 1737 onward, although we need not sacrifice the tetrameters of Oidipous.[307]

In this play, too, scholars have searched for political allusions; Polyneikes has even been seen as Alkibiades. Here J. de Romilly (op. cit.) has settled the matter in a way that is exemplary for the interpretation of all Greek tragedy. She rightly rejects the assumption that individual personalities are portrayed and specific events are reflected in the play. Just as rightly, however, she reckons with the far-reaching influence of the pressing problems of the age. In this view the *Phoinissai* represents the tragedy of the φιλοτιμία and φιλοκερδία (ambition and profit-seeking) which increasingly undermined Athenian democracy. Comparisons with Thukydides are instructive. The antitype is Menoikeus, one of those Euripidean characters who outshines all others in an unstable world.

The Theban cycle of legends also gave Euripides the source material for his *Antigone* (see our commentary on the *Hippolytos*) as well as for his *Oidipous*.[308] Long trochaic lines and the numerous resolutions indicate that this play belongs to the later phase of the poet's career. Its reconstruction is extremely difficult. Neither the fact that fr. adesp. 378N (which Meineke already allotted to this drama) is now confirmed as the opening verse by *P. Oxy.* 2455, fr. 4, nor the five new fragments (*P. Oxy.* 2459, ed. Turner) provide substantial help. Fr. 541N, which is the most important but also the most difficult to place, speaks of the blinding of Oidipous by the servants of Laios. That he is there called the son of Polybos shows that the blinding (apparently the punishment for Laios's murder) preceded and so was separated from the disclosure of his true parentage. It speaks against L. Deubner's reconstruction (op. cit.), which is based on the Pisander scholium to *Phoin.* 1760, that he is obliged to athetize this very fragment. That the Sphinx and her riddle played an important role, either in the plot itself or as part of the background, is indicated by the remark of Malalas (53. 12) that the drama concerned Oidipous, Iokaste, and the Sphinx. This agrees with the first of the new fragments, which features a description of the beast, the iridiscence of whose wings is depicted in a way that anticipates the coloristic effects of the Hellenistic period. Hyginus, *Fab.* 66 f., remains a doubtful source.

The *Orestes*, according to the scholium on v. 371, was produced by Euripides in 408, shortly before his departure for Makedonia.[309] This popular play, later to be assumed into the Byzantine triad, was given a repeat performance by the actor Neoptolemos in 341 (attested by *IG* II² 2320), who in the previous year had performed the *Iphigeneia*.

Like the plays that dramatize a flight to sanctuary, the *Orestes* begins with a tableau. Webster (*Eur.*, 247) believes it was rolled out on the ekkyklema, and thus avoids the notion that the actors arranged themselves before the eyes of the spectators. Orestes lies asleep on a cot, attended by Elektra. She delivers the prologue speech, which begins with a general maxim about man's capacity for suffering (Johansen, 74) and then immediately switches to the genealogy of the Atreidai. With maidenly bashfulness she passes over erotic entanglements (14, 26), but connects the matricide with the command of Apollo. When she speaks of the god's ἀδικία (injustice; 28), this is a shade clearer than the aposiopesis in the *Elektra* (1245). Here the poet introduces a theme that runs throughout the play, but it is in no sense the central motif.[310] The Aischylean questions regarding the dissolution of the ancestral curse, the abolition of the code of blood for blood, and the dual aspect of Orestes' deed are here relegated to the background.

The situation that Elektra now recounts is the same as the one developed in Euripides' *Elektra*, up to the point when the Dioskouroi intervene.

Six days have passed since the cremation of Klytaimestra's corpse; the goddesses whom Elektra fears to name torment Orestes with attacks of madness, between which he lies in tears, covered in his bed. The Argives have expelled the siblings and set a trial for this very day, threatening them with death by stoning. A single hope yet remains. After many wanderings Menelaos has landed at Nauplia (*Odyssey* 3. 311 has him arrive on the day of the funeral banquet); now Elektra anxiously watches for his arrival.

Her speech also brings in two characters decisive for the later course of events. Helen, preceding Menelaos, has come to the palace by night, she the disastrous woman who shuns the families of the victims who fell at Troy for her sake. She weeps for her murdered sister, but she has a consolation in her daughter Hermione, who grew up in Argos while she was living with Paris.

The prologue section dispenses with lyric, but, as in other instances, it does introduce the party of the opposition. Helen emerges from the palace and joins Elektra in conversation. Longer passages of dialogue frame a stichomythy.[311] A hopeless situation! Offerings must be made at Klytaimestra's tomb, but which one of them could do it? Helen dreads the anger of the Argives and must hear Elektra's bitter confirmation of her fear (99). But her presumption that Elektra should bring the offerings to her dead mother betrays a total lack of consideration. Finally Elektra suggests that Hermione run the errand. She reasons plausibly that Klytaimestra raised the girl, but Hermione's temporary absence and her return from the grave are of the utmost importance for the plot. Helen summons her daughter, gives her the offerings, and returns to the palace. The words of hate and contempt that Elektra now speaks reveal the true relationship between these two women, who were careful to observe the forms of courtesy in their conversation. The negative characterization of Helen must be considered when we evaluate the later attack on her.[312]

In our discussion of the *Ion* we were able to establish the poet's tendency in his later works to present the entrance of the chorus in some form of mime. The parodos of the *Orestes* (140–207) offers an especially impressive example. The two predominantly dochmiac strophic pairs are so constructed that in each part a lively dialogue between Elektra and the chorus of Argive women is followed by a passage given exclusively to Elektra. In content the two strophes correspond to one another, as do the antistrophes, the former being filled with concern for the sleep of the ailing Orestes, the latter singing of the distress of the children and the house. In both antistrophes (161, 191) Elektra denounces Apollo as the cause of this misery.

The first epeisodion (208–315) begins with the awakening of Orestes. The blessings of liberating sleep, the process of coming to oneself again from the depths of forgetfulness have rarely been so movingly portrayed as in these six verses. A fairly long distichomythy between brother and sister follows: Elektra's loving care for the sick Orestes is both tenderly and realistically drawn. The motif of hope from the prologue now grows stronger: Menelaos has landed at Nauplia, Menelaos who owes so much to Agamemnon. If only he had come alone! Orestes too hates Helen. His agitation at hearing her name plunges him again into distraction. At the end of the section his madness returns; he takes Elektra for one of the Erinyes. In a long scene he first imagines himself in possession of a bow given him by Apollo, with which he tries to fend off the avenging spirits. This recalls a motif from the *Oresteia* of Stesichoros. Elektra covers her face in grief. The attack passes as swiftly as it came, and now Orestes speaks of his misery and his horrible deed. He denounces Loxias both in his madness (276) and when he regains his senses (285). He goes so far as to say that Agamemnon himself, had he been able to ask him, would have pleaded with him to spare his mother. The principal accent of this masterful scene, which depicts the situation of the siblings, is on their relationship to each other. In a sea of pain and hostility they have only each other; alone they are nothing. Thus Orestes demands that his sister get some rest, and thus Elektra hesitates to leave her brother, until she finally yields to his wish. The tenderness of this scene must not be forgotten in the tumult of the wild events to come. Elektra's οὔτοι μεθήσω (I shall not leave you; 262) recalls Apollo's οὔτοι προδώσω (I shall not betray you) in the *Eumenides* (64). But here a human speaks the helping word.

The first stasimon (316–347) is one of those short and generally pertinent odes that occur beside the "dithyrambic" stasima, particularly in the later plays. The single pair of strophes concludes the presentation of the siblings' condition—suffering, danger, madness, and the bond between brother and sister—before livelier movement begins. The chorus appeals to the Erinyes (α) and Zeus (α'), pleads for Orestes, and bemoans the fate of the House of Tantalos.

The second epeisodion (356–806) leads Orestes out of his sickness and torments and through remorse sets him on the road to action. In Menelaos he meets with the world that opposes him; in Pylades, a helpful friend joins his side.

Menelaos comes in with an entrance monologue that portrays him, just returned home, under the impression of the news of the recent events. At Cape Malea the sea-daimon Glaukos (a duplicate of Proteus in the *Odyssey*) announced to him Agamemnon's death, and on landing in Nauplia he learned of Orestes' matricide. In a long stichomythy framed by the boy's fervent pleas, Menelaos is made aware of the situation. In this sickly and haggard young man he was unable to recognize his nephew, who was only a child when the fleet left for Troy. Now he learns of Orestes' pangs of conscience, how he imagined the vision of the three malevolent goddesses (he avoids their name), when by night he and his helper Pylades collected his mother's bones from the ashes. Menelaos shrinks back from the stricken youth: It is not terrible for one to suffer who has done terrible deeds (413). We note a first intimation of his later retreat. But Orestes defends himself by invoking the command of the god, who now admittedly tarries with his aid. But such is the way of the gods, by whom man finds himself abandoned (420).

Menelaos is a cautious man and a good reckoner. He wants to know how the city stands on Orestes' case. Here the news is all bad. The father of Palamedes (the audience would recall the second play of the trilogy of 415) and the followers of Aigisthos are inciting the townspeople; Orestes has no prospect for the scepter of Argos (Menelaos takes note that the leadership is open), and he must stand trial for his and Elektra's life. Menelaos's last word is one of regret (417). We cannot say how he would decide if forced to make an immediate decision, but at this moment Tyndareos enters, the father of Klytaimestra.

Orestes is overcome with shame before this man, who once lavished love on him and whose daughter he slew. The old man immediately reproaches Menelaos for speaking with the murderer, but here he meets with opposition and an appeal to the bonds of family. Now a strange agon begins. Tyndareos wants to destroy Orestes, but his words are addressed to Menelaos, who is given the role of umpire, from which, however, he shrinks back.

Klytaimestra's father does not conceal her immorality, but he makes his claim as the defender of nomos. This would have demanded that Orestes banish his mother from the house and bring her to trial. Disregard for the law must lead to an endless chain of murder upon murder. Only near the end, overwhelmed by emotion does he turn to Orestes: How did you feel when your mother bared her breast in supplication? Then again with a harsh warning to Menelaos: Take not his side, or you will never see Sparta again! Addressed in such a way Menelaos maintains an eloquent silence. After two dividing verses of the chorus leader, Orestes begins a long speech in his own defense. Masterfully Euripides conjures up a man who must overcome serious misgivings, but whose passion increases steadily as he speaks; Orestes shifts from the acknowledgment of the ambiguous nature of his deed (546, 563) to the assertion of its absolute justice, even of its advantages for all of Greece (564–572). How differently Orestes speaks in this battle for his life from when he was alone with his conscience—this becomes clear if we compare the verses about Agamemnon mentioned above (288 ff.) with 580, in which he speaks of the rancor with which his father would have persecuted him, had he not avenged his death.[313]

This Orestes, who grasps at every argument, invokes the greater value of the father, like Apollo and Athena in the trial of the *Eumenides*; cites his mother's infidelity with Aigisthos; and goes so far as to impute the guilt for the whole disaster to Tyndareos, who begot such daughters. His strongest defense, Apollo's command, he saves for the end. The divine sphere is no more excluded in this play than in the *Hippolytos*, but here the course of events unfolds on the human plane.

The chorus leader wanly supports his speech with a condemnation of women (605 f.), but Tyndareos bursts into a rage. Now he himself will exhort the Argives to stone Orestes and Elektra, who spurred her brother on. To Elektra he allots the greater share of guilt, a reminiscence of her role in the earlier play. Once more he intimidates Menelaos with dire threats: He must choose between friendship and hatred. If he chooses the second, he will never reach Sparta again.[314]

The "arbiter" Menelaos paces back and forth, pondering the situation. He has still not reached a decision, or does not know how to express it. It is an extraordinarily fine touch that in his indecisiveness the cowardly Menelaos demands that Orestes speak, since he cannot endure the youth's silence that awaits his decision. A sort of post-agon now takes place, in which Orestes breaks into the silence of Menelaos with a long speech (640–679). Now he presses his claims with insistence. He demands χάρις (an act of kindness) for χάρις, as Hekabe did of Odysseus. The accounts he draws up are strange: Granted, his deed involves him in injustice, but Agamemnon, his father, also took injustice upon him when he marched on Troy for the sake of a woman. Ten years! He only needs help for a single day! Nor need Hermione be sacrificed, as Iphigeneia was (for Menelaos). Then, seeing resistance in the looks or gestures of Menelaos, he implores him in the name of Helen—himself stung with shame at such a plea—and again in the name of the shade of Agamemnon.

The chorus leader seconds his request, but Menelaos responds with a speech that is a masterpiece of characterization; a timeless exemplar of the speeches of all those who shrink from straightforward action: He would gladly help, if he only had the resources. As it is, however, he uses images of fire and seafaring to demonstrate the necessity of abandoning all hope of force and trying instead friendly persuasion. Then he leaves.

Orestes knows where he stands. The only attempt at salvation that he believed possible, the first to be undertaken in this drama, has proved a failure because of Menelaos's worthlessness. The fate of the siblings appears sealed, when suddenly Pylades enters, a true friend after the traitorous relative. It is significant that here, where the plot is forcibly lifted up from an absolute nadir (προδέδομαι, 722), the meter changes to trochaic tetrameter.

Brief speeches surround a long stichomythy, whose last third is broken into antilabai. First, Orestes describes the situation to his friend and recounts the collapse of his one hope. Pylades inquires about Helen; we are reminded of her presence throughout the play. He himself tells how he was banished by his father, Strophios, for participating in the matricide. Their deliberations begin with the antilabai. Orestes' decision to speak before the Argive assembly gives cause for renewed hope. And should the road not lead to salvation, then at least it would lead to an honorable death.

The poet does not wish the transition from the image of the ailing Orestes to that of the ruthless man of action to appear too abrupt. So in the conclusion of this scene Orestes expresses his anxiety that an attack of madness might thwart his plan. The motif also serves another function: These words of concern elicit from Pylades an affirmation of loyal friendship that forms the sharpest possible contrast to the failure of Orestes' blood relative.

The second stasimon (807–843) is again short and contains but one triad. The ancient prosperity of the Tantalids has vanished since the quarrel over the golden ram and the banquet of Thyestes (α); terrible is the deed of matricide, despite all its ambiguity (α'); he who spilt such blood has fallen victim to the Eumenides (ep.).

Since the lyrical section starting with v. 960 assumes the place of a stasimon, the messenger act may be defined as the third epeisodion (844–959).

The opening is composed as an encounter scene. Elektra emerges from the house, anxious to know where Orestes is, when the messenger comes in to report the unhappy news of the death sentence. The description of the popular assembly with its succession of speakers is an outstanding achievement. The messenger is an honest peasant, a devoted member of Agamemnon's household, who reports from a sound point of view.

First to speak was Talthybios, the herald, who curried favor with the powerful, who spoke sinuously and was in league with Aigisthos's friends. Then Diomedes tried to achieve a just verdict by suggesting exile. But a smooth-talking speaker, no true Argive (a double of the townsman in the *Bakchai*; 717), whom Tyndareos sent to the gathering, declared that Orestes and Elektra should be stoned. He was opposed by a stout-hearted man, an αὐτουργός (one who lives by his work), who seldom visits the city, one of those who preserve the strength of the land. He makes the challenging proposal that they should crown Orestes for his deed, for no man will wish to go off to war if he knows his wife will be seduced by those who stay at home. The detailed, positive characterization of this man, who reminds us of the αὐτουργός in the *Elektra* and puts us in mind of the praise for the middle class in the *Suppliants* (244), is of great importance for our evaluation of the play. Of course the matricide should not be considered vindicated or unproblematic, but the fact remains it is so judged by a man of preeminent worth.[315] The dialectic must be kept open; we must not view Orestes simply as a guilty criminal.

The emissary of Tyndareos has carried the vote; Orestes can only persuade the assembly to spare Elektra and himself from stoning, that they might take their own lives.

The report is followed by a triad (960–1011) which is best allotted exclusively to Elektra, in accordance with the MSS.[316] She begins with wild gestures of lamentation, bewails the race of Pelops, which is perishing utterly through divine disfavor and the death sentence of the citizens (dual motivation), and, in the highly elaborate verses of the lengthy epode, she traces their catastrophic history from Tantalos to herself.

The conclusion is divided by the lyric dialogue (1246–1310) and repeats in the section just before this (1018–1245) the vigorous movement before the messenger act, but now the tone is greatly heightened: deep depression and the certainty of death are succeeded by new confidence and a new will to action.

Choral anapests announcing Orestes introduce a distichomythy with a concluding speech of Orestes (1018–1068), in which moving gestures reveal the inner bonds between the siblings marked for death. Orestes first recoils from touching his sister; he will not soften in the face of death. When Elektra asks to be killed by him he, who earlier had spilt his mother's blood, shrinks back. But his hardness has finally dissolved, and the siblings unite in a fervent embrace.

Still within the distichomythy, as it is drawing to a close, a new movement is foreshadowed in Elektra's question about Menelaos's behavior at the assembly. Orestes informs her that their uncle failed to appear and sees himself faced with certain death. He is about to deliver the fatal blow—already he requests that his friend tend to their corpses when Pylades intercedes with an ἐπίσχες (stop! 1069). In a short stichomythy followed by paired speeches, he declares that he will die with his friend. Orestes refuses. When he says that Pylades still has a house and a homeland (1076), the poet counts on our forgetting that Strophios banished his son. The motif could not be used in this brief friendly agon.

At the close of this section Pylades gives the dialogue a decisive turn: Since we must die, then we should devise some way for Menelaos to share in our misfortune. In a fairly long stichomythy (1100–1131), in which Pylades takes the lead, they develop a plan to kill Helen. As if in supplication, but with swords hidden under their garments, the friends will enter the palace; the cowardly Phyrgian slaves will present no obstacle. This prepares us for the long scene with the Phrygian.

It is characteristic of the formal elements of tragedy that the plan is first developed in a stichomythy, and then evaluated in a speech by Pylades. No longer branded a matricide, no, but as killer of the despised Helen, Orestes will be celebrated. The conclusion of the speech is noteworthy. If the plot to kill Helen fails, then the friends will burn down the palace and die in the flames (1050). For the first time smoke rises between the verses. But at the end another aspect emerges, perhaps already intimated in v. 1141. The deed will not only wreak revenge on Menelaos; it might mean certain death, but it might also bring salvation. The chorus leader indicates agreement by condemning Helen, but Orestes praises his friend who (a new thought) once also contrived the destruction of Aigisthos. At the end of his speech the idea recurs that, beyond revenge on Menelaos, this path could lead to their rescue.

It would be a sharp deviation from the Euripidean style of intrigue if the plotting were left to men alone. Elektra steps in. First in a stichomythy, then in a lengthy dialogue with Orestes (Pylades joins in at v. 1209), she unfolds a plan to take Hermione hostage when she returns from Klytaimestra's grave. The girl will protect the three from the wrath of Menelaos. Elektra's suggestion also aims at escape: Menelaos will submit and intercede to have the death sentence annulled.

Now Orestes, wholly bent on action, gives the orders. Elektra must remain before the house to guard the friends and wait for Hermione. Then he prays to Agamemnon, and all three voices unite in an invocation to the dead man.[317] Motifs from the great scene of the *Choephoroi* are here combined within a very short space.

The following lengthy melodramatic dialogue between Elektra and the chorus (1246–1310, composed as a triad) is so closely drawn into the course of the plot that it cannot truly be called a substitute for a stasimon, despite its transitional function.

Strophe and antistrophe are again strongly suggestive of mime. In excited dochmiacs (trimeters are inserted twice in each strophe), Elektra stations the two semi-choruses at the parodoi to guard the entrances to the house. The antistrophe presents their scouting, an alarm, and then reassurance. The epode is constructed as a triptych. Elektra expresses impatience and concern—excitedly she echoes Helen's fearful cries from within—and then accompanies the deed with wild shouts of encouragement. The dactyls in v. 1303 create a special effect.

A brief Hermione scene (1311–1352) interrupts the broad lyric passages of this section of the drama. Skillfully Elektra averts possible danger. Hermione has heard a scream from the house, but Elektra tells her that the friends are inside imploring Helen to help them. Again a motif serves a double function. Hermione's fear is allayed; unsuspecting she walks into the house and into the jaws of the trap; but at the same time the poet uses this opportunity to characterize the pure young girl as sympathetic, obliging, and sensitive. In such characters Euripides distilled what was left of his faith in humanity; they shine like crystal amongst the bleak rubble.

What the poet daringly pulled off with the greatest success in the *Bakchai* is avoided in this play. He does not present two messenger-speeches in trimeter; instead, he composes the second, reporting the attack on Helen, as a bizarre lyric passage of richly varied meters. A strophe and antistrophe of the chorus (1353–1365, 1537–1549a) surround the extensive monody of the Phrygian slave with the subsequent trochaic scene between him and Orestes.

The strophe of the chorus, as is generally the case in this play, is integrated into the plot. With noise and shouting the women try to drown out the events inside the house so that the Argives will not interfere. Just punishment has been meted out to Helen.

The entrance of the Phrygian slave, who is fleeing in panic from the violence within, has caused a widespread misconception that arose in antiquity and persisted long thereafter. Today, we would like to think the problem has been solved once and for all by A. M. Dale.[318] The Phrygian tells (1371) of his escape over the cedar rafters and out between the triglyphs. From this the scholiast concluded that such acrobatics were visible, and that lines 1366–1368, which suggest the slave's entrance through the door, were only added later by a more cautious actor. Murray and now W. Biehl agree with the athetesis. N. Wecklein and others believed the scholiast and drew the conclusion that the Phrygian jumped down from the roof of the skene. A. M. Dale rightly defended the questionable verses and refers the slave's words to his path of escape within the house.

The aria of the Phrygian is divided by trimeters of the chorus leader into six perikopai. The richly ornamental style, with its numerous repetitions and its exaggerated commotion, points in the direction of the new Attic dithyramb and the *Persians* of Timotheos.[319]

The first two parts of the great Phrygian aria are filled with fear and lamentation; in the third he begins his dramatically constructed narrative: How the friends came up to Helen, Orestes leading her to the hearth of her ancestor Pelops while Pylades chased off the Phrygian slaves and locked them in, and how Helen seemed doomed to fall by the sword of her enemies. The Phrygians broke down the doors where they were confined, but Pylades proved the superiority of the Greeks in the ensuing battle. With skillful timing Euripides here inserts the arrival of Hermione. The friends fall upon her, capture her, but when they turn again to Helen, she has vanished. The Phrygian has escaped in confusion.

The chorus leader sees Orestes coming from the house, and now the poet appends to this peculiar messenger-speech a burlesque scene in trochaic tetrameters, which exists mostly for its own sake, since the removal of the Phrygian might have been accomplished much more simply without this cat-and-mouse game that Orestes plays with him. He makes the panic-stricken slave swear that he despises Helen, and terrifies him with threats of death. When Orestes asks him whether he fears he will turn to stone at the sight of his sword, as if it were some Gorgon, and the slave replies that what a Gorgon is he doesn't know, but what he's afraid of is turning into a corpse, the grotesque joke seems better suited to comedy. Orestes lets the wretch scamper off and waits for Menelaos. Here again the hope of rescue overshadows the revenge motif: if Menelaos wants to avenge Helen and refuses to save the three, he will see Hermione's corpse as well.

Here follows the antistrophe of the chorus, in which they oddly consider informing the city but finally decide to keep quiet. From the house they see smoke rising, for torches are being lit within to set the palace on fire. The god will decide the issue; a curse lies on the house since the fall of Myrtilos.

In five trochaic tetrameters (1549–1553) the chorus leader announces the approach of Menelaos and the danger to the conspirators. Menelaos enters in a rage; he has heard from some panic-stricken fellow (probably the Phrygian) that Helen is not dead, but has been whisked away; however, he imagines that this is some trick of the matricidal Orestes. He is about to have his servants batter down the doors, but there on the roof stands Orestes with Pylades;[320] he holds his sword to the throat of Hermione. He warns Menelaos not to touch the door, for he is prepared to smash in his head with a piece of masonry. A stichomythy (1576–1617) develops, whose tempo accelerates with the antilabai. Orestes is now master of the situation. He regrets that he was unable to kill Helen; he has banished all remorse for the matricide, and the impotent threats and deprecations of the furious Menelaos at the locked door he answers blow for blow. He threatens two things: to burn the palace and to kill Hermione. His demands are quite clear: Menelaos must go to the Argives and persuade them to revoke the death sentence. Trapped, Menelaos can see no way out and finally surrenders: ἔχεις με (you have me; 1617). We might expect Orestes to snatch up this confession eagerly, but he speaks only words of contempt: You've caught yourself by your own wickedness. He orders Elektra and Pylades to set the building on fire. Enraged, Menelaos calls for the help of the Argives, from whom the matricide would wrest his life by force. Of the prevailing confusion here of opposing motives, we shall speak later.

Apollo appears just in time. He can hardly be imagined at the same level on the roof as the group around Orestes, but on a theologeion raised above them.[321] The machine is another possibility that cannot be excluded. The god has Helen next to him, for Menelaos addresses her at v. 1673. Therefore, we cannot follow Murray and Paley in deleting lines 1631 f. as an actor's interpolation; thus it becomes understandable that Apollo speaks of Helen's departure in the future tense (1637, 1684). She is still visible. But the end of verse 1631 ἐν αἰθέρος πτυχαῖς (in the clefts of the aether) cannot be retained, since according to v. 1636 Helen has not yet been brought there.[322]

With swift strokes Apollo gives everything a different appearance—in fact, he very nearly turns it all upside down. Helen, maligned throughout the whole play, is united as a goddess with Kastor and Polydeukes into a trinity that actually had a cult.[323] Now we learn that the gods needed her only to instigate a war for the purpose of relieving the earth of excess population, a motif familiar from the opening of the *Kypria*.

Orestes is to dwell for a year in Arkadian Parrhasia, but then he is to go to Athens, where a tribunal of the gods (not of the polis) will exonerate him. Hermione, whose life he just threatened, he will take to wife, for Neoptolemos, who will demand that the god account for his father's death, is doomed to die. Elektra and Pylades will become a happily married couple; Menelaos will rule in Sparta, Orestes in Argos. As if the god had just remembered that the Argive citizens had wanted to stone Orestes only hours before, he adds that he will put everything in order, for it was he who ordered the matricide.

Orestes recants his doubts about the god, releases Hermione, and immediately asks for her hand. Everyone is obedient and all goes rather quickly. With anapests exhorting them all to honor Eirene, most beautiful of the goddesses (Athens had been at war for an endlessly long time), and again proclaiming the apotheosis of Helen, Apollo takes his leave. The familiar request for victory (*Iph. T., Phoin.*) concludes the play.

After the broad depiction of the terrible situation in which the siblings find themselves (1–347), the structure of the play is determined by three attempts at escape. Already in the exposition (52, 67, 241) the coming of Menelaos is announced; they expect help from him as their nearest blood relative. This hope is thwarted by the intervention of Tyndareos; after his departure the first low mark is reached: οἴμοι προδέδομαι (alas, I am betrayed; 722). A new path is opened by Pylades. Orestes must prevail over the Argive assembly. Here the plot advances behind the scenes, and in the messenger act his failure becomes apparent; again all hope seems shattered and death inevitable: ἐπ' ἔργον ... πορεύομαι (I go to do the deed; 1068). And again Pylades provides the impetus for new movement. Revenge on Menelaos is what he first suggests, but it soon becomes clear that this very revenge can lead to rescue. The turbulence of the conclusion results from the entanglement of these two viewpoints. To extort the saving intercession of Menelaos, it would suffice to threaten Helen and Hermione, but the traitorous relative must also be punished by the death of his wife. Thus a situation arises that is only set right by the sheer force of Apollo's intervention.

The concluding remark of the hypothesis was long regarded as authoritative for the evaluation of the play: it was a great theatrical success (which we can easily believe), but it portrayed only evil characters, with the exception of Pylades. The dark shadow cast over the trio of supposed desperadoes was happily dispelled by W. Krieg's dissertation. Long before, Jakob Burckhardt had protested against a one-sided interpretation of the play, but one must read how Pohlenz (1. 420) still could rebuke him to gauge the distance that had yet to be covered. When W. Schmid (3. 609) speaks of the sympathetic characterization of brother and sister, and Rivier (141) designates as the central theme "la lutte pour la vie des trois êtres abandonnés dans une cité hostile," the influence of the mistaken judgment of the hypothesis seems at an end. Of course we should not fall into the opposite extreme and fail to recognize that the characters of this play are far removed from the grand gestures of a time when heroic sensibilities were more demanding. But the fervent love of Orestes and Elektra, the self-sacrificing friendship of Pylades, the upright stance of the countryman at the assembly, the unblemished childlike nature of Hermione, shine out the more brightly through the smoky gloom of a world burning with hatred and revenge. The pessimism with which Euripides observes the broad landscape of humanity clearly intensified before his departure from Athens. The most evil character in the play is Menelaos. Aristotle (*Poet.* 15, 1454a) saw in him the paradigm of a character unnecessarily portrayed as base. A strange misunderstanding, for it is just his human failing that functions in the play as igniting the will to live, to resist, in an Orestes who has been shattered by the murder of his mother.

The section just before the appearance of Apollo poses the most difficult problem of the play. First of all, the situation must be grasped clearly. Orestes has put Menelaos under intense pressure and has left no doubt that Hermione's life is at stake. Faced with this threat, Menelaos's ἔχεις με (you have me) is a total capitulation. It must not be minimized by the assertion that Menelaos is only conceding that his back is to the wall and shows no trace of submission (Strohm, 88. 2; similarly W. Krieg, op. cit., 27; now G. A. Seeck, op. cit., 13). Nor can we agree with A. Spira that he collapses without having made a decision.[324] This ἔχεις με cannot be separated from the previous, extremely concrete demands of Orestes. And even if Menelaos were only saying that his back is to the wall, we should still expect that Orestes would now exploit this admission and ask how far his opponent would be willing to go. Instead he gives the order to burn down the palace.

The scholars of the nineteenth century, always handy with scissors and paste, knew exactly what to do here: they cut verses 1618–1620 from the play. Page (54) concurred and counted the lines among the actors' interpolations *spectaculi causa.* Recently, in a thorough and quite clever study, Seeck (op. cit.) experimentally tried to solve the problem with atheteses. He shows that in order to deal with the fire motif, one must also remove the earlier passages in which it was foreshadowed (1149 f., 1541–1544, 1573, 1593–1596). Seeck presents all the arguments against each individual passage, but we are pleased to find that the results of this experiment (expressly designated as such) led him to conclude that the problem cannot be solved in this manner.

Just as little, however, can be accomplished through a purely psychological interpretation. This is especially true of Pohlenz's explanation (1. 419; 2. 172) that Orestes rejects the possibility of escape because of his overwhelming lust for revenge.[325] And it is not for us to interpolate a thought of Orestes—never once intimated in the text—that no help could be expected from this miserable Menelaos anyway.[326] Did he not undertake the entire affair for the express purpose of forcing Menelaos to intercede? A more reasonable solution is offered by Strohm (88. 2), now followed also by Steidle (116). The threat of arson pushes the extortion of Menelaos one step further. But if this step swiftly and without hesitation "must lead to the complete submission of a Menelaos who was already convinced of his defeat," then we would expect that his reaction would be to yield even further in that direction, not to call to the Argives for help in an angry outburst (1621–1624). Then, too, he would appear to act quite incomprehensibly, for in sharp contrast to his ἔχεις με, he now risks the life of Hermione. Orestes can thrust at any moment.

After all these deliberations we stand by a technical explanation, unburdened by psychological complications.[327] With an instinctive flair for theatrical effect the poet carries all the conflicting elements in the situation to their extreme, and there seems to be no viable way to resolve them. No such way is needed either, of course, for just then Apollo arrives and provides a solution by force.

Again we must deal with the problem of the mythical world's relationship to the reality of life as represented in the play. Steidle strongly emphasized the god's role in the drama. In his view, Orestes' and Elektra's special situation is based on the very fact that they believe Apollo abandoned them long ago. This is undoubtedly correct. But we think that it is no mere quibble over words if we assert that while the god's behavior does belong to the mythical background of the play, which Conacher (218) also stresses, it is not the main subject. That human fates are determined by the basic incommensurability of unfathomable divine will (Steidle, 114) certainly provides a backdrop for Euripidean tragedy; but unlike in Sophokles, it is no more than this. What this play tries to show has been excellently formulated by Pohlenz (1. 412) in the title "Man in the struggle against his fellow men." Again we find that the mythical element can be detached (a situation unthinkable in Sophokles), for the drama might just as easily be presented as the struggle of a murderer fighting for his life against the world around him. Of course this does not hold for the conclusion— which we describe only as brought about by force, but which certainly allows one to understand why recent scholars see only irreality and irony in Euripides' denouements. Our opinion was also expressed by Webster (Eur., 252): "Here Euripides reserves traditional mythology for prologue, lyric and epilogue."

Euripides produced *Orestes* in the spring of 408, while still in Athens; very soon after this he left for the court of Archelaos in Makedonia. The news of his death reached Athens before the Dionysia of 406. But this short span of time was an extremely productive one for the poet, and from it we possess two of his greatest works. Of course we can little regret the loss of the *Archelaos*, which, according to Zielinski's conjecture, formed a trilogy with the *Temenos* and the *Temenidai*.[328] Of these two plays we can only say that their plot was taken from the legend of the return of the Herakleidai. It can be conjectured that the murder of Temenos by his sons played some role. They felt wronged by their father, who preferred their brother-in-law Deiphontes, the husband of Hyrnetho. The story in Pausanias (2. 28) of the attempt of Temenos's sons (the youngest, Agraios, did not join in the plot) to separate Hyrnetho from her husband by slandering Deiphontes and afterward to abduct her, all of which resulted in their death as well as that of their sister, might be based on the *Teme-nidai*.

We know more about the *Archelaos*, from whose prologue we possess two fragments separated by a short lacuna, with a long genealogical list (fr. 228N and *P. Hamb.* 118a).[329] The speaker was Archelaos, an invented ancestor of the Makedonian king, who in this genealogy proves to be the son of Temenos and a descendant of Herakles. Like the ancestor, the plot was probably also invented; it can be reconstructed confidently from Hyginus, *Fab.* 219. There we learn that Archelaos, expelled by his brothers, is received in Thrace by King Kisseus, who was hard pressed by his enemies. Archelaos liberates him in return for the promise of the king's daughter in marriage. But when he comes for his reward, Kisseus tries to kill him in a camouflaged pit filled with fire. However, a servant of the king reveals the trickery and Kisseus himself falls victim. We would also extract from Hyginus Apollo as deus ex machina who sent Archelaos to Makedonia. A goat shall guide him and he will name his city Aigai in its honor.

The scholium on Aristoph. *Ran.* 67 states with reference to the didaskaliai that after the poet's death his son produced the plays *Iphigeneia at Aulis, Alkmeon*, and the *Bakchai*. According to the *Suda* (s.v. Euripides) it was his nephew, also named Euripides, who won a posthumous prize for the poet with these plays.

It is as if Euripides in these three dramas once again displayed the entire incredible range of his creative powers. The plot of the *Alkmeon in Korinth*,[330] thus designated to distinguish it from the *Alkmeon in Psophis* that we mentioned in connection with the *Alkestis*, is given by Apollodoros (3. 7. 7), who specifically cites Euripides as his source. Alkmeon has left Amphilochos and Tisiphone, his two children by Manto, in Korinth with King Kreon, whose wife later sells the girl to her own father as a slave. Alkmeon returns to Korinth with Tisiphone, where they meet Amphilochos; thus we have three immediate kinfolk, none of whom knows of his or her close bond to the others. How Alkmeon was threatened by Kreon and how the anagnorisis took place, we cannot say. The allotment of individual fragments, all carefully discussed by Van Looy, to one of the *Alkmeon* dramas remains problematic. In our play Apollo spoke the prologue, and perhaps also appeared at the end. Although much remains unclear, the *Alkmeon in Korinth* clearly belongs among the dramas of the poet's later career, in which mortals must endure the many vicissitudes of Tyche.

In the later plays of Euripides we have often been able to discern a new instability within the human psyche, and this factor determines to an especial degree his *Iphigeneia at Aulis*.[331] Aischylos and Sophokles had dealt with the subject before him. We know that in Sophokles' drama Odysseus played an essential role in the plot to sacrifice Iphigeneia, and this is also the version that is presupposed in the *Iphigeneia in Tauris* (24). The fact that Odysseus remains in the background in Euripides' play makes possible the role of Menelaos in the opening section.

In its transmitted form the prologue of the play poses a difficult problem. In an anapestic section (1–48) Agamemnon summons an aged servant from his tent in the middle of the night, bewails the care-worn lot of great men, and is questioned by the old man about the cause of his anxiety and his strange doings with a writing tablet, which he inscribes and then erases, seals and then reopens. This is followed by an iambic prologue in the usual form (49–114), in which Agamemnon recounts at some length the events leading up to the expedition against Troy and reveals the background information essential to the plot: Kalchas's announcement that Artemis demands the sacrifice of his daughter Iphigeneia, then the trick devised under the pressure of Menelaos that the girl be summoned to the camp under the pretext of marriage to Achilleus, finally Agamemnon's remorse and his attempt to prevent the arrival of Iphigeneia by sending a second letter countermanding the first.

Now anapests begin again (115–163), in which Agamemnon discloses the contents of his letter to the servant and orders him to make haste.

It has often been asserted that Euripides actually wrote this prologue in the form transmitted by the manuscripts, but the stylistic break between the individual sections seems simply too harsh.[332] The authenticity of the anapests, which Murray ascribed to the younger Euripides without mistaking their great beauty, was successfully defended by E. Fraenkel (op. cit.). The anapestic prologue of the *Andromeda* shows that Euripides experimented in his later plays. Of course the two anapestic passages do not form a complete prologue; we must assume with Fraenkel that a middle section, with the information about the intrigue, has somehow been lost. The iambic prologue is perhaps best explained by the conjecture that two different versions were found among the poet's manuscripts after his death. Conacher makes a similar point (253. 11).[333]

The parodos (164–302) is the longest in any extant tragedy. In form and content it falls into two parts. In a triad in aeolic meters the women of Chalkis sing of their desire to see the Greek army in Aulis. They have already recognized some of the famous heroes, including Achilleus, as he competed in a race with his chariot. The entire epode is devoted to him, corresponding to his later importance for the plot.

This section is followed by a catalogue of ships in trochaic strophic pairs, with a long epode that should not be forced into a strophic arrangement. The poetic quality of this passage is below standard.[334] The depiction of the ornamentation on some of the ships' sterns was modeled on the description of the shields' blazonry in Aischylos's *Seven*. The expansive survey of the Greek troops does serve a real purpose. The will of the army and the respect it demands are present as important factors from the very start and maintain their significance as events unfold.

The first epeisodion (303–542) begins with the entrance of two characters involved in a violent dispute—a technique of scene opening that is quite common later in comedy. Menelaos has caught the servant on his way to Mykenai, and at the end of a short stichomythy he snatches from him the letter intended for Klytaimestra. Hearing his cries, Agamemnon comes out of his tent and a quarrel develops between the two brothers. In the familiar schema, two stichomythies frame the agon speeches, but while the meter already shifts to trochaics at the beginning of the first, the concluding stichomythy returns to iambic trimeters, as the heat of the fight cools.

Menelaos was watching for the arrival of Iphigeneia, so impatiently does he await the victim. Now he brings the old man to call Agamemnon to account. We must simply accept the fact that he only takes away the letter before our eyes (314), yet, from the next verses, already knows the contents. He will publicize it to the whole Greek army, and in a long speech, he reproaches his brother for his blind ambition and his feeble inconstancy: He curried favor to win the generalship of the army, but then turned against his old friends; he despaired at being stranded in Aulis and greeted the oracle of Kalchas as a solution. He himself used trickery to bring Iphigeneia to the camp, though no one forced him to do so (360). The contradiction between this and the iambic prologue (97) is obvious.

Agamemnon has a ready reply for his brother. Menelaos' only real reason for the expedition is Helen, whom this uxorious husband wants to have back. Twice Menelaos asserts that the mission against Troy was undertaken for the sake of all the Greeks (370, 411). The first statement is wholly ignored by Agamemnon; the second statement he dismisses with vehemence: A god has willed that Greece share your sickness!

In parting, Menelaos threatens to seek other means and other friends, when suddenly a messenger arrives. His entrance is all the more dramatic for coming in mid-verse. The messenger announces the approach of Iphigeneia, who—quite contrary to the plan of the king—is accompanied by Klytaimestra and the infant Orestes. With good reason the poet lingers over the broad description of the soldiers' jubilation and their eager attempts to explain her arrival. For the second time after the parodos we see the masses, ready at any moment to assume a decisive role in the course of events. The irony of the situation is also played out at some length: everyone expects a feast; fortunate people in the fullness of life naturally attract the eyes of all. In the anapests of the prologue (22) we heard Agamemnon bemoan the deceptive luster of high honors, and soon (446) he will speak poignantly of the advantages of ignoble birth.

Agamemnon curtly dismisses the messenger and then breaks into bitter complaints. Klytaimestra has come along against his will. How can he face her? But the encounter with his daughter will also be unbearable. What was planned at a distance as a trick becomes in actuality an unspeakable horror.

The chorus leader joins in the lament, explaining that she is touched by the suffering of strangers. Then suddenly Menelaos asks for the hand of his brother, and we hear from his speech that he too is deeply moved by the king's plight. This Menelaos is as soft as his brother—it should not be thought that he is being hypocritical. He is serious about abandoning the sacrifice of Iphigeneia and giving her back to her father. Let Agamemnon dismiss the army!

The chorus leader praises his words, as does his brother. But then comes the surprise: Agamemnon now declares that the sacrifice is inevitable. He feels constrained by an ananke, a secularized ananke, which is no longer the great force imbued with divinity, as in Aischylos, but one resulting from external circumstances.[335] The following stichomythy with a concluding speech by the king shows how the sides have been completely reversed in this world of unstable characters and wavering decisions. Now the army emerges as the decisive factor. Kalchas will not keep silence, and, even if he is eliminated, Odysseus will betray the secret. Here we catch a glimpse of the role Odysseus once played as the instigator of the plan. The multitude will demand Iphigeneia's death. If Agamemnon refuses, they will act without regard for him, his position, or his life. The plan to save his daughter has failed miserably; only one thing remains in his power; Klytaimestra must learn nothing of the intended sacrifice; he wants to spare himself her tears.

The first stasimon (543–589) consists of a single triad. Strophe and epode correspond loosely in content, in that the strophe weighs the joys and disasters connected with the gifts of Kypris, while the epode sings of Paris, who won Helen and plunged the nations into war. In the intervening antistrophe Euripides returns to an idea that once captivated him (Hek., Suppl.). He now sees man's physis and his upbringing in a certain balance as the deciding factors constituting his moral worth; τό τε γὰρ αἰδεῖσθαι σοφία (to feel awe is wisdom) sounds like the wisdom in restraint praised in the Bakchai.

The second epeisodion (607–750) is introduced by anapests that pose some difficulty. The second verse group (598–606) is easily comprehensible. The women of Chalkis bid each other (or are bidden by the chorus leader) to help Klytaimestra out of her carriage. However, the previous anapests (590–597) call Iphigeneia "my mistress" and are markedly different in tone. With the praise of noble women and the announcement of future happiness, they echo the jubilant spirit of the army, which the messenger described at length. All attempts to uphold the allotment of these lines to the chorus are unsatisfactory. The solution of Murray, in whose text they are given to a secondary chorus of soldiers, has much to recommend it. Evidently, great stress was to be laid on the arrival of the women. Whether this was added for a later production, thus justifying the athetesis of the lines, or whether Euripides himself chose to magnify the effect of the scene in this way, it is difficult to decide. Yet one should not be too rash in striking verses from a play in which the poet elsewhere shows his willingness to innovate.[336]

The weight of the second epeisodion lies on two long stichomythies framed by shorter speeches, in which Agamemnon confronts first Iphigeneia, then his wife.

Klytaimestra greets the welcome offered her by the women of the chorus as a good omen and with many gestures bids them assist her. Agamemnon comes out of his tent; Iphigeneia runs to meet him and displays in the following stichomyth the full extent of her childlike tenderness and devotion, which must be unbearable torture for Agamemnon. In dark hints he refers to the fate that awaits her. His inner conflict becomes visible when to be rid of her he sends her into the tent, and yet first requests her childlike embrace. Here (681) he bids her a painful yet tender farewell that vividly recalls the words of Medeia.

Now he is alone with Klytaimestra. To allay suspicion, he attributes his sorrow to his impending separation from Iphigeneia by her marriage. Klytaimestra wants to know more about the future bridegroom; this should not be misconstrued as mere vanity on her part. A stichomyth develops in which Agamemnon recounts the lineage of Achilleus and elaborately describes the marriage of Peleus and Thetis. But when Klytaimestra asks about the day of Iphigeneia's wedding and the arrangements for the feast, Agamemnon interrupts the conversation, issuing an order (725).

In the course of the dialogue, we become aware that any discussion of the fictitious marriage is pure torture for him, so that he finally blurts out what lies foremost on his mind: Klytaimestra must return to Argos immediately. But his wife opposes this affront to her maternal rights. Who will wave the bridal torch? Agamemnon's helpless reply that he will do it himself is grotesque. When he tries to accomplish his purpose with a gruff πιθοῦ (obey!) Klytaimestra leaves the stage, assuring her husband that she will not neglect her proper duties. Agamemnon remains alone in his distress, and he could not sum up the outcome of all his μηχανήματα (intrigues) better than with the phrase πανταχῇ νικώμενος (everywhere defeated; 745). He now goes to consult with Kalchas about the details of the sacrifice.

The second stasimon (751–800), again one triad, sets the events in Aulis within the broader context of the expedition against Troy. In the epode the chorus sings of the fear and misery of the Trojan women. All the guilt is borne by Helen, begotten of the swan. Here however the Chalkidian women show themselves to be a true Euripidean chorus, in that they express doubts about this report of Helen's lineage: Is it true or merely the invention of poets? Mistrust of traditional myth was expressed even more firmly by the chorus in the *Elektra* (737).

Formally the third epeisodion (801–1035) is so constructed that after the entrance speech of Achilleus, misunderstanding and enlightenment are contained in a stichomythy, followed by two lengthy speeches in which the characters express their agitation on learning the true situation.

Achilleus comes on stage looking for Agamemnon to demand his reasons for delaying the fleet. The call for a servant is but a thin disguise for the monologue form of his entrance speech. He introduces an important motif (808) when he speaks of the fervent desire for the expedition that has seized the army—surely not without divine influence. Agamemnon earlier (411) spoke of a sickness to describe the irrational aspect of the masses' yearning. It is significant for later events that Achilleus depicts the stormy impatience of his Myrmidons in particular.

No servant emerges from the hut in response to his call, but Klytaimestra does instead. Now in the form of a distichomythy a scene of misunderstanding is developed that has since been repeated countless times in the situation humor of comedy. Achilleus is rather embarrassed by her royal presence and tries to withdraw, but Klytaimestra greets him heartily as Iphigeneia's bridegroom. At this he becomes even more perplexed, which she first attributes to the shyness of youth, until both must realize that they are tangled in an elaborate deception. They are about to part when the old servant, whom Agamemnon tried to send with his letter, carefully opens the door (doubtless he has been eavesdropping for some time) and stops them.[337] In the following strongly accentuated stichomythy, which brings the old man first into conversation with Achilleus, then with Klytaimestra, the meter shifts to trochaic tetrameter. From the anapests of the prologue we already know that this servant came to the house as part of Klytaimestra's dowry; now his loyalty to the queen is stressed once again (860, 867 ff.), to account for his betrayal of Agamemnon. After a lengthy assertion of his fidelity, the old man reveals the terrible truth in one verse (873): Agamemnon plans to kill his own daughter. Then he recounts the whole story, step by step. At the end of the stichomythy Klytaimestra turns to Achilleus, falls at his feet, and begs him to help, for he alone can save her child. His name has been abused, and this obliges him to lend his assistance.

Now it is his turn to speak. For the evaluation of his speech it is important to note that the two dividing verses of the chorus already mark the change to iambic trimeters as the suitable medium for more strongly rationalistic statements.

The opening of the long speech of Achilleus is almost insufferable, so much so that one is tempted to find an excuse for athetesis, but Murray's warning in his apparatus cannot be taken lightly. Achilleus begins by saying that he knows moderation in joy and sorrow, as if attempting to quote Archilochos (fr. 67aD). The simple ways of life he learned from Cheiron. Not until the middle of the speech does he turn to Klytaimestra and with great pathos promise to rescue her child, whom, he says, no one shall touch. His reasons for doing so—as he explains in the conclusion of his speech, which, like the opening, is more of a monologue—are quite sobering. Only because he was left out of the plot is he moved to resist; if Agamemnon had taken him into his confidence (in Sophokles' play this appears to have been the case), he would have been ready and willing to hand over Iphigeneia to the Greeks. The final lines present another address to Klytaimestra and a pathetic touch of conceit: for her he will be a god of salvation. If we add to this what Achilleus considers the pinnacle of wisdom, before the final crisis (1366 ff.)—which is decided by Iphigeneia alone—then we can only conclude with Reinhardt that the nature of heroism has become suspect even in this character.[338]

Klytaimestra has heard only his promise to help; to her thanks she adds another urgent plea and asks if Iphigeneia should grasp the knees of her savior. This, Achilleus refuses, but, starting up again, pledges to forfeit his own life if he fails to save the girl (1006 f.). However, in the following short stichomythy and adjoining speech his tone changes. It would be better—and would spare Achilleus the reproaches of the army—if Klytaimestra could change Agamemnon's mind and bring about an amicable settlement for all. The queen agrees, but asks for his reassurance of aid and concludes the epeisodion with a statement of resignation that anticipates events to come: If the gods exist, they will stand by the just cause; if they do not, why all the bother! Here and there in the poet's works such doubts repeatedly break through, doubts with which he himself grappled throughout his creative life.

By recalling the splendid marriage of Peleus and Thetis, which the gods themselves attended, the strophe and antistrophe of the third stasimon (1036–1097; one triad) reflect the glory of the hero who sprang from their union. The epode, however, looks ahead and bewails the fate of Iphigeneia, whose sacrifice is an outrage in sharp contrast to the bright image just developed.

If we follow Kranz (229) in allotting to Iphigeneia's aria (1279–1335) the divisional function of a choral ode, we may designate the section 1098–1275 as the fourth epeisodion. Klytaimestra steps out of the lodging to look for Agamemnon, whom she knows to be outside. Thus, for the sake of the πιθανόν (plausible), the coincidence of a chance meeting is avoided. We learn that Iphigeneia knows the whole truth and has collapsed in tears. Convincingly Euripides has Klytaimestra confront her husband in a way quite different from her encounter with Achilleus. No suppliant speaks here, but a woman wounded to the heart, superior because of her awareness of the injustice she has suffered. Nowhere does Agamemnon appear so miserable as here, when he tries to trick Klytaimestra (who knows his real purpose) into surrendering Iphigeneia to him under the pretext of offering wedding sacrifices. The mother understands that in reality all has meanwhile been prepared for the sacrifice of her daughter. She knows how to unmask Agamemnon in the most painful way possible: she summons Iphigeneia, who is to come carrying the infant Orestes in her arms. In a brief stichomythy, emotional and highly irregular in form, Agamemnon learns to his dismay that the secret is out. Thus, even his final attempt to avoid the worst has failed. He can say nothing (1144). And then his assurance that he will not add lies to compound the disaster sounds most untrustworthy after his behavior at the beginning of the scene. He says no more, for he has no more to say. Not so Klytaimestra—on the contrary. Her speech that now follows is a good example for Strohm's perceptive observation (145. 1) that the Euripidean agon uses the opponent's whole bios as the background for the particular case. Klytaimestra begins with a strange motif. She claims that Agamemnon killed her first husband, Tantalos, tore their child from her breast, and dashed it to the ground. Despite this she was a good wife to him, and now see the thanks she gets! In threatening tones, the idea of retribution begins to take shape in her words. Again the myth plays along, evoking between the lines the image of future events after Agamemnon returns from Troy. In concluding, she adds the thought—as in other cases involving such sacrifices—that a substitute could be found, here by a lottery. Since the situation precludes such a solution, it is passed over without reply.

The chorus leader insists that Agamemnon save his child, but he remains silent. Then Iphigeneia throws herself at his feet. Klytaimestra accused and demanded, but her daughter storms Agamemnon's heart with moving, childlike pleas, with tender memories, finally enlisting the infant Orestes as her ally. Her whole speech is filled with the horror of death and culminates in the statement: Anyone who wants to die is mad. Better to live wretchedly (poverty and disgrace are both implied in κακῶς) than die nobly. This flies momentarily in the face of any notion of heroic conduct (Soph. *Ai.* 479!) but should be understood as a contrast to the Iphigeneia we will see at the end of the play.

Two verses of the chorus leader (1253 f.) call to mind Helen as the cause of all the misery; then follows a speech of Agamemnon that in its brevity is as peculiar as it is decisive for the course of the plot. Agamemnon asserts that he is not cruel, that he loves his children. But the army, the violent multitude, demands her sacrifice and there is no way out. In terms of the external plot, we are now exactly at the point we were at the end of Agamemnon's speech (528) concluding the first epeisodion. But the next three lines (1264–1266) mark an extremely concise and neatly executed turning point. The first two verses say what we have already heard twice before (411, 808): The army is gripped by the passionate desire to move against Troy. The third verse, however, offers an explanation that is new to us: There must be an end to the abduction of Greek women. The inescapable constraint that lay on Agamemnon's shoulders now becomes the great Hellenic cause; indeed, nothing less is at stake than the freedom of Greece, whose women must not be stolen by barbarians. This is Agamemnon's final word in the drama, after which he leaves the stage.

But his speech has not yet inflamed the others. After a brief lament by Klytaimestra, Iphigeneia begins a lengthy aria, in which she bewails her destiny. She still deplores her sacrilegious slaughter by her sacrilegious father (1318); but the fact that Paris, his judgment, the fleet at Aulis, and the obstacle to sailing (here the work of Zeus) now stand in the foreground, connects this lament with Agamemnon's words at the end of his speech. To be sure, we hear nothing yet in this song that might indicate Iphigeneia's willingness to die.

After two trimeters, in which the chorus leader professes her sympathy, an agitated scene begins whose trochaic tetrameters are soon broken into antilabai. Achilleus enters with a band of followers in a state of great commotion. Iphigeneia tries to withdraw from the men's sight, but Klytaimestra bids her stay. Achilleus reports how the army is violently demanding the sacrifice, how his resistance led to threats of stoning, and his Myrmidons were the first to oppose him. He is resolved to fight, but when he replies to Klytaimestra's anxious question "So my child won't be killed?" with "At least not if I can help it," announces the imminent approach of Odysseus and his brutal grip, and advises Klytaimestra to cling to her daughter, it becomes obvious that his opposition will prove futile.

Then, in mid-verse Iphigeneia interrupts, a different Iphigeneia from the one who sang the lamentation aria before this scene. She asks her mother to harbor no resentment against her father. The will of the army is too powerful, and the eyes of Greece are upon her. She wishes to put off all traces of ignobility and suffer a glorious death. Now she picks up on Agamemnon's words: The whole expedition to avenge the abduction of Helen depends on her sacrifice; by her death she will liberate Hellas. But Achilleus must not perish on her account. For one man is worth much more than countless women! Once again, in a sort of rapture, she returns to the lofty significance of her sacrifice. Thus she will gain a lasting memorial, her noble deed will compensate for the loss of marriage and children.

This turnabout, which resolves a completely hopeless situation, is sudden and unexpected. More on this later. Two verses of the chorus leader (transition to trimeters) combine admiration and sorrow. But now, in this drama so filled with psychological reversals, Achilleus recognizes the greatness of the girl with whom he was united, if only through deception. Though earlier he was concerned only with the honor of his name, now he wants to rescue Iphigeneia from her fate to preserve for himself such a precious possession. But his offer is refused: Enough misery has already come to men through Helen. Let me save Greece! Achilleus admires such greatness and submits. So that he does not appear too shabby beside Iphigeneia, the poet has him say in parting that he will guard the altar with his men and intervene should she change her mind. A pitifully disguised retreat.

Now Iphigeneia is alone with Klytaimestra. She is the strong one as she comforts her weeping mother and has her promise that neither she nor her daughters will dress in mourning. Only one request cannot be fulfilled: Klytaimestra will not lay aside her bitterness against Agamemnon; his deceit was too vile.

And so there remains only the painful farewell, for Iphigeneia forbids her mother to accompany her on her final path. Then she bids the women sing a paean to Artemis, to whom she is sacrificing herself, and strikes up the song herself. The chorus joins in and celebrates the glory of her noble decision after she departs.

The finale as preserved in the Laurentian MS leaves us in great uncertainty.[339] A messenger calls Klytaimestra from the lodging and reports the preparations for, and execution of, the sacrifice, at which Achilleus dutifully assists, as is consistent with the downgrading of his heroic attitude. But when Kalchas delivers the fatal blow, a doe lies bloodied on the altar. Iphigeneia has been snatched away, Artemis is appeased. Quite superfluously Agamemnon comes in and declares that all is well.

This concluding section from v. 1570 onward shows signs of disrupted transmission and arouses the suspicion of Byzantine interpolation, especially in the passage after 1578. For the previous portion Euripides cannot simply be excluded as the author. But matters are further complicated by the quotation in Ailian's *De nat. an.* 7. 39 (fr. 857N) of three verses from Euripides' *Iphigeneia* in which Artemis promises (to Klytaimestra) that she will send a doe to the Achaians, which they will slaughter in the belief that they are sacrificing Iphigeneia. Page's reasons (200) do not suffice to question the authenticity of the lines. Since it is possible that Euripides never completed the play, the two versions might represent sketches for the conclusion, but it is more probable that the drama ended with the appearance of Artemis ex machina, and only the verses in Ailian belong to the genuine finale. The messenger-speech in its well-preserved sections might then stem from an addition composed for the posthumous performance.

The *Iphigeneia at Aulis* is for the most part a play of intrigues, but it differs from other Euripidean dramas in that here the emphasis is on the failure of all the cleverly laid plans. This Agamemnon succeeds at just about nothing. It is partly for this reason that in the first four-fifths of the play, despite much movement back and forth, the plot is not advanced in the slightest. Set above all this is the demand of Artemis for sacrifice, the basis of the plot supplied by myth, whose deeper religious problems are not touched upon. And few today will agree with Hegel that Iphigeneia and Agamemnon embody the antithesis between family and state.[340] The myth provides a partial situation as the framework within which human nature is revealed in a new breadth of variation. The psychological instability that is observable in the later plays becomes here the basic principle that determines events on stage.[341]

The first scene complex, which runs until v. 542, presents the collapse of the letter intrigue. The coincidence that permits Menelaos to seize the letter, his wrathful intervention, Klytaimestra's unforeseen arrival, the sudden change in Menelaos's attitude, and Agamemnon's realization that now it is too late—these form an exciting sequence of scenes, but the result of it all is entirely negative. At the end we hear Agamemnon say that he has but one hope left: Klytaimestra must not discover before the sacrifice what is really happening.

Despite much vigorous movement, the second expansive scenic block, extending from v. 607 to v. 1275, presents nothing more than the collapse of this hope. Here the poet does not neglect the opportunity to play out at some length the difficulty of

Agamemnon's situation. He labors in vain to persuade Klytaimestra to return home; and when the old servant brings the truth to light, he is spared no shame before his wife, no pain before his daughter. When he leaves the stage (1275) he is firmly resolved to sacrifice Iphigeneia, as at the end of the first scene complex (542). With the introduction of Achilleus in the second part, a real dilemma develops. The sacrifice seems inevitable. But will it be possible to carry it through? Have we not just heard Achilleus decide to prevent it? But did not much appear doubtful about this promise, so that we can hardly be sure of its fulfillment?

At this point all problems are solved by a changed Iphigeneia, who has left all fear of death behind her and takes the sacrifice upon herself for the glory of her country. Here again, as so often, Euripides, who had become so skeptical in his judgment of human nature, has the self-sacrificing enthusiasm of unblemished youth provide the solution to a gloomy situation that seemed well-nigh insoluble.

Wilamowitz called the *Iphigeneia at Aulis* an "unrealistic sentimental melodrama" (*Herakles* 2. 133); it is heartening that more recent critics have judged the work more fairly, and we are pleased to read what Zuntz (*Inquiry*, 102) has written lately of this "beautiful play." And yet even today the drama still suffers from the authoritarian censure of Aristotle. In the *Poetics* (15, 1454a 26) he demands as the fourth element necessary for the portrayal of ἤθη (character) the quality of τὸ ὁμαλόν (consistency), citing the Iphigeneia of our play, who first begs for her life and then behaves so differently, as the prime example of the ἀνώμαλον (inconsistent).[342] H. Funke (op. cit.) sought to corroborate this verdict with detailed evidence. In his view, Iphigeneia's great decision is unmotivated and unbelievable, since she was only repeating rhetorical phrases that she had just heard from Agamemnon. The change in her decision is thus completely incomprehensible and derives solely from the desire for dramatic effect.

We do not believe that this judgment does justice to Euripides, but welcome the opportunity thus presented for a new discussion of the problem.

First of all, it is perfectly correct that the national-Hellenic aspect of the sacrifice remain wholly in the background until the abrupt switching of motifs in the final words of Agamemnon (1260). In the lengthy dispute between the brothers, Menelaos makes two attempts to bring Hellas into consideration (370, 410). The first time Agamemnon ignores him completely, the second statement elicits only a sharp rebuff. Not until Agamemnon's last speech does the motif receive its full weight. In our analysis we attempted to show with what skill the poet accomplishes the transition. There, too, we established that the new viewpoint in no way immediately caused the change in Iphigeneia. Between the aria in which she bewails her life (and also admittedly brings Troy more vividly into the picture) and her great speech of resolution, there is only the brief Achilleus scene (1338–1368). To what extent does it provide the basis for Iphigeneia's decision? She, who expresses as her firm conviction (1394) that one man is worth more than ten thousand women, comes to realize how seriously Achilleus's life is threatened. She must also realize that the sacrifice for which he is prepared will be in vain, according to his own words of resignation (1368). Of special importance is the reply (1352) she hears Achilleus give to Klytaimestra's question: Who would dare to lay a hand on him? πάντες Ἕλληνες, he says: all the Greeks. Here the lines converge: the threat to Achilleus proceeds from the fixed resolve of all the Greeks to make the expedition against Troy, to which Agamemnon has given a new, noble aspect. In the short scene before Iphigeneia's decision, the vast multitude of the army, to which our attention has been called repeatedly during the course of the play from the parodos on, emerges as the decisive factor.[343] But Iphigeneia recognizes the army not only as a superior force, but also, through Agamemnon's final words, as the representative of a national idea.

One certainly cannot say that Euripides introduces Iphigeneia's self-sacrificing decision without preparation or motivation. Nor, of course, can one assert that he depicts for us the development of this decision in the girl's soul. A master in portraying psychological conditions, he was not equally concerned with describing how these conditions came about. It is a curious paradox that the magnificent portrayal of a development within the soul, as exemplified in Klytaimestra at the conclusion of the *Agamemnon*, has no parallel in the much acclaimed "psychodrama" of Euripides.

At the end of Euripides' career there stands a play of elemental magnificence, more difficult for us to understand than any other: the *Bakchai*.[344] The Theban myth of defiance against Dionysos was already dramatized by Aischylos in a tetralogy that contained a *Pentheus*.[345] We know next to nothing about the play and must rely on the remark of Aristophanes of Byzantium (in the hypothesis to the *Ba.*) that it dealt with the same material as Euripides' play. The other tetralogy of Aischylos, the *Lykourgeia*, had for its subject the Thracian king's opposition to the god and his consequent punishment. E. R. Dodds has argued persuasively that individual motifs of the *Bakchai*—the capture of Dionysos, interrogation of the god disguised as a stranger, mockery of his effeminate appearance—derived from the *Lykourgeia* of Aischylos.

The prologue of this play is formed solely by a speech of Dionysos. The god states his name and lineage, and informs us emphatically (4. 53 f.) that he has assumed human form for his mission of punishment.[346] He speaks of his long journey through Asia, and of how having left Lydia, he is now coming to Thebes, his birthplace, as the first city in Greece. He sees that the grave of his mother, Semele, who was killed by lightning, has been well tended, and praises Kadmos. We should recall this at the end of the play, when, for all his pious submission, the aged Kadmos also becomes a victim of the catastrophe.

The sisters of Semele have seriously offended the god by denying the truth of his descent from Zeus. Therefore, Dionysos has filled them and all the Theban women with bakchic frenzy and driven them into the mountains. Here at once the ambivalence of Dionysian ecstasy becomes visible in its full extent: the god possesses the women to punish them, and terrible events will ensue. At the same time, however, the messenger-speeches will show us how these same women, admitted into the deepest peace and the miracles of nature, experience a bliss that only this god can bestow. Indeed, if Pentheus, Kadmos's grandson, who now rules Thebes, wants to mobilize his army against the mainads, the god will prove to be their powerful ally, will not abandon those whom he really is punishing. Once again a Euripidean prologue introduces the possibility of a development that will not be realized.

The god summons the thiasos of women who have followed him from Asia; he himself hastens to Mount Kithairon to participate in the dances of the Bakchai, again in his strange double role as punisher and bringer of Dionysian jubilation.

The parodos (64–169) consists of a prelude, two strophic pairs, and an epode. Until the end of the first antistrophe the meter is ionic, and ionics also appear in the remaining sections. In the manner of a leitmotif they will recur in the later odes of the Bakchai. The conjecture that cult songs provided the model seems probable enough.[347]

In the prelude the Asian women solemnly announce their hymn to the god. The strophe describes the blessedness of the mystai who devote their lives to Dionysos; the antistrophe relates his double birth from the womb of lightning-struck Semele and from the thigh of Zeus. The second strophe calls all of Thebes to join in the mountain revelries of the god; the antistrophe presents valuable evidence for the amalgamation of orgiastic cults from the border areas of the Aegean. The very first strophe named the Great Mother Kybele together with Dionysos; now we hear of Kuretes and Korybantes, who invented the tympana for the Great Mother (here called Rhea) at the birthplace of Zeus in Krete. From her the satyrs received the resounding tambourines in which Dionysos rejoices and which the chorus beats now. The epode offers a deeply felt and beautifully composed song praising bakchic ecstasy, with all the elements of the cult: the oreibasia (mountain revels), and the sparagmos and omophagia (the dismembering of an animal in which the god's force dwells, and the consumption of its flesh). But again, foreshadowing the two messenger-speeches, the double nature of the cult is revealed. Next to orgiastic savagery, which culminates in the horrible demise of Pentheus, stands the intimate union with nature that causes milk, honey, and wine to spring from the earth for the mystai.

The first epeisodion (170–369) comprises a Teiresias-Kadmos-Pentheus act. The aged seer, decked out like a Dionysian initiate with garland, thyrsos, and nebris, comes before the palace to summon Kadmos to the service of the god. Teiresias, as the prophet of Thebes, is a sort of timeless character. When he appears here as the near contemporary of Kadmos, we are not meant to compute how old he must have been as Kreon's adviser in the Phoinissai. His entrance poses a minor problem of staging. As often, Teiresias is here thought to be blind (210). How does he come on stage? It has been suggested that he is led by a boy or servant.[348] Against this we must consider that the departure of the two old men, who go off leaning against each other, one leading the other, does not allow for a mute character of this type. That one entered and then departed without being mentioned is improbable. Perhaps we might conjecture that the god is the guiding force (189) in this blind man who finds his way alone.

From the palace comes Kadmos, all ready to dance for Dionysos. In a short stichomythy between the speeches of the old men, they both decide to forgo the use of a chariot and to walk out to the mountain woods, they who alone of Theban men know what befits the god's worship. In a speech rounding off this part of the scene, Teiresias gives his reasons for wanting to dance the round despite his gray hair. Important is his reference to the tradition handed down by the fathers, as old as time itself (201). This obviously conflicts with the newness of the Dionysos cult, which has just now come to Thebes, but it is also obvious that the poet wanted us to understand this cult as a part of religious tradition. The opponents of this tradition may resort to σοφίζεσθαι (sophistic quibbling), but: οὐδεὶς αὐτὰ καταβαλεῖ λόγος (no speech will overthrow it).[349] There can be little doubt that this passage refers to Sophism and the καταβάλλοντες ("overthrowing" speeches) of Protagoras.

Kadmos informs the blind Teiresias that his grandson Pentheus, who rules Thebes, is approaching in great haste. We are thus prepared for the following agon.

In the appearance of these two elderly initiates, whose frailty contrasts grossly with their bakchic inspiration, it was long thought that the decisive element was grotesque comedy.[350] The case is similar to the rejuvenation of Iolaos in the *Herakleidai*, which also borders on the grotesque, but the meaning of the scene is not limited to that side alone, as we saw. Euripides' purpose with these two old men was certainly not to expose the objectionable folly of the god's cult, but instead to enrich and expand in a different direction the image of Dionysian power that was presented in the parodos. Above all, however, one must consider the necessity of the scene in its dramatic context. Euripides had to develop the character of Pentheus before staging his confrontation with Dionysos. But for this he needed foils, for which the two old men were especially suited, because they represent borderline cases of Dionysian influence and make use of apologetic arguments of a special type.

Pentheus's speech is first (until 247) an entrance monologue (cf. *Hel.* 386, *Or.* 356), in which he vents his anger at the bakchic pestilence that has infected the women of the city. Some of them he has already caught and imprisoned; now he is after the stranger who is spreading this new religion. His passionate and suspicious nature leads him to a distorted impression of the cult: the charge that the women steal out of the city to seek the pleasures of Aphrodite is totally without grounds.

In a stage convention that became stylized in comic drama, the speaker of the monologue does not see the other persons present for quite some time. Incensed at the unworthy mission of the old men, Pentheus immediately accuses Teiresias of furthering the Dionysian craze for personal gain. After three indignant lines from the chorus leader, the prophet answers him with a speech in defense of the god. It contains many peculiar features and has often led to the denigration of Teiresias as a vain priest who resorts to sophistic argumentation. The prophet explains that the goddess Demeter is really the earth—call her whatever name you wish. She gives dry nourishment to men, but Dionysos bestows the moist juice of the grape, the reliever of cares—indeed, he himself is in the drink and thus as a god is offered to the gods. This represents neither a criticism nor a rejection of tradition; it is simply another case in which the myths were given an allegorical explanation, a development that began with Theagenes of Rhegion in the sixth century and which later would help the Stoics to make their peace with tradition. The prophet tries to circumvent the old story of the birth of Dionysos from the thigh of Zeus—which the chorus regards as sacred history (94)—with an etymological explanation: Zeus, after saving Dionysos from the flames of the lightning blast, protected the child from Hera by breaking off a piece of the aether that surrounds the earth (cf. Empedokles DK 31, B 38) and giving it (probably in the form of Dionysos) to his jealous wife as a hostage (ὅμηρος). Thus, from a misinterpretation of the word, the story was started about the birth from Zeus's thigh (μηρός!). Here again we must be careful in speaking of a rationalization of myth. In accepting the murderous lightning bolt of Zeus and the jealousy of Hera, Teiresias remains firmly on the ground of tradition; he merely wishes to eliminate a detail that seems obviously unbelievable. This is basically the same attitude that Pindar takes in *Olympian* 1. 46 when he declares that the story of Pelops's dismemberment was a malicious rumor, since in reality Poseidon abducted the handsome youth. But we may confidently assume that both the allegorizing and the smoothing out of motifs reflect the trends of an age that was deeply concerned with the questions of myth.

Continuing his speech in defense of Dionysos, Teiresias speaks of the god's other ἀρεταί (excellences): From him comes prophetic inspiration, but also the fear that can intimidate a whole army; great is he throughout Greece; in Delphi too he will be celebrated. He is not responsible for the women's sexual behavior, where their physis is the deciding factor. This idea has its roots in ancient Greek thought.[351]

The speech of Teiresias has ended nicely with the admonition to think sensibly and yield to the god (313). The mention of the women, the remark that the god enjoys respect just like the king, the prophet's insistence on his own piety, and the coarse rebuke at the end—all this reads strangely like a postscript. Today we are not as quick to athetize as were our predecessors, but it should be noted that the two verses of the chorus leader (328 f.) about the honor that Teiresias gives equally to Apollo and Dionysos, directly picks up what the prophet said about Dionysos in Delphi (306).

In a shorter speech Kadmos tries to win over his grandson to the new cult. His utilitarian suggestion that Pentheus should acknowledge Bakchos, even if he weren't a god, for the sake of family honor, is surely not very uplifting; nor does it make Kadmos into an unbelieving hypocrite. Neither his previous statements nor his warning about the punishment of Aktaion would fit such an image. Teiresias and Kadmos have themselves surrendered totally to Dionysos, but they try to persuade the doubting Pentheus by any means available, so that he might escape a fatal clash with the invincible god.

Pentheus scorns their efforts. When Kadmos tries to crown him with ivy, he pushes his hand away: He will have the prophetic seat of Teiresias destroyed, and the foreigner who seduces Theban women must be caught and imprisoned. With this Pentheus leaves the stage.[352] Teiresias calls out after him with harsh words of rebuke for his delusion, then he goes on his way with Kadmos, and we have seen and heard our last of him.

The first stasimon (370–433) is composed of two strophic pairs, of which the first again displays ionic meters, the second glyconic. The subject of the ode is determined by the previous scene. Teiresias's rejection of σοφίζεσθαι (200) and his praise for the wine-giving god are echoed. Formally the strophes deal with the situation at hand; the antistrophes branch out into generality. The chorus calls to the goddess Holiness (Ὁσία) to take notice of Pentheus's blasphemy (α). Unbridled speech ends in disaster; peace and discretion guard the home. Gods watch over men. Tὸ σοφὸν δ᾽ οὐ σοφία (wit is not wisdom). Only a fool pursues the unattainable, for man's life is short (α΄). While the previous strophe praised the joyful release of Dionysian worship, the antistrophe provides the transition to the image of moderation and inner tranquillity—sung by the same chorus that in the parodos proclaimed the delights of oreibasia and sparagmos.[353] Somewhat abruptly the next strophe presents their wish to be carried away: to Kypros, Paphos, or Pieria (β).[354] Then the ode returns to the god who gladdens rich and poor with his gifts, and hates all those who in their intellectual arrogance scorn the peaceful pleasures of life. The chorus prefers the faith and way of life of the plain folk (β΄). If it were still necessary to do so, then these last words alone would show that this ode does not simply represent the beliefs of the poet.

In the short second epeisodion (434–518), the two opponents confront each other. A servant brings in the "stranger," now a bound prisoner. His report about how the latter quietly and good-naturedly let himself be captured (we recall the proud confidence of the god in the seventh *Homeric Hymn*), how the bonds fell from the captive bakchants, and the door opened by itself is the first warning given to Pentheus through the miracles of the god. In a long stichomythy, he interrogates the prisoner with a mixture of spiteful indignation and impatient curiosity (469, 471, 485). The god replies calmly, not without playing on his true identity (500, 518). Pentheus has him locked up in the stables; the women of the chorus he threatens to sell abroad or keep as his own slaves.

The second stasimon (519–575) is composed of one triad; again ionics dominate the meter, until the final verses. In fear the chorus appeals to Dirke, who once received the child Dionysos in her streams when Zeus saved him from the flames and sewed him in his thigh. Unlike Teiresias, the women of the chorus believe that the nativity story is true (α). Pentheus, the monster who threatened them and locked up their leader, proves his descent from the earth-born. Dionysos must help (α΄). The epode summons the god from his favorite haunts. The special emphasis on Pieria (already mentioned earlier; 410) reminds us that Euripides wrote the play in Makedonia.

The third epeisodion (576–861) forms the great central section of the drama; it consists of three parts, the first of which, the liberation of the captive god, is again tripartite.

A lyric section directly follows the choral ode. Dionysos has heard the cry of his followers; his voice resounds from within the palace. He bids the forces of earthquake and lightning to devastate the palace of Pentheus. The chorus sees how the architrave is shaken and flames blaze up from Semele's grave. The motif is used here as it was in the *Herakles*. It has its meaning for a particular scene in the play and is then forgotten. When the chorus exclaims that the beams of the architrave are split asunder, that suffices for the illusion. The collapse mentioned by Dionysos in v. 633 may be imagined behind the facade of the palace. The blazing fire at Semele's grave may have been represented—already at v. 8 we heard that flames burn there constantly—but even this is uncertain.[355]

In the second scene (604–641; composed in trochaics) of the first part of the epeisodion the god appears in his human form to the women of the chorus, allays their fear, and reports the miraculous events inside the house: how Pentheus bound a bull instead of him in the stall, how the god (Dionysos speaks in the mask of the "stranger") caused the house to shake and the fire to blaze up, and how the king battled with a phantom in the courtyard of the collapsing palace.

In the third scene of this section Pentheus rushes out of the palace and is furious to find that the stranger is free. A short stichomythy does not yet clarify what he intends to do, but then a messenger arrives, whose report forms the second part of this epeisodion.

Here the usual introductory dialogue cannot anticipate the gist of the speech, as is the case elsewhere and in the second messenger-report of the *Bakchai*; instead, we find merely a reference to "strange deeds surpassing wonder." The passage contains an indirect characterization of Pentheus, when the messenger, fearful of the king's rash nature, asks if he may speak freely.

In the two messenger-reports of the *Bakchai*, the epic skill of the poet reached its final pinnacle. The wonders of Dionysian ecstasy, above all the contradictory nature of this cult, are expressed with the immediacy of shattering experience.

As often, the beginning is calm, idyllic. At sunrise the herdsmen are driving the cattle up the mountain, when the messenger catches sight of the three thiasoi of bakchants, led by Agaue, Ino, and Autonoe.[356] The women repose in peaceful slumber. The messenger makes use of his requested freedom of speech to correct the king's opinion about the immoral activities of the inspired women. When Agaue wakes them they show signs of an intimate union with nature. Snakes lick their cheeks, they offer their breasts to does and young wolves, they strike water from stones and springs of wine from the ground, the earth yields milk, and honey drips from their wands. A second time the messenger warns the king (712): Had you been there, you'd have learned to pray to the god!

The shepherds discuss the marvelous sights; one of them, a smooth-talking townsman, suggests that they abduct Pentheus's mother and so earn the king's thanks.[357] This plan meets with approval and it is the messenger himself who tries to capture Agaue when the women, filled with Dionysos, begin their joyous revelry. But Agaue calls the mainads to battle, they break out in a raging fury, scatter the men, and fall upon the herds. The scenes of sparagmos, to which even bulls fall victim, form a grisly prelude to the fate of Pentheus. The women then rush down to the plains, storm villages, and, themselves invulnerable, put to flight armed men with their wands. After their terrible outbreak of fury, they return to the tranquillity of nature, from which they were startled by the curiosity of the herdsmen.

The speech of the messenger, in which the actions of the Bakchai reflect the forces of nature, at once profoundly peaceful and horribly destructive, ends with a third and final warning to the king: Receive this mighty god!

The third part of this lengthy central epeisodion (775–861) frames a lively "persuasion" stichomythy, which shifts from double to single verses, with shorter passages of trimeter. Here we see the first signs of the decisive turn toward Pentheus's destruction and the god's triumph. The motivation in this section is so complex that the one-sided emphasis of individual factors has led to long and basically unnecessary controversies.

After three trimeters by the chorus leader, in which praise for the god overcomes her fear of Pentheus, the latter, unmindful of the miracles related by the messenger, bursts into a rage. The possibility considered in the prologue (perhaps a survival from the *Pentheus* of Aischylos) seems about to be realized now: The king intends to mobilize his entire army to battle the mainads. The stranger warns that Bromios will not endure an attack on the Bakchai (again the women punished by the god with madness [32, 35] are seen to be under his protection), but Pentheus rejects this with the brusque remark that he should be happy to be free of his bonds. In this way Euripides glosses over the somewhat surprising fact that Pentheus does not order the stranger to be seized a second time. Furious, the king proclaims his wild plan to murder the women on Mount Kithairon; once again he rebuffs the stranger's bothersome warning, but when the god (802) in friendly tones mentions the possibility of setting all in order, Pentheus pricks up his ears. Dionysos promises to deliver the women on the spot—and without weapons. What this suggestion means it is difficult to say. That it might be some trick of the god is nowhere made clear, so we follow Dodds and others in interpreting it as an earnest attempt at mediation whose function is to emphasize once more the obstinacy of the god's adversary. Pentheus calls for arms for his march against the Bakchai, and silences the protests of the stranger. But now a decisive turn is marked by one of the strongest interjections in tragedy (810). Here begins the path which leads first to the psychic and then to the physical annihilation of Pentheus. The god asks him if he would like to see the women as they sit together in the mountains. The king jumps at this offer with passionate eagerness, as he later also (820) urges haste. These two passages are of key importance in deciding which impulses lead Pentheus on the track to the mainads, whose victim he becomes.[358] Following others, R. P. Winnington-Ingram (op. cit.) has gone especially far in supposing that the Dionysian, which Pentheus suppressed in his heart, breaks out here, and so the god's opponent proves to be essentially his follower. H. Diller (op. cit.) has opposed an extremist interpretation along this line (without, however, rejecting the basic assumption) and has seen as the decisive factor the desire of Pentheus to verify his ideas about the women's activity by spying on them. A third interpretation, supported by Rosenmeyer (147) and H. Merklin (op. cit., 156), puts all the weight on the overpowering of man by the superior force of god, who strikes his victim with madness.

We do not believe that the problem can be solved with any one-sided interpretation. The eagerness with which Pentheus picks up Dionysos's suggestion to spy on the mainads, the discord between this desire and the assertion (814) that the sight of the drunken women would cause him pain—all this shows that the psychological interpretation supported of late, especially by Schwinge and Rohdich, is quite justified, at least within limits, as Conacher (68) well emphasizes. But the motif that Pentheus plans military action against the women is not dropped—in fact, in his last words of this scene (845), he still considers armed intervention as an alternative. And besides the impulses at work in Pentheus himself, it is also advisable to take into account, on a corresponding level, the influence of the god as he presses on toward his goal.

Dionysos plans to make his opponent's demise into a horrible grotesque by persuading Pentheus to spy on the women disguised in the garb and attributes of a mainad. Pentheus is still only half-decided; he refuses flatly, then expresses misgivings (828, 836, 840). His last words before departing leave open whether he will venture out in arms or in the suggested disguise.[359] And yet his fate has already been decided, as Dionysos says to the chorus: The man is caught in the nets. The stranger plays once more on his dual identity, calling on the god to send madness on Pentheus. He will lead him to his doom through the streets of Thebes, a laughingstock for the citizens. Again we become aware of the polarity of the god and his world when Dionysos appears as the god who is at once most terrible and friendliest to mortals.

The triad of the third stasimon (862–911) is noteworthy, both for its content and its great poetic beauty.[360] The women of the chorus now feel safe from the threats of the god's enemy; through the image of the fawn who escapes the nets and the pack, they sing of their happiness. Then follows a refrain that is repeated after the antistrophe. The question τί τὸ σοφόν (What is "wise"?) recalls the τὸ σοφὸν δ' οὐ σοφία (wit is not wisdom) of the first stasimon (395). Instead of a direct answer, however, a new question follows: Or what gift of the gods is more beautiful than to hold your hand over an enemy's head in triumph? This is an answer of sorts, clearly referring to Pentheus. Senseless and futile is all σοφίζεσθαι (sophistry), such as Teiresias condemned (200), but joyous the victory over the blasphemer.

The antistrophe picks up this thought directly and announces the late but sure revenge of the insulted divinity. It takes little effort to believe in its power. Dodds compares fr. trag. adesp. 350N. This is the chorus speaking and not a recanting Euripides, who does, however, add a brief word of his own (894): ὅ τι ποτ' ἄρα τὸ δαιμόνιον (whatever divinity might be). It is significant that in the pious faith of this chorus the antithesis between nomos and physis is resolved: that which is sanctified by tradition is identical with what grows naturally (895).[361] Only with this type of insight (thus our own interpretation runs) can one attain the happiness of quiet contentment praised in the epode. Again we note the variety in the concept of happiness in the *Bakchai*; it is intimately connected with the polarity of the Dionysian. The bliss of a tranquil harbor is celebrated by the same chorus that praised the raptures of bakchic ecstasy in the parodos.

In the short fourth epeisodion (912–976) Dionysos comes on stage with Pentheus, whom he, true to his promise, has stricken utterly with divinely ordained madness, and with whom he now plays his cruel game. In his derangement, Pentheus sees the sun and Thebes doubled, but at the same time he perceives the terrible reality behind appearances, for he sees the god in his most powerful form, the bull. ῎Αξιε ταῦρε (worthy bull) he is called by the women of Elis (Plut. *Quaest. Graec.* 36; 299A). The grotesqueness of the scene is carried to extremes in Pentheus's concern about the correctness of his bakchic garments, in the god's scornful willingness to help him. Irrational surges of power fill the young king's mind; in reality, the god has rendered him utterly helpless. Mount Kithairon, together with the Bakchai, he would lift on his shoulders. Here reappears in distorted form the motif of fighting with the mainads. But Pentheus is swiftly dissuaded: it is better to spy on the women. In dark words the god hints at the coming catastrophe. The distichomythy breaks into antilabai, in which the stranger promises that Pentheus will return home in his mother's arms, as indeed he will, but with a final horrible twist.

Pentheus leaves first, while Dionysos calls on Agaue and her sisters to do their work and seal the victory of Bromios.

The fourth stasimon (977–1023) again consists of one strophic pair with refrain and a short epode; its dochmiac rhythms express great agitation. The strophe picks up the summons of Dionysos: The swift hounds of Lyssa, bringer of rabid madness, should hasten to the mountains. The gist of the following messenger-speech is anticipated by the chorus when they declare that Agaue will catch sight of her prowling son, but will mistake him terribly. In the ode the actual event is intimated as one of several possibilities: Pentheus will scout from a cliff or a tree, his mother will take him for the offspring of a lioness or of Libyan Gorgons.[362] The refrain calls on Dike to punish the godless one with death. This thought is at first continued in the antistrophe, but soon gives way to the general idea that pious contentment alone assures human happiness. The concept recurs in the odes like a leitmotif, and so too the textually difficult verse 1605 must be understood from the parallels with 395 and 877. The epode calls on Dionysos, whether in the form of a bull, snake, or fire-snorting lion, to lay the fatal trap for Pentheus.[363]

We may count the following scene with the messenger-report (1024–1152) as the fifth epeisodion, and the short lyric passage of the chorus (1153–1164) as the fifth stasimon, but one should bear in mind that the formal delineation is weak, and essentially the exodos has already begun at this point.

The introductory dialogue of the messenger-speech is here especially animated, since the messenger is taken aback when the chorus rejoices at his mournful news. That he delivers his entire report to the chorus despite his bitterness at this is only thinly excused by his conciliatory remark at vv. 1039 f.

The second messenger-report, another masterpiece of epic narration, follows the basic outlines of the first. Again, the tranquil beginning, with the journey to the mountains and the description of the forest valley shaded with pines and nourished by gushing streams. Again we find the women in the calm but joyful service of Bakchos, though here described in less detail. Here Pentheus himself must provoke the storm. With miraculous strength the stranger bends down the crest of a pine tree, sets Pentheus on top, and carefully raises him back on high. Then the god disappears, but from the aether his voice resounds, delivering Pentheus to the revenge of the mainads. A miracle of flashing light confirms the will of Dionysos. With consummate skill the poet inserts a moment of terrifying silence—all nature is hushed—before the storm breaks loose. As yet the Bakchai have not understood the divine voice; they stand still, watching and listening, but when the god calls again they rush forth. Filled with Dionysos they storm through the valley (which with the attribute χειμάρρους, put into turmoil by raging waters, participates in the wildness of the scene). They catch sight of Pentheus, and after vain attempts to strike him with stones and branches, they rip the tree up by its roots. His mother is the first to fall on Pentheus, who tears the bands from his head and begs her not to kill him for his ἁμαρτίαι (mistakes). This statement stands in complete isolation and makes it difficult to decide whether Pentheus, having awakened from his delusion, now feels genuine remorse, or merely recognizes his mistake in opposing a superior power.

Agaue tears his arm and shoulder from his body, the other women complete the gruesome sparagmos. She impales her son's head on her thyrsos and hastens toward the city. Her sisters remain with the mainads. Agaue's isolated entrance, so important to the poet, is carefully motivated (1143).

This messenger-speech is also concluded with a gnome, which again strikes up the leitmotif of the chorus: Pious reverence for the gods remains the best σοφία.

As in the *Hippolytos* (1268) and the *Ion* (1229), at the height of dramatic tension—here before Agaue's entrance—the chorus is given only one short strophe. The horror that mounted in the messenger-report is now answered by the savage joy of satisfied revenge. Then anapests of the chorus leader announce Agaue, who rushes on stage with Pentheus's head stuck on her thyrsos. An amoibaion between Agaue and the chorus in the form of a strophic pair (1168–1199) plays out at length the triumph of insanity, which the chorus further intensifies with questions and encouragement. But when Agaue invites the women to eat raw flesh, to eat *this* raw flesh, even they draw back in revulsion (1184). And when the chorus leader drives Agaue further on in the display of her delusion, she offers also a word of pity: ὦ τάλαινα (poor woman! 1200).

Agaue exhorts all Thebes to share in her triumph. She calls for Kadmos, and wants Pentheus to nail the precious trophy to a triglyph of the palace. Kadmos comes in with the remnants of the corpse that he and his servants have laboriously collected on Mount Kithairon. In the dialogue that now develops, he encounters Agaue, still triumphant and glorifying her deed. The horror of Kadmos she misconstrues as the morose temper of old age, and again she calls for her son to witness her success at the hunt. Her return to consciousness, her recognition of the terrible truth, is presented by the poet in a stichomythy (1263–1301). The form proves to be especially effective for the process of gradual awakening. Kadmos first bids Agaue to look up to the sky, to lead her back to clarity. Her slowly returning awareness is subtly intimated by a double verse (1269 f.). Now Kadmos, recalling memories of her earlier life, leads Agaue completely back to reality. She recognizes the hand of Dionysos; her ἄρτι μανθάνω (only now do I realize it; 1296) echoes the words with which Admetos spoke of his ruined life (940). Kadmos bursts into a stirring lament for his grandson, who was the prop of his old age. In tones of great tenderness, which Euripides can evoke as no other tragedian, the old man recalls the loving care he received from Pentheus.

Both the beginning and the end of this speech (1302–1326) contain a confession of guilt toward the god. Kadmos spoke this way even earlier in the stichomythy (1249, 1297), and will speak this way to the god later (1344, 1347; see below at 1377 f.). With due caution, we would like to connect these passages with the ἁμαρτίαι (mistakes) that Pentheus confesses at the hour of his death (1121).

In the earliest of these statements by Kadmos (1249), besides avowing his own guilt, he also accuses the god of punishing to excess. He repeats this before Dionysos (1346), and then adds the thought, sprung from a purified conception of divinity, that gods should not imitate the wrath of men. So spoke the old man to Aphrodite in the *Hippolytos*, and so spoke the messenger in the *Andromache* about Apollo.

After two verses of the chorus leader, who calls Pentheus's demise just, but pities Kadmos, and one verse beginning a speech of Agaue, there follows in the MS (P) a lacuna of at least fifty lines, in which stood the speech of Agaue and the opening words of Dionysos. Apsines' remarks on the scene (*Rhetores Graeci*, ed. Walz, 9. 587), as well as verses of the *Christus Patiens*, permit us to reconstruct the content. Agaue bewails her dead son and embraces in a painful farewell each part of his dismembered body in turn.

From the speech of Dionysos (who, according to a tempting conjecture of Webster, *Eur.*, 269, wears a bearded mask), the last fourteen lines, with the prediction of Kadmos's fate, are preserved. In the form of snakes, he and his wife, Harmonia, will journey abroad among barbarians, by whom the Enchelians (Herodotos 5. 61) are probably meant. The ὄχος μόσχων (ox-cart) mentioned in this context may be connected with the city of Βουθόη (Budua) on the southern Dalmatian coast, which Kadmos supposedly founded, after arriving there with a team of oxen (*Etym. Magnum*, s.v.). He shall lead an army of barbarians, so the god continues, which will destroy many cities, but suffer an evil return after plundering Delphi. Nonetheless, Ares will save Kadmos and Harmonia and settle him in the Fields of the Blessed. This is ancient tradition (Pindar, *Ol.* 2. 78) that seems rather out of place here, since neither Dionysos in his final chastening words, nor Kadmos himself, in his lamentations, pays any attention to his final exaltation.

A brief stichomythy follows between him and the god, in which Kadmos impotently protests against the excessive harshness of the punishment. With the invocation of Zeus, Dionysos puts the stamp of irrevocability on his decision, as Agaue realizes (1350). The god concludes the dialogue with the utmost severity: Why do you delay to submit to the inevitable? Now follows the lament of Kadmos, which is continued in a short stichomythy with Agaue, whom the god doomed to banishment in the lost portion of his speech. In the anapestic finale they bid each other a painful farewell before leaving for strange lands; Agaue's last words are a passionate rejection of Dionysos: Never more will she gaze on Kithairon, never again recall the thyrsos!

A difficulty is presented by lines 1377 f., in which, according to the MSS, the god again asserts that his greatness was slighted. In that case, either he must have remained on stage, although his departure seems likely after v. 1351, or else only his voice is meant to be heard. We prefer the solution of Hermann and others who read ἔπασχεν and give the verse to Kadmos.

The chorus closes with the verses familiar from *Alk.*, *Andr.*, *Hek.*, and (with slight variation) *Medeia*. Here they are surely misplaced.

More so than with other plays we have already been obliged to include questions of structure and meaning in the course of our analysis of the *Bakchai*. Thus stress has been placed on the central importance of the lengthy tripartite third epeisodion (576–861), which presents the decisive turning point. The previous sections develop in dialogue and song the image of Dionysian influence in its full breadth, until the second epeisodion confronts the two adversaries and leads to the apparent defeat of the god and his followers. Further, it is the function of these scenes to show how obstinately Pentheus persists in opposing Dionysos, despite all the opportunities he has to comprehend the god's greatness. By the end of the third epeisodion his defeat is assured. It is drawn out at length in the dressing scene, then made manifest through the messenger-speech and in the final scenes with the collapse of the royal house. The strongly emphasized role of the chorus contributes greatly to the unity of the composition; the choral odes broadly depict the world opposed to Pentheus.

Reinhardt concludes his essay "Die Sinneskrise bei Euripides" with a sentence about the *Bakchai*: "Even today the guesswork continues." The intense and direct power of this play contrasts strangely with the difficulty of determining its meaning.[364] For a long while the interpretation was dominated by extremists, some of whom saw in the drama a sort of palinode by Euripides, who supposedly returned to traditional belief in the gods, while others perceived only the protest of an enlightened poet: tantum religio potuit suadere malorum! Both viewpoints are all but abandoned in more recent interpretations.[365] The change, which E. R. Dodds introduced in his brilliant essay "Euripides the Irrationalist," was carried further with great success in his edition of the play.[366] R. P. Winnington-Ingram (op. cit.) assisted in establishing the conviction that in this drama we possess Euripides' direct encounter with a phenomenon that moved him to the very depths of his soul. The poet's interest in the irrational aspect of mystical cults is attested relatively early. An ode of the *Helena* (1358) presents orgiastic motifs with a Dionysian coloring; in the *Antiope* Dirke appears with a swarm of mainads (schol. *Hipp.* 58), and the choral odes of the *Phoinissai* are repeatedly interwoven with bakchic elements (226, 649, 784). However, Makedonia brought the poet in contact with much more primitive forms of the ecstatic cult than Attika could offer.

At the end of his career Euripides captured the force of the tragic and the ruthless consistency of its logic in a way scarcely equalled in his other creations. Euripides is neither Pentheus nor a Dionysian initiate. He is neither, and yet both at once, in the splendid immediacy with which he presents, to use Goethe's phrase, the "irreconcilable opposition" of two worlds. He does not describe them as a dispassionate observer, but rather bears them in his own soul as the forces determining life itself. Pentheus is the Man of Reason, as H. Diller (op. cit.) has neatly characterized him. He embodies the belief that life can be mastered by the rational manipulation of its data, and so one's own existence can be upheld against all the powers of darkness. Such a belief easily becomes a substitute for religion and begets in its representative an intolerance of any other type of fanaticism. To Pentheus is contrasted the superior force of Dionysos, which, in an enigmatic polarity, offers man just those extremes that lie outside the bounds of an existence determined solely by reason: the profoundly satisfied peace of one who rests secure in the faith of tradition, and the orgiastic outburst into infinity. The unparalleled intensity with which Euripides depicts this polarity—ultimately the polarity of the forces of nature and life—must not lead us into the misconception that he identifies himself with the Dionysian. He was able to bring all this to fulfillment in his soul, for he knew of the conflict of these two worlds, and how deeply it strikes in the life of any human being who does not merely vegetate. To present this perennial conflict within man was the poet's real concern.

Today it is considered questionable to draw biographical conclusions, and in fact many sins have already been committed on this score; yet we believe that access to this drama is denied to anyone who fails to recognize its conflict as one that Euripides experienced in his own thought.

This conflict, which forms the basis of the play, is insoluble. The god triumphs, but in the final words of Agaue, who hopes never to see Kithairon again, never again to recall the thyrsos, there persists some of the opposition of Pentheus, whom the god made his victim.

Dionysos was the starting point for Attic tragedy, and with him too it ends for us in the *Bakchai*, a work that burns like a flaming sunset on the horizon of classical poetry in this great century.

The *Kyklops* is the only satyr play that has come down to us in its entirety.[367] It was long thought to be an early work of the poet. In the introduction to his translation, Wilamowitz proposed a date soon after the *Hippolytos*;[368] recently Conacher (320) goes back even further, "perhaps before 438." But nowadays a later date, first postulated by Marquart, has won general acceptance.[369] We still cannot accept structural and thematic parallels with the *Iph. T.* and *Hel.* as decisive, nor are we convinced by A. M. Dale's suggestion that the cave of Kyklops, with its double entrance, imitated a similar construction in the *Philoktetes*, thus indicating 408 as the year of production. But the frequency of resolutions and the use of three-part dialogue and antilabai do speak in favor of a late date for the play. The exact limits remain arbitrary, since we cannot say for sure how far the formal development of the satyr play corresponded to that of tragedy. The close, genetic relationship of the two genres makes significant differences improbable, to be sure.

The dramatization of the Kyklops adventure in the *Odyssey* presented the poet with the difficult task of making a visible stage play out of the incidents in the monster's cave. A further drastic alteration was necessary to accommodate the presence of the chorus of satyrs. In the prologue Silenos tells how they came into the service of the Kyklops. Just as in the seventh *Homeric Hymn*, here, too, Tyrrhenian pirates have abducted Dionysos. To search for him, the aged Silenos set out with his satyr children but, as happened once to Odysseus, an easterly gale caught them at Cape Malea and drove their ship to the foot of Aitna, where Polyphemos made them his slaves. That the satyrs lose their way and thus are removed from the service of Dionysos or else run away from him, that they must serve strange masters until they attain their freedom—these are constant themes of the satyr play.

The parodos introduces the satyrs dancing a sikinnis and driving a flock of sheep on stage. Servants accompany them, herding the animals into the cave (82). In the first epeisodion, Odysseus arrives with his men, and, in a comical scene that also introduces the play's main theme, Odysseus peddles wine to Silenos, who offers in exchange generous provisions from the supplies of the Kyklops.[370] The curious chorus leader inquires about Troy and Helen, adding his own satyr-like speculations about the soldiers' treatment of their lovely prize. His wish—If only the race of women had never been created, except for me alone (186 f.)—is a humorous parody of those utopian wishes for improving the world that Euripidean characters are fond of uttering.

The gaiety is cut short by the approach of Polyphemos. When Silenos advises Odysseus and his men to hide in the recesses of the cave, we recall the situation in the *Odyssey*. Of course the advice must be rejected—Odysseus's boast of heroism before the walls of Troy provides a good excuse—because in fact he must remain on stage. A brief dialogue between the Kyklops and the chorus leader shows the monster's gluttony; then he perceives the Greeks in possession of his supplies. The wine-flushed visage of Silenos he attributes to blows that the old satyr must have received, and so gives him a splendid cue for cowardly betrayal and palpable lies. Silenos claims he was attacked, and what's more, the strangers threatened to do their worst to the Kyklops. He swears to all possible gods, and not by his own life but by the lives of his children instead (269)! For their part the satyrs betray Silenos without hesitation, and swear by the life of their worthy father.

A short introductory dialogue marks the transition to the agon between Odysseus and the monster. For all his bestiality Polyphemos possesses enough natural sensitivity that he calls war for the sake of a woman shameful.

Mistaking the ogre's true nature, Odysseus first tries to win over Polyphemos by recalling the pious services rendered to his father Poseidon—he even appeals to common Greek sentiment (297). When Odysseus realizes his words are having no effect, he invokes the nomos that protects suppliants. The poet adds a tragic accent to the speech (as far as we can make out, the great figures of myth are not ridiculed in the satyr play) when Odysseus declares that enough victims have fallen before Troy.

Silenos's three dividing verses parody this rhetorical display in the most insolent manner. The reply of the Kyklops is an impressive self-description. The gods don't bother him, neither Poseidon nor Zeus when he thunders. He can do that, too, when his belly is stuffed. To eat and drink your way through life each day, that is the real Zeus for any reasonable man. The devil take those people who complicate life with their νόμοι (laws)! Thus these νόμοι are man's contrivance, mere trifles, to be ignored by one who truly understands, who has the necessary power at his command. These statements carry some weight. They should not be overemphasized and made the basis of interpretation,[371] but there is no doubt that the passage betrays the influence of those extreme Sophists for whom νόμος is merely a fetter invented by the masses. It must also be said that Euripides has here somewhat overburdened his comic play.

A choral ode (356–374) follows; it divides the play into two nearly equal halves. The Kyklops may glut his belly with human flesh, but the satyrs—for all their worthlessness, they are still Greek satyrs—are repulsed by such a meal.

Odysseus emerges from the cave, functioning as a messenger. As is the rule in tragedy, he informs the chorus leader in the opening dialogue that the Kyklops has slaughtered two of his companions. His report, from which every trace of comedy is absent, describes all this in gruesome detail, but also presents the beginning of Odysseus's counterattack. He has made the monster drunk with wine and has now slipped out of the cave so as to plan his revenge with the satyrs. Revenge is the main concern (422). To this is added (less convincingly, considering the situation) the thought of rescue and escape (427, 441 f.). This was important in the *Odyssey*; here we must overlook the fact that no mention is made of a rock blocking the cave. Nor should we ask why the Greeks cower inside, instead of fleeing. After all, Odysseus has come out and it does not sound convincing when he says (480) that he didn't want to run away and leave his companions behind.

Odysseus now develops his plan to blind the drunken Kyklops after he falls asleep. Gleefully, the satyrs agree. Their anapests announce the entry of the monster, whom Euripides, unlike Homer, has to bring out onto the stage. Again, we may not ask why Odysseus's men remain in the cave. Three individual strophes, the second of which belongs to the Kyklops, celebrate the joys of the komos. In a stichomythy with Polyphemos, Odysseus describes the power of the god in the wineskin, and endeavors to dissuade the drunken monster from sharing the gift of Bakchos with his one-eyed friends. Silenos also advises him to stay and acts as a thieving cupbearer, who deceitfully pours wine down his own throat. In an enthusiastic description of his drunken ecstasy, the Kyklops professes to be a zealous devotee of pederastic pleasures and drags old Silenos into the cave to be his Ganymede. Odysseus concludes the scene with a prayer that strikes a note of genuine tragedy: Now the gods must help, or else be proved less than merest chance (τύχη).

In a brief little ode (608–623), the satyrs carouse in anticipation of revenge and their return to Dionysos. Odysseus comes out of the cave and orders the θῆρες (animals; at 590 he addressed them as sons of Dionysos, well-born children) to be quiet. Now they must act and burn out the eye of the Kyklops. Here ends the heroism of the satyrs, however, who find the most amusing excuses to avoid the vengeful deed. A brief song is all they can contribute to the blinding, which Odysseus and his men carry out in the cave.

The finale unrolls in swift tempo; Homeric motifs whiz past. The blinded Kyklops appears in the mouth of the cave and cries that "no one" stole his eye. The οὔτις motif (briefly introduced at 549) is used here, but the meaning that the trick had in the old folk tale has been lost. The chorus leader toys with the Kyklops for a while as he blindly gropes for his enemies; then Odysseus reveals who he is. Now the Kyklops recognizes the fulfillment of an ancient oracle, but promises also that Odysseus will long wander miserably. The final scene of the adventure in the *Odyssey* is summed up in all of four verses. Only now do we learn of the double entrance to the cave; an earlier reference would have further increased the difficulties discussed above.[372] Here, however, it serves a dramatic purpose: The Kyklops can disappear into the cave, threatening to climb out the other side and throw rocks at the fleeing band. Everyone in the audience would know from the *Odyssey* that this plan failed.

The play has its humorous moments, like the wine sale, Silenos's actions as cupbearer, and the cowardly dodges of the satyrs. For all their incompetence, these enchanting creatures amuse us here as they do on countless vase-paintings. And yet! Since we have come into possession of large sections of Sophokles' *Ichneutai* and now have some idea of the *Diktyoulkoi* and *Isthmiastai* of Aischylos, we have set new standards for the Attic satyr play, and in comparison the *Kyklops* is a disappointing specimen. We can understand why Euripides occasionally avoided it and, as in 438, substituted a play with a happy ending at the conclusion of a tetralogy.

Of Euripides' other satyr plays we know at least that the overpowering of a monster was a popular motif. This was undoubtedly so in the *Busiris*;[373] in the *Syleus* Herakles was supposed to perform forced labor for that evil master, but instead plundered his supplies, certainly with the assistance of the satyrs, and destroyed his house. From the *Skiron*, in which the evil son of Poseidon assuredly got his just desserts, we now possess fragments of the hypothesis, but these pose more questions than they answer.[374] In the first verse Hermes is addressed, then we learn that Skiron entrusted the guarding of the road to someone else, and went away. E. G. Turner suggested Hermes, W. S. Barrett (in Austin) plausibly conjectured Silenos. From fr. 675N and the new fragment of the hypothesis, Bruno Snell (op. cit.) has reconstructed a business venture involving the satyrs, who appeared with hetairai whom they bought at Korinth and wanted to deliver in Athens for a profit. If Barrett has correctly identified fr. 5 of the papyrus as the end of the hypothesis, Herakles appeared at the conclusion—though not, in a satyr play, as deus ex machina. He may have come as the friend of Theseus, who was probably here too the victor over Skiron.

If *P. Oxy.* 2455 fr. 7 (Austin, p. 93) comes from the hypothesis of the *Sisyphos*, which seems quite probable, then Hermes (Psychopompos) played a role in the play, and Sisyphos, having escaped from Hades, terrified the cowardly satyrs by his appearance.

Little can be said about the *Autolykos*. The utilization of Hyginus, *Fab.* 201, as a source is quite precarious. Perhaps this master thief was outdone by the thieving satyrs. Noteworthy is fr. 282N with its detailed criticism of worthless athletes. In the *Eurystheus* Herakles appeared of course, as is confirmed also by fr. 371N; the *Theristai* remains no more than a title.

ON SOME FRAGMENTS

As we already remarked in the section "Manuscript Transmission and Editions," a number of plays of Euripides that are known to us only through fragments bear such a thematic similarity to the extant works that I have thought it best to deal with both groups together. Here are just a few additions.

An early date has been suggested for the *Alkmene*,[1] based on the absence of resolutions in the scanty fragments in Nauck, but this evidence, weak enough as it is, will not stand if Austin is correct in assigning the third column of *P. Hamb.* 119 to the prologue of this play. There we find mention of Alkmene's oath to follow only the man who would avenge the death of her brothers in their quarrel with the sons of Taphios. The subject of the play seems to have been the birth of Herakles and the complications which then resulted. With Webster we can conjecture from fr. 90N that Alkmene sought refuge at an altar (as reported by a messenger), that Amphitryon tried to chase her away with fire, and that Zeus intervened. Zeus could also have spoken the epilogue.

For the *Thyestes*,[2] a terminus ante of 425 is provided by Aristophanes' *Ach.* 433, from which we also learn that Thyestes appeared on stage in rags, like Telephos. The revenge of Atreus on his brother by serving him the gruesome meal of his sons' flesh will have been the main theme. H. J. Mette (*Lustrum* 1964/9, 65) and Webster (*Eur.*, 114) have made a strong case for Ennius' use of Euripides as the model for his *Thyestes*. In an early article I tried to prove this for the *Thyestes* of Seneca, at the same time distinguishing Euripides' play from the two *Thyestes* dramas of Sophokles. H. J. Mette cautiously proposed that col. ii of *P. Hamb.* 119 (Austin no. 151) might represent fragments from the prologue of the play: A father (Thyestes?) wants to see his children, but another person (Atreus?) prevents him from entering the house.

The *Oineus*, since Aristophanes *Ach.* 418 refers to it, was produced before 425.[3] The scholium on that passage, which largely agrees with Hyginus, *Fab.* 175, and Apollodoros 1. 8. 6, furnishes a clue to the theme, although only in its broadest outlines. The sons of Agrios usurped the throne of Oineus, who had been left helpless after the death of his son Tydeus and the revolt of his grandson Diomedes against Thebes, and drove him into misery. But Diomedes came back to Kalydon, killed Agrios, and restored Oineus to power.

The following three plays may be assigned with relative certainty to the later phase of Euripides' career.

According to Philochoros (Diog. Laert. 9. 55) Euripides alluded to the death of Protagoras in the *Ixion*.[4] True or not, this presupposes that the play was produced after the Sophist met with disaster on his flight from Athens, which Jacoby (*FGrH* III b. Suppl. 1. 584) dates at 412/411, others (see Webster, *Eur.*, 160) around 420. The blasphemy and punishment of Ixion were the subject of the play. This is confirmed by the anecdote in Plutarch *Mor.* 19e, that Euripides answered the protests against the portrayal of such a blasphemer by saying that, after all, he nailed him to the wheel before his role was ended. If this occurred on stage (Webster considers the possibility of the ekkyklema) this would provide a certain parallel to the opening of the *Prometheus*.

The *Polyidos* is numbered among the later works based on the frequency of resolutions (three in one verse: fr. 641N).[5] Hyginus, *Fab.* 136, recounts the story of Polyidos, who solves the riddle of a magic calf that can change its color and therefore is chosen by Minos to locate his dead son Glaukos. He not only finds him, but, after many dangers, brings him back to life. Since the tricolored cow is attested for Euripides (schol. Aristid. p. 728f.) as is the bird which points out the way (Ailian, *De nat. an.* 5. 2), we can confidently derive the basic elements of the plot from Hyginus. Bruno Snell's supplement to Nauck offers as a new fragment (645a) anapests that seem to indicate a female chorus.

A much fuller picture can be gained from the remnants of the *Phaethon*, which was probably one of Euripides' most impressive plays.[6] Metrical observations place it in the time period 415–409. Our most valuable aids for the reconstruction are two parchment pages from the codex Par. Claromontanus 107 (see V) that provide fragments from the beginning and end of the drama. It was set in the Far East, close to the palace of Helios, whence he rises (Mimnermos fr. 11). There, near the land of the Aithiopians, King Merops lives with Klymene, who conceived a son by the sun-god and raised him in the house of Merops.[7] This was long conjectured for the prologue and is now confirmed by the remnants of the hypothesis P. Oxy. 2455 fr. 14 col. xv. Thanks to this papyrus we are also certain of the reconstruction of a scene near the beginning of the play, in which Klymene tells her son of a planned marriage and in this context reveals to him who his father is. She herself advises him to go to the palace of Helios, where he is promised the fulfillment of a wish; thus, he can verify his parentage.

A lucky chance has preserved for us the parodos of the chorus of maidservants, a lovely lyric passage describing the awakening of man and beast in the freshness of morning. The fragments also indicate an agon between Merops and Phaethon, who persists in his refusal to marry. We may surmise that he shared some of the characteristics of Hippolytos.

The central portion of the play is missing, but through the second page of the Claromontanus we can form some idea of the conclusion, in which contrast seems to have played a large role. A messenger recounts the fatal ride of Phaethon in the chariot of the sun, and his fall. The corpse is brought in and hidden in the treasure chamber by Klymene. Then Merops enters in procession with an auxiliary chorus of maidens who sing the hymenaios for the coming wedding.[8] But a servant reports smoke pouring from the chamber; Merops finds the corpse and learns how the boy died, and, undoubtedly, also that Phaethon was not his real son. Helios probably appeared as deus ex machina, rescuing Klymene from her threatening husband.

The most difficult question involves the identity of the divine bride meant for Phaethon. All arguments lead back to the solution proposed by Wilamowitz (first in Hermes 18 [1883], 413), that it was Aphrodite herself. We cannot overlook the bold conjecture of Webster (Eur., 230), though it remains unsupported by tangible evidence. In his view Aphrodite, whose intentions were unknown to Merops, was planning to destroy the son of the despised Helios (Od. 8. 270), who spurned her gifts. If only we knew more about this curious wedding arrangement!

The Kadmos remains for us a mere title.

DRAMATIC FORM AND LANGUAGE

Much more so than his predecessors', the work of Euripides is marked by contradictions. This can be seen immediately in the architectonics of his dramas. Certain typical elements such as prologue, agon, rhesis, messenger-speech, divine epilogue, choral ode, and monody are more sharply distinguished and tend toward greater independence. With Euripides it becomes easier to mark off individual "acts."[1] Yet it would be wrong to assert that Euripidean tragedy falls apart neatly into the aforementioned parts. Rather, its structure is as a rule extraordinarily taut, and the inner relationship between these elements is carefully considered, as we have endeavored to show in our analyses. Often one can perceive a balanced symmetry of construction: not seldom a large central section can be set off, enclosed by a beginning and end section.[2] This sort of triptych-like arrangement is repeated in individual scenes.

If our view of the ancient prologue is correct (see above under Thespis), the expository opening speech represents a return to an old and primitive form of introducing subject matter.[3] The idea, first formulated by Lessing (*Hamb. Dram.* no. 48), that Euripides anticipated coming events in order to devote full attention to the execution of the plot by removing the element of suspense, is valid, if at all, for the prologues delivered by gods. But even in these much is left open; indeed, the audience's expectations are sometimes purposely led astray. The *Ion* is a good example of this. Euripides did not consider the prologue speech merely a convenient way of clarifying the complex background information presupposed by the plot; its sober declarative tone, free of strong emotion, allows for effective crescendi in the subsequent odes and speeches.

The agons emerge as structures clearly set apart both in content and form.[4] They possess something like an internal logic, since each partner brings to bear all the arguments at his disposal. Here the basic dialectical feature of the Greek character found suitable room for expression. For this reason the greatest caution is necessary when one attempts to evaluate the statements in the agon for the interpretation of the play as a whole. We need only recall the problems involved with the *Alkestis*. In this and other plays, to name only *Med.*, *Herakles*, *El.*, the conflict is brought to a pinnacle in the agon, after which the forces, now clearly delineated, are released, or else a turning point is reached. The formal structure is based on the careful balance between self-contained speeches separated by choral verses (usually doublets) and spirited stichomythies, in which the opponents frequently run in place after their arguments have been exhausted.

Stichomythy is given especially wide play in the works of Euripides. No other element of his tragedies has received such an excellent and productive analysis as Schwinge's of this one. He has corrected the error of A. Gross, who believed that stichomythies were used only to express excitement, and showed the whole range of its functions in counsel, persuasion, and narration.[5] Euripides demonstrated high artistic skill in this difficult form of dialogue, and although lame passages and empty verses are certainly not entirely absent, they are nevertheless extremely rare.

Outside the agon, too, Euripides composed his great set speeches with the utmost care. The new significance of rationality in arguments based on proof, probability, and contradiction, the importance of the εἰκός (probable), which F. Solmsen has demonstrated for Antiphon, now play a decisive role.[6] The ancients could also praise such rhetorical skill (Dio Chrys. 52. 11) or condemn it as a corrupting influence on the city (Aristoph. *Ran.* 1069). When the *Vita* of Aischylos asserts that this poet strictly avoided τὸ πανοῦργον κομψοπρεπές τε καὶ γνωμολογικόν (wicked witticism and sententiousness) in his works, the slap at Euripides is unmistakeable. But it is wrong to make Euripides into a mere pupil of rhetoric. Views like those propounded by Miller in his *Euripides Rhetoricus* (Göttingen 1887) have been corrected and considerably modified by Tietze.[7] Interpretation shows that the appearance of rational elements in the speeches is determined by the specific situation and does not adhere to any fixed set of principles. Of course we cannot rule out all contacts with the art of rhetoric that was developing so vigorously during the poet's lifetime. The careful designation of theme at the beginning of certain speeches (e.g. *Herakles* 170, 1255; *Suppl.* 426; *Tro.* 916, 969) and the emphasis on organizational elements point in this direction. It is understandable that Quintilian (10. 1. 68) singles out Euripides as the most useful of the tragedians for the aspiring orator and stresses the forensic character of his speeches.

Connected with the emergence of rational elements is the poet's special consideration for the πιθανόν (plausible), the careful motivation of the comings and goings of his characters, of their action and inaction. Recall, for instance, the painstaking way in which the pedagogue of the *Phoinissai* (95, 142) explains his knowledge of the situation in the enemy camp! More on this in Schadewaldt, *Mon.* 8. 4. Dio Chrys. (52. 6) already pointed out this preoccupation of the poet, which to be sure might also occasionally lead to added complications. In the *Andromache* (1085) the poet has Neoptolemos spend three days in Delphi, for Orestes needs this time to prepare his attack. And so we must simply accept the fact that Neoptolemos whiles away these three days sightseeing instead of getting on with his pressing business.

In the course of our analyses we judged the messenger-speeches of Euripides to be epic masterpieces, an estimation requiring qualification only in the case of battle descriptions. As a rule, the messenger reports the most important facts in a brief introductory dialogue (often with the chorus leader), after which he develops the full picture in a broad flowing speech—essentially repeating, mutatis mutandis, the relationship of the prologue speech to the following succession of scenes. Above all in these messenger-speeches, Euripides develops a realism that is also in evidence elsewhere in his work, as for example in his portrayal of elderly persons.[8]

In keeping with the character of these narratives, we find in them numerous echoes of epic language. The less frequent use of the article belongs in this context, as well as the epic flourish to introduce an anonymous speaker (e.g., *Andr.* 1104; *Herakles* 951; *Hel.* 1589).[9]

The dramatist shapes a piece of life, whether it be taken from myth, history, or everyday life. To cut off this piece of life at a certain point, to make an ending that is truly final and does not leave the audience with unanswered questions—this has always been the playwright's most difficult task. In the majority of his extant works, Euripides chose for his conclusion the god from the machine, who surveys past and future at once. There is no deus in *Alk.*, *Herakles*, *Tro.*, and *Phoin.*, since in the *Alkestis* all turns out well anyway, while in the other three, no reversal is possible and no clarification necessary. In *Med.*, *Hek.*, and *Herakleidai*, however, some figure with prophetic powers appears in the role of a deus ex machina. Since in recent years the discussion of this device of dramatic technique has focused on the question of its meaning, and this in turn is closely bound up with the significance of the traditional gods for Euripides, we will investigate this problem further in the next section.

No sweeping generalization can do justice to Euripides' choral odes,[10] not even when made by Aristotle, who demands (*Poet.* 1456a) that the chorus participate in the action as a part of the whole, and contrasts with Sophokles the bad example of Euripides. The closeness of the chorus to the plot is entirely variable in Euripides and is adapted to the conditions of the particular play. Also, the individual odes of a play are frequently connected to each other, as in the *Phoinissai*, in which the choral songs add the background of Thebes' mythical history to the action of the drama. Often Euripides will capture the atmosphere of a scene in the subsequent choral ode.

In Euripides' odes we can clearly perceive a development that derives from the new Attic dithyramb.[11] Kranz (282) has spoken of the "new ode" when dealing with the final decades of Euripides' career. This development must have had a great effect especially on the musical side of drama. The mimetic element played an important role, which agrees with the fact that the late choral odes of Euripides seem to invite such a display of gesture. In view of the preponderance of the new music, the separate value of the text sometimes becomes questionable. Sentence elements are strung together in a loose sequence; participles and relative clauses often pile up to the point where all shape and meaning are lost. Wilamowitz, who compares the style of Timotheos, phrases it neatly: "The structural framework is only there, like the rods of a trellis, to support the intertwining tendrils of extravagant ornamentation." Aristophanes directed all his rancor against this new style, and his parodies (esp. *Ran.* 1309) provide valuable assistance in grasping its characteristics.

In the multiplicity of Euripides' choral odes we can perceive one more development which, according to Aristotle (*Poet.* 18, 1456a 29), begins with Agathon: the ode is simply an interlude, an ἐμβόλιμον, foreshadowing the χοροῦ (the mere direction "for the chorus" in place of a choral ode) of comedy. In Euripides we find examples of lyric narrative which, while not completely irrelevant to the drama, do have an independence of their own, so that Kranz, comparing the poetry of Bakchylides, could speak of dithyrambic stasima. *Hek.* 905 illustrates this in rudimentary form; the other examples are *Tro.* 511; *El.* 432, 699; *Iph. T.* 1234; *Hel.* 1301; *Phoin.* 638, 1019; *Iph. A.* 164, 751, 1036.

Besides the choral songs, actor's arias gain increasing importance in the dramas of Euripides, and similar formal observations can be made about them. While the linguistic expression may occasionally seem bombastic, not a few of these monodies are imbued with a direct pathos arising from genuine emotion. This is true both for the jubilation of reunited siblings or lovers and for the grievous pain that Kreusa pours forth in her aria (859), one of Euripides' most magnificent songs.

The inner contradictions of Euripides' work are also evident in his choice of language.[12] The ornamentation of the lyric passages, exaggerated to the point of bombast, contrasts with that σαφές (clarity) in the spoken verse that Aristotle (*Rhet.* 3. 2; 1404b 1) designates as the special advantage of λέξις (speech) in general. Also in this connection belongs that approximation to the language of everyday life which, as Aristotle (op. cit., 1404b 26) notes, appears first in Euripides. In addition to his praise of Euripides' language, Satyros (col. vii) quotes the enthusiastic judgment of Philemon. This is understandable, since Euripides prepared the way for New Comedy with his language as well as with his themes. It is telling that scholars vacillated for quite some time between him and Menander for the authorship of the Didot Papyrus. Here too the author of *On the Sublime* (40) proves himself an astute critic, when he offers examples to show how Euripides, with a very ordinary vocabulary, achieved a certain solemnity in spoken verse through word order alone. Modern scholars could learn much from such observations.

The tables in Smereka (op. cit., esp. 1. 238) list numerous words that are found only in Euripides, or are used by him for the first time. As we might expect, examples from the lyric passages predominate. But there is hardly a trace left of the rugged creative power of Aischylos's language; rather with Euripides we find mostly nominal and verbal composite formations whose expressive force is relatively slight. In dialogue passages, Euripides' language grips us through its sheer simplicity, which never descends to the level of triviality. There is a clear trend toward abstraction, and a related phenomenon, the delight in carefully worked out conceptual antitheses. The ὄνομα-ἔργον antithesis has been well treated by F. Heinimann;[13] for the sharp contrast between εἷς (one) and plural expressions, we have assembled material in the *Anz. Ak. Wien* 1947, 109. 2 = *Ges. Schr.*, 151. 15.

The greater freedom taken by Euripides in his handling of iambic trimeter is revealed, above all, in the number of resolutions, which, in general, increase steadily as the years go by. We have already made frequent mention of this; here we recall the fundamental studies by T. Zielinski, *Tragodumenon Libri Tres*, Cracow 1925, and E. B. Ceadel, "Resolved Feet in the Trimeters of Euripides," *Class. Quart.* 35 (1941), 66, as well as the contributions of Matthiessen, *El., Taur. Iph. u. Hel.*, Hypomn. 5 (1964) 168, and A. M. Dale in her edition of the *Helena* (Oxford 1967, xxv).

In the extant works, trochaic tetrameters occur for the first time in the *Troiades* of 415, after which they become standard (on the problem of the *Elektra* see the commentary on the play above).[14] One may attribute their use to the poet's archaizing tendency, another provocative contradiction to the internal development of his works.

POET AND PHILOSOPHER

The title of this section expresses a perennial problem of Euripidean interpretation.[1] Scholars have always tended to play off the thinker against the poet; some have even made Euripides into a philosopher of the stage.[2] Rivier's book was a necessary protest against the one-sidedness of this picture. To give the poet his due remains the primary task of any interpreter of Euripides. Conversely, however, this is not possible without a historical context, and herein lies the problem. Sophokles, Herodotos, and Euripides were contemporaries of the Sophistic movement and thus, in a city that united far-reaching intellectual trends within a very small area, they witnessed the upheaval of all tradition. While the reaction of the first two men was primarily one of resistance, the case is very different with Euripides. To be sure, a long-championed error can now be considered outdated. Euripides is not the "poet of the Greek Enlightenment," as the title of Wilhelm Nestle's book (1901) claimed; he was in no sense the "herald" or the "mouthpiece" for the Sophistic view of life.[3] But of course he did not ignore it. Euripides' whole work betrays a profound unrest caused by the new ideas, and his highly differentiated reaction to them. Yet it would be altogether wrong to piece together the poet's "world view" from a mosaic of individual passages. Not only in the fragments is it usually (but not always) impossible to decide whether we hear Euripides speaking through his characters. But often their statements would have been inconceivable before the emergence of Sophism, and could only have been written by a dramatist who found himself in a continual dialogue with the new movement.

A fragment from the *Antiope* (189N) says if one were truly capable of speaking, one could undoubtedly unleash a battle of δισσοὶ λόγοι (opposite arguments) for any given subject. The phrase belongs to the intellectual domain of the Sophists, and in that context it can mean nothing other than that the skilled orator knows how to debate—under certain circumstances even how to make the weaker cause appear the stronger. But on a deeper level it can also mean that in a world of contradictions, there are two different viewpoints on every matter, and here we find ourselves wholly in the sphere of Protagoras's *Antilogoi*. The confidence that rested on and was guaranteed by tradition has been replaced by a suspension of belief that gives voice to doubts that once were unthinkable. An uneasiness has possessed the mind of the intellectuals, and this is reflected in the work of Euripides. Reinhardt spoke of a "crisis of meaning," which is valid so long as we bear in mind that Euripides did not despair of life's meaning but was engaged in a constant struggle to discover it. It is from this standpoint that his characters speak, and the paradoxes of a world recognized as contradictory find expression in what they say. For this we offer two examples.

The ancient scholiast on *Med.* 665 already noticed that σοφός (clever, wise) was one of the poet's favorite words, and σύνεσις (reason), which Aristophanes has him invoke before the agon in the *Frogs* (893), is also a word that appears frequently in his dramas.[4] Whoever spoke the lines of fr. 910N, with their praise of the happiness that knowledge can bring, they could only have been written by a poet who himself was capable of experiencing such happiness in rigorous mental activity. Noteworthy is the consonance with the proud assertion of Anaxagoras (DK 59A 30) that θεωρία (contemplation) is the meaning of human existence. To this we add the song of praise for Athens (*Med.* 824), which, in highly poetic form, takes up ideas about the environment, such as those presented in the medical writings of the time, and which twice (827, 844) sings the high praise of σοφία (wisdom). In the same play, however, the messenger harshly condemns (1225) "the sophists and false philosophers of Eur. own day" (Page in his comm.). Similar sentiments are found in frr. 913 and 924. All this may depend on the particular context, but in the *Bakchai* the chorus sings of the bliss of a peaceful soul and of intellectual renunciation (395: τὸ σοφὸν δ' οὐ σοφία— wit is not wisdom) with an immediacy attainable only by a poet whose spiritual potential included such sentiments. Not that we claim to hear here a confession representing the aged Euripides' last word on wisdom.[5] We do, however, maintain that the poet was acutely aware of the irreconcilable antinomy between the restlessness of inquisitive meditation and the peace for which the human heart yearns.

In the *Iph. T.* (678), Euripides has Pylades say, as if he were saying something perfectly obvious, that the many are bad; *Iph. Aul.* 1357 expresses a similar sentiment. In contrast to this, however, under the influence of new ideas, Euripides tore down social barriers and repeatedly demonstrated the ethical potential of people from the lower classes. There is the auxiliary chorus of shepherds in the *Alexandros* (fr. 52N; further, fr. 54); there are characters like the stouthearted but impoverished farmer in the *Elektra* (note the thoughtful reflection of Orestes, 367), or the upright fellow in the *Orestes*, who intercedes on Orestes' behalf, one who seldom comes to the city and numbers among those who alone preserve the land! His counterpart is found in the glib city dweller who offers the fatal advice in the *Bakchai* (717). Even to the slave Euripides concedes the possibility of moral bearing actually superior to that of a free man.[6]

That Euripides, as a concerned witness to such a manifold new upheaval, occasionally let his dramatic figures speak out of character, was a criticism leveled against him even in antiquity (Plutarch, *Mor.* 539B; cf. on fr. 978). And E. R. Dodds remarks on *Hek.* 603: "Euripides the philosopher, who must then make his excuses as best he can to Euripides the dramatist."[7] When, for example, Medeia (230) bemoans the unworthy lot of women, this pertains far more to the wife of the Attic citizen than to the Kolchian heroine.

A few examples can offer a picture of the widely diverse and occasionally contradictory opinions expressed by Euripidean characters on questions that concerned the poet's own time. However, the utmost caution is necessary in attempting to derive a partial biography of the poet by arranging differences of this type chronologically. Thus, it remains doubtful whether we should assume with Goossens a period from 410 onward, in which the poet regarded all human reasoning with great skepticism. In one case, however, we believe that it is possible to fix roughly in time the poet's preoccupation with a problem of enormous contemporary significance. Three passages in plays that belong quite close together in the decade 430–420 (*Hipp.* 79; *Hek.* 592; *Suppl.* 913) illustrate how Euripides gradually dropped the old concept of the sole and decisive importance of φύσις (inborn character) in favor of a new educational optimism propounded by the Enlightenment.[8]

But Euripides' reaction to the ideas of his time has its most far-reaching consequences in his treatment of the gods, who appear on stage in his plays no less frequently than in those of his predecessors. The contradictions of his work emerge more sharply than elsewhere in religion, and it is understandable that we find a corresponding polarity among scholarly opinions on this point. In the introduction to his edition of the *Ion* (1926, 18), Wilamowitz designates the prologue and Athena's final speech as concessions of the poet to the very faith in the gods that he was attacking through his manipulation of the plot. M. Imhof, however, in his study (Bern 1966) attempts to derive from these same sections the basis of a profoundly religious interpretation of the play. In various passages in his book on Euripides, Conacher expresses his basic view that the purpose behind the poet's portrayal of the gods was to destroy belief in them, but B. M. W. Knox in his critique upholds not only the reality of the Euripidean gods, but actually sees in them a return to the Homeric divinities that went beyond the theological conceptions developed by his two predecessors. These two examples will stand for many others.[9]

Euripides the dramatist did not write religious manifestos designed to liberate his Athenian audience from their beliefs. But so often and so harshly do his characters criticize traditional conceptions that the poet's own misgivings are undeniable. What gods are these, who take note of the slightest annoyance in their petty vindictiveness and punish mortals for personal motives (*Hipp.* 117 with 1420; *Andr.* 1161; *Ba.* 1348)! And even if Apollo in the *Ion* arranges everything neatly at the end, yet he remains the god whose game was almost spoiled by Tyche, who palms off a son on the Athenian king, who cannot undo Kreusa's suffering, and has good reasons for sending his sister, Athena, ahead to speak with the parties involved. But Athena is also the object of reproach; Auge (fr. 266N) complains that she delights in the weapons of the slaughtered in her temple, but that a birth desecrates the place. This is similar to the rebuke voiced by Iphigeneia among the Taurians (380) against an Artemis who shuns all impurity and yet delights in human sacrifice. The latter passage is rendered strangely ambiguous by a twist typical of Euripides' notions of divinity. Thus Iphigeneia begins to criticize τὰ τῆς θεοῦ σοφίσματα (the deceitful devices of the goddess) but then (385) refuses to believe such things about the daughter of Zeus and Leto, as she also rejects the story of the gods' banquet with Tantalos. It is the barbarians in this land who have imputed to the goddess such a wicked custom.

Here we must add the passages that cast doubt on various features of myth, as on Helen's birth from Leda (*Hel.* 21; *Iph. Aul.* 794) or the change in the sun's course caused by Zeus because of Thyestes' outrage (*El.* 737). Hekabe's criticism of the story about the judgment of Paris (*Tro.* 969), which was among the arguments Helen used in the agon, is characteristic in its sort of double reasoning. Hekabe proves the legend to be nonsense, but not with the intent of undermining belief in the goddesses; on the contrary, she perceives herself as their σύμμαχος (ally) when she contradicts a story that is unworthy of their greatness.

It was inevitable that the criticism of the gods and myths in Euripides' plays was taken to imply that the poet himself was an atheist. Thus the garland seller in the *Thesmophoriazusai* (445) complains that she has been losing business since Euripides convinced the people through his tragedies that the gods do not exist. In truth, however, behind all these criticisms lies the poet's search for a purified divine image. Thus Iphigeneia concludes her above-mentioned speech about human sacrifice with the assertion that no god could be evil (391). In a fragment from the *Bellerophontes* (292N) we find the laconic phrase: If gods do something shameful, they are not gods. Curious lines from the *Melanippe* (fr. 506N), in which the belief in the tablets of Zeus with the notation of mortal transgressions is rejected, sound like a correction of Aischylos (*Eum.* 275; fr. 530, 21M). What replaces this belief we learn at the verse's end: Dike is here close to us, if only we wish to see her (cf. fr. 151N)! A similar yearning for justice in the world is voiced by Elektra (*El.* 583): Belief in the gods would crumble if injustice were stronger than justice. The chorus leader in *Suppl.* 564 speaks of the light of Dike.

In searching for a concept of divinity without the dross, the dramatizer of traditional myths was bound to come into conflict with his material. As a result, Euripides' work is filled with shrill dissonances, and few as shrill as Herakles' words to

Theseus after murdering his family (1341): Never could gods engage in illicit love affairs or fight with each other. These are the poets' wretched tales! We might be listening to Xenophanes (DK 21B 11). And yet in the play we have seen Lyssa and Iris enter the palace to fulfill Hera's command. Their arrival, however, contrasts harshly with the previous choral ode with its pious praise of divine justice (772). Truly: πολὺς ταραγμὸς ἔν τε τοῖς θεοῖς ἔνι / κἀν τοῖς βροτείοις (great confusion reigns among gods and among men; *Iph. T.* 572)!

As an alternative to the traditional anthropomorphism that he rejected, Xenophanes developed a deeply spiritual concept of a single god separated from everything human (DK 21B 23–26). Euripides never reached such a goal. Two things stood in his way. Myth remained the only source from which he could draw his material; he could strain against these bonds, but never break them. But what life showed him, with all the unaccountability of those forces to which man remains exposed and helpless despite all his plans and devices—this least of all could lead the poet to enlightenment. Variations, which are caused by the restlessness of his search, surround an essentially unified line of agnosticism. Here the choral lines 1104 ff. in the *Hippolytos* offer a striking example. The opening words recall the hymn to Zeus in the *Agamemnon* (165); reflection on "the god's care for men" provides release from pain.[10] But then we hear that this profound hope for understanding crumbles in the face of the sufferings and deeds of men. Hardly anywhere can we see so deeply into the turmoil of this search as in Hekabe's prayer (*Tro.* 884). The formula ὅστις ποτ᾽ εἶ σύ (whoever you may be), referring to Zeus, again recalls the hymn of Aischylos. But while the earlier poet used the phrase to express the insufficiency of language to grasp the greatness of his god, in Euripides the words are spoken out of deep uncertainty and probing doubt. What is this Zeus, δυστόπαστος εἰδέναι (hard to fathom), who supports the earth and has his seat upon it? Is he the necessity of natural law or the spirit that rules in man (cf. fr. 1018)? It has long been recognized that this passage was greatly influenced by the speculative thought of the time, in particular that of Diogenes of Apollonia and Anaxagoras.[11] Of course this does not represent any "profession of faith" on the poet's part, a notion against which Rohdich (21, 27) protests, but it does bear witness to his search for the essence of divinity, a search determined by the ideas of his age. That he intended with this prayer to characterize Hekabe as a queen with philosphical aspirations that have nothing to do with his own ideas, is rather improbable.

The ὅστις formula recurs in different variations (*Herakles* 1263; *Or.* 418; *Ba.* 894, here in the midst of the chorus's profession of humility in accepting the ancient and honorable traditions; fr. 480N[12]), always as an expression of our limited ability to comprehend divinity. "Radical agnosticism concerning the divine" (Zuntz) is voiced in the choral stanza *Hel.* 1137. Confronted with the changeable destinies ordained by the gods, who could attempt to explain their nature?[13] Here also we find the phrase τὰ θεῶν (the divine), which occurs with especial frequency from the 420s onward, as E. Heitsch has demonstrated; he interprets it well as a neutral-indefinite expression.[14] One of the numerous Euripidean rejections of prophetic wisdom is connected, in fr. 795N, with contempt for all those who claim to possess knowledge about the gods.[15]

Indeed, the old man's statement in the *Helena* (711 f.) could stand as a motto for the poet's work: ὁ θεὸς ὡς ἔφυ τι ποικίλον καὶ δυστέκμαρτον (God is something intricate and hard to interpret).

When speaking of the agnosticism professed again and again by Euripidean characters, one thinks naturally of Protagoras, whom the *Vita* connects with the poet in a teacher-pupil relationship, and who is supposed to have declaimed his work *On the Gods* in Euripides' house (DK 80A 1). But Kannicht in his commentary on the *Helena* (p. 296) skillfully shows that the agnosticism of Euripides, in contrast to that of Protagoras, is only apparently destructive, "since it does not concern the existence of divine authority as such, but only the constitution of its nature and the meaning of its actions."

Even so, there are some passages in which the incomprehension of the gods' nature also approaches the question of their existence. Of course one should not quote in this context fr. 286N, from the *Bellerophontes*, with its radical denial of the gods, since it is clearly spoken by someone who brings up the question that the ride to heaven on Pegasos is to solve. It is more indicative of the poet's personal agnosticism when in the *Iph. Aul.* (1034 f.) Klytaimestra, in a remark not demanded by the context, juxtaposes the existence or nonexistence of the gods as equal possibilities. The verses spoken by Hekabe (*Hek.* 800) are difficult: ἀλλ' οἱ θεοὶ σθένουσιν χὡ κείνων κρατῶν / νόμος· νόμῳ γὰρ τοὺς θεοὺς ἡγούμεθα (But the gods too are mighty and the nomos that rules over them; for by nomos we believe in the gods). Their meaning cannot be explained with certainty, but it seems to us that F. Heinimann has proposed the most probable interpretation.[16] He believes that the first line echoes Pindar's fr. 169 about nomos as king over all (this latter passage in itself presents serious problems), but then Euripides turns the thought around, takes νόμος in the sense of that which is valid by convention, subsuming under this notion both belief in the gods and the concepts of justice mentioned in the next verse. Νόμος would then be understood not much differently from in the fragment from the *Auge* (920N = 265a Suppl.), which is wholly based on the Sophistic antithesis: ἡ φύσις ἐβούλεθ', ᾗ νόμων οὐδὲν μέλει (So it was willed by nature, which cares naught for laws).

From this brief overview emerges the picture of an unappeased and also unappeasable unrest. Furthermore, it is clear that we cannot follow those scholars who attempt to portray Euripides as a man for whom the dissonances of life are ultimately resolved in a meaningful rule of the gods.[17] Understandably the deus ex machina plays a significant role in such discussions. The interpretation of this device reveals once again the problematical nature of Euripidean studies. While A. Spira and M. Imhof (both op. cit.) believe that the divinity at the end of the play establishes a genuine reconciliation and real order, von Fritz (312) in particular supports the view that Euripides tended more and more (the *Orestes* being the extreme case) to emphasize the irreality of the happy endings. The deus ex machina represents for him an ironic technique by which Euripides himself can boldly underline the contrast to the plot, as he saw and shaped it. We prefer not to go this far, but one should recognize the tacked-on character of most Euripidean machine-gods, as opposed to Herakles in the *Philoktetes*. Nowhere is this so evident as in the *Iph. T.*, in which a wind must drive the successful escapees back to shore so that Athena can make her appearance. There also it becomes especially clear what a large role the cult aitia play in these final speeches. They are present in nearly every play, and if gods do not appear, a mortal must do the honors (*Hek.*, *Hkld.*). That the poet lays such great stress at the end of plays on a connection with cult tradition that often appears suspect in other passages, is one of the contradictions deeply rooted in his work. Human inadequacy and divine caprice lead events into an apparently inescapable confusion. The means by which Euripides restores some semblance of order must necessarily be violent. Regard for the traditional material, consideration for his public, and the fact that tragedy still remained a sacred performance at the Festival of Dionysos—all these may have had an equal share in this.

An essential feature of Euripidean tragedy has recently been summed up in a phrase by de Romilly (*Time*, 131): "what has been lost for theological consideration . . . has been gained for the study of man himself." Recent studies allow us to recognize more clearly the techniques of characterization peculiar to Euripides, thus giving new meaning to the formulation of Jakob Burckhardt: "While Sophokles is always concerned with the whole of a character, Euripides occasionally has a way of exploiting to the fullest the emotion of a certain character in a particular scene."[18]

The unity and consistency of the ethos of the great Sophoklean figures is not repeated to the same extent in Euripides. The powerful flood of outpouring emotion heralds a new sentimentality in drama. The *Vita* of Aischylos (7), with clear sarcasm toward Euripides, stresses that the elder tragedian refused to cater to the maudlin sensibilities of his audience. Quintilian, however (10. 1. 68), admires Euripides primarily because of his portrayal of the emotions that arouse our sympathy. As the creator of a new style in representing pathos, Euripides shows himself once again as the precursor of Hellenism. The treatise *On the Sublime* (15. 3) credits him with the masterly depiction of the emotional states of love and madness, and these are two spheres that dominate in Hellenistic poetry. The new importance of children's roles also belongs in this context.

And so there is some justification for Zürcher's basic thesis that the poet was primarily concerned with the isolated psychic phenomenon and its motivation, course, and effect. But in following the lead of Tycho von Wilamowitz he has gone so far as to deny that Euripides was capable of drawing individuals at all; both the scholium on *Med.* 922 (similarly the hypothesis), which criticizes the disintegration of the title figure, and Aristotle's objection to the portrayal of the *Iphigeneia at Aulis* (*Poet.* 1454a 31) are the starting points for his interpretation. In our analyses of the individual plays, we opposed this view, and see that today the correct mean has been reached. Despite sharp accentuation of the isolated psychic phenomenon, the figures of Euripidean tragedy are so clearly characterized as individuals that there can be no talk of a disintegration of character.

Distinguishing himself from his predecessors, Euripides added new features to the tragic portrayal of man. While the characters of the two earlier dramatists tread unswervingly the path imposed by fate or their own conscience, the figures of Euripides often display a new fluidity of opinion and decision.[19] The first part of the *Iph.*

A. is filled with this sort of movement; one μεταβολή (change) follows the other until Iphigeneia's heroic decision puts an end to all the confusion. This too must be said of Euripides' portraits of humanity: Above all the frailty and inadequacy of his now questionable heroes, above the petty hatred and selfishness, there rises again and again the pure self-sacrificing courage of young men and women who do not yet carry the world's poison within them. In these characters the poet invested the remnants of his faith in ethical conduct.

Euripides was a master in the representation of emotional states, but he was not so interested in showing the path from one to the other. The abruptness of Iphigeneia's decision to die has caused consternation ever since Aristotle. Not that the change in her would be totally incomprehensible, but something comparable to Klytaimestra's transition in the *Agamemnon*, from jubilation over her deed to fear-stricken insight into its implications, is not to be found in the works of the great dramatizer of stationary emotion.

Regarding certain difficulties of interpreting Euripides, H. D. F. Kitto made a statement that we might resignedly set over the poet's entire work: "You never know where you are."[20] But who could leave it at that? And so we too are unable to give up the search for the key that unlocks the innermost meaning of Euripides' works. *Euripides the Rationalist*, the title of A. W. Verrall's book (1905), has been challenged by E. R. Dodds with "Euripides the Irrationalist," *Class. Rev.* 43 (1929), 97, and his brilliant introduction to the *Bakchai*. In fact, Euripides was both, and to a degree that does not permit us to draw a sharp dividing line but merely to state that the two were indissolubly fused. He was quite aware of man's imperative task (never to be mastered despite his irrepressible hopes and endeavors) of controlling his world by means of reason and shaping it into a meaningful cosmos that satisfies his needs; but he also possessed the other insight that man, for all his search and struggles, remains helpless before unaccountable powers that at any moment might smash to pieces all that he has accomplished. Thus Herakles perishes, the great man of action, and in this perspective the *Bakchai* does not stand isolated at the end of Euripides' career but represents the genuine portrayal of a conflict that to a great extent determines the poet's whole work. The *Bakchai* is neither a recantation nor a protest but rather a depiction of that enigmatic force which human *ratio* has never matched and never will match.[21]

So much for the tragic Euripides, who composed tragedy in the sense of that "irreconcilable opposition" that Goethe spoke of to Chancellor von Müller (6 June 1824). We encounter something altogether different in the dramas dominated by the caprices of Tyche, in which long-separated couples are reunited, and human (especially feminine) cleverness finds a way out of every danger. For these *pièces roses*, which can only be called tragedies in the ancient sense of the word, and which foreshadow the secularization of drama in New Comedy, the concept of *salvazione* in the sense of σωτηρία is quite apt, and Garzya (*Pensiero*) has focused on this in his interpretations. Here the irrational no longer appears as the opposing force that overwhelms all but instead as Tyche, whose whims arbitrarily confuse the paths and destinies of man and can even endanger the designs of a god (*Ion*). Despite the force of chance, it is possible to maintain one's existence by planning and daring.

Aischylos and Sophokles were also aware of the overwhelming power of the irrational, but this was for them beyond all doubt identical with the rule of the gods as presented by tradition. Modifications of ancient belief (e.g., *Ag.* 750) signify a deepening, not a rejection, of faith. The case is different with Euripides. Again we are confronted with a contradiction that is decisive for his entire work. For him the gods of the old faith are no longer the great forces of reality. His search ends in agnosticism. But what forms can he use to express his beliefs about the adversaries of rational man? In what garb, in what masks can he have them appear on stage? Until the complete triumph of philosophical thought and speech, a Greek author could express his significant ideas about the world and the driving forces behind it only with the help of myth. Just as one speaks of the intermediate world of language, so too, for broad segments of Greek creativity, we can speak of an intermediate world of myth, especially in poetry.[22] Euripides too had no other mode of expression, unless he wished to dramatize philosophical treatises. Zuntz rightly says: "To him the traditional figures offered wide and wonderful aesthetic possibilities."[23] We would like to extend these possibilities beyond the realm of aesthetics to the existential statements of the poet.

Thus we have confirmed the problems posed by Euripides' gods from a new perspective. Although basically a skeptic, who basically could speak with as little certainty about the gods as Protagoras, he was obliged to deal with them through his artistic medium, which as a poet he could not escape. Of course, one could remove Aphrodite and Artemis from the *Hippolytos*, or Iris and Lyssa from the *Herakles*, and the plots could run almost wholly much as they do without these mythical figures, but then the great forces of opposition to which the protagonists succumb would remain without expression; tragedy would become the presentation of mere intrigues or regrettable accidents.

At the end of Euripides' work stands the great and fearful figure of Dionysos. In the *Bakchai* the man who tries to assert the power of his rational thought is brought to destruction by the overwhelmingly higher and contrary force of the god; the way in which this action is portrayed reaches far beyond all the other statements of the poet. In this last play we perceive the consummation of the conflict that pervades Euripides' work and was ultimately the existential conflict within his own soul.

7

ION, AGATHON, AND KRITIAS

Nauck's collection of fragments preserves a great many names of tragedians, some of which can be fleshed out here and there by a few fragments. Nothing gives us cause to believe that manuscript transmission has deprived us of any particularly outstanding works. Of the predecessors of the three great tragedians, we have already made mention; we also observed that within their families there developed something like a poetic succession, and among their descendants can be found many a tragic poet. Here, too, fifth-century comedy offers much in the way of evidence, to mention only the striking passage in the *Frogs* (72), in which the desolation of the Athenian tragic stage caused by the death of the great tragedians is described with very specific references.

The three men to whom this chapter is devoted all wrote at the time when Attic tragedy was still at its height. Ion of Chios has already been mentioned in connection with Sophokles' visit to that island. He was actively involved with Athens and her leading personalities, especially Kimon, and spent several portions of his life in the city. T. B. L. Webster suggests for his visits the years ca. 470–461, 451–443, and 433 until sometime after 428.[1] From the *Suda's* article on Ion, we learn that he produced his first play in the 82d Olympiad (452–449). The same source lists the number of his plays as twelve or thirty or forty. The last two estimates can easily be understood as ten trilogies with or without satyr plays, while twelve might represent the works possessed by the Alexandrians. That we know titles and fragments from eleven dramas agrees with this, more or less. The fragments with commentary are in *Ion von Chios* by A. von Blumenthal, Stuttgart 1939, 27. A deep insight into the technique and ability of Ion is denied us. The Ionic element seems to have been prominent in his work. The author of the treatise *On the Sublime* (33. 5) says that Ion's faultless elegance is to the fire of Sophokles what Bakchylides is to Pindar. A certain rationalism is unmistakable, if not in the few surviving lines from his tragedies then at least in the opening of his treatise *Triagmos* (fr. 20Bl.), in which arete is defined as the trinity σύνεσις καὶ κράτος καὶ τύχη (reason, power, and luck). Webster (op. cit.) has shown that in Ion's fragments we can discern references to the earlier plays of Sophokles. The two poets also share a certain preference for tripartite form in their speeches.

We can form some idea, albeit a predominantly negative one, of the artistic personality of Agathon.[2] According to Athenaios 5. 217a, he won his first tragic victory at the Lenaia in 416. The celebration of this victory provides the background for Plato's *Symposion*, in which Agathon delivers the fifth speech on Eros, with its playful Gorgianisms and rather flat content. Next to Euripides, Aristophanes had an especially critical interest in Agathon. The parodies in the first part of the *Thesmophoriazusai* are instructive.[3] A monody (39) and an astrophic choral song with solo part (101) exemplify the art of Agathon, as Aristophanes saw it. The free ionics of the choral ode find a parallel, characteristically enough, in Timotheos. It is also significant that the comic poet (156) has Agathon place particular emphasis on the importance of mimesis; Ἀγάθωνος αὔλησις (Agathon's flute music) is described by ancient critics as μαλακὴ καὶ ἐκλελυμένη (soft and relaxed; *Suda*). It is quite clear that Agathon was especially open to the influences of the new dithyramb, of which we also found traces in Euripides. The development of a highly trained virtuosity in the musical sections of tragedy was bound to lead to their independence from the dramatic structure. We noted strong tendencies in this direction in Euripides as well. Thus we understand the remark in the *Poetics* (18, 1456a 30) that Agathon began the practice of having the chorus sing pure interludes (ἐμβόλιμα).

Aristotle's statement in *Poet.* 9, 1451b 21 is important and difficult: ἐν τῷ Ἀγάθωνος Ἄνθει (in the *Anthos* of Agathon) the πράγματα (plot) as well as the ὀνόματα (names) were freely invented; nonetheless the drama was enjoyable. First of all, we must confess that in the manuscripts that have come down to us it is utterly impossible to decide whether the reading should be Ἀνθεῖ[4] or Ἄνθει, and therefore whether the play should be titled *Antheus* or *Anthos*. In his commentary on the *Poetics* (Berlin 1934) A. Gudeman suggested Ἄνθη and the corresponding title *Anthe*. This is connected with the special significance he accords to the Arabic translation.[5] Since Aristotle explicitly states that the plot and names were invented, it is inadmissible to search for a mythical character to explain the title. Thus we cannot follow Schmid (3. 849. 4), who suggests the son of Antenor slain by Paris, nor S. M. Pitcher,[6] who thinks of the Ἄνθος (masc. irreconcilable with Ἀνθεῖ) who, according to Antoninus Liberalis *Met.* 7, was torn apart by horses and transformed into a bird.

More important is the question whether Agathon, with his freely invented plot, abandoned the common ground of myth and created something like bourgeois drama. Here I share Ziegler's doubts (2050) completely. Such a wholly unique renunciation of the traditional framework is quite unlikely.

At the time of the *Frogs*, Agathon had left Athens and, like Euripides, had taken up residence at the court of Archelaos of Makedonia. It is to be feared that the ridicule of him in comedy has tarnished his image overmuch. The friendly manner in which Aristotle (loc. cit.) speaks of his play should give us second thoughts, and so, too, should the characterization of the poet in the *Frogs*, written when he was already gone from Athens (84): ἀγαθὸς ποιητὴς καὶ ποθεινὸς τοῖς φίλοις (a good poet and missed by his friends).

Kritias, the tyrant, tried his hand at various literary genres; thus he is the last known representative of the old political elegy. He also wrote tragedies, and since Wilamowitz's *Analecta Euripidea* (Berlin 1875, 161) it has been customary to allot four titles of tragedies to a tetralogy by Kritias.[7] According to the *Vita* of Euripides, the plays *Tennes*, *Rhadamanthys*, and *Peirithoos* were regarded as spurious; in all likelihood they formed a trilogy. The *Peirithoos* was thought by some to be the work of Kritias, as Ath. 11, 496b, attests. Opinion also varied in assigning the satyr play *Sisyphos* to either Euripides or Kritias; in Sext. Emp. 9. 54, it is ascribed to the latter. If we limit the dramatic production of Kritias to these four plays, the *Sisyphos* is joined with the others automatically to form a tetralogy. Yet these conclusions merit no more than some probability.

The *Tennes* introduced the title character in a plot employing the motif of Potiphar's wife and thus displays a great thematic similarity to a series of Euripidean dramas. The end of the hypothesis of the *Rhadamanthys* was found in a Florentine papyrus, but it does not help us much.[8] The play made reference to the battle of the Apharetidai with the Dioskouroi, in which the latter were defeated. The daughters of Rhadamanthys played some role in the piece. The third play presented the Hades adventure of Peirithoos and Theseus, who wished to abduct Persephone. Herakles freed the rash heroes; in the course of the plot, the confirmation of the friendship between Theseus and Peirithoos seems to have played a significant role. A papyrus find has yielded portions of a dialogue between Herakles and Theseus.[9] The dialogue between Aiakos, the underworld's gatekeeper, and the newly arrived Herakles (DK 88B 16) belongs to the prologue.

From the *Sisyphos* stems the large fragment preserved by Sextus Empiricus (1 N; DK 88B 25) with the explanation that Sisyphos gives for the origins of religion. In the course of expounding a theory of the origins of culture filled with the spirit of Sophism, he describes law as a human invention for overcoming the primeval state of chaos in the world. In order to thwart transgressions of the law under cover of darkness, some clever fellow devised the concept of all-knowing and all-seeing gods. Wilhelm Nestle (op. cit., 416), following others, advocated the view that Kritias, with this radical atheism most uncommon in antiquity, was influenced by Diagoras of Melos. The two appear together in ancient tradition (late, to be sure), and the connection maintained by Nestle must at least be regarded as a possibility.

8

DECLINE

Dramatic contests were held regularly in Athens until the first century B.C.; however, to gain an accurate picture of their substance even for the fourth century is an extraordinarily difficult task.[1] To this earlier period we allot with relative confidence the *Rhesos*, a dramatization of the Doloneia transmitted among the works of Euripides.[2] The first hypothesis reveals that the debate over the play's authenticity was already heated in antiquity.[3] Even today the question has not been completely settled. Wilamowitz (*Anal. Eurip.*, Berlin 1875, 198) justified the athetesis anew, and his opinion stood for a long while. Then at the beginning of the 1930s, the Belgian school of philology, on the basis of alleged historical references, strongly supported the play's authenticity, which today is defended only by occasional rearguard skirmishes, without success.[4] Details like the Boiotianism in v. 523, the greeting of Rhesos as Zeus Phanaios in v. 355 (unthinkable in the fifth century; cf. Wilamowitz, *Glaube der Hell.* 2. 262), the absence of gnomai, the sporadic use of short stichomythies, and above all the disjointed construction of the plot, which is wholly dependent on the epic model—all this conclusively rules out Euripidean authorship. The hypothesis offers the counterargument that the *Rhesos* was listed as a drama of Euripides in the didaskaliai. Thus, we are obliged to assume that in our tradition the extant play was somehow substituted for the lost work of Euripides.

The *Rhesos*, whose author sought lively dramatic movement at any price, begins with the excited entry of the chorus of camp guards.[5] In an anapestic scene they awaken Hektor, but it takes some time before we learn from their agitated cries that fires have been lit in the Greek camp and that the army is pressing round Agamemnon's tent. Hektor concludes that the Greeks intend to flee and, in a swaggering speech, proposes an immediate attack on their camp, since only darkness and the prophets' warnings had prevented him from utterly destroying the enemy army with his spear. Constantly intent on contrast, the poet first juxtaposes him with the chorus leader, then with Aineias, both of whom advise caution. Finally Hektor yields and decides to dispatch a spy. Dolon volunteers for the mission and demands the horses of Achilleus as his reward after the Greeks have been defeated. Hektor agrees, although he himself desires them. (The dramatist is fond of touching up his picture with fine details.) The chorus sends Dolon off with good wishes, with praise for his courage, and a hubristic prediction of the heroic exploits he will accomplish. A shepherd enters to announce the approach of Rhesos with his Thracian troops. Again and again small flames are kindled, but the whole never really catches fire. The hasty Hektor first quarrels with the messenger since he believes the man wants to report about the flocks, but then he is again the proud hero, confident of victory, who will tolerate the tardy Rhesos merely as a spectator of his own bold exploits. The chorus leader and shepherd must entreat him before he swiftly changes his mind (339) and declares himself ready to accept Rhesos as an ally in battle. A choral song full of hopes for victory greets the Thracian king as he enters. Hektor cannot refrain from harshly scolding Rhesos for his late arrival. The king excuses himself, as he had to fight Skythian tribes along the way; his speech proves him Hektor's equal in boastfulness. Indeed, he goes him one better with a plan that staggers even Hektor: to devastate Greece after Troy's liberation. Then he demands the first among the Greek heroes as his adversary and enters the camp with Hektor.

The poet has skillfully separated this section from the following one, which contains the decisive action, by the dawn song of the guards, the finest ode in the play, which recalls similar verses in the *Phaethon* of Euripides.[6] The guards are restless because Dolon has been away for so long; their decision to wake the Lykians provides the opportunity for removing the chorus from the scene.

Odysseus and Diomedes come to Hektor's tent on their nocturnal mission. They have captured and killed Dolon; Hektor is to be their next victim. Since they cannot find him, again one of the play's many small conflicts breaks out: Diomedes still wants to do something noteworthy: to kill Aineias; Odysseus, whose very first words (565) characterize him as cautious, urges their immediate return. The still undecided quarrel is settled by Athena, who sends the heroes on the way to Rhesos and his white steeds. She herself screens her protégés in a self-contained episode that merely bridges a span of time. Alexandros has heard a rumor that enemy spies are in the camp, and he wants to alarm Hektor. Athena, however, pretending to be Kypris, allays his fears with a deceitful speech and persuades him to turn back. He does not appear again in the play.

The poet of the *Rhesos* composes according to the dictum of Astydamas (fr. 4N) that the dramatist must provide his audience with a diversified meal. Intent on ποικιλία (variety, diversity), he now presents a highly agitated scene in which guards rush in after Odysseus, since the murder of Rhesos has been discovered. However, Odysseus is able to deceive them in the darkness; he knows the password, which he extracted from Dolon, and sends his pursuers off in the wrong direction. A portion of the soldiers (probably mute extras) hurry off, the chorus remains on stage, and Odysseus makes his escape. The motif of the horse theft (619, 624) is here dropped; it returns later, but only in allusions (781, 839). In a scene that is mostly divided among individual voices, the chorus guesses at the identity of the culprit, suspects Odysseus, and fears the reproach of Hektor. At this point Rhesos's charioteer enters, pours out laments in turbulent anapests, and then delivers a set speech. Again, it is characteristic for this play of great and small misunderstandings, of the playful confusion of appearance and reality, that the chorus leader first believes they have caught an enemy (730). While the messenger of earlier tragedy, despite his sympathies, nonetheless stands at a certain distance from what he reports, here the charioteer, himself wounded, is much more directly involved. In his agitation he succumbs to the most serious misunderstanding of the play. When Hektor comes and first severely rebukes the guards, who can cite their prompt reporting of the unrest in the Greek camp, the charioteer cuts him short and accuses him of killing his master. The quarrel ends inconclusively; Hektor has the man brought into his house and arranges the burial of the murdered king.

At the end appears one of the Muses, the mother of Rhesos by the river Strymon, at the point where the deus ex machina generally enters in Euripides. The execution of the scene is different, however. With her dead son in her arms she presents a touching image, but after a partly lyrical threnos she switches to a lengthy report in which only the determination of Odysseus's and, on another plane, Athena's, guilt (already known to the audience) and the explanation of Rhesos's hesitant expedition (his mother forbade it) have any importance for the play. Her speech does not lack a prophecy, which again corresponds to Euripidean technique: Rhesos will not dwell in Hades, but in the grottoes of his homeland as an ἀνθρωποδαίμων (deified man).

Bruno Snell has determined that approximately thirty years passed from the end of the Peloponnesian War until really noteworthy tragic performances began to be held again.[7] We are also indebted to him for a masterly study that confirmed a few dates for the younger and better known Alkidamas.[8] He belongs to the succession Philokles,[9] Morsimos, Alkidamas I, Alkidamas II; of his fifteen victories we can distinguish those at the Dionysia of 372, 341, and 340. He won special acclaim with his *Hektor*, which Plutarch (*De gloria Athen.* 7; 349F) places on a level with Aischylos, Sophokles, and the *Aerope* of Karkinos. This Karkinos was a contemporary of Astydamas and won the first of his eleven victories at the Dionysia shortly before 373.

From the Hellenistic age we possess three papyri with fragments of a *Hektor* drama, which Snell for good reasons assigns to the play of Astydamas: *P. Amh.* 2. 10 (169 Pack); *P. Strasbourg* WG 304. 2 (*Herm.* Einzelschriften 5 [1937], 84; 170 Pack); *P. Hibeh* 2. 174 (171 Pack).[10] Welcker (*Gr. Trag.*, 1059) makes it seem probable that the *Hector proficiscens* of Naevius was adapted from Astydamas's work.

In this play about Hektor's departure from Troy it seems that special emphasis was laid on the fact that the hero bore the arms of Achilleus after he had stripped them from the fallen Patroklos. Unlike in the *Iliad*, his departure and farewell to Andromache must be set after the slaying of this opponent, but this presents no serious difficulty. Snell rightly points out that the young Astyanax's alarm at the sight of his father's helmet in Astydamas (schol. *Il.* 6. 472) thus acquires special meaning.

The *Hermes* of Astydamas was probably a satyr play.[11]

Modesty was not one of Astydamas's virtues. In the *Bibliotheca* of Photios (502. 21; *Anth. Lyr.* D 1, 3d ed., p. 113; Snell, *Trag. Min.* 60T 2) we find two distichs in which he regrets not having lived at the time of the great tragedians. His rivalry would have proved dangerous to them.

His contemporary Chairemon appears in the *Rhetoric* of Aristotle (3. 12; 1413b

13) as ἀναγνωστικός (suitable for reading).[12] It is important to know that a reading public acquired an ever increasing importance for the circulation and influence of tragedy, but we should not jump to the conclusion that a poet like Chairemon wrote solely for such a following. Live performance was still of primary concern.[13] Compositions such as the tragedies of the Cynic Diogenes of Sinope or Timon of Phleius presumably stood on the extreme borderline of the genre and were genuine closet dramas.

Bruno Snell has pointed out new tones of a simultaneously playful and refined sensuousness and, related to this, a great delight in flowers in the fragments of Chairemon. All this is a prelude to Hellenistic poetry. E. G. Turner successfully identified a fragment of Chairemon among the Hibeh papyri (2. 224; now *Brit. Mus.* 2989), which comprises the beginning sections of eight verses, probably hexameters. Aristotle reports (*Poet.* 1, 1447b 21) that Chairemon wrote *Kentauros*, a rhapsody in a medley of all meters. The content of our fragment fits this perfectly: it is composed wholly of moralizing maxims, one of Chiron's specialties. We need only recall the Χίρωνος ὑποθῆκαι (*Precepts of Chiron*) ascribed to Hesiod. The extent to which Chairemon also took readers into consideration is shown by the acrostic discovered by Kannicht: the first letters of the verses spell out the poet's name.

Our possibilities for forming a clear picture of fourth-century tragedy are meager enough. Many names like Karkinos or Antiphon remain wholly insubstantial. But in this context the *Poetics* of Aristotle is of great importance. Not that it might provide us with concrete information about poets and works—Ziegler (1965) weighs with requisite caution the possibility that some dramas listed without authors' names could belong to this period—but the vital point to grasp is that tragedy is considered from now on as an independent art form with its own technical rules of composition, and is released from the determinative bonds of its early development and prime. The classical form of the polis belongs to the past and so also does the soil from which tragedy had drawn much of its power. Walter Jens sums it up well: "But where a firmly established system of order no longer exists as a premise, there can be no tragedy, only, as in the fourth century, a theater play."[14]

This period also saw the culmination of a process of expansion that had already begun under the classical tragedians. It is no coincidence that among the scanty reports about fourth-century tragedy a relatively large number refer to productions outside of Athens (Ziegler, 1964).

This separation from the polis was already foreshadowed in Euripides, as was another highly significant process. Myth was stripped of its inner content and became essentially mere stock material. As before, poets continued to employ predominantly the old traditional myths, but the great ideological questions that stirred the fifth century retreated completely into the background. Instead, dramatists sought to contrive effective new situations from the old materials and to augment the cast of characters. For the predominance of this interest in myth as raw subject matter, the remarks of Aristotle (*Poet.* 1450a 25, 37) about the priority of μῦθος (plot) over ἦθη (character), indeed, on the absence of the latter in later tragedy, are important. Of course Aristotle uses this to support his argument that in drama μῦϑος takes precedence over ἦϑη.

An important source, although difficult to evaluate without careful analysis, is the mythological handbook of Hyginus. That he makes abundant use of tragedy is well known, but modern scholars (C. Robert in particular) have often been too hasty in connecting the individual fabulae with the great names of the fifth century, without taking later tragedy properly into account. Stories like that of Iphigeneia in Delphi, which made such a strong impression on Goethe, show the games of Tyche escalated to extremes. Nothing speaks against the view that the plots in this and similar cases are drawn from later tragedies, which in suspenseful situations (here again following Euripides' lead) give wide play to sentimentality. T. B. L. Webster refers the decoration on a silver cup in the British Museum to a late tragedy, a continuation of the *Iph. T.*: the original of Pacuvius's *Chryses*, with the rescue of the fugitives by Chryses, the son of Chryseis.[15]

If our judgment of these sources is correct, we can see in them a strong preference for the suspenseful and the gruesome, and in this connection a significant heightening of pathos was inevitable. Undoubtedly, we are also justified in assuming that diction became more heavily rhetorical, and that further advances were made in the line of musical virtuosity, which Plato (*Laws* 3, 700d) condemned as the main reason for the corruption of theater.

For the developmental trend of tragedy in its decline it is instructive to note the shift in meaning of the word τραγικός (tragic). Plato and after him Aristotle already use the word in the sense of "solemn," but also of "exaggerated," where often the secondary meaning of "bombastic" is unmistakable. "Tragic" in this strongly external sense is no longer limited only to tragedy: it now exerts a powerful influence on the writing of history; indeed to a great degree it dominates the historical style of the Hellenistic age.[16]

From such connections it is understandable that now historical subjects were again occasionally chosen for tragedies. Theodektes of Phaselis wrote a *Maussolos*; a *Themistokles* and *Pheraioi* (probably about the violent death of the tyrant Alexandros of Pherai) were composed by Moschion, although some scholars place him in the third century (*RE* 16. 345). Of course exotic subjects now hold a special fascination. The elder Dionysios of Syracuse composed an *Adonis* tragedy (Ath. 9. 401 f.),[17] and at the court of Philip of Makedon a *Kinyras* was performed (Suet. *Calig.* 57; Jos. *Ant. Jud.* 19. 1. 13).

The first production of an old drama from the time that was perceived as "classical" is attested for 386, and the shifting program of the festivals made room more and more often for a παλαιά (old play) before the new dramas. The discovery of inscriptions from the Athenian agora has shown us that in the middle of the third century regular contests of actors performing older plays were held.[18]

This leads us to a further sign of the fading inner force of tragic composition: the predominance of the director's and actors' performance. For the first, the scholium on *Or.* 57 offers an excellent example: a later stage manager had a mute Helen

enter the palace with the Trojan booty at the beginning of the play. The revue elements of the Roman stage fit well in this context, for which Bieber (*Hist.*) has collected the evidence. Already in classical times accomplished actors were singled out
by name, thus Kleandros and Mynniskos in the *Vita* of Aischylos, Tlepolemos (schol.
Ar. *Nub.* 1266) and Kleidemides (schol. *Ran* 791) for Sophokles. For his own time,
however, Aristotle (*Rhet.* 3, 1403b 33) complains that more attention was paid to the
actors than to the poets. Much evidence sheds light on the increasing importance
that was now attached to the skill of the performers.[19] Theodoros brought the wicked
Alexandros of Pherai to tears (Ail. *Var. Hist.* 14. 40); Polos, in the role of Sophokles'
Elektra, had presented to him the urn with the ashes of his recently deceased son
(Gell. *N. A.* 6. 5); Thessalos was held in special esteem by Alexander the Great (Plut.
Alex. 10 and 29). How important the actors were can be seen from the care with
which they were assigned to the plays occasionally in the fourth century. Each protagonist had to play in one drama of the three competing poets in turn (Pickard-Cambridge, *Festivals*, 94). T. B. L. Webster has conjectured a similar procedure for a certain period of the fifth century (see under Fragments section of chapter 5).

By and large, interest seems to have dwindled in the satyr play during the
course of the fourth century. The "didaskaliai" for the Dionysia of 341–339 b.c. (*IG*
II² 2320) record at the beginning of the list only a single satyr play in each year.[20]

Yet we have evidence for a "unique sort of satyr play" (to repeat the phrase of
Bruno Snell, who has also made decisive contributions toward its interpretation): the
Agen.[21] All that we know of it comes from Athenaios, who quotes eighteen lines
from the play (13. 586: 14–18; 13. 596: first 1–8a, then 8b–18) and offers a few remarks. The verses are taken from two sections that are not immediately consecutive,
but both belong to the exposition.

Concerning the date of production we find two contradictory statements in
Athenaios. According to the first, the satyr play was performed during a festival of
Dionysos at the Hydaspes in India, when Alexander's march had reached its furthest
limit; but according to the other it was only after Harpalos, fearful because of his
mismanagement, fled from Asia after Alexander's return. K. J. Beloch (*Griech. Gesch.*
IV² 2. 434) based his dating of 324 on the second of these two alternatives, and this
has been widely accepted.[22] However, Snell has brought forward cogent arguments for
the earlier date of 326.

As the author, Athenaios names an unidentifiable Python from Katane or Byzantium. It has even been attributed to Alexander himself.

The scanty remnants do allow a reconstruction of setting and plot in broad
outlines. The stage showed on the left the famous temple of prostitution built by
Pallides. Harpalos, Alexander's licentious and extravagant favorite, appears in the
play under this name.[23] Among the honors that he lavished on his concubine Pythionike was a temple dedicated to her when she died. On the other side of the stage
were reeds, concealing an entrance to the Underworld. The brief text reveals a great
deal more. The satyrs appear here as a chorus of Persian magi who have promised to
retrieve Pythionike from Hades for Harpalos-Pallides. This undoubtedly occurred in
the form of a necromancy, and Pythionike, rising up out of the reeds, must have up-

braided her former lover for replacing her with Glykera, acquired from Athens at great cost. The play is called *Agen* (a *nomen agentis* derived from ἄγω), which has rightly been referred to Alexander. He must have appeared at the end to settle matters.

Snell has shed much light on the background of the play by adducing information (likewise preserved in Athenaios, 13. 586C, 595A) about Theopompos's *Letter from Chios*. This open letter from the historian to Alexander contained serious charges against Harpalos, who developed an extravagant and expensive cult with Pythionike and Glykera that aroused much displeasure. It also mentions that Glykera was worshipped in Tarsos with proskynesis. It remains doubtful, however, whether on this account we can read between the lines of the *Agen* a deep political significance in the struggle over new forms of ruler veneration alien to the West.

For Hellenistic tragedy, our fragments are just as scanty as for the fourth century (besides *Alexandra* and *Exagoge*, we have nine fragments with twenty-two verses), and it is little consolation that we know the names of some sixty poets.[24] The seven most important tragedians at the court of Ptolemaios Philadelphos were united to form the Pleiad, but the exact list varies. The following names are always listed: Alexandros Aitolos, Lykophron of Chalkis, Homeros of Byzantium, Philikos of Kerkyra, Sositheos, probably from the Troad. In different versions we also find Sosiphanes, Aiantiades, Dionysiades, and Euphronios.

For a clearer picture of Hellenistic tragedy, we must examine two works, although both occupy a peculiar position. The *Alexandra* of Lykophron is a single artificially obscure speech of Kassandra with prophecies about the fall of Troy and the future destinies of the Greeks.[25] There is no attempt at a plot, and one can only marvel at what was sometimes called tragedy without being one. The dating problem is connected with historical allusions that are especially abundant for the West and have as their source especially Timaios of Tauromenion. Alexander, "the lion from the stock of Aiakos and and Dardanos" (1440), will end the battle between East and West; after the sixth generation, a man of Kassandra's blood will fight with the wolf of Galadra (= Makedonia?), but then both will share in the spoils. Since the prophecy of Rome's dominion is unthinkable in the time of Ptolemaios Philadelphos it is probable that, as Niebuhr suggests, the work belongs to the early second century, after the victory of T. Quinctius Flamininus, and was written by another Lykophron, perhaps a grandson of the tragedian.

We are in a somewhat better position to evaluate the celebrated remains of the *Exagoge* preserved by Eusebios in the ninth book of the *Praeparatio Evangelica*.[26] This Moses drama, which dramatizes portions of the Old Testament, was written by a Jew named Ezechiel in the second century B.C. Technically remarkable in the play are two scene changes and the condensation of rather widely separated time periods, but of course we cannot say whether this was unique or indicates greater technical freedom in Hellenistic tragedy. It accords well with Horace's theory in the *Ars Poetica*, which itself uses Hellenistic sources, that we can probably postulate five acts and do without a fourth actor (*Ars P.* 189, 192). Unfortunately, we cannot determine from what has survived whether the *Exagoge* had a chorus. Since, however, the theory of Horace and the practice of Roman tragedy both maintain the use of the chorus, it is highly probable that Hellenistic tragedy did too.[27] The question whether the drama was meant to be performed or recited must remain open.[28]

For the rest we may surmise basically the same trends for the tragedy of Hellenistic times as for that of the fourth century. The delight of this age in esoteric subjects is clearly expressed in the drama titles, of which a considerable number refer to themes hitherto unknown in dramatic literature. Again we find exotic motifs, like an *Adonis* of Philikos from the Pleiad and of Ptolemaios Philopator, and again historical matter like the *Themistokles* of Philikos, and even contemporary subjects like Lykophron's Κασσανδρεῖς. Such compositions already look ahead to the Roman praetextata. Phanis J. Kakridis would assign the enigmatic *P. Osl.* 1413 to the realm of Hellenistic tragedy and the *tragoedias cantare* that also played an important role in Rome.[29] In his view it represents a narrative addressed to Deidameia concerning the slaying of Penthesileia by the resurrected Achilleus, and the latter's command to bring Neoptolemos to Troy, told on the occasion of his summoning. The papyrus is full of difficulties.

Quite a stir was raised by the discovery of a papyrus with fragments of a *Gyges* tragedy, which E. Lobel published in 1950.[30] The sixteen quite well preserved verses of the middle column belong to a speech of the queen in which she recounts the nocturnal events in her bedroom. We can still just make out that she sent Kandaules out of the palace early on some pretext and then summoned Gyges. The close parallel to the report of Herodotos is unmistakable, the discrepancies that do exist are trifling, and an independent coexistence of the two versions is inconceivable. In all likelihood the composition belongs to the Hellenistic age and represents a dramatization of the story in Herodotos. For the reconstruction we must allow for the possibility of several scene changes, as was the case with the *Exagoge* of Ezechiel, which was also a dramatization of a historical narrative. The fragment offers no solid evidence for the question of the chorus in Hellenistic drama.[31]

An age that from its glutted urban culture learned to appreciate the crude nature of rural life was bound to take delight in the satyr play. Thus an epigram of Dioskorides (*Anth. Pal.* 7. 707) celebrates Sositheos as the renovator of the old-style satyr play. We can form some idea of his *Daphnis* (or *Lityerses*), in which Herakles slew the monster Lityerses and freed Daphnis, who then married Thaleia.[32] A trend begun in the *Agen* is continued here in the elements of personal abuse, the stock-in-trade of Old Comedy. Sositheos appears to have gone after philosophers primarily. According to Diog. Laert. 7. 173, he directed a rather crude attack against Kleanthes. There we also find the delightful story that Kleanthes was present in the theater, but did not bat an eye on hearing an especially aggressive line (fr. 4N). This won him the audience's sympathy and Sositheos a flop. Lykophron composed a *Menedemos*, about which we have two contradictory accounts. According to Athenaios 2. 55D, this satyr play ridiculed the founder of the Eretrian school, but Diog. Laert. 2. 140 calls it an encomium. It is not difficult to conceive of a form of mockery from which one might also extract a sort of appreciation as is the case with Aristophanes' treatment of the tragedians.[33]

Evidently under the influence of the satyr play, in the Hellenistic age a development in the meaning of the word σατυρικός from "burlesque" to "mocking," "satyric," in our sense of the word, can be observed.

The history of Greek tragedy ends for us in a darkness illuminated only sparsely here and there.[34] We regret the paucity of our knowledge about Hellenistic tragedy for many reasons, not least because its influence on Roman drama is beyond doubt. We would also understand many passages in Seneca better, although in general he strives to imitate the classical dramatists. At the time of Hellenism, however, another widely influential strain had already branched off from tragedy, and this we are better able to grasp and follow. As the Satyros *Vita* of Euripides shows, even the ancients clearly understood the debt of New Comedy to this tragedian especially. Since we now possess originals of Menander, we can evaluate the extent and the limits of this influence. And finally, with New Comedy and Senecan tragedy, we have named the two literary spheres that absorbed the direct influence of the ancient tragic play, transmitting it in diverse ways to the cultures of the West and thus playing a decisive part in the genesis and elaboration of their dramatic forms.

NOTES

CHAPTER 1

1. For the earlier period, the survey of E. Tièche remains worthwhile: "Der Ursprung der Tragödie," *Jahrb. d. Ver. schw. Gymnasiallehrer*, Aarau 1915. For more recent works, Webster in *Fifty Years*; del Grande offers a wide-ranging and richly documented overview in ΤΡΑΓ., 293–358; Patzer discusses the modern hypotheses, 39–88.

2. Munich 1955, 572. He refers to his work "Der Ursprung der Tragödie," *N. Jb.* 27 (1911), 609 and 673 = *Opusc.*, I, 62, and 111, that appeared one year before the essay by Wilamowitz on the *Bloodhounds* of Sophokles, which relied entirely on the ancient tradition. *N. Jb.* 29 (1912), 449 = *Kl. Schr.*, I, 347.

3. *Journ. Hell. Stud.* 26 (1906), 191.

4. *Ann. Br. Sch. Ath.* 16 (1909/10), 244.

5. *Gesch. d. griech. Lit.*, 3d ed., Stuttgart 1876, 2. 26.

6. *Themis: A Study of the Social Origins of Greek Religion*, Cambridge 1912; 2d ed., 1927.

7. In *Themis* (see previous note), Excursus on chap. 8, 341. Taken up again in *Aeschylus*, Oxford 1940, 4 ff., 146, and *Euripides and His Age*, 7th ed., Oxford 1955. Also to be kept in mind is L. R. Farnell, *The Cults of the Greek States*, Oxford 1896–1909, 5. 234. Further literature in Patzer 41. 3. The best overview of the material is now in Guépin.

8. In the first edition of his book *Dithyramb, Tragedy and Comedy*, 185.

9. *Class. Quart.* 37 (1943), 46.

10. "Some Thoughts on the Pre-History of Greek Drama," *Bull. Inst. Class. Stud.* 5 (1958), and in the revision of the book by Pickard-Cambridge, 128.

11. The foreword to the German edition discusses the numerous translations of this book. Important for the fundamentals of Thomson's theories is his book *Studies in Ancient Greek Society: The Prehistoric Aegean*, London 1949.

12. Well handled by H. J. Rose, *Mnem.* 4, v. 3 (1950), 281.

13. *Gesch. d. griech. Religion*, I, 2d ed., 11.

14. *Vortr. d. Bibl. Warburg* 7 (1930), 1. Ziegler (1949) is correct and decisive.

15. K. Meuli, *Schweizer Masken*, Zurich 1943, 58.

16. "Satyrtänze und frühes Drama," *Sitzb. Bayer. Ak. Phil.-hist. Kl.*, 1943/5, 5.

17. Cf. W. Wrede, "Der Maskengott," *Ath. Mitt.* 53 (1928), 66.

18. In M. P. Nilsson, *Gesch. d. griech. Rel.*, I, 2d ed., pl. 31. 2. In view of the musicians, there is no reason to doubt the existence of mask dances. On the cults, see R. Stiglitz, "Die grossen Göttinnen Arkadiens," *Sonderschr. Öst. Arch. Inst.* 15 (1967).

19. Besides his article "Maske" in the *Handb. des deutschen Aberglaubens*, 1933, there is the introduction to *Schweizer Masken*, Zurich 1943, and the study "Altrömischer Maskenbrauch," *Mus. Helv.* 12 (1955), 206.

20. Rather too confident, F. Speiser, "Schreck- und Scherzmasken," *Schw. Volksk.* 37 (1947), 92: "No one will dispute the fact that the anthropomorphic masks originate in animistic conceptions." Cf. K. Kerényi, "Uomo e maschera," *Dioniso* 12 (1949), 17.

21. The story of the thirteenth man among the player devils in K. Paulin's *Tiroler Sagen* is part of the same tradition, Innsbruck 1940, 32. Bieber, *Hist.*, 28, rightly emphasizes the importance of costume for the act of tragic transformation.

22. Bieber, *Maske*, 2072. On the εὑρετής question, see A. Kleingünther, Πρῶτος εὑρετής, *Phil.* Suppl. 26, 1933.

23. "Die Entstehung der Tragödie," *Kl. Schr.*, Leipzig 1911, 414. He arrived at the Eleusinian mysteries through E. Rohde, *Kl. Schr.*, Tübingen 1901, 2. 361. Ziegler (col. 1951) also considers Eleusinian influence. A mediating position is assumed by P. Amandry, "Eschyle et Eleusis," *Mel. Grégoire*, I, 1949, 27. More generally on mysteries and tragedy, M. Untersteiner, 201, who considers an influence through the spirit of the mysteries. On the ceremony at Eleusis, see M. P. Nilsson, *Gesch. d. griech. Rel.*, I, 2d ed., 469.

24. The problems of the origin of drama have been dealt with extensively by Italian scholars. Besides the books of R. Cantarella (now also in *Storia della letteratura greca*, Milan 1962, 226, and in *Letteratura greca classica*, Florence 1967, 171; see also n. 1); Peretti, Untersteiner, and del Grande (also: *Intorno alle origini della tragedia ed altri saggi*, Naples 1936), there are: F. Gagliuolo, "Sul problema di Thespis e l'origine del dramma satiresco," *Riv. Indo-greco-ital.* 13 (1929), 1; B. Stampo, "Le origini della tragedia," Milan 1935 (in an anti-philological stance), and *Dioniso* 6 (1937), 143; G. Perrotta, "Tragedia: origine," *Encicl. Ital.* 34 (1937), 146.

25. *Gli Eraclidi el il Filottete di Eschilo*, Florence 1942. Especially extreme in the use of the "Mediterranean element" is G. Patroni, "Studi di mitologia mediterranea ed Omerica," *Ist. Lombardo* 25/2, Milan 1951.

26. This meaning seems to me not so well proven as Patzer (217. 4) assumes, but he likewise rejects the attempt of Schreckenberg.

27. TEXT: R. Kassel, Oxford 1965. COMMENTARIES: J. Bywater, Oxford 1909; A. Rostagni, Turin 1928; A. Gudeman, Berlin 1934. INTERPRETATION: G. F. Else, *Aristotle's Poetics: The Argument*, Cambridge, Mass. 1957; D. W. Lucas, Oxford 1968; L. Cooper–A. Gudeman, *A Bibliography of the Poetics of Aristotle*, Cornell Stud. in English 11, New Haven 1928, with the supplement of M. T. Herrick, *Am. Journ. Phil.* 52 (1931), 168.

28. "[Tragedy] originated in improvisation, just as comedy did—the one beginning with the leaders of the dithyramb, the other with the leaders of the phallic songs that still persist as institutions in many cities—and grew bit by bit as they developed whatever appeared in it. Having gone through many changes, tragedy stopped [developing], since it had attained its own nature. Aischylos was the first to increase the number of actors from one to two, diminish the role of the chorus, and make the dialogue play a major part. Sophokles introduced the third actor and the painted skene. Then there is [external and internal] magnitude: leaving behind small matters and comic diction in the course of its transformation from the satyric it at last achieved seriousness, and the trochaic meter gave way to iambics. Trochaic tetrameter had been used because the poetry was satyric and more connected with dancing; but as the dialogue developed, nature itself found the proper meter, since iambic is the closest meter to speech. . . . Next there is the number of episodes—but as for the rest, let them be accepted as stated, since it would be quite laborious to go through each of them."

The text is R. Kassel's, whom we also follow in accepting the reading πρωταγωνιστεῖν of Sophianus (*Rhein. Mus.* 105 [1962], 117). Less certain is his rejection of the restoration ἐκ ⟨τοῦ⟩ σατυρικοῦ. The article is attested in the Syrian-Arabian translation. Cf. also Patzer 53. 1. The attempt of G. F. Else, "Aristotle and Satyr-Play," *Trans. Am. Phil. Ass.* 70 (1939), 139, to delete everything from τρεῖς δέ to ἀπεσεμνύθη must be rejected.

29. *I primordi della tragedia*, Salerno 1936; *Eschilo*, I, Florence 1941; finally, "Alcune considerazioni sul teatro greco," *Dioniso* 37 (1963), 3.

30. "Dithyrambos und Tragödie," *Glotta* 40 (1962), 183.

31. In the section "Geburt und Wiedergeburt der Tragödie" in *Streifzüge eines Hellenisten*, Zurich 1960, 38.

32. Op. cit., p. xxv.

33. Op. cit., 38.

34. *Phil. Woch.* 50 (1930), 284.

35. Cf. H. Frisk, *Griech. Etym. Wörterb.* s.v. Further, see H. Färber, *Die Lyrik in der Kunsttheorie der Antike*, Munich 1936, 32, with supplements *Phil. Woch.* 1942, 99, 3; Pickard-Cambridge, *Dith.*, 1. Del Grande, ΤΡΑΓ, 26, seems to me incorrect in interpreting the dithyramb as originally a processional song.

36. In Pickard-Cambridge, *Dith.*, 5, fig. 1.

37. *Marm. Par.* ep. 46. On the dating problem, see Jacoby's commentary, *FGrH* 11 D 692; Pickard-Cambridge, *Dith.*, 15, and *Festivals*, 72.

38. The source material in H. Schönewolf, *Der jungattischen Dithyrambos*, Giessen 1938.

39. "Satyrspiele," *Bull. van de Vereenigung tot Bevordering der Kennis van de Antieke Beschaving te's Gravenhage* 17 (1942), 1.

40. We have already strongly emphasized this argument in the first edition of *Griech. Trag.*, Stuttgart 1938, 8.

41. Comic poetry too is recorded for Ion of Chios by schol. Aristophan. *Pax* 835 and *Suda* s.v. διθυραμβοδιδάσκαλοι. With good reason A. von Blumenthal, *Ion von Chios*, Stuttgart 1939, doubts the report for a poet of the fifth century, even though he considers a tragedy as the source of fr. 118. Reports of a poet Timokles, who supposedly wrote in both categories, have come to nothing. It is of course another matter when Homer appears in Aristotle, *Poetics* 4, 1448b 34, as the precursor of tragedy and comedy. On this see R. van Pottelberg, "Bij een aristoteliaansche Aporie," *Ant. Class.* 10 (1941), 83.

42. J. D. Beazley, *Attic Red-fig. Vase-painters*, 2d ed., Oxford 1963, 1258. 1; cf. 1055. 76, 1258. 2. H. Herter *RE* 6 A (1937), 1897.

43. Q. Cataudella, "Satyrikon," *Dioniso* 39 (1965), 3 = *Saggi sulla tragedia greca*, Messina 1969, 9, speculates on the nature of these presentations. He considers them, as does Aristotle, an early form of tragedy, but wants to separate the satyrikon as scherzoso, salace, burlesco from any firm connection with the satyrs, which passages of later times cannot support.

44. Cf. M. Gabathuler, *Hellenistische Epigramme auf Dichter*, St. Gall 1937, esp. 85 with an invalid polemic against Pohlenz (see below). Also see Ziegler, 1925.

45. "Das Satyrspiel und Pratinas von Phleius," *GGN* 1926/3, 298, and *Griech. Trag.* 2. 7. The opponents of Aristotle necessarily reject the picture offered by Pohlenz.

46. "Tragedy is very ancient to this place, begun not by Thespis, as is thought, nor by Phrynichos; but if you wish to investigate, you will find that it is a very old invention of this city."

47. The evidence is in Ziegler, 1924.

48. Hyginus, *De Astr.* 2. 4. Powell, *Coll. Alex.*, fr. 22, who prefers Hiller's Ἰκαριοῖ to the accentuation Ἰκάριοι (Maas) on the basis of Steph. Byz. (s.v. Ἰκαρία). On Eratosthenes, see F. Solmsen, *Trans. Am. Phil. Ass.* 73 (1942), 192. On Erigone, see R. Merkelbach, *Miscellanea di studi Alessandrini in memoriam di Aug. Rostagni*, Turin 1963, 469. On the theory of Eratosthenes, see K. Meuli, "Altrömischer Maskenbrauch," *Mus. Helv.* 12 (1955), 206. F. Rodríguez Adrados (see bibliography) approaches this theory when he assumes the κῶμος as the common ground on which the dramatic types grew.

49. F. Jacoby, *FGrH* 2. 239, A 43.

50. *Primordi*, 53; *Eschilo*, 200.

51. A collection of the evidence is in O. Crusius-R. Herzog, *Phil.* 79 (1924), 401.

52. *Thespis*, Leipzig 1933.

53. *Anth. Lyr.* 2. 5. 154D; *Poetae Mel. Gr.* fr. 708, p. 367P. Literature in Ziegler, 1936; E.

Roos. *Die tragische Orchestik im Zerrbild der attischen Komödie,* Lund 1951, 209. 3, and 232. 1; F. Stoessl, *RE* 22/2 (1954), 1722.

54. Among others, M. Pohlenz, *GGN* 1926, 317; *Griech. Trag.,* 1. 3b; Ziegler, 1936; C. del Grande, *Note filologiche,* Naples 1942, 39; E. Diehl in the *Anth. Lyr.;* E. Roos, op. cit., 232; Patzer 130. 2: "surely a fragment from a satyr play."

55. Cf. A. E. Harvey, "The Classification of Greek Lyric Poetry," *Class. Quart.* 5 (1955), 157; Pickard-Cambridge, *Festivals,* 256.

56. "Stasimon and Hyporcheme," *Eranos* 48 (1950), 14, and *Words, Music and Dance,* London 1960.

57. In the second edition of Pickard-Cambridge, *Dith.,* 20.

58. Op. cit., 209.

59. Lloyd-Jones (15) rejects any connection between the "hyporchema" and the history of drama and even considers the possibility of two different poets named Pratinas.

60. Patzer, 83. 2.

61. V. Jarcho emphasizes this well in his discussion, *DLZ* 84 (1963), 570.

62. Zemmaro Toki orients the reader quickly; *Japanese Nō-Plays,* Tokyo 1954. Cf. A. Lesky, *Maia* 15 (1963), 38 = *Ges. Schr.,* 275.

63. M. Imhof shows this, "Tetrameterszenen in der Tragödie," *Mus. Helv.* 13 (1956), 125. Against Aristotle's testimony on the meters, Patzer, 79.

64. Surveys in Flickinger, 13, with *Class. Phil.* 8 (1913), 269; Patzer, 131. 2.; Burkert, 88. 2, who interprets the τραγῳδοί as a group of masked men who performed the sacrifice of a goat in spring.

65. Thus Schmid 2. 47; Flickinger, 14; Pickard-Cambridge in the first edition of *Dith.,* 165, while Webster in his revision tends toward the interpretation offered here; Burkert, 115.

66. From *Herakles* to *Glauben der Hellenen* 1. 1931, 199.

67. *Ann. d. Inst.* 1877, 225; *Der Satyr aus Pergamon,* Vierzigstes Programm zum Winckelmannsfeste, Berlin 1880 (*Kl. Schr.,* I, 134, 190). The goat attributes of the satyrs mentioned by Dion. Hal. 7, 72. 10 and Diodorus 1. 88. 3 also belong in this Hellenistic development.

68. No satisfactory etymology for silenos or satyros has been found. Cf. Frisk, *Gr. Etym. Wörterb.* We need not bother with the late equation σάτυρος = τίτυρος; cf. Brommer, *Sat.,* 5.

69. H. Lattermann in "Arkadische Forschungen," *Abh. Preuss. Ak.* 1911, 24, 41, plate 13, 3a.

70. *Gymn.* 72 (1965) 77.

71. *Att. Red-fig. Vas.* 420. 21. Illustrations in Bieber, *Hist.,* fig. 16. Pickard-Cambridge, *Dith.,* plate 15a, with bibliography, p. 314.

72. "Zur Vorgeschichte der attischen Tragödie," *Festschr. Gomperz* 1902, 451. The essay is still important, but we cannot agree with everything in it. On the Pandora krater, see Webster in Pickard-Cambridge, *Dith.,* 117.

73. "But you are still a child; as a young man you behave like a goat, taking pride in your yellow beard."

74. Kuhnert, 527.

75. Examples for such usage from the tragedians in G. Thomson, *Oresteia,* Prague 1966, on *Ag.* v. 395; cf. also P. Groeneboom on the verse in his *Agamemnon* commentary.

76. *Ath. Mitt.* 19 (1894), 522.

77. Bieber, *Hist.,* fig. 132.

78. *Vom dionysischen Tanz zum komischen Spiel,* Iserlohn 1947, 13. Refutation also in Pohlenz 2. 11.

79. In Pickard-Cambridge, *Dith.,* 303, no. 19.

80. *Gnomon* 19 (1943) 27. 1.

81. " . . . or because the choruses for the most part were composed of satyrs, humorously called goats either because of their hairy bodies or their sexual appetite, both like a goat's; or because the choreutes plaited their hair and thus imitated the goat style."

82. Characteristically Dion. Hal. 7. 72. 10, in which the satyrs are equipped with goat skins

according to the Hellenistic development and are distinguished from silenes. Yet nothing is emphasized in the silenes that would connect them with horses. They are characterized by their shaggy dress, the μαλλωτὸς χιτών.

83. Furtwängler-Reichhold, *Griech. Vasenm.*, plates 143–45 with Buschor's text. Bieber, *Hist.*, figs. 31–33. Pickard-Cambridge, *Dith.*, plate 13, no. 85; *Festivals*, fig. 49.

84. *Arch. Jahrb.* 14 (1899) 63 f. with fig. 4. Staatl. Mus. Berlin, Ant. Abt. Inv. 3364.

85. Brommer, op. cit., 110. 3.

86. *Ichn.* 141, 215; *Kykl.* 624.

87. Bieber, *Hist.*, fig. 48. The centaurs: *Die Antike* 5 (1929) 269, fig. 5.

88. "He was the first among men to compose dithyrambs, so far as we know, and he named them and produced them in Korinth."

89. "He is also supposed to have been the originator of the tragic mode, to have been the first to assemble a chorus and to have it sing a dithyramb, and he named the song performed by the chorus and introduced satyrs who spoke in verse."

90. "Arion of Methymna introduced the first tragic drama, as Solon taught in his poems called elegies. But Charon of Lampsakos says that drama was first produced in Athens and had Thespis as its author."

91. Kalinka, 38, is overconfident in ascribing the phrase to Solon himself. H. Kolleritsch, "Konnte Solon von Tragödien Arions sprechen?" *Eranos* 66 (1968), 1.

92. Thus Schmid 2. 44, who even considered a historical basis; thus also Pickard-Cambridge, *Dith.*, 77. Patzer, 127, set the date for the introduction of the speaker around the middle of the century. Tièche, 10. 10, recognizes the chronological difficulties, but does not believe them to be decisive. Diogenes Laertios (1. 59) expanded the Thespis anecdote to the prohibition of tragedy by Solon.

93. See on this point Pickard-Cambridge, *Festivals*, 56.

94. "Alcune considerazioni sul teatro greco," *Dioniso* 37 (1963), 3.

95. On the Dionysos festivals, L. Deubner, *Attische Feste*, Berlin 1932; Pickard-Cambridge, *Festivals.*

96. On Webster's theory of the distribution of the plays, see chap. 5, under Fragments. For the days of the performances, see Pickard-Cambridge, *Festivals*, 66.

97. The problems with this date are discussed in the chapter on Thespis.

98. Pickard-Cambridge, *Festivals*, 108.

99. Cf. Pollux 7. 125; Eustath. *Od.* 3. 350; Hesychios s.v. ᾠδεῖον. The passages for a place named ὀρχήστρα in the agora are in Pickard-Cambridge, *Festivals*, 37. 6. Bieber (*Hist.*, 54) is problematical; cf. also Gerkan, *Gnom.* 14 (1938), 238.

100. Thus also F. Brommer, *Arch. Ang.* 1964, 112.

101. By the editors of Pickard-Cambridge, *Festivals*, 200, in contrast to the agreement in the first edition, 213. Dingel, 26, also rejects it.

102. Xen. *Hell.* 2. 3. 31, 47. Plut. *Nikias* 2; εὐμεταβολώτερος κοθόρνου: Zenob. 3. 93. On the actors' costumes, Bieber, *Hist.*, 24; Pickard-Cambridge, *Festivals*, 197. On the kothornos, Pickard-Cambridge, *Festivals*, 204, with bibliography.

103. Still worth reading are Jane Harrison's remarks (*Proleg. to the Study of Gr. Rel.*, 2d ed., 1908, 568) on the Dionysian transformation. For the category of reality in the tragic play: B. Snell, "Mythos und Wirklichkeit in d. gr. Trag.," *Die Antike* 20 (1944), 115 = *The Discovery of the Mind*, New York 1960, 90.

104. Evidence in H. Herter, *RE* 6A (1937) 1897.

105. *Suda* and Photios, s.v., Plut. *Quaest. Conv.* 1. 1. 5, 615a; Ps. Plut. *De Proverbiis Alexandrinorum* 30; Apostolios 13. 42; Zenobios 5. 40. Further, Pohlenz, *GGN* 1926, 299; Ziegler, 1933; Pickard-Cambridge, *Dith.*, 124.

106. For example, see K. Deichgräber, *Nachr. Gött.* 1 (1938/9), 244; Murray, *Aesch.*, 145.

107. The Sikyonians honored Adrastos in other ways, too, but especially, they celebrated his terrible πάθεα with tragic choruses, which were not to honor Dionysos, but Adrastos. Kleis-

thenes, however, gave the choruses to Dionysos, but the rest of the sacrificial ceremony to Melanippos.

108. The evidence is in Peretti, 281; Pickard-Cambridge, *Dith.*, 105; M. P. Nilsson, *Gesch. d. Gr. Rel.*, 1, 2d ed., 187.

109. On this important point there is general agreement with Schmid, 1. 632; Ziegler, 1914; Pickard-Cambridge, *Dith.*, 104. That ἀπέδωκε in the Herodotos passage does not mean "give back," but expresses the fact that the τραγικοὶ χοροί came to the position that in Herodotos's opinion, was properly theirs has been often stated correctly; see A. von Blumenthal, *Gnom.* 19 (1943) 28. 1. Also pertinent is A. Gitti, "Clistene di Sicione e le sue reforme," *Mem. Ac. Lincei* 1926, 539.

110. Also on the relation of hero saga to the dithyramb, see Patzer, 94, 121.

111. On the role of the myth, A. M. G. Little, *Myth and Society in Attic Drama*, New York 1942; A. Lesky, "Der Mythos im Verständnis der Antike," *Gymn.* 73 (1966) 27 = *Ges. Schr.*, 422.

112. Important for the historical drama is B. von Wiese, *Deutsche Vierteljahrschr.* 20 (1942) 412, esp. 423. For the significance of myth in tragedy there are also Kommerell, 131; del Grande, ΤΡΑΓ., 59.

113. *The Origin of Tragedy*, Cambridge 1910. M. P. Nilsson, "Der Ursprung d. Trag.," *N. Jb.* 27 (1911) 609, 673, assigns central importance to the dirge in his theory of tragic origins. For the connection of the heroic myth with the Dionysian, there is an important contribution of W. Schmid, *Zur Gesch. d. gr. Dithyrambos*, Program Tübingen 1901. For the persistence of cult forms in tragedy, R. Hölzle, "Zum Aufbau der lyrischen Partien des Aischylos," Diss. Freiburg im Breisgau 1934.

114. This goes considerably beyond Plutarch (*Pyrrhos*, 11), cited by Pickard-Cambridge, *Dith.*, 102.

115. For the meaning "tragic", Schmid 1. 408n., 631. 2. 47n.; Pickard-Cambridge, *Dith.*, 1st ed., 138. Webster differs, 2d ed., 103. Blumenthal, *Soph.*, II, 22; Peretti, 281; Bickel, 76; *Rhein. Mus.* 91 (1942), 130; Patzer, 59. For the "goat choruses" meaning, Wilamowitz, *Einl. in d. gr. Trag.*, Berlin 1910, 84; *Kl. Schr.*, 1. 376; Kalinka, 39; Pohlenz, *GGN* 1926, 301. 1; *Gr. Trag.*, 2. 9; Howald, 30; Brommer, *Satyroi*, 35, 59; Untersteiner, 85. Flickinger, 11, 15, wished to explain the τραγικοὶ χοροί, like the Alexandrians with τραγῳδία from a goat prize, which he thought was introduced in Sikyon when Dionysos took over the choruses.

116. "Geistererscheinungen bei Aischylos," *Rhein. Mus.* 91 (1942) 123.

117. Before the book mentioned in the bibliography, Else discussed this problem: *Aristotle's Poetics: The Argument*, Cambridge, Mass. 1957. Further, *Trans. Am. Phil. Ass.* 76 (1945), 1; *Herm.* 85 (1957), 19; *Wien. Stud.* 72 (1959), 75.

118. Additions to the bibliography: F. Gagliuolo, "Sul problema di Thespis e l'origine del dramma satiresco," *Riv. Indo-greco-ital.* 13 (1929), 1; B. Stampo, *Le origini della tragedia*, Milan 1935, and *Dioniso* 6 (1937), 143; G. Perrotta, "Tragedia: origine," *Encicl. It.* 34 (1937), 146; A. C. Mahr, *The Origin of Gr. Tragic Form*, New York 1938; F. Robert, *Sur l'origine du mot tragédie*, Mél. Ch. Picard, II, Paris 1949, 872; W. F. Otto, *Ursprung der Tragödie: Das Wort der Antike*, Stuttgart 1962, 162; K. Kerényi, "Naissance et Renaissance de la Tragédie," *Diogène* 28 (1959), 22; F. Rodríguez Adrados, "Κῶμος, κωμῳδία, τραγῳδία: Sobre los origines del teatro," *Emerita* 35 (1967), 249.

119. On this point, R. van Pottelbergh, *Ant. Class.* 10 (1941), 83.

CHAPTER 2

1. 328 (in the following verse κούρη Ἰκαρίοιο); 8, 498; 17. 385; also *Homeric Hymn to Hermes* 442. Else, 52, seeks to exploit this for his theory of the origins of tragedy in the performance of epic.

2. Evidence in Pickard-Cambridge, *Dith.*, 69. Tièche treats the poet intelligently and usefully. G. Rudberg, "Thespis und die Tragödie," *Eranos* 45 (1947), 13, betrays a certain lack of enthusiasm for his subject. Gaster proceeds from ethnological considerations.

3. Dioskorides, *Anth. Pal.* 7. 410, 411. Horace, *Ars Poet.* 275 ff. In the *Marm. Par.* ep. 43, the goat prize is mentioned, but the place of the agon was Athens. On the verse of Eratosthenes, cf. n. 48, chap. 1.

4. According to Wilamowitz, *Hom. Unters.*, 248. 13, on the basis of the restoration of the numbers in the *Marm. Par.* ep. 43, and of the name of Thespis in Eusebios. Cf. also T. J. Cadoux, *Journ. Hell. Stud.* 68 (1948), 109.

5. *Herm.* 85 (1957), 19. 1.

6. Text of the fragments in Nauck.

7. Wehrli, besides on Aristoxenos fr. 114, also in the commentary on Chamaileon, p. 124.

8. "Die Urform der attischen Tragödie and Komödie," *N. Jb.* 43 (1919), 145; *Stasimon*, 14. *Gesch. d. gr. Lit. Samml. Dieterich* 42. 114.

9. Ziegler, 1960, note 26, also considers this inconceivable, and even assumed that I had misunderstood Kranz on this point. I have shown in *Phil. Woch.* (1937), 1404, that this is not the case.

10. Lammers also followed this path. Despite much criticism of Kranz, the lyric dialogue of the double chorus is, for him at least, one of tragedy's original components.

11. Decidedly in favor at the time were Wilamowitz, *Einl. in die gr. Trag.*, 1910, 87, and *Gr. Trag.* 14, Berlin 1923, 22, and E. Bethe, *Proleg. zur Gesch. d. Theaters im Altertum*, 1896, 36. Further quotes in A. Lesky, *Wien. Stud.* 47 (1929), 4 = *Ges. Schr.*, 84.

12. We do not hold Aristotle's opinion that first the chorus entered and sang a song to the gods, then Thespis invented the prologue and speech, and Aischylos the third actor and the kothornos, while we owe everything else in tragedy to Sophokles and Euripides.

13. Thus, we cannot follow Patzer (27), who explains the remark of Themistios as a later interpolation into the Aristotelian schema.

14. For the inclusion of the Themistios passage in our picture of this development, A. Lesky, *Wien. Stud.* 47 (1929), 3 = *Ges. Schr.*, 83; E. Fraenkel, *Phil.* 86 (1930), 9; Tièche, 7; Schmid, 2.39n., more cautious 45. 6; Flickinger, 298; Ziegler, 1930. Peretti, who (64) polemizes well against Kranz and remarks (66.1) that the term ὀκρίβαντες does not occur in the *Poetics*, which points to another source for Themistios, that could have been the lost dialogue περὶ ποιήτων. In the same vein, Pickard-Cambridge, *Dith.*, 78 (first ed., 109); cf. *Festivals*, 130. Buschor, 76, without referring to Themistios, speaks of the art of Thespis, who opposed an actor to the chorus. Kranz (270) had to deny the credibility of Themistios because of his theory discussed above. He maintains a contradiction between Aristotle and Themistios that does not exist. Untersteiner follows him (*Origini*, 281) and carries on the argument given up by Kranz; that the prologue meant "the part before the logos" and thus could not be very old. Pohlenz, 2. 15, wishes to exclude the Themistios passage as "a very fleeting remark."

For the information that Aischylos introduced the third actor, we must consider that Themistios is relying on a tradition different from that of the *Poet.* 1449a, which is also present in the *Vita* of Aischylos (15). It can also refer to Aischylos's taking over of the third actor from Sophokles. Of course one can assume a copying error in the numbers, as Patzer (27. 4) does. Pickard-Cambridge, *Festivals*, 130, follows yet another path, separating τρίτον from ὑποκριτάς (Med.) and interpreting this as the third phase of development. The explanation of the questionable numerals, which rests on the differentiation of τραγῳδός and ὑποκριτής, in G. F. Else, *Trans. Am. Phil. Ass.* 76 (1945), 1; *Wien. Stud.* 72 (1959), 75. *Origin and Early Form*, 59, 86, leads to no solution. Cf. A. Lesky, *Ges. Schr.*, 241. Pickard-Cambridge, *Festivals*, 130; B. M. W. Knox, "Aeschylus and the Third Actor," *Am. Journ. Phil.* 93 (1972), 104.

15. I elaborated on this theory in *Wien. Stud.* 47 (1929), 3; an excerpt from a paper on this subject already in 1926 in *Mitt. d. Ver. kl. Phil. in Wien* 3, p. viii; cf. also *DLZ* 1933, 2316; *Phil. Woch.* 1937, 1404. Walter Nestle came independently to the same conclusion. A. Körte, *Phil.*

Woch. 1928, 1297, reported favorably in a discussion of Nestle's unpublished dissertation about his evaluation of the prologue; Nestle elaborated this view in the excellent book on the structure of the introduction in Attic tragedy (1930). The function of such a prologue is well illustrated by the announcer who introduces the following pantomime in Xenophon's *Symposion* (9. 2).

16. Webster in Pickard-Cambridge, *Dith.* 2, 61; on the beginning of *Suppl.* and *Pers.*: "an innovation rather than a survival." This is true in the sense that in both cases the chorus has taken over the exposition of the material.

17. The attempt of F. Marx, *Rhein. Mus.* 77 (1928), 337 to devaluate the passage was unsuccessful.

18. The archaic character of the Euripidean prologue was emphasized by O. Krausse, "De Euripide Aeschyli instauratore," Diss. Jena 1905, 192. J. M. Stahl, *Rhein. Mus.* 69 (1914), 591; Flickinger, 299; and Walter Nestle, op. cit., 124, among others. A different view is taken by Schmid, 3. 772. When Pohlenz, 1. 432, shows that the undramatic formation of the prologue is not fully realized until the later dramas of Euripides, this can be added to the other archaisms in his work of this period.

19. On the interpretation of the individual passages with an attempt to show a development of meaning, see A. Lesky, *Studi in onore di Enrico Paoli*, Florence 1955, 469 = *Ges. Schr.*, 239.

20. *Aischylos als Regisseur und Theologe*, Bern 1949, 10. Earlier bibliography in A. Müller, *Lehrbuch der griech. Bühnenaltertümer*, 1886, 170, and in Schmid 2. 58. In favor of "interpreter" are A. Lesky, *Wien. Stud.* 47 (1929) 13. 33 = *Ges. Schr.*, 91. 33, and in the study mentioned in the previous note; G. Thomson, *Aeschylus and Athens*, London 1941 (German edition, Berlin 1957, 190), with a problematical extension into ethnology; H. Koller, "Hypokrisis und Hypokrites," *Mus. Helv.* 14 (1957), 100; H. Schreckenberg, Δρᾶμα, Würzburg 1960, 111, who errs, however, with his thesis that tragedy long remained a pure dance form; B. Zucchelli, Ὑποκριτής: *origine e storia del termine*, Studi grammaticali e linguistici 3, Paideia 1963 (published in 1962 as a paper of the Istit. di filol. class. of the University of Genoa), who gives a good overview of the problem, but would like the "interprete" to refer to the role and thus to the word of the poet; J. Rode, "Untersuchungen zur Form des aischyleischen Chorliedes," Diss. Tübingen 1965, 216. Pickard-Cambridge proceeded doubtfully in the first edition of *Dith.* (Oxford 1927, 110); in the first ed. of *Festivals* (Oxford 1951, 131), he supported more confidently the meaning "answerer." Differently, if also hesitantly, the revisers of the new edition of *Festivals* (126. 5, with bibl.; 131) also prefer the meaning "interpreter," "expounder." Others in favor of "answerer" are Patzer, 127. 4, and Else, 58. Separate are A. von Blumenthal, *Gnom.* 19 (1943), 33. 2, who rejects "answerer" but offers an unacceptable explanation for Thuk. 7. 44. 5, and K. Kerényi, *Streifzüge eines Hellenisten* (Zurich 1960, 43), who assumes as the original meaning of ὑποκρίνεσθαι: "the answering—speech and behavior, according to one's true nature, to one's genuine character, the inner, hidden truth."

21. Other possibilities in Pickard-Cambridge, *Dith.*, 79.

22. Webster (op. cit., 80) offers a list of monuments with different costumes from the time of Thespis; see his *Monuments*. Less convincingly, the passage in the *Suda* is taken as a reference to the different attempts of Thespis to appear before the chorus, which had always been masked, as an actor, also masked (Pickard-Cambridge, *Festivals*, 191).

CHAPTER 3

1. The discussion of Wilhelm's book by E. Reisch, *Ztschr. f. öst. Gymn.* 58 (1907), 289, still offers the best introduction to this difficult material. Cf. also Flickinger, 318. A. Körte, *Herm.* 73 (1938), 124, and especially Pickard-Cambridge, *Festivals*, 101.

2. Cf. Pickard-Cambridge, *Dith.*, 68.

3. On the form of the name, Schmid, 2. 170. 8. The *Suda* names as variants of the father's

name Minyros and Chorokles; this is not certain, since the son of Phrynichos, Polyphrasmon, was, of course, named after the grandfather.

4. On this, R. Cantarella, *Esch.*, 288, and A. von Blumenthal, *RE* 20 (1941), 911.

5. *Rhein. Mus.* 77 (1928), 340.

6. Thus, albeit with a "perhaps," Howald, 45. Similarly, A. von Blumenthal, *RE* 20 (1941), 913, with the suggestion Δανάη ἢ Περσεὺς ἢ Σύνθωκοι. Cantaralla, *Esch.*, 230, transposes the second ἢ, but the resulting Σύνθωκοι ἢ Δαναΐδες destroys the alphabetical order. The Πέρσαι is supposedly identical with the Μιλήτου ἅλωσις, which was a general description of content, not a title, in Herodotos.

7. The argumentation is unacceptable in Arnott's attempt, *Scen. Conv.*, 70, to interpret away the prologue of the eunuch.

8. The subject is the casualties of early and late afternoon. Restoration attempts in H. Diels, *Rhein. Mus.* 56 (1901), 29. F. Marx (see following n.), 357. A. von Blumenthal, *RE* 20 (1941), 916. I am grateful to H. Erbse for pointing out that his new comparison of the papyrus yielded decisive objections against the previous restorations. For the Ionicisms, the explanation of H. Diels, who considers them the archaisms of a poet influenced elsewhere too by Ionic elements, is preferable to that of F. Marx, who assumes the speaker to be an Ionian loyal to the Persians.

9. *Rhein. Mus.* 77 (1928), 337.

10. Thus Lammers (60) in his detailed treatment of the *Phoinissai*, which quotes much older bibliography. T. B. L. Webster, in Pickard-Cambridge, *Dith.*², 65, considers the less attractive possibility that the councillors composed the main chorus, the Phoinikian women the second chorus.

11. *Essays in Greek History*, Oxford 1958, 177.

12. W. G. Forrest, *Class. Quart.* n.s. 10 (1960), 235, has shown how improbable this is.

13. Thus also Podlecki, 14.

14. Cf. Lloyd-Jones, 22. G. Freymuth denies any political intention in the piece. "Zur Μιλήτου ἅλωσις von Phrynichos," *Phil.* 99 (1955), 51.

15. Aristoph. *Ran.* 1299. On the whole question: P. Wiesmann, "Das Problem der tragischen Tetralogie," Diss. Zurich 1929; M. Delcourt, "La tétralogie et la trilogie attique," *Ant. Class.* 7 (1938), 31; Untersteiner, *Orig.*, 285; Del Grande, *Hybris*, 120; T. Krischer, "Das Problem der trilogischen Komposition und die dramaturgische Entwicklung der attischen Tragödie," Diss. Frankfurt am Main 1960; H. Steinmetz, *Die Trilogie: Entstehung und Struktur einer Grossform des deutschen Dramas nach 1800*, Heidelberg 1968.

16. "*Alkestis*, der Mythus und das Drama," *Sitzb. Wien* 203/3 (1925), 63. L. Weber, *Euripides Alkestis*, Leipzig 1930. "Φρυνίχου Ἄλκηστις," *Rhein. Mus.* 79 (1930), 35, has not taken the question further. We have no occasion to presume that the long period of time that passes between the sacrificial vow and its fulfillment in the Euripidean version already existed in Phrynichos's play. Fr. 2N is a reference to the wrestling match between Herakles and Death, as maintained by Hermann and Welcker, against Schmid (2. 172. 1).

17. *Esch.*, 234; also Schmid, 1. 636, dated at 500.

18. Also on the vase paintings: Brommer, *Satyrspiele*, and L. Campo, *I drammi satireschi della Grecia antica*, Il pensiero Greco 15, Milan 1940.

19. A tragedy title is missing for one tetralogy. Garrod, *Class. Rev.* 34 (1920), 130, wished to restore (after Bergk) Ἀνταίῳ as the third tragedy, which is paleographically attractive.

20. This form seems preferable to the Δύσμαιναι suggested by Meineke.

CHAPTER 4

Biographical Notes

1. Radermacher's commentary (3d ed. prepared by W. Kraus, Vienna 1967) is also important for this.

2. *Ges. Abh.* 1. 153. 1. So too Wilamowitz, *Glaube der Hellenen.* 2. 221. 1. The initiation of Aischylos is maintained among others by O. Kern, *RE* 16 (1935), 1249 and recently by B. M. W. Knox (see bibliography on Soph.), 174. 82.

3. Thus especially A. Dieterich, "Die Entstehung der Tragödie," *Kl. Schr.*, Leipzig 1911, 414; cf. also E. Rohde, *Kl. Schr.*, Tübingen 1901, 2. 361.

4. *Ion von Chios*, Stuttgart 1939, 1.

5. The Armenian version names the previous year, the fourth year of the seventieth Olympiad, which coincides better with the *Suda*.

6. For the problems involved with the title and other questions connected with the play, see the section on the fragments.

7. On the question whether two versions are involved here, see the discussion of the play. On Aischylos in Sicily: M. Bock, "Aischylos und Akragas," *Gymn.* 65 (1958), 402; Q. Cataudella, *Eschilo in Sicilia: Saggi sulla tragedia Greca*, Messina 1969, 67; C. J. Herington, "Aeschylus in Sicily," *Journ. Hell. Stud.* 87 (1967), 74.

8. What is the meaning of *Vita* 11, in which it states that the pilgrims ὑπεϰρίνοντο there? Are these actual performances or recitations?

9. Further passages: Philostratos, *Vita Apollonii* 6. 11; schol. Aristoph. *Ach.* 10, *Ran.* 868 (ἐψηφίσαντο). All the material connected with such repeat performances was collected by R. Cantarella (who seeks to draw conclusions from vase-paintings), "Aristoph. *Plut.* 422–425 e le riprese Eschilee," *Acc. dei Lincei. Rendic. d. Classe di Scienze morale, stor. e fil.* ser. 8, vol. 20, 363.

10. On the documents of dramatic performances, *Nachr. Ak. Gött. Phil.-hist. Kl.* 1966/2.

11. F. Poulsen, *Ny Carlsberg Glyptothek. Katalog over antike skulpturer*, Copenhagen 1940, no. 421; L. Laurenzi, *Ritratti Greca*, Florence 1941, 99; K. Schefold, *Die Bildnisse der antiken Dichter, Redner und Denker*, Basel 1943, 88. 207; id., *Griechische Dichterbildnesse*, Zurich 1965, 24, plate 14b; V. Poulsen, *Les portraits Grecs*, Cophenhagen 1954, no. 8; A. Hekler, *Bildnisse berühmter Griechen*, 3d ed. by H. von Heintze, Berlin 1962, p. 61. The most comprehensive overview is given by G. M. A. Richter, *The Portraits of the Greeks*, London 1965, 121, illus. 577–610.

K. Schefold, *Gnom.* 34 (1962), 585, describes a head published in the *Jahrb. d. Arch. Inst.* 70 (1955), 105, as a "horrible pastiche," while L. Laurenzi in the *Enc. Arte Ant. s. Eschilo* (1960) assumes that the poet is intended.

For information concerning the recent portrait literature on the tragedians I must heartily thank Dr. Friedrich Brein.

Manuscript Transmission and Editions

1. *Quaestionum trag. cap. tria*, Poznan 1939 (1 ff., "De Aeschyli fabularum catalogo"). M. Untersteiner tries to answer the question with drastic alterations of the transmitted text of the *Vita*, "Quanti drammi scrisse Eschilo?" *In memoriam A. Beltrami*, Univ. Genova Inst. di filol. class. 1954, 244.

2. *Rhein. Mus.* n.s. 48 (1893), 141 = *Kl. Schr.*, 111; cf. on this Mette, *Fragm.*, p. 258.

3. Thus W. B. Sedgwick, *Class. et Med.* 9 (1947), 1; E. G. Turner, *Athenian Books in the 5th and 4th Centuries B.C.*, London 1952, 21; C. F. Russo, *Belfagor* 23 (1968), 317. A different verdict was reached by Wilamowitz, *Einleitung in die griech. Trag.*, repr. 1959, 121. On this ques-

tion also D. L. Page in the introduction to Eur. *Med.*, xxxvii. H. J. Newiger, *Herm.* 89 (1961), 429. 3. Webster, *Soph.*, 101.

4. Little can be made of *Ran.* 1114, which Wilamowitz, *Einl.* 124, cited in this connection; cf. Radermacher's commentary on the verse.

5. Cf. E. Nachmanson, "Der. griech. Buchtitel," *Göteborgs Högskolas Årsskrift* 47 (1941), 6.

6. J. Vürtheim offers in his edition of the *Suppl.* of Aischylos, Amsterdam 1928, 231, a section on ancient actors' texts. The major work is Page's book, listed in the Bibliography. In the Quintilian passage quoted at note reference 9 in the biographical section, *correctas* must refer to the fact that later poets worked on the Aischylean plays in order to smooth over the difficult spots. We know nothing of the details involved and decline to make any speculations.

7. Cf. R. Böhme, *Gnom.* 15 (1939), 353.

8. On the numbers allotted in the hypotheseis to some plays, see the section on the *Antigone*.

9. In his treatment of this papyrus, *Hermes* Einzelschriften 5 (1937), 69; the quoted sentence, 78. A series of other papyri of this sort is described by Zuntz, *Inquiry*, 250.

10. On this, Zuntz, *Inquiry*, 253.

11. Further, W. S. Barrett, *Eur. Hipp.*, 52, and Zuntz, op. cit., 254.

12. H. Hunger in *Geschichte der Textüberlieferung*, Zurich 1961, 47.

13. H. Hunger, op. cit., 94. Zuntz offers (*Inquiry*, 262 n.) a short doxography of the question of when the transcription of poetic texts began. Against the later estimates of Dain and Irigoin, he chooses the time of Arethas, in any case at least that of Photios, who brings us into the second half of the ninth century.

14. *Inquiry*, 204, in which may also be found the information about the opposing evaluation of these manuscripts by A. Turyn and E. Fraenkel.

15. "Contributions to the Study of the Thoman Recension of Aeschylus," Diss. Univ. of Illinois 1956.

16. *Gnom.* 25 (1953), 441.

17. Special studies on individual manuscripts: G. Pasquali, "I codici inferiori della tril. Eschilea," *Rendiconti Ac. Lincei* 6 (1930), 35 in the Bibl. Vitt. Emman. 5; S. G. Peppink, *Athenaei Dipnosoph. Epit.*, I, Leyden 1937, 177 ("Spicilegium Aeschyleum") on cod. Vat. 1332. An Athous (Iviron cod. 209, olim 161) was first referred to by Dawe (p. 28). H. F. Johansen, *Codex Scurialensis*, pl. I 15 and the "Transmission of Aeschylus' Suppliants," *Greek, Roman and Byzantine Stud.* 9 (1968), 359, offers a collation of this manuscript from the sixteenth century, which contains the *Dionysiaka* of Nonnos and the *Suppliants* of Aischylos, by the same hand. He shows that for this drama the manuscript is in no way directly dependent on M.

18. Wilamowitz's verdict is scathing (ed. maior, xiii) nor has he any praise for Dähnhardt. On the scholia Romagnoli, *Atti Istit. Veneto* 75 (1915), 16.

19. Not much work has been devoted to the life of the plays after the poet's death. B. Costantini, "La fortuna di Eschilo in Italia," *Dioniso* 12 (1949), 148; F. M. Pontani, "Eschilo nella poesia neo-greca," *Maia* 2 (1949), 53; cf. also Sheppard.

The Extant Tragedies

1. For an example, see especially G. Müller, "De Aeschyli Supplicum tempore atque indole," Diss. Halle 1908; F. Focke, *GGN* 1922, 183, who wanted to go as far back as ca. 499. Authors who stand by the early dating are listed in the next note.

2. The view proposed above and in expanded form in *Herm.* 82 (1954), 1 = *Ges. Schr.* 220 is still the subject of heated controversy, in which nevertheless the scales tilt toward the later date. An overview is *Anz. f. d. Altertumsw.* 12 (1959), 10; extensive bibliography also in H. Lloyd-Jones in the appendix to the second edition of Aischylos in the Loeb Class. Libr., Cambridge, Mass. 1957, 595. Also in Mette on fr. 122. The following scholars have declared them-

selves for the late dating suggested by the papyrus: D. L. Page, *Agamemnon*, Oxford 1957, xix. Galiano, 97, with good bibliography and careful deliberation; T. B. L. Webster in Pickard-Cambridge, *Dith.*², 60; H. Lloyd-Jones, "The *Supplices* of Aeschylus: The New Date and Old Problems," *Ant. Class.* 33 (1964), 356; I. Trencsényi-Waldapfel, "Les *Suppliantes* d'Eschyle," *Acta Antiqua Ac. Scient. Hungar.* 12 (1964), 259; J. A. Davison, *Ancient Society and Institutions*, Oxford 1966, 95; H.-J. Newiger, *GGA* 219 (1967) in a very substantial discussion of the book by Koster; G. Salanitro, "La data e il significato politico delle *Supplici* di Eschilo," *Helikon* 8 (1968), 311.

The following scholars still hold to the early dating with the arguments discussed above: V. Ehrenberg, *Sophokles und Perikles*, 4. 2. A Diamantopoulos, "The Danaid Tetralogy of Aeschylus," *Journ. Hell. Stud.* 77 (1957), 220, suggesting 492/491 on the basis of assumed political allusions; E. Wolff, "The Date of Aeschylus' Danaid Tetralogy," *Eranos* 56 (1958), 119, and 57 (1959), 6; Del Grande, TPAΓ., 144, with the assumption of a repeat performance; and W. J. W. Koster, "Welke is de oudste bewaard gebleven tragedie?" *Ned. AB. Afd. Letterkunde*, n.s. 29, no. 4, 1966. Attempting to solve the problem by assuming that a long period of time elapsed between composition and performance is R. Cantarella, *Rendicotti della Classe di Scienze morali, stor. e filol. dell' Accademia dei Lincei*, s. 8, 20 (1965), 371. Extensive bibliography recently in H. Van Looy, "Aeschyli *Supplices . . . und ein Ende?*" *Ant. Class.* 38 (1969), 489.

3. On the restoration see B. Snell, *Gnom.* 25 (1953), 438. On the reading of the fragments involving the Danaid trilogy: F. Lasserre, *Herm.* 83 (1955), 128; G. Freymuth, *Phil.* 99 (1955), 64. 1; H. J. Mette, *Gymn.* 62 (1955), 397; Podlecki, 163. 7.

4. In the prefatory remarks to the translation of the play (see above); cf. *Struktur des Eingangs*, 15. 1; *Menschliche Existenz* 11. 2; *Gnom.* 10 (1934), 413. Late datings of the Danaid trilogy can be traced as far back as A. Boeckh, *Tragoediae Graecae principum rel.*, 1808, 54, and K. O. Mueller, *Eumenides*, 1833, 123; *Griech. Lit. Gesch.*, 3d ed., 2. 88. The decisive factors were assumed political references. The dating to 476 of J. Vürtheim in his edition, which W. J. Koster, op. cit., follows, never gained acceptance.

5. We preface the bibliographical notes with the statement, valid for all three tragedians, that the treatment of the individual plays in the monographs listed in the bibliography is rarely listed. Correspondingly we will not repeat in the list of editions those contained in complete editions.

ANNOTATED EDITIONS: P. Groeneboom, Groningen 1930, valuable edition is translated into German in the student-texts III/1 and 2 edited by B. Snell and H. Erbse, Göttingen 1960; Inama-Colonna, Turin 1948; M. Pontani, Rome 1951; G. Italie, Leyden 1953; H. D. Broadhead, *The Persae of Aeschylus*, Cambridge 1960, currently the leading edition with extensive bibliography; L. Roussel, *Eschyle: Les Perses*, Presses Univ. de France 1960, without apparatus, highly problematic; D. Korzeniewski, text and preparatory material, Bamberg 1966. INTERPRETATION: K. Deichgräber, "Die *Perser* des Aisch." *Nachr. Gött. Phil.-hist. Kl.* 1/4 (1941), 155, a complete and well-thought-out analysis, id., *Der listensinnende Trug des Gottes*, Göttingen 1952; J. Bidez, "A propos des *Perses* d'Eschyle," *Bul. Ac. Belg.* 1937, 206; M. V. Ghezzo, "I *Persiani* di Esch.," *Atti Ist. Ven.* 98 (1938/1939), 427; R. Lattimore, "Aisch. on the Defeat of Xerxes," in *Class. Stud. in Honor of W. A. Oldfather*, Univ. of Illinois 1943; Kaufmann-Bühler, 107; F. Stoessl, "Die *Phoinissen* des Phrynichos und die *Perser* des Aischylos," *Mus. Helv.* 2 (1945), 148; R. D. Dawe, "Inconsistency of Plot and Character in Aesch.," *Proc. Cambr. Phil. Soc.* no. 189 (1963), 27; D. Korzeniewski, "Studien zu den *Pers.* des Aisch," I, *Helikon* 6 (1966), 548; and II, 7 (1967), 27; W. Kierdorf, *Erlebnis und Darstellung der Perserkriege*, Hypomn. 16, Göttingen 1966; L. Golden, *In Praise of Prometheus*, Chapel Hill, North Carolina 1966, 31; B. Alexanderson, "Darius in the *Persians*," *Eranos* 65 (1967), 1; E. B. Holtsmark, "Ring Composition and the *Persae* of Aeschylus," *Symb. Osl.* 45 (1970), 5; R. P. Winnington-Ingram, "Zeus in the *Persae*," *Journ. Hell. Stud.* 93 (1973), 210; RELATION TO HISTORY: R. Lattimore (see above), 82; Podlecki, 8. GERMAN TRANSLATIONS (collected): A. Mundhenk, *N. Jahrb.* 2 (1939), 74; (individual): O. Werner, Frankfurt am Main 1940; E. Buschor, Munich 1953; R. Borchardt, Stuttgart

1958; W. Schadewaldt, *Griech. Theater*, Frankfurt am Main 1964, 7. ENGLISH VERSE TRANSLA-
TION: G. Murray, London 1939. ITALIAN TRANSLATION: E. Bignone, Florence 1950.

6. *Herm.* 32 (1897), 382; *Aisch. Int.*, 42.

7. We must reject the attempt of W. Riemschneider, *Herm.* 73 (1938), 347, to remove the
difficulty by postulating a silent scene. On the motif, Wilamowitz, *Aisch. Int.*, 42, and F.
Stoessl, op. cit., 150.

8. A lengthy discussion of the question in H. D. Broadhead, op. cit., xliv. Further, Webster,
Greek Theatre Production, 8; Arnott, *Scenic Conventions*, 57; W. Kierdorf, op. cit., 53; Dingel,
83, who rightly rejects the equation of stage altar and the tomb of Dareios by Arnott, but incorrectly reverts to the hypothesis of A. M. Harmon, *Trans. Am. Phil. Ass.* 63 (1932), 7, that the
play was set in front of a city gate. Cf. also W. Barton, "Schauplatz und Bühnenvorgänge bei
Aisch." Diss. Jena 1951.

9. Similarly Webster (see previous note), who believes the tomb was a part of the vaguely
described structure, but we cannot accept his argument when he demands as early as the *Persians* the existence of a door, a roofed area, and the ekkyklema (*Gr. Bühnenaltert.*, 19). A skene-
wall as background is proposed by Dr. Korzeniewski, op. cit. ("Studien"), 549.

10. On this W. Süss in his edition of the *Frogs*, Kl. Texte 66.

11. On this Wilamowitz, *Aisch. Interpret.*, 44; H. D. Broadhead, op. cit., li; R. D. Dawe, op.
cit., 27; B. Alexanderson, op. cit., who also intelligently handles the unnecessarily controversial question of how far Dareios's knowledge extends.

12. πειράσομαι; we would not like to change this to πορεύσομαι with H. D. Broadhead.
Atossa does in fact miss her son insofar as he first meets the chorus.

13. For the evaluation of the messenger's report, J. Keil, *Herm.* 73 (1938), 333, and Appendix
VI in the edition of H. D. Broadhead.

14. 471 according to the most probable estimate.

15. Other arguments of Podlecki such as the emphatic use of the Ionian name or the role of
the daimon have no weight in this context.

16. *Dioniso* 19 (1956), 229.

17. E. Siegmann, "Die neuen Aischylos Bruchstücke," *Phil.* 97 (1948), 62; Galiano, 110, with
extensive bibliography; Z. K. Vysoký, "Zu den neuentdeckten Bruchstücken der Tragödie
Glaukos Potnieus von Aisch.," *Charisteria Novotný*, Prague 1962, 13 (on the role of Glaukos's
wife and her dream); Mette, *Verl. Aisch.*, 7. H. D. Broadhead, op. cit., lvii with older, now obso-
lete, hypotheses.

18. *P. Oxy.* 20 (1952), 2245. On this E. Fraenkel, *Proc. Brit. Ac.* 28 (1942), 13; B. Snell, *Gnom.*
25 (1953), 435, who considers the relationship of *P. Oxy.* 2256 fr. 59 f. and 2252; A. Lesky,
Gymn. 61 (1954), 302; R. Stark, *Maia* n.s. 8 (1956), 8; H. Lloyd-Jones, Appendix to the Aischylos of the Loeb Class. Libr. 1957, 562; Galiano, 250, with good bibliography. In Mette, frr. 343–
350.

19. J. D. Beazley, *Am. Journ. Arch.* 43 (1939), 618; ibid., 44 (1940), 212. Several vase-paintings with Prometheus bringing fire amidst the satyrs are listed by Brommer, *Satyrspiele* no. 9,
187–199a, probably, like the Ashmolean krater, an aftereffect of a repeat performance of the
Aischylean play.

20. *Riv. di Fil.* n.s. 32 (1954), 337. That the chiton mentioned in fr. 1, col. 2, v. 3, of the
papyrus could not have been a garment of satyrs is incorrect, according to the evidence of
the vases. Besides this, Snell's restoration, *Gnom.* 25 (1953), 435, establishes a reference to
the nymphs.

21. *Der. Verl. Aisch.* 27. Rose Unterberger, "Der *gefesselte Prometheus* des Aisch.," *Tüb.
Beitr.* 45 (1968), 134, now joins him.

22. A careful discussion of the question by H. D. Broadhead, op. cit., lix.

23. ANNOTATED EDITIONS: P. Groeneboom, Groningen 1938. G. Italie, Leyden 1950; Q. Cataudella, Florence 1966, and the introduction in *Saggi sulla tragedia Greca*, Messina 1969, 169.
ON TEXT AND INTERPRETATION: O. Regenbogen, "Bemerkungen zu den *Sieben* des Aisch. II: Zu

Eteokles Entschliessungsszene, 631 ff.,"*Herm.* 68 (1933), 63 = *Kl. Schr.*, 1961, 49; J. Mesk, "Die Parodos der *Sieben gegen Theben*," *Phil.* 89 (1934), 454; F. Solmsen, "The Erinyes in Aischylos' *Septem*," *Trans. Am. Phil. Ass.* 68 (1937), 197; E. van Veen, "Interpolaties in Aeschylus' *Zeven gegen Thebe*," Diss. Groningen 1938; A. Lesky, "Aisch. *Septem*, 576 ff.," *Studi in onore di G. Funaioli*, Rome 1955, 163 = *Ges. Schr.*, 233; Kaufmann-Bühler, 50; Q. Cataudella, "Emendamenti ai *Sette contro Tebe*," *Riv. fil. class.* 1956, 45 = *Saggi sulla tragedia Greca*, Messina 1969, 187; E. Fraenkel, "Die sieben Redepaare in Thebanerdrama des Aeschylus," *Sitzb. Bayer. Ak. Phil.-hist. Kl.* 1957/3 = *Kl. Beitr.*, I, 273, E. Wolff, "Die Entscheidung des Eteokles in den *Sieben gegen Theben*," *Harv. Stud.* 63 (1958), 89; H. Patzer, "Die dramatische Handlung der *Sieben gegen Theben*"; ibid., 97; B. Otis, "The Unity of the *Seven against Thebes*," *Greek, Roman and Byz. Stud.* 3 (1960), 153; A. Lesky, "Eteokles in den *Sieben gegen Theben*," *Wien. Stud.* 74 (1961), 5 = *Ges. Schr.*, 264; G. R. Manton, "The Second Stasimon of the *Seven against Thebes*," *Bull. Inst. Class. Stud.* 8 (1961), 77, precursor of an edition prepared for the Oxford Press, for which he has access to sixteen new manuscript collations by R. D. Dawe; K. von Fritz, "Die Gestalt des Eteokles in Aeschylus' *Sieben gegen Theben*," in *Antike und moderne Trag.*, Berlin 1962, 193; R. D. Dawe, "Inconsistency of Plot and Character in Aesch., "*Proc. Cambr. Philol. Soc.*, no. 189 (1963), 31; H. Erbse, "Interpretationsprobleme in den *Septem* des Aischylos," *Herm.* 92 (1964), 1; L. Golden, "The Character of Eteokles and the Meaning of the *Septem*," *Class. Phil.* 59 (1964), 79; A. J. Podlecki, "The Character of Eteokles in Aischylus' *Septem*," *Trans. Am. Phil. Ass.* 95 (1964), 283; W. Jarcho, "Nochmals über die Gestalt des Eteokles in Aisch. Trag. *Sieben gegen Theben*," *Inasemna philologija* 9/5 (1966), 107 (Russ. with German summary); L. Golden, *In Praise of Prometheus*, Chapel Hill, N.C. 1966, 42; S. Benardete, "Two notes on Aeschylus' *Septem*," *Wien. Stud.* n.s. 1 (1967), 22 and 2 (1968), 5; C. W. W. Willink, "A Problem in Aesch. Septem," *Class. Quart.* n.s. 18 (1968), 4; B. Borecký, "Bemerkung am Rande des Bruderstreites in den *Sieben gegen Theben*," *Antiquitas Graeco-Romana et tempora nostra*, Prague 1968, 263; G. N. Kirkwood, "Eteocles Oiakostrophos," *Phoenix* 23 (1969), 9; F. Ferrari, "La decisione di Eteocle e il tragico dei *Sette contro Tebe*," *Annali della Scuola Normale Superiore di Pisa, Classe di lettere e filosofia*, ser. 3, vol. 2/1 (1972), 141; id., "La scelta dei difensori nei *Sette contro Tebe* di Eschilo," *Studi Classici Orientali* 19/20 (1970/71); O. L. Smith, "The Father's Curse—Some Thoughts on the *Seven against Thebes*," *Class. et Mediev.* 30 (1974), 27. ON THE QUESTION OF THE CONCLUSION: H. Lloyd-Jones, "The End of the *Seven against Thebes*," *Class. Quart.* n.s. 9 (1959), 80; E. Fraenkel, "Zum Schluss der *Sieben gegen Theben*," *Mus. Helv.* 21 (1964), 58; R. D. Dawe, "The End of *Seven against Thebes*," *Class. Quart.* n.s. 17 (1967), 16; Schwinge (see bibl. on Eur.), 39. 6, with further bibliography; H. Petersmann, "Zum Schluss von Aischylos' *Sieben gegen Theben*," *Ziva Antika* 22 (1972), 25. INDIVIDUAL TRANSLATIONS: G. Murray, Oxford 1935; K. Schilling, Munich 1940; W. Schadewaldt, *Griech. Theater*, Frankfurt am Main 1964, 49.

24. "Religiöse Kunst im Zeitalter der Tragödie," *Antike* 5 (1929), 259.

25. E. Howald's suggestion in his Zürich Rector's speech (1939) that the material was derived from a myth about the departure of the underworld demons is not convincing.

26. *Die Trilogie des Aischylos*, Baden bei Wien 1937, 171. Mette, *Verl. Aisch.*, 31, stays within the necessary limits with his suggestions.

27. "Oedipus-Probleme," *Sitzb. Preuss. Ak.* 1942, 40.

28. Thus, for example, Kenner, 107.

29. This view has a long history; see, N. Wecklein in the introduction of his explanatory edition. It also may be found in Tucker and in the translations of G. Murray and W. Schadewaldt.

30. H. Hunger, "Eine spieltechnische Beobachtung im Texte des Euripides," *Wien. Stud.* 65 (1952), 19.

31. Wilamowitz, *Aisch. Int.*, 76; P. Groeneboom, op. cit., 136; G. Italie, op. cit., on v. 286. Cf. A. Lesky, op. cit. (*Wien. Stud.*), 8 = *Ges. Schr.*, 266; R. D. Dawe, op. cit., 36 agrees with the interpretation proposed there.

32. "Der Parallelismus der sieben Redepaare in den *Sieben gegen Theben* des Aeschylus," *Opuscula*, I, 300.

33. It is regrettable that Dawe argues for this in his valuable study.

34. Thus H. Bogner, *Das Neue Bild der Antike*, I, Leipzig 1942, 187; H. Patzer, op. cit., 113 f., 119, 24, for whom the explanation of the chorus completely misses the point; K. von Fritz, op. cit., 214; G. Müller, *Sophokles*, Wege der Forschung 95, 1967, 236.

35. More detailed comments in A. Lesky, op. cit., 13 = 271. W. Jarcho. op. cit., correctly sees the effectiveness of the confrontation between Eteokles' subjective impulses and objective necessity. De Romilly, *Time*, 149. 13, excellently evaluates the change in the chorus's attitude; also R. D. Dawe, op. cit., 31.

36. *Eschyle*, 1922, 122; P. von der Mühll, "Der Zweikampf der Oidipussöhne in den *Septem*," *Mus. Helv.* 21 (1964), 225.

37. "Die Wappnung des Eteokles," *Eranion. Festschr. Hommel*, Tübingen 1961, 105. H. J. Rose also argues for a panoply in his commentary, but inserts the donning of the arms in other passages.

38. Bibliography with reasoned evaluation in Podlecki, 31.

39. INTERPRETIVE EDITIONS: J. Vürtheim, Amsterdam 1928; M. Untersteiner, Naples 1935 (sections of the introduction with interpretations, *Dioniso* 6 [1937], 24). For a dual-language edition with explanatory essay see W. Kraus, Frankfurt am Main 1948, and Stuttgart 1966 (the Reclam edition). An edition with a treatment of the foundations of the text, English translation, and the scholia edited by O. Smith: H. F. Johansen's, Copenhagen 1970 (commentary to follow). The bibliography related to the dating problem is listed in chap. 4 in "The Extant Tragedies" section. CONTENT AND INTERPRETATION: Anna Elisei, "Le Danaidi nelle *Supplici* di Eschilo," *Stud. It.* n.s. 6 (1928), 197; von Fritz, 160; Peretti, *Epirrema*, 81 and passim; Cantarella, *Eschilo*, 105; O. Hiltbrunner, *Wiederholungs- und Motivtechnik bei Aischylos*, Bern 1950, 7; H. F. Johansen, "Some Features of Sentence Structure in Aeschylus' *Suppliants*," *Class. et Mediaev.* 15 (1954), 1; id., "Progymnasmata," *Class. et Mediaev.* 27, (1966), 39 (with treatment of individual passages); Kaufmann-Bühler, 38; R. D. Murray, *The Motif of Io in Aeschylus'* Suppliants, Princeton 1958; G. R. Manton (see on the *Seven*), 80; Helen H. Bacon, *Barbarians in Greek Tragedy*, New Haven 1961, passim; I. Trenscényi-Waldapfel, "Les *Suppliantes* d'Eschyle," *Acta Antiqua Ac. Scient. Hungar.* 12 (1964), 259; H. Lloyd-Jones, "The *Supplices* of Aeschylus: The New Date and Old Problems," *Ant. Class.* 33 (1964), 356; F. Wehrli, "Io, Dichtung und Kultlegende," *Festschrift Schefold*, 1967, 196; J. Alsina, "Etapas en la visión trágica de Esquilo," *Boletin del Inst. de Estudios Helenicos* 2 (1968), 9. Bibliography related to the problem of Eteokles' decision will be found in the section "Destiny and Guilt."

On the reconstruction of the trilogy, besides the important essays of K. von Fritz and W. Kraus (both op. cit.), see A. Diamantopoulos, "The Danaid Tetralogy of Aeschylus," *Journ. Hell. Stud.* 77 (1957), 222; R. P. Winnington-Ingram, "The Danaid trilogy of Aischylus," ibid. 81 (1961), 141; G. Salanitro, "La date e il significato politico delle *Supplici* di Eschilo," *Helikon* 8 (1968), 311; A. F. Garvie, *Aeschylus'* Supplices: *Play and Trilogy*, Cambridge 1969; Christina Gülke, *Mythos und Zeitgeschichte bei Aischylos: Das Verhältnis von Mythos und Historie in* Eum. *und* Hik., Meisenheim 1969; H. Van Looy, *Ant. Class.* 38 (1969), 489, and "Aeschyli Suppl. ... und kein Ende," *Anamnesis: Gedenboek Prof. Leemans*, Ghent 1970, 369; K. A. Neuhauser, "Tereus und die Danaiden bei Aisch.," *Herm.* 97 (1969), 167; F. Ferrari, "Il coro delle ancelle nell'esodo delle *Supplici* di Eschilo," *Maia* n.s. 24 (1972), 353.

40. On the difficult nautical image in 438 and 440 f.: D. van Nes, *Die maritime Bildersprache des Aischylos*, Groningen 1963, 89.

41. S. Eitrem, *RE* 9 (1916), 1733; Wilamowitz, *Aisch. Int.*, 15; F. Wehrli, op. cit., gives an epic basis, developed from ancient cult presentations, for the Io story in Aischylos (*Suppl.* and *Prom.*).

42. *Epilegomena to the Study of Greek Religion and Themis*, New York, 1962, 530; I. Trenscényi-Waldapfel, op. cit., 267.

43. E. Benveniste, "La légende des Danaides," *Rev. Hist. Rel.* 139 (1949), 129; Thomson *Aeschylus and Athens*, 289–290; I. Trenscényi-Waldapfel, op. cit., 268. Differently, H. G. Macurdy, "Had the Danaid Trilogy a Social Problem?" *Class. Phil.* 39 (1944), 95. A euhemeristic explanation was attempted by M. P. Nilsson, *Homer and Mycenae*, London 1933, 108: captured Danaid women killed their Egyptian masters; it was rightly opposed by H. Hommel, *N. Jb.* 1940, 291. 90.

44. Schol. Eur. *Hek.* 886; Apollod. *Bibl.* ii.i.4.5; Hyginus, *Fab.* 168; Servius on Verg. *Aen.* 10. 497. A variant in the scholia on *Il.* 1. 42 and Eur. *Or.* 872.

45. Op. cit., 202; W. Schadewaldt, *Gnom.* 8 (1932), 10, explains Hermann's text as follows: "rejecting the incestuous and godless marriage with the sons of Aigyptos."

46. "Nota Eschilea," *Phil.* 108 (1964), 293.

47. *Aisch. Int.*, 15, and ed. maior, p. 335: quia mares devitare nati sumus.

48. This was correctly argued especially by A. Elisei, op. cit.; von Fritz, 183, is good on this; cf. also J. Alsina, op. cit., 11.

49. On the *Suppl.*, A. Lesky, *Herm.* 72 (1937), 126 = *Ges. Schr.*, 142.

50. *Die frühe Klassik der Griechen*, Stuttgart 1966, 143, outstanding for its reasonable treatment of the questions involving tragedy and politics; F. Stoessl, "Aischylus As a Political Thinker," *Am. Journ. Phil.* 73 (1952), 113; V. Ehrenberg, "Origins of Democracy: The Constitution in Aeschylus' *Suppliants*," *Historia* 1 (1950), 517 = *Polis und Imperium*, Zurich 1965, 266; J. A. Davison, "Aeschylus and Athenian Politics," *Festschr. Ehrenberg*, Oxford 1966, 95.

51. G. Salanitro, "L'*Orestea* e la politica estera di Atene," *Siculorum Gymn.* n.s. 19 (1966), 158. 20, conjectures that the alliance with Argos after Kimon's failure also had support in the conservative camp.

52. E. Cavignac, "Eschyle et Themistocle," *Rev. phil.* 45 (1921), 103; W. G. Forrest, "Themistocles and Argos," *Class. Quart.* n.s. 10 (1960), 221; Podlecki, 56, should have been more cautious; I. Trenscényi-Waldapfel, op. cit., considers various references to Themistokles in the play. More important is his conjecture that special interest in Egypt may have been connected with the preparation of the Athenian expedition for Inaros; cf. also Deichgräber, *Gött. Nachr. Phil.-hist. Kl.* 1/3 (1939), 284.

53. Thus M. L. Cunningham, *Rhein. Mus.* 96 (1953), 223, and with an evaluation of a restoration by B. Snell (*Gnom.* 25 [1953], 436) in *Rhein. Mus.* 105 (1962), 189. In Mette, fr. 496 of unknown origin.

54. Pohlenz 1. 51; W. Kraus, op. cit; M. L. Cunningham, see previous note.

55. Of course the same is true of the attempt to connect with our play a kalpis in Boston, which depicts theater satyrs carrying pieces of furniture; cf. Mette, *Verl. Aisch.*, 183, following T. B. L. Webster, *Journ. Hell. Stud.* 70 (1950), 86.

56. The other passages in Wilamowitz, *Aisch. Int.*, 23. 2.

57. F. Brommer, *Ath. Mitt.* 63/64 (1938/9), 171, has assembled the vase pictures on this subject. They begin after 440 and can be connected with the reawakened interest in Aischylos in the final third of the fifth century.

58. An edition with commentary for all three plays using material of W. G. Headlam by G. Thomson, 2 vols., Cambridge 1938. A revision without the translation but with the scholia and a presentation of Headlam's critical methods: *The Or. of Aesch.*, 2 vols., Czechoslovak Academy, Prague 1966. Older bibliography, besides Schmid, also in W. Morel, *Bursians Jahresb.* 259 (1938), 1. INTERPRETATION: A. Lesky, "Die *Orestie* des Aisch.," *Herm.* 66 (1931), 190 = *Ges. Schr.*, 92; A. Setti, *L'Or. di Esch.*, Florence 1935; J. T. Sheppard, *Aesch., the Prophet of Greek Freedom: An Essay on the* Or. *Tril.*, London 1943; P. B. R. Forbes, "Laws and Politics in the *Oresteia*," *Class. Rev.* 62 (1948), 99; R. P. Winnington-Ingram, "Clytemnestra and the Vote of Athena," *Journ. Hell. Stud.* 68 (1948), 130; Kaufmann-Bühler, 59; E. R. Dodds, "Morals and Politics in the *Oresteia*," *Proc. Cambr. Phil. Soc.* 186 (1960), 19 (especially to be recommended); G. del Estal O. S. A., "La *Orestiada* y suo genio juridico," *El Escorial* 1962 (with translations of considerable portions); von Fritz, *Die Orestessage bei den drei grossen grie-*

chischen Tragikern, 113; J. J. Peradotto, "Cledonomancy in the *Oresteia*," *Am. Journ. Phil.* 90 (1969), 1; M. Leaky, "The Role of Cassandra in the *Oresteia* of Aeschylus," *Bull. of the John Rylands Libr.* 52 (1969), 145; A. Lebeck, *The Oresteia: A Study in Language and Structure*, Cambridge, Mass. 1971. By itself stands R. Böhme, *Bühnenbearbeitung aischyleischer Tragödien*, Basel 1956; second part, 1959. He comes to the conclusion that the *Oresteia*, which Swinburne considered calling the "greatest achievement of the human mind," was the result of a far-reaching stage revision from the years 408–405, and is basically a hybrid monster! GERMAN TRANSLATIONS: O. Werner, Munich 1948 (with Greek text, now replaced by his Aisch. translation, see above); E. Buschor, Munich 1953; E. Staiger, Stuttgart 1959 (the Reclam edition); a shorter theater version by W. Jens, Hersfeld n.d. ITALIAN TRANSLATION: M. Untersteiner, Ed. Mondadori 1951. ENGLISH TRANSLATIONS: R. Lattimore, Chicago 1953; H. Lloyd-Jones, Englewood Cliffs, N.J. 1970.

59. On this see chap. 5, in the "Dramatic Form and Language" section.

60. A. Lesky, op. cit., and "Die Schuld der Klytaimestra," *Wien. Stud.* n.s. 1 (1967), 5. There too on the question of whether Pindar, *Pyth.* 11. 17, was a source for Klytaimestra as the sole culprit of the *Oresteia*. This is certain if the poem is dated to 474, which is supported by many scholars, but even with the date 454, defended by C. M. Bowra in *Pindar* (Oxford 1964, 404), there remain features to be considered in Pindar's ode that point to a tradition independent of Aischylos.

61. On this motif M. Bock, "Die Schlange im Traum der Klytaimestra," *Herm.* 71 (1936), 230, is good, rightly recognizing Agamemnon in the Pleisthenides into whom the δράκων is transformed.

62. Bibl. in A. Lesky, *Wien. Stud.* n.s. 1 (1967), 7, 7 f.

63. Such is imagined by P. Zancani Montuoro, *Rendic. acc. Napoli* 26 (1951), 270, in connection with the interesting metope from the Heraion at the mouth of the Sele, depicting Orestes encircled by a snake.

64. The monumental three-volume edition by E. Fraenkel, Oxford 1950, with introduction, translation, and commentary is one of the most important works for all aspects of scholarship on tragedy. An attractive and fruitful situation results from the fact that D. L. Page in his edition of the commentary left by J. D. Denniston, Oxford 1957, repeatedly takes up the debate with Fraenkel. Next to these the edition of P. Groeneboom, Groningen 1944, is of lasting value. TEXT, TRANSLATION AND COMMENTARY: J. C. Lawson, Cambridge 1932. A. Y. Campbell's treatment of the text (London 1936) is thoroughly arbitrary. TEXT WITH BRIEF COMMENTARY: E. Janssens, Namur 1955. INTERPRETATION: R. Daube, "Zu den Rechtsproblemen in Aisch. *Ag.*," Diss. Basel 1939 (further, the studies named for the *Oresteia*); H. Bogner, "Der *Ag.* des Aisch.," *N. Jb.* 3 (1940), 1; A. Ardizzoni, *Studi Eschilei*, I, L'*Ag.*, Catania 1946; F. Fletcher, *Notes to the* Ag., Oxford 1949; E. Fraenkel, *Der Ag. des Aesch.: Ein Vortrag*, Zurich 1957 = *Kl. Beitr.*, Rome 1964, I, 329, and "Die Kassandraszene der *Orestie*," *Kl. Beitr.*, 375; J. Alsina, "Observations sobre la figura de Clitemestra," *Emerita* 27 (1959), 297; H. Gundert, "Die Stichomythie zwischen Agamemnon und Klytaimestra," *Theoria, Festschr. Schuchardt*, Baden-Baden 1960, 69; R. Kuhns, *The House, the City and the Judge: The Growth of Moral Awareness in the Oresteia*, Indianapolis, Ind. 1962; R. D. Dawe, "Inconsistency of Plot and Character in Aesch.," *Proc. Cambr. Phil. Soc.* 189 (1963), 43; W. H. Friedrich, "Schuld, Reue and Sühne der Klytaimestra," in *Vorbild und Neugestaltung*, Göttingen, 1967, 140; J. de Romilly, "L'évocation du passé dans l'*Ag.* d'Eschyle," *Rev. Et. Gr.* 80 (1967), 93; H. Lloyd-Jones, "Agamemnonea," *Harv. Stud.* 73 (1969), 97; O. L. Smith, "Once Again: The Guilt of Agamemnon," *Eranos* 71 (1973), 1. INDIVIDUAL TRANSLATIONS: New edition of the Wilamowitz translation by E. Kappus, Berlin 1940; A. Stauffenberg, Delfinverlag 1951. English: T. G. Tucker, Melbourne 1935; L. MacNeice, London 1936; E. Hamilton, in *Three Greek Plays*, New York 1937; A. Y. Campbell, Liverpool 1940.

65. When the hypothesis mentions a second vehicle with Kassandra and the spoils following the king's chariot, we may think of the director of a later performance, in the manner of the

play director who, according to schol. *Or.* 57, at the beginning of the *Helena* had the queen silently enter the palace with the booty.

66. Aristoph. *Ran.* 911; *Vita* 6.

67. Kraus, 91, is careful and thorough on this question.

68. E. Fraenkel, "Der Zeushymnos im *Ag.* des Aisch.," *Phil.* 86 (1931), 1 = *Kl. Beitr.*, Rome 1964, 353; W. Ferrari, "La parodos dell'*Ag.*," *Ann. Scuola Norm. Sup. di Pisa*, 1938, 7, 355; C. H. Reeves, "The Parodos of the *Ag.*," *Class. Journ.* 55 (1959/60), 165; Eug. Grassi, "La parodos dell'*Ag.*," *At. e Roma* 6 (1961), 138; M. Treu, "Der Zeushymnos im *Ag.* des Aisch." Ἐπιστημονικὴ ἐπητερίς 1965, 207; M. Fernandez Galiano, "Los dos primeros coros del'*Agamemnon* de Esquilo," *Estudios sobre la trag. Griega*, Madrid 1966, 37.

69. R. D. Dawe, "The Place of the Hymn to Zeus in Aesch. *Ag.*," *Eranos* 64 (1966), 1. Opposed by Leif Bergson, "The Hymn to Zeus in Aesch. *Ag.*," *Eranos* 65 (1967), 11. Recently Dawe has offered reasons for his transposition in *Harv. Stud.* 72 (1968), 110.

70. Further, besides the studies mentioned in the previous two notes, W. Whallon, "Why is Artemis angry?" *Am. Journ. Phil.* 82 (1961), 78. Dawe argues well against this contrived interpretation in the article just cited (*Eranos* 64 [1966], 14); he substantiates the interpretation presented in the commentary of Denniston-Page and here in the text with good arguments.

71. H. Lloyd-Jones (see next note) searches for the solution in this direction.

72. The difficult passage has sparked a lively debate in recent years. In addition to the bibl. in n. 68: H. Lloyd-Jones, "The Guilt of Agamemnon," *Class. Quart.* 56 (1962), 187; N. G. L. Hammond, "Personal Freedom and Its Limitations in the *Oresteia*," *Journ. Hell. Stud.* 85 (1965), 42; A. Lesky, "Decision and responsibility in the tragedy of Aeschylus," *Journ. Hell. Stud.* 86 (1966), 78; A. Rivier, "Rémarques sur le nécessaire et la nécessité chez Eschyle," *Rev. Et. Gr.* 81 (1968), 15. Most of these studies reach beyond the *Ag.* and will be complemented by further notes in the section "Destiny and Guilt."

73. Galiano (see n. 68) also supports Fraenkel's view.

74. "Ekkyklema und Thyroma," *Rhein. Mus.* 83 (1934), 21.

75. In his lecture on the *Ag.* (op. cit., 35 = 349), E. Fraenkel simply states: "The door of the house opens." Webster, *Greek Theater Prod.*, 9, 17, assumes the existence of the ekkyklema for all the plays of Aischylos; *Griech. Bühnenaltert.*, 19. Also, A. M. Dale in her interesting study "Seen and Unseen on the Greek Stage," *Wien. Stud.* 69 (1956), 98. Dingel, x, 3, who gives further bibliography, seems to judge correctly when he holds the question open until new arguments are brought forward.

76. Thus also Reinhardt, 106.

77. Here I must correct the statements published in *Herm.* 66 (1931), 193 = *Ges. Schr.*, 94. The sword appears as Klytaimestra's weapon in the *Odyssey* 11. 424, and on an archaic bronze plate from a shield strap of the second quarter of the sixth century: E. Kunze, *Olympische Forschungen* 2, Berlin 1950, 167, plate 18 = *Neue Meisterwerke griech. Kunst aus Olympia*, Munich 1948, fig. 46; cf. A. Lesky, *Wien. Stud.* n.s. 1 (1967), 18. E. Fraenkel, in his commentary 809. 1, seems to me overconfident in rejecting the view of C. Robert and others that the axe as the murder weapon was derived from the version of Stesichoros. That κάρα βεβροτωμένος (bloodstained head) is said of the δράκων in the dream (*PMG* fr. 42) does point to axe blows.

78. EDITIONS: Wilamowitz, *Das Opfer am Grabe*, Berlin 1896; M. Untersteiner, *Como* 1946 (a second part with comm., *Dioniso* 12 [1949], 171, 250); M. Valgimigle-M. V. Ghezzo, Messina 1947; G. Ammendola, Florence 1948. TO BE RECOMMENDED: W. Schadewaldt, "Der Kommos in Aisch. *Choe.*," *Herm.* 67 (1932), 312 = *Hellas und Hesperien*, 106; A. Lesky, "Der Kommos der. *Choe.*," *Sitzb. Ak. Wien* 221/3, 1943; R. D. Dawe, "Inconsistency of Plot and Character in Aesch.," *Proc. Cambr. Phil. Soc.* 189 (1963), 52; H.-J. Dirksen, *Die aischyleische Gestalt des Orest*, Nürnberg 1965; On the role of Pylades: H. J. Rose, *Ann. Br. School Ath.* 37, 1936/1937 (1940), 201. For bibliographical information on the recognition scene, see below.

79. Aristoph. *Ran.* 1126–8, 1172 f., schol. Pind. *Pyth.* 4. 145; schol. Eur. *Alk.* 768.

80. How Reinhardt 167. 16, could object to this interpretation on the grounds that it transformed Orestes into the "godless Germanic hero" will never be clear to me.

81. The paraphrase explains sufficiently why the transposition of the two sections of the third strophic pair supported by Rose in his commentary (following Preuss) must be rejected. The interpretation of particulars is difficult, but v. 638 sounds like a reply to the ἀκαίρως in v. 624.

82. The arrangement of the passage basically derived from Weil and accepted by Murray, Thomson, and Rose corresponds best to Aischylean diction. The suggestion of Wilamowitz καίπερ αἰνῶν ἐπίμομφον ἄταν, taken over by P. Groeneboom, also is consistent with our interpretation.

83. *Rein. Mus.* 58 (1903), 546. R. Böhme, "Aisch. und der Anagnorismos," *Herm.* 73 (1938), 195; cf. *Gnom.* 15 (1939), 350.

84. Reinhardt, 111, treats the motif without misgivings, as did Pohlenz, who recommends the arrangement 228, 227, 230, 229 found in the editions of Groeneboom and Murray; cf. also L. Gernet, "Droit et prédroit dans la Grèce ancienne," *L'Année Sociologique* ser 3 (1949), 77; G. Freymuth, *Gnom.* 31 (1959), 395; A. D. Fitton-Brown, "The Recognition Scene in *Choe.*," *Rev. Et. Gr.* 74 (1961), 363; H. Lloyd-Jones, "Some Alleged Interpolations in Aesch. *Choe.* and Eur. *El.*," *Class. Quart.* 55 (1961), 171; H.-J. Newiger, *Herm.* 89 (1961), 427. 8; K. Matthiessen, "*Elektra, Taurische Iphigenie* und *Helena*," *Hypomn.* 4 (1964), 110; Dingel 127. 4 with further bibliography; and especially F. Solmsen, "Electra and Orestes," *Meded. Nederl. Ak.* n.s. 30/2 (1967), 36 with a fine analysis of the questionable scene. P. Pucci, "Euripides Heautontimoroumenos," *Trans. Am. Phil. Ass.* 98 (1967), 365.

85. *Comment. philol. in honorem T. Mommseni* 1877, 291.

86. Perhaps we can escape this consideration with K. Matthiessen (see n. 84) by referring Orestes' words not to verses 201–204 but to 124–148. In fact the first words of Elektra are probably a call to the gods, but not a specifically directed prayer; this is contained in the second passage mentioned (138 f.).

87. Wilamowitz supported it in his commentary, then also in *Griech. Trag.* 2: *Orestie*, Berlin 1901, 148, and *Aisch. Int.*, Berlin 1914, 205.

88. Von Fritz, 125. Reinhardt, 165, 12, completely agrees with W. Schadewaldt's interpretation, while himself offering a thorough analysis (112). In his edition (p. 155) P. Groeneboom interprets the kommos very much as we do. O. Hiltbrunner, *Wiederholungs- und Motivtechnik bei Aisch.*, Bern 1950, 69, also agrees. See also E. R. Dodds, *Proc. Camb. Philol. Soc.* 186 (1960), 29; H.-J. Dirksen, op. cit., 23. 11; R. Lennig, "Traum und Sinnestäuschung bei Aisch., Soph., Eur.," Diss. Tübingen 1969, 66.

89. Supported by Schütz, Wecklein, and Weil (who then changed his opinion), then by Wilamowitz, joined by Snell, 130, and A. Lesky, op. cit., 101. Kraus, 100, offers detailed argument for the transposition. Murray in his apparatus and Groeneboom in his commentary are hesitant. The opposing points are developed by W. Schadewaldt, op. cit., 338 = 127 (with further bibl.). Pohlenz, 2. 60, thinks he has solved the problem by leaving 434–438 in its place but assuming that a strophe has been lost after 455.

90. The history of this error, which dates back to the Aldine edition, is given by W. A. McDonald, *Class. Journ.* 1960, 367.

91. ANNOTATED EDITIONS: F. Blass, Berlin 1907; P. Ubaldi, Turin 1931; P. Groeneboom, Groningen 1952; G. Pompella, Naples 1972. On the meaning of a codex in Salamanca for the *Eum.* See Dawe, 189. INTERPRETATION: H.-J. Dirksen, *Die Aischyleische Gestalt des Orest.*, Nürnberg 1965; H. D. Robertson, "The Hybristes in Aesch.," *Trans. Am. Phil. Ass.* 98 (1967), 373 (esp. on the second stasimon). See also the expansive bibliography on the historical references, below.

92. This recurs in the Paean of Limenios (D. 2. 6. 175. Powell, *Coll. Alex.*, 149), v. 11. Further passages in the study of C. Gülke, 46. 3 mentioned in the discussion of the *Suppliants*;

there too on the Pythaïs, a sacrificial procession that went from Athens to Delphi and preserved the memory of the journey of Apollo from Delos to Delphi by way of Athens.

93. In fr. 530 (probably from the *Aitnaiai*), vv. 5 f., Dike announces that Zeus overcame Kronos in a just manner.

94. Erna Lesky, "Die Zeugungs- und Vererbungslehren der Antike," *Ak. Mainz. Geistes- u. sozialw. Kl.* 1950/19, 1278, shows clearly how wide the cultural context is in which this passage stands. The same idea is plainly evident in fr. 145M 8 f. in the opposition between ἄρουρα and σπέρμα (soil and seed).

95. Much has been written about the "calculus Minervae." Again Aylen, 349, supports the theory that an additional voting stone is added to break the tie after the others had been cast. He also cites passages that attest to the variety of opinion even in antiquity. Since in vv. 711–733 each of the doublets probably accompanies the casting of a vote, Aylen must argue that the first judge cast his vote in silence. This is possible, but the explicit and final statement of Athena (753) that the number of the stones is equal and her solemn reference to the ἰσόψηφος δίκη (795) when calming the Erinyes point rather to the view that the equality of the votes only resulted when the goddess cast her stone.

96. On the view explained here with a Hittite parallel, A. Lesky, *Eranos* 52 (1954), 10 = *Ges. Schr.*, 374.

97. H.-J. Dirksen, op. cit., 20 (cf. 81 ff.), misinterprets the meaning of Hermes as escort. It is very risky to try to make "ethically vulnerable Olympians" of Hermes and Apollo (8). On the role of Apollo see also R. P. Winnington-Ingram, "The Role of Apollo in the *Oresteia*," *Class. Rev.* 47 (1933), 97. The difficulties indicated here are correctly dealt with by R. D. Dawe in the article cited for the *Lib. Bearers*, "Inconsistency . . . " (58). That the expiation by pig's blood at the omphalos has no place in the play was already noticed by F. Hauser in Furtwängler-Reichhold, *Griech. Vasenmalerei* 2. 332; cf. also A. Lesky, *Herm.* 66 (1931), 209 = *Ges. Schr.*, 106. Differently now R. R. Dyer, "The Evidence for Apolline Purification Rituals at Delphi and Athens, *Journ. Hell. Stud.* 89 (1969), 38.

98. Wilamowitz stood by this judgment also in his *Erinnerungen*, 255.

99. For the text I would simply like to assume an anacoluthon, as considered by P. Groeneboom in his commentary.

100. Surveys are found in Podlecki's notes on the *Oresteia*, and in the article by C. Gülke cited for the *Suppliants*, 28. 1. See also F. Stoessl, "Aeschylus As a Political Thinker," *Am. Journ. Phil.* 73 (1952), 113; K. J. Dover, "The Political Aspect of Aesch. *Eum.*," *Journ. Hell. Stud.* 77 (1957), 230; F. Jacoby, *FGrH* III b, Suppl. 1, 22; H. T. Wade-Gery, *Essays in Greek History*, Oxford 1958, 176, 183. 2, with the conjecture that the trial in the play reflected a new order according to which civil officials themselves no longer judged, but assigned the cases to specific courts; S. J. Lurje, "Die politische Tendenz der Tragödie *Die Eum.*," summary in *Bibl. Class. Or.* 1960, 295; S. Mazzarino, "Eschilo, Pericle e la storia dell'Areopago," *Riv. de cult. class. e mediev.* 2 (1960), 301; H. Quincey, "Orestes and the Argive Alliance," *Class. Quart.* n.s. 14 (1964), 190; G. Salanitro, "L'*Orestea* e la politica estera di Atene," *Siculorum Gymn.* n.s. 19 (1966), 153; F. Schachermeyr, *Die frühe Klassik der Griechen*, Stuttgart 1966, 145.

101. See previous note, 146.

102. On the material that preceded Aischylos's drama, see F. Solmsen, *Hesiod and Aeschylus*, Ithaca 1949, 124; J. H. Finley, *Pindar and Aeschylus*, Cambridge, Mass. 1955, 220; Reinhardt, *Aisch.*, 29; U. Bianche, "Prometheus der titanische Trickster," *Paideuma* 7 (1961), 414; A. Garzya, "Le tragique de *Prométhée Enchaîné* d'Eschyle," *Mnem.* 4. 18 (1965), 113; Mette, *Verl. Aisch.*, 16.

103. On the discoveries of recent times that show the Oriental connection with the succession myth, cf. the articles assembled in A. Lesky, *Ges. Schr.* 356, 372, 379; P. Walcot, *Hesiod and the Near East*, Cardiff 1966.

104. The most important edition with commentary is by P. Groeneboom, Groningen 1928. Older editions and translations in the edition of E. Rapisarda, Turin 1936. Further, G. Thom-

son, Cambridge 1932 (with comm. and transl.); W. Buchwald, Bamberg 1962 (with a preparatory volume). INTERPRETATION: W. Kraus, *RE* 23 (1957), 666; K. Reinhardt, "Prometheus," *Era-
nos-Jahrb.* 25, Zurich 1957, 241 = *Tradition und Geist*, Göttingen 1960, 191; S. Long, "Notes
on Aesch. *Prom. Bound*," *Proc. Am. Phil. Soc.* 102/3 (1958), 229; K. Kerényi, *Prometheus*,
Hamburg 1959; J. Granera, "Esquilo *Prometeo Encadenado*," Mendoza 1963; S. Benardete,
"The Crimes and Arts of Prometheus," *Rhein. Mus.* 107 (1964), 126; L. Golden, *In Praise of
Prometheus: Humanism and Rationalism in Aeschylean Thought*, Chapel Hill, N.C. 1966.
Older essays on myth and drama by N. Terzaghi in the volume *Prometeo*, Turin 1966; Irin
Zawadzka, *Das Altertum* 12 (1966), 210; Rose Unterberger, "Der *Gefesselte Prometheus* des
Aischylos," *Tüb. Beitr.* 45 (1968), with comprehensive bibliography; E. Dolin, "Prometheus
Psellistes," *Calif. Stud. in Class. Antiquity* 2 (1969), 85; C. J. Herington, *The Author of the
Prom. Bound*, Austin and London 1970. TRANSLATIONS: W. A. Roth, Berlin 1936 (there were
once chemistry professors who could produce such translations of Aischylos); H. Bogner, Hei-
delberg 1949 (with Greek text); at the top stands W. Kraus, Stuttgart 1965 (Reclam) with an
excellent afterword. ENGLISH: T. G. Tucker, Melbourne 1935; E. Hamilton in *Three Greek Plays*,
New York 1937; R. C. Trevelyan, Cambridge 1939. ITALIAN: E. Fumi, Florence 1936; more in
the edition of Rapisarda. Articles on the authenticity question are cited below.

105. Passages like 110, 123, 235, 250 ff., are important for the change in the motif.

106. Thus 96, 149, 163, 186, 310, 389, 439, 942, 955.

107. This syncretism stands in opposition to the speech of the prophetess (*Eum.* 2), in which
Themis succeeds her mother Gaia as the keeper of the oracle.

108. The sentiment appears strange in the context, since trust is not the issue at all. But the
rule of Zeus is characterized as a tyranny like those Aischylos knew in Sicily. The phrase and
related expressions recur constantly: 310, 324, 357, 402 ff., 736, 756, 761, 909, 942, 958.

109. A. Kleingünther, Πρῶτος εὑρετής, *Phil.* Suppl. 26/1, 1934.

110. Later material for comparison in W. Schmid, "Untersuchungen zum *Gefesselten Prometheus*," *Tüb. Beitr.* 9 (1929), 92. 2; cf. also G. Rudberg, *Symb. Osl.* 1940, 1 ff.

111. A carefully considered structure 2–7–2–7. In her first doublet Io asks about the Titan's
fate, in the second about her own.

112. On the Aithiopians who dwelt close to the sun as the paradigm of the geographical
arrangement of an originally purely mythical conception: A. Lesky, *Herm.* 87 (1959), 27 = *Ges.
Schr.*, 410.

113. "Das Prometheusproblem," *N. Jahrb.* 45 (1920), 201. A very substantial survey of the
problems involved in J. Coman, *L'authenticité du Prométhée Enchaîné*, Bucharest 1943. One
of the latest thorough treatments is in Podlecki, 101, with bibl.

114. "Untersuchungen zum *Gefesselten Prometheus*," *Tüb. Beitr.* 9 (1929). W. Schmid, "Epi-
kritisches zum *Gef. Prom.*," *Phil. Woch.* 51 (1931), 218, opposes the primarily negative criticism of his book.

115. Nestle, *Menschl. Existenz*, vii.

116. "Die Stichomythie in der früh. griech. Trag.," *Zetem.* 11 (1955), 33. Previously the authenticity of the play had been rejected by E. Busch, *N. Jahrb.* 1941, 283. 50, and F. Heinimann,
Nomos und Physis, Basel 1945, 44. 5, who claims to be able to discover so many stylistic and
intellectual peculiarities as to preclude the assumption of a revision of the play.

117. "The Structure of Imagery in Aeschylus," *Class. et Mediev.* 26 (1965), 12. 8. Comm. on
the *Antigone*, 26.

118. *Heroic Temper*, 50. That the *Prometheus* was close to Sophokles in the frequency of
enjambments was proved by E. C. Yorke, "The Date of the *Prom. Vinctus*," *Class. Quart.* 30
(1936), 153. The same direction was taken by J. D. Denniston, "Pauses in the tragic senarius,"
Class. Quart. 30 (1936), 73, 192.

119. In the article cited at the *Lib. Bearers*, 25. But the numerous mirabilia of the play cannot be brought to bear against its authenticity.

120. It might give an idea of the nature of such objections that the ἔργῳ–λόγῳ antithesis ap-

pears in Aischylos only in the *Prom.* (336, 1080), or that φύσις designates the whole of certain creatures only at *Prom.* 489. A collection of quotes for similar observations in A. Lesky, *Gnom.* 19 (1943), 198. Further, C. J. Herington, "A Unique Technical Feature of the *Prom. Bound*," *Class. Rev.* n.s. 13 (1963), 5; I. Zawadzka, "Die Echtheit des *Gefesselten Prometheus*: Geschichte und gegenwärtiger Stand der Forschung," *Das Altertum* 12 (1966), 210, who herself believes the play spurious. Cf. also B. Gladigow, *Phil.* 111 (1967), 20. 1, and E. R. Schwinge, *Rhein. Mus.* 112 (1969), 6. 18.

121. Besides A. Körte and J. Coman (already cited), the following scholars also support the play's authenticity: C. del Grande, *Hybris*, Naples 1947, 435; L. Séchan, *Le Mythe de Prométhée*, Paris 1951; G. Méautis, *L'Authenticité et la Date du* Prom. Enchaîné *d'Eschyle*, Geneva 1960. On the basis of metrical and stylistic details E. C. Yorke places the *Prom.* closer to the other plays of Aischylos: "Trisyllabic Feet in the Dialogue of Aesch.," *Class. Quart.* 30 (1936), 116 (of course some details remain without parallels). J. D. Denniston, *Greek Particles*, 2d ed., Oxford 1954, lxviii, demonstrated the greater variation of the particles in the *Prom.* and the *Oresteia*. On the similarities in the construction of the choral language in both plays: C. J. Herington, "A Unique Technical Feature of the *Prom. Bound.*," *Class. Rev.* n.s. 13 (1963), 5.

122. Cf. for example F. R. Earp, *Journ. Hell. Stud.* 65 (1945), 11, who nonetheless does not conclude that the play is inauthentic.

123. O. J. Todd, "The Character of Zeus in Aeschylus' *Prom. Bound*," *Class. Quart.* 19 (1925), 67; H. Bogner, "Die Stellung des Zeus im *Prom. Desm.*," *Phil.* 87 (1932), 469, and *Das Neue Bild der Antike*, I, Leipzig 1942, 186. The unique quality of the drama and of its image of Zeus was heavily emphasized by L. R. Farnell, "The Paradox of the *Prom. Vinctus*," *Journ. Hell. Stud.* 53 (1933), 40. Against his view is H. D. F. Kitto, "The *Prom.*," *Journ. Hell. Stud.* 54 (1934), 14; W. J. K. Knight, "Zeus in the *Prometheia*," *Journ. Hell. Stud.* 58 (1938), 51; D. Grene, "*Prom. Bound*," *Class. Phil.* 35 (1940), 22; Murray, *Aesch.*, 99; A. Peretti, "Zeus und Prometheus bei Aisch.," *Die Antike* 1944, 1, and "Religiosità Eschilea nel *Prometeo*, *Maia* 4 (1951), 3. H. Lloyd-Jones tries to prove that the image of Zeus in Aischylos is unified: "Zeus in Aeschylus," *Journ. Hell. Stud.* 76 (1956), 55.

124. Nestle, *Menschl. Existenz*, 34, nicely interprets the *Prometheia* along these lines. Reinhardt protests in his book on Aischylos against the assumption of a development of Zeus. The Titanic and the Olympian are antithetical and limit one another, as also violence and mercy are inextricably intertwined. W. Kraus, in the afterword to his abovementioned translation, understands the *Prometheia* as the path to harmony from primeval opposites; thus also F. Schachermeyr, *Die frühe Klassik der Griechen*, Stuttgart 1966, 166. Important is the remark of de Romilly, *Time*, 68, that in *Prom.* 982 learning through time is directly applied to Zeus. Inappropriately, it seems to us, Rosenmeyer, 73, doubts the possibility of a reconciliation with a Zeus whom Aischylos needed simply as "a supreme and comprehensive focus for cruelty and irresponsibility." Nor can we agree with L. Golden, op. cit., 124, who interprets Zeus as "an impersonal, amoral force representing universal power in its fullest, most naked form."

125. Supporters of this view may be found in H. Lloyd-Jones (see n. 123), 56. 21.

126. Eirik Vandvik, "The Prom. of Hesiod and Aesch.," *Ak. Oslo* 1942/2, 1943; H. Dörrie, "Leid und Erfahrung," *Abh. Ak. Mainz. Geistes- und sozialwiss. Kl.* 1956/5, 328.

127. E. Cassirer, "Logos, Dike, Kosmos," *Göteborgs Högskolas Årsskrift* 47 (1941/6), 16.

128. We would have additional proof if fr. 336—with the taming of useful animals—(referred without further information to Prometheus) could be confirmed for the *Lyomenos*.

129. II. v. 4 and 11. On the difficulties connected with this motif: W. Kraus, *RE* 23 (1957), 679 f.

130. Earlier bibl. in Schmid 3. 299. 2. Besides Pohlenz, the trilogy is also thought to have begun with the *Pyrphoros* by A. D. Fitton-Brown, "*Prometheia*," *Journ. Hell. Stud.* 79 (1959), 52, and K. Kerényi, *Prometheus*, London 1963, 75.

131. *Prol. zu Aisch. Trag.*, Leipzig 1869, Appendix 206. Also, among others, Murray, Coman,

recently Podlecki (176. 9), R. Unterberger (op. cit., 133). With especially detailed argumentation, Reinhardt (58, 163, as well as in the study mentioned in our discussion of the play) makes a case for the *Pyrphoros* as the final play.

132. K. Reinhardt's attempt, with a bold restoration of *P. Heidelb.* 185 (fr. 323aM under *Lyomenos*) to include the anodos of Pandora in the plot, is unwarranted: "Zum Prometheus," *Herm.* 85 (1957), 12, 125 = *Tradition und Geist*, Göttingen 1960, 182. If the papyrus really belongs to the *Pyrphoros*, this would add weight to the observation of I. Trenscényi-Waldapfel, "Mythologie und Gnosis," in *Studi di storia religiosa della tarda antichità*, Messina 1968, 59; in line 9 the word ἄγαλμα appears and according to a note in Fulgentius (*Myth.*, II, 6) Prometheus was the first to create statues of the gods. This could have been evidence of his reconciliation with the Olympians that occurred in the third play. A problematic attempt at a reconstruction of the trilogy is in C. J. Herington, "A Study of the *Prometheia*," *Phoenix* 17 (1963), 180, 236.

133. This view was favored by H. J. Mette in the foreword in his *Suppl. Aeschyleum*, Berlin 1939 (with older bibl.) but was later dropped in his two books dedicated to the Aischylean fragments. It was emphatically supported by F. Focke, "Aischylos' Prom.," *Herm.* 65 (1930), 259. W. Kraus seeks the solution along these lines in his *RE* article "Prometheus," but is more hesitant in the afterword of his translation (58).

134. Besides the studies mentioned for the problem of authenticity, there is a careful evaluation in Podlecki, 142. Rose Unterberger, op. cit., 14. 2, also judges the alternatives carefully.

135. This also speaks against a date in the final years of the poet in Sicily. Thus, G. Méautis (see n. 121); H. J. Rose, *Eranos* 45 (1947), 99; J. A. Davison, *Trans. Am. Phil. Ass.* 80 (1949), 66, and *Studies Presented to V. Ehrenberg*, Oxford 1966, 98, in which the dilogy theory is offered with the suggestion that Aischylos never completed the third play.

136. This is opposed to Reinhardt, 63, 77, who accepts the puppet without question and denies that the act of releasing the bonds took place on stage.

137. "Der Einzug des Chores im *Prometheus*," *Ann. Scuola Norm. Sup. Pisa* 23 (1954), 269.

138. The attempt of E. Baglio, *Il Prometeo di Eschilo alla luce delle storie di Erodoto*, Rome 1952, to interpret the drama as a projection of the Persian Wars, should be quickly forgotten. Unfortunately, the same may be said of J. A. Davison's theory (see above), according to which we should see Perikles and Protagoras behind the opponents in the *Prom.*

Fragments

1. Comprehensive bibl. in H. Lloyd-Jones's appendix to the Aischylos of the Loeb Class. Libr. Further, H. Pfeufer, "Die Gnomik in der Trag. des Aisch.," Diss. Munich 1940, 119. Del Grande, *Hybris*, 126.

2. Reinhardt was also unsuccessful in assigning *P. Oxy.* 2, 213 (Mette, *Verl. Aisch.* 46), most often ascribed to Sophokles (*Niobe* or *Tantalos*), to the *Niobe* of Aischylos, although Pohlenz (2. 65) enthusiastically supported this. It was opposed by R. Pfeiffer, *Sitzb. Bayer. Ak. Phil. hist. Kl.* 1938/2, 21. 1, who discusses the possibilities of interpretation.

3. This was contradicted by H. Kloesel, *Herm.* 72 (1937), 468. 5, and H. Pfeufer (see n. 1), 120. 10.

4. R. Stark, "Ein neuer Aischylosprolog," *Herm.* 82 (1954), 372, wanted to ascribe it to the *Iphigeneia* of Aischylos with Kalchas as the speaker, as did Kakridis in a letter. On the reconstruction of the trilogy, Z. K. Vysoký, "Aischylova *Achilleis*," *Listy Filologické* 81 (1958), 147. The extensive fragment from the *Kares* or the *Europa* preserved in *P. Didot* (fr. 145M) seems likewise to stem from a prologue. If this conjecture is correct, then this speech of Europa anticipates features of the Euripidean prologue speeches.

5. W. Schadewaldt (*Herm.* 71 [1936], 52. 3 = *Hellas und Hesperien*, 194. 3) rightly insists on the exact translation as "slices," not scraps or crumbs.

6. Thalia P. Howe, "The Style of Aesch. as Satyr-playwright," *Greece and Rome* 6 (1959/1960), 150.

7. The *Phorkides* probably dealt with the Gorgon adventure of Perseus, the *Polydektes* with his return to Seriphos and the rescuing of Danae from the attack of the king.

8. Further, A. Barigazzi, *Ann. Scuola Norm. Sup. di Pisa* 22 (1954), 1; R. P. Winnington-Ingram, *Gnom.* 32 (1960), 316; Mette, *Verl. Aisch.*, 164.

9. T. B. L. Webster, *Journ. Hell. Stud.* 70 (1950), 86, and K. Kerényi, *Röm. Mitt.* 68 (1961), 164, believe that a bell krater from Ancona illustrates this legend.

10. A. Greifenhagen, "Ein Satyrspiel des Aischylos?" 118th *Winckelmanns Progr.*, Berlin 1963, considers a possible connection between a chous obtained for the Berlin Museums and decorated by the Altamura painter with four satyr boys at a torch race before an enlarged figure of Dionysos, and the *Prometheus Pyrphoros*, which then would be a satyr play. We have seen the satyrs as athletes in the *Isthmiastai* and the representation of the runners as children may be connected with the nature of the chous pots. An allusion to some satyr play cannot be excluded, but the specific reference assumed by Greifenhagen cannot be sufficiently supported.

11. Further, R. P. Winnington-Ingram, *Bull. Inst. Class. Stud.* 6 (1959), 58. Z. K. Vysoký, *Listy Filologické* 82 (1959), 1.

12. Equally attested in the tradition is the form of the title Αἶτναι, which was defended by Wilamowitz, *Aisch. Int.* 242. 1. Opposed by P. Mazon in his edition, iv n. 2; Schmid 2. 189. 2. Αἰτναῖαι is the more probable form, but E. Fraenkel prefers to leave the question open. The Αἰτναῖαι νόθοι, listed in the manuscript catalogue, shows what interest was aroused by this festival play.

13. On the play also F. C. Görschen, *Dioniso* 19 (1956), 217 and 22 (1959), 147.

14. An overview of what has been confirmed and what remains hypothetical is easily accessible in Mette, *Verl. Aisch.* An older compilation in Schmid, 2. 188. 8.

15. "Die *Lykurgie* des Aischylos. Versuch einer Wiederherstellung der dionysischen Tetralogie," *Nachr. Gött. Phil.-hist. Kl.* 1/3 (1938/9), 231; with (244. 2) older bibl. On individual fragments, see A. von Blumenthal, *Herm.* 77 (1942), 106; Z. K. Vysoký, "Aischylova *Lykurgeia*," *Listy Filologické* 82 (1959), 177 and 83 (1960), 45 and 199; S. Oświecimski, "Quo tempore Aeschyli *Lycurgia* primum acta sit," *Eos* 54 (1964), 33.

16. Bibl. in H. Lloyd-Jones in the appendix to the Aischylos of the Loeb Class. Libr., 586; on fr. 110M. Further, E. G. Turner on *P. Oxy.* 27, 2454; Mette, *Verl. Aisch.*, 149.

17. "Il papiro Ossirinchita 2454 e gli Eraclidi di Eschilo," *Rev. Et. Gr.* 79 (1966), 38 = *Saggi sulla tragedia Greca*, Messina 1969, 135.

Dramatic Form and Language

1. Here are assembled works not found in the bibliography that are important for the motifs, technique, and language of all three tragedians.

Thilde Wendel, "Die Gesprächsanrede im griech. Epos und Drama der Blütezeit," *Tüb. Beitr.* 10, Stuttgart 1930; E. Pfiffner, "Die Götteranrufungsformeln in den Werken der drei Tragiker," Diss. Freiburg/Schweiz 1931; W. Hörmann, "Gleichnis und Metapher in der griech. Trag.," Diss. Munich 1934 (with good basic comments); G. Capone, *L'arte scenica degli attori tragici Greci*, Padua 1935; R. M. Hickmann, "Ghostly Etiquette on the Class. Stage," Diss. Iowa 1938; N. T. Pratt, *Dramatic Suspense in Seneca and his Greek Precursors*, Princeton 1939; W. B. Stanford, *Ambiguity in Greek Lit.*, Oxford 1939.

R. T. Weissinger, *A Study of Act Divisions in Class.* Drama, Iowa Stud. in Class Phil. 9, 1940; W. Nauhardt, *Das Bild des Herschers in der griech. Dichtung*, N. D. Forsch, 255, Berlin 1940; B. A. van Groningen, "Βασιλεύς, de alleenheerscher op het trag. toneel der Grieken," *Nederl. Ak.* 1941; T. B. L. Webster, "A Study of Greek Sentence Construction," *Am. Journ. Phil.* 1941, 385; H. W. Miller, "Medical Terminology in Trag.," *Trans. Am. Phil. Ass.* 75 (1944); J. Duchemin, *L'AΓΩN dans la trag. Gr.*, Paris 1945; A. Spitzbarth, "Untersuchungen zur Spieltechnik der griech. Trag.," Diss. Zurich 1946; R. Butts, *The Glorification of Athens in Greek Drama,* Iowa Stud. in Class. Phil. 11, 1947; J. Myres, "The Structure of Stichomythia in Attic Trag.," *Proc. Brit. Ac.* 35 (1949); G. Björk, *Das alpha impurum und die trag. Kunstsprache,* Uppsala 1950; W. Helg, "Das Chorlied der griech. Trag. in seinem Verhältnis zur Handlung," Diss. Zurich 1950; W. Jens, *Die Stichomythie in der frühen griech. Trag.,* Zetemata 11, Munich 1955; F. Zucker, "Formen gesteigerter affektiver Rede in Sprechversen der griech. Trag.," *Ind. Forsch.* 62 (1955), 62; Leif Bergson, *L'épithète ornamentale dans Esch., Soph. et Eur.,* Uppsala 1956; T. B. L. Webster, "Some Psychological Terms in Greek Trag.," *Journ. Hell. Stud.* 77 (1957), 149; D. M. Clay, *A Formal Analysis of the Vocabularies of Aesch., Soph. and Eur.,* ii, Am. School of Class. Stud., Athens 1958, and i., Minneapolis 1960 (statistical classification according to suffixes within the parts of speech); J. Keller, "Struktur und dramatische Funktion des Botenberichtes bei Aisch. und Soph.," Diss. Tübingen 1959; C. J. Classen, "Untersuchungen zu Platons Jagdbildern," *D. Ak.* Berlin 1960 (with a section on tragedy); J. Kazik-Zawadzka, *Les hapax eiremena et les mots rares dans les fragments papyrologiques des trois grands tragiques Greks,* Archiwum Filologizcne 5, Varsovie 1962; G. Kiefner, "Die Versparung: Untersuchungen zu einer Stilfigur der dichterischen Rhetorik am Beispiel der griech. Trag.," *Klass. Phil. Stud.* 25, Wiesbaden 1964. The bibliography on imagery in antiquity produced under the direction of V. Pöschl by Helga Gärtner and Waltraut Heyke (Heidelberg 1964) is also a useful aid for tragedy. Material on tragic metaphors also in M. M. Kokolakis, Μορφολογία τῆς κυβευτικῆς μεταφορᾶς, Athens 1965; L. di Gregorio, *Le scene d'annuncio nella tragedia Greca,* Milan 1967; J. Duchemin, "Le déroulement du temps et son expression théatrale dans quelques tragedies d'Eschyle," *Dioniso* 41 (1967), 197; J. Kopperschmid, "Die Hikesie als dramatische Form," Diss. Tübingen 1967. An extensive bibliographical index on the symmetrical arrangement of dialogue and scene in Schwinge (*Eur.*), 11. 3, 12. 4; D. Fehling, *Der Wiederholungsfiguren und ihr Gebrauch bei den Griechen vor Gorgias,* Berlin 1969.

For tragic meters there is still the great thesaurus of Wilamowitz, *Griech. Verskunst,* Berlin 1921. Also B. Snell, *Griech. Metrik.,* Studienhefte zur Altertumswiss, 1, 3d ed., Göttingen 1962; A. M. Dale, *The Lyric Metres of Greek Drama,* 2d ed., Cambridge 1968; M. Kaimio, *The Chorus of Greek Drama within the Light of the Person and Number Used,* Helsinki 1970; T. B. L. Webster, *The Greek Chorus,* London 1970. Individual references may be found in E. Kalinka, "Griech.-röm. Metrik und Rhythmik im letzten Vierteljahrh (1909–1935)," *Jahresber. f. Altertumsw.* 250, 256, 257. For many of the questions involving trimeter, see J. Descroix, *Le trimètre iambique,* Macon 1931; A. Wifstrand, "Eine Versregel für die Anapäste der griech. Trag.," *Herm.* 69 (1934), 210; J. B. Denniston, "Lyric Iambics in Greek Drama," *Gr. Poetry and Life: Essays Pres. to G. Murray,* Oxford 1936; M. Imhof, "Tetrameterszenen in der Trag.," *Mus. Helv.* 13 (1956), 125; Kraus, see bibliography.

2. Thus also T. B. L. Webster, "The Order of Tragedies at the Great Dionysia," *Hermathena* 6 (1965), 21, who claims content trilogies existed for the last eleven years of Aischylos's career. This would be invalid if S. Oświecimski (see n. 15 of previous section) were correct in dating the *Lykourgeia* to 485, but this is completely uncertain. On the question of trilogy/tetralogy (where external unity is not always clearly differentiated from unity of content), see P. Wiesmann, "Das Problem der trag. Tetralogie," Diss. Zurich 1929; A. von Blumenthal, "Tetralogie," *RE* 5 A (1934), 1077; M. Delcourt, "La tétralogie et la trilogie attique," *Ant. Class.* 7 (1938), 31; M. Untersteiner, *Origini,* 285; Del Grande, *Hybris,* 120. Older bibl. in A. Szantyr, *Phil.* 93 (1938), 292. 21. The term *trilogy* is attested in early Hellenistic times: schol. Ar. *Ran.* 1124.

3. The claim of K. Deichgräber, *Nachr. Gött. Phil.-hist. Kl.* 1/3 (1938/9), 252. 1, that the trochaic tetrameter (not especially common in Aischylos, incidentally) is always found in a dialogue of the actor with the chorus needs to be modified in view of *Pers.* 703.

4. On the question of assignment of roles to the actors, Flickinger's third chapter remains instructive. But the spurious conclusion of the *Seven* must be excluded.

5. Wilamowitz, *Aisch. Int.,* 1, is recommended. On the development from the first division

into acts to the five-act rule of the *Ars Poet.* 189, R. T. Weissinger (see n. 1 of this section).

6. The judgments about Aischylos in antiquity can be found in A. de Propris, *Eschilo nella critica dei Greci*, Turin 1941. For the aesthetic evaluation of the agon in the *Frogs*, see M. Pohlenz, "Die Anfänge der griech. Poetik," *Nachr. Gött.* 1920, 142; J. Coman, *Le concept de l'art dans les* Grenouilles *d'Aristophane*, Bucharest 1941; F. Wehrli, "Der erhabene und der schlichte Stil in der poetisch-rhetorischen Theorie der Antike," *Phyllobolia*, Basel 1946, 23. On comedy as a distortion of tragic language, see P. Rau, *Paratragodia: Untersuchung einer komischen Form des Aristophanes*, Zetemata 45, Munich 1967.

7. Besides the studies listed above, on tragedy in general, see J. A. Schuursma, *De poetica vocabulorum abusione apud Aesch.*, Amsterdam 1932; R. Hölzle, "Zum Aufbau der lyrischen Partien des Aisch.," Diss. Freiburg im Breisgau 1934; H. Mielke, "Die Bildersprache des Aisch.," Diss. Breslau 1934; J. Dumortier, *Les images dans la poésie d'Esch.*, Paris 1935; id., *Le vocabulaire médical d'Esch. et les écrits Hippocr.*, Paris 1935; W. Ficker, "Vers und Satz im Dialog des Aisch.," Diss. Leipzig 1935; J. Seewald, "Unters. zu Stil und Kompos. der aisch. Trag.," Diss. Greifswald 1936; W. A. A. van Otterlo, "Beschouwingen over het archaische element in den stijl van Aesch.," Diss. Leyden 1938; B. G. Freymuth, "Tautologie und Abundanz bei Aisch.," Diss. Berlin 1939; H. G. Robertson, "Legal Expressions and Ideas of Justice in Aesch.," *Class. Phil.* 34 (1939), 209; H. Pfeufer, "Die Gnomik in der Trag. des Aisch.," Diss. Munich 1940; W. B. Stanford, "Traces of Sicilian Influence in Aesch.," *Proc. Irish Ac.* 44C 8 (1938), 229, and *Aesch. in His Style: A Study in Language and Personality*, Oxford 1942; F. R. Earp, *Some Features in the Style of Aesch.*, Cambridge 1948; H. J. Rose, "On an epic idiom in Aesch.," *Eranos* 45 (1947), 88 (on the idiom of the type ἴς Τηλεμάχοιο); P. T. Stevens, "Colloquial Expressions in Aesch. and Soph.," *Class. Quart.* 39 (1945), 95; J. F. Johansen, "Some Features of Sentence-structure in Aesch. *Suppliants*," *Class. et Mediaev.* 15 (1954), 1; V. Citti, *Il linguaggio religioso e liturgico nelle tragedie di Eschilo*, Bologna 1962; D. van Nes, *Die maritime Bildersprache des Aisch.*, Groningen 1963; S. Srebrny, *Wort und Gedanke bei Aisch.*, Archiwum Filologiczne 7, Wroclaw 1964; Ole Smith, "Some Observations on the Structure of Imagery of Aesch.," *Class. et Mediaev.* 26 (1965), 10; A. Sideras, *Aeschylus Homericus: Untersuchungen zu den Homerismen der aischyleischen Sprache*, Hypomn. 31, 1971; R. Schweizer-Keller, "Vom Umgang des Aischylos mit der Sprache: Interpretationen zu seinen Namensdeutungen," Diss. Zurich, Aarau 1972.

8. This is well handled by E. Neustadt, "Wort und Geschehen in Aisch. *Ag.*," *Herm.* 64 (1929), 243.

9. Collected in Schmid, 2. 297. 3; cf. E. Neustadt (see previous note).

10. Cf. W. Breitenbach, "Unters. zur Sprache der eurip. Lyrik," *Tüb. Beitr.* 20, Stuttgart 1934, 117.

11. See J. A. Schuursma, op. cit.

12. This thought determines large sections of W. Porzig's book, *Die attische Tragödie des Aisch.*, Leipzig 1926, but the application overshoots the mark. Cantarella, *Eschilo*, 266, has tabulated assonance, alliteration, homoioteleuton, and word repetition in the *Suppliants*. It turns out (278) that these techniques are distributed rather equally over lyric sections and spoken verse.

13. Critics have learned to watch for such things, thus, e.g., B. Kranz, 276; K. Deichgräber, *Nachr. Gött. Phil.-hist. Kl.* 1/4 (1940/1), 25. 1; cf. also the index in A. Lesky, "Der Kommos der Choe.," *Sitzb. Ak. Wien. Phil.-hist. Kl.* 221/3, 1943, under "Wortanklänge."

14. This observation was made independently of Dumontier also by H. Rahner, *Zeitschr. f. kath. Theol.* 66 (1942), 211; cf. also A. Lesky, *Thalatta: Der Weg der Griechen zum Meer*, Vienna 1947, 232. In the seventh chapter of this book there is a discussion of the elements of tragic language that refer to the sea and its creatures. O. Hiltbrunner's study, *Wiederholungs- und Motivtechnik bei Aisch.*, Bern 1950, is excellent.

15. The study of J. Seewald (see n. 7 of this section) makes a good start.

16. In general, see W. A. A. van Otterlo, *Unters. über Begriff, Anwendung und Entstehung*

der griech. Ringkomposition, Nederl. Ak. 1944. For tragedy, see Pohlenz 2. 47; H. Pfeufer (see n. 7 of this section), 89; P. Groeneboom, *Agamemnon,* 362. Peretti's assumption (253) that the stereotyped structure of the archaic rhesis gave rise to Aristotle's statement about λέξις γελοία, and σατυρικόν is untenable.

17. *Untersuchungen zur Form des aischyleischen Chorliedes,* 1965.

18. See F. Wehrli, "Der erhabene und der schlichte Stil in der poetisch-rhetorischen Theorie der Antike," *Phyllobolia,* Basel 1946, 13. It seems strange that the gifted author of the treatise *On the Sublime* still felt somewhat oppressed by the weight of Aischylean φαντασίαι; cf. 15. 5. For the criticism of the poet in the Greek world, see A. de Propris, *Eschilo nella critica dei Greci,* Turin 1941.

19. A noteworthy reflection of the ancient report is given by the profound words that Ludwig Tieck in his novella *Dichterleben* has Marlowe speak specifically about the tragic poet. The motif of unconscious creativity also occurs here.

Destiny and Guilt

1. "Zeus in Aeschylus," *Journ. Hell. Stud.* 76 (1956), 55.

2. In the introduction to his edition of the *Agamemnon,* Oxford 1957.

3. There has been no lack of contradiction. Thus in T. B. L. Webster in *Fifty Years (and Twelve) of Class. Scholarship,* Oxford 1968, 113. The religious thought of the poet is sharply differentiated from the general trends of his time by de Romilly (*Time,* 84). L. Pearson assumes the correct stance in the chapter on Aischylos in his book *Popular Ethics in Ancient Greece,* Stanford 1962, 90, in that he does not find in Aischylean tragedy "a mere reflection of popular morality," but also does not separate Aischylos from his time as an isolated individual. L. Golden, *In Praise of Prometheus: Humanism and Rationalism in Aeschylean Thought,* Chapel Hill, N.C. 1966, 100, in his study of the statements about Zeus, comes to the conclusion (only satisfactory in the positive sense) that Aischylos is concerned with the designation of a power that effected all action yet was separated from ethical principles, "a spiritual conception in that he symbolizes all of the effecting, all of the accomplishing forces in the universe" (123). E. Fraenkel in his commentary on *Ag.* 757–762 has shown that the poet's protest against the general belief is not contradicted by the θεῶν φθόνος of *Pers.* 362, and that we are not obliged, with Wilamowitz, to assume a theological development.

4. Some studies on thought content to be added to those already mentioned are J. Coman, *L'idée de la Némésis chez Eschyle,* Paris 1931; M. Delcourt, "Orient et Occident chez Eschyle," *Mél. Bidez,* 1934, 233; A. Bonnard, "La pensée relig. d'Eschyle," *Rev. de Théol. et de Philos.* n.s. 21 (1935), 192; W. F. J. Knight, "The Tragic Vision of Aesch.," *Greece and Rome,* 1935, 29, and "The Aeschylean Universe," *Journ. Hell. Stud.* 63 (1943), 15; G. Richard, "L'impurité contagieuse et la magie dans la trag. Gr.," *Rev. Et. Anc.* 37 (1935), 301; A. Setti, *L'Orestea di Eschilo,* Bibl. di cultura, Florence 1935; F. Campanella, *Il genio di Esch.: Le sue idee morali e religiosi,* Naples 1936; D. Bassi, "La divinità nei tragici Greci," *Dioniso* 8 (1941), 239; E. Busch, "Religion und Tragik im Drama des Aisch.," *N. Jahrb.* 1941, 273; A. Kollmann, "Sophrosyne," *Wien. Stud.* 59 (1941), 12; R. Couffignal, "Sur l'Εὐσέβεια d'Esch.," *Rech. de science rel.* 34 (1947), 128; W. Dekker, "Het Godsbesef bij Aeschylus," in *De Antieke Tragedie,* Leyden 1947; W. Schadewaldt, "Das Drama der Antike in heutiger Sicht," *Universitas* 8 (1953), 591 = *Hellas und Hesperien,* 99; H. D. F. Kitto, "The Idea of God in Aeschylus and Sophocles," in *La notion du divin.,* Vandoeuvres 1954, 169; H. Dörrie, "Leid und Erfahrung," *Abh. Ak. Mainz. Geistes- und sozialw. Kl.* 1956/5; F. Rodríguez Adrados, "Die Gestalt des griech. Helden im griech. Drama," *Das Altertum* 10 (1962), 215; P.-R. Schulz, "Göttliches und menschliches Handeln bei Aisch.," Diss. Kiel 1962; W. Rösler, *Reflexe vorsokratischen Denkens bei Aischylos,* Meisenheim 1970; H. Lloyd-Jones, *The Justice of Zeus,* Berkeley 1971, chap. IV; A. Wartelle, "La pensée théologique d'Eschyle," *Bull. Ass. G. Budé* 1971, 535; V. N. Jarcho,

"Zum Menschenbild der Aischyleischen Tragödie," *Phil.* 116 (1972), 167; de Romilly, *Time*, 66, shows well the role of time in the theodicy of Aischylos. Also worthy of mention are the books mentioned in the bibliography: Nestle, *Menschl. Existenz.*; Maddalena, *Interpr.*; Kaufmann-Bühler; de Romilly, *La crainte*; Fischer; Kiefner. The bibliography of the problem of personal decision in Aischylos follows later. The question of the influence of political events on the work of Aischylos is taken up under the individual plays, where Podlecki dominates the field. We add F. Stoessl, "Aesch. as a Political Thinker," *Am. Journ. Phil.* 73 (1952), 113, and the chapter in F. Schachermeyr, *Die frühe Klassik der Griechen*, Stuttgart 1966, 139 (also important for the religion of the poet).

5. Thus, G. Thomson, "Mystical Allusions in the *Oresteia*," *Journ. Hell. Stud.* 55 (1935), 20, and in the commentary on the *Oresteia*; cf. also M. Bock, "De Aesch. Poeta Orphico et Orpheopythagoreo," Diss. Jena 1914. Echoes of Orphism seem most probable in the references to judgment in the afterlife, *Suppl.* 230, 416; *Eum.* 274, 339, as pointed out by K. Latte, *Arch. Rel. Wiss.* 20 (1920/21), 281 = *Kl. Schr.*, 23. More examples of Orphic influence upon the poet are claimed by H.-J. Dirksen: *Die aischyleische Gestalt des Orest.*, Nürnberg 1965, 33, note 45.

6. G. Pasquali, "L'origine dei concetti morali nella Grecia antichissima," *Civiltà Moderna* 1 (1929), 343.

7. B. Gladigow, "Aischylos und Heraklit: Ein Vergleich religiöser Denkformen," *Arch. Gesch. d. Philos.* 44 (1962), 225. Solmsen, 222. 166, is cautious in his judgment; Aylen, (346) is skeptical about a connection with Xenophanes.

8. On the passage, *Sitzb. Ak. Vienna* 221/3 (1943), 27. The key word already in *Ag.* 533, 1564, 1658. Parallels from Greek literature in G. Thomson's commentary on the *Oresteia*, s.v. 312. In Plato, *Laws* 9, 872e, the word stems from old priests. For the entire subject see K. Latte, "Schuld und Sühne in der griech. Religion," *Arch. Rel. Wiss.* 20 (1920/21), 254 = *Kl. Schr.*, 3.

9. An old proverbial saying was elevated into the realm of religious thought; cf. H. Dörrie (see note 4 of this section), also important for the interpretation of the hymn to Zeus (22). Cf. de Romilly, *Time*, 67.

10. On the text, see E. Fraenkel's commentary, which should be consulted for the whole section. On the opening of the hymn to Zeus, in which an ancient formula became the mainstay of the monotheistic thought that Aischylos strives for most decisively in fr. 105M from the *Heliades*: K. Latte, *Arch. Rel. Wiss.* 20 (1920/21), 275. 2 = *Kl. Schr.*, 19. 27; cf. also R. Hölzle, "Zum Aufbau der lyrischen Partien des Aischylos," Diss. Freiburg im Breisgau 1934. On the attempt to transpose the hymn, see n. 69 in "The Extant Tragedies" section.

11. More material in W. Haedicke, "Die Gedanken der Griechen über Familienherkunft und Vererbung," Diss. Halle 1936, 56. Cf. especially Herodotos, 6. 86.

12. The thought is continued along these lines in the magnificent conversation between the Pope and Medardus in E. T. A. Hoffman's *Elixiere des Teufels* (second part, third section, beginning), where the question of responsibility too is examined most keenly.

13. On αἰτία, in which *cause* and *guilt* are not separated: J. Stenzel, "Die Entwicklung des griechischen Geistbegriffs," *Die Antike* 1 (1924), 244. O; Regenbogen, *Die Antike* 6 (1929), 247. Fundamental is K. von Fritz, "Tragische Schuld und poetische Gerechtigkeit in der Griech. Trag.," *Studium Generale* 8 (1955), 194, 219 = *Antike und moderne Tragödie*, Berlin 1962, 1 (with older bibl. in n. 1). R. D. Dawe, "Some Reflections on Ate and Hamartia," *Harv. Stud.* 72 (1968), 89, is important for the affinity of the two concepts. J. M. Bremer, *Tragic Error in the Poetics of Aristotle and in Greek Tragedy*, Amsterdam 1968.

14. See K. Deichgräber, "Der listensinnende Trug des Gottes," *Nachr. Ak. Göttingen. Phil.-hist. Kl.* 1/4 (1940), 1, then, in the book of the same title, Göttingen 1952, 108; H. Hommel, *N. Jahrb.* 1940, 287. 74. This conception is paralleled in Herodotos 7. 12 ff., with the dream apparition that drives Xerxes to Ate. The closeness of some sections of Herodotos to Aischylos is well handled by M. Pohlenz, *Herodot*, Leipzig 1937, 117.

15. On the problems associated with μεταίτιος, E. Fraenkel's commentary (*Ag.* 811) is excellent.

16. "Eschyle et le tragique," *Bull. de la Fac. de Lettres de l'Univ. Lausanne et de la Soc. des Et. de Lettres*, ser. 2, 6, (1963), 73, and "Un débat sur la tragédie Grecque: Le héros, le 'nécessaire' et les dieux," *Rev. de théol. et de philos. Lausanne* 99 (1966), 233. Here Rivier opposed R. Schaerer, who in the same journal (98 [1965], 241) responded to the criticism of his book *Le héros, le sage et l'événement dans l'humanisme Grec.*, Paris 1964, by J. Sullinger in the same volume (172). A. Rivier has now summarized his interpretation in the study cited in note 72 of "The Extant Tragedies" section. We append the following to the studies cited there, as well as to those in notes 34 f. and 72 of "The Extant Tragedies" section: A. W. H. Adkins, *Merit and Responsibility: A Study of Greek Values*, Oxford 1960; P. R. Schulz, "Göttliches und menschliches Handeln bei Aisch.," Diss. Kiel 1962; U. Fischer, *Der Telosgedanke in den Dramen des Aisch.*, Spudasmata 6, Hildesheim 1965.

17. The sharply diverging opinions in A. Lesky, *Journ. Hell. Stud.* 86 (1966), 81.

18. *Harv. Stud.* 63 (1958), 89.

19. Well put by A. G. Fuller, *Harv. Theol. Rev.* (1915), 460: " . . . dilemma where there is a conflict of duties such that while a choice is morally imperative none is morally possible."

20. Wilamowitz, *Herm.* 26 (1918), 227.

21. Cf. the chapter "Zum Problem des Tragischen" in A. Lesky, *Die griech. Trag.*, 11.

CHAPTER 5

Biographical Notes

1. A. Dain, "La 'Vie' de Sophocle," *Lettres d'Humanité* 17 (1958), 4, has published the translation of the *Vita* by P. Mazon and added some comments on the text.

2. These aspects of his character are described by W. Schadewaldt, *Sophokles und Athen*, Frankfurt am Main 1935.

3. However, there remain for Lampros chronological difficulties, which von Blumenthal, *RE* 1043, and Webster, *Soph.*, 179, could not completely resolve.

4. C. M. Bowra, "Soph. on his own Development," *Am. Journ. Phil.* 61 (1940), 385, accepts the passage as genuine, probably rightly, and suggests Ion of Chios as the source. Likewise A. von Blumenthal, *Ion von Chios*, Stuttgart 1939, fr. 9. Perrotta (7) also believes the remark is authentic. Cf., too, L. A. Post, "Aeschylean Onkos in Sophocles and Aristotle," *Trans. Am. Phil. Ass.* 88 (1947), 242.

5. Schmid, 2. 313, has Sophokles produce his first play "in the 77th Olympiad (472–469)," which is given by Eusebios, *Chron. Ol.* 77. However, A. von Blumenthal, *Burs. Jahresber.* 259. 68, wishes to follow Plutarch rather than Eusebios. But there is no real contradiction, because the Dionysia of 468 belongs in the 77th Olympiad. F. Jacoby is correct, *FGrH* 239, A 56.

6. Athenaios apparently still possessed an unabridged version of the *Vita*. The Thamyris vase in the Vatican is depicted in K. Schefold, *Die Bildnisse der antiken Dichter, Redner, und Denker*, Basel 1943, 58. On the mask of Thamyris with different-colored eyes, see A. Lesky, *Anz. Österr. Ak. Phil.-hist. Kl.* 1951, 101 = *Ges Schr.*, 169.

7. Remnants of elegies and a paean to Asklepios (or Koronis) in Diehl, *Anth. Lyr.*, 3d ed., 1. 79. For the epigraphical remains of the paean (O. Kern, *Inscriptiones Graecae*, Berlin 1913, plate 45), which was still sung in Athens at the time of the Antonines (Philostratos, *Vita Ap.* 3.17; Philostratos Junior, *imag.* 13); see especially S. H. Oliver, "The Serapion Monument and the Paean of Sophocles," *Hesperia* 5 (1936), 91, and E. Diehl in the supplement to *Anth. Lyr.* 4. 57.

8. G. Müller, *Herm.* 89 (1961), 398, considers it probable that Sophokles discussed the function of the chorus.

9. Von Blumenthal, *RE* 1050; Perrotta, 12. If the treatise did exist, then it was probably

more concerned with the chorus itself than with tragedy in general, as Webster (*Soph.*, 7) imagines.

10. Fr. 2D. The connection with Herodotos is attested by many reminiscences in the poet's work, collected in Schmid, 2. 318. 3, with a supplement by P. Keseling, *Phil Woch.* 57 (1937), 910. These are all individual parallels; intellectually Herodotos is closer to Aischylos, as M. Pohlenz has well shown in his *Herodot* (1937). Fr. 1D offers a pentameter line in which Sophokles endeavors with some difficulty to fit the name Archelaos (of Miletos) into the meter. On the two spurious and foolish distichs (fr. 3D) that polemize against Euripides with a reference to pandering, see F. Wehrli in the commentary on Hieronymos of Rhodes (*Die Schule des Aristoteles*, 10) frr. 35 f.

11. On the strategoi of this time, F. W. Lenz, "The Athenian Strategoi of the Years 441/440 and 433/432," *Trans. Am. Phil. Ass.* 72 (1941), 226.

12. The numerical references in the *Vita* are admittedly confused. That Sophokles was sixty-nine years old at the time agrees with the date of the war against the Anaians, but an election date seven years before the Peloponnesian disorders fits better with his first term as strategos. It remains questionable whether, with Webster (12), we should conjecture a third term on the basis of an anecdote in Plutarch (*Nikias* 15. 2) that joins him with Nikias as strategos and describes him as humble. On this, see H. D. Westlake, "Sophocles and Nicias as Colleagues," *Herm.* 84 (1956), 110. When the *Vita* (1) reports that the poet was strategos not only with Perikles but also with Thukydides, this must refer to the son of Melesias, who was ostracized from 443 to 433. If we assume that he was elected strategos after his return, then the war against the Anaians would be a possibility.

13. The Sophokles who is named as an attorney in a hubris-trial (Aristot. *Rhet.* 1. 14; 1374b 36) could also have been the poet. He is certainly the one meant in the reference to a Sophokles (ibid., 3. 15; 1416a 15) who denies the reproach that he is simulating the trembling of an old man. A. von Blumenthal correctly emphasizes, against Perrotta (48), that this passage has nothing to do with the alleged trial of Iophon against his father.

14. "Das Priestertum des Sophokles," *Festschrift Keramopullos*, Athens 1953, 469.

15. Webster considers the whole story an invention of comedy, which is quite possible. (Likewise W. C. Helmbold, "The Mad Sophocles," *Class. Journ.* 45 [1950], 342). But the connection with the *Phratores* of Leukon produced in 421 is as ingenious as the attempt to construct a parallel to the *Pytine* of Kratinos. There Iophon supposedly accused Sophokles of abandoning his lawful wife, Theoris (Art), in favor of his mistress, Nikostrate (Glory of War). The women's names must have been reversed in the tradition. P. Mazon, "Sophocle devant ses juges," *Rev. Et. Anc.* 47 (1945), 82, conjectures that at a meeting of the phratriai Sophokles introduced to the rolls his like-named grandson over Iophon's protest, but this is not the solution.

16. The most comprehensive overview of all identifiable types is offered by G. M. A. Richter, *The Portraits of the Greeks*, London 1965, 124; figs. 611–716.

17. The bibliography is the same as that cited above for the Aischylos portrait. The original of this type is dated at 400–390 by Laurenzi, op. cit., 92, and at approx. 380 by Schefold, op. cit. (*Bildnisse der antiken Dichter*), 72. Bibliography on the replicas is in both these authors and in Richter.

18. Laurenzi, op. cit., 99. Hekler, op. cit (2d ed.), 24. Schefold, op. cit., 90, 207, offers an especially fine illustration of the head before its restoration. Another example is in Schadewaldt, *Sophokles und das Leid*, Potsdam 1944 = *Hellas und Hesperien*, 231 = *Gottheit und Mensch in der Tragödie des Sophokles*, Darmstadt 1963, with penetrating evaluation. Now also in K. Schefold, *Griechische Dichterbildnisse*, Zurich 1965, 23, plate 14a.

19. Laurenzi, op. cit. (2d ed.), 24. Schefold, op. cit., 158, 214. V. Poulsen, *Les portraits Grecs*, Copenhagen 1954, nos. 9 f. As a second reproduction of the portrait of the aged Sophokles, Laurenzi, op. cit., 136, designates the Sophokles Arundel (Brit. Mus. no. 2320), whose archetype he dates at 50–25 B.C. Finally, we mention the mosaic in Cologne (Schefold, op. cit., 154),

where the inscriptions beneath the portraits have been confused. "Sophocles" is written under a head of Euripides, and the one identified as Sokrates is probably supposed to represent our poet.

Manuscript Transmission and Editions

1. The remark in A. von Blumenthal, *RE* 1080, that Wilamowitz identified this Sallustios with the friend of the emperor Julian, is incorrect. Wilamowitz calls the identification more than doubtful.

2. A. Turyn, "The Manuscripts of Sophocles," *Traditio* 2(1944),1; "The Sophocles Recension of Manuel Moschopulus," *Trans. Am. Phil. Ass.* 80 (1949), 94; *Studies in the Manuscript Tradition of the Tragedies of Sophocles*, Illinois Studies in Language and Literature 36/1–2, Urbana 1952. V. de Marco, "Sulla tradizione manoscritta degli scolii Sofoclei," *Stud. It.* n.s. 13 (1936), 3; "De scholiis in Sophoclis tragoedias veteribus," *Mem. Acc. Lincei*, ser. 6, 6 (1937), 105; "Gli Scolii all'*Edipo a Colono* di Sofocle e la loro tradizione manoscritta," *Rendiconti Acc. Napoli* 26 (1951), 1; "Intorno al testo di *Edipo a Colono* in un manoscritto romano," ibid., 260; *Scholia in Sophoclis* Oedipum Coloneum, Rome 1952. R. Aubreton, *Démétrius Triclinius et les recensions médiévales de Sophocle*, Paris 1949. R. D. Dawe, *Studies in the Text of Sophokles.* I: *The manuscripts and the Text of Sophokles;* II: *The Collations*, Leyden 1973. The tradition is represented most accurately by the texts of *Aias*, *Elektra*, and *Oid. Tyr.*

3. *De arte interpretandi*, 1847, 103.

4. J. Vurtheim, *Der Leidener Sophoclespalimpsest zum ersten Male vollständig untersucht*, Leyden 1926; H. J. Scheltema, "De codice Sophocleo Lugdunensi," *Mnem.* ser. 4, 2 (1949), 132; J. Irigoin, "Le palimpseste de Sophocle," *Rev. Et. Gr.* 64 (1951), 443.

5. J. Irigoin, *Rev. Et. Gr.* 67 (1954), 507, objected to Turyn's view that the "Laurentian family" and the "Roman family" could be traced back to a source in minuscules that came from a single transcription. P. E. Easterling, *Class. Quart.* 61 (1967), 63, correctly asserts the impossibility of determining the exact time when the two branches of the tradition separated.

6. This question was emphatically put by P. Maas, *Gnom.* 25 (1953), 441 f., and H. Lloyd-Jones, *Gnom.* 28 (1956), 105 ff.; 31 (1959), 478 ff.

7. "Sophokles' *Ajax*: Collation of the manuscripts G, R, and Q." *Class. Quart.* 61 (1967), 52.

8. "The Manuscript A of Soph. and its Relation to the Moschopulean Recension," *Class. Quart.* 54 (1960), 51; cf. also H. Lloyd-Jones, *Gnom.* 28 (1956), 107. J. C. Kamerbeek, "De Soph. memoria," *Mnem.* ser. 4, 11 (1958), 25; W. J. W. Koster, "De codicis Par. Gr. 2712 aetate," *Mnem.* ser. 4, 12 (1959), 135; V. de Marco, *Scholia in Sophoclis* Oed. Col., Rome 1952, viii, has also expressly emphasized the value of the Parisinus.

9. "Koine," *Sitzb. Ak. Wien. Phil.-hist. Kl. 1947*, 69.

The Extant Tragedies

1. For text, interpretation, and translation for all plays consult the books and essays cited in the bibliography, as well as in the summary sections. Here are listed materials specifically for the *Aias.*

ANNOTATED EDITIONS: M. Untersteiner, Milan 1943; A. Willem and C. Josserand, Liège 1940; V. de Falco, 3d ed., Naples 1950; A. Colonna, 2d ed., Turin 1951; G. Ammendola, Turin 1953. The leading edition is that of J. C. Kamerbeek, Leyden 1953 (without text). See also W. B. Stanford, London 1963; K. Holeschofsky, Paderborn 1965. The translation of E. Staiger is also published separately in the Europa-Reihe of the *Sammlung Klosterberg*, Basel 1942. *Aias*, *El.*, *Trach.*, *Phil.* were translated by E. F. Watling, Penguin Classics 28, London 1953. ON INTERPRE-

TATION: G. Dalmeyda, "Soph. *Ajax*," *Rev. Et. Gr.* 46 (1933), 1; K. von Fritz, "Zur Interpretation des *Aias*," *Rhein. Mus.* 83 (1934), 113 = *Antike und moderne Tragödie*, 241; F. Dirlmeier, "Der *Aias* des Soph.," *N. Jahrb.* 1938, 297; G. Perrotta, "L'*Aiace* di Sof.," *Dioniso* 7 (1939), 135; R. Ebeling, "Missverständnisse um den *Aias* des Soph.," *Herm.* 76 (1941), 283; G. Pavano, L'*Aiace* di Sof.," *Atti Acc. Palermo*, ser. 4/3/2/3 (1942), 539; K. Reinhardt, "*Aias* Vers 131," *Herm.* 78 (1943), 111 (against Ebeling); L. Massa-Positano, *L'unità dell'*Aiace *di Sof.*, Naples 1946. Opposed by A. de Propris, *Dioniso* 12 (1949), 123; R. Camerer, "Zu Soph. *Aias*," *Gymn.* 60 (1935), 289; I. M. Linforth, *Three Scenes in Soph.* Ajax, Univ. Calif. Public. in Class. Phil. 15/1, Berkeley 1954; S. M. Adams, "The *Ajax* of Soph.," *Phoenix* 9 (1955), 93; I. Errandonea, Les quatre monologues d'*Ajax* et leur signification dramatique," *Et. Class.* 26 (1958), 21; B. M. W. Knox, "The *Ajax* of Soph.," *Harv. Stud.* 65 (1961), 1; G. Grossmann, "Das Lachen des Aias," *Mus. Helv.* 25 (1963), 65; E. Fraenkel, "Zwei *Aias*-Szenen hinter der Bühne," *Mus. Helv.* 24 (1967), 79. See also M. Simpson, "Soph. Ajax: His Madness and Transformation," *Arethusa* 2 (1969), 88; M. Sicherl, "Die Tragik des Aias," *Herm.* 98 (1970), 14. The treatment of this play by O. Becker, *Das Bild des Weges*, *Hermes* Einzelschriften 4 (1937), 204, is noteworthy.

2. The old late dating by Wilamowitz (e.g., Berl. Klassikert. 5. 2. 71) is accepted by Perrotta, *Sofocle*, 163. He conjectures 431 and competition with the *Medeia* of Euripides. His argument that the trimeter scenes of *Antigone* contain no antilabai, while the *Aias* has them at 591–594 and 981–985, might seem important, but the corresponding proofs for older dramas of Euripides given by Perrotta himself (173) invalidate his conclusion. For the inconclusiveness of such observations, H. D. F. Kitto, *Am. Journ. Phil.* 60 (1939), 178, is important. Another argument of Wilamowitz, that *Aias* 1102 was dependent on Eur. fr. 723N from the *Telephos*, has been picked up and reinforced by Buchwald (49). Reinhardt correctly opposes him. Further attempts at a late dating were undertaken by H. Grégoire ("La date de l'*Ajax* de Soph.," *Bull. Ac. Belgique* 41 (1955), 187), who arrives at 424, since Aias supposedly represents Alkibiades, who began his political career in 425. Also B. Stumpo, "L'*Aiace* di Sof.," *Aevum* 30 (1956), 1, who discovers similarities between Aias and Perikles and dates the piece at 425 because such a pessimistic play would be inconceivable in the previous years. Both theories are regrettable examples of a method that constantly searches through the plays for contemporary references. Persuasively, C. M. Bowra (*Am. Journ. Phil.* 61 [1940], 385) conjectures that the *Aias* be assigned to the second of the three periods of Sophokles' development differentiated by the poet himself according to Plutarch (*De prof. in virt.* 7. 79b).

3. Max Scheler, *Die weissen Blätter*, 1911, 768, evaluated the apparently favorable change as a means of excluding for the tragic action every appearance of calculability.

4. The lost *Teukros* of Sophokles probably dealt with his banishment by Telamon.

5. In the Tusculum edition of Willige the verses 1028–1037 are placed in brackets and 1038 f. printed beneath the main text; the athetesis of 1028 by Morstadt and Nauck was rejected by Jebb in an appendix to his edition. The motif of Hektor's fatal gift appears at 661 ff. and 817 f. Its brief resumption at 1026 f. is quite effective; the long continuation of the theme that follows is far less so. Also, αἰέν in v. 1031 is colorless, and the reference of ἐκεῖνος (1035, occurring in a zeugma) to v. 1030 is harsh. But the chorus leader's injunction μὴ τεῖνε μακράν (don't prolong your speech; 1040) indicates a certain verbosity in Teukros's speech and argues against the assumption of an actor's interpolation.

6. Even Reinhardt does not quite do justice to the conclusion in his book on Sophokles.

7. For the instability of opinion on this problem, two statements by Wilamowitz are representative. In *Gr. Verskunst*, 1921, 507, it was "short-sighted" not to recognize that Aias prepares his own destruction by boasting to Athena; in the introduction to his translation of *Oidipous* (new edition, Berlin 1939, 7. 1) it is "painful to see" that guilt should be interpreted into the character of Aias. He is very specific in *Glaube der Hell.* 2. 233: After all, "was Aias a κακός?" In agreement with F. Dirlmeier, H. Hommel, *N. Jahrb.* 1940, 288. 76 is against an overvaluation of the guilt motif, while Perrotta (633) actually would like to separate *Aias* and *Ant.* as Dike dramas from the others as Ate dramas. The guilt of Aias is also mentioned by R.

Ebeling, op. cit., and Bowra in his analysis. But both refer this to the mistake of a great man who can be exalted after his death. M. Pohlenz, *Herm.* 78 (1943), 270, speaks of Aias's guilt, but cf. *Trag.* 1. 181. Recently the question of guilt was treated by Funke, 76. 146, who proceeds from a statement by Wilamowitz, *Glaube der Hell.* 2. 233. 2, and sees in the hubris motif of the play an attempt to justify the gods who send destruction.

8. This was shown by F. Dirlmeier, op. cit., who also (307. 17, 308) points to the thematic Hubris-Menis relationship in the *Aias Lokros, Thamyris, Niobe*, and *Laokoon* of Sophokles. In every case the guilt motif stems from later epic. Pohlenz, 1. 181, disagrees.

9. This recalls the odd limitation in the oracle in *Trach.* 164 ff.; cf. de Romilly, *Time*, 17. A problematic reading of the Kalchas speech is in M. M. Wigodsky, "The 'Salvation' of Aias," *Herm.* 90 (1962), 149.

10. *Rhein. Mus.* 3 (1829), 68. We judge Aias on the basis of the characteristics of the Sophoklean hero so accurately described by Knox in *The Heroic Temper.*

11. *Three Scenes in Soph.* Aiax, Univ. of Calif. Publ. in Class. Phil. 15/1 (1954), 1. I. Errandonea, op. cit., 21, believes that Aias does deceive the chorus, but also that he speaks the truth at the beginning of the speech insofar as he, under Tekmessa's influence (as if this were anywhere apparent in the play!), rejects killing the Atreidai and decides to destroy himself.

12. "The *Ajax* of Soph.," *Harv. Stud.* 65 (1961), 1.

13. *Neue Wege zur Antike* 8, Leipzig 1929; cf. *Hellas und Hesperien*, 304.

14. *Rhein. Mus.* 83 (1943), 113 = *Ant. u. mod. Trag.*, 241.

15. F. Grob, "De scena Soph.," *Mél Navarre*, Toulouse 1935, 245.

16. The view of P. Mazon that the oldest play was the *Trach.*, followed by *Ant., Aias, Oid. Tyr.*, as a distinct group, has no chance of being accepted.

17. *Die Stellung der* Trach. *im Werk des Soph.*, Hypomn. 1 Göttingen 1962, 16.

18. *Herakles*, 1. 137, 152. Elaborated by A. Dieterich, *Rhein. Mus.* 46 (1891), 25 = *Kl. Schr.*, 48, and T. von Wilamowitz, *Die dramatische Technik des Soph.*, Phil. unters. 22 (1917), 90.

19. Bibliography is in E. R. Schwinge, 15.

20. The appendix of his book on Sophokles (289), listed in the bibl., appears translated into German in the anthology *Sophokles*, Wege der Forschung 95, Darmstadt 1967, 183.

21. There remained scattered supporters of a late dating. Most extreme is Perrotta (544), who would like to go down as far as 407/406. H. D. F. Kitto, "Soph., Statistics and the *Trachiniai*," *Am. Journ. Phil.* 60 (1939), 178, wants to set the play around 420, while G. Schiassi, "La figura di Ipsipile nell' omonima tragedia euripidea e le *Trachinie*," *Riv. di Filol.* 32 (1954), 1, arrives at 414–410 on the basis of a completely hypothetical comparison of the two plays.

22. His arrangement of the plays agrees with that of G. M. Kirkwood (see above); S. G. Kapsomenos, *Soph.* Trach. *und ihr Vorbild*, Athens 1963, who carefully tries to prove that the *Trach.* was written before the *Alkestis*; J. Goth, "Soph. *Ant.*," Diss. Tübingen 1966, 210.

23. *Der Tod des Herakles*, Zurich 1945.

24. *Herm.* 75 (1940), 180. See also his edition of Bakchylides, 7th ed. 1958, 47 and 53 of the preface. Likewise K. Thomamüller, "Die aiolischen und daktyloepitritischen Masse in den Dramen des Soph.," Diss. Hamburg 1965, 12 (with bibl.).

25. With good criticism of this view, S. G. Kapsomenos (see above) comes to the conclusion that Sophokles knew the poem of Bakchylides. J. C. Kamerbeek in the introduction to his commentary (28) does not believe that a relative chronology can be established in this case.

26. "Göttliches und menschliches Wissen bei Soph.," *Kieler Universitätsreden* 1 (1950), 15 = *Gottheit und Mensch in der Tragödie des Soph.*, Darmstadt 1963, 11; id., "Über das Selbstbewusstsein der soph. Personen," *Wien. Stud.* 69 (1956), 81.

27. Reinhardt in his book on Sophokles, 66 and 257 f. of the 3d ed., and J. C. Kamerbeek in the introduction to his commentary, 28.

28. Leipzig 1930, 49, 108.

29. "Zur Datierung der *Trach.*," *Herm.* 72 (1937), 270.

30. *Herm.* 80 (1952), 66 = *Hellas and Hesperien*, 334 (cf. also 298).

31. Thus also *Gesch. d. Griech. Lit.*, 2d ed., Bern 1963, 312; *Griech. Tragödie*, 4th ed., Stuttgart 1968, 145.

32. W. M. Calder III, *Greek, Rom. and Byz. Studies* 9 (1968), 398. On the basis of metrical analysis, H. A. Pohlsander, *Am. Journ. Phil.* 84 (1963), 280, and D. S. Raven, ibid. 86 (1965), 225, have placed the *Trach.* closer to the *Oid. Tyr.*, which agrees with our own estimate. L. Sirchia, "La Cronologia delle *Trachinie*," *Dioniso* 21 (1958), 59, dates the play especially close to the *Oid. Tyr.*

33. C. de Vleminck-R. van Compernolle, "Bibliographie analytique de l'*Antigone* des Soph." *Phoibos* 2 (1947/8), 85. Recent Annotated Editions: A. Tovar, Madrid 1942; J. C. Kamerbeek, Leyden 1945; A. Willem, 2d ed., Liège 1945; C. Riba, Barcelona 1951 (with *Trach.*; in a Catalan transl.); A. Colonna, 2d ed., Turin 1951; A. Anania, Florence 1957; F. Chuytens-V. Daenen, Antwerp 1957. TEXT: B. Wyss, Ed. Helv. 6, Basel 1946; E. Pilch, Berlin 1949 (with verse transl.). WITHOUT TEXT: the great commentary of G. Müller, Heidelberg 1967, a work equally valuable for the language and interpretation of the play, but which often provokes opposition by its exaggerated hunt for double meanings: cf. further the detailed discussion of B. M. W. Knox, *Gnom.* 40 (1968), 747, and H. Flashar, *Poetica* 2 (1968), 558. ESSAYS: K. von Fritz, "Haimons Liebe zu Antigone," *Phil.* 89 (1934), 19 = *Ant. u. mod. Trag.*, 227; M. K. Flickinger, "The ἁμαρτία of Soph. *Ant.*," Diss. Iowa 1935; K. Kerényi, *Dionysos und das Tragische in der* Ant., Frankf. Stud. 13, Frankfurt am Main 1935; E. della Valle, *Saggio sulla poesia dell'*Ant., Bari 1935; R. Bultmann, "Polis und Hades in der Ant. des Soph.," *Theol. Aufs., K. Barth zum 50. Geburtst.*, Munich 1936, 78 = *Sophokles*, Wege der Forschung 95 (1967), 311; L. Bieler, *Antigones Schuld im Urteil der neueren Sophoklesforschung*, Vienna 1937; E. Bignone, "L'*Ant.* di Sof.," *Riv. It. del Dramma* 2 (1937), 13; G. Méautis, "La psychologie de l'*Ant.* de Soph.," *Rev. Phil.* 14 (1940), 25; G. Rudberg, "Zu Soph. *Ant.*," *Symb. Osl.* 21 (1941), 1; T. B. L. Webster, *Greek Interpretations*, Manchester 1942, 45; R. F. Goheen, *The Imagery of Soph.* Ant., Princeton 1951; A. Bonnard, *La tragédie et l'homme*, Neuchâtel 1951, 19; A. Lesky, "Zwei Soph.-Interpretationen," *Herm.* 80 (1952), 91; W. Jens, "Ant.-Interpretationen," *Satura: Festschr. Weinreich*, Baden-Baden 1952, 43 = *Sophokles*, Wege der Forschung 95 (1967), 295; I. Errandonea, "Das 4. Stasimon der Ant. von Soph.," *Symb. Osl.* 30 (1953), 16; S. M. Adams, "The Ant. of Soph.," *Phoenix* 9 (1955), 47; H. J. Mette, "Die Ant. des Soph.," *Herm.* 84 (1956), 129; F. Pérez Ruiz, "Antigona," *Humanidades* 9 (1957), 7; W. Schadewaldt, "Einl. zur. Ant. des Soph. von Hölderlin in der Vertonung von Carl Orff," *Hellas und Hesperien*, Zurich 1960, 247 (further, 861); E. Eberlein, "Über die verschiedenen Deutungen des tragischen Konfliktes in der Trag. Ant. des Soph.," *Gymn.* 68 (1961), 16; I. M. Linforth, *Antigone and Creon*, Berkeley 1961; S. Bradshaw, "The Watchman Scenes in the Ant.," *Class. Quart.* n.s. 12 (1962), 203; F. R. Adrados, "Religion y politica en la *Antigona*," *Revista Univ. Madrid* 13 (1964), 493; H. Funke, "Κρέων ἄπολις," *Ant. und Abendl.* 12 (1966), 29; J. Goth, "Soph. *Ant.* Interpretationsversuche und Strukturuntersuchungen," Diss. Tübingen 1966; W. M. Calder III, "Sophocles' Political Tragedy, Ant.," *Gr., Rom. and Byz. Studies* 9 (1968), 389; J. S. Lasso de la Vega," 'La *Antígona* de Sófocles' por Bertolt Brecht," *Cuadernos, Hispanoamericanos* 1968, 228. FROM THE NUMEROUS TRANSLATIONS: E. Staiger, Zurich 1944; R. Woerner, Leipzig 1947; K. Reinhardt, 3d ed., Göttingen 1961; W. Schadewaldt in *Griech. Theater*, Frankfurt 1964, 90; Bertolt Brecht, "Die Ant. des Soph." (adapted for the stage from the translation of Hölderlin, with C. Neher as collaborator); *Material on the* Ant., collected by W. Hecht, 2d ed., Frankfurt 1967. ENGLISH: D. Fitts and R. Fitzgerald, New York 1939; L. J. Morrison, London 1939; G. Murray, Oxford 1941; F. K. Smith, London 1950. FRENCH: P. Waltz, Paris 1941. ITALIAN: M. Untersteiner, Modena 1937; E. della Valle, Bari 1951; E. Pettine, Salerno 1968.

34. Flickinger, *Greek Theater*, 331; Goossens, *Eur.*, 25. 10, who supports the view that the number referred not to the plays preserved in Alexandria, but to all the plays known to the grammarians through the didaskaliai; A. M. Dale, *Alkestis*, Oxford 1954; V. Zuntz, *Inquiry*, 251; T. B. L. Webster, *Wien. Stud.* 79 (1966), 115.

35. Ismene can say ἐν νυκτὶ τῇ νῦν (on this night; 16). On the determination of the time see S. Bradshaw, op. cit., 203; Knox, *Heroic Temper*, 180. 43.

36. G. Müller rightly prefers the reading πόλεως for v. 187, which is also attested by the scholium. So too Reinhardt, and Schadewaldt in his translation.

37. In such poetry we are obliged simply to accept the fact that the corpse of Polyneikes, who died the day before, is already in decay and gives off an unbearable odor.

38. Verse 572 is difficult. Scholars have objected to the fact that in the stichomythy Antigone speaks only this one verse, and so they give it to Ismene; thus E. Fraenkel, "Die *Phoin.* des Eur.," *Bayer. Ak.* 1963, 114 and H. F. Johansen, *Lustrum* 1962/7 (1963), 194, both with bibl. But in his commentary G. Müller has rightly pointed out that v. 572 stands not within the stichomythy between Kreon and Ismene, but at its end, as do the verses of the chorus leader immediately afterward. Reinhardt and Schadewaldt in their translations also give the verse to Antigone.

39. The emendation of κόνις to κοπίς is obvious. Dust that cuts would be too much even for Aischylos.

40. The arrangement of the difficult verses 854 f. has always seemed impossible to me, since the same chorus that (872) admitted Antigone's εὐσέβεια (which, to be sure, would never conflict with power), is made to say of her that she has fallen at the steps of Dike (or even dashed her foot against them)! Cf. *Herm.* 80 (1952), 93 = *Ges. Schr.*, 177. In agreement J. Goth, op. cit., 157 n. Against the objection of Müller (op. cit., 191), who himself suggests an interesting interpretation of the lines, to the use of πολύ that I have assumed, stand passages like *Oid. Tyr.* 743, 786.

41. Kreon's words to Haimon (1228), οἷον ἔργον εἴργασαι, (What have you done?), are strange, but they cannot support the conjecture of Adams (58) that Kreon believes his son (who is armed with a sword) has killed Antigone with a noose. W. M. Calder iii, "Was Antigone murdered?" *Gr., Rom. and Byz. Stud.* 3 (1960), 31, considers this; recently also in *Gr., Rom. and Byz. Stud.* 9 (1968), 402.

42. It is natural that the messenger who (1255) entered the house with some anxiety brings the news, and not just any servant.

43. G. Müller, op. cit., 270, may be correct in assuming that a verse is missing in the section 1301–1305 responding to the six trimeters 1278–1283.

44. Thus also the newest interpretation of W. M. Calder iii, *Gr., Rom. and Byz. Stud.* 9 (1968), 402, who sees in the play only the drama of Kreon the politician, whom he exonerates to a great extent.

45. The devaluation of the final section by Wilamowitz, *Griech. Trag.*, 4. 348, taken over by W. M. Calder iii (see previous note; Reinhardt also has objections), is difficult to understand and misinterprets the poet's statement.

46. *Ästhetik* 2. 2, sect. 1. Bowra, 65, well demonstrates how Hegel's interpretation fits into his overall conception of history. H. Oeben, "Hegels *Antigone*-Interpretation," Diss. Bonn 1953.

47. A good overview of the question is in L. Bieler, op. cit., who still wishes to see a sort of guilt in her overstepping the given boundaries. Earlier bibl. in M. K. Flickinger, op. cit. H. Kleinknecht, in the article "Nomos" in Kittel's *Theologisches Wörterbuch* 4. 1020, sees the drama as a struggle of nomos against nomos. W. Schadewaldt, in an earlier work (Neue Wege zur Antike 8, Leipzig 1929), thought that Antigone, when faced with death, realized that she could safeguard the rights of her dead brother only by fighting against the state, but he later supported the interpretation outlined here (*Universitas* 8 [1953], 596 = *Hellas und Hesperien*, 104; further, 264 and, with some restriction, 273). W. Jens, op. cit., 56 = 308, considers Antigone partially guilty because of her total exclusion of other individuals. S. M. Adams, op. cit., believes the final verdict of the chorus refers to Kreon and Antigone. Knox, 62, reads the play politically and sees in Kreon the representative of a democratic principle akin to that of Kleis-

thenes, opposed by the defender of the ancient clan relationships. W. Elliger, "Sophokles und Apollon," *Synusia für W. Schadewaldt*, Pfullingen 1965, 98, emphasizes in Antigone a trait of hubris and will for self-destruction. Conflicting traits are also seen in the verdict of F. Rodríguez Adrados, op. cit.

48. An overview of the discussion in the nineteenth century in H. Meyer-Benfey, Soph. *Ant.*, 1920, 31. More recent are C. Hoeg, *Antigone og eftertiden*, Copenhagen 1949; E. Eberlein, op. cit.; and H. Funke, op. cit.

49. On these, see esp. Ehrenberg, 22 (25 of the German ed.). It is with some justification that A.-J. Festugière, *Personal Religion among the Greeks*, Berkeley 1954, 52, sees a connection with the ideas of Plato. Despite all reservations against the inclusion of Christian concepts, we cannot dispute the right of F. Sengle in his very interesting essay "Vom Absoluten in der Tragödie," *D. Vierteljahrsechr.* 20 (1942), 272, to introduce the concept of martyrdom into the discussion of Antigone.

50. On the basic concepts involved, see H. Höppener, "Het begrafenisverbod in Soph. *Ant.*," *Hermeneus* 9 (1973), 73; Goossens, 631. 121; Funke, 34. 30. J. Goth, op. cit., 44. 3 is very good. Cf. Herod. 9. 79: τὰ πρέπει μᾶλλον βαρβάροισιν (these things rather befit barbarians); Thuk. 1. 138. Xen. *Hell.* 1. 7. 22; Phylarchos, *FGrH* 81, fr. 45. Also important are Goethe's statements about Kreon to Eckermann on March 28, 1827.

51. I. Errandonea has made this a system of interpretation: *Emerita* 10 (1942), 28; *Humanidades* 5 (1963), 199: and the book: *Sofócles: Investigaciones sobre la estructura dramática de sus siete tragedias y sobre la personalidad de sus coros*, Madrid 1958.

52. Whitman, 135 (*Oid. Tyr.*); Waldock, 112 (*Ant.*); F. Egermann, "Vom att. Menschenbild," 76 (*Oid. Tyr.*); G. Zuntz, "Ödipus und Gregorius," *Ant. u Abendl.* 4 (1954), 191 = *Sophokles*, Wege der Forschung 95, Darmstadt 1967, 348; J. C. Kamerbeek, "Comments on the Second Stasimon of the *Oid. Tyr.*," *Wien. Stud.* 79 (1966), 80 (*Oid. Tyr.*). G. Müller supports this interpretation, not only in his commentary on *Ant.*, but also in a series of articles: "Überlegungen zum Chor der *Ant.*," *Herm.* 89 (1961), 398; *Sophokleische Theologie in der Tragik Antigones*, Der Humanismus und die Auslegung klass. Texte, Frankfurt 1965, 14; "Chor und Handlung bei den griech. Tragikern.," *Sophokles*, Wege der Forschung 95, Darmstadt 1967, 212; "Das zweite Stasimon des *König Ödipus*," *Herm.* 95 (1967), 269. The opposing view: A. Lesky, "Der Herren eigener Geist: Das Altertum und jedes neue Gute," *Festschr. Schadewaldt*, Stuttgart 1970, 79. On the problems of the chorus: C. A. Uhsadel, "Der Chor als Gestalt: Seine Teilnahme am Geschehen sophokleischer Stücke," Diss. Tübingen 1969. For the performance of the choruses, T. B. L. Webster, *The Greek Chorus*, London 1970, is important.

53. *Herm.* 69 (1934), 61. The one-sidedness that denies any possible contemporary references has not gone without opposition: Funke, *Trag. Schuld* 95. 3, who believes that a reference to Kreon is intended (see his essay cited for the play). J. Goth, op. cit., 64, esp. 67. 1, is excellent. J. Burckhardt, *Griech. Kulturgesch.* 2. 285 (in the Kröner edition) rightly said that Sophokles "treats the chorus alternately as a real and as an ideal component." Ehrenberg (61 = 75) carefully illuminates the problems of the ode. In the foreword to the anthology *Sophokles* cited in the previous note, H. Diller (5) rejects elements of personality in Sophokles, but limits this exclusion with an "almost always."

54. Thus Ehrenberg (see previous note).

55. B. Alexanderson, "Die Stellung des Chores in der *Ant.*," *Eranos* 64 (1966), 85.

56. Recently: E. J. Messmer, "The Double Burial of Polyneices," *Class. Journ.* 37 (1941/42), 515; J. L. Rose, "The Problem of the Second Burial in Soph. *Ant.*," *Class. Journ.* 47 (1951/52), 219; E. Struck, "Der zweimalige Gang der Antigone zur Leiche des Polyneikes," *Gymn.* 60 (1953), 327; I. Errandonea, "La doble visita de Antigona al cadaver de su hermano Polinices," *Est. Clás.* 3 (1955), 111; W. M. Calder iii, *Gr., Rom. and Byz. Stud.* 9 (1968), 391, with much older bibl.

57. For the almost unmanageable bibliography on the subject, an overview is given by M. Duvoisin, "A propos des vers 903–915 de l'*Antigone* de Sophocle," *Mem. de Fac. des. Lett. de*

Lausanne, 1965 (typ.) For further help we refer the reader to H. F. Johansen, *Lustrum* 1962/7 (1963), 198, who also offers good criticism of the curious attempts to explain the verses as a result of Antigone's mental derangement.

58. *La tragédie et l'homme*, Neuchâtel 1951, 92. Though not decisive for the question, the parallels from the East and from modern popular poetry offered by J. T. Kakridis, *Homeric researches*, Lund 1949, 152, are interesting.

59. Thus, we cannot consider, with E. de Strycker, "Het eerste stasimon van Soph. *Ant.*," *Miscellanea J. Gessler* II, Louvain 1948, 1168, a reference in lines of this ode to the foundation of Thurioi.

60. In contrast to this, it is a less important question whether we should think of Perikles at v. 8 (στρατηγός), as Ehrenberg cautiously proposes (105; 129 in the Germ. ed.). Opposed by H. Funke. op. cit., 39, 49, and F. Schachermeyr, *Wien. Stud.* 79 (1966), 54. Cf. further Goossens, *Eur.*, 26. 22. H. Lloyd-Jones, *Journ. Hell. Stud.* 76 (1956), 113; F. Wehrli, *Mus. Helv.* 15 (1958), 246.

61. ANNOTATED EDITIONS: R. Cantarella, Naples 1926; D. Bassi, Naples 1931; J. C. Kamerbeek, Leyden 1946 (his large commentary, without text), Leyden 1959; C. Riba (with the *Ant.* in a Catalan translation), Barcelona 1951; G. Ammendola, Florence 1953; G. Schiassi, Torino 1953; G. Norcio, Florence 1966. ON INTERPRETATION (in addition to the articles mentioned for the dating problem): 1. Errandonea, "Deianeira vere ΔHI-ANEIPA," *Mnem.* 55 (1927), 145, and "El 'problema' de las *Traquinas*," *Actas del I. Congreso Español de Est. Clas.*, Madrid 1958, 472; T. B. L. Webster, "Soph. *Trach.*," *Greek Poetry and Life: Essays Pres. to G. Murray*, Oxford 1936, 164; F. R. Earp, "The *Trachiniae*," *Class. Rev.* 53 (1939), 113; G. M. Kirkwood, "The Dramatic Unity of Soph. *Trach.*," *Trans. Am. Phil. Ass.* 72 (1941), 203; F. Stoessl, *Der Tod des Herakles*, Zurich 1945; V. Ehrenberg, "Tragic Heracles," *Aspects of the Ancient World*, Oxford 1945, 144; G. Murray, "Heracles, The best of men," *Greek Studies*, Oxford 1946, 106, and, in German, in *Sophocles*, Wege der Forschung 95, Darmstadt 1967, 325; G. Carlsson, "Le personnage de Déjanire chez Sénèque et chez Sophocle," *Eranos* 45 (1947), 59; J. M. Linforth, *The Pyre on Mount Oeta in Soph.* Trach., Univ. of Calif. Publ. in Class. Phil. 14/7 (1952), 255; A. Beck, "Der Empfang Ioles," *Herm.* 81 (1953), 10; E. R. Schwinge, *Die Stellung der* Trach. *im Werk des Soph.*, Hypomn. I, Göttingen 1962 (with comprehensive bibl.); S. G. Kapsomenos, *Soph.* Trach. *und ihr Vorbild*, Athens 1963. TRANSLATIONS: E. S. Barlow, Manchester 1938; G. Murray, London 1947; L. J. Morrison, Eton 1951; E. F. Watling, see on the *Aias*.

62. F. Stoessl, op. cit. is much more confident.

63. On this, see E. R. Schwinge, op. cit., 25. 3, with bibl.

64. Except for Hyllos, they have no role in the play. The poet later (1153) gives reasons for their absence.

65. If 88 f. and 90 f. really are doublets, as Kamerbeek assumes with good reason in his commentary, then this, too, points to the sketchy character of the section.

66. In vv. 171 f. the prophetic oak and a pair of doves are mentioned. It is difficult to decide whether prophesying birds or priestesses, who are called doves, are meant here.

67. On the allotment of lines in this whole section see Kraus, 137.

68. Such an explanation seems to me (Kamerbeek agrees) more probable than the assumption that Hyllos comes out of the house.

69. Kraus (138) has an excellent treatment of the section and also explains the unavoidable but not drastic textual emendations. His schema: Herakles, ABCA; the old man and Hylos, C; Herakles, DBCD.

70. Important for the oracles in the play and in Sophokles generally is H. Diller, "Göttliches und menschliches Wissen bei Soph.," *Kieler Universitätsreden* 1, 1950 = *Gottheit und Mensch in der Tragödie des Soph.*, Darmstadt 1963 (on the *Trach.*, p. 15); E. R. Schwinge, op. cit., 95.

71. Thus especially Johanna Heinz in the article mentioned above at n. 28; and Kirkwood 290, now also in "*Sophokles*," Wege der Forschung 95, Darmstadt 1967, 184.

72. E. R. Schwinge, op. cit., 27, is good; however, I cannot agree with his view, adopted by K. Matthiessen, Hypomn. 4 (1964), 22. 1, that Euripides was decisively influenced in his technique of introduction and construction of the intrigues by the *Trach.* The differences are simply too great.

73. E. R. Schwinge, op. cit., 27, and Funke, 114, are good; also J. Carrière, *Rev. Et. Gr.* 79 (1966), 15. 36. Opposed: I. Errandonea, *Sófocles,* Madrid 1958, 205 (cf. p. 208); now M. P. Houghton, *Pallas,* 1962, 71.

74. Reinhardt's interpretation has given rise to numerous debates, whose particulars may be found in H. F. Johansen, *Lustrum* 1962/7 (1963), 265.

75. Op. cit.

76. "Un debat sur la tragédie Grecque," *Rev. de Theol. et de Philos.* 99 (1966), 252.

77. ANNOTATED EDITIONS: A. Verhoven, Turnhout 1939; L. Roussel, Paris 1940 (learned but problematic); W. Schmitz, Paderborn 1946; A. Willem, 5th ed., Liège 1949; D. Pieraccioni, Florence, 1966; E. Janssens, Namur 1953 (modest) and 1956; G. Ammendola, Turin 1954; G. Schiassi, Bologna 1967. THE LEADING COMMENTARIES (without text): J. C. Kamerbeek, Leyden 1967; T. M. Gould (ed. and transl.), Prentice-Hall, 1970; O. Longo, Florence 1972. Wilamowitz's translation was published by K. Kappus, Berlin 1939 (1949) with a Greek text that attempts to reproduce that used by Wilamowitz. B. Wyss prepared the text for the Ed. Helv.; O. Regenbogen, 1949, for the Heidelberg edition; F. Salomon, Vienna 1950, for the Austrian Gymnasien. TEXT AND TRANSLATION with *Oid. Kol.*: I. Errandonea, Barcelona 1959. A useful aid is offered by R. Schmidt, Frankfurt 1959. ESSAYS: M. Croiset, *Oedipe-roi de Sophocles,* Paris, n.d., E. Bignone, "Introd. all'*Ed. re,*" *At. e Roma* 5 (1937), 3; M. Delcourt, *Oed. ou la légende du conquérant,* Bibl. de la Fac. de phil. Liège, fasc. 104, Paris 1944; R. A. Pack, "Fate, Chance, and Trag. Error," *Am. Journ. Phil.* 60 (1939), 350; E. T. Owen, "Drama in Soph. *Oed. Tyr.,*" *Univ. of Toronto Quart.* 10 (1940/41), repr. in Twentieth Century Interpretations (see below); L. Deubner, *Oedipusprobleme,* Abh. Preuss. Ak. Phil.-hist. Kl. 1942/4; K. Reinhardt, *Geist. Überlief.* 2 (1942), 53 (synopsis of individual sections with Goethe's *Tasso*); A. Wilhelm, "Zu Soph. *K. Oid.,*" *Herm.* 78 (1934), 204; O. Küster, *Über die Schuld des Königs Oed.: Beitr. zur geistigen Überlieferung,* Godesberg 1947, 167; E. Schlesinger, *El Edipo rey de Sof.,* Univ. Nac. de la Plata, 1950; W. C. Helmbold, "The Paradox of Oedipus," *Am. Journ. Phil.* 72 (1951), 293; C. Diano, "Edipo, figlio della τύχη," *Dioniso* 15 (1952), 56; I. Errandonea, "Das zweite Stasimon des *König Oed.* von Soph.," *Herm.* 81 (1953), 129; G. Zuntz, "Oedipus und Gregorius," *Ant. und Abendl.* 4 (1954), 191 = *Sophokles,* Wege der Forschung 95, Darmstadt 1967, 348; B. M. W. Knox, "Why is Oed. called Tyrannus?" *Class. Journ.* 50 (1954/55), 97; "The Date of the *Oed. Tyr.,*" *Am. Journ. Phil.* 77 (1956), 133, and *Oed. at Thebes,* New Haven, Conn. 1957, repr. 1966; J. Carrière, "Ambiguité et vraisemblance dans *Oedipe-Roi,*" *Pallas* 4 (1956), 5; H. Drexler, "Die Teiresiasszene des *König Oed.,*" *Maia* 8 (1956), 3; W. Schadewaldt, "Der *König Oed.* des Soph. in neuer Deutung," *Schweiz. Monatsh.* 36 (1956), 21 = *Hellas und Hesperien,* 277; H. Musurillo, "Sunken Imagery in Soph. *Oed.,*" *Am. Journ. Phil.* 78 (1957), 36; P. W. Harsh, "Implicit and Explicit in the *Oed. Tyr.,*" *Am. Journ. Phil.* 79 (1958), 243; M. Ostwald, "Aristotle on ἁμαρτία and Soph. *Oed. Tyr.,*" *Festschr. E. Kapp,* Hamburg 1958, 93; A. Maddalena, "L'*Edipo Re,*" *Filosofia* 9/3 (1958); W. M. Calder III, "The Staging of the Prologue of *Oed. Tyr.,*" *Phoenix* 13 (1959), 121, and "The Blinding, *Oed. Tyr.* 1271–1274," *Am. Journ. Phil.* 80 (1959), 301; id., "*Oed. Tyr.* 1515–1530," *Class. Phil.* 57 (1962), 219; Thalia P. Feldman, "Taboo in the Oed. Theme," *Trans. Am. Phil. Ass.* 93 (1962), 124 (German in *Sophockles,* Wege der Forschung 95, Darmstadt 1967, 370). Important for the interpretation of the play is von Fritz, 1; G. Kremer, "Strukturanalyse des *Oid. Tyr.* von Soph.," Diss. Tübingen 1963; Funke, 54, 73. P. H. Vellacott, "The Guilt of Oed.," *Greece and Rome* 11 (1964), 137, and *Sophocles and Oedipus,* London 1971; W. Elliger, "Soph. und Apollon," *Synusia,* Pfullingen 1965, 79; E. R. Dodds, "On Misunderstanding the *Oed. Rex.,*" *Greece and Rome* 13 (1966), 37; G. Greifenhagen, "Der Prozess des Ödipus," *Herm.* 94 (1966), 147; J. C. Kamerbeek, "Problemen van de Eenheid en de Zin van Soph. *Oed. Tyr.,*" *Meded. Nederl. Ak. Afd. Letterkunde,* n.s. 29/6 (1966), and "Comments on the Second Stasimon of the

Oed. Tyr.," Wien. Stud. 79 (1966), 80; G. Müller, "Das zweite Stasimon des *König Öd.*," *Herm.* 95 (1967), 269; *Twentieth Century Interpretations of* Oed. Rex, ed. by M. J. O'Brien, Prentice-Hall 1968; A. Cameron, *The Identity of Oedipus the King: Five Essays on the* Oed. Tyr., New York 1968; A. S. McDewitt, "Dramatic Imagery in the Parodos of *Oed. Tyr.*," *Wien. Stud.* n.s. 4 (1970), 28; R. P. Winnington-Ingram, "The Second Stasimon of the *Oed. T.*," *Journ. Hell. Stud.* 91 (1971), 119; E. Staiger, "Soph: *König Öd.*," *Scheidewege* 3 (1973), 74. TRANSLATIONS: K. Schilling, Munich 1941; Donner's transl. newly edited by G. Diener, Bamberg 1949; E. Buschor, Munich 1954; W. Schadewaldt, Frankfurt 1955, now *Griech. Theater*, Frankfurt 1964, 141; K. A. Pfeiff, Göttingen 1969; H. Frey, *Deutsche Sophoklesübersetzungen: Grenzen und Möglichkeiten des Übersetzens am Beispiel der Trag.* König Oed. von Soph., Winterthur 1964; D. Fitts-R. Fitzgerald, New York 1949, London 1951 (on this and other English translations M. J. Costelloe, *Class. Bull.* 26 [1950], 61); B. M. W. Knox, New York 1959; A. Bonnard, Lausanne 1946; S. Quasimodo, Milan 1947; F. Rodríguez Adrados, Madrid 1956.

78. A debate concerning the nature of the plague developed between M. Delcourt, "Les suppliants et leurs rameaux au début d'*Oed. R.*," *Ant. Class.* 6 (1937), 63, and *Stérilités mysterieuses et naissances maletiques*, Bibl. de la Fac. de phil. Liège, fasc. 83, Paris 1938, and G. Daux, "Oed. et le fléau," *Rev. Et. Gr.* 53 (1940), 97. The parallel to the Erinyes' threats in the *Eumenides* was also drawn by M. E. Hirst, "The *Eum.* and the *Oid. Tyr.*," *Class. Rev.* 48 (1934), 170. The reference to the Athenian plague is maintained by W. Schadewaldt, *Soph. u. Athen*, Frankfurt 1935, 18 = *Hellas und Hesperien*, 228, and B. M. W. Knox, op. cit., among others. Cautious judgments are given by H. F. Johansen, *Lustrum* 1962/7 (1963), 229, and J. C. Kamerbeek in his commentary, 28. Untenable is the late date 411 by Perrotta, 257, and C. Diano, op. cit., who operates with political allusions.

79. *Der Mythos von König Oedipus*, 2d ed., Mainz 1964.

80. C. Robert, *Oedipus*, Berlin 1915; L. Deubner, op. cit.; F. Wehrli, "Oidipus," *Mus. Helv.* 14 (1957), 108. The limits of our knowledge are cautiously defined by J. C. Kamerbeek in the introduction to his commentary.

81. J. C. Kamerbeek lists the pertinent passages in his commentary (24).

82. The transmitted text of vv. 227 f. is difficult; ὑπεξέλοι in Dain is an unsatisfactory solution. Among J. C. Kamerbeek's suggestions are an unresolved corruption or a lacuna. The greatest difficulty lies in the contrast between the mild form of banishment in our passage and the violent cursing of the guilty party in v. 246.

83. On the problems of some individual passages see W. Schadewaldt, "Zum zweiten Stasimon des *König Öd.*," *Stud. It.* 27/28 (1956), 489 = *Hellas und Hesperien*, 287; H. F. Johansen, *Lustrum* 1962/7 (1963), 242; J. C. Kamerbeek in his commentary.

84. Reprinted from *Studium Generale* 8 (1955), 195, 229. Cf. further M. Ostwald, op. cit., 93; Funke, 73; R. D. Dawe, "Some Reflections on Ate and Hamartia," *Harv. Stud.* 72 (1968), 89. The subtitle of E. Janssens's older edition (op. cit), "le péché d'intelligence," characterizes a belated straggler.

85. Not to mention the mistake of speaking of a tragedy of resignation, as did R. Müller-Freienfels, *Psychologie der Kunst*, 1, 3d ed., 1923, 228. Well put by H. Pongs, "Psychoanalyse und Dichtung," *Euphorion* 34 (1933), 54: "*Oedipus* is, like every great tragedy, a tragedy of both fate and character at once."

86. Bowra, 210, saw that Oidipous, struck down by the gods, comes close to them in his very fall. Similarly A. Rivier. *Rev. de Theol. et de Philos.* 99 (1966), 253 f.

87. This was already established by Nietzsche in his lecture on King Oidipous. Bowra, 163, is also good.

88. Since the problems involved are similar to those of the first stasimon of the *Ant.*, cf. the bibl. cited there (note 52 above). In particular, we mention the studies of the ode by J. C. Kamerbeek and G. Müller. The latter excludes any reference to the poet's time and claims to see here also a foolish misconception on the part of the chorus, who misinterpret Iokaste's fear as godlessness and express superficial and in fact impious half-truths. The hidden meaning in-

tended by the poet would then become clear if δικαίως (889) were separated from the negation and made the main concept: "when he, i.e., Oidipous, in a just manner, i.e., guiltlessly, achieves no success . . . etc." Thus with an allusion to the guiltless Oidipous, Sophokles would be contradicting the guilt-sin theodicy of Aischylos. It should be clear from our analysis above that we are unable to follow even a single step of this interpretation. Cf. further our study listed for the *Ant.* Extensive bibl. in H. F. Johansen, *Lustrum* 1962/7 (1963), 242. Cf. note 83 above.

89. E. R. Dodds's (op. cit., 46) agreement on this point is especially important to us.

90. There is little hope for I. Errandonea's suggestion (op. cit.) that Laios is intended.

91. Important for the text is A. Wilhelm, op. cit. Bibl. in H. F. Johansen, *Lustrum* 1962/7 (1963), 247, who speaks of a "miserable ending." Further, W. Pötscher, "Soph. *Oid. Tyr.* 1524–1530," *Emerita* 38 (1970), 149.

92. The authenticity of the verses in the *Phoinissai* was challenged by E. Fraenkel, "Zu den *Phoen.* des Eur.," *Sitzb. Bayer. Ak.* 1963/1, 117.

93. ANNOTATED EDITIONS: Still important is G. Kaibel, Leipzig 1896 (1911); M. Untersteiner, Milan 1932; P. Groeneboom, Groningen 1935; G. Ammendola, Florence 1951; text in the Ed. Helv., no. 11; J. H. Kells, Cambridge Greek and Latin Classics, 1973. ESSAYS: L. Roussel, "Le rôle de Pylade," *Et. Class.* 9 (1940), 328; W. Wuhrmann, "Strukturelle Untersuchungen zu den beiden *Elektren* und zum eurip. *Or.*," Diss. Zurich 1940; P. Suys, "Recherches sur l'*El.* de Soph.," *Et. Class.* 10 (1941), 117, 275, and 11 (1942), 73, 204, 355; G. M. Kirkwood, "Two Structural Features of Soph. *El.*," *Trans. Am. Phil. Ass.* 73 (1942), 86; A. Colonna, "Il volto di Elettra nel dramma di Sofocle," *Dioniso* 19 (1956), 14; R. P. Winnington-Ingram, "The *El.* of Soph.: Prolegomena to an Interpretation," *Proc. Cambr. Phil. Soc.* 183 (1954/55), 20; W. Corrigan, "The *El.* of Soph.," *Tulane Drama Review* 1/1 (1955), 36 (short doxography); I. Errandonea, "Le choeur dans l'*El.* de Soph.," *Et. Class.* 23 (1955), 367, and "El coro de la *El.* de Sóf.," La Plata 1968; J. Alsina, "Observaciones sobre la figura de Clitemestra," *Emerita* 27 (1959), 297; W. M. Calder III, "The End of Soph. *El.*," *Gr., Rom. and Byz. Stud.* 4 (1963), 213; I. M. Linforth, *Electra's Day in the Tragedy of Soph.*, Univ. of Calif. Publ. in Class. Phil. 19/2 (1963), 89; H. F. Johansen, "Die *El.* des Soph.: Versuch einer neuen Deutung," *Class. et Med.* 25 (1964), 8; T. M. Woodard, "*El.* by Sophocles. The Dialectical Design," *Harv. Stud.* 68 (1964), 163; and 70 (1965), 195; R. M. Torrance, "Soph.: Some Bearings," *Harv. Stud.* 69 (1965), 307; B. Alexanderson, "On Soph. *El.*," *Class. et Med.* 27 (1966), 79; A. M. Dale, "The *El.* of Soph.," *Essays in honor of Fr. Letters*, Melbourne and Cheshire 1966, 71; C. P. Segal, "The *El.* of Soph.," *Trans. Am. Phil. Ass.* 97 (1966), 473; F. Solmsen, "Electra and Orestes: Three Recognitions in Greek Tragedy," *Meded. Nederl. Ak. Afd. Letterkunden* n.s. 30/2 (1967); Steidle, 91. TRANSLATIONS: Verses 1098–1231 were translated by M. Kommerell, "Werke und Tage," *Festschr. R. A. Schröder*, Hamburg 1938, 88; W. Schadewaldt, *Griech. Theater*, Frankfurt 1964, 201; E. F. Watling, see under *Aias*; L. Traverso, Mazara 1956.

94. Thus in W. Theiler, "Die ewigen Elektren," *Wien. Stud.* 79 (1966), 110. Various dates are discussed by C. P. Segal, op. cit., 533. 77. Further, A. Colonna, "Sulla cronologia dell'*Elettra* di Sof.," *Dioniso* 10 (1947), 204, who suggests a date between 424 and 417, which is too early. A. Vögler is very thorough on the dating question in *Vergleichende Studien zur soph. und eur. El.*, Heidelberg 1967, 86. He considers 415 the earliest possible date and sees a terminus ante in Eur. *Hel.* 1049 f., since in his opinion the passage presupposes Soph. *El.* 56–64 (so also A. M. Dale in her commentary on *Helena*). H. Lloyd-Jones, *Class. Rev.* 83 (1969), 37, correctly maintains the skepticism he proposed in *Ant. Class.* 33 (1964), 372, against a precise dating. For "at the earliest ca. 419" see E. R. Schwinge, *Rhein. Mus.* 112 (1969), 11. The dating question is discussed in the essays on the chronological relationship between the two *Elektra*s, q.v. under Eur. *Elektra*.

95. Fine analysis of this section, as of the rest, in Kraus, 148.

96. Here Klytaimestra and Aigisthos are both presented as the culprits. The epic tradition

allowed for such a variation; cf. A. Lesky, "Die Schuld der Klytaimestra," *Wien. Stud.* n.s. 1 (1967), 5.

97. Not maidens; cf. V. Coulon, *Rev. Et. Gr.* 52 (1939), 1.

98. Verse 199 is odd: "Was it a god or some mortal who did this?" An echo of the double motivation that played a large role in earlier Greek thought.

99. Incomprehensible is I. Errandonea's attempt (op. cit) to make the chorus the driving force in contrast to a more sensitive Elektra.

100. Valuable interpretations in F. Solmsen, op. cit., and Steidle, 94.

101. Responsion surely exists, but its exact determination is complicated by lacunae in the antistrophe; cf. Kraus, 157.

102. Sophokles is less scrupulous than Euripides in matters of probability, but his characters' motivations are occasionally more convincing.

103. Of course it is quite possible that single spoken lines should be assigned to one of the women of the chorus. The distribution in this passage is very uncertain.

104. Was the opening of the door sufficient to reveal the group? Or did servants carry the bier to the front of the house? It is inadvisable to belabor the oft-invoked ekkyklema.

105. C. P. Segal, op. cit., 480, offers an instructive schema that well amplifies earlier statements of my own.

106. Some recent opinions: von Fritz (139), who follows Reinhardt (149); Hans Diller in *Gottheit und Mensch in der Tragödie des Soph.*, Darmstadt 1963, 3; Funke, 151; K. Matthiessen, *El., Taur. Iph., und Hel.*, Hypomn. 4 (1964), 114. 2; A. M. Dale, *Helen*, Oxford 1967; X. A. Vögler, op. cit., 22. 32, with bibliography.

107. "Electra: A Defense of Soph.," *Class. Rev.* 41 (1927), 2 and 163. Opposed by J. D. Denniston, *Eur. El.*, Oxford 1939, xxv. 1. We should also mention Steidle, 91, A. Wasserstein, *Gnom.* 32 (1960), 178, and A. Salmon, "L'ironie tragique dans l'exodos de l'*El.* de Soph.," *Et. Class.* 29 (1961), 269.

108. ANNOTATED EDITIONS: A. Anarratone, Milan 1933; A. Manzoni, Turin 1940; J. C. Kamerbeek, Leyden 1946; A. Taccone, Florence 1948; T. B. L. Webster, Gr. and Latin Class. I, 1969. ESSAYS: N. T. Pratt, "Sophoclean 'Orthodoxy' in the *Phil.*," *Am. Journ. Phil.* 70 (1949), 273; K. I. Vourveris, "Τὸ πρόβλημα τῆς παιδείας εἰς τὸν Φιλ. τοῦ Σοφ.," *Platon* 1 (1949), 129, and Σοφοκλέους Φιλ., Athens 1966; id., Ὁ Φιλ. τοῦ Σοφ.: ἡ αἰωνία τραγῳδία τοῦ ἐφήβου, Athens 1966; L. Radermacher, "Anmerkungen zum *Phil.* und *Oed. Col.*," *Rhein. Mus.* 93 (1950), 158; I. Errandonea, "*Filoctetes*," *Emerita* 23 (1955), 122; 24 (1956), 72; M. H. Jameson, "Politics and the *Phil.*," *Class. Phil.* 51 (1956), 217; I. M. Linforth, *Phil.: The Play and the Man*, Univ. of Calif. Publ. in Class Phil. 15/3 (1965), 95; B. Stumpo, "Il *Filottete* di Sof.," *Dioniso* 19 (1956), 89; R. Muth, "Gottheit und Mensch im *Phil.* des Soph.," *Studi in onore di L. Castiglioni*, Florence 1959, 641; P. W. Harsh, "The Role of the Bow in the *Phil.* of Soph.," *Am. Journ. Phil.* 81 (1960), 408; K. Alt, "Schicksal und Physis in *Phil.* des Soph.," *Herm.* 89 (1961), 141; H. Erbse, "Neoptolemos und Philoktet bei Soph.," *Herm.* 94 (1966), 177; A. E. Hinds, "The Prophecy of Helenus in Soph. *Phil.*," *Class. Quart.* 61 (1967), 169; E. Schlesinger, "Die Intrige im Aufbau von Soph. *Phil.*," *Rhein. Mus.* 111 (1968), 97, 156. ON THE STAGING: A. M. Dale, *Wien. Stud.* 69 (1956), 104. TRANSLATIONS: W. Willige, Stuttgart 1957; E. F. Watling, see under *Aias*.

109. Evidence in Mette, *Verl. Aisch.*, 100.

110. *Hellenika* 14 (1955/56), 449.

111. Reconstruction attempts in Mette, *Verl. Aisch.*, 104; *Lustrum* 1967/12 (1968), 266; Webster, *Eur.*, 58.

112. In the *Little Iliad* Diomedes took Philoktetes away from Lemnos; cf. W. Kullmann, *Die Quellen der Ilias*, Hermes Einzelschriften 14 (1960), 54 (72). He also played a role in Euripides' drama. In Sophokles he appears in the fiction of the emporos.

113. As Steidle, 175, nicely points out, the conviction that Philoktetes' personal intervention is part of the divine plan is already foreshadowed in the words of Neoptolemos, vv. 191 ff.

114. In agreement on this point are Reinhardt, 198; H. Erbse, op. cit., 184; and I. M. Linforth, op. cit., who believes Odysseus knows that Philoktetes must follow him of his own free will, and thus rejects the possibility of ordering his men to drag him to the ship. We doubt that the audience was able to consider this possibility in a scene so full of dramatic movement, and thus to interpret Odysseus in such a manner. Sophokles certainly offers no assistance on the point. Further bibliography on interpreting the passage as a trick in Steidle, 171. 10, who does not, however, share this opinion.

115. Knox, 187. 21, taking issue with Kitto, offers a thorough discussion of the question of Neoptolemos's knowledge; cf. also H. Erbse, op. cit., 184. 2.

116. H. Erbse, op. cit., 178, considers Neoptolemos of lesser importance, but it is revealing how large a role he still plays in Erbse's analysis.

117. The word and related terms: 79, 88, 874, 902, 950, 1014, 1284, 1310, 1372. On the concept of φύσις see F. Heinimann, *Nomos und Physis*, Basel 1945.

118. Goethe, in a Pindaric moment: "Only the acquired side of human nature frequently breaks down in contradictions; what is inborn is ever capable of finding an opening and overcomes its opposition quite often with the greatest success." Quoted by E. Grumach, *Goethe und die Antike*, 2, 1949, 795.

119. If we interpret Odysseus's threat to sail off alone with the bow as a mere bluff, it becomes irrelevant to our question.

120. In the 2d edition of this book, 130, and *Anz. f. d. Altertumsw.* 14 (1961), 19.

121. Opinion is sharply divided. Whitman, 186, interprets the apparition psychologically, Linforth, op. cit., 151, from the necessities of the plot.

122. "Chor und Handlung bei den griech. Tragikern.," *Sophokles*, Wege der Forschung 95, Darmstadt 1967, 215.

123. The same position is now taken also by Uhsadel, 36.

124. ANNOTATED EDITIONS: M. Untersteiner, Turin 1929; D. Bassi, Naples 1935; G. Ammendola, Turin 1953; D. Pierraccioni, Florence 1956. DUAL-LANGUAGE EDITION: J. T. Sheppard, Cambridge 1949. SCHOLIA: V. de Marco, Rome 1952, and, on the MS tradition, "Intorno al testo dell'*Edipo a Colono* in un manoscritto Romano," *Rend. Acc. di Arch. Napoli* 26 (1951), 260. ESSAYS: P. E. Arias, "L'*Ed. a Colono* e l'*Ippolito* nel mito e nell'arte," *Dioniso* 5 (1935/6), 183, on vase-paintings relevant to the play; E. Bignone, "Introduzione all'*Ed. a Col.*," ibid., 149; Walter Nestle, *Gnom.* 14 (1938), 427; R. Camerer, *Gnom.* 15 (1939), 633; G. Méautis, *L'Oedipe à Colone et le culte des héros*, Neuchâtel 1940; A. von Blumenthal, *Herm.* 78 (1943), 276; L. Radermacher, see under *Philoktetes*; I. M. Linforth, *Religion and Drama in Oed. at Colonus*, Univ. of Calif. Publ. in Class. Phil. 14 (1951), 75; A. Lesky, "Zwei Soph.-Interpretationen," *Herm.* 80 (1952), 99; T. G. Rosenmeyer, "The Wrath of Oed.," *Phoenix* 6 (1952), 92; S. M. Adams, "Unity of Plot in the *Oed. Col.*," *Phoenix* 7 (1953), 136; I. Errandonea, "La personalidad del coro base de la unidad en *Edipo en Colono*," *Humanidades* 5 (1953), 199; R. P. Winnington-Ingram, "A Religious Function of Greek Tragedy," *Journ. Hell. Stud.* 74 (1954), 16; E. Fantato Zborowski, "La funzione del coro nell'*Edipo a Colono* di Sof.," *Riv. Stud. Class.* 4 (1956), 99; H. W. Schmidt, "Das Spätwerk des Soph.: Eine Strukturanalyse des *Oid. auf Kol.*," Diss. Tübingen 1961. ON THE STAGING: A. M. Dale, *Wien. Stud.* 69 (1956), 102. TRANSLATIONS: R. Bayr, Krefeld 1948 (adaptation); E. Buschor, Munich 1954; R. Fitzgerald, New York 1941, London 1957; R. C. Trevelyan, Cambridge 1946; G. Murray, London 1948; M. Meunier, Paris 1945; A. Nucciotti, Milan 1933; D. Sarros, Athens 1937.

125. Thus Schmid, 2. 407; Goossens, 717. 47. Opposed is Pohlenz, 2. 138.

126. The responsion relationships are difficult. We should probably assume a lacuna of four verses after v. 183; cf. Kraus, 170.

127. While at v. 440 it was the city that expelled him, the sons incurring guilt only because of their refusal to help, here (similar to 1356) they must bear the entire burden of the accusation. Yet another version at v. 770.

128. Antilabai are employed with special frequency in *Oid. Kol.* to loosen up the dialogues.

129. Indeed, the similarity extends to addressing the warned party as a child (1420, 1431). Cf. *Seven* 686.

130. Timid people might be calmed by the thought that Theseus took care of these things. Sophokles was not timid.

131. "Nachlese zu Aristoteles' Poetik," *Jub. Ausg.* 38. 83. Noteworthy are the remarks of F. J. Brecht, *Die Antike* 7 (1931), 213, on the work of Count Paul York von Wartenburg, *Die Katharsis des Aristotles und der* Oedipus Coloneus *des Sophokles*, Berlin 1866 (reprinted by K. Gründer, *Zur Philosophie des Grafen Paul York von Wartenburg*, Göttingen 1970, 154–186).

132. *Disputatio de distributione personarum inter histriones in tragoedia Graeca*, Marburg 1840, 42.

133. "The Division of Parts among the Actors in Soph. *Oed. Col.,*" *Class. Quart.* 35 (1941), 139. In his version a parachoregma would take over a few verses of Antigone and Ismene. Among earlier works, we mention H. Kaffenberger, "Das Dreischauspielergesetz in der griech. Trag.," Diss. Giessen 1911; among those more recent, H. W. Schmidt, op. cit., who supports the division of the parts (twice for Theseus).

Fragments

1. E. Siegmann, "Unters. zu Soph. *Ichn.,*" *Hamb. Arb. z. Altertumsw.* 3, Hamburg 1941. TEXT (with apparatus): D. L. Page, *Greek Lit. Pap.* 1950, 26, and V. Steffen, *Satyrographorum Graec. fragm.*, 2d ed., Poznan 1952, 172; he also has the fragments of the other satyr plays. EDITION (with comm. and transl.): D. Ferrante, *I Braccatori*, Naples 1958. TRANSLATIONS: P. Menge, *N. Jahrb.* 2 (1939), 108; two scenes are done by E. Siegmann, *Ant. u. Abendl.* 1 (1945), 18; O. Werner, Stuttgart 1958, with an attempt at poetic restoration. ENGLISH: R. L. Green, Penguin Classics 76, 1957 (with the *Kyklops*). ITALIAN: B. Marzullo in *La Commedia Classica*, Florence 1955; M. Pasquale, *Clizia* (Bari) 4 (1958), 1099. ESSAYS: G. Conflenti, "Il *Ciclope*, gli *Ichneutai* e il dramma satiresco," Rome 1932; A. W. Pickard-Cambridge, "The *Ichn.* of Soph." in *New Chapters in the History of Greek Lit.*, Oxford 1933, 87; V. Steffen, *Studia satyrica* 1, Poznan 1933, and "De Sophoclis Indagatoribus quaestiones aliquot," *Pozn. Towarz. Przyi. Nauk, Prace Kom. Filol.* 11 (1949), 83; C. T. Murphy, "Quae ratio inter fabulas satyricas et comoediam antiquam intercedat," *Harv. Stud.* 46 (1935), 206; E. Bignone, "Saggio sui 'Satiri segugi' di Sof.," *At. e Roma* 7 (1939), 77. We are much indebted to H. F. Johansen, *Lustrum* 1962/7 (1963), 278, for assembling recent suggestions on individual passages.

2. *N. Jahrb.* 29 (1912), 461.

3. *Ant. u. Abendl.* 6 (1957), 161. 12 = *Sophokles*, Wege der Forschung 95, Darmstadt 1967, 198. 12.

4. The history of the legend is very well presented by L. Radermacher, "Der. hom. Hermeshymnus," *Sitzb. Ak. Wien* 213/1 (1931), 181.

5. *Sitzb. Bayer. Ak. Phil.-hist. Kl.* 1938/2, 23, and ibid., 1958/6. A satyr play is also conjectured by J. T. Kakridis, Ὁ ῎Ιναχος τοῦ Σοφοκλῆ, *Wiss. Jahrb. d. Phil. Fak. Thessalonike* 7 (1960), 101, and C. Pavese, "L'*Inaco* di Sof.," *Quaderni Urbinati* 3 (1967), 31. Such an allotment is preferable to the attempt of W. M. Calder III, "The Dramaturgy of Soph. *Inachus,*" *Gr. and Byz. Stud.* 1 (1958), 137, to prove the lines the remnants of a tragedy. Thus also N. E. Collinge, "Some Reflections on Satyr-plays," *Proc. Cambr. Phil. Soc.* 1958/59, 28. For other satyr plays of Soph.: V. Steffen, "De Sophoclis *Dionysisco,*" *Munera philol., L. Cwiklinski oblata*, Poznan 1936, 84, and *Studia satyrica* 2, Poznan 1934, on the *Herakles*. A. von Blumenthal, *Ion von Chios*, Stuttgart 1939, 56, wishes to see a satyr play in *P. Oxy.* 8, 1083 as had Hunt. The allotment to the *Phoinix* is problematic. On the satyr play *Krisis* with the judgment of Paris: B. Snell, *Die Entdeckung des Geistes*, 3d ed., Hamburg 1955, 327. On the Ἀχιλλέως ἐρασταί, V. Steffen, *Eos* 41 (1940/46), 114.

6. *IG* II², 3091. Pickard-Cambridge, *Festivals*, 54.

7. A. W. Pickard-Cambridge, "The Inscription of Aexone and the Story of Telephus in Sophocles' Plays," *New Chapters in the History of Gr. Lit.*, Oxford 1933, 69. P. Mazon, "Inscription chorégique d'Aixoné," *Mél. Navarre*, Toulouse 1935, 399. On the reconstruction of the trilogy see A. Szantyr, "Die Telephostrilogie des Soph.," *Phil.* 93 (1938), 287 (with older bibl.); S. Srebrny, "Studia Scaenica," *Pol. Ak. Nauk. Arch. Fil.* 5, 1960; E. W. Handley and J. Rea, *The* Telephus *of Eur.*, *Bull. Inst. Class. Stud.*, Suppl. 5, 1957, with the important assignment of *P. Berol.* 9908 (*Berliner Klassikertexte* 5/2, p. 64) and *P. Ryl.* 482 to the *Telephos* of Euripides; Pickard-Cambridge, *Festivals*, 55, 81.

8. See B. Snell, "Zu den Urkunden dramatischer Aufführungen," *Nachr. Ak. Göttigen. Phil.-hist. Kl.* 1966/2, 21.

9. "The Order of Tragedies at the Great Dionysia," *Hermathena* 100 (1965), 21; cf. *Wien. Stud.* 79 (1966), 118.

10. A. Lesky, *RE* 17 (1936), 653; V. Steffen, "Miscellanea tragica," *Tragica* ii, Wroclaw 1954, 73; Akiko Kiso, "The *Niobe* of Soph.: A Glimpse of Soph. as a Young Dramatist," *Journ. Class. Stud.* 13 (1965), 51 (Japanese with English summary).

11. *Neue Fragm. des Aisch. u. Soph.*, Hamburg 1936, 41. O. Skutsch, "Der ennianische Soldatenchor," *Rhein. Mus.* 96 (1953), 193, has strengthened the case that this chorus belongs to the play of Sophokles.

12. *Phil.* 88 (1933), 1. W. Schubart, *Griech. lit. Pap.*, Verh. Sächs, Ak. Phil.-hist. Kl. 97/5, Berlin 1950, 45, conjectures that the remains of a narrow strip of parchment from a codex are fragments of a commentary on this play. The uncertainty of this assumption is emphasized by L. Alfonsi, "Sui Papiri Schubart," *Aegyptus* 33 (1953), 299. Cf. further C. E. Fritsch (see previous note), 54.

13. "A Reconstruction of Soph. *Polyxena*," *Gr., Rom. and Byz. Stud.* 7 (1966), 31.

14. On this, Webster, *Eur.*, 75.

15. *Eur.* Hippolytos, Oxford 1964, 22; on Seneca, 30. Snell, *Scenes*, 46, correctly stresses that we know next to nothing about the nature of the Sophoklean *Phaidra*. On the play also, Goossens, *Eur.*, 150; H. Herter, *Rhein. Mus.* 114 (1971), 44.

16. F. Stoessl, *Apollonios Rhodios*, Bern 1941, 120, goes rather far in setting up a complete scenario of this play.

17. A date of about 429 is given by I. Cazzaniga, *La saga di Itis nella tradizione letteraria e mitografica greco-romana*, i, Milan 1950, and G. Mihailow, "Sur le *Téré* de Soph.," *Ann. mus. nat. arch. Plovdiv* 2 (1950), 39; id., "La légende de Téré," *Ann. Univ. Sofia Fac. de Phil.* 50/2 (1956), 88. In a thorough analysis of the question with much older bibliography, Goossens, *Eur.*, 295. 18, arrives at the period 431–424, which he then narrows down to 428–425. Cf. Aristoph. *Av.*, esp. 100 f. (pointed out by W. Kraus).

Dramatic Form and Language

1. To the works cited in the bibliography and those listed under Aischylos are added: H. C. Jaene, "Die Function des Pathologischen im Aufbau soph. u. eur. Trag.," Diss. Kiel 1929; W. M. A. van de Wijnpersse, *De Terminologie van het Jachtwezen bij Soph.*, Amsterdam 1929; S. Rieger, "Die Bildsprache des Soph.," Diss. Breslau 1934; T. B. L. Webster, "Soph. and Ion of Chios," *Herm.* 71 (1936), 263, and "A Study of Greek Sentence Construction," *Am. Journ. Phil.* 62 (1941), 385; V. de Falco, *L'evoluzione tecnica nelle parodoi e negli stasimi di Sof.*, Naples 1937; I. Errandonea, "Il coro como elemento integrante en la tragedia de Sof.," *Emerita* 10 (1942), 28, and "La constanzia personal del coro sofocleo en sus siete tragedias," *Helmantica* 7 (1956), 401; id., *Sófocles: Investigaciones sobre la estructura dramática de sus siete tragedias y sobre la personalidad de sus coros*, Madrid 1958; F. R. Earp, *The Style of Soph.*, Cambridge 1944; P. T. Stevens, "Colloquial Expressions in Aischylos and Soph.," *Class. Quart.* 39 (1945),

95; J. C. F. Nuchelmans, "Enige opmerkingen over de taal van de Attische tragedie," in *De Antiecke Tragedie*, Leyden 1947, 122; id., *Die Nomina des soph. Wortschatzes*, Utrecht 1949; R. F. Goheen, *The Imagery of Soph.* Antigone: *A Study of Poetic Language and Structure*, Princeton 1951; G. M. Kirkwood, "The Dramatic Role of the Chorus in Soph.," *Phoenix* 8 (1954), 1; H. Diller, "Menschendarstellung und Handlungsführung bei Soph.," *Ant. u. Abendl.* 6 (1957), 157 = *Sophokles*, Wege der Forschung 95, Darmstadt 1967, 190; R. B. Moulin, "L'élément homérique chez les personnages de Soph.," *Ann. Fac. de lettres Aix-en-Prov. Série travaux et mémoires* 40 (1966), 251; H. Musurillo, *The Light and the Darkness: Studies in the Dramatic Poetry of Soph.*, Leyden 1967; A. A. Long, *Language and Thought in Soph.: A Study of Abstract Nouns and Poetic Technique*, London, 1968. The works of G. Müller on Soph. choruses were cited in connection with the *Ant.* U. Parlavantza-Friedrich, *Täuschungsszenen in den Trag. des Soph.*, Berlin 1969. On metrics see A. M. Dale, "Lyrical Clausulae in Soph.," *Greek Poetry and Life: Essays Pres. to G. Murray*, Oxford 1936, 181; H. M. Macomber, "De licentiis metricis quae in canticis Soph. reperiuntur," *Harv. Stud.* 48 (1937), 203; D. Korzeniewski, "Interpretationen zu soph. Chorliedern," *Rhein. Mus.* 104 (1961), 193, and "Zum Verhältnis von Wort und Metrum in soph. Chorliedern," ibid. 105 (1962), 142; H. A. Pohlsander, *Metrical Studies in the Lyrics of Soph.*, Leyden 1964; K. Thomamüller, *Die aiolischen und daktyloepitritischen Masse in den Dramen des Soph.*, Hamburg 1965; P. E. Easterling, "Repetitions in Soph.," *Herm.* 101 (1972), 14; Kraus, see bibliography.

2. On this, T. Krischer, "Das Problem der trilogischen Komposition und die dramaturgische Entwicklung der attischen Tragödie," Diss. Frankfurt 1960.

3. On the passages, see chapter 2, note 14, and Pickard-Cambridge, *Festivals*, 139. On the text of Aristotle see R. Kassel, *Rhein. Mus.* 105 (1962), 117.

4. Good observations on the three-part dialogue are in J. Heinz, "Zur Datierung der *Trach.*," *Herm.* 72 (1937), 273.

5. *Journ. Hell. Stud.* 67 (1947), 13. Cf. Webster, *Gr. Theatre Prod.*, 13, and *Gr. Bühnenaltertümer*, 23; Arnott, *Gr. Sc. Conv.*, 93. Kenner, 155, reconciles the differences (as does Bulle) and provides older bibliography.

6. Sophokles as the representative of pure classicism: K. Reinhardt, "Die klass. Philologie und das Klassische," *Geistige Überlieferung* 2 (1942), 54. On his canonical reputation in the fourth century: Xen. *Mem.* 1. 4. 3.

7. In this analysis, which identifies ἦθος and πάθος as the cardinal features of tragic poetry, we cannot help but recognize the polemic against the supremacy of μῦθος supported by Aristotle.

8. Material in Schmid, 2. 486, in the notes and in Webster, 145. F. R. Earp, op. cit., follows closely the development from a style closer to Aischylos to a later idiom.

9. For the relationship to Homer: H. W. Miller "Ὁ Φιλόμερος Σοφοκλῆς and Eustathius," *Class. Phil.* 41 (1946), 99.

10. Also in Dion. Hal. Περὶ μιμ. 2. 11 we read about criticism of the διάκενος κόμπος (vacuous boasting).

11. An observation on the occasional use of a popular expression in L. Radermacher, "Koine," *Sitzb. Ak. Wien. Phil.-hist. Kl.* 1947, 9. 1.

12. On the prevalence of abstract nouns, see esp. A. A. Long, op. cit.

13. "Sophocles and the Perfect Number," *Proc. Brit. Ac.* 16 (1930).

14. Cf. L. Radermacher on *Ai.* 986. He also discusses rhetorical doubling (on 1215) and the polar method of expression (on 1284).

15. Cf. A. Lesky, *Thalatta*, Vienna 1947, 227.

The Interpretation of Sophokles Today

1. A fine discussion of the various schools of Sophoklean interpretation in the early nineteenth century is offered by H. Schrader, *Hölderlins Deutung des* Oed. *und der* Ant., Bonn 1933. He distinguishes three viewpoints: the aesthetic, that of classicism and romanticism

(though differences exist between them); the ethical view of Hegel; and the religious view of Hölderlin.

2. Schwinge, *Stich.*, 24, correctly opposes a prevalence of plot over character (he uses the term without misgivings). Older views opposed to Tycho's partiality: E. Wolff, "Sophokles," *N. Jahr.* 7 (1931), 393; K. von Fritz, ibid. 8 (1932), 339; A. Lesky, ibid., 400. Good discussion of Sophoklean interpretation in L. Bieler, "Antigones Schuld," Vienna 1937, 4.

3. H. Diller, "Über das Selbstbewusstsein der soph. Personen," *Wien. Stud.* 69 (1956), 70, distinguishes φύσις, a conscious possession that puts its bearer under an obligation, from the τρόποι with which Aischylean characters confront their tragic situations.

4. Additions to the works listed in the bibliography and the bibl. on the individual plays: R. Camerer, "Zorn und Groll in der soph. Trag.," Diss. Freiburg im Breisgau 1936; M. Untersteiner, "La religiosità di Sof.," *Religio* 12 (1936), 1; A. von Blumenthal, "Die Erscheinung der Götter bei Soph.," *Welt als Geschichte* 3 (1937), 137; P. Donnini, *Il dramma di Sof.*, Naples 1937; S. Fiorini, *Elementi di umanità nel teatro di Sof.*, Rome 1938; J. A. Moore, *Soph. and Arete*, Cambridge, Mass. 1938; E. Busch, "Die Religion des Soph.," *Ztschr. f. Missionskunde und Rel. Wiss.* 54 (1939), 210; P. Tournaud, "Essai sur Soph." (cf. *Et. Class.* 12 [1943], 57); J. C. Opstelten, "De tragische held bij Soph. en zijn dichter," *De Antieke Tragedie*, Leyden 1947, 56, and "Humanistisch en religieus standpunt in de moderne beschouwing van Soph., *Meded. Nederl. Ak. Afd. Letterkunde* n.s. 17/1, Amsterdam 1954; W. Schadewaldt, *Soph. und das Leid*, 4th ed., Potsdam 1948 = *Hellas und Hesperien*, 231. The essay is joined with those of Diller and Lesky (below) in *Gottheit und Mensch in der Trag. des Soph.*, Darmstadt 1963; H. Diller, *Göttliches und menschliches Wissen bei Soph.*, Kiel 1950; A. Lesky, "Soph. und das Humane," *Alman. Öst. Ak.* 101 (1951), 222 = *Ges. Schr.*, 190; H. W. van Pesch, "De idee van de menselijke beperktheid bij Soph.," Diss. Leyden 1953; R. Schaerer, *L'homme antique et la structure du monde intérieur d'Homère à Socrate*, Paris 1958, 171; Goossens, 146; J. C. Kamerbeek, "Individu et norme dans Soph.," *Le théâtre tragique* i: *Le monde antique*, Paris 1962, 29; R. P. Winnington-Ingram, "Tragedy and Greek Archaic Thought," *Festschr. Kitto*, London 1965, 31; F. Rodríguez Adrados, "Sófocles y su época," *Cuadernos de la "Fundación Pastor"* 13, Madrid 1966, 77; S. Melchinger, *Sophokles*, Velber b. Hannover 1966 (Friedrich's *Dramatiker der Weltlit.*, 12); J. S. Lasso de la Vega, "El dolor y la condición humana en le teatro de Sóf.," *Asclepio* 20 (1968), 3; G. Germain, *Sophocle, Ecrivains de toujours*, Paris 1969. A valuable survey of the recent controversial opinions on the Sophoklean image of divinity and mankind is offered by H. F. Johansen, *Lustrum* 1962/6 (1963), 152; H. Lloyd-Jones, *The Justice of Zeus*, Berkeley 1971, chap. 5.

5. "You could not learn divinity, if the gods conceal it, even if you were to set out and examine everything."

The warning about impertinent inquiries into the unknowable is repeated in fragments 80N, 83 P; 671N, 747P; 759N, 834P, but we must bear in mind that in all these cases the context is unknown.

6. *Vita* 12: θεοφιλής . . . ὡς οὐκ ἄλλος (reverent . . . like no other); schol. *El.* 823: εἷς ἦν τῶν εὐσεβεστάτων (He was one of the most pious men). Although these statements refer to various biographical details, nonetheless they reflect the impression of his work.

7. Schmid, 2. 375. 3, interprets the words as blasphemy and counts them among the "Euripidean" elements. Evidently he assigns them to Hyllos. G. Murray, "Heracles, 'The best of men,'" *Greek Studies*, Oxford 1946, 122, assigns the lines to the chorus but believes them to be an indictment of Zeus. It is inconceivable that Sophokles concluded a play in such a way. The right solution is to assign the verses to the chorus or chorus leader and interpret them as a correction of the accusation in Hyllos's words. Thus Pohlenz, 2. 89, and others, among them Bowra, 158, with excellent reasoning, and J. C. Kamerbeek in his commentary. Fragment 103N, 107P, with a criticism of the gods and a statement about how things *should* be, sounds Euripidean, but we do not know the context.

8. Kirkwood, 176, 274 ff., is good on the harshness of this world view; also G. Müller in the comm. on *Ant.* 273.

9. Jones's warning (172) is justified, but not his attempt to eliminate from Sophokles' world view the concept of the gods as a guiding force (though not comprehensible to man).

10. *The Greeks and the Irrational*, Berkeley 1951, 49.

11. Op. cit., 31.

12. F. Rodríguez Adrados, op. cit., who correctly places Sophokles next to Herodotos as the bearer of a theonomic world view and points out that the tragic situations involving decisions that we saw in Aischylos do not recur in his work, is excellent on this.

13. Cf. on this Funke, 87.

14. "I learn what can be learned, I seek what can be found; but what can be done by prayer I request from the gods."

15. An important chapter, "Die dramatische Verwendung der Orakel," is contained in E. R. Schwinge's *Die Stellung der* Trach. *im Werk des Soph.*, Hypomn. 1, Göttingen 1962, 93.

16. Excellent on this is F. Dirlmeier, "Der *Aias* des Soph.," *N. Jahrb.* 1938, 317. In a few pages, J. C. Kamerbeek, op. cit., impressively outlines the characteristics of Sophokles' image of man. Whitman, in his book on Sophokles, is the most radical in his one-sided interpretation of the tragedies from the standpoint of the heroic figures.

17. W. Schadewaldt's essay *Sophokles und das Leid* (see n. 4 above) is among the finest statements ever made about the poet.

18. J. C. Kamerbeek, "Sophocles et Héraclite," *Studia varia C. W. Vollgraff oblata*, Amsterdam 1948, 84. From an article in *Ant. u. Abendl.* by E. Dönt, I have taken the following parallels: *Ai.* 674–676 ~ *DK* 22B 67, 111. fr. 771P ~ *DK* 22 B 93; fr. 919P ~ *DK* 22B 45. fr. 923P ~ *DK* 22B 34. Herakleitan thought is also echoed by fr. 576, 871P.

19. Cf. A. Lesky, *Herm.* 80 (1952), 95 = *Ges. Schr.*, 180.

20. Schmid provides sections with rich material on the later influence of the tragedians. For Soph. we add the tenth chapter in Perrotta and G. L. Luzzatto, "Traduzioni e imitazioni antiche di Sof.," *Dioniso* 6 (1937/8), 109, 180, 253. For a collection of the material, K. Heinimann, *Die trag. Gestalten der Griechen in der Weltlit.*, Leipzig 1920, is still useful. Excellent, too, is Käte Hamburger; see bibliography.

CHAPTER 6

Biographical Notes

1. Murray, *Eur.* 65 f., takes it for granted that the poet saw combat as a soldier. But since all evidence is lacking, Schmid's opposing view (3. 318. 10) appears justified. The report that Eur. took part in an embassy to Syrakuse (a scholiast's inference from Aristot. *Rhet.* 1348b 15) is very uncertain. Cf. Goossens, 671. 4, who also correctly casts doubt on the stories of Eur.'s journeys in Athen. 2. 61B (to the isle of Ikaros) and Diog. Laert. 3. 6 (to Egypt, with a foolish tale about *Iph. T.* 1193).

2. The best edition of the poet's *genos* with its many appendixes, preserved in several MSS, is in the Eur. scholia edited by E. Schwartz, Berlin 1887/91, from which our references are taken. The other sources (particularly important are the *Suda* article and Gell. *Noct. Att.* 15. 20) are collected in the edition of A. Nauck, Leipzig 1871, I. x. Further, M. Delcourt, "Biographies anciennes d'Eur.," *Ant. Class.* 2 (1933), 271; P. T. Stevens, *Journ. Hell. Stud.* 86 (1956), 87. Instructive—though not for the life of the poet—are the remains from the end of the sixth book of *Bioi* by the Peripatetic Satyros, in which Euripides is discussed in dialogue form: *P. Oxy. 9* (1912), 1176; J. von Arnim, *Suppl. Eurip.*, Bonn 1913, 3; G. Arrighetti, "Satiro. Vita di Euripide," *Studi Class. e Orient.* 13 (1964); I. Gallo, *La vita di Eur. di Satiro e gli studi sulla*

biografia antica. Parola del passato 1967, 134; F. Schachermeyr, "Zur Familie des Euripides," *Antidosis: Festschr. W. Kraus*, Vienna 1972, 306.

3. The complicated business of synchronization was demonstrated and explained with great erudition by F. Jacoby, *FGrH* in the comm. on 239A 50, 63 and 244F 35.

4. Thus in the declamation against the athletes, fr. 282N from the satyr play *Autolykos*, for which Athen. 10. 413C claims dependency on Xenophanes. Further, in a similar attitude, fr. 199, 201N (different in subject but comparable in spirit, fr. 369N). At *El.* 883 there is a possible polemical reference to sports, although Denniston in his comm. (Oxford 1939) is skeptical.

5. The evidence of his relationship with Sokrates has been examined with positive results by Goossens, 182, 70. Cf. the discussion of the *Hipp.*

6. Wilamowitz, *Herakles* 1. 2d ed., 135, and Murray, *Eur.* 72, date the victory to 420.

7. A thorough treatment with much bibl. in E. Heitsch, "Τὰ θεῶν: Ein Epigramm des Eur.," *Phil.* 111 (1967), 21.

8. Thus Goossens, 195, 340. Webster, *Eur.*, 7, 8, correctly remains skeptical; he also distrusts the late account in *P. Oxy.* 2400 about a trial for impiety because of the *Herakles.*

9. *Vita*, Satyros col. ix. Gellius was shown the "dark and gloomy grotto" during his stay in Athens. The cave of the creative intellectual is a recurring motif: H. Gerstinger, *Wien. Stud.* 38 (1916), 65. 3, with Schmid, 3. 313. 7. Poets and philosophers were commonly pictured by the sea: C. Schneider, *Arch. Rel. Wiss.* 36 (1939), 322; cf. too the lovely passage in Tacitus, *Dial.* 12. Euripides' cave need not for that reason be a fiction. But it is childish of the *Vita* to assert that the poet's favorite haunt produced the wealth of his images taken from the sea. On the closeness to the sea in the language of the three tragedians, cf. *Thalatta*, Vienna 1947, 224.

10. On the problems involved with this number, cf. Webster, *Eur.* 5.

11. Goossens, 661, suggests that the journey to Makedonia was undertaken for the purposes of propaganda, which is highly improbable.

12. As so often in Euripides, the other λόγος appears in frr. 777 and 1047N, which have a cosmopolitan ring, but we do not know their contexts.

13. For the bibl, cf. the material cited for the portrait of Aischylos. Further, for Eur.: V. Poulsen, *Les portraits Grecs*, Copenhagen 1954, nos. 11, 23, 24; A. Hekler, *Bildnisse berühmter Griechen*, 3d ed. by H. von Heintze, Berlin 1962, 59 f., plates 32–35. Once again, the most comprehensive overview is offered by G. M. A. Richter, *The Portraits of the Greeks*, London 1965, 133 ff., ill. 717–779.

14. F. Poulsen, op. cit., no. 414, in B. Laurenzi, op. cit., 100; K. Schefold, *Die Bildnisse der antiken Dichter*, 88. 3, 207.

15. Op. cit., 207.

Manuscript Transmission and Editions

1. C. F. Russo, "Eur. e i concorsi tragici lenaici," *Mus. Helv.* 17 (1960), 165, attempts to make the case that Euripides did not produce any plays at all for the Lenaia.

2. Details in Schmid, 3. 824. 3.

3. W. S. Barrett, op. cit. 51. 1, assumes there was an uncial MS with these plays (though the alphabetical order, certainly intended but quite inexact, presents problems), and considers two codices with five plays each as the source of our group; his position is similar to Snell's. There is no serious difficulty involved in assuming the loss of a container or codex with six plays (*Theseus, Thyestes, Ino, Ixion*, and the two *Hipp.*) between the two groups listed above.

4. W. S. Barrett, op. cit. 59. 1 mentions E. Fraenkel's interesting remark that Wilamowitz occasionally doubted his theory: *Sitzb. Preuss. Ak.* 1911, 505 = *Kl. Schr.*, 1. 322.

5. In his discussion of Turyn's book, *Dioniso* 20 (1957), 115 f.

6. In *Geschichte der Textüberlieferung der antiken und mitteralterlichen Literatur* 1, Zurich 1961, 274.

7. "De codicis Euripidei fragmento nuper reperto," *Latinitas* 4 (1966), 284; "A Fragment of a Euripides Manuscript in the John Rylands Library," *Bull. of the John Ryl. Libr.* 49 (1967), 497.

8. Photographic reproduction: J. A. Spranger, Florence 1920. Turyn offers a thorough description and bibliography for all the MSS mentioned here.

9. Photographic reproduction: J. A. Spranger, Florence 1937. S. G. Daitz, *A Facsimile Edition with Commentary*, Berlin 1970. On the history of this witness, cf. di Benedetto, 73.

10. Photographic reproduction: J. A. Spranger, Florence 1935.

11. Cf. also T. W. Allen, *Journ. Hell. Stud.* 57 (1937), 109.

12. In his critique of Turyn, *Gnom.* 30 (1958), 502.

Dramatic Works

1. T. Zielinski, *Tragodumenon libri tres*, Cracow 1925; C. B. Ceadel, "Resolved Feet in the Trimeter of Euripides and the Chronology," *Class. Quart.* 35 (1941), 66. But it is impossible to use the progression of resolutions as the basis for mathematically precise conclusions, as A. Vögler has correctly pointed out: cf. *Studien zur soph. und eur. El.*, Heidelberg 1967, 61. 26.

2. This applies especially to the works influenced by H. Grégoire, such as those of Delebecque. Despite his greater caution, Goossens, in his book on Euripides, also belongs in this camp. The inevitable reaction set in with the *Political Plays* by Zuntz and his lecture at the Congressus Madvigianus 1954 (1956). But in our discussion of the plays it will be seen that the baby is occasionally thrown out with the bathwater.

3. Chronological synopses in Webster (3), who also expressed his views on the question in "Chronological Notes on Eur.," *Wien. Stud.* 79 (1966), 112. Further, F. Stoessl's "Nachtrag zu Eur.," *RE* S 11 (1968), 658. An attempt to arrange a large number of plays chronologically was made by W. Theiler, "Die ewigen Elektren," *Wien. Stud.* 79 (1966), 102. M. Fernandez-Galiano, "Estado actual de los problemas de cronologia euripidea," *Actas del III congreso español de estud. clas.*, Madrid 1968, 1. 321.

4. M. Papathomopoulos, *Recherches de Papyrologie* 3 (1964), 40.

5. On the history of the myth: A. Lesky, "Alkestis, der Mythus und das Drama," *Sitzb. Ak. Wien. Phil.-hist. Kl.* 203/2, 1925; G. Megas, *Arch. Rel. Wiss.* 30 (1933), 1. A. Wesselsky, "Das Geschenk der Lebensjahre," *Arch. Orientálni* 10 (1937), 79; M. Gaster, "Zur Alkestis-Sage," *Byz. Neugr. Jahrb.* 15 (1939), 66.

ANNOTATED EDITIONS: L. Weber, Leipzig 1930; A. Maggi, Naples 1935; D. F. W. van Lennep, Leyden 1949; A. M. Dale, Oxford 1954 (the standard edition); G. Paduano (I classici della nuova Italia 59), Florence 1969. WITH TRANSLATION: J. Alsina, Barcelona 1966. INTERPRETATION: L. Séchan, *Le dévouement d'Alceste*, Paris 1927; M. Valgimigli, *Atti Ven.* 92 (1932/33), 111; Van Lennep, 33; H. Dörrie, "Zur Dramatik der eur. Alk.," *N. Jahrb.* 1939, 176; D. M. Jones, "Eur. Alc.," *Class. Rev.* 62 (1948), 50; C. del Grande, "Interpretazione dell'*Alcesti* di Eur.," *Rendiconti Acc. Bologna* 1949/50; G. Italie, "De Euripide Aeschyli imitatore," *Mnem.* ser. 4, 3 (1950), 177; K. von Fritz, "Eur. Alk. und ihre modernen Nachahmer und Kritiker," *Ant. u. Abendl.* 5 (1956), 27 = *Ant. u. mod. Trag.*, 256; A. J. Festugière, "Vraisemblance psychologique et forme litéraire chez les anciens," *Phil.* 102 (1958), 21 (on the farewell scene); C. R. Beye, "Alcestis and her Critics," *Gr., Rom. and Byz. Stud.* 2 (1959), 109; O. Vicenzi, "Alkestis und Admetos," *Gymn.* 67 (1960), 517; W. D. Smith, "The ironic structure in Alc.," *Phoenix* 14 (1960), 127; U. Albini, "L'*Alc.* di Eur.," *Maia* n.s. 13 (1961), 3 (also on the later versions of the story); Garzya, *Pensiero*, 15; E. R. Schwinge, *Die Stellung der Trach. im Werk des Soph.*, Hypomn. 1, Göttingen 1962, 42, and "Verwendung der Stich.," 36; L. Torraca, *Note criticoesegetiche all'Alc. di Eur.*, Naples 1963; Rosenmeyer, *Masks*, 229; A. Lesky, "Der angeklagte Admet.," *Maske und Kothurn* 10 (1964), 203 = *Ges. Schr.*, 281; Anne P. Burnett, "The Virtues of Admetus," *Class. Phil.* 60 (1965), 240; Conacher, 327; Webster, *Eur.*, 48; Chromik, 3; W. Kullmann, "Zum Sinngehalt der eur. Alk.," *Ant. u. Abendl.* 13 (1967), 127; A. Rivier, "Sur un motif de l'*Alc.* d'Eur.," *Actas del III congreso español de estud. clas.*, Madrid 1968, 2. 286; Rohdich, 23; Steidle, 132; Margret Dietrich in the collection of seven Alkestis plays in *Theater der Jahr-hunderte*, Munich-Vienna 1969, 9; G. Paduano, *La formazione del mondo ideologico e poetico di Eur.* Alc.-Med., Pisa 1968; J. R. Wilson, *Twentieth Century Interpretations of Eur.* Alc.: *A Collection of Critical Essays*, Englewood Cliffs, N.J. 1968; C. M. J. Sicking, "Eur. *Alk.*," *Lampas* 2 (1970), 322; E. R. Schwinge, "Zwei sprachliche Bemerkungen zu Eur. *Alk.*," *Glotta* 48 (1970), 36; A. Rivier, "En marge d'*Alc.* et de quelques interpretations récentes," *Mus. Helv.* 29 (1972), 124 and 30 (1973), 130; A. Lesky, "Alkestis und Deianeira," *Miscellanes Tragica in honorem J. C. Kamerbeek*, 1976, 273. TRANSLATIONS: L. Wolde's version was chosen by M. Dietrich for the *Alk.* volume mentioned above. Engl.: D. Fitts-R. Fitzgerald, New York 1936. D. W. Lucas, London 1951. Ital.: Eug. della Valle, Urbino 1956. Dutch: J. M. van Buytenen, Amsterdam 1943.

For an evaluation of the statement in the hypothesis that the *Alk.* was the seventeenth play Euripides composed, cf. our remarks on the *Antigone*, note 34.

6. Cf. Lloyd-Jones, 20.

7. This eliminates the argument of O. Vincenzi, op. cit., that Admetos knew nothing of his wife's promise.

8. The athetesis of the second anapestic passage suggested by Wilamowitz has been rightly rejected by A. M. Dale in her comm.

9. On the uncertainty, see Buchwald, 47. On the play, see Webster, *Eur.* 97; H. J. Mette, *Lustrum* 1967/12 (1968), 216.

10. References to the recent debate can be found in A. Lesky, op. cit. ("Der angeklagte Admet."). Here we can only touch on a few essential points. Especially noteworthy, however, is A. Rivier, op. cit., who has removed any possible stigma from προδοῦναι (250, 275) by comparison with *Hipp.* 1456.

11. A. Lesky, op. cit. ("Der angeklagte Admet."), 293; W. Kullmann, op. cit., 143.

12. Garzya, 15, lays great stress on the motif of salvazione.

13. J. Schmitt, "Freiwilliger Opfertod bei Euripides," *Rel. Vers. u. Vorarb.* 17 (1921); H. Förs, "Dionysos und die Stärke des Schwachen im Werk des Eur.," Diss. Tübingen 1964, 87; Valgiglio, 63. For the *Phrixos* (on both plays with this title see at note reference 284 in Dramatic Works section of this chapter), the sacrifice motif was inferred by W. Schadewaldt, *Herm.* 63 (1928), 1. Also, van Looy, 177, and Webster, *Eur.*, 136, include the motif in their reconstructions of *Phrixos* B.

14. For the category of admiration and its significance in baroque poetry, see esp. Kommerell, 88, 276. The connection between self-sacrifice and admiration was already pointed out by P. Decharme, *Eur.*, Paris 1893, 295.

15. The uncertainty of the hypothesis is emphasized by H. J. Mette, *Lustrum* 1967/12 (1968), 156.

16. W. Schadewaldt, *Herm.* 80 (1952), 46, who assigned PSI 13/1 (1949), 1302 to the play. Webster, *Eur.*, 41, and H. J. Mette (see previous note), 33, follow him. Doubts were raised by van Looy, 127, in his thorough treatment of all the fragments of both Alkmeon tragedies.

17. Printed in Austin, 66, listed by H. J. Mette, *Lustrum* 1967/12 (1968), 235, who discusses the most important fragments in *Verl. Aisch.*, 81. On the reconstruction: H. Metzger, "Apollon 'Lycien' et Télèphe, *Mél. Charles Picard* II, Paris 1949, 746. D. L. Page, *Lit. Pap.*, 130. Webster, *Eur.*, 43, 302.

18. *The* Telephus *of Eur.*, *Bull. Inst. Class. Stud.* Suppl. 5, London 1957.

19. A new hypothesis on a papyrus in Paris in A. Blanchard-A. Bataille, *Recherches de Papyrologie* 3 (1964), 37. ANNOTATED EDITIONS: D. L. Page, Oxford 1938, repr. with corrections, 1952; A. Balsamo, Florence 1943; U. Brella, Turin 1950; J. C. Kamerbeek, Leyden 1950; G. Ammendola, Florence, 1951; E. Valgiglio, Turin 1957. TEXT: E. Diehl, Bonn 1911 (with scholia); E. Tièche, Ed. Helv. 5, Basel 1944; G. Busch, Heidelberger Texte 3, 1950; J. Kaiser, Bamberg 1956. INTERPRETATION: J. Caimo, "Umanità e verità della figura di Med. in Eur.," *Dioniso* 6 (1937/8), 89;

Zürcher, 43; O. Regenbogen, "Randbemerkungen zur *Med.* des Eur.," *Eranos* 48 (1950), 21; G. Müller, "Interpolationen in der *Med.* des Eur.," *Studi ital. di filol. class.* n.s. 25 (1951), 65; R. B. Palmer, "An Apology for Jason: A Study of Eur. *Med.*," *Class. Journ.* 53 (1957), 49; H.-D. Voigtländer, "Spätere Überarbeitungen im grossen Medeamonolog.," *Phil.* 101 (1957), 217; K. von Fritz, "Die Entwicklung der Iason-Medea-Sage und die *Med.* des Eur.," *Ant. u. Abendl.* 8 (1959), 33 = *Ant. u. mod. Trag.*, 322; W. H. Friedrich, "Medeas Rache," *Nachr. Ak. Göttingen. Phil.-hist. Kl.* 1960/4, 67 = *Vorbild und Neugestaltung*, Göttingen 1967, 7; W. H. Friedrich, "Med. in Kolchis," *Ant. u. Abendl.* 12 (1966), 3 = *Vorbild und Neugestaltung*, 57. These last three essays offer valuable aid in interpreting the drama and are also the best accounts of its later influence. Further, A. Bloch, "Medea-Dramen der Weltlit.," Diss. Göttingen 1957 (typescript). Here too we note Käte Hamburger's book (see Bibl.) and the synopses in H. Hunger's *Lex. d. gr. u. röm. Mythologie*. (5th ed., Vienna 1959), which supplements the "Med." of W. H. Friedrich, op. cit., 54; D. Ebener, "Zum Motiv des Kindermordes in der *Med.*," *Rhein. Mus.* 104 (1961), 213; E. Christmann, "Bemerkungen zum Text der *Med.* des Eur.," Diss. Heidelberg 1962; H. Diller, "Θυμὸς δὲ κρείσσων τῶν ἐμῶν βουλευμάτων," *Herm.* 94 (1966), 267; H. Musurillo, "Eur. *Medea*: A Reconsideration," *Am. Journ. Phil.* 87 (1966), 52. E. Schlesinger, "Zu Eur. *Med.*," *Herm.* 94 (1966), 26; H. Erbse, "Über die Aigeusszene der eurip. *Med.*," *Wien. Stud.* 79 (1966), 120; Conacher, 183; Webster, *Eur.*, 52; Steidle, 152; B. Meissner, "Eur. *Med.* 1236–1250," *Herm.* 96 (1968), 155; G. A. Seeck, "Eur. *Med.* 1059–68: A Problem of Interpretation," *Gr., Rom. and Byz. Stud.* 9 (1968), 291; G. Paduano, *La formazione del mondo ideologico e poetico di Eur. Alc.-Med.*, Pisa 1968; Rohdich, 44. RECENT TRANSLATIONS: G. Lange, Munich n.d. (1941); L. Wolde, as stage-manuscript, 1943 in Ralf Steyer Verlag; E. Buschor, Munich 1952; R. C. Trevelyan, Cambridge 1939; D. W. Lucas, London 1949; A. Taccone, Modena 1936; L. Cammelli, Milan 1940.

20. *Herm.* 15 (1880), 406. Earlier bibl. in Goossens, 118. 14. The opposing view (that the motif existed before Euripides) is supported by Steidle, 154. 16, but his arguments are far from decisive. The history of the source material is in A. Lesky, *RE* 15 (1930), 29, and D. L. Page in the preface to his edition. Page considers it possible that Eur. knew of a version in which the Korinthians falsely ascribed the murder of the children to Medeia. This remains uncertain, as does Zürcher's (45) conjecture that Iason's betrayal was also an innovation of Eur. If so, one would have to derive Paus. 2. 3. 6 from Eur., which is not easy; cf. D. L. Page op. cit., xxv.

21. Who, according to Wilamowitz, *Herm.* 15 (1880), 487, is dependent on Antigonos of Karystos.

22. On the problem: E. A. Thompson, "Neophron and Eur. *Med.*," *Class. Quart.* 38 (1944), 10 (Neophron before Eur.); A. Colonna, "Testimonianza Aristotelica su Neofrone?" *Dioniso* 13 (1950), 36. The priority of Euripides was asserted by, among others, Wilamowitz, *Herm.* 15 (1880), 487 = *Kl. Schr.*, 1. 23, who thought rather unconvincingly of a "malicious tendentious Peloponnesian forgery"; Séchan, 593 (with older bibl.); Schmid, 3. 371; F. Wehrli on Dikaiarchos fr. 63. The possibility of Neophron's priority was proposed by von Fritz, 335; he is followed by E. Christmann, op. cit., 105, who supports the same arrangement as Elmsley, Welcker, and Weil. These are opposed by H. Erbse, *Euphorion* 58 (1964), 192. Cf. H. Lloyd-Jones, *Gnom.* 34 (1962), 743. My acquaintance with Snell's discussion is due to his kindness in sending me the proofs for the German translation of his *Scenes*. In his second appendix he concludes the priority of Neophron on the basis of the passages that refer to θυμός.

23. The children go into the house with the old man after v. 105. The address in 118 is directed to them in their absence.

24. The athetesis of 355 f. by Nauck is unjustified.

25. On their interpretation, Schadewaldt, *Monolog*, 190.

26. Here, as in similar instances, the argumentation is very carefully arranged: 475, 545, 548 f. But such observations should not lead us to exaggerate the influence exerted by rhetoric on Euripides. A sober judgment is offered by E. Tietze, "Die eurip. Reden und ihre Bedeutung," Diss. Breslau 1933.

27. On the dating of the *Aigeus*, Buchwald, 42, who leans toward the early estimate of Wilamowitz, which is also favored by F. Solmsen, *Herm.* 69 (1934), 407. 2 and recently T. B. L. Webster, *Wien. Stud.* 79 (1966), 116; *Ant. Class.* 34 (1965), 519; and *Eur.* 77, 297, in which he uses vase-paintings to support an early date (soon after 450). Cf. B. B. Shefton, *Am. Journ. Arch.* 60 (1956), 159; H. J. Mette, *Lustrum* 1967/12 (1968), 12.

28. The question of when Medeia poisons the gifts must remain unanswered if we assume that she does not leave the stage during the whole of the following choral ode; the chorus's addresses in the second strophic pair can hardly be directed to Medeia in absentia, and she is already there to receive Iason in the following scene. D. L. Page on v. 789, and J. D. Denniston on *El.* vv. 948–949, do not consider the possibility that Medeia went into the house during the first and longer strophic pair.

29. D. L. Page correctly interprets v. 1058; ἐκεῖ could lead to the assumption of an ambiguity, but surely Medeia does not wish to live with her children in Hades.

30. D. L. Page on v. 1166 refers well to Aristainetos 1. 25. One might also imagine the position of the so-called Aphrodite Kallipygos, although there the interest is not exactly in the drapery.

31. Page follows Wilamowitz, probably rightly, in athetizing vv. 1233–35.

32. On the interpretations of this speech B. Meissner, *Herm.* 96 (1968), 155–166; however, he underestimates the emotional factor.

33. We quote from the book cited in the bibl. Rohdich (58) sees in Iason the idea of sophistic-intellectual world dominion brought to the stage.

34. E. Bethe's attempts (*Sitzb. Leipzig* 70 [1918], 1) to distinguish different strata in the play on the basis of such arguments need no longer be considered.

35. On this, A. Lesky, "Zur Problematik des Psychologischen in der Trag. des Eur.," *Gymn.* 67 (1960), 19 = *Ges. Schr.*, 256.

36. But there is general agreement on the athetesis of verses 1062 f., a doublet of 1240 f.

7. Steidle's abundant bibliography supplements the doxography presented by G. A. Seeck, op. cit.

38. Seeck, op. cit., 306. 27 also lays great stress, correctly, on οὐκ ἐκφεύξεται, which is syntactically very difficult. He translates "there is no escape"; cf. Steidle, 160. 51.

39. Op. cit., 137, offering a valuable survey of various interpretations and on the basis of F. Dirlmeier, *Gymn.* 67 (1960), 26.

40. On the finale cf. also M. P. Cunningham, "Medea ἀπὸ μηχανῆς," *Class. Phil.* 49 (1954), 151. Cf. *Entretiens sur l'ant. class.* 6 (1960), 32 f.

41. Von Fritz, W. Kullmann, see on the *Alk.*

42. Webster, *Eur.*, 61. H. J. Mette, *Lustrum* 1967/12 (1968), 107.

43. ANNOTATED EDITIONS: Wilamowitz, Berlin 1891; A. Taccone, Florence 1942; G. Ammendola, Florence 1946; W. S. Barrett, Oxford 1964, a monumental edition, richly annotated, with a text compiled on a broad base of manuscript comparison. INTERPRETATION: L. Méridier, *Hipp. d'Eur.* Paris n.d. (1931); S. M. Adams, "Two plays of Eur., I: The Final Scene of the *Hipp.*," *Class. Rev.* 49 (1935), 118; M. Tierney, "The *Hipp.* of Eur.," *Proc. Ir. Ac.* 44 C 2, 1937/8, 59; U. Boella, "Il dramma del dubbio in Eur.: Osserv. a prop. di Ippolito," *Mondo Class.*, 1938, 42; D. Grene, "The Interpretation of the *Hipp.* of Eur.," *Class. Phil.* 34 (1939), 45; A. R. Bellinger, "The *Bacchae* and *Hipp.*," *Yale Class. Stud.* 6 (1939), 15; H. Emonds, *Zweite Auflage im Altertum*, Leipzig 1941, 342; G. Soury, "Eur. rationaliste et mystique d'après *Hipp.*," *Rev. Et. Gr.* 56 (1943), 29; A. Bonnard, "L'*Hipp.* d'Eur. et le drame de la passion refoulée," *Bull. Soc. des Et. de Lettres*, Lausanne 1944, 1; W. B. Stanford, "The *Hipp.* of Eur.," *Hermathena* 63 (1944), 11; D. W. Lucas, "*Hipp.*," *Class. Quart.* 40 (1946), 65; B. M. W. Knox, "The *Hipp.* of Eur.," *Yale Class. Stud.* 13 (1952), 1; Friedrich, 110; R. Y. Hathorn, "Rationalism and Irrationalism in Eur. *Hipp.*," *Class. Journ.* 52 (1956/57), 211; L. G. Crocker, "On interpreting *Hipp.*," *Phil.* 101 (1957), 238; E. Valgiglio, "L'*Ipp.* di Eur.," Turin 1957; R. P. Winnington-Ingram, "*Hipp.*: A Study in Causation," *Entretiens sur l'ant. class.* 6, (1960), 171; G. Devereux, "The Enetian Horses of

Hipp.," Ant. Class. 33 (1964), 375; Snell, *Scenes,* 23, 47; H. Merklin, "Gott und Mensch im *Hipp.* und den *Bakchen* des Eur.," Diss. Freiburg im Breisgau 1964 (with a thorough doxography on interpretation); Lasso de la Vega, "Hipólito y Fedra en Eur.," *Estudios clás.* 46 (1965), 361; C. P. Segal, "The Trag. of *Hipp.*: The Waters of Ocean and the Untouched Meadow," *Harv. Stud.* 70 (1965), 117; C. P. Segal, "Eur. *Hipp.* 108–112: Tragic Irony and Tragic Justice," *Herm.* 97 (1969) 297; C. P. Segal, "Shame and Purity in Eur. *Hipp.*," *Herm.* 98 (1970), 288, and "Oath in Eur. *Hipp.*," *Ramus* 1 (1972), 165; Gisela Berna, "Nomos and Physis: An Interpretation of Eur.," *Herm.* 101 (1973), 165; Conacher, 27; Webster, *Eur.,* 64; Chromik, 31. TRANSLATIONS: E. Buschor, Munich 1952; L. Traverso, Urbino 1956; J. A. Ross, Amsterdam 1940 (a Dutch translation in verse with an introduction).

44. "Hippolytos und Thekla," *Ak. Wien. Phil.-hist. Kl.* 182/3 (1916). On Hippolytos: L. Séchan, "La légende d'Hippolyte dans l'antiquité," *Rev. Et. Gr.* 24 (1911), 105; P. E. Arias, "L'*Ed. a Col.* e l'*Ippolito* nel mito e nell'arte," *Dioniso* 5 (1935/36), 183; H. Herter, "Theseus und Hipp.," *Rhein. Mus.* 89 (1940), 273 (with extensive bibl.). A valuable overview is in the preface to W. S. Barrett's edition (see note 43, above). The legend, its adaptations in antiquity, and subsequent influence are thoroughly treated by H. J. Tschiedel, "Phaedra und Hippolytos: Variationen eines tragischen Konfliktes," Diss. Erlangen 1969. W. Fauth, "Hipp. und Phaidra," *Ak. Mainz. Geistes- und sozialw. Kl.* 1958/9 and 1959/8, goes too far when he claims to recognize behind the conflict of the play the relationship of a Mediterranean mother goddess to her paredros. H. Petriconi also goes astray in his article "Die verschmähte Astarte," *Roman. Jahrb.* 13 (1962), 149, according to which Euripides must have been familiar with the epic of Gilgamesh.

45. Friedrich, 148, concludes that the first *Hipp.* was performed in 434, on the basis of Seneca, *Phaed.* 788 ff., with its mention of a lunar eclipse. W. S. Barrett rejects this date. Its value depends on the extent to which Euripides can be reconstructed from Seneca. On the dating see also Wilamowitz, *Kl. Schr.,* 1. 19, and Buchwald, 47. On the play, see W. H. Friedrich, *Untersuchungen zu Senecas dram. Technik,* Leipzig 1933, 38; C. Zintzen, *Analytisches Hypomnema zu Senecas* Phaedra, Meisenheim/Glan 1960; Snell, *Scenes,* 23. Further, H. Lloyd-Jones, *Journ. Hell. Studies* 85 (1965), 164, and *Gnom.* 38 (1966), 14; W. S. Barrett, op. cit., 10, with a compilation of the evidence; J. Dingel, "Ἱππόλυτος ξιφουλκός: Zu Senecas *Phädra* und dem ersten *Hipp.* des Eur.," *Herm.* 98 (1970), 44.

46. The possibility of also using Ovid, *Heroides* 4 was discussed by F. Leo in his edition of Seneca's tragedy, in connection with the reconstruction problem.

47. E.g. *Nem.* 3. 41.

48. Quite correctly, W. S. Barrett (op. cit., 318) excludes the use of the ekkyklema here, despite Aristophanes of Byzantium. The opposing view is taken by T. B. L. Webster, *Gnom.* 45 (1973), 613, with reference to A. M. Dale, *Collected Papers,* Cambridge 1969, 121.

49. That the second section is sung by Phaidra alone supports Barrett's view that the earlier passage was intended as a monody of the chorus leader. He rejects, probably rightly, Murray's assignment of the lines to individual members of the chorus.

50. With Wilamowitz and Barrett we interpret v. 492 to mean that Phaidra and the nurse should speak in undisguised terms, not that Hippolytos should be informed.

51. In v. 514 it seems necessary to accept Reiske's πλόκον for λόγον, as much as we would like to see in the word an announcement of the nurse's conversation with Hippolytos.

52. Allusions in Aristoph. *Thesm.* 275, *Frogs* 101, 1971. Cf. Aristot. *Rhet.* 1416a 28.

53. Here Barrett, op. cit., 318, considers the ekkyklema indispensable. But would seeing a corpse hanging just behind the door have been so difficult for the audience that Phaidra would have to be rolled into view? We prefer to leave the question open.

54. Vv. 877 f.: lyric iambics.

55. The abrupt σέ at the beginning has a good parallel in *Med.* 271.

56. Cf. H. Herter, *Rhein. Mus.* 89 (1940), 289.

57. A survey of various opinions is in Chromik, 73.

58. Thus B. Snell, *Die Entdeckung des Geistes*, 3d ed., Hamburg 1955, 176; *Scenes*, 69.

59. In his discussion of the play, R. P. Winnington-Ingram (op. cit.) shows well how the abundance of human relations in the drama cannot be satisfactorily explained through the influence of the goddesses.

60. A different view, opposing Winnington-Ingram, is offered by H. Merklin, op. cit., 87.

61. H. Merklin, op. cit., 84, offers a valuable summary of opinions.

62. On this, H. Merklin, op. cit., 83.

63. "Das früheste Zeugnis über Sokrates," *Phil.* 97 (1948), 125, and *Scenes*, in the two important chapters "Passion and Reason," I and II, in which he points out (59) that T. Barthold, in his edition of *Hipp.*, 1880, 39, already remarked the reference to Sokrates' teachings. Snell also gives additional bibl. The connection is denied by Barrett, 229, and Lloyd-Jones, *Journ. Hell. Stud.* 85 (1965), 161, and *Gnom.* 38 (1966), 15. In agreement are, among others, R. P. Winnington-Ingram, op. cit., 174, and A. Carlini, "Due note Euripidee," *Studi Class. e Orient.* 14 (1965), 7, who assumes a similar reference for v. 358 f. as well.

64. On the secondary chorus, see Lammers, 88, who discusses the important scholium on *Hipp.* 58, which lists similar occurrences in Euripides.

65. D. L. Page, *Lit. Pap.*, 126, with earlier references and a reproduction of the prologue; see also: Johansen, 134. B. Zühlke," Eur. *Sthen.*," *Phil.* 105 (1961), 1 and 198; D. Korzeniewski, "Zum Prolog der *Sthen.* des Eur.," *Phil.* 108 (1964), 45; Webster, *Eur.*, 80, 301; H. J. Mette, *Lustrum* 1967/12 (1968), 221.

66. A. Carlini, "Due note Euripidee," *Studi Class. e Orient.* 14 (1965), 3, defends the assignment of fr. 68N (Nauck assigns it to the *Alkmeon*) to the *Bellerophontes* by Michael Ephesius; he includes earlier bibliography on reconstruction attempts. Webster, *Eur.*, 109, shows how strictly limited we are in reconstructing this play. H. J. Mette, *Lustrum* 1967/12 (1968), 93, with a new fragment from Herodian.

67. Webster, *Eur.*, 84; H. J. Mette (see previous note), 272; Austin, 101, with the beginning verse from *P. Oxy.* 2455 fr. 14. Since these texts are of great importance for numerous questions of reconstruction, we cite for all the following: E. G. Turner, "Euripidean Hypotheses in a New Papyrus," *Proc. IX Int. Congr. of Papyrology, Oslo 1958* (1961), 1.

68. Webster, *Eur.*, 85; H. J. Mette (see note 66, above), 208. I must correct my conjecture about this play (*RE* 19 [1936], 305), which, however, would be unnecessary if D. G. Harbsmeier, "Die alten Menschen bei Eur.," Diss. Göttingen 1968, 19, were correct in his conjecture that fr. 619N was spoken by an old Peleus. But this point remains uncertain, and even the circumstance that in the *Peleus* of Sophokles the title figure was old can prove nothing about Euripides.

69. Webster, *Eur.*, 15, 303. H. J. Mette (see note 66, above), 16.

70. Suet. *Nero* 21; Cass. Dio 63. 10. 2; A. Lesky, *Ges. Schr.*, 342.

71. Fragments and the evidence of mythographers in Austin, 49. See also H. J. Mette, *Lustrum* 1967/12 (1968), 157. RECONSTRUCTION: A. Rivier, "Eur. et Pasiphaé: Lettres d'Occident," *Festschr. Bonnard*, Neuchâtel 1958, 51; H. J. Mette, "Eur. κρῆτες," *Herm.* 91 (1963), 256, and *Lustrum* 1964/9 (1965), 140; H. Lloyd-Jones, *Gnom.* 35 (1963), 447; R. Cantarella, *Eur.* I Cretesi: *Testo e comm.*, Milan 1963; D. W. Lucas, *Gnom.* 37 (1965), 455; Webster, *Eur.*, 87, 299 (with earlier bibl.).

72. L. Deubner, *Sitzb. Berlin* 1942/4, 9; F. Wehrli, *Mus. Helv.* 14 (1957), 108; Snell, *Scenes*, 63; H. J. Mette, *Lustrum* 1964/9 (1965), 136, and *Lustrum* 1967/12 (1968), 286; Webster, *Eur.*, 111, 298, and *Wien. Stud.* 79 (1966), 114, dates the play early in Euripides' career, but here as in many other cases the remnants are too scanty to admit conclusions drawn on the basis of trimeter technique. *P. Oxy.* 2455 fr. 17 (Austin, 103) consists of only two letters from the first verse.

73. J. Mesk, "Die *Ant.* des Eur.," *Wien. Stud.* 49 (1931), 1, who definitively excluded the seventy-second fable of Hyginus for the reconstruction; Webster, *Eur.*, 181; H. J. Mette, *Lustrum* 1967/12 (1968), 58.

74. A. Körte, *Herm.* 69 (1934), 1. H. J. Mette, *Lustrum* 1964/9 (1965), 148, and 1967/12 (1968), 229. See also *Verl. Aisch.* 105, 1; F. Jouan, "Eur. et les légendes des Chants Cypriens," Paris 1966, 204; Webster, *Eur.*, 95, 301. In *Eur.*, p. 4, and *Wien. Stud.* 79 (1966), 116, 119, he posits a very early date.

75. H. J. Mette, *Lustrum* 1964/9 (1965), 138, and 1967/12 (1968), 175. Webster, *Eur.*, 233, 306. B. Gentili, *Gnom.* 33 (1961), 341, pursued A. M. Dale's idea that an annotated fragment (*P. Oxy.* 25 [1959], 2436) might come from a monody of Althaia, but this is unlikely.

76. EDITIONS: J. T. Sheppard, Oxford 1924; A. Taccone, Turin 1937; W. King, London 1938; T. T. Jeffrey, London n.d.; M. Tierney, Dublin 1946; A. Garzya, Rome 1955; S. G. Daitz, Leipzig 1973; K. Matthiessen is preparing an annotated edition. INTERPRETATION: G. Méautis, *Mythes inconnues de la Grèce antique*, Paris 1944; G. Kirkwood, "Hecuba and Nomos," *Trans. Am. Phil. Ass.* 78 (1947), 61; E. L. Abrahamson, "Eur. Tragedy of Hecuba," *Trans. Am. Phil. Ass.* (1952), 120; Friedrich, 30; W. Biehl, "Die Interpolationen in Eur. *Hek.* v. 59–215," *Phil.* 101 (1957), 55, and "Das Kompositionsprinzip der Parodos in Eur. *Hek.* (98–135)," *Helikon* 6 (1966), 411; D. J. Conacher, "Eur. *Hecuba*," *Am. Journ. Phil.* 82 (1961), 1, and *Eur. Drama*, 146; L. Pearson, *Popular Ethics in Ancient Greece*, Stanford 1962, 144, 247. 10; D. Lanza, "Νόμος ε ἴσον in Eur.," *Riv. di filol.* 91 (1963), 416; A. W. H. Adkins, "Basic Values in Eur. *Hecuba* and *Hercules Furens*," *Class. Quart.* 16 (1966), 193; W. Steidle, "Zur *Hek.* des Eur.," *Wien. Stud.* 79 (1966), 133, and *Studien*, 44; Webster, 121; K. Matthiessen, "Manuscript Problems in Eur. *Hec.*," *Gr. Rom. and Byz. Stud.* 10 (1969), 293; Q. Cataudella, *L'Ecuba di Eur. Saggi sulla trag. Greca*, Messina 1969, 263. TRANSLATION: S. Quasimodo, Urbino 1962.

77. An extensive reconstruction attempt was made by W. M. Calder III, *Gr., Rom. and Byz. Stud.* 7 (1966), 31. Schol. *Hek.* 1 also suggests Sophokles.

78. In the *Iliad* (20. 407), Polydoros appears as the youngest son of Priam and is slain by Achilleus. Of course we cannot rule out the possibility that Euripides was dealing with a local legend, but, despite H. Weil, this cannot be maintained with the certainty that Pohlenz (2. 116) professes.

79. Cf. H. Emonds, *Zweite Auflage im Altertum*, Leipzig 1941, 277. A date before 423 is also suggested by Pohlenz, 2. 116 (probably 424). Goossens, 309, suggests a time between 425 and 423. See also Webster, *Wien. Stud.* 79 (1966), 116, and *Eur.*, 101. W. Theiler, *Wien. Stud.* 79 (1966), 109, dates the play at 420 and holds to the assignment of the Aristophanes passages to the second version of the *Clouds*.

80. Attempts to discern different stages of composition based on this discrepancy are, we hope, a thing of the past. Bibl. in Conacher, 151. 15.

81. Friedrich, 45, has brought forward cogent reasons for deleting the hexameters 74 f. (with the badly mangled v. 76) and 90 f. that are interspersed among Hekabe's anapests. Yet I would not like to extend the athetesis to 92–98, as does W. Biehl (see note 76, above), "Interpolationen". The chorus leader expressly (v. 110) assumes that Hekabe knows about Achilleus's appearance.

82. G. Hermann believed he was able to demonstrate such an arrangement. Murray followed in his edition, with some misgivings. In any case we must then delete the expendable verses 175 f.

83. The desire to see Helen punished forms the subject of an entire agon in the *Troades*.

84. A. Lesky, "Erbe und Erziehung im griech. Denken des 5. Jh.s.," *N. Jahrb.* 2 (1939), 361, and "Eur. und die Pädagogik," *Wien. Human. Bl.* 11 (1968), 16.

85. Expressions of sympathy: 732, 763, 783, 785.

86. Bibl. in Conacher, 146. 1.

87. Bibl. in L. Pearson, *Popular Ethics in Ancient Greece*, Stanford 1962, 248.

88. ANNOTATED EDITIONS: J. C. Kamerbeek, Leyden 1944; U. Scatena, Rome 1956; A. Garzya, 2d ed., Naples 1963; P. T. Stevens, Oxford 1971. INTERPRETATION: M. Delcourt, "Eur. et les événements de 431–424," *Bibl. fac. de phil. Liège*, 44 (1930), 117; R. Sauer, "Untersuchungen zu Eur.," Diss. Leipzig, Würzburg 1931, 43; D. L. Page, "The Elegiacs in Eur. *Andr.*," *Greek*

Poetry and Life, Oxford 1936, 206; J. C. Kamerbeek, "L'*Andromaque* d'Eur.," *Mnem.* ser. 3, 11 (1942), 47; Rivier, 171; A. Lesky, "Der Ablauf der Handlung in der *Andr.* des Eur.," *Anz. Ost. Ak. Phil.-hist. Kl.* 84 (1947), 99 = *Ges. Schr.,* 144; A. Garzya, "Interpretazione dell'*Andr.* di Eur.," *Dioniso* 14 (1951), 109; Friedrich, 47; H. Erbse, "Eur. *Andr.," Herm.* 94 (1966), 276; Steidle, 118; Conacher, 166; Webster, 118; F. Ferrari, "Struttura e personaggi nell'*Andr.* di Eur.," *Maia* n.s. fasc. 3, 23 (1971), 209. TRANSLATION: R. Cantarella, Urbino 1964.

89. Webster, *Eur.,* 118 (also *Wien. Stud.* 79 [1966], 115 f.) considers the years from 428 to 424. Ca. 425 is suggested by L. Méridier in the edition of the Budé series and van Lennep, 81; see also M. Delcourt and J. C. Kamerbeek (both op. cit.). The arguments with which Goossens, 377 and note 5 (with earlier bibl.), supports a later date (423 or 422) are inconclusive.

90. Various suggestions for the site of production, e.g., Argos (D. L. Page, op. cit., 221), a city in the Chalkidike (M. Delcourt, op. cit., 117), somewhere in Thessaly (Goossens, 412. 23), or the court of the Molossian king (Schmid 3. 405; see also Conacher, 180. 16) remain of course quite uncertain. We add one more conjecture, equally as tentative: Might it have been produced in Sikyon, thus leading to the play's ascription to Demokrates (schol. *Andr.* 445)? A tragedian, Demokrates of Sikyon, appears in a list of tragic poets of the third century B.C. (*P. Tebt.* 695).

91. An ancient mythological basis for the hostility between Neoptolemos-Pyrrhos and Orestes, who was associated with Delphi, was uncovered by L. Radermacher, *Das Jenseits im Mythos der Hellenen,* Bonn 1903, 51.

92. Strohm, 3, is especially helpful on the altar motif.

93. The athetesis of verses 668–677 should be rejected because their deletion would severely damage the external balance of the speeches.

94. A fairly comparable instance occurs in the οὕτω παῖδας εὖ παιδεύετε of Adrastos, *Hik.* 917.

95. Thus Menelaos is charged more seriously here than in Sophokles, where the two different promises of Tyndareos and Menelaos are opposed to one another.

96. Steidle neatly points to v. 967, where the pronoun refers to the absent Neoptolemos. Cf. H. Hunger, *Wien. Stud.* 65 (1950/51), 19.

97. A. Lesky, op. cit., 99 and 144 respectively, with bibl. The same interpretation also in J. C. Kamerbeek, op. cit. J. Pouilloux in J. P. and G. Roux, *Enigmes à Delphes,* Paris 1963, 102, interprets section 1085–1157 in terms of Delphian topography.

98. "Lesefrüchte," *Herm.* 60 (1925), 284.

99. With reference to P. N. Boulter, *Phoenix* 20 (1966), 51. On the entire set of problems involved with detecting contemporary influences, an extensive bibliography is offered by D. G. Harbsmeier, "Die alten Menschen bei Eur.," Diss. Göttingen 1968, 132. 4. For the *Andr.* he recognizes passages with an anti-Spartan tendency, without exaggerating their importance.

100. ANNOTATED EDITIONS: A. C. Pearson, Cambridge 1907; B. Calzaferri, Florence 1939; A. Maggi, Turin 1943. INTERPRETATION: G. Zuntz, "Is the *Heraclidai* Mutilated?" *Class. Quart.* 41 (1947), 46. On this point, cf. his book cited in the Euripides bibliography (*Pol. Plays*), which offers a comprehensive and outstanding analysis, as well as critical treatment of individual sections. F. Stoessl, "Die *Herakl.* des Eur.," *Phil.* 100 (1956), 207; J. W. Fitton, "The *Suppliant Women* and the *Herakleidai* of Eur.," *Herm.* 89 (1961), 430; H. Förs, "Dionysos und die Stärke des Schwachen im Werk des Eur.," Diss. Tübingen 1964, 95; Conacher, 109; Webster, 102; D. G. Harbsmeier, "Die alten Menschen bei Eur.," Diss. Göttingen 1968, 38; A. Greifenhagen, *Frühhellenistischer Kolonettenkrater mit Darstellung der* Herakliden *123,* Winkelmannsprogramm der Archäologischen Gesellschaft, Berlin 1969; A. Lesky, "On the *Heraclidae* of Euripides," *Yale Class. Stud.* 25 (1977), 227.

101. Mette, *Verl. Aisch.,* 149.

102. Conacher agrees in his discussion of the problem; he also offers a large bibliography.

103. *Wien. Stud.* 79 (1966), 116.

104. Zuntz, *Pol. Plays*, 109, rightly accepts Reiske's conjecture of a lacuna after v. 2, in order to establish the necessary stylistic balance in the antithesis.

105. The localization in Marathon could go back to the time when Theseus was not yet the Athenian, but lord of Aphidnai, adjacent to the Tetrapolis; cf. H. Herter, "Theseus der Ionier," *Rhein. Mus.* 85 (1936), 197.

106. This is repeatedly mentioned with the same purpose; 183, 193, 305. With especial emphasis, 329.

107. Goossens, 199, recalls the speech of Nikias on the aid given Egesta (Thukydides 6. 13. 2).

108. Its significance for this play has been worked out especially vigorously by Conacher.

109. D. G. Harbsmeier, op. cit., 40, argues well against the athetesis of 221–225 supported by Pohlenz (2. 146).

110. Philostratos, *Vita Soph.* 2. 1. 8; differently in Goossens, 229, note 42.

111. Niejahr's athetesis of vv. 299–301 is rightly supported by Zuntz, *Pol. Plays*, 110, against Pohlenz 2. 145. 1. A line has been lost after v. 311. The plurals of 304 f. and 307 take into account the presence of Akamas, but in the highly emotional conclusion of his speech Iolaos appeals to Demophon alone.

112. On such scenes of collapse see the fine excursus in D. G. Harbsmeier, op. cit., 114.

113. On the correct arrangement of lines 682–694, see Zuntz, *Pol. Plays*, 113, and Schwinge, 60. 7, with bibl.

114. On the interpretation of the strophe, which is filled with unsolved problems, see Zuntz, *Pol. Plays*, 115.

115. The τρίτη φθίνοντος (third day of the waning moon) was considered Athena's birthday.

116. If a further argument were necessary it could be pointed out that Hyllos's servant certainly did not leave the side of Iolaos, with whom he departed, while the messenger knew of the miraculous rejuvenation only from hearsay (847). The ὅδε of line 793 has caused difficulties. Murray's overbold suggestion "praeterducitur, ni fallor, in pompa Iolaus iuvenis factus" (unless I am mistaken, Iolaos is led forth in a procession, rejuvenated) was correctly rejected by Zuntz, *Pol. Plays*, 122. Either one must follow Elmsley in substituting οὖν (or better: ἆρ') for οὐκ, and ἔτι for the ὅδε, or one must leave the demonstrative alone, which is possible in view of our statements in note 96 above.

117. Zuntz, *Pol. Plays*, 125; Conacher, 119. 17; Schwinge, 59. 4, with bibl.

118. Op. cit. ("Is the *Heracl.* mut.?"). Rejected also by Martinazzoli, 124; L. Méridier in the French ed. Schmid, 3. 422; Pohlenz, 2. 144. Grube, 174, confessed " . . . we are here on very uncertain ground." With detailed argumentation, Page, 32, supported the assumption of a later abridgment. R. Guerrini, "I frammenti degli *Eraclidi* di Eur.," *Studi Classici e Orientali* 19/20 (1970/71), 15, and "La morte di Macaria," *Stud. It.* 45 (1973), 46.

119. H. Förs op. cit., 103, interprets the lines confidently.

120. Zuntz, *Pol. Plays*, 30, takes Iolaos quite seriously, but considers the ridiculous element as a stage that the old man must overcome along the way. A detailed discussion of the scene in D. G. Harbsmeier, "Die alten Menschen bei Eur.," Diss. Göttingen 1968, 44, who offers the interesting thought that the elements that appear ridiculous should at the same time provoke the audience's pity.

121. ANNOTATED EDITIONS: A. C. Pearson, Pitt Press 1907; T. Nicklin, London 1931; N. Wecklein, Berlin 1972; G. Ammendola, Palermo 1922; G. Italie, Groningen 1951. INTERPRETATION: C. Kuiper, "De Eur. *Suppl.*," transl. by J. J. Hartmann, *Mnem.* n.s. 51 (1923), 102; W. J. W. Koster, "De Eur. *Suppl.*," *Mnem.* ser. 3, 10 (1942), 161; B. Lavagnini, "Echi del rito Eleusinio in Eur.," *Am. Journ. Phil.* 68 (1947), 82; Norwood, 112; G. Zuntz, "Über Eur. *Hik.*," *Mus. Helv.* 12 (1955), 20, and *Pol. Plays*, 3, 71, 88; D. J. Conacher, "Religious and Ethical Attitudes in Eur. *Supp.*," *Trans. Am. Phil. Ass.* 87 (1956), 8; H. Diller, *Gnom.* 32 (1960), 229; J. Fitton, "The *Suppliant Women* and the *Herakleidai*," *Herm.* 89 (1961), 430; G. Paduano, "Interpretazione

delle *Suppl.* di Eur.," *Ann. Scuola Normale Superiore, Pisa*, ser. 2, 35 (1966), 193; W. D. Smith, "Expressive Form in Eur. *Suppl.*," *Harv. Stud.* 71 (1967), 151; Conacher, 93; Webster, *Eur.*, 124. For a metrical analysis see Wilamowitz, *Gr. Versk.*, 155.

122. Fr. 54N; 267–270M; Mette, *Verl. Aisch.*, 40.

123. A thorough discussion of the question in Lammers, 94.

124. Vv. 12, 102, 755, 963.

125. Earlier interpretations in Conacher, 100. 14. The explanation supported by many scholars (G. Hermann, H. Grégoire, T. Nicklin, Grube, 231. 1), that Theseus contrasts the obedience to Apollo's word to the disregard for Amphiaraos, is untenable. This would leave the insoluble contradiction that Theseus in one case sharply reproves obedience to a divine order (222) but in the other demands it just as forcefully for the prophecy. In reality Theseus reprimands Adrastos because he felt bound to Apollo's word, yet interpreted it falsely. In v. 221 ὡς ζώντων θεῶν cannot be maintained. Even if one understands it *e sententia Adrasti*, the connection with the following reproach is lost. Markland's δόντων is excellent. The pointed repetition of the verb would then mean: In your error you gave your daughters to the men, as if it were the gods who did it. However, Markland's interpretation of the passage as an attack on Apollo seems to us totally unnecessary. In the mouth of the Theseus of this play this would sound incomprehensibly dissonant.

126. With others, Goossens, 459. 2, takes as terminus post quem the Theban victory over the Athenians at Delion in 424, when the Thebans refused to surrender the dead, but he will not accept a date much later than this. Pohlenz, 2. 148, dates the play to the Dionysia of 421, directly before the official conclusion of the war, which is too late. Zuntz eliminated the argument about Delion by pointing out that Aischylos had already dealt with the same material. He also emphasizes correctly that the alliance with Argos promised in the finale can in no way be connected with a specific treaty date, since this question was constantly under discussion. He makes a good case (88) for the year 424. This coincides well with Webster, *Eur.*, 124 (cf. *Wien. Stud.* 79 [1966], 115 f.), who places the drama close to the *Hekabe* on the basis of metrics.

127. In our passage v. 195 clearly indicates that controversial questions are at issue here.

128. Elmsley's ἥμαρτον in v. 250 has much to recommend it. Matthiae's athetesis of v. 252 is unconvincing.

129. On this idea in Eur., cf. v. 1140 of this play; further, *Hel.* 1016; fr. 839N; *Hypsipyle* fr. 60, 93 Bond. That this belief, though undoubtedly first developed in philosophy, was nonetheless fairly widespread is shown by the epigram on the fallen soldiers of Potidaia *IG* I² 945. How easily different eschatological concepts may exist side by side is demonstrated by v. 1140 (aether) next to 1142 (Hades).

130. None of the transpositions suggested by Murray is mandatory.

131. The MSS here incorrectly make the chorus leader the partner of Adrastos. Stoessl follows this in his translation, but, for reasons deriving from the history of our tradition (paragraphos), we can have little confidence in the allotment of lines as they appear in the manuscripts. After v. 763 a verse of Adrastos is missing.

132. Norwood, 159, went so far as to explain the Euadne scene as a later interpolation because of its complex staging problems. Webster, *Eur.*, 126, imagines that the grave, the cliff, and Euadne were all rolled out on the ekkyklema. The solution suggested above agrees with that of Hourmouziades, 32, and de Romilly, *L'évolution*, 37, who should also be consulted on other aspects of the scene.

133. It is better to assume a secondary chorus than to assign, with Webster, the singing of the boys' part to the mothers. Similarly, Webster imagines that the children's passages in *Alk.* and *Andr.* were sung by a cantor, while the boy, as actor, supplied the gestures. To add Adrastos as a partner in the kommos, as the MSS suggest on v. 1145, is inadvisable.

134. It is useless to ask why Theseus has not done this before.

135. Delebecque, a scholar well respected in other fields, has as the exponent of an entire school gone especially far.

136. A good survey of recent interpretations in G. Paduano, op. cit., who himself successfully continues the line initiated by Zuntz.

137. On earlier interpretations see also Norwood, in his radical analysis of the speech (126).

138. Goossens, 468; Webster, *Eur.*, 127; C. Austin, "De nouveaux fragm. le l'*Erechth.* d'Eur.," *Recherches de Papyrologie* 4, 1967, and *Nova Fragm. Eur.*, 22; H. J. Mette, *Lustrum* 1967/12 (1968), 112; W. M. Calder III, "The date of Eur. *Erechth.*," *Gr., Rom. and Byz. Stud.* 10 (1969), 147 (also on the Latin spelling *Erectheus*, which Austin also prefers in the *Nova Fragm.*); J. C. Kamerbeek, "Remarques sur les fragments de l'*Erechtée* d'Eur.," *Mnem.* ser. 4, 23 (1970), 113.

139. *Analecta Euripidea*, Berlin 1875, 151; *K. Schr.* 1. 72. Calder (op. cit., 153 f.) cites later opinions.

140. H. Herter, *Rhein. Mus.* 91 (1942), 234 with bibl. Webster, *Eur.*, 106, considers the assignment of *P. Oxy.* 2452 (cited above under the fragments of Sophokles) to Eur. *Theseus*, while E. G. Turner in his edition and H. Lloyd-Jones, *Gnom.* 35 (1963), 436, suggested Sophokles. Webster points out the anadiplosis in fr. 5. 11 of the papyrus.

141. Wilamowitz's edition remains irreplaceable: 2d rev., 2 vols., Berlin 1895, reprinted Darmstadt 1959. INTERPRETATION: J. T. Sheppard, "The Formal Beauty of the *Hercules Furens*," *Class. Quart.* 10 (1916), 72; Perrotta, *Sof.*, 527; A. Ardizzoni, "L'*Eracle* di Eur.," *At. e Roma* (1937), 46; E. Kroeker, "Der *Her.* des Eur.," Diss. Leipzig 1938; H. Drexler, "Zum *Her.* des Eur.," *Nachr. Gött. Phil.-hist. Kl.* 1943/9; H. O. O. Chalk, "Aretê and Bia in the *Herakles*," *Journ. Hell. Studies* 82 (1962), 7; F. Stoessl, "Zur Iris-Lyssa-Szene in Eur. *Her.*," *Serta Philol. Aenipontana*, Innsbruck 1962, 117; A. W. H. Adkins, "Basic Values in Eur. *Hecuba* and *Herc. Furens*," *Class. Quart.* 16 (1966), 193; J. C. Kamerbeek, "Unity and Meaning of Eur. *Her.*," *Mnem.* ser. 4, 19 (1966), 1; J. Carrière, "Autour des dernières réponses aux problèmes de l'*Her.* d'Eur.," *Information littéraire* 1967, 1 (earlier *Ann. de la Fac. des Lettres de Toulouse* 1 [1952], 2); Chromik, 92; Conacher, 78; Webster, *Eur.*, 188; Rohdich, 71. TRANSLATION: E. Buschor, Munich 1952; S. Quasimodo, Urbino 1964. For assigning the date 424, Goossens (371. 1) proceeds from the baseless assumption that Aristoph. *Clouds* 1048 ff. depends on *Herakles* 1335, as well as from speculations about historical references. The estimate between 421 and 415 in Wilamowitz's edition is still valid, but today, on the basis of metrical analyses, we are more inclined to consider the later years of this period; cf. A. M. Dale, *Helen*, Oxford 1937, xxvii. 1, who also considers 414, and T. B. L. Webster, *Wien. Stud.* 79 (1966), 115. W. Theiler, ibid., 109, dates the play to 417.

142. The transposition of v. 87 after v. 89 (Wil.) is necessary.

143. One thinks of the constant rivalry between infantry and artillery in World War I—the parallel could not be more striking.

144. The tradition allots it to *Amphitryon*, which F. Stoessl adopts in his translation despite vv. 266, 270, and 275.

145. Wilamowitz, *Griech. Verskunst*, 243.

146. On the concept, O. Weinreich, "Gebet und Wunder," *Tüb. Beitr.* 5 (1929), 175. A fine later example is offered by the inscription *TAM* III/1, no. 103, where one of the citizens who has deserved well of the grain supply chases the λιμός (famine) into the sea.

147. Cf. *Hipp.* 616 and 940, with W. S. Barrett's commentary; *Suppl.* 1080.

148. Amphitryon goes into the house after v. 731, so it is impossible for him to speak the trimeters in the kommos, as the tradition on v. 740 falsely claims.

149. Vv. 739, 757, 772, 798.

150. Hourmouziades, 162, also must leave the question open. One is tempted, with Webster, *Eur.*, 190, to eliminate the problem entirely by taking Lyssa's chariot metaphorically. But the description in v. 880 is really too concrete for this. Occurrences in the *Peace* of Aristophanes

(421), which is not too distant in time from our play, offer a certain parallel.

151. The transmitted assignment of speakers amounts to nonsense and was corrected by Musgrave. Another view is taken by F. Stoessl, op. cit.; cf. A. Lesky, *Anz. f. d. Altertumsw.* 16 (1963), 153. In the choral passage 875 ff., too, the allotment of single exclamations to Amphitryon is necessary, as indicated by Murray following the procedure of others. The assignment of vv. 904–908 is especially difficult. Murray assigns 904 f. to the chorus, as one must (note the ἰδού, ἰδού), the rest to Herakles, who addresses this call to Athena. Her intervention is accompanied by the shaking of the house.

152. A detail shows us the limits beyond which we may not go when analyzing poetry. At v. 942 Herakles, already deranged, demands his bow and club. No mention is made of anyone giving him the weapons. The servants laugh or are afraid. But later he has them to perform his awful deed.

153. The chorus sings (1029) of the opening door. Thus, in their translations, E. Buschor, F. Stoessl, and R. Kannicht (transl. Donner) believe that the audience was given a glimpse of the interior at this point. But several considerations suggest the use of the ekkyklema, rolled through the door as Hourmouziades (98) believes. Amphitryon, noticing that Herakles awakes, wants to flee ὑπὸ μέλαθρον (inside; 1070); Herakles sees the sky, the earth, and the sun (1090); later he instructs his father to "bring in" the dead children (1422). Cf. A. Lesky, *Gnom.* 38 (1966), 745.

154. The entire section receives excellent treatment in Schwinge (414). We take this occasion to recommend the abundance of valuable interpretation in this book, which, as opposed to earlier schemas, has helped us to understand the Euripidean stichomythy in all its richness of form and content.

155. Many dochmiacs. On a peculiarity in the sequence, see Dale, *Lyric Metres*, 174.

156. The manuscripts assign them to Theseus, whose following speech is marred by a lacuna at the beginning.

157. Besides the well-known fragments, see esp. DK 21A 32.

158. βίοτον (life) is the conjecture of Wecklein and Wilamowitz; the MSS have θάνατον (death). But only the conjecture yields the sense demanded by the context and recommended by *Androm.*, 262. If we keep the MS reading, as many scholars do, we must assume that Euripides used the verb in two different places with the exact opposite meaning. Supporters of both sides are cited in Chromik, 141, note 152; cf. W. Kranz, *Studien* 1967, 307.

159. Thus Schmid (3. 440), Pohlenz (1. 229); and even Kamerbeek's excellent study (op. cit.) betrays the influence of the psycho-pathological interpretation when he speaks of "madness as the violent reaction to the overstrain of burdensome life." However, he correctly sees in the drama a gripping symbol of man's helplessness.

160. E. Peterson, *Die attische Tragödie als Bild- und Bühnenkunst*, Bonn 1915, 42; Schadewaldt, *Monolog*, 253; Perrotta, 527; E. Kroeker, op. cit., 114 (with a survey of the problem); H. Drexler, op. cit.; Rivier, 116; Zürcher, 92; Greenwood, 80; K. Matthiessen, *El., Taur. Iph. und Hel.*, Hypomn. 4 (1964), 79; Chromik, 105. Martinazzoli (148), who reports Wilamowitz's old interpretation inaccurately and describes it as "astrattismo germanico", stands alone in his own view that Eur. was representing in Herakles' madness the inner inadequacy of physical force, but in fact he comes quite close to what Wilamowitz meant. A valuable survey of the history of *Herakles* interpretations is in Rohdich, 73.

161. Cf. L. Deubner, "Oedipusprobleme," *Sitzb. Berlin* 1942/4, 12.

162. On this, H. Herter, *Rhein. Mus.* 88 (1939), 313, and 91 (1942), 234.

163. "The Order of Tragedies at the Great Dionysia," *Hermathena* 6 (1965), 21; also *Eur.*, 8.

164. Standard text by B. Snell, *Eur. Alexandros und andere* Strassburg. *Pap. mit Fragm. griech. Dichter. Hermes* Einzelschriften 5. Berlin 1937; F. Scheidweiler, "Zum *Alex.* des Eur.," *Phil.* 97 (1948), 321; W. Strzelecki, *De Senecae* Agamemnone *Euripidisque* Alexandro, Breslau 1949; D. Lanza, "L'*Alessandro* e il valore del doppio coro Euripideo," *Stud. It.* 34 (1963), 230;

J. O. de G. Hanson, "Reconstruction of Eur. *Alex.*," *Herm.* 92 (1964), 171; K. Matthiessen, *El., Taur. Iph. und Hel.*, Hypomn. 4 (1964), 125; F. Jouan, *Eur. et les légendes des Chants Cypriens*, Paris 1966, 113; H. J. Mette, *Lustrum* 9 (1964), 69, and 1967/12 (1968), 22, with bibl; Webster, *Eur.*, 165, with bibl.

165. On the secondary chorus, see Lammers, 88 and D. Laura, op. cit.

166. F. Stoessl, "Die Palamedestragödien der drei grossen Tragiker," *Wien. Stud.* 79 (1966), 93; F. Jouan, op. cit., 339; Webster, *Eur.*, 174; H. J. Mette, *Lustrum* 1967/12 (1968), 195.

167. ANNOTATED EDITIONS: L. Cammelli, Milan 1933; A. Taccone, Turin 1937; G. Martelotti, Rome 1948; G. Schiassi, Florence 1953; A. G. Westerbrink (Gr. en Lat. schrijvers 69), Leyden 1968. TEXT: W. Biehl, Leipzig 1970. HISTORY OF THE LEGEND: T. C. W. Stinton, *Eur. and the Judgement of Paris*, London 1965 (he treats the passages from *Andr., Hek., Tro., Iph. A.*); F. Jouan, op. cit. INTERPRETATION: H. Steiger, "Warum schrieb Eur. seine *Troerinnen?*" *Phil.* 59 (1900), 362; C. Robert, "Zu Eur. *Tro.*," *Herm.* 56 (1921), 302; L. Parmentier, "Notes sur les *Troyennes* d'Eur.," *Rev. Et. Gr.* 1923, 46; M. Vincieri, *La ragione storica delle* Troadi *di Eur.*, Padua 1937; Friedrich, 61; H. D. Westlake, "Eur. *Troades* 205–99," *Mnem.* ser. 4, 6 (1953), 181; D. Ebener, "Die Helenaszene der *Tro.*," *Wiss. Ztschr. d. Univ. Halle. Ges.-Sprachw.* 3/4 (1954), 691; W. S. Maguinness, "Eur. *Tro.* 1180–88," *Bull. Inst. Class. Stud.* 12 (1965), 27; Chromik, 181; Conacher, 127 (with discussion of the trilogy); Webster, 177, (with special treatment of the possible connections to the two preceding plays); J. R. Wilson, "An interpolation in the prologue of Eur. *Tro.*," *Gr., Rom. and Byz. Stud.* 8 (1967), 205; D. G. Harbsmeier, "Die alten Menschen bei Eur.," Diss. Göttingen 1968, 71; Steidle, 50; Wilamowitz, *Gr. Verskunst*, 163, is still important for the metrical analysis. TRANSLATION (as stage manuscript): L. Wolde, Leipzig 1942; E. Buschor, Munich 1957; E. Hamilton, *Three Greek Plays* (*Prom., Ag., Tro.*), New York 1937; F. K. Smith, London 1951; Calogero de Caro, Urbino 1959.

168. The athetesis of 48–49 proposed by J. R. Wilson, op. cit., strikes to the very heart of the play. That disaster threatens the victors as well is explicitly proclaimed in the drama (Kassandra act) and reveals the whole insanity of the war. Moreover, Poseidon gives Athena her cue clearly enough at v. 47.

169. Cf. Steidle, 50. In her excellent study *L'Evolution du path.*, de Romilly examines Euripides' use of characters sinking onto the earth or lying on it as an expression of pathos; on the *Tro.*, p. 80.

170. Friedrich, 61, is good on this.

171. Chromik, 194, is good on this.

172. Thus Friedrich is probably right to interpret the passage in this way (in disagreement with Chromik, 232. 38): Kassandra takes off the fillets before disgrace and death in order to preserve them from desecration.

173. We must assume a lacuna after v. 434 unless we follow Wilamowitz in deleting 435–443. Recently Chromik (232. 37) favored the athetesis, but v. 444, in which Kassandra refrains from describing Odysseus's sufferings at greater length, does point to a more detailed description in the previous section.

174. Cf. Steidle, 51.

175. Thus, Seidler's athetesis of lines 647–656, mentioned in Murray's apparatus, is superfluous.

176. As Herwerden points out, the deletion of 862 f. is necessary in view of 869 f.

177. Chromik (206) carefully examines all the elements of this peculiar composition and offers numerous other passages for comparison.

178. This probably refers to a character who appeared in the *Alexandros*, and not to Priamos.

179. Cf. the debate in "Euripide," *Entretiens sur l'ant. class.* 6 (1960), 155. See also Steidle, 54.

180. Passages in Chromik, 230. 25.

181. In the play complaints against the gods, who send disaster or indifferently allow it to

occur, are voiced with increasing intensity. Andromache: 775; chorus: 597, 599, 858, 1060; Hekabe: 696, 1240, 1242, 1280.

182. A poignant touch was provided by W. S. Maguinness's emendations λέχος (1181) and ὕπνοι τε κοινόι (1188).

183. Odysseus is occasionally made the son of Sisyphos when his unscrupulous cleverness is under attack. It must remain uncertain whether there was a connection along these lines to the *Palamedes*, in which Odysseus's cunning was a main theme.

184. On this, Goossens, 507; Conacher, 136.17.

185. Thus, as a recent example, Steidle, 55, with bibl.

186. "That the theater works presented the stage, or rather a tableau on the proscenium, actually being consumed by flames, is beyond doubt." *Commentariola metrica*, Göttingen 1895 = *Gr. Versk.*, 165.

187. The extent to which drama can make such demands on the public is shown by the Japanese Noh plays; cf. A. Lesky, *Maia* n.s. 15 (1963), 41 = *Ges. Schr.*, 278. But of course this does not prove anything about the Athenian theater.

188. ANNOTATED EDITIONS: J. D. Denniston, Oxford 1939; G. Schiassi, Bologna 1956 (1963). INTERPRETATION: W. Wuhrmann, "Strukturelle Untersuchungen zu den beiden *El.* und zum eurip. *Or.*," Diss. Zurich, 1940; Friedrich, 76; F. Stoessl, "Die *El.* des. Eur.," *Rhein. Mus.* 99 (1956), 47; José Alsina, "Observaciones sobre la figura di Clitemestra," *Emerita* 27 (1959), 297; U. Albini, "L'*Elettra* di Eur.," *Maia* 14 (1962), 85; K. Matthiessen, *El., Taur. Iph. u. Hel.*, Hypomn. 4, 1964; Chromik, 143; Conacher, 199; M. Kubo, "The Norm of Myth: Eur. *El.*," *Harv. Stud.* 71 (1967), 15; A. Vögler, *Vergl. Studien zur soph. und eurip.* El., Heidelberg 1967; Webster, 143; Steidle, 63; J. Dingel, "Der 24. Gesang der *Od.* und die *El.* des Eur.," *Rhein. Mus.* 112 (1969), 103. Especially recommended is Zürcher's analysis (108). TRANSLATIONS: E. Buschor, Munich 1957; D. W. Lucas, London 1951. The extensive literature on the dating problem, the relationship of the two *Elektras*, and Euripides' criticism of Aischylos is assembled in separate footnotes below.

189. *Pol. Plays*, 64. Zuntz is followed by, among others, H. J. Mette, *Gymn.* (1959), 151; H. J. Newiger, *Herm.* 89 (1961), 427; Von Fritz, 476, 24; K. Matthiessen, op. cit., 52; T. B. L. Webster, *Wien. Stud.* 79 (1966), 116, and *Eur.*, 4, with the dating 421–415; A. M. Dale, *Helen*, Oxford 1967, xvii; Steidle, 82. Recently E. R. Schwinge, "Abermals: *Die Elektren*," *Rhein. Mus.* 112 (1969), 6, speaks of "The *Elektra* of 418." For the earlier dating, see Goossens, 562. A. Vögler, op. cit., reattempts to prove this correct. He offers extensive bibl. Tentatively, H. Diller, *Serta Philol. Aenipontana*, Innsbruck 1962, 96, and A. Lesky, *Gesch. d. gr. Lit.*, 2d ed., Bern 1963, 420. A compromise solution based on the "theory of the drawer" is sought by W. Theiler, *Wien. Stud.* 79 (1966), 103.

190. Does the word choice in πρῴρας ἐνάλους (prows in the sea) have special significance? Are we supposed to see the prows of the ships calmly plowing the sea? Certainly there is no hint of distress.

191. Many good and liberating comments are in G. Zuntz, "Contemporary Politics in the Plays of Eur.," *Acta Congressus Madvigiani* i, Copenhagen 1958, 155.

192. T. Zielinski, *Tragodumenon libri tres*, Cracow 1925, 133; J. M. Descroix, *Le trimètre iambique*, Macon 1931; C. B. Ceadel, "Resolved Feet in the Trimeters of Eur.," *Class. Quart.* 35 (1941), 66. Recently in the introduction to her *Helen* (Oxford 1967, xxv ff.), A. M. Dale has offered a number of careful observations; cf. further, K. Matthiessen, op. cit., 168. We have omitted several other theories on the dating that rely on structural considerations because they led to no trustworthy results and operate on the basis of a very narrow concept of development.

193. We use the table in K. Matthiessen, op. cit., 170, based on the figures of C. B. Ceadel. His principle of excluding from consideration trimeters in a lyric context and proper names is in our opinion correct. The statistics in Webster, *Eur.*, 3 ff., following Zielinski, show some deviation, but here too the regressive movement from *Med.* (6.5%) to *Hipp.* (5.6%) may be clearly discerned.

194. Op. cit., 103. He was anticipated by T. Zielinski, 185; J. M. Descroix, 58, 171; E. B. Caedel, 76 (all three op. cit.).

195. A good observation in K. Matthiessen, op. cit., 62.

196. For the opposition to social prejudices, cf. *Hipp.* 1249; *Andr.* 638; *Hel.* 729, 1640; frr. 52, 495. 40, 831N. A new evaluation of country dwellers is also expressed in *Or.* 917 and *Ba.* 717. For questions of this sort the collection of passages in Wilhelm Nestle's *Eur. der Dichter der griech. Aufklärung*, Stuttgart 1901, offers convenient reference material.

197. The curious form of address, which sounds as if it were addressed to the audience, recalls the conclusion of the funeral speech of Adrastos.

198. Steidle, 72, offers much in support of the scene, but K. Matthiessen's judgment (op. cit., 121) is essentially correct.

199. The complaints of old people about the toils of travel recur elsewhere in Euripides; cf. *Herakles*, 119.

200. E. R. Schwinge, *Rhein. Mus.* 112 (1969), 9. 19, correctly follows Strohm (78), as opposed to K. Matthiessen (op. cit., 124), who believes that Euripides was here trying to avoid the traces of the Sophoklean drama. The composition of the scene is to be explained from the requirements of the play itself. On the short dochmiac system of the chorus, cf. *Hipp.* 362, *Rhes.* 131.

201. The MSS assignment of the lines is much confused; J. D. Denniston, in his commentary, correctly defends Murray's separation into triads.

202. The section poses a number of individual questions. The entrance of the victors is not designated as precisely as is usually the case. It must have occurred during the antistrophe of the chorus, between στέψω (872) and δέξαι (882). Elektra briefly went into the house to bring the garlands.

Unlike J. D. Denniston, I would prefer to see in v. 883 οὐκ ἀχρεῖον ἔκπλεθρον δραμὼν ἀγῶνα (running a difficult two-hundred-meter course), a disdainful judgment of victories in sports because of the precise notation of the stadion course. Such an attitude may already be expressed in vv. 862 f.

Aigisthos's corpse is brought on stage. This is confirmed by v. 959. I believe 895 also refers to this, while Denniston thinks it refers to the head, which would then have been separated from the trunk. Is this a necessary inference from the messenger's statement (856), or can we also interpret it to mean that Orestes, with Aigisthos's corpse, will confront Elektra with a sight that has an effect different from that of the Gorgon's head? Note that the κάρα Γοργόνος (Gorgon's head) is contrasted to ὃν στυγεῖς Αἴγισθον (Aigisthos, whom you hate).

Elektra crowns both with garlands. Here Steidle (83) correctly remarks that they can hardly have gone to kill Klytaimestra while still wearing the garlands, and he makes the ingenious suggestion that they take off the wreaths during the verses of Orestes (890 ff.)—which grant to the gods the honor of the victory—and dedicate them (on an altar?).

203. The assignment of lines 959–966 is difficult. In opposition to the changes suggested by Camper and accepted by Murray and Denniston, Steidle (74) defends the manuscript assignment with good reasons. Thus 959–961 belong to Orestes together with the beginning of the stichomythy (962) with Elektra. However, I cannot imagine Orestes speaking both 965 and 967, despite Steidle. The transposition of 965 and 966 recommended by Kirchhoff results in a smooth sequence of thought. The juxtaposition of 965 and 967 is quite effective.

204. The old question: Did an opening door suffice to show the two corpses, pointed out by Orestes (1178), or was it necessary to employ the ekkyklema? After the remarks on the *Herakles* I cannot refute the latter assumption.

205. Cf. A. Lesky, "Psychologie bei Eur.," *Entretiens sur l'ant. Class.* 6 (1960), 147, and "Zur Problematik des Psychologischen in der Trag. des Eur.," *Gymn.* 67 (1960), 24 = *Ges. Schr.*, 261.

206. The change in the chorus's verdict has a parallel in the *Choephoroi*, but there it involves the double aspect of the deed, which Euripides can explain but not morally justify.

207. Steidle, 90, discusses the assignment of speakers in the kommos.

208. Steidle, 85, takes an opposing view. But it seems unbelievable that in this situation

Kastor would call the siblings οὐ μυσαροὶ τοῖσδε σφαγίοις (not polluted by this slaughter). Conversely it is clear that he expressly bases his exception for the previous questioner (probably Elektra) on the grounds that Apollo was the real instigator (1296).

209. *Pol. Plays*, 69. 1; now also Steidle, 81, with further bibl. Kitto's interpretation of the *El.* as a melodrama is rightly contradicted by Conacher, 200.

210. A brief summary of other positions: for the priority of Eur. once decreed by Wilamowitz, *Herm.* 18 (1883), 214: H. F. Johansen, *Class. e. Mediaev.* 25 (1964), 11 (cautiously); H. J. Newiger, *GGA* 219 (1967), 190, with a polemic against Matthiessen (see below); F. Solmsen, "Electra and Orestes. Three Recognitions in Gr. Trag.," *Meded. Nederl. Ak. Afd. Letterkunde* 30/2 (1967), 51; W. Theiler, "Die ewigen *Elektren*," *Wien. Stud.* 79 (1966), 102, whose dating sequence we append here, without identifying ourselves with it (423 *Kresphontes*; 423/2 *Andr.*; 420 *Hek.*; 419 *Suppl.*; 419/8 *El.* (consigned to the drawer); 417 *Herakles*; 416 Soph. *Trach.* [quite rightly with a question mark!]; 415 *Alex., Palam., Tro.*; 414 *Iph. T.*; 413 Eur. *El.* [finally produced]; 412 *Hel., Andromeda*; 411 *Ion*? Soph. *El., Phaethon*; 410 *Antiope*; 409 *Phoin.*; 408 *Or., Hypsipyle*); Webster, *Eur.*, 15.

The priority of Sophokles, which W. Kranz (*Sokrates* n.s. 6 [1918], 334 = *Studien* 1967, 304) believed to be beyond doubt, has won increasing support: Friedrich, 76; von Fritz, 143; K. Matthiessen, op. cit. 81; A. Vögler, op. cit.; E. R. Schwinge, *Rhein. Mus.* 112 (1969), 1.

211. R. Böhme, "Aischylos und der Anagnorismos," *Herm.* 73 (1938), 195; E. Fraenkel, *Aesch. Ag.*, vol. 3, Oxford 1950, 821, with a careful discussion of the problem.

212. Thus H. Lloyd-Jones, *Class. Quart.* n.s. 11 (1961), 172; H. J. Newiger, *Herm.* 89 (1961), 427. 5, with bibl; H. Diller, *Serta Philol. Aenipontana* 1962, 95. 5, with bibl; K. Matthiessen, op. cit., 122; F. Solmsen (see note 210), 36, 43.

213. On the form of the title, see M. Platnauer, xvi, and K. Matthiessen, op. cit. The local designation added to the name is of course secondary and serves to differentiate the play from the *Iph. at Aulis*. Our abbreviation *Iph. T.* stands for *Iphigeneia Taurica*.

214. Thus, M. Platnauer, xvi, and K. Matthiessen, 63 (for both, see next note); A. M. Dale, *Helen*, Oxford 1967, xxviii, on the basis of very subtle metrical observations, with a justified mistrust of the decisiveness of structural comparisons.

The priority of the *Helen* was supported by T. von Wilamowitz; followed by Zielinski; Perrotta (quoted in K. Matthiessen, op. cit., 57. 1); G. Mathieu, "Peut-on dater l'*Iph. en Taur.*?" *Ant. Class.* 10 (1941), 77; Zürcher, 150. 3, and Pohlenz, 2. 164; and finally, K. Alt, "Zur Anagnorisis der *Hel.*," *Herm.* 90 (1962), 6.

215. ANNOTATED EDITIONS: M. Platnauer, Oxford 1938; J. D. Meerwaldt, 2 vols., 4th pr., Leyden 1970; G. Ammendola, Turin 1948; H. Strohm, Munich 1949 (on p. 211 is a list of older editions). On the History of the Legend: A. Baschmakoff, "Origine Taurienne du mythe d'Iph.," *Bull. Ass. Budé* 64 (1939), 3; G. McCracken, *Mnem.* ser. 3, 9 (1941), 161. INTERPRETATION: G. Perrotta, "L'*Elena* e l'*If. Taur* di Eur.," *Stud. It.* n.s. 6 (1928), 5; F. Solmsen, "Zur Gestaltung des Intrigenmotivs in den Tragödien des Soph. und Eur.," *Phil.* 87 (1932) 1, and "Eur. *Ion* im Vergleich mit anderen Tragödien," *Herm.* 69 (1934), 390; G. Zuntz, "Die *taur. Iph.* des Eur.," *Die Antike* 9 (1933), 245; C. del Grande, *Note fil.*, Naples 1942, 63; J. C. Kamerbeek, *Mnem.* ser. 3, 12 (1944), 44 (on 1010 f.); K. Matthiessen, *El., Taur. Iph. und Hel.*, Hypomn. 4, Göttingen 1964; Conacher, 303; Webster, 184. TRANSLATIONS: E. Buschor, Munich 1946 (1957); E. Bossi, Urbino 1957; K. H. de Raaf, Zutphen 1939; J. Humblé, Antwerp 1941.

On the many forms of the intrigue motif, in addition to the studies by Solmsen (above), Mette, *Verl. Aisch.*, 57. 2, offers much bibl. Especially recommended is H. Strohm, "Trug und Täuschung in der eurip. Dramatik," *Würzburg. Jahrb.* 4 (1949/50), 140; see also his book on Euripides.

216. Thus already Wilamowitz, *Herm.* 18 (1883), 249. On the extent of Euripidean invention, A. Lesky, *RE* 18 (1939), 997 ff.

217. The reference of the relative ἧς in v. 36 to ἑορτῆς and not to Artemis seems more certain to Platnauer than it does to me. After all, Artemis is called Καλή and Καλλίστη, and what

was the name of the festival supposed to be, and why the aposiopesis? Conacher (311. 11) suggests an intentional ambiguity.

218. The overlong sentence ending in an anacoluthon (77 ff.) seems peculiar. Is it supposed to indicate the despair of the speaker?

219. *Med., El., Tro., Hel., Or., Hypsipyle.*

220. In v. 336 Meckler's ηὔχου instead of the εὔχου of the MSS adds an unnecessary touch of cruelty to Iphigeneia's character.

221. We prefer this divison to Platnauer's, who separates the section into two epeisodia divided by the kommos (643–657).

222. Here again we emphasize the excellent discussion of the passage by Schwinge (270), as by rights we should whenever the subject of Euripidean stichomythy arises.

223. Cicero, *Lael.* 7. 24, tells us of an effective scene in Pacuvius in which Pylades pretended before the king to be Orestes so as to be sacrificed in place of his friend, but Orestes insisted on his own identity.

224. Cf. Schwinge, 201. 13, with bibl.

225. G. Zuntz is good on this line, *Die Antike* 9 (1933), 251.

226. See the black-figured lekythos in *Corp. Vas. Paris Bibl. Nat.* III J a plate 86, figs. 2 and 6–8.

227. In his commentary M. Platnauer adduces weighty evidence that ἐκπέμπειν here means "escort out of" and that the command is directed not to Thoas but to Orestes. The πέμψω of Thoas in v. 1482 would then only indicate his agreement. Thus, too, K. Matthiessen op. cit., 59. 1, who rightly rejects Grégoire's notion that directions were given in the lacuna ascertained by Reiske to send the chorus to Delos. Lines 1097 ff. are insufficient support for this.

228. K. Matthiessen, op. cit., has many good comments.

229. ANNOTATED EDITIONS: A. C. Pearson, Cambridge 1903; N. Wecklein, Leipzig 1907; N. Terzaghi, Florence 1919; A. Taccone, Naples 1931; G. Italie, Groningen 1949; A. Y. Campbell, Liverpool 1950; G. Ammendola, Turin 1954; R. Argenio, Rome 1956; A. M. Dale, Oxford 1967; R. Kannicht, 2 vols., Heidelberg 1969, the most penetrating commentary on the play, with valuable introduction and bibliography. A NEW TEXT: K. Alt, Leipzig 1964. INTERPRETATION: G. Perrotta, "L'*Elena* e l'*If. Taur.* di Eur.," *Stud. Ital.* n.s. 6 (1928), 5; P. Maas, "Epidaurische Hymnen," *Schr. d. Königsberger Gel. Ges.* 9/5 (1933), 141 (on the stasimon, 1301); F. Solmsen, "Onoma and Pragma in Eur. *Helen,*" *Class. Rev.* 48 (1934), 119, and the studies cited for the *Iph. T.;* J. Griffith, "Some Thoughts on the *Hel.,*" *Journ. Hell. Stud.* 73 (1953), 36; A. N. Pippin, "Eur. *Helen*: A Comedy of Ideas," *Class. Phil.* 55 (1960), 151; G. Zuntz, "On Eur. *Helen*: Theology and Irony," *Entretiens sur ant. class.* 6 (1960), 199, and *Inquiry,* passim; K. Alt, "Zur Anagnorisis der *Helena,*" *Herm.* 90 (1962), 6, with much bibl., and "Bemerkungen zum Text der *Hel.,*" *Phil.* 107 (1963), 30, 173; K. Matthiessen, *El., Taur. Iph. u. Hel.,* Hypomn. 4, 1964, and "Zur Theonoeszene der eurip. *Hel.,*" *Herm.* 96 (1968), 685; A. Tovar, "Aspectos de la *Hel.* de Eur.," *Estudios sobre la trag. griega,* Madrid 1966, 107; Conacher, 286; Webster, 199.

Further bibl. on the interpretation of the play is in D. G. Harbsmeier, "Die alten Menschen bei Eur.," Diss. Göttingen 1968, 148. 1. On the MS tradition exhaustively treated by R. Kannicht, cf. V. di Benedetto, "Sul codice L e L'*Elena* di Eur.," *Phil.* 108 (1962), 138.

230. Thus, R. Kannicht, op. cit., 1. 30. Cf., too, C. M. Bowra, "The Two Palinodes of Stes.," *Class. Rev.* n.s. 13 (1963), 245; J. A. Davison, "De *Helena* Stesichori," *Quad. Urbinati* 2 (1966), 80.

231. This need not be doubted (as Conacher does, 286) because the passage in Plato *Phaidr.* 243a (*PMG* 192) states that Helen never boarded a ship. Besides, it is just as probable that she was whisked away by a god.

232. Thus, J. Schwartz, *Pseudo-Hesiodea,* Leyden 1960, 554; A. Tovar, op. cit., 118. 34; Conacher, 287; R. Kannicht, op. cit., 24. 5.

233. Cf. K. von Fritz, *Die griech. Geschichtsschreibung,* Berlin 1967, 1. 162. We can also forget the speculations of F. Iesi, "L'Egitto infero nell'*Elena* d'Eur.," *Aegyptus* 45 (1965), 56.

234. The attempt of P. Gilbert, "Souvenirs de l'Egypte dans l'*Hél.* d'Eur.," *Ant. Class.* 18 (1949), 79, to identify the characters of Proteus and Theonoe with historical persons is unfounded.

235. Passages now in K. Matthiessen, *Herm.* 96 (1968), 699.

236. The athetesis of lines 257–259 by Badham does not seem as certain to me as it does to R. Kannicht. The doubts about myth go well with v. 21. A. M. Dale believes them to be genuine. Conversely, there is much to be said for deleting 299–302 with Hartung, since they interrupt the flow of the speech.

237. G. Zuntz, op. cit. (*Entretiens*, 214) rightly protests against designating the man a messenger. He is a servant of Menelaos (728), here appearing, to be sure, in the function of a messenger.

238. The parallel to the corresponding section of the *Iph. T.* is obvious. It extends into details. Just as Iphigeneia in her joy turns to the captive Greek women of the chorus (842), so does Helen (627, 648). The textually difficult passage 630–651, for which *P. Oxy.* 22 (1954), 2336, provides further evidence, was thoroughly treated by Zuntz, *Inquiry*, 217. See further R. Kannicht's commentary. Cf., too, K. Matthiessen, *Hypomn.* 4 (1964), 136; W. Biehl, "Das Problem der Textreconstruction in Eur. *Hel.* 635–641," *Phil.* 116 (1972), 201.

239. Cf. W. Nestle, *Vom Mythos zum Logos*, Stuttgart 1940, index.

240. A thorough doxography on the passage is in R. Kannicht; he does not favor athetesis (cf. G. Zuntz, op. cit., *Entretiens*, 207), but rather the assumption of a lacuna, supposing that the text once contained a portrayal of the alternatives that endanger Theonoe herself: exposure or silence? This is a satisfactory solution, but A. M. Dale in her commentary makes do without such an assumption, thinking to see in 892 f. a command—never carried out—to inform her brother. In that case one might reasonably expect Helen to begin her speech differently, with a μη δῆτα (*Don't!*) or the equivalent. Recently K. Matthiessen, *Herm.* 96 (1969), 689. 2, also seeks an alternative to the lacuna theory.

241. It seems certain that v. 1150 is meaningless here in the form given by the MSS. The most recent suggestion, οὐδ' ἔχω τί τὸ σαφὲς ὅ τι ποτ' ἐν βροτοῖς / ἀμφὶ θεῶν· οὐδὲν ἀλαθὲς ηὗρον (I do not know for certain what there is among men from the gods; I have found nothing sure), by Kannicht results in a nice ring-composition for the strophe.

242. Important is P. Maas's treatment, op. cit., which compares it with the epigraphic hymn to the Mother of the gods IG ιν. 1², 131.

243. On this manner of praying and on the passage, cf. A. M. Dale, *Maia* 15 (1963), 314 and R. Kannicht in his commentary.

244. In discussing the old problem of whether an anonymous servant must be added here because of v. 1630, A. M. Dale and R. Kannicht in their commentaries rightly decide in favor of the chorus or its leader.

245. K. Matthiessen, *Herm.* 96 (1969), 699, is all too quick to dismiss such references, but he is perfectly right in distinguishing the role of the gods here from apparently comparable instances in Sophokles (697).

246. H. Grégoire and R. Goossens, "Les allusions politiques dans d'*Hél.* d'Eur.," *Compt. rend. de l'Ac. des Inscr.* 1940, 206, and H. Grégoire in the Eur. edition of the Budé series (V, 17). Both refer to the Teukros episode. P. Gilbert (see note 234, above) conjectures historical persons behind Proteus and Theonoe.

247. "Intrigenbildung in der att. Tragödie," *Anz. Ak. Wien. Phil.-hist. Kl.* 1932, 4.

248. G. Busch, "Unters. zum Wesen der τύχη in der Trag. des Eur.," Diss. Heidelberg 1937, goes too far in depreciating its importance. Passages like those assembled by Schadewaldt, *Monolog*, 257, and F. Solmsen, *Herm.* 69 (1934), 400. 2, cannot be lightly dismissed. A sober judgment appears in Zürcher, 149. The main example is *Ion* 1512.

249. W. Mitsdörffer, "Das Mnesilochos-Lied in Aristoph. *Thesm.*," *Phil.* 98 (1954/55), 59; P. Rau, *Paratragodia*, Munich 1967, 65; T. B. L. Webster, *The Andromeda of Eur.*, 192, 304; H. J. Mette, *Lustrum* 1967/12 (1968), 47. Sophokles too composed an *Andromeda*.

250. ANNOTATED EDITIONS: Wilamowitz, Berlin 1926; A. S. Owen, Oxford 1939; G. Italie, Leyden 1948; G. Ammendola, Florence 1951. INTERPRETATION: F. Solmsen, "Eur. *Ion* im Vergleich mit den anderen Tragödien," *Herm.* 69 (1934), 390; F. M. Wassermann, "Divine Violence and Providence in Eur. *Ion*," *Trans. Am. Phil. Ass.* 71 (1940), 587; F. Scheidweiler, "Textkritisches zum *Ion* des Eur.," *Rhein. Mus.* 92 (1943), 179; Friedrich, 10; D. J. Conacher, "The Paradox of Eur. *Ion*," *Trans. Am. Phil Ass.* 90 (1959), 20, and *Eur. Dr.*, 267; A. Spira, *Untersuchungen zum deus ex machina bei Soph. und Eur.*, Kallmünz 1960, 33; Q. Cataudella, "Lettura dello *Ione* euripideo," *Dioniso* 36 (1962), 15 = *Emerita* 26 (1958), 47 = *Saggi sulla trag. Greca*, Messina 1969, 235; Anne P. Burnett, "Human Resistance and Divine Persuasion in Eur. *Ion*," *Class. Phil.* 57 (1962), 58; C. Wolff, "The design and myth in Eur. *Ion*," *Harv. Stud.* 69 (1965), 169; A. Imhof, *Eur. Ion*, Bern 1966; Webster, *Eur.*, 202; S. L. Radt, *Eur. Ioon*, Amsterdam 168; Rohdich, 105; R. F. Willets, "Action and Character in the *Ion* of Eur.," *Journ. Hell. Stud.* 93 (1973), 201. TRANSLATION: E. Staiger, Bern 1947; D. W. Lucas, London 1949; L. Volpis, Milan 1939; Q. Cataudella, Urbino 1962.

251. H. Grégoire in the edition of the Budé series, 167; Delebecque, 225; Goossens, 478; A. S. Owen, xxxvi; Conacher, 271, also supports the early date.

252. F. Solmsen, op. cit., 404, makes some progress but in our opinion goes too far (cf. the remarks above). He dates the *Ion* after the *Helena*, on the basis of the use of anagnorisis and mechanema. It is difficult to contradict Conacher (274) when he explains the difference of the *Ion* from *Iph. T.* and *Hel.* not so much from the progressive development of the poet as from the demands of the material. K. Matthiessen, Hypomn. 4 (1964), 89, 138, dates the *Ion* to 413 after the *Iph. T.* (414); he offers a good survey of the whole problem. T. B. L. Webster, *Wien. Stud.* 79 (1966), 115, and A. M. Dale, *Helen*, Oxford 1967, xxviii, date the *Ion* close to the *Hel.*; Webster, *Eur.*, 192, believes it was produced together with the *Andromeda* and *Helena* in 412, which poses problems because of the thematic similarity between *Ion* and *Helena*; S. L. Radt, op. cit., 24, follows the metrical criteria for the later date.

253. Cf. Conacher, 271. Of special importance is Plato, *Euthyd.* 302d.

254. The τάδε in v. 76 need not mean that the δαφνώδη γύαλα (laurel-wooded dells) were visible (though a paraskenion decorated with laurel is conceivable); an explanatory gesture of the god would suffice.

255. Only in this way does the difficult verse 68, to which S. L. Radt, op. cit., 26, 34, devotes a thorough discussion, yield an acceptable sense. But then it is a nice touch that it is precisely the secretive actions of his brother that arouse Hermes' curiosity.

256. The *Erechtheus* of Eur. preceded the *Ion* and was fresh in the minds of the Athenian audience.

257. It is very strange that after Ion remarks that his mother was probably the earth, Xouthos says (542) that children do not grow from the ground. Is this supposed to contradict the legend about the birth of Erichthonios, Kreusa's ancestor (cf. 267, 1000)?

258. On 642 ff., cf. F. Heinimann, *Nomos und Physis*, Basel 1945, 167.

259. A nice list has been assembled by A. S. Owen, op. cit., on v. 661. Hermes had already made a preliminary reference to Ion's future name (v. 80).

260. On the assignment of parts in the opening section, see Schwinge, 78. On recognizable responsions in the lyric verses, see A. S. Owen, op. cit., on v. 763.

261. Schwinge is excellent on this, 129, 216.

262. Vv. 1112 and 1237 must be understood in this way, and the same goes for πετρορριφῆ (1222), although it is translated in LSJ as "hurled from a rock"; but cf. A. S. Owen on 1112 and *Or.* 50. Conversely *Ion* 1268 speaks of a fall from a cliff, which also appears in the Aesop romance as the punishment for the blasphemer. It is highly questionable whether one can reconcile the two with Owen's suggestion that the stoning took place before or after the fall.

263. Somewhat obtrusively the poet seeks an ironic effect in v. 1307, in which Kreusa replies to Ion's command to leave the altar: Go give orders to your mother, wherever she may be.

264. K. Matthiessen, Hypomn. 4 (1964), 134, compares the amoibaia in the plays listed. In v.

1441 Kreusa switches suddenly from spoken trimeters to a sung iambelegus. The coexistence of sung and spoken parts in a verse is found again at 1452, 1481, and (according to the transposition suggested by Wilamowitz) 1496. A. S. Owen is certainly incorrect to eliminate it in 1481.

265. In v. 1570 Athena speaks of her chariot. Figurative usage cannot be ruled out, but is less probable.

266. In his edition of the *Ion*, Cambridge 1890, and in *Euripides the Rationalist*, Cambridge 1913. In his edition (xxxii) A. S. Owen points to a predecessor of Verrall in an H. B. L., who published a translation of the *Ion* with notes in 1889. A good survey of the history of this interpretation is in Rohdich, 105.

267. F. M. Wassermann, op. cit; A. Spira, *Untersuchungen zum deus ex machina bei Soph. und Eur.*, Kallmünz 1960, 33; Q. Cataudella, op. cit.; Anne P. Burnett, op. cit.; C. Wolff., op. cit.; and especially M. Imhof, op. cit., following Spira. Recently also Steidle, 113. 94.

268. The relationship between Tyche and the gods bothers the speaker of the five trimeters from the second *Phoinix* in H. J. Mette, *Lustrum* 1967/12 (1968), 281, no. 1158; cf. Austin, 86, no. 154.

269. Ion's criticism: 436, but cf. also passages like 355, 370, 1497, 1537.

270. A. S. Owen, op. cit., xxi; Rosenmeyer, 119; Conacher, 279. Now S. L. Radt, op. cit., 17, offers a moderate and reasonable judgment. During the Peloponnesian War, Delphi assuredly was no favorite of Athens. From this, F. Schachermeyr, "Religionspolitik und Religiosität bei Perikles," *Sitzb. Öst. Ak. Phil-hist. Kl.* 258/3 (1968), 22, explains the negative features in the portrait of Apollo.

271. *Griech. Kulturgesch.*, 2. 306 (Kröner). On the motifs of Kreusa's attack, cf. Schwinge, 219. 58, who offers a different opinion.

272. E. G. Turner on *P. Oxy.* 2458 (27 [1962], 73), *Hermes* 93 (1965), 256, and "The prologue to Eur. *Cresphontes*," *Aegyptus* 46 (1966), 93; E. J. Jory, *Bull. Inst. Class. Stud.* 10 (1963), 65; H. J. Mette, *Herm.* 92 (1964), 391, and *Lustrum* 1964/9 (1965), 66, and 1967/12 (1968), 148; Hourmouziades, 105; Webster, *Eur.*, 136; Austin, 41.

273. H. Schaal, "De Euripidis *Antiopa*." Diss. Berlin 1914; D. L. Page, *Lit. Pap.*, London 1950, 60; P. Frassinetti, *Antidoron Paoli*, Genoa 1956, 96; R. Argenio, *Riv. Stud. Class.* 6 (1958), 50 (on the *Antiopa* of Pacuvius); U. Haussmann, *Ath. Mitt.* 73 (1958), 50; H. J. Mette, *Lustrum* (see previous note) 88 and 62; Snell, *Scenes*, 70; T. B. L. Webster, "Three Plays by Eur.," *Studies in Honor of H. Caplan*, Ithaca, N.Y. 1966, 95, and *Eur.*, 205, 305; Z. K. Vysoký, "Euripidova *Antiopa*," *Listy Filologické* 91 (1968), 371 (with German summary); J. Kambitsis, *L'Antiope d'Euripide: edition commentée des fragments*, Athens 1972. On the brothers' agon see also E. K. Borthwick, *Class. Quart.* n.s. 17 (1967), 41.

274. Webster, *Eur.*, 98; H. J. Mette, *Lustrum* 1967/12 (1968), 132.

275. Webster, *Eur.*, 236; H. J. Mette (see previous note), 210.

276. D. L. Page, *Lit. Pap.*, London 1950, 116; *P. Oxy.* 27 (1962) 2455 frr. 1 f. (E. G. Turner); Van Looy, 185; Z. K. Vysoký, *Listy Filologické* 87 (1964), 17; Webster, *Eur.*, 147; H. J. Mette, *Lustrum* 1964/9 (1965), 72, and 1967/12 (1968), 168.

277. The studies listed in the previous note discuss this play also. D. L. Page, op. cit., 108, offers the two substantial fragments: Berl. Klass. Texte 5. 2, 1907, p. 125 (vv. 1–12 also in *P. Oxy.* 1176 fr. 39) with the defense of women, probably spoken by Melanippe, and the parchment text, ibid., 5. 2. 84 with a section from the messenger-report.

278. B. Borecký, "La tragédie *Alope* d'Eur.," *Festschrift A. Salač.*, Prague 1955, 82; Webster, *Eur.*, 94, 305; H. J. Mette, *Lustrum* 1967/12 (1968), 42. The doubts of Wilamowitz (*Das Schiedsgericht*, Berlin 1925, 127) about using Hyginus *Fab.* 187 to reconstruct the play were refuted by F. Wehrli (*Motivstudien zur griech. Kom.*, Zurich 1936, 119).

279. Goossens, 596, following Zielinski, dates it to 411 or 410, Webster, *Eur.*, 238, to 408, together with *Oidipous* and *Orestes*. Sources in H. J. Mette, *Lustrum* 1967/12 (1968), 85.

280. See also F. Heinimann, *Nomos und Physis*, Basel 1945, 132.

281. Webster, *Eur.*, 94; H. J. Mette (see note 279), 102. The remnants of a *Danae* composed by a late Byzantine humanist are of no use for Euripides. Cf. Schmid, 3. 595.

282. After the edition of G. Italie (Berlin 1923) and the publication of *P. Oxy.* 852 by D. L. Page, *Lit. Pap.*, London 1950, 76 (with earlier bibl.), G. W. Bond, *Eur.* Hypsipyle, Oxford, 1963, subjected the fragments to a thorough and beneficial revision. In an addendum H. Lloyd-Jones considers attributing *P. Hamburg* 118b to the prologue of the play. Bond dates the drama to 408 or 407. H. Van Looy, *Ant. Class.* 35 (1966), 574, suggests 409. A. M. Dale, *Journ. Hell. Stud.* 84 (1964), 166; T. B. L. Webster, "Three Plays by Eur.," *Studies Caplan*, Ithaca, N.Y. 1966, 83 and *Eur.*, 211, 306; F. C. Görschen, "Der Hypsipyleprolog," *Herm.* 94 (1966), 297; H. J. Mette (see previous note), 254.

283. Cf. the remarks on the *Ion* (note 264 above). The four trimeters that G. W. Bond, op. cit., 48, cites as "Fr. apud Lydum," now prove to be a quote from the second *Phrixos*.

284. W. Schadewaldt, "Zum *Phrixos* des Eur.," *Herm.* 63 (1928), 1 = *Hellas und Hesperien*, 305; D. L. Page, *Lit. Pap.*, London 1950, 170; K. Schauenburg, "*Phrixos*," *Rhein. Mus.* 101 (1958), 41; Van Looy, 132; T. B. L. Webster, *Wien. Stud.* 79 (1966), 114 (also on the uncertainty of the dating) and *Eur.*, 131; H. J. Mette, *Lustrum* 1967/12 (1968), 278.

285. V. Bartoletti, *Maia* 17 (1965), 388; Austin, 86, no. 154; H. J. Mette (see previous note), 281, no. 1158.

286. INDIVIDUAL EDITIONS: A. C. Pearson, London 1909; J. A. Powell, London 1911; C. H. Balmori, Tucumán, Argentina 1946. INTERPRETATION: H. O. Meredith, "The End of the *Phoen.*," *Class. Rev.* 51 (1937), 97; W. H. Friedrich, "Prolegomena zu den *Phoen.*," *Herm.* 74 (1939), 265; H. D. F. Kitto, "The Final Scenes of the *Phoen.*," *Class. Rev.* 53 (1939), 104; W. Riemschneider, "Held und Staat in Eur. *Phoen.*," Diss. Berlin, Würzburg 1940; Schmid, 3. 862; Ludwig, 130; B. Snell, "Zu Eur. *Phoen.*," *Herm.* 87 (1959), 7 = *Ges. Schr.*, 178; T. Krischer, "Das Problem der tril. Komposition und die dram. Entwicklung der eur. Trag.," Diss. Frankfurt 1960, 109; E. Valgiglio, *L'esodo delle* Fenicie *di Eur.*, Turin 1961; A. J. Podlecki, "Some Themes in Eur. *Phoen.*," *Trans. Am. Phil. Ass.* 93 (1962), 355; E. Fraenkel, "Zu den *Phoen.* des Eur.," *Sitzb. Bayer. Ak. Phil.-hist. Kl.* 1963/1 (earlier: "A Passage in the *Phoen.*," *Eranos* 44 [1946], 81). See also H. Diller, *Gnom.* 36 (1964), 641; D. Ebener, "Die Phönizierinnen des Eur. als Spiegelbild geschichtlicher Wirklichkeit," *Eirene* 2 (1964), 71; W. S. Barrett, "The Epitome of Eur. *Phoinissai*: Ancient and Medieval Versions," *Class. Quart.* n.s. 15 (1965), 58; J. de Romilly, "Les *Phéniciennes* d'Eur. ou l'actualité dans la trag. Grecque," *Rev. Phil.* 39 (1965), 28; H. Erbse, "Beiträge zum Verständnis der eur. *Phoin.*," *Phil.* 110 (1966), 1; D. J. Conacher, "Themes in the Exodus of Eur. *Phoen.*," *Phoenix* 21 (1967), 92, and *Eur. Dr.*, 227; Webster, 215.

287. Cf. Goossens, 628. 62, and Conacher, 228. 2. The archon Nausikrates cited in Aristophanes' hypothesis must be an error, since there was no such person. We cannot follow Wilamowitz in referring the name to the choregos, or Schmid, 3. 569. 9, who suggests an ἐπιλαχών (potential officer, who takes office in the event of a vacancy). According to the hypoth. Soph. *Phil.*, the archon at the time of the Dionysia in 409 was Glaukippos.

288. H. J. Mette, *Lustrum* 1964/9 (1965), 123, and 1967/12 (1968), 192; Webster, *Eur.*, 115.

289. Hourmouziades (31) is good on the scenic arrangements. A ladder visibly attached to the skene is quite impossible.

290. A passage like 145, where in the same sentence lyrics follow a trimeter verse, again poses questions about the manner of performance. Probably an elevated spoken style here broke into sung recitative.

291. That the girls sailed from Tyre with the west wind over the Ionian Sea was correctly explained by Wilamowitz, *Gr. Verskunst*, 278. 1, as the natural route into the Korinthian Gulf.

292. So now E. Fraenkel, op. cit., 25, following Hartung and Robert; opposed by H. Erbse, op. cit., 3.

293. 28 : 27 : 58 is the relationship given by the transmitted text, which changes slightly if

we accept the atheteses of 548 and 555–558 suggested by Fraenkel, op. cit., 28. Just in case a warning is needed against attempts to establish an exact numerical corresponsion by any conceivable artifice, we issue that warning now for this and all similar cases.

294. Here Euripides uses an Aischylean motif: *Seven*, 576; cf. A. Lesky, "Aischylos *Septem* 576 ff.," *Studi in onore di Funaioli*, Rome 1955, 163 = *Ges. Schr.*, 223.

295. The commentary on this by Wilamowitz is important, *Gr. Verskunst*, 279.

296. A different view is taken by Pohlenz, 2. 156; H. Erbse is more cautious, op. cit., 5. 1; H. Diller, op. cit., 644, speaks of an "agonal" motif.

297. The rather strange reason why the betrothed Haimon could not be sacrificed has been neatly explained from Athenian law by H. Erbse, op. cit., 13.

298. Op. cit., 271; on the athetesis, also E. Fraenkel, op. cit., 53; H. Diller, op. cit., 644.

299. E. Fraenkel, op. cit., 71, has deleted it; H. Diller, op. cit., 648, and H. Erbse, op. cit., 18, defend it, rightly. Under no circumstances can Kreon enter bearing the corpse of Menoikeus. From v. 1317 it is clear that he has brought the body inside the house and is now looking for Iokaste to wash and lay out the corpse. That Kreon remains mute on stage for an unusual length of time we must simply accept as H. Erbse, op. cit., 16, suggests.

300. The athetesis of lines 1595–1614 by E. Fraenkel, op. cit., 89, is refuted by H. Diller, op. cit., 645, and H. Erbse, op. cit., 20, with an excellent evaluation of the passage.

301. Line 1634, which intensifies the decree and is clearly an imitation of *Ant.* 29, was already deleted by Valckenauer, and rightly so.

302. We shall first analyze the final section without discussing the question of authenticity.

303. Following Wilamowitz, H. Diller, op. cit., 646, supports the authenticity of these lines, which would then attest to the legend before Sophokles; also H. Erbse, op. cit., 30.

304. Quite conservative views are held by Perrotta (*Sof.*, 572 n.) and H. O. Meredith; recently also Webster, *Eur.*, 219. Conacher, 243, does not wish to eliminate any of the major themes from the exodos. More in the text.

305. *Euripides restitutus*, II, Hamburg 1844, 465.

306. Thus, W. Riemschneider, op. cit., 50; Schmid 3. 867; Ludwig, 134.; H. Diller, op. cit., 650, also speaks of Antigone's failure. The possibility of such a solution is doubted by Erbse, op. cit., 28, who retains the entire conclusion.

307. If others wish to delete only after v. 1742 in the amoibaion, this may also be correct. So W. Riemschneider, op. cit., 53. 92, with quotes from C. Robert, *Oidipous*; Schmid 3. 867; Pohlenz 2. 158. The Strasbourg papyrus of tragic odes (B. Snell, *Herm.* Einzelschriften 5 [1937], 69) breaks off at v. 1736. But one must concede to H. Erbse, op. cit., 30. 2, that because of the nature of these texts, this does not yield reliable proof.

308. C. Robert, *Oidipous*, Berlin 1915, 1. 305; L. Séchan, *Etudes sur la Tragédie Grecque*, Paris 1926 (1967), 434; L. Deubner, "Oedipusprobleme," *Sitzb. Berlin* 1942/44, 19; F. Wehrli, "Oidipus," *Mus. Helv.* 14 (1957), 108; B. Snell, "Der Anfang von Eur. Oid.," *Herm.* 91 (1963), 120; H. Lloyd-Jones, *Gnom.* 35 (1963), 446; J. Vaio, "The New Fragments of Eur. Oed.," *Gr., Rom. and Byz. Stud.* 5 (1964), 43; Webster, *Eur.*, 241, 307; H. J. Mette, *Lustrum* 1967/12 (1968), 183; Austin, 59; J. Dingel, "Der Sohn des Polybos und die Sphinx," *Mus. Helv.* 27 (1970), 90, with good arguments for reversing the order of fragments 1 and 2 in Turner and Austin. He ascribes both to a messenger-report, which has far-reaching consequences for the reconstruction of the play.

309. ANNOTATED EDITIONS: N. Wecklein, Leipzig 1906; A. M. Scarcella, Rome 1958; V. di Benedetto, Florence 1965; W. Biehl, Berlin 1965 (without text). On these last two editions see E. Degani, *Boll. del Comit. per la preparazione della Ed. Naz. dei Class. Gr. e Lat.* n.s. 15 (1967), 17. INTERPRETATION: W. Krieg, "De Eur. Or.," Diss. Halle 1934; A. Lesky, "Zum Or. des Eur.," *Wien. Stud.* 53 (1935), 37 = *Ges. Schr.*, 131; H. G. Mullens, "The Meaning of Eur. Or.," *Class. Quart.* 34 (1940), 153; W. Wuhrmann, "Strukturelle Untersuchungen zu den beiden *Elektren* und zum euripid. *Orestes*," Diss. Zurich 1940, 99; F. Daraio, "L'*Oreste* di Eur.," *Dioniso* 12 (1949), 92; W. Biehl," Textprobleme in Eur. Or., "Diss. Jena 1955; V. di Benedetto, "Note

critico-testuali all'*Or.* di Eur.," *Studi Class. e Orient.* 10, 1961; K. von Fritz, 145; N. A. Green-berg, "Eur. *Or.*: An Interpretation," *Harv. Stud.* 66 (1962), 157; D. Ebener, "Zum Schluss des *Or.*," *Eirene* 5 (1966), 48; W. Biehl, "Gedanken zu einem Eur.-Kommentar," *Helikon* 7 (1967), 466; Conacher, 213; W. D. Smith, "Disease in Eur. *Or.*," *Herm.* 95 (1967), 291; Webster, *Eur.*, 247; Steidle, 96; W. Biehl, "Zur Darstellung des Menschen in Eur. *Or.*," *Helikon* 8 (1968), 197; G. A. Seeck, "Rauch im *Or.* des Eur.," *Herm.* 97 (1969), 9; H. Parry, "Eur. *Or.*: The Quest for Salvation," *Trans. Am. Phil. Ass.* 100 (1969), 337. ON THE VIENNESE PAPYRUS (*P. Rain.* G 2315) (with verses 338–344 and musical notation): E. G. Turner, *Journ. Hell. Stud.* 76 (1956), 95; D. D. Feaver, *Am. Journ. Phil.* 81 (1960), 1; G. A. Longman, *Class. Quart.* n.s. 12 (1962), 61; H. Hun-ger-E. Pöhlmann, *Wien. Stud.* 75 (1962), 76; cf. also the bibl. on Greek music in A. Lesky, *Gesch. d. gr. Lit.*², 813. 6 (English translation, *A History of Greek Literature*, London 1966, 761. 3). TRANSLATION: E. Buschor, Munich 1960.

310. Vv. 76, 121, 161, 191, 276, 285, 329, 416, 596, 956.

311. Here again we refer to Schwinge, 64.

312. "Did you see how careful she was to cut off only the tips of her hair for the sacrifice?" (128). This line, addressed to no one in particular, we prefer to imagine (with Schadewaldt, *Monolog*, 10. 2) spoken to the audience, rather than interpreting it as a mere colloquialism (as does Fraenkel, *Sitzb. Bayer. Ak. Phil.-hist. Kl.* 1963/1, 111).

313. We prefer not to speak of a contradiction in the play, but rather of a changed attitude under changed circumstances. The disparity appears greater to us, however, than to Steidle (96. 5).

314. With Murray we accept the duplication 536 f. = 625 f. as genuine, but serious doubts should not be suppressed in dealing with the text of this play, which contains other interpola-tions elsewhere (schol. 57, 268, 1366). Wilamowitz, *Herm.* 59 (1924), 258, deleted v. 537 and v. 625. V. di Benedetto would athetize only v. 537, W. Biehl only v. 626.

315. In discounting his judgment, both G. Perrotta, *Stud. It.* 6 (1928), 89, and H. von Arnim, *Zwölf Trag. d. Eur.*, Vienna 1931, 450, go astray.

316. Thus Murray and also V. di Benedetto in his commentary; against H. Weil's assignment of the strophic pair 960–981 to the chorus: G. Pasquali and W. Biehl (in his commentary).

317. On the assignment of the parts, A. Lesky, *Wien. Stud.* 53 (1935), 44 = *Ges. Schr.*, 136.

318. In her essay, important for many questions about staging, "Seen and Unseen on the Greek Stage," *Wien. Stud.* 69 (1956), 103. She is followed by V. di Benedetto and W. Biehl in their commentaries, the latter, however, with the then unnecessary athetesis of lines 1366–1368. V. di Benedetto has also offered much to support the retention of v. 1384.

319. On Euripides and Timotheos see E. K. Borthwick, *Herm.* 96, (1968), 69.

320. It is difficult to decide whether Elektra is present in the group as a mute figure (like Pylades). Steidle (109) rightly remarks that one might expect her appearance in accordance with the design of the play, but the text at v. 1618 raises some doubts: ὑφάπτειν means "to ignite something from below," as one sets fire to a funeral pyre (Thuk. 2. 52). This suggests that Elektra is inside the house and that Orestes calls the command down to her. On the other hand, he orders Pylades to ignite the eaves, which would be of little use in burning down the palace, but what else can his friend do up on the roof? Of course it is also possible that Orestes sends Elektra, standing near him with a burning torch, down inside the palace.

321. Thus, we arrive at a stage with three levels, as did A. Frickenhaus, *Die altgriech. Bühne*, 1917, 15, and H. Bulle, *Unters. an griech. Theatern*, 1928, 225, against M. Bieber, *Gnom.* 8 (1932), 480.

322. On the conjecture that a later director who had Helen appear on the machine thus re-vised the genuine line, cf. A. Lesky, *Wien. Stud.* 53 (1935), 46 = *Ges. Schr.*, 137.

323. F. Chapoutier, *Les Dioscures au service d'une déesse*, Paris 1935.

324. *Untersuchungen zum deus ex machina bei Soph. und Eur.*, Kallmünz 1960, 144.

325. Similarly Grube, 395; W. Wuhrmann, op. cit., 116; Reinhardt, *Sinneskrise*, 255.

326. Thus Garzya, *Pensiero*, 114, and W. Biehl in his commentary, 169, 175, 177.

327. Cf. *Wien. Stud.* 53 (1935), 43 = *Ges. Schr.*, 135. *Gesch. d. gr. Lit.*², Bern 1963, 432 (English translation, *A Hist. of Gr. Lit.*, London 1966, 395). Now also V. di Benedetto on v. 161: "Ai personaggi si sovrappone lo schema."

328. On the reconstruction of the three plays, see Webster, *Eur.*, 252. H. J. Mette, *Lustrum* 1967/12 (1968), 251, 248, 76. The new papyrus fragments are *P. Oxy.* 27 (1962), 2455, frr. 8–11 (further, E. G. Turner, p. 58); *P. Hamburg* 118a (further, E. Siegmann, *Griech. Pap. der Hamburger Staats-und Universitätsbibl.*, Hamburg 1954, 1). Austin, 11, 97 f. On the prologue of the *Archelaos*: F. Stoessl, *Almanach der Stadt Wien*, 1958, 1, and see "Prologos" in *RE*.

329. Fr. inc. 846N = Aristoph. *Ran.* 1206 claims to belong to the prologue. According to the scholiast, Aristarchos could not find the verses. Nauck correctly infers that either a lost duplicate version or simply an error is the reason for this.

330. T. Zielinski, "De Alcmeonis Corinthii fabula Euripidea," *Mnem.* 50 (1922), 305; Van Looy, 103; Webster, *Eur.*, 265; H. J. Mette, *Lustrum* 1967/12 (1968), 34.

331. ANNOTATED EDITIONS: E. B. England, London 1891; G. Ammendola, Turin 1939; A. Willem, Liège 1952. INTERPRETATION: L. Parmentier, "L'*Iph. à Aulis* d'Eur.," *Ac. Belg. Bull. de la classe des lettres*, ser. 5, 12 (1926), 266; Snell, *Aisch.*, 148; Page, 122; A. N. W. Sounders, "A Modern Play by Eur.," *Greece and Rome* 6 (1937), 156; A. Bonnard, "*Iph. à Aulis*: Tragique et poésie," *Mus. Helv.* 2 (1945), 87; V. Frey, "Betrachtungen zu Eur. *Iph. Aul.*," *Mus. Helv.* 4 (1947), 39; F. M. Wassermann, "Agamemnon in the *Iph. at Aulis*," *Trans. Am. Phil. Ass.* 80 (1949), 174; Friedrich, 89; S. Lyritzès, "Ὁ φόβος τοῦ θανάτου εἰς τὴν Ἰφ. τὴν ἐν Αὐλίδι τοῦ Εὐρ.," *Platon* (1954), 57; E. Fraenkel, "Ein Motiv aus Eur. in einer Szene der Neuen Kom.," *Studi U. E. Paoli*, Florence 1955, 293 = *Kl. Schr.*, 487; E. Valgiglio, "L'*If. in Aulide* di Eur.," *Riv. di studi class.* 4 (1956), 179; H. Vretska, "Agamemnon in Eur. *Iph. in Aulis*," *Wien. Stud.* 74 (1961), 18; H. M. Schreiber, "Iphigenies Opfertod," Diss. Frankfurt 1963; H. Förs, "Dionysos und die Stärke der Schwachen im Werk des Eur.," Diss. Tübingen 1964, 131; H. Funke, "Aristoteles zu Eur. *Iph. in Aulis*," *Herm.* 92 (1964), 284; R. Bogaert, "Le revirement de Menélas," *Et. Class.* 33 (1965), 3; Conacher, 249; Webster, 258; G. Mellert-Hoffmann, *Untersuchungen zur Iph. Aul. des Eur.*, Heidelberg 1969. TRANSLATIONS: E. Buschor, Munich 1960; F. M. Stawell, London 1929 (with an introduction by Gilbert Murray); J. Humblé, Antwerp 1942.

332. W. H. Friedrich, *Herm.* 70 (1953), 73; and more recently, Webster, *Eur.*, 258.

333. H. M. Schreiber, op. cit., takes the anapests for the original, the iambic prologue for a later substitute. He can refer to the hypothesis of the *Rhesos*, which speaks of two iambic prologues, while the play begins with anapests. Also in Schrieber (86. 2) are references to actual or supposed ancient quotes from both prologues.

334. However, its deficiencies probably do not warrant athetesis, as Page would have it (145). Wilamowitz, *Gr. Versk.*, 282, with an analysis of the parodos, Kranz (257), and now H. M. Schreiber (op. cit., 99) take opposing views.

335. H. Vretska, op. cit., 32, is good on this.

336. For the assignment to the chorus, see Lammers, 103, and recently H. M. Schreiber, op. cit., 104. Athetesis is suggested by Page, 160 (vv. 590–606), and Webster, *Eur.*, 260 (598–606), while Wilamowitz, *Herm.* 54 (1919), 52, claimed to recognize in the verses the remnants of a revision, in which Greek soldiers supposedly formed the chorus, as was the case in the *Iphigeneia* of Ennius. In further support of assigning the passages to an auxiliary chorus of warriors, there is the correspondence between lines 428 f. and 596 f.

337. The scenic arrangement is difficult here. When Klytaimestra bids farewell, she evidently will go into the house, but this is just where Achilleus was going to look for Agamemnon, as he explicitly states (854). Also, the old man's words give the impression that he stopped Achilleus as the latter was moving away from the door. Hourmouziades, 21, identifies the problems well and considers either several doors of the skene or a lacuna. But perhaps we should not be too concerned with the movements of the two dialogue partners, since the call of the servant checks them before they start to leave.

338. *Die Sinneskrise bei Euripides*, 240.

339. On the conclusion see Page, 207. Schreiber, op. cit., 92; cf. Zuntz, *Inquiry*, 102.

340. *Philosophie der Religion*, Jub. Ausg. 16, 133.

341. A. Lesky, *Entretiens sur l'ant. class.* 6, 1958 (1960), 143, and "Zur Problematik des Psychologischen in der Trag. des Eur.," *Gymn.* 67 (1960), 22 = *Ges. Schr.*, 259; B. M. W. Knox, "Second Thoughts in Greek Trag.," *Gr. Rom. and Byz. Stud.* 7 (1966), 213.

342. Aristotle was extremely strict on this point and discerned an ἀνώμαλον also in the Achilleus of the last book of the *Iliad*: fr. 168R, schol. *Il.* 24. 569.

343. H. Diller is correct in his essay, valuable for other plays of Euripides as well: "Umwelt und Masse als dramatische Faktoren bei Eur.," *Entretiens sur l'ant. class.* 6, 1958 (1960), 89 (104). In down-playing the army as mere rabble, H. Funke, op. cit., 292, goes astray. At v. 1372 Iphigeneia does not warn her mother about the slanders of the mob; she merely wishes her to avoid becoming involved in a fatal opposition to the army. The parallel with Soph. *Phil.* 582 clarifies the passage. The will of the army becomes one with that of Iphigeneia in her heroic decision.

344. ANNOTATED EDITIONS: E. Bruhn, 3d ed., Berlin 1891; N. Wecklein, 2d ed., Leipzig 1903; L. Cammelli, Milan 1932; E. R. Dodds, Oxford 1944, 2d ed. 1960 (with Murray's text and excellent introduction and commentary); A. Nucciotti, Florence 1947; G. Ammendola, 2d ed., Turin 1948; A. Maggi, Naples 1948; P. Scazzoso, Milan 1957; J. Roux, Bibl. de la Fac. des Lett. de Lyon 21. On the transmission of the play, which must be counted among the dramas of the selection despite the lack of evidence, Zuntz, *Inquiry*, 110. INTERPRETATION: G. Méautis, "Les *Bacchantes* d'Eur.," *Acropole* 3 (1928), 153, and *Mythes inconnus de la Grèce antique*, Paris 1944; M. R. Glover, "The *Bacchae*," *Journ. Hell. Stud.* 49 (1929), 82; F. M. Wassermann, "Die *Bakchantinnen* des Eur.," *N. Jahrb.* 5 (1929), 272, and "Man and God in the *Bacchae* and in the *Oed. at Col.*," *Studies presented to D. M. Robinson*, St. Louis 1953, 2. 559; K. Deichgräber, "Die Kadmos-Teiresiasszene in Eur. *Bakchen*," *Herm.* 70 (1935), 322; G. M. A. Grube, "Dionysus in the *Bacchae*," *Trans. Am. Phil. Ass.* 66 (1935), 37; A. R. Bellinger, "The *Bacchae* and *Hippolytus*," *Yale Class. Stud.* 6 (1939), 17; J. C. Kamerbeek, "Eur. en het probleem der *Bacchen*," *De antieke Tragedie*, Leyden 1947, 96; R. P. Winnington-Ingram, *Eur. and Dionysos: An Interpretation of the* Bacchae, Cambridge 1948, repr. 1969; E. R. Dodds, "Maenadism," *The Greeks and the Irrational*, Sather Class. Lectures 25 (1951), 270; H. Diller, "Die *Bakchen* und ihre Stellung im Spätwerk des Eur.," *Abh. Ak. Mainz. Geistes-und sozialwiss. Kl.* 1955/5 = *Eur.*, Wege der Forschung 89, Darmstadt 1968, 469; Norwood, 52 (with partial correction of earlier opinions influenced by Verrall in: *The Riddle of the* Bacchae, London 1908); A. J. Festugière, "La signification religieuse de la parodos des *Bacchantes*," *Eranos* 54 (1956), 72, and "Eur. dans les *Bacchantes*," *Eranos* 55 (1957), 127; B. Stumpo, "Le *Baccanti di Eur.*," *Dioniso* 20 (1957), 75; J. Carrière, "Théocrite et les *Bacchantes*," *Pallas* 6 (1958), 7, and "Sur le message des *Bacchantes*," *Ant. Class.* 35 (1966), 118; J. Roux, "Sur la parodos des *Bacchantes*," *Rev. Et. Gr.* 75 (1962), 64; W. J. Verdenius, "Notes on Eur. *Bacchae*," *Mnem.* ser. 4, 15 (1962), 337; J. de Romilly, "Le thème du bonheur dans les *Bacchantes*," *Rev. Et. Gr.* 76 (1963), 361; H. Förs, "Dionysos und die Stärke der Schwachen im Werk des Eur.," Diss. Tübingen 1964; H. Merklin, "Gott und Mensch im *Hippolytos* und in den *Bakchen* des Eur.," Diss. Freiburg im Breisgau 1964; R. R. Dyer, "Image and Symbol: The Link between the Two Worlds of the *Bacchae*," *Aumla* no. 21 (1964), 15; C. W. Willink, "Some Problems of Text and Interpretation in the *Bacchae*," I, *Class. Quart.* 16 (1966), 27, and II, ibid., 220; Chromik, 241; Conacher, 56; V. Lejnieks, "Interpolations in the *Bacchae*," *Am. Journ. Phil.* 88 (1967), 332; Webster, 268; Rohdich, 131; Steidle, 32; G. Devereux, "The Psychotherapy Scene in Eur. *Bacchae*," *Journ. Hell. Stud.* 90 (1970), 35. TRANSLATIONS: E. Buschor, Munich 1960; O. Werner, Stuttgart 1968; F. A. Evelyn, London 1936.

345. On the composition of the two tetralogies, and other thematically related dramas, see E. R. Dodds in the introduction to his edition (xxviii). See also Mette, *Verl. Aisch.*, 136, and K. Deichgräber, *Nachr. Gött. Phil.-hist. Kl. Fachgr.* 1, vol. 3, 1938/39, 306. We know nothing of a *Pentheus* by Thespis; even the authorship is disputed.

346. How Rohdich (151 f.) can doubt the exclusively divine nature of the stranger is incomprehensible to me.

347. Interesting comparisons are offered by Philadamos's Delphic hymn to Dionysos and the Iakchos ode in the *Frogs* (324).

348. So D. G. Harbsmeier, "Die alten Menschen bei Eur.," Diss. Göttingen 1968, 52, in a reasonable treatment of the entire scene; for Teiresias's entrance he makes use of the stage directions in Wilamowitz's translation.

349. A valuable summary of the use of σοφός and related words in the play may be found in Conacher, 73. See also, R. P. Winnington-Ingram, "Eur.: Poietes Sophos," *Arethusa* 2 (1969). We cannot concur with the athetesis of lines 201 f. by C. W. Willink, op. cit., 39.

350. K. Deichgräber, op. cit., goes quite far in his depreciation of the two characters, in whom he sees the ludicrous and the repulsive combined. Numerous supporters of a similar interpretation are listed in Rohdich, 144. 40, who includes too hastily my statement in the *Gesch. d. Gr. Lit.*², 437 (in the English translation, *A History of Greek Literature*, 399). When I spoke of "a scene which borders on the grotesque," I meant much the same as Conacher's (61) "comic overtones," and did not mean to imply that the comic element was dominant.. Rivier (88 f.) early and rightly objected to a one-sided interpretation of the scene as comic; the same line with variations is taken by H. Merklin (op. cit., 128), Conacher (62), Rohdich (144), Steidle (33), and at least partially by Webster (271).

351. V. 316 need not be deleted, and perhaps we need not even replace the MS ἐν with Porson's εἰ in v. 315. On the other hand, 314 disturbs the train of thought.

352. In his commentary on 434–518, E. R. Dodds suggests that Pentheus might have remained on stage during the first stasimon. The address in v. 434 sounds abrupt; nonetheless we prefer, with Steidle (35), to have Pentheus depart at the end of the first epeisodion.

353. J. de Romilly, op. cit., has penetratingly analyzed the different aspects of the concept of happiness in the *Bakchai*.

354. On the puzzling connection between Paphos and the Nile, cf. the suggestions in Dodds's commentary.

355. Very reasonable discussions of the general lack of illusionistic effects are in Wilamowitz, *Gr. Versk.*, 581, and E. R. Dodds, in his commentary, p. 148. Steidle (27. 23) leaves open the extent to which such means were employed but does not believe that everything could have been mere illusion. The rationalistic explanation of A. W. Verrall and G. Norwood tried to interpret the events as a delusion of the chorus induced by suggestion. This was incorporated into Rohdich's theory (135) that Euripides used the very fact that the supposed miracle did *not* occur to depict the Dionysian as a problem of the human soul which concerns the skeptic as well. This is surely asking too much of the passage. Earlier bibl. on the "palace miracle" can be found in Schwinge, 370. 51.

356. The three thiasoi also appear elsewhere in the cult, as an inscription from Magnesia (Kern, 215) shows.

357. If we recall the episodic figures of the stout countryman in the *El.* and the speakers at the popular assembly in the *Or.*, their traits, insofar as they are not wholly determined by their situations, allow us to draw conclusions about the poet's specific views of city people and country people.

358. On this, H. Merklin, op. cit., 154; an especially thorough doxography is in the excellent discussion of the passage by Schwinge, 378.

359. Dingel (157), followed by Schwinge (395), believes that the final vacillation of Pentheus is caused by servants, who at this very moment bring on stage the weapons requested at v. 809. This remains a possibility, although it is conceivable that this order was never carried out. In Dingel there is also bibl. on the scene of the dressing of Pentheus.

360. On this, Rohdich, 156, at times oversubtle.

361. A good discussion of the passage in F. Heinimann, *Nomos und Physis*, Basel 1945, 166.

362. On the difficult σκόλοπος (983), see E. R. Dodds in his commentary.

363. The evidence for these forms of epiphany is collected in Dodds.

364. The history of interpretation is well summarized by R. Nihard, "Le problème de *Bacchantes* d'Eur.," *Musée Belg.* 16 (1912), 91, 297; H. Merklin, "Gott und Mensch im *Hipp.* und den *Bakchen* des Eur.," Diss. Freiburg im Breisgau 1964, 30; Chromik, 241; Rohdich, 132.

365. The "conversion theory" was still emphatically supported by Goossens, 724; a similar position is taken by H. Grégoire in the introduction to his edition in the Budé series. Conversely, W. Nestle, *Vom Mythos zum Logos*, Stuttgart 1940, 498, saw depicted in the drama the terrible effects of fanaticism. K. Deichgräber, *Nachr. Gott. Phil.-hist. Kl. Fachgr.* 1, vol. 3 (1938/39), 309, and ibid., vol. 4 (1940/1), 31, also wished to recognize criticism in the spirit of the Enlightenment.

366. *Class. Rev.* 43 (1929), 97; further, the introduction to his edition of the *Bakchai*.

367. ANNOTATED EDITIONS: J. Duchemin, Paris 1945; G. Ammendola, Florence 1952. INTERPRETATION: F. Hahne, "Zur ästhetischen Kritik des eurip. *Kyklops*," *Phil.* 66 (1907), 36; P. Waltz, "Le drame satyrique et le prologue du *Cyclope* d'Eur.," *L'Acropole* 5 (1930), 278; R. Kassel, "Bemerkungen zum *Kykl.* des Eur.," *Rhein. Mus.* 98 (1955), 279; D. Ferrante, "Il *Ciclope* di Eur. e il IX dell'*Odissea*," *Dioniso* 34 (1960), 165; P. D. Arnott, "The Overworked Playwright: A Study in Eur. *Cycl.*," *Greece and Rome* 8 (1961), 164; R. St. Pathmanathan, "A Playwright Relaxed or Overworked?" ibid., 10 (1963), 123; H. Förs, "Dionysos und die Stärke der Schwachen im Werk des Eur.," Diss. Tübingen 1964; W. Wetzel, *De Eur. fabula satyrica, quae Cyclops inscribitur cum Homerico comparata exemplo*, Wiesbaden 1965. TRANSLATIONS: S. Ferlini, Vittoria 1951; U. Albini, Florence 1955.

368. *Griech. Trag.*, III, 6th ed., Berlin 1926, 13.

369. "Die Datierung des eurip. *Kyklops*," Diss. Leipzig 1912. For a late date see A. M. Dale, *Wien. Stud.* 69 (1956), 105; K. Joerden, "Hinterszenischer Raum und ausserszenische Zeit," Diss. Tübingen 1960, 262; K. Matthiessen, *El., Taur. Iph. und Hel.*, Hypomn. 4 (1964), 91, 171; Webster, *Eur.*, 18. A survey of the various conjectures is offered by W. Wetzel, op. cit., 151, who does not commit himself.

370. From v. 147 we are obliged, with Murray (in the apparatus), to imagine a miraculous inexhaustible wineskin, although the motif remains completely isolated; cf. Conacher, 318.

371. As Arrowsmith does in the introduction to his translation of the play in *The Complete Greek Tragedies*, Chicago 1959/60; he also claims to see sophistic humbug in Odysseus.

372. O. Zwierlein, *Gnom.* 39 (1967), 453, correctly underscores the contradiction between 195 ff., 666 ff., and 707, but incorrectly wishes to perceive a special design of the poet: the audience is supposed to realize that Euripides is pulling their leg.

373. The opening verse in *P. Oxy.* 2455 fr. 19; Austin, p. 90. An insignificant fragment from the *Syleus* in *P. Oxy.* 2455 fr. 8; Austin, p. 96. The pre-Euripidean tradition was reconstructed from vase-paintings by F. Brommer, *Arch. Jahrb.* 59/60 (1944/45), 69.

374. *P. Oxy.* 2455 fr. 6. 5 init. See also E. G. Turner (also earlier in *Proc. of the IX. Int. Congress of Papyrology*, Norw. Univ. Press 1961, 16); Austin, p. 18; B. Snell, "Zu Eur. Satyrspiel *Skiron*," *Aegyptus* 47 (1967), 184. H. J. Mette also includes *P. Amherst* 2. 17, and offers a new supplement in *Mus. Helv.* 21 (1964), 71. This evaluation of the papyrus had been opposed by Zuntz (*Pol. Plays*, 134. 3) and E. G. Turner (*P. Oxy.* 27, 1962, 57); Austin, p. 95, remains doubtful.

On Some Fragments

1. J. Schwartz, "Sur l'*Alcmène* d'Eur.," *Bull. Fac. des Lettres Strasbourg* 30 (1951/52), 277; T. B. L. Webster, *Studies in Later Greek Comedy*, Manchester 1953, 87 and *Eur.*, 92, 298; G. Arrighetti, *Studi Class. et Or.* 13 (1964), 110; H. J. Mette, *Lustrum* 1967/12 (1968), 38; Austin, p. 84.

2. A. Lesky, "Die griech. Pelopidendramen und Senecas *Thyestes*," *Wien. Stud.* 43 (1922/

23), 172 = *Ges. Schr.*, 519; H. J. Mette, *Lustrum* 1964/9 (1965), 65, and 1967/12 (1968), 128; Webster, *Eur.*, 113.

3. H. J. Mette (see previous note), 91 and 188 respectively; Webster, *Eur.*, 113.

4. Webster, *Eur.*, 303; H. J. Mette, *Lustrum* 1967/12 (1968), 138.

5. H. J. Mette (see previous note), 212; Webster, *Eur.*, 161.

6. H. Volmer, "De Euripidis fabula quae ΦΑΕΘΩΝ inscribitur restituenda," Diss. Münster 1930; A. Lesky, "Zum *Phaethon* des Eur.," *Wien. Stud.* 50 (1932), 1 = *Ges. Schr.*, 111; N. Wilson, *Class. Quart.* 10 (1960), 199; H. J. Mette, *Lustrum* 1967/12 (1968), 261; Webster, *Eur.*, 220; J. Diggle, *Euripides' Phaethon*, Cambridge 1970. A scenario of the play was reconstructed by Goethe, "Sophienausgabe" 41. 2. 32 ff.

7. Merops is not king of Aithiopia; cf. A. Lesky, *Wien. Stud.* 63 (1948), 29 = *Ges. Schr.*, 31.

8. Cf. W. S. Barrett, *Eur. Hipp.*, Oxford 1964, 167, who refers to the auxiliary choruses in *Hipp.*, *Antiope*, and *Alexandros*.

Dramatic Form and Language

1. On the question of the development of act division, which only became completely standardized in New Comedy, see R. T. Weissinger, *A Study of Act Divison in Classical Drama*, Iowa 1940.

2. Ludwig's *Sapheneia* remains important; Friedrich, *Eur. und Diph.*, has made valuable observations on the structure of individual plays; an exhaustive bibliography on the question of symmetrical composition is offered by Schwinge, 11. 3.

3. Besides the material on Eur.'s technique listed in the general bibliography, see also J. Gollwitzer, "Die Prolog- und Expositionstechnik der griech. Trag. mit bes. Berücksichtigung des Eur.," Diss. Munich 1937; A. Todesco, "I prologhi Euripidei," *Dioniso* 6 (1937/38), 83; N. Terzaghi, "Finali e prologhi Euripidei," ibid., 304; G. Erdmann, "Der Botenbericht bei Eur.: Struktur und dramatische Funktion," Diss. Kiel 1964.

4. Jacqueline Duchemin, *L'ΑΓΩΝ dans la trag. Gr.*, Paris 1945; G. Graf, "Die Agonszenen bei Eur.," Diss. Göttingen 1950; E. Epke, "Über die Streitszenen und ihre Entwicklung in der griech. Trag.," Diss. Hamburg 1951; R. Senoner, "Der Redeagon im eurip. Drama," Diss. Wien 1961. See also Kretz, 20; W. J. Proleykes, "Der Ἀγὼν λόγων," Diss. Bonn 1973, 320.

5. *Die Stichomythie in der griech. Trag. u. Kom.*, Berlin 1905.

6. "Antiphon-Studien," *N. Phil. Unters.* 8, Berlin 1931; commentary there (54) and in W. Kroll, *RE* S 7, 1042, also on the influence on Euripides of the new movements developed by the Sophists.

7. "Die eurip. Reden und ihre Bedeutung," Diss. Breslau 1933.

8. D. G. Harbsmeier, "Die alten Menschen bei Eur.," Diss. Göttingen 1968.

9. A. Svensson in ΔΡΑΓΜΑ *Martino P. Nilsson*, Lund-Leipzig 1939, 449.

10. The basic work is still Kranz's *Stasimon*. Further, C. Möller, "Vom Chorlied bei Eur.," Diss. Göttingen 1933; L. Stella, "Eur. lirico," *Atene e Roma*, 1939 and 1940; V. di Benedetto, "Responsione strofica e distribuzione delle battute in Eur.," *Herm.* 89 (1961), 298; N. C. Conomis, "The Dochmiacs of Greek Drama," *Herm.* 92 (1964), 23; A. M. Dale, "The Chorus in the Action of Gr. Trag.," in *Classical Drama and its Influence* (in honor of H. D. F. Kitto), London 1965, 15; H. Neitzel, "Die dramatische Funktion des Chorliedes in den Trag. des Eur.," Diss. Hamburg 1967.

11. H. Schönewolf, "Der jungattische Dithyrambos," Diss. Giessen 1938.

12. W. Breitenbach, "Unters. zur Sprache der eur. Lyrik," *Tüb. Beitr.* 20, Stuttgart 1934, with a discussion of vocabulary, tropes, figures of speech, word order, and echoes of the other poets, restricted to the lyric sections of Eur.; J. Smereka, *Studea Euripidea* I and II/1, Leopoli 1936/37, with tables and statistics on dialect forms, vocabulary, word order, epithets, figures of speech, and linguistic form of the individual parts of tragedy. Thorough sections also in Schmid 3. 790;

K. Pauer, "Die Bildersprache des Eur.," Diss. Breslau 1934; P. T. Stevens, "Colloquial Expressions in Eur.," *Class. Quart.* 31 (1937), 182 (now in German in *Euripides*, Wege der Forschung 89, Darmstadt 1968, 104); J. E. Nussbaumer, "Die Figuren des Gleichklangs bei Eur.," Diss. Fribourg 1938; E. E. Pot, "De maritieme Beeldspraak biy Eur.," Diss. Utrecht 1943; I. Kazik-Zawadska, "Les hapax eiremena et les mots rares dans les fragments papyrologiques des trois grands tragiques grecs," Warsaw 1962; S. A. Barlow, *The Imagery of Euripides: A Study in the Dramatic Use of Pictorial Language*, London 1971. As always, see in addition the works cited in the bibliography and under Aischylos.

13. *Nomos und Physis*, Basel 1945, 52; ibid., 56. 30 f. on similar studies.

14. M. Imhof, "Tetrameterszenen in der Trag.," *Mus. Helv.* 13 (1956), 126.

Poet and Philosopher

1. A few surveys with much bibl. are found in M. Croiset, "Euripide e ses plus récents critiques," *Journ. des Savants*, n.s. 7 (1909), 197, 245; J. C. Kamerbeek, *Entretiens sur l'ant. class.* 6 (1960), 3; H. M. Schreiber, "Iphigenies Opfertod," Diss. Frankfurt 1963, 1; Rohdich, 13; E. R. Schwinge, *Euripides*, Wege der Forschung 89, Darmstadt 1968, introd. Besides the works listed in the bibl. see S. Melchinger, *Euripides*, Velber by Hannover 1967 (Friedrich's *Dramatiker des Welttheaters*, 41); H. Lloyd-Jones, *The Justice of Zeus*, Berkeley 1971, chap. 6.

2. Ancient opinions in Schmid, 3. 318. 5. A cautious and balanced evaluation in R. P. Winnington-Ingram, "Euripides: Poietes Sophos," *Arethusa* 2 (1969), 127.

3. W. Nestle, *Vom Mythos zum Logos*, Stuttgart 1940, 496; Schmid, 3. 332. Cf. N. Petruzellis, "Eur. e la sofistica," *Dioniso* 39 (1965), 356.

4. Cf. Wilamowitz, *Herakles*, 655, and L. Radermacher in his commentary on the passage.

5. On the difficulty of interpreting the passage, see E. R. Dodds in his commentary, p. 117. Important remarks on the problem of knowledge in Eur. are in Snell, *Aisch.*, 157, and B. M. W. Knox, "New Perspectives in Euripidean Criticism," *Class. Phil.* 67 (1972), 270.

6. *Hel.* 728, 1640; *Ion* 854; *Or.* 868; *Ba.* 1027; Frr. 495. 40, 511, 831N.

7. "Euripides the Irrationalist," *Class. Rev.* 43 (1929), 97.

8. A. Lesky, "Euripides und die Pädagogik," *Wiener Human. Bl.* 11 (1968), 16.

9. *Univ. of Toronto Quart.* 1968, 395. For further lit. besides bibl., cited under note 1 of this section, T. Zielinski, "L'évolution religieuse d'Eur.," *Rev. Et. Gr.* 36 (1923), 459; A. J. Festugière, "La religion d'Eur.," *L'enfant d'Agrigente*, 2d ed., Paris 1950; F. Chapoutier, "Eur. et l'accueil du divin," *Entretiens sur l'ant. Class.* 1 (1954), 204; M. P. Nilsson, *Gesch. d. gr. Rel.*, I, 2d ed., Munich 1955, 771; Reinhardt, *Sinneskrise*; D. Diano, *Eur., auteur de la catharsis tragique, Numen* 8, Leyden 1961, 117; K. Matthiessen, *El., Taur. Iph. und Hel.*, Hypomn. 4, Göttingen 1964; Chromik, 173.

10. The phrase is from the commentary of W. S. Barrett on this passage.

11. Chromik, 206, has a thorough analysis of the section. According to Diogenes the air (ἀήρ) supports the spiritual principle of νόησις (~Anaxagoras's νοῦς). He is supposed to have identified this with Zeus (DK 64 A 8). The principle supporting the earth was probably the αἰθήρ, according to frr. 919, 941, 944N. This appears in Euripides often as a divine power, occasionally connected with Zeus or even identified with him (frr. 877, 941). Passages are cited in K. Matthiessen, "Zur Theonoeszene der eurip. *Helena*," *Herm.* 96 (1969), 699 ff., who does not believe that the αἰθήρ represents a divine essence above the sphere of the Olympian gods. We agree with him, but primarily because for Euripides the Olympians themselves are no longer essences in the ancient sense. With Zeus-Aether, Euripides was moving along a path that reached its goal in the Zeus hymn of the Stoic Kleanthes.

12. On the variations in the tradition, cf. Pickard-Cambridge, *Festivals*, 274. 10.

13. That in the final verse (1150) the MSS reading with the positive belief in the "word of

the gods" cannot be maintained, was shown first by G. Zuntz, *Entretiens sur l'ant. Class.* 6, 1958 (1960), recently also by R. Kannicht in his commentary. Both rightly reject the evasion of Wilamowitz, *Gr. Versk.*, 456. 1, who claims that Euripides first spoke as a disciple of Protagoras, but then redeemed himself by adding a passage to appease the dullards.

14. *Phil.* 111 (1967), 24.

15. For this and related aspects, W. Nestle, *Eur., der Dichter der griech. Aufklärung*, Stuttgart 1901, offers abundant material.

16. *Nomos und Physis*, Basel 1945, 121. F. Chapoutier, *Entretiens sur l'ant. Class.* 1, 1952 (1954), 235, takes a different view. Cf. D. Lanza, "Νόμος e ἴσον in Eur.," *Riv. Fil.* 91 (1963), 416.

17. A. Spira is especially radical, "Untersuchungen zum deus ex machina bei Soph. und Eur.," Diss. Frankfurt, Kallmünz 1960. The same line is taken by H. M. Schreiber, "Iphigenies Opfertod," Diss. Frankfurt 1963, and M. Imhof, *Eur. Ion*, Bern 1966. Cautious but similar reflections in Patzer, 162, 172. Individual interpretations of Spira are rightly contradicted by Webster, *Eur.*, 146, 251. See also W. Schmidt, "Der deus ex machina bei Eur.," Diss. Tübingen 1963. Of course in this context Reinhardt's essay on the crisis of meaning in Eur. is important as an antidote.

18. Zürcher's book remains an important basis for debate. Deserving of special mention is de Romilly, *L'évolution du pathétique*. Cf. also F. Will, "Remarks on Counterpoint Characterization in Eur.," *Class. Journ.* 55 (1960), 338, and "The concept of χαϱακτήϱ in Eur.," *Glotta* 39 (1960/61), 233. The quote from Burckhardt is in *Griech. Kulturgesch.* 2. 306 (Kröner).

19. A. Lesky, *Entretiens sur l'ant. Class.* 6, 1958 (1960), 143 = *Euripides*, Wege der Forschung 89, Darmstadt 1968, 94, and "Zur Problematik des Psychologischen in der Trag. des Eur.," *Gymn.* 67 (1960), 22 = *Ges. Schr.*, 259; B. M. W. Knox, "Second Thoughts in Greek Trag.," *Gr., Rom. and Byz. Stud.* 7 (1966), 213.

20. *Entretiens sur l'ant. class.* 1, 1952 (1954), 228.

21. Our interpretation coincides with that of Rohdich on many points. Yet in his important book he seems to us to have been too rigid in identifying one pole of the fundamental antithesis with Sophism, great as its influence was. But it is not enough to say that Iason is the representative of sophistic planning, and this does not apply to Herakles at all.

22. A. Lesky, "Der Mythos im Verständnis der Antike," *Gymn.* 73 (1966), 40 = *Ges. Schr.*, 434.

23. *Entretiens sur l'ant. class.* 6, 1958 (1960), 212.

CHAPTER 7

1. "Sophocles and Ion of Chios," *Herm.* 71 (1936), 263.

2. P. Lévèque, *Agathon*, Ann. Univ. de Lyon, 3d ser., 26. Les Belles Lettres, Paris 1955; J. Waern, "Zum Tragiker Agathon," *Eranos* 54 (1956), 87.

3. On this, see H. Schönewolf, *Der jungattische Dithyrambos*, Giessen 1938, 45. Source material on the musical innovations of Agathon is in H. Färber, *Phil. Woch.* 1942, 103. Characteristic of Agathon's affected style is the way in which he tries to outdo with six virtuoso lines (fr. 4N) the eleven verses of Euripides with the description of the letters in Theseus's name by an illiterate (fr. 382N). B. Snell is excellent on this in the additional chapter "Agathon, Chairemon" in the German translation of his *Scenes from Greek Drama*, Berlin 1971.

4. This reading does not originate with Wilamowitz, as Schmid (3. 849. 4) asserts; Welcker already considered it (*Griech. Trag.* 3. 995); cf. Gudeman on the passage in the *Poetics*. P. Lévèque (op. cit.) decides in favor of *Anthos*.

5. The Latin translation of W. de Moerbeke also has *anthe*, however.

6. *Am. Journ. Phil.* 60 (1939), 145. C. Corbato, "L'*Anteo* di Agatone," *Dioniso* 11 (1948), 163, considers whether we should perceive an echo of the play in the *Apollo* of Alexander Aetolus (Powell, *Coll. Alex.*, 122).

7. Sources and bibl. are in A. von Blumenthal, *Der Tyrann Kritias als Dichter und Schrift-steller*, Stuttgart 1923; Wilhelm Nestle, *Vom Mythos zum Logos*, Stuttgart 1940, 411; Schmid, 3. 176; M. Untersteiner, *Sofisti: testimonianze e frammenti*, fasc. 4, Florence 1962, 274.

8. C. Gallavotti, *Riv. Fil.* n.s. 11 (1933), 177; A. Körte, *APF* 11 (1935), 277; *PSI* 12/2 (1951), no. 1286.

9. *P. Oxy.* 17. 2078; A. Körte, *APF* 10 (1932), 50; Page, *Lit. Pap.*, London 1950, 120, who stresses the uncertainty of Kritias's authorship.

CHAPTER 8

1. T. B. L. Webster, *Art and Literature in Fourth Century Athens*, London 1956, and "Fourth Century Tragedies and Poetics," *Herm.* 82 (1954), 294. Kitto, *Form and Meaning*, 231. Aylen, 150. The few well-attested names are in Ziegler (1963, 1967). F. Leo's statements on post-Euripidean tragedy (*Gesch. d. röm. Lit.* 1. 228) are still worth reading.

2. A dual-language edition (Greek-German) with a good introduction and brief notes by D. Ebener, Berlin 1966. B. Fenik, "*Iliad* x and the *Rhesus*: The Myth," *Latomus* 73 (1964). H. Parry, "The Approach of Drama in the *Rhesus*," *Phoenix* 18 (1964), 283. In a letter K. Matthiessen informed me that working through Murray's apparatus showed him twenty instances in which P against L either has the correct reading or agrees in its mistakes with another MS. He prefers to assume for the *Rhesus* that P is independent of L.

3. In *PSI* 12/2 (1951), 1286 (cf. C. Gallavotti, *Riv. Fil.* 11 (1933), 177) are found portions of the hypothesis with considerable textual deviations. The papyrus belongs to a collection of hypotheseis to Euripides' plays arranged in alphabetical order.

4. On earlier stages of the debate see J. Geffcken, "Der *Rhesos*," *Herm.* 71 (1936), 394. Defenders of authenticity are R. Goossens, "La date du *Rhesos*," *Ant. Class.* 1 (1932), 93, who suspects the Thracian king Sitalkes behind Rhesos and also in his book on Euripides (252) dates the play ca. 425; H. Grégoire, "L'authenticité du *Rh.* d'Eur.," *Ant. Class.* 2 (1933), 91; the 3d volume of the same journal contains the criticism of T. Sinko (233, 411) and the responses of the two authors mentioned above (431); Buchwald, 50 (assumes an early drama of Eur.; cf. G. Björck, "*Rhesos*," *Arctos* n.s. 1 (1954), 16, and "The Authenticity of Rhesos," *Eranos* 55 [1957], 7); C. B. Sneller, *De Rheso tragoedia*, Amsterdam 1949; further, A. Lesky, *Gnomon* 23 (1951), 141; Silvia Compagno, "Sull'authenticità del *Reso* di Eur.," *Atti Acc.* Turin 98 (1963/64), 1; W. Ritchie, *The Authenticity of the* Rhesos *of Euripides*, Cambridge 1964. These are opposed by E. Fraenkel, *Gnom.* 37 (1965), 228, with arguments that could really settle the problem. Recently authenticity was defended by Q. Cataudella, "Vedute vecchie e nuove sul *Reso* Euripideo," *Saggi sulla trag. Gr.*, Messina-Florence 1969, 315. Important reasons for rejection can be found in H. Strohm, "Beobachtungen zum *Rhesos*," *Herm.* 87 (1959), 257.

5. The first hypothesis offers two other trimetric openings that do not fit the transmitted play, a verse quoted from Dikaiarchos (fr. 81 W) that sounds Euripidean, and eleven trimeters from an address by Hera to Athena, rightly criticized in the hypothesis as prosaic and un-Euripidean.

6. G. H. Macurdy, "The Dawn Songs in *Rhesus* (527–556) and in the Parodos of *Phaethon*," *Am. Journ. Phil.* 64 (1943), 408.

7. In the fifth chapter, "Astydamas' Hektor," of the German edition of his *Scenes from Greek Drama*, Berlin 1971.

8. "Zu den Urkunden dramatischer Aufführungen," *Nachr. Ak. Gött. Phil.-hist. Kl.* 1966/2, 11.

9. On his trilogy *Pandionis*, between 430 and 414, cf. T. B. L. Webster, *Wien. Stud.* 79 (1966), 117.

10. The first two papyri are also in D. L. Page, *Lit. Pap.*, London 1950, 160, with misgivings about Snell's attribution.

11. Cf. B. D. Meritt, *Hesperia* 7 (1938), 116.

12. In the additional chapter "Agathon, Chairemon" of the German edition of his *Scenes*, Snell derives essential features of this dramatist from the meager fragments and data; cf. C. Collard, "On the Tragedian Chairemon," *Journ. Hell. Stud.* 90 (1970), 22.

13. O. Crusius, "Die Anagnostikoi," *Festschrift für Th. Gomperz*, 1902, 381. F. Mehmel, *Virgil und Apollonius Rhodius*, Hamburg 1940, 20, 23. O. Zwierlein, *Die Rezitationsdramen Senecas*, Meisenheim 1966. R. Pfeiffer, *History of Classical Scholarship*, Oxford 1968, 29.

14. In "Antikes und modernes Drama," *Eranion: Festschr. H. Hommel*, Tübingen 1961, 43.

15. In *Fifty Years (and Twelve) of Classical Scholarship*, Oxford 1968, 116.

16. Source material on τραγικός in J. Geffcken, *Der Begriff des Tragischen in der Antike*, Vortr. Bibl. Warburg 1927/28, Berlin 1930, 120, 123. J. H. Waszink, in the excellent essay "Die griech. Trag. im Urteil der Römer und der Christen," *Jahrb. f. Ant. u. Christent.* 7 (1964), 144. 24, quotes J. Stille's *Staatsexamensarbeit* for A. Dihle, "Die Bedeutung des Wortes τραγικός seit Platon und Aristoteles." Xen. *Eph.* 3. 1. 4 will suffice as example of what τραγῳδία can mean in later times. On the position of Kallimachos with regard to tragedy: E. Howald, *Der Dichter Kallimachos von Kyrene*, Erlenbach-Zurich 1943, 16. On the "tragic" style of Hellenistic historical writing, some references are in J. Geffcken, op. cit., 139. 5. V. Fritz's chapter "Entstehung und Inhalt des neunten Kapitels von Aristoteles *Poetik*" is important for these questions.

17. W. Suess, "Der ältere Dionys als Tragiker," *Rhein. Mus.* 109 (1966), 299.

18. *Hesperia* 7 (1938), 116 nr. 22. A. Körte, *Herm.* 73 (1938), 123. For questions of this nature, A. Wilhelm, *Urkunden dram. Aufführungen in Athen*, Vienna 1906, is still important, but see now esp. Pickard-Cambridge, *Festivals*. Everything we can know about the individual poets is in T. B. L. Webster, *Art and Literature in Fourth Century Athens*, London 1956, and "Fourth Century Tragedies and Poetics," *Herm.* 82 (1954), 294.

19. Gone Capone, *L'arte scenica degli attori tragici greci*, Padua 1935. Also instructive is the treatment of the Würzburg vase-fragment (Pickard-Cambridge, *Festivals*, fig. 54a) with an actor holding his mask, by H. Bulle in the *Festschrift für James Loeb*, Munich 1930, 5, and *Corolla Curtius*, Stuttgart 1957, 151.

20. Pickard-Cambridge, *Festivals*, 124. C. A. van Rooy, *Studies in Classical Satire and Related Literary Theory*, Leyden 1965, 126.

21. On the interpretation of the fragments see W. Suess, *Herm.* 74 (1939), 210; A. von Blumenthal, ibid., 216; H. Hommel, *Herm.* 75 (1940), 237, 335; W. Steffen, "Aus der Altertumswiss.," *Arbeit Volkspolens*, 1955, 36; S. Schiassi, *Dioniso* 21 (1958), 83 and now esp. Snell, *Scenes*, 99.

22. So too C. A. van Rooy in the above-mentioned *Studies*, 127, and H. Lloyd-Jones, *Gnom.* 38 (1966), 16.

23. A. Meineke thought he heard an echo of "phallos" in the name. Snell, *Scenes*, 104. 9, supports this with sound linguistic arguments.

24. Listed in Ziegler, 1970. The fragments without Ezechiel in F. Schramm, "Tragicorum Graec. hellenisticae quae dicitur aetatis fragmenta eorumque de vita atque poesi testimonia collecta et illustrata," Diss. Münster 1929. G. M. Sifakis, *Studies in the History of Hellenistic Drama*, London 1967 (in particular about performances in Delos and Delphi). On the Pleiad, see W. Steffen, *Quaest. trag. capita tria*, Poznan 1939; J. H. Waszink, "Die griech. Tragödie im Urteil der Römer und der Christen," *Jahrb. f. Ant. u. Christent.* 7 (1964), 139; P. Boyancé, "On the Position of the Epicureans against tragedy," *Rev. Et. Anc.* 49 (1947), 90.

25. EDITIONS: C. von Holzinger, Leipzig 1895, repr. 1968 (with comm.); E. Scheer, 2d ed., 2 vols. (vol. 2 contains the scholia), Berlin 1958; L. Mascialino, Leipzig 1964. INTERPRETATION: Wilamowitz, *Hellenistiche Dichtung*, 2d ed., Berlin 1962, 145; K. Ziegler, *RE* 13, 2336; St. Josifović, "Zur Quellenkunde von Lykophrons *Alexandra*," *Jahrb. Phil. Fak. Novi Sad* 5 (1960), 283.

26. J. Wieneke, "Ezechielis Judaei poetae Alexandrini fabulae quae inscr. ΕΞΑΓΩΓΗ fragmenta," Diss. Münster 1931 (comm.). See the text also in the edition of the *Praeparatio Evan-*

gelica of K. Mras. INTERPRETATION: A. Kappelmacher, "Zur Tragödie der hellenistischen Zeit," *Wien. Stud.* 44, (1924/25), 69; I. Trencsényi-Waldapfel, "Une tragédie Grecque à sujet biblique," *Acta Orientalia* II/2–3 (1952/53), 143; A. Lesky, *Herm.* 81 (1953), 3 = *Ges. Schr.*, 206; M. Hadas, *Hellenistic Culture*, New York 1959, 99; B. Snell, "Ezechiel's Moses-drama," *Ant. u. Abendl.* 13 (1967), 150 (chap. 7 in the German edition of *Scenes from Greek Drama*).

27. G. M. Sifakis, *Studies in the History of Hellenistic Drama*, London 1967, 122, conjectures that there was a chorus of sisters of Sepphora.

28. Snell thinks there was a performance, which we also consider quite possible, while O. Zwierlein, in his book *Die Rezitationsdramen Senecas*, Meisenheim 1966, in a chapter devoted to the *Exagoge*, tries to prove that the piece was written to be read rather than staged.

29. "Frauen im Kampf," *Wien. Stud.* 77 (1964), 5.

30. "A Greek Historical Drama," *Proc. Brit. Ac.* 35 (1950), 1. Bibl. in the research reports of *Anz. f. d. Altertumsw.* 5 (1952), 152 and 7 (1954), 150; further, in A. E. Raubitschek, "Gyges in Herodotus," *Class. Weekly* 48 (1955), 48 (with an attempt to ascribe the work to Ion of Chios). The view proposed by D. L. Page, *A New Chapter in the History of Greek Tragedy*, Cambridge 1951, that the Gyges tragedy was written by a tragedian before Herodotos (Phrynichos), has recently received support from Lloyd-Jones, *Problems*, 25. Q. Cataudella, "Sulla cronologia del cosidetto 'Frammento di Gige'" *Studi Calderini e Paribeni* II, Milan 1957, 103 = *Saggi sulla tragedia Greca*, Messina 1969, 43. 411, also considers a poet (of lesser quality) before Herodotos. We believe firmly in the later date: K. Latte, "Ein antikes Gygesdrama," *Eranos* 48 (1950), 136 = *Kl. Schr.*, 585; A. Lesky, "Das hellenistische Gyges-Drama," *Herm.* 81 (1953), 1 = *Ges. Schr.*, 204; B. Snell, "Gyges und Kroisos als Tragödienfiguren," *Ztschr. f. Pap. u. Epigr.* 12 (1973), 197.

31. On the supposed reading of a γλεφ[, which would suggest lyric, cf. *Anz. f. d. Altertumsw.* 7 (1954), 151.

32. C. A. van Rooy in the above-mentioned *Studies*, 134, considers the influence of contemporary bucolic poetry.

33. J. Wikarjak, *Eos* 43 (1949), 127, assumed "subtle mockery," probably rightly. W. Steffen, *Charisteria Th. Sinko oblata*, Warsaw 1951, 331, objected and suggested an elogium. Conversely C. A. van Rooy (see above), 127, prefers to side with Athenaios. Id., 136, for an excellent treatment of the development of the meaning of the word σατυρικός.

34. For Greek tragedy in imperial times see: K. Latte, "Zur Gesch. der griech. Trag. in der Kaiserzeit," *Eranos* 52 (1954), 125 = *Kl. Schr.*, 590; M. Kokolakis, *Lucian and the Tragic Performances in his Time*, Athens 1961. On the interesting phrase περιόδων τὰ ἰαμβεῖα, cf. A. Lesky, *Anz. f. d. Altertumsw.* 20 (1967), 81.

BIBLIOGRAPHY

ON TRAGEDY (GENERAL)

Arrowsmith, W. "A Greek Theater of Ideas." In *Ideas in the Drama*, edited by J. Gassner. New York, 1964.

Aylen, L. *Greek Tragedy and the Modern World*. London, 1964.

Baden, H. J. *Das Tragische*. 2d ed. Berlin, 1948.

Baldry, H. C. *The Greek Tragic Theater*. London, 1971.

Bergson, L. *L'épithète ornamentale dans Esch. Soph. et Eur.* Uppsala, 1956.

Bickel, E. *Die griechische Tragödie*. Bonn, 1942.

Bogner, H. *Der tragische Gegensatz*. Heidelberg, 1947.

Bonnard, A. *La tragédie et l'homme*. Neuchâtel, 1951.

Bremer, J. M. *Hamartia: Tragic Error in the* Poetics *of Aristotle and in Greek Tragedy*. Amsterdam, 1969.

Broadhead, H. D. *Tragica: Elucidations of Passages in Greek Tragedy*. Christchurch: Univ. of Canterbury, 1968.

Buchwald, W. *Studien zur Chronologie der attischen Tragödie 455 bis 431*. Königsberg, 1939.

Dale, A. M. *The Lyric Metres of Greek Drama*. 2d ed. Cambridge, 1968.

———. *Metrical Analyses of Tragic Choruses, I: Dactylo-Epitrite. Bull. Inst. Class. Stud.* Suppl. 21, 1. London, 1972.

Ferguson, J. *A Companion to Greek Tragedy*. Austin and London, 1972.

Friedrich, W. H. *Vorbild und Neugestaltung: Sechs Kapitel zur Geschichte der Tragödie*. Göttingen, 1967.

Fritz, K. v. *Antike und moderne Tragödie: Neun Abhandlungen*. Berlin, 1962.

Funke, H. "Die sogennannte tragische Schuld." Diss. Cologne, 1963.

Grande, C. del. *Hybris: Colpa e castigo nell'espressione poetica e letteraria degli scrittori della Grecia antica da Omero a Cleante*. Naples, 1947.

———. ΤΡΑΓΩΙΔΙΑ. *Essenza e genesi della Tragedia*. 2d ed. Naples, 1962.

Greene, W. C. *Moira: Fate, Good and Evil in Greek Thought*. Cambridge, Mass., 1944.

Guggisberg, P. *Das Satyrspiel.* Zurich, 1947.

Hamburger, K. *Von Sophokles zu Sartre.* 3d ed. Stuttgart, 1965.

Harsh, P. W. *A Handbook of Classical Drama.* Stanford, 1948.

Howald, E. *Die griechische Tragödie.* Munich, 1930.

Jackson, J. *Marginalia Scaenica.* Oxford, 1955.

Jens, W. *Die Bauformen der gr. Tragödie.* (With contributions from K. Aisele et al.) Poetica Beiheft 6. Munich, 1971.

Johansen, H. F. *General Reflection in Tragic Rhesis.* Copenhagen, 1959.

Jones, J. *On Aristotle and Greek Tragedy.* London, 1962.

Kitto, H. D. F. *Greek Tragedy: A Literary Study.* 3d ed. London, 1961.

———. *Form and Meaning in Drama: A Study of Six Greek Plays and of Hamlet.* London, 1956.

Kommerell, M. *Lessing und Aristoteles: Untersuchung über die Theorie der Tragödie.* Frankfurt am Main, 1940.

Kott, J. *The Eating of the Gods: An Interpretation of Greek Tragedy.* Transl. by B. Taborski and E. J. Czerwinski. New York, 1973.

Kranz, W. *Stasimon: Untersuchungen zu Form und Gehalt der gr. Tragödie.* Berlin, 1933.

Kraus, W. "Strophengestaltung in der gr. Tragödie. I. Aischylos und Sophokles." *Sitzb. Öst. Akad. Phil.-hist. Kl.* 231/4, 1957.

Lammers, J. "Die Doppel- und Halbchöre in der antiken Tragödie." Diss. Münster. Paderborn, 1931.

Lattimore, R. *The Poetry of Greek Tragedy.* Baltimore, 1958.

———. *Story Patterns in Greek Tragedy.* London, 1964.

Lennig, R. "Traum und Sinnestäuschung bei Aischylos, Sophokles, Euripides." Diss. Tübingen, 1969.

Lesky, A. *Die griechische Tragödie.* 4th ed. Stuttgart, 1968 (English: 2d ed. London, 1967; Spanish: Barcelona, 1966; Norwegian: Oslo, 1971; Portuguese: São Paulo, 1971).

———. *Geschichte der gr. Literatur.* 2d ed. Bern, 1963 (English: London, 1966).

Lucas, D. W. *The Greek Tragic Poets.* 2d ed. London, 1959.

Nebel, G. *Weltangst und Götterzorn: Eine Deutung der gr. Tragödie.* Stuttgart, 1951.

Nestle, W. *Die Struktur des Eingangs der attischen Tragödie.* Tüb. Beitr. 10. Stuttgart, 1930.

Norwood, G. *Greek Tragedy.* 4th ed. London, 1948.

Pack, R. A. *The Greek and Latin Literary Texts from Greco-Roman Egypt.* 2d ed. Ann Arbor, 1965.

Page, D. L. *Actors' Interpolations in Greek Tragedy.* Oxford, 1934.

Pohlenz, M. *Die griechische Tragödie.* 2 vols. 2d ed. Göttingen, 1954.

Post, L. A. *From Homer to Menander.* Berkeley, 1951.

Raphael, D. D. *The Paradox of Tragedy.* London, 1959.

Rodríguez Adrados, F. *El heroe tragico y e filosofo Platonico.* Cuadernos de la fundación Pastor 6. Madrid, 1962.

Romilly, J. de *L'évolution du pathétique d'Eschyle à Euripide.* Paris, 1961.

———. *La tragédie grecque*. Paris, 1970.

———. *Time in Greek Tragedy*. Ithaca, 1968.

Rosenmeyer, T. G. *The Masks of Tragedy: Essays on Six Greek Tragedies*. Austin, 1963.

Schadewaldt, W. *Monolog und Selbstgespräch*. N. Phil. Unters. 2. Berlin, 1926.

———. "Furcht und Mitleid?" *Hermes* 83 (1955): 129 = *Hellas und Hesperien*, 346. Zurich, 1960.

Schlesinger, A. C. *Boundaries of Dionysos*. Cambridge, Mass., 1963.

Schmid, W. and Stählin, O. *Geschichte der gr. Literatur*. (*Handb. d. Altertumswiss.* Section 7). 1st Part: *Die klassische Periode der gr. Literatur*, W. Schmid. 1, Munich, 1929; 2, 1934; 3, 1940.

Séchan, L. *Etudes sur la tragédie Grecque dans ses rapports avec la ceramique*. Second printing. Paris, 1967.

Snell, B. *Scenes from Greek Drama*. Sather Class. Lectures 34. Berkeley and Los Angeles, 1964 (German: Berlin, 1971).

Steidle, W. *Studien zum antiken Drama*. Munich, 1968.

Vickers, B. *Towards Greek Tragedy*. London, 1973.

Weber, A. *Das Tragische und die Geschichte*. Hamburg, 1943.

Webster, T. B. L. "Greek Tragedy." In *Fifty Years (and Twelve) of Classical Scholarship*. 2d ed. Oxford, 1968.

Wolf, E. *Griechisches Rechtsdenken*. 1, Frankfurt am Main, 1950; 2, 1952.

Ziegler, K. "Tragoedia." *RE* 6 A, 1937, 1899–2075.

For specialized studies relating to all three tragedians, see the chapter on Aischylos. For further bibliographical data on the concept of tragedy, see A. Lesky, *Die griechische Tragödie*, 4th ed., 269.

Two recent publications contain several articles on tragedy: *Miscellanea Tragica in honorem J. C. Kamerbeek*, and *Yale Classical Studies* 25 (1977): 227.

ON THE ANCIENT STAGE

Arnott, P. *An Introduction to the Greek Theatre*. London, 1959.

———. *Greek Scenic Conventions in the Fifth Century B.C.* Oxford, 1962.

Bieber, M. "Maske." *RE* 14, 1930, 2070–2120.

———. *The History of the Greek and Roman Theater*. 2d ed. Princeton, 1961.

Dingel, J. "Das Requisit in der gr. Tragödie." Diss. Tübingen, 1967.

Fiechter, E. R. *Antike griechische Theaterbauten*. Stuttgart, 1930–1950.

Flickinger, R. C. *The Greek Theater and Its Drama*. 4th ed. Chicago, 1936. Repr., 1960.

Gerhäuser, M. F. "Untersuchungen über die Spielmöglichkeiten im gr. Theater." Diss. Hannover, 1959. Special edition, Darmstadt, 1964.

Gerkan, A. v. *Das Theater von Priene*. Munich, 1921.

———. *Das Theater von Epidauros*. Stuttgart, 1961.

Hourmouziades, N. C. See under Euripides.

Jobst, W. "Die Höhle im gr. Theater des 5. und 4. Jhs. v. Chr." *Sitzb. Öst. Akad. Phil.-hist. Kl.* 268/2, 1970.

Kenner, H. *Theater und Realismus in der gr. Kunst.* Vienna, 1954.

Lesky, A. "Noh-Bühne und griechisches Theater." *Maia* n.s. 15 (1963): 38 = *Ges. Schr.* Bern, 1966, 275.

Melchinger, S. *Das Theater der Tragödie.* Munich, 1974.

Pickard-Cambridge, A. W. *The Theater of Dionysos in Athens.* Oxford, 1946.

———. *The Dramatic Festivals of Athens.* 2d ed., revised by J. Gould and D. M. Lewis. Oxford, 1968.

Simon, E. *Das antike Theater.* Heidelberger Textedidaktische Reihe 5. Heidelberg, 1972.

Snell, B. "Zu den Urkunden dramatischer Aufführungen." *Nachr. Akad. Gött. Phil.-hist. Kl.* 1966/2.

Spitzbarth, A. *Untersuchungen zur Spieltechnik der gr. Tragödie.* Zurich, 1946.

Trendall, A. D., and Webster, T. B. L. *Illustrations of Greek Drama.* London, 1971.

Webster, T. B. L. *Greek Theater Production.* 2d ed. London, 1970.

———. *Griechische Bühnenaltertümer.* Studienh. z. Altertumsw. 9. Göttingen, 1963.

———. "On the Dramatic Terracottas of Lipari." *Meligunìs Lipára* 2 (1965): 319.

———. *Monuments Illustrating Tragedy and Satyr Play.* 2d ed. with appendix. *Bull. Inst. Class. Stud.* Suppl. 20 (1967).

———. *The Greek Chorus.* London, 1970.

ON THE EARLY HISTORY OF TRAGEDY

Björck, G. *Das Alpha impurum und die tragische Kunstsprache.* Acta Societatis Litterarum Humaniorum Regiae Upsaliensis 39, 1. Uppsala, 1950.

Brommer, F. *Satyroi.* Wurzburg, 1937.

———. "Σιληνοί und σάτυροι." *Phil.* 94 (1940): 222.

———. *Satyrspiele: Bilder griechischer Vasen.* 2d ed. Berlin, 1959.

Burkert, W. "Greek Tragedy and Sacrificial Ritual." *Greek, Rom. and Byz. Stud.* 7 (1966): 87.

Buschor, E. *Satyrtänze und frühes Drama.* Sitz. Bayer. Akad. Phil.-hist. Kl. 1943/5.

Cantarella, R. *I primordi della tragedia.* Salerno, 1936 (essentially repeated in *Eschilo*; see below under Aischylos).

Else, G. F. *The Origin and Early Form of Greek Tragedy.* Cambridge, Mass., 1965.

Gallo, I. *Il teatro greco: letture critiche e testimonianze.* Rome, 1971.

Gaster, T. H. *Thespis: Ritual, Myth and Drama in the Ancient Near East.* 2d ed. New York, 1961.

Guépin, J. P. *The Tragic Paradox.* Amsterdam, 1968.

Hartmann, A. "Silenos und Satyros." *RE* 3 A, 1927, 35.

Kalinka, E. *Die Urform der griechischen Tragödie.* Commentationes Aenipontanae 10, 1924.

Kuhnert, E. "Satyros und Silenos." *Myth. Lex.* 4 (1909/15): 444.

Lindsay, J. *The Clashing Rocks: A Study of Early Greek Religion and Culture and the Origins of Drama.* London, 1965.

Lloyd-Jones, H. "Problems of Early Greek Tragedy." *Estudios sobre la tragedia Griega.* Cuadernos de la fundación Pastor 13. Madrid, 1966, 11.

Patzer, H. *Die Anfänge der griechischen Tragödie.* Wiesbaden, 1962.

Peretti, A. *Epirrema e tragedia.* Florence, 1939.

Pickard-Cambridge, A. W. *Dithyramb, Tragedy and Comedy.* 2d ed., revised by T. B. L. Webster. Oxford, 1962.

Robert, F. "Les origines de la tragédie Grecque." In *Le théâtre tragique,* I: *Le monde antique.* Paris, 1962.

Rodríguez Adrados, F. "Sobre los origines del teatro: κῶμος, κωμῳδία, τραγῳδία." *Emerita* 35 (1967): 249.

Schreckenburg, H. Δρᾶμα. *Vom Werden der griechischen Tragödie aus dem Tanz.* Wurzburg, 1960.

Thomson, G. See under Aischylos.

Tièche, E. *Thespis.* Leipzig, 1933.

Untersteiner, M. *Le origini della tragedia e del tragico.* Turin, 1955.

AISCHYLOS

Blumenthal, A. von. *Aischylos.* Stuttgart, 1924.

Cantarella, R. *Eschilo I.* Florence, 1941.

Dawe, R. D. *The Collation and Investigation of Manuscripts of Aeschylus.* Cambridge, 1964.

———. *Repertory of Conjectures on Aeschylus.* Leyden, 1965.

Finley, J. H., Jr. *Pindar and Aeschylus.* Martin Class. Lect. 14. Cambridge, Mass., 1955.

Fischer, U. *Der Telosgedanke in den Dramen des Aischylos.* Spudasmata 6. Hildesheim, 1965.

eim, 1965.

Galiano, M. F. "Les papyrus d'Eschyle." *Proc. of the IX Int. Congr. of Papyrology.* Norw. Un. Press, 1961, 81.

Hommel, H., ed. *Wege zu Aischylos,* I and II. Darmstadt, 1974 (forty-seven essays with select. bibl.).

Kaufmann-Bühler, D. "Begriff und Funktion der Dike in den Tragödien des Aischylos." Diss. Heidelberg. Bonn, 1955.

Kiefner, W. *Der religiöse Allbegriff des Aischylos.* Spudasmata 5. Hildesheim, 1965.

Maddalena, A. *Interpretazione Eschilee.* Turin, 1951.

Méautis, G. *Eschyle et la trilogie.* Paris, 1936.

Mette, H. J. *Die Fragmente der Tragödien des Aischylos.* Berlin, 1959.

———. *Der Verlorene Aischylos.* Berlin, 1963.

Murray, G. *Aeschylus: The Creator of Tragedy.* Oxford, 1940. Paperback, 1962.

Nestle, Walter. *Menschliche Existenz und politische Erziehung in der Tragödie des Aischylos.* Tüb. Beitr. 23. Stuttgart, 1934.

Owen, E. T. *The Harmony of Aeschylus*. London, 1952.

Podlecki, J. *The Political Background of Aeschylean Tragedy*. Ann Arbor, 1966.

Porzig, W. *Die attische Tragödie des Aischylos*. Leipzig, 1926.

Reinhardt, K. *Aischylos als Regisseur und Theologe*. Bern, 1949.

Riele, G. J. M. J. te. *Les femmes chez Eschyle*. Proefschrift Utrecht. Groningen, 1955.

Romilly, J. de. *La crainte et l'angoisse dans le théâtre d'Eschyle*. Paris, 1958.

————. "Ombres sacrées dans le théâtre d'Eschyle." In *Le théâtre antique*, I: *Le monde antique*. Paris, 1962.

Sheppard, J. T. *Aeschylus and Sophocles: Their Work and Influence* (Our Debt to Greece and Rome). New York, 1963.

Snell, B. *Aischylos und das Handeln im Drama*. Phil. Suppl. 20/1. Leipzig, 1928.

Solmsen, F. *Hesiod and Aeschylus*. New York, 1949. Repr., 1967.

Thomson, G. *Aeschylus and Athens*. 2d ed. repr. London, 1966 (German: Berlin, 1957).

Untersteiner, M. *See under Early History of Tragedy*.

Wilamowitz-Moellendorff, U. von. *Aischylos. Interpretationen*. Berlin, 1914.

SPECIAL LEXICON: W. Dindorf, Leipzig, 1873.

INDEX VERBORUM: G. Italie, Leyden, 1955. Additions in Mette's collection of the fragments (see above).

SOPHOKLES

Adams, S. M. *Sophocles the Playwright*. Toronto, 1957.

Bates, W. N. *Sophocles: Poet and Dramatist*. London, 1964.

Blumenthal, A. von. "Sophokles." *RE* 3 A (1927), 1040–1094.

————. *Sophokles: Entstehung und Vollendung der griechischen Tragödie*. Stuttgart, 1936.

Bowra, C. M. *Sophoclean Tragedy*. Oxford, 1944. Repr., 1947. Paperback, 1965.

Diller, H.; Schadewaldt, W.; Lesky, A. *Gottheit und Mensch in der Tragödie des Sophokles*. (Three lectures.) Darmstadt, 1963.

————. *Sophokles*. Wege der Forschung 95 (twenty-two essays by various authors, with an introduction and bibliography after 1960 by H. Diller). Darmstadt, 1967.

Egermann, F. *Vom attischen Menschenbild*. Munich, 1952.

————. "Arete und tragische Bewusstheit bei Sophokles und Herodot." In *Vom Menschen in der Antike*. Munich, 1957/5.

Ehrenberg, V. *Sophocles and Pericles*. Oxford, 1954 (German: Munich, 1956).

Eicken-Iselin, E. "Interpretationen und Untersuchungen zum Aufbau der Sophokleischen Rheseis." Diss. Basel. Dortmund, 1942.

Fochi, F. *Il valore drammatico dell'opera di Sofocle*. Turin, 1946.

Kamerbeek, J. C. *Studien over Sophocles*. Amsterdam, 1934.

Kirkwood, G. M. *A Study of Sophoclean Drama*. Cornell Studies in Class. Phil. 31. Ithaca, New York, 1958.

Kitto, H. D. F. *Sophocles: Dramatist and Philosopher*. London, 1958.

Knox, B. M. W. *The Heroic Temper: Studies in Sophoclean Tragedy.* Sather Class. Lect. 35. Berkeley, 1964.

Letters, F. J. H. *The Life and Work of Sophocles.* London, 1953.

Maddalena, A. *Sofocle.* 2d ed. Turin, 1963.

Méautis, G. *Sophocle: Essai sur le héros tragique.* Paris, 1957.

Opstelten, J. C. *Sophocles and Greek Pessimism.* Amsterdam, 1952.

————. *Humanistisch en religieus standpunt in de moderne beschouwing van Sophocles.* Mededelingen der Koninklijke Nederl. Akad. n.s. 17/1. 1954.

Perrotta, G. *Sofocle.* Messina/Milan, 1935. Repr., 1963.

Reinhardt, K. *Sophokles.* 3d ed. Frankfurt am Main, 1948.

Ronnet, G. *Sophocle poéte tragique.* Paris, 1969.

Sheppard, J. T. *The Wisdom of Sophocles.* London, 1947.

————. See under Aischylos.

Trencsényi-Waldapfel, J. *Sophoklés.* Budapest, 1964.

Turolla, E. *Saggio sulla poesia di Sofocle.* Bari, 1934.

Uhsadel, C. A. "Der Chor als Gestalt: Seine Teilnahme am Geschehen sophokleischer Stücke." Diss. Tübingen, 1969.

Untersteiner, M. *Sofocle: Studio critico.* 2 vols. Florence, 1935.

Waldock, A. J. A. *Sophocles the Dramatist.* Cambridge, 1951. Repr., 1966.

Webster, T. B. L. *An Introduction to Sophocles.* 2d ed. London, 1969.

Weinstock, H. *Sophokles.* 3d ed. Wuppertal, 1948.

Whitman, C. H. *Sophocles: A Study of Heroic Humanism.* Cambridge, Mass., 1951.

Wilamowitz-Moellendorff, T. von. *Die dramatische Technik des Sophokles.* Phil. Unters. 22. Berlin, 1917.

SPECIAL LEXICON: F. Ellendt and H. Genthe. Berlin, 1872.

EURIPIDES

Austin, C. *Nova Fragmenta Euripidea in papyris reperta.* Kl. Texte 187. Berlin, 1968.

Barlow, S. A. *The Imagery of Euripides.* London, 1971.

Bates, W. N. *Euripides, A Student of Human Nature.* Philadelphia, 1930.

Benedetto, V. di. *La tradizione manoscritta Euripidea.* Proagones. Studi 7. Padua, 1965.

————. *Euripide: teatro e società.* Turin, 1971.

Blaiklock, E. M. *The Male Characters of Euripides: A Study in Realism.* Wellington, 1952.

Burnett, A. P. *Catastrophe Survived: Euripides' Plays of Mixed Reversal.* Oxford, 1971.

Chromik, C. "Göttlicher Anspruch und menschliche Verantwortung bei Euripides." Diss. Kiel, 1967.

Conacher, D. P. *Euripidean Drama: Myth, Theme and Structure.* Toronto, 1967.

Delebecque, E. *Euripide et la guerre du Péloponnèse.* Paris, 1951.

————. "Euripide et l'actualité de son temps." In *Le théâtre tragique*, I: *Le monde antique*. Paris, 1962.

Friedrich, W. H. *Euripides und Diphilos*. Zetemata 5. Munich, 1953.

Garzya, A. *Studi su Euripide e Menandro*. Naples, 1961.

————. *Pensiero e tecnica drammatica in Euripide*. Naples, 1962.

Goossens, R. *Euripide et Athènes*. Acad. Royale de Belgique, 1962.

Greenwood, L. H. G. *Aspects of Euripidean Tragedy*. Cambridge, 1953.

Grube, G. M. A. *The Drama of Euripides*. 2d ed. London, 1961.

Hourmouziades, N. C. *Production and Imagination in Euripides*. Athens, 1965.

Kretz, L. "Persönliches bei Euripides." Diss. Zurich, 1934.

Laugholf, V. *Die Gebete bei Euripides und die zeitliche Folge der Tragödien*. Göttingen, 1971.

Lennep, D. F. W. Van. *Euripides* ΠΟΙΗΤΗΣ ΣΟΦΟΣ. Amsterdam, 1935.

Looy, H. Van. *Zes verloren tragedies van Euripides*. Vlaamse Acad. Kl. d. Letteren 26 (1964), no. 51.

Ludwig, W. "Sapheneia. Ein Beitrag zur Formkunst im Spätwerk der Euripides." Diss. Tübingen, 1954.

Martinazzoli, F. *Euripide*. Rome, 1946.

Meissner, B. "Mythisches und Rationales in der Psychologie der euripideischen Tragödie." Diss. Göttingen, 1951.

Murray, G. *Euripides and His Age*. 7th ed. Oxford, 1955 (German: Darmstadt, 1957).

Norwood, G. *Essays on Euripidean Drama*. Berkeley and London, 1954.

Prieto, M. H. U. *Da esperanca na obra de Euripides*. Lisbon, 1966.

Reinhardt, K. "Die Sinneskrise bei Euripides." *Neue Rundschau* 68 (1957): 615 = *Tradition und Geist*. Göttingen, 1960, 227 = *Euripides*. Wege der Forschung 89 (see under Schwinge), 507.

Reverdin, O., *Euripide*. Fondation Hardt. Entretiens VI. Vandoeuvres-Geneva 1958/1960 (J. C. Kamerbeek: "Mythe et realité dans l'oeuvre d'E." A. Rivier: "L'élément démonique chez E." H. Diller: "Umwelt und Masse als dramatische Faktoren bei E." A. Lesky: "Psychologie bei E." R. P. Winnington-Ingram: "Hippolytos: A Study in Causation." G. Zuntz: "On E.'s *Helena*: Theology and Irony." V. Martin: "E. et Menandre face à leur public").

Rivier, A. *Essai sur le tragique d'Euripide*. Lausanne, 1944.

Rohdich, H. *Euripideische Tragödie. Untersuchungen zu ihrer Tragik*. Bibl. d. klass. Altertumswiss. n.s. 2, 24. Heidelberg, 1968.

Schwinge, E. R. *Die Verwendung der Stichomythie in den Dramen des Euripides*. Bibl. d. klass. Altertumswiss. n.s. 2, 27. Heidelberg, 1968.

————. *Euripides*. Wege der Forschung 89 (twenty-one essays by various authors, with a bibliography after 1960 provided by E. R. Schwinge). Darmstadt, 1968.

Segal, E., ed. *Euripides: A Collection of Critical Essays*. Englewood Cliffs, 1968.

Strohm, H. *Euripides*. Zetemata 15. Munich, 1957.

Tuilier, A. *Recherches critiques sur la tradition du texte d'Euripide*. Etudes et commentaires 68. Paris, 1969.

Turyn, A. *The Byzantine Manuscript Tradition of the Tragedies of Euripides.* Urbana, 1957.

Valgiglio, E. *Il tema della morte in Euripide.* Biblioteca della rivista di studi classici. Turin, 1966.

Webster, T. B. L. *The Tragedies of Euripides.* London, 1967.

Zuntz, G. *The Political Plays of Euripides.* 2d ed. Manchester, 1963.

————. *An Inquiry into the Transmission of the Plays of Euripides.* Cambridge, 1965.

Zürcher, W. *Die Darstellung des Menschen im Drama des Euripides.* Schweiz. Beitr. z. Altertumswiss. 2. Basel, 1947.

INDEX VERBORUM: J. T. Allen and G. Italie, *A Concordance to Euripides.* Berkeley, 1953. Additions in Austin (see above) and C. Collard, *Supplement to the Allen and Italie Concordance to Euripides.* Groningen, 1971.

Scholarly work on Greek tragedy and its poets from 1948 on is periodically reviewed in the *Anzeiger für die Altertumswiss.*, continued by H. Strohm. *Bibliografia del dramma antico* by V. Bonajuto, R. Cantarella, A. Colonna, A. Garzya from 1947 on in the journal *Dioniso.* In *Fifty Years (and Twelve) of Classical Scholarship,* 2d ed. Oxford, 1968, T. B. L. Webster offered a survey of the bibliography on tragedy.

For the fragments: A. Nauck, *Tragicorum Graecorum Fragmenta.* Reprint of the 2d ed. Hildesheim, 1964. With a supplement by Bruno Snell. Id., *Trag. Graec. Fragmenta,* vol. I. (*Didascaliae Tragicae, Catalogi Tragicorum et Tragoediarum, Testimonia et Fragmenta Tragicorum Minorum*). Göttingen, 1971.

The extremely valuable *Lustrum* volumes by H. F. Johansen on Sophokles (1962/7) and H. J. Mette on the fragments of Euripides (1967/12) are listed under their respective authors.

INDEX